Cases in Managing
Financial Resources

CASES IN MANAGING FINANCIAL RESOURCES

IKE MATHUR
Southern Illinois University at Carbondale

DAVID LOY
Illinois State University

RESTON PUBLISHING COMPANY, INC.
A Prentice-Hall Company
Reston, Virginia

Library of Congress Cataloging in Publication Data

Mathur, Iqbal.
    Cases in managing financial resources.

    1. Corporations—Finance—Case studies. 2. Business
enterprises—Finance—Case studies. 3. Corporations,
Nonprofit—Finance—Case studies. I. Loy, David.
II. Title.
HG4015.5.M37 1984   658.1'5   83-21313
ISBN 0-8359-0709-0

Editorial/production supervision and
interior design by Camelia Townsend

© 1984 by Reston Publishing Company, Inc.
A Prentice-Hall Company
Reston, Virginia 22090

10 9 8 7 6 5 4 3 2 1

PRINTED IN THE UNITED STATES OF AMERICA

To Our Families

Contents

Acknowledgments

No project of this nature is successful without the generous help and cooperation of many individuals. We gratefully acknowledge the generosity of the following who so kindly consented to having their cases included in this casebook.

M. Edgar Barrett, Southern Methodist University
Brian Belt, University of Missouri—Kansas City
William O. Cain, Jr., Execucom, Austin, Texas
W. R. Cozens, Honolulu Children's Treatment Center
Kenneth W. Cubbage, Pacific Lutheran University
John R. Darling, Texas Tech University
Steven M. Dawson, University of Hawaii
Bruce H. Fairchild, Financial Concepts and Applications, Inc.
Jack D. Ferner, Wake Forest University
Kenneth R. Ferris, Southern Methodist University
John D. Forsyth, Duke University
John R. Grady, Public Service Commission of Maryland
H. James Graham, Montgomery County Hospital
James A. Hoeven, Colorado State University
Charles F. Hoitash, Eastern Michigan University
IMEDE, Lausanne, Switzerland
Frank Keller, University of Houston at Clear Lake City
James A. Largay, III, Lehigh University
Allen Michel, Boston University
Mike E. Miles, University of North Carolina at Chapel Hill
Paul A. Mueller, Bowling Green State University
Jerome S. Osteryoung, Florida State University
Jim Puhl, Honolulu, Hawaii
Ira W. Pyron, Troy State University
Linda M. Roush, Illinois State University
Burton F. Schaffer, California State University, Sacramento

Frederick C. Scherr, West Virginia University
David J. Springate, Southern Methodist University
Clyde P. Stickney, Jr., Dartmouth College
Russell A. Taussig, University of Hawaii
George W. Trivoli, Nova University
William L. Weis, Seattle University
James A. Wilbur, Seattle, Washington
Richard E. White, University of North Florida
John D. Williams, The University of Akron
Charles W. Young, University of North Florida

We express our thanks to our colleagues at Southern Illinois University at Carbondale and Illinois State University, as well as at other institutions, who were supportive of this project and whose comments and suggestions were constructive and helpful in expediting completion of this project.

Preface

We have yet to find a student who does not face the problem of having to relate classroom concepts, techniques, and theories to real-life situations. The astute student recognizes that ultimately his or her value in an institutional setting is going to be dependent on his or her ability to understand, analyze, and solve problems and to implement appropriate remedial strategies. Additionally, most firms appreciate those individuals who can not only apply the "received doctrine" well enough but who also are capable and willing to look at more innovative approaches to problem solving. Cases allow students to apply their knowledge of business concepts to real-life problems. More importantly, in considering alternative solutions and their impacts on the firms, it is not uncommon to see the students coming up with new, creative solutions to age-old problems.

Students, in looking at cases from a managerial perspective, begin to develop a feel for the decision-making environments in which executives exist. This simulative exposure to the business environment helps sensitize them to the types of issues and opportunities that they are going to face in the future. In using cases students learn to communicate and provide hard support for their decisions. These, as well as other, factors argue for the use of cases in intermediate- and advanced-level courses in business.

The purpose of this casebook is to put together in one package financial cases representing a variety of business settings. The cases are designed to expose the student to different financial issues in different settings. Cases are based on real firms and real data, although on occasion the name of the company or organization has been disguised in deference to their managers' desires. The cases are designed for discussion and analysis in the classroom and are not meant to be illustrative of either effective or ineffective handling of administrative situations.

The cases in this casebook vary in length as well as in complexity. All have been thoroughly classroom tested to assure their readability and amenability to financial problem solving. In addition, the cases presented in this book do a diligent job of preserving the business decision-making environment without overwhelming the reader with extraneous data. This assures that viable solutions can be derived in reasonable amounts of time, without unduly frustrating the case user, and still have real-life relevance. A computer-assisted instruction package is available.

Cases in this book have been organized along the lines of asset management and liabilities management. We have found this sequencing to be useful in conducting our own case-oriented classes. Needless to say, each case in this book can be worked on and solved independently of other cases. Consequently, nonsequential use of these cases would in no way detract from their usefulness in the classroom.

Our experience in teaching indicates that more and more business majors are considering positions in the not-for-profit sector of the economy. Inclusion of some cases on not-for-profit institutions here not only shows the universality of financial management concepts but also serves to stimulate student interest in these institutions.

We realize that any project of this nature can be further improved. Your comments, corrections, and suggestions for improvements are cheerfully and actively solicited.

PART ONE

Financial Analysis

CASE 1

Children's Toy Industry

In January 1982 Mr. Stephen Kolbach, vice-president of the Chicago National Bank, was becoming concerned about the increasing number of problem loans his bank had in its portfolio. He was particularly worried about loans to two companies in the children's toy industry —Leisure Dynamics, Inc., and Mego International, Inc. On January 10, 1982, he had called a newly hired staff member, Mr. Michael DiLeonardi, and had asked him to prepare a report on the status of the two companies. Mr. Kolbach had begun the discussion by saying, "Mike, I want to know what shape these two companies are in. Here are our files on Leisure Dynamics and Mego International. Run some financial ratios and report back to me tomorrow on what you find."

Mr. DiLeonardi returned to his small office and began working on the report.

The files Mr. Kolbach had given to him contained, among other items, financial statements for both companies covering the most recent five-year period and financial ratios for the children's toy industry as compiled and reported by Robert Morris Associates in their *Annual Statement Studies* (see Exhibits 1 to 8). An analysis of the economic outlook for the children's toy industry had been prepared on January 5, 1982, and had been placed in the file. Mr. DiLeonardi was able to piece together a brief history of the two companies from their loan applications and from clippings of recent newspaper articles.

THE CHILDREN'S TOY INDUSTRY*

The children's toy industry was highly competitive. Industry sales were distrib-

---

This case was prepared by and used with the permission of Linda M. Roush, Illinois State University.

*Information in this section was derived from *Standard & Poor's Industry Survey* (1982), pp. L25–L27. Albert F. Shaw, Leisure Time Analyst.

uted among four segments: (a) six large publicly held companies, (b) four conglomerates with large subsidiaries in the toy business, (c) 1000 or more small independently owned companies, and (d) an undetermined number of foreign manufacturers. In recent years, foreign toy manufacturers had captured an increasing share of the U.S. toy market by exporting large volumes of low-priced toys.

Retail sales of toys were highly seasonal, with over 60 percent of annual sales occurring during the Christmas shopping season. Most retailers were ordering toys from manufacturers during the first four months of the year, and manufacturers were making delivery on these orders in the four months preceding Christmas.

Companies were setting production schedules, in part, on the basis of orders received early in the year. In order to achieve production efficiency and provide inventory control, most companies were also producing toys in anticipation of demands that they hoped would develop in the last half of the year. In the event that the anticipated sales were not realized on a given toy line, manufacturers were left with large inventories that were liquidated at prices far below cost. If demand for a given toy line was greater than anticipated, manufacturers were often unable to produce and deliver additional toys in time to meet the demand.

Sales of toys were strongly affected by consumer "fads." In any one year over 50 percent of all toys produced were new items, and of these, over 80 percent were unprofitable. New toy lines that were popular and profitable in one year were oftentimes unprofitable and unpopular the following year. The large toy manufacturers were marketing a few well-established products, such as "Monopoly" and "Barbie" dolls, that maintained their popularity and provided stable sales year after year.

Industry sales were continuing a long trend of slow but steady growth in 1981. The growth was primarily a result of the aggressive marketing strategies used by the toy companies and by their frequent introduction of new products. An additional factor contributing to sales growth was the renewal in the rate of births in the U.S., which adds new customers for children's toys.

By 1981 the electronic video games' segment of the toy market was experiencing a rapid growth in sales. Competition from the electronic video games was taking sales away from some of the more traditional toy lines, such as power-driven toys and nonelectronic games. Other toy lines were unaffected by the growing market share captured by electronic video games. These lines were stuffed animals, dolls, crafts, puzzles, and nonpowered transportation toys.

LEISURE DYNAMICS, INC.

Leisure Dynamics, Inc. was established in 1946. By 1981 the company was operating facilities in Minnesota, California, Canada, and England. Their major toy items were games, engine-powered model airplanes, power-driven toy cars, and hobby products. The company's most popular products were the strategy game "Aggravation" and "Cox" model airplanes.

In October 1981 Leisure Dynamics arranged a two-year loan and security agreement with a group of lenders that would provide up to $18 million in borrowing at an average interest rate of 4¼ percent above the prime rate. The Chicago National Bank's participation in the loan was limited to 20 percent of the loan balance. This loan agreement replaced a secured credit agreement that Leisure Dynamics had previously obtained from the Chicago National Bank. The new loan agreement was secured by all of the company's assets. As of December 31, 1981, Leisure Dynamics had taken down slightly more than $6 million on the loan.

MEGO INTERNATIONAL, INC.

Mego International, Inc., was organized in 1969 with the merger of Mego Corporation and Lion Rock Trading Company, Ltd. Mego International's operations were based in New York and Hong Kong. The company was distributing its products—dolls, costumes, electromechanical toys, and games—through discount stores, mail order houses, and supermarkets. Many of the company's products carried names and titles of popular television programs, for example, "Star Trek" and "World's Greatest Heros."

In April 1981 Mego International entered into a three-year credit agreement with a lending group to provide $36.5 million in credit. Advances against the credit line were secured by inventory and accounts receivable. As a part of the credit agreement, the Chicago National Bank was extending a $4 million loan to Mego International through October 1983.

The auditor's report on Mego International's financial statements, dated February 28, 1981, stated:

> Continuity of future operations will be dependent upon substantially achieving sales projections and ultimately attaining profitability, as well as maintaining new financial arrangements. . . . The Company is in a highly seasonal business, and it is too early in the business cycle to determine whether sales and profit projections will be achieved. . . . Should projections not be substantially achieved or new financing not be maintained, future operations may be interrupted which may result in adjustments to both realizability of asset values and classification of liabilities. . . .

Interim financial statements for the nine months ending November 30, 1981, were

Net sales	$59,144,000	
Income before taxes	(10,877,000)	
Income taxes	57,000	dr
Net income	($10,934,000)	

Comparable figures for the nine months ending November 30, 1980, were

Net sales	$61,428,000	
Income before taxes	(14,617,000)	
Income taxes	2,198,000	cr
Net income	($12,419,000)	

EXHIBIT 1

Children's Toy Industry
Leisure Dynamics, Inc.

Balance Sheets
(dollar figures in thousands)

	As of December 31				
	1977	*1978*	*1979*	*1980*	*1981*
Assets					
Current assets:					
Cash & temporary investments	$ 4,980	$ 4,159	$ 5,687	$ 2,820	$ 1,214
Accounts receivable (net)	13,059	13,598	15,909	12,231	13,781
Inventory	7,726	9,304	12,800	10,947	10,128
Income tax recovery	—	—	—	4,820	45
Other current assets	503	512	1,777	903	706
Total Current Assets	26,268	27,573	36,173	31,721	25,874
Net property, plant & equip.	6,960	6,721	7,053	6,225	5,765
Excess purchase price over net assets of acquisitions	2,010	2,000	2,133	1,899	1,781
Trademarks & patents	514	501	484	476	471
Other assets	571	893	2,340	2,972	3,012
Total Assets	$36,323	$37,688	$48,183	$43,293	$36,903
Liabilities & Owners' Equity					
Current liabilities:					
Notes payable & current debt	$ 1,608	$ 760	$ 596	$10,513	$ 6,820
Accounts payable	1,681	1,560	2,859	2,612	3,487
Accruals	5,618	5,419	7,125	6,309	6,294
Income tax payable	1,730	1,890	701	900	622
Dividend payable	262	204	232	—	—
Total Current Liabilities	10,899	9,833	11,513	20,334	17,223
Long-term debt	8,962	8,918	19,210	16,730	15,145
Deferred income taxes	196	289	276	—	—
Total Liabilities	20,057	19,040	30,999	37,064	32,368
Owners' equity:					
Common stock ($1 par)	2,624	2,746	2,776	2,777	2,797
Capital surplus	9,159	9,229	9,381	9,381	9,058
Retained earnings	5,228	7,646	8,432	(2,454)*	(4,546)
Less treasury stock	—	109	2,642	2,787	2,249
Less stock in ESOT	745	864	763	688	525
Total Owners' Equity	16,266	18,648	17,184	6,229	4,535
Total Liabilities & Owners' Equity	$36,323	$37,688	$48,183	$43,293	$36,903

*Restated to show an additional $273,000 reduction in retained earnings.

EXHIBIT 2

Children's Toy Industry
Leisure Dynamics, Inc.

Income Statements
(dollar figures in thousands)

	For Period Ending December 31				
	1977	*1978*	*1979**	*1980*	*1981*
Net sales	$51,453	$50,329	$59,791	$47,349	$46,482
Cost of goods sold	30,639	27,759	33,875	34,707	29,962
Selling, general & admin. exp.	15,705	17,391	22,517	24,424	15,358
Interest expenses (net)	1,390	1,455	2,075	3,762	4,648
Other income	7	542	677	551	1,613
Income before income taxes and extraordinary items	3,726	4,266	2,001	(14,993)	(1,873)
Provision for income taxes	1,800	2,041	740	(4,380)	219
Income before extraordinary items	1,926	2,225	1,261	(10,613)	(2,092)
Extraordinary items	(33)	601	—	—	—
Net Income	$ 1,893	$ 2,826	$ 1,261	($10,613)	($2,092)
Depreciation & amortization	$ 2,664	$ 1,841	$ 2,126	$ 3,065	$ 1,894
Dividends	392	408	475	—	—

*Changed to LIFO method for domestic games, hobby, and toy product inventories that reduced net income by $201,000 or $0.08 per share.

EXHIBIT 3

Children's Toy Industry
Mego International, Inc.

Balance Sheets
(dollar figures in thousands)

			As of February 28		
	1977	*1978*	*1979*	*1980*	*1981*
Assets					
Current assets:					
Cash & marketable securities	$ 2,681	$ 1,331	$14,070	$10,374	$ 2,884
Accounts receivable (net)	7,482	10,995	13,732	15,659	8,382
Inventories	14,891	14,536	18,293	27,347	20,477
Income tax recovery	—	1,965	117	4,478	712
Other current assets	1,353	1,527	2,316	2,012	1,567
Total Current Assets	26,407	30,354	48,528	59,870	34,022
Net property, plant & equip.	7,970	8,444	9,364	11,226	8,926
Deferred charges & other assets	411	300	5,204	1,838	3,413
Total Assets	$34,788	$39,098	$63,096	$72,934	$46,361
Liabilities & Owners' Equity					
Current liabilities:					
Notes payable & current debt	$ 9,228	$10,643	$10,680	$21,905	$14,746
Accounts payable	5,363	6,346	8,695	7,088	3,480
Accruals & other liabilities	1,592	2,243	2,454	2,944	3,643
Income taxes	289	55	2,446	878	446
Deferred income taxes	390	302	236	94	—
Total Current Liabilities	16,862	19,589	24,511	32,909	22,315
Long-term debt	313	1,498	14,909	14,521	27,264
Deferred income taxes	765	856	1,266	2,036	187
Total Liabilities	17,940	21,943	40,686	49,466	49,766
Owners' equity:					
Common stock ($0.10 par)	209	209	225	227	227
Paid in surplus	3,076	3,106	4,336	4,390	4,390
Retained earnings	13,563	13,840	17,849	18,851	(8,022)
Total Owners' Equity	16,848	17,155	22,410	23,468	(3,405)
Total Liabilities & Owners' Equity	$34,788	$39,098	$63,096	$72,934	$46,361

EXHIBIT 4

Children's Toy Industry
Mego International, Inc.

Income Statements
(dollar figures in thousands)

	1977	1978	1979	1980	1981
			For Period Ending February 28		
Net sales	$67,235	$73,726	$91,946	$105,206	$66,949
Cost of sales	36,690	43,241	51,668	62,640	56,999
Selling, administrative & advertising expenses	23,070	28,370	30,340	38,190	32,484
Interest expense (net)	530	1,825	2,691	5,231	6,999
Income before income taxes and extraordinary items	6,945	290	7,247	(855)	(29,533)
Equity in earnings of unconsolidated affiliates	—	—	—	343	—
Provision for income taxes	2,497	(468)	2,734	(2,101)	(2,156)
Income before extraordinary items	4,448	758	4,513	1,589	(27,377)
Extraordinary items	—	—	—	—	820
Net income	$ 4,448	$ 758	$ 4,513	$ 1,589	($26,557)
Depreciation & amortization	$ 837	$ 2,068	$ 2,370	$ 3,226	$ 3,830
Dividends	394	481	504	587	316

EXHIBIT 5

Children's Toy Industry

Financial Statement Classifications

Balance Sheet	
Total Assets	
Total current assets	
Cash & equivalents	Cash, marketable securities, and other near-cash items, excluding sinking funds
Accounts & notes receivable (net)	Trade accounts and notes receivable, minus allowance for doubtful accounts
Inventory	Inventory items
All other current assets	Other current assets, excluding prepaid items
Fixed assets (net)	Property, plant, and equipment plus leasehold improvements less accumulated depreciation and depletion
Intangibles (net)	Intangible assets less accumulated amortization
All other noncurrent assets	Prepaid items and other noncurrent assets
Total Liabilities & Net Worth	
Total current liabilities	
Notes payable	Short-term notes, excluding trade notes payable
Current maturities long-term debt	Portion of long-term debt due within one year
Accounts & notes payable	Trade accounts and notes payable
Accrued expenses	Accrued expenses including income taxes
All other current liabilities	Other current liabilities
Long-term debt	Senior debt including bonds, debentures, bank debt, mortgages, and deferred portions of long-term debt
All other noncurrent liabilities	Noncurrent liabilities including subordinated debt, deferred taxes, and liability reserves
Net worth	Total assets minus total liabilities

Income Statement	
Net sales	Gross sales, minus returns and discounts
Cost of sales	Cost of goods sold (includes depreciation)
Gross profit	Net sales, minus cost of sales
Operating expenses	Selling, general and administrative expenses including depreciation, excluding interest expense
Operating profit	Gross profit, minus operating expenses
All other expenses (net)	Miscellaneous other income and expenses (net) including interest expense, minus interest income and dividends received
Profit before taxes	Operating profit minus all other expenses (net)

Source: Derived from Robert Morris Associates, *Annual Statement Studies.*

EXHIBIT 6

Children's Toy Industry

Definition of Financial Ratios Used in the Industry Analysis

Ratio	Definition
Current ratio	Current assets/current liabilities
Quick ratio	(Cash & equivalents + accounts & notes receivable)/total current liabilities
Sales/receivables	Net sales/accounts & notes receivable
Cost of sales/inventory	Cost of sales/inventory
Sales/working capital	Net sales/net working capital
Interest coverage ratio	Earnings before interest & taxes/annual interest expense
Fixed assets/net worth	Net fixed assets/net worth
Leverage ratio	Total liabilities/net worth
Return on equity	(Profit before taxes/net worth) × 100
Return on assets	(Profit before taxes/total assets) × 100
Fixed asset turnover	Net sales/net fixed assets
Total asset turnover	Net sales/total assets
Percent depreciation, depletion & amortization to sales	(Depreciation + amortization + depletion) × 100/net sales

Source: Derived from Robert Morris Associates, *Annual Statement Studies.*

EXHIBIT 7

Children's Toy Industry

Industry Analysis
Games, Toys & Children's Vehicles
Financial Ratios

		For Sample Firms with Annual Reports Dated Between				
		6/76– 3/77	6/77– 3/78	6/78– 3/79	6/79– 3/80	6/80– 3/81
Current ratio	*High	12.8	10.4	11.9	10.9	10.3
	*Median	7.1	6.2	6.9	7.2	6.6
	*Low	4.8	5.1	5.0	4.3	4.7
Quick ratio	High	1.4	1.5	1.4	1.4	1.4
	Median	1.0	1.0	1.0	.8	.9
	Low	.6	.7	.6	.5	.6
Sales/receivables	High	12.8	10.4	11.9	10.9	10.3
	Median	7.1	6.2	6.9	7.2	6.6
	Low	4.8	5.1	5.0	4.3	4.7
Cost of sales/inventory	High	7.0	6.4	6.2	5.6	5.7
	Median	3.5	4.6	4.1	3.3	4.0
	Low	2.7	3.2	3.1	2.5	2.7
Sales/working capital	Low	4.3	4.5	4.2	4.2	4.0
	Median	7.4	6.0	6.2	6.7	6.2
	High	12.9	11.5	16.5	10.2	10.3
Interest coverage ratio	High	10.5	11.0	11.5	5.4	5.3
	Median	5.3	4.5	3.7	2.6	2.9
	Low	2.4	2.3	2.1	1.2	1.5
Fixed assets/net worth	Low	.2	.2	.2	.1	.3
	Median	.4	.4	.4	.4	.5
	High	.9	.8	.8	.9	.8
Leverage ratio	Low	.7	.7	.6	.6	.6
	Median	1.2	1.8	1.3	1.4	1.4
	High	2.7	3.3	2.7	3.1	3.7
Return on equity	High	41.9	38.9	39.0	41.0	38.3
	Median	31.7	26.5	19.7	21.4	23.3
	Low	12.5	15.4	10.7	3.0	6.2
Return on assets	High	20.3	19.2	14.8	13.6	15.9
	Median	11.8	10.6	9.6	8.6	9.7
	Low	4.3	4.7	5.0	.7	2.5

EXHIBIT 7 (Continued)

		For Sample Firms with Annual Reports Dated Between				
		6/76–3/77	6/77–3/78	6/78–3/79	6/79–3/80	6/80–3/81
Fixed asset turnover	High	26.3	42.1	31.7	40.0	21.6
	Median	10.7	12.2	15.6	13.8	9.1
	Low	6.4	7.7	6.4	6.8	6.4
Total asset turnover	High	2.7	2.7	2.9	2.6	2.5
	Median	2.0	2.2	2.1	2.0	1.9
	Low	1.4	1.7	1.7	1.5	1.3
Percent depreciation, depletion, & amorti- zation to sales	Low	.8	.7	.8	.7	1.0
	Median	1.4	1.4	1.3	1.4	1.9
	High	2.8	2.0	2.1	2.3	2.8

Source: Derived from Robert Morris Associates, *Annual Statement Studies*.
*Ratios were calculated for each company in the sample and rank ordered from the highest to lowest values. "High" represents the value ranked at the third quartile, "median" at the second quartile, and "low" at the first quartile. Of the 70 sample firms for the period 6/80 through 3/81, 8 were in the $50 to $100 million sales range.

EXHIBIT 8

Children's Toy Industry

Industry Analysis
Games, Toys, & Children's Vehicles
Common Size Analysis

	For Sample Firms with Annual Reports Dated Between				
	6/77– 3/77 (%)	6/77– 3/78 (%)	6/78– 3/79 (%)	6/79– 3/80 (%)	6/80– 3/81 (%)
Balance Sheet **(% of Total Assets)**					
Current Assets					
Cash & equivalents	5.7	6.3	7.4	7.2	9.5
Accounts receivable/notes receivable	29.1	35.7	31.3	30.2	28.5
Inventory	34.6	34.0	36.6	39.1	34.5
All other current assets	1.2	1.0	.9	1.1	2.2
Total Current Assets	70.7	76.9	76.2	77.6	74.7
Fixed assets (net)	19.8	18.1	18.1	17.0	19.3
Intangible assets (net)	2.6	1.7	.7	1.1	.5
All other noncurrent assets	6.9	3.3	5.0	4.3	5.6
Total Assets	100.0	100.0	100.0	100.0	100.0
Current Liabilities					
Notes payable	12.9	14.1	15.8	14.5	10.2
Current maturity—long-term debt	3.9	1.8	1.4	2.7	3.3
Accounts & notes payable—trade	15.0	18.4	14.5	15.7	15.1
Accrued expenses	6.2	5.5	6.7	5.7	7.8
All other current liabilities	2.6	3.1	3.7	4.5	5.0
Total Current Liabilities	40.6	42.9	42.2	43.0	41.5
Long-term debt	13.8	12.2	11.7	12.8	13.5
All other noncurrent liabilities	2.0	2.7	2.0	.9	1.4
Net worth	43.6	42.2	44.1	43.2	43.6
Total liabilities & owners' equity	100.0	100.0	100.0	100.0	100.0
Income Statement **(% of Net Sales)**					
Net sales	100.0	100.0	100.0	100.0	100.0
Cost of sales	67.1	69.1	69.8	69.2	69.0
Gross profit	32.9	30.9	30.2	30.8	31.0
Operating expenses	24.7	24.5	24.0	24.6	25.0
Operating profit	8.2	6.4	6.2	6.2	5.9
All other expenses (net)	2.1	1.0	1.2	2.3	2.3
Profit before taxes	6.1	5.4	4.9	3.8	3.7

Source: Derived from Robert Morris Associates, *Annual Statement Studies.*
*Percentages represent average values for the sample firms. Of the 70 sample firms for the period 6/80 through 3/81, 8 were in the $50 to $100 million sales range. Totals may be subject to slight rounding errors.

CASE 2

The Martin Luther Home

The Martin Luther Home (the Home), a division of Lutheran Community Services, Inc. (LCS), was planning to build a new nursing home and retirement center. The Home operated a 139-bed nursing facility in Spokane on a five-year lease ending on July 31, 1978. During the period 1938 to 1973, the Home had operated 20 cottages and a 39-bed nursing care center in Greenacres, a suburb of Spokane. Its former three-story building in Greenacres could not economically be brought up to new state health care standards, so the Home sold its nursing home and cottages to East Valley Hospital (another LCS division) in 1973. The Home's Board of Governors since that time had been planning to build a new facility which would serve the total Spokane County community; the board viewed its goal to be to minister to all elderly people—not just those of the Lutheran faith.

Though the members of the board of governors believed their program to be ambitious, they were convinced the Lutheran community could be called upon to provide the necessary assistance and financial contribution to get the new nursing home built. After that, all services would have to be self-sustaining. The Home had a strong financial position. Its financial and operating statements for recent years are presented in Exhibits 1 through 5.

Jim Odin, president of the Home's Board of Governors, called a special meeting of the board's executive committee for Monday, November 24, 1975. His agenda stated that the committee should be prepared to discuss all facets of the proposed nursing and retirement center. Specifically, the committee would help decide what information should be included in two reports to be presented in early December. These reports were (1)

This case was prepared by and used with the permission of professor Kenneth W. Cubbage of Pacific Lutheran University.

an application for Certificate of Need (CN), which the State Department of Social and Health Services (DSHS) required for all organizations wanting to construct new nursing care facilities that would also serve public assistance residents, and (2) a report by Ken Christensen to the quarterly meeting of the Board of Trustees of LCS.

BACKGROUND OF THE ORGANIZATION

Lutheran Community Services, Inc., provided various social services to the people of Spokane, Washington, and its environs since 1922. It was originally incorporated as Lutheran Welfare Society (LWS) and offered counseling and related social services. LWS moved into care for the elderly in 1938. In 1957 it combined two small, failing hospitals to form East Valley Hospital in Greenacres. Shortly after, LWS raised approximately $350,000 through its 34 Lutheran congregation constituency to pay off the debts of the former hospitals.

The three divisions of LWS (the service center, the Home, and the hospital) provided quality services through the years—each developed unique areas of service. Only the service center was not self-sustaining. Some of its support had come from the community's United Way fund drive, and it had also received contributions from Lutheran churches and individuals to meet its budget.

In the early 1970s LWS changed its name to Lutheran Community Services and shortly thereafter brought in three young administrators to head its operations. Bob Gubbrud was elected executive director of LCS and director of the service center. He was a pastor and had

seven years' experience in social work in Minneapolis and Chicago. Dave Hammer was chosen to administer the hospital. In January 1974 Don Crippen was chosen to direct the Lutheran Home which had just recently moved from Greenacres to Spokane. Don had five years' experience in directing homes for the elderly: two as administrator of a 120-bed home in Yakima, Washington, and three years as a regional director of several homes operated by the Good Samaritan Society of Sioux Falls, South Dakota.

ACTIONS LEADING TO THE PRESENT DECISION SITUATION

The Board of Governors of the Home selected a local architect in August 1973 to design a new cottage and nursing home complex. Preliminary sketches were drawn, but the board could not find suitable land. The architect apparently did not have the expertise to design nursing homes, so the board dropped these plans, which cost $4600, in January 1974.

At the February 1974 annual meeting of LCS, the elected delegates of LCS's 34 member churches selected 11 new trustees to serve on its 27-person board of trustees. These trustees also served on the board of governors of one of the three divisions. The division to which a trustee would be assigned depended upon the expertise each trustee had and the needs of the individual boards. This was particularly true for CPAs, attorneys, and business executives.

At the February meeting of the Home board, new officers were elected, and a long-range planning committee (LRPC) was selected. The goal of the LRPC was to program, within a time sequence, the steps the Home board must take to ensure that a new facility was available when the lease expired in July 1978.

The LRPC was not only to state what steps should be taken and by what date but also to coordinate all activities. It was to report all its activities to the entire board and define the situations so that the board could review and act upon all steps programmed in the long-range plan. In summary the long-range plan was to

1. Select an architect by October 1974.

2. Select, with the architect's help, and sign an option on a prime building site by April 1975.

3. After securing the site promptly apply for a Certificate of Need from the state (it takes about 120 days to get state approval).

4. Seek financing for the program, considering all possible sources: April through August 1975.

5. Select, if necessary, a fund organizer by September 1975 to generate a fund drive for the new nursing home.

6. Select contractors to build the nursing home-apartment complex, after the architect has drawn the appropriate plans. This should be done by July 1976.

7. Start construction on the retirement living units (cottages and/or apartments) by September 1976.

8. Start construction on the nursing home by May 1977 (the state generally allows two years for an organization to start building after receiving a Certificate of Need).

9. Ready nursing home for occupancy by May 1978. Allow three months to move in the present 139 residents, plus fill any additional beds the home may be granted in its Certificate of Need.

By late November 1975, the LRPC had accomplished two goals: selected an architect and taken an option on a desirable piece of land. The committee also had looked into several alternative sources of financing in the private and governmental sectors. The LRPC wrote to more than 20 architectural firms asking for interest on the Home project and for documentation of each firm's experience in building health care facilities. Three firms were asked to make presentations before the board of governors. In October 1974 the board selected Rich Ditterman of Seattle. He had designed over 150 facilities similar to the nursing home being planned. He was selected not only for his experience in the field but also because he held a philosophy of care similar to that of the board members and was a small operator. That is, he would be the architect responsible for all phases of planning, drawing, and supervising the project.

The architect's job was to be done in two phases. Phase I was to help select the building site and to make drawings required for the state's application of Certificate of Need. Phase II was to make drawings for the city of Spokane regarding zoning and schematics for the state health planners. In Phase II he was also responsible for producing working drawings and for coordinating construction. His fees would be $20,625 for Phase I and, if Phase II were undertaken, his fee would be 6 percent of the land development, construction, equipment and furnishing costs for the retirement center.

The members of the LRPC and the architect established the criteria for site selection. The board of governors concurred. After four months of searching through more than 50 sites, the LRPC and architect found 21 acres of land in a transition area between apartments and single-family dwellings. The latter were built around a nine-hole golf course. After five months of bargaining a 180-day option was signed in October 1975. The purchase price was $400,000 plus commission, which was negotiated at $15,000. Terms were $40,000 down ($20,000 over the option price), $60,000 one year after closing, and $100,000 each year for three years. Interest was to be paid monthly, 6 percent for the first two years and 10 percent thereafter.

Tentatively, the LRPC had recommended that the Home consider conventional financing through a savings and loan association or consortium of S & Ls. Terms would probably be 9½ to 9¾ percent interest and 25 years to maturity, with about a 20 percent down payment. The architect and members of the LRPC had visited many newly constructed nursing homes. All these owners recommended avoiding the time and "red tape" involved in all government financing. They agreed to the person, that any interest saved by government financing would be more than offset by deferred, and therefore higher, construction costs. Having received a favorable response on possible financing from Spokane's largest savings and loan association, the LRPC felt comfortable with its recommendation to the board.

THE EXECUTIVE COMMITTEE MEETING

Jim Odin called the meeting to order promptly at seven o'clock. Those attending the meeting were

1. Werner Wulf: vice-president and a practicing attorney
2. Al Fruehauf: treasurer and a staff auditor for DSHS
3. Bill Wahl: secretary and a junior high principal
4. Ken Christensen: chairman of LRPC and a CPA
5. Don Crippen: administrator of the Home
6. Rich Ditterman: architect

Jim made introductory comments, then explained his agenda and why the Home needed immediate action. He stated, "We need enough new beds to care for our present 139 residents when we leave this leased building. Also, we have to have additional beds to operate as an efficient unit and to provide the types of service we plan in our 'total-care'[1] concept. In short, we need to state our program clearly and prove that it is financially feasible—to the State and to our Board of Trustees. I believe that we can readily get the approval of the Trustees. However, the State is something else. What comments do you have on how we should approach the State DSHS?"

The administrator stated, "I have been drafting and re-drafting the narra-

---

[1] "Total care" is a program by which the elderly can, within one care facility, move from independent living in apartments through several steps of care to skilled care. The purpose is to minimize elderly persons' uncertainties and anxieties concerning their own care.

tive portions of the Certificate of Need since October. County and regional health planners have helped me tremendously. And I believe we have documented our current care capabilities well. Also, the health planners say we should plug our concept of 'total care' to the hilt—which I have done. What I need now is the number of beds we plan to apply for. From that we can determine financial feasibility."

"The number of beds you seek," responded the architect, "must be based on how you plan to develop the land. Over the past 3 or 4 months, the LRPC and I have discussed how we could best do this. As you know all the land is zoned for multiple-dwelling housing. Preliminary plans of the former owner, approved by the city, called for 265 apartments. Because of the nature of our nursing home and apartments, I believe the zoning code will allow us not only 300 nursing care beds but also well over 200 units of apartments, townhouses, and/or cottages. And of course, we must, and will, have about 35 percent of the acreage for open space."

"You aren't suggesting that we apply for 300 beds now are you?" asked Al Fruehauf, the treasurer. "Personally I can see nothing but trouble ahead for the whole project. Though I'm just new at DSHS, I know that the executive director of DSHS wants to slow the movement of the elderly to care institutions. That's in line with his personal philosophy. Also, the State cannot afford to support all the elderly who quickly use up their personal savings and soon become, in effect, wards of the State. Social security and pensions of these folks just don't go far toward nursing care bills. In addition, our (that is DSHS) view is that Spokane

County needs only about 50 more beds. You can ask for all you want, but you won't get 50 in my opinion."

The architect responded to the treasurer's remarks noting that he too had been aware of the DSHS' view on certifying new beds. In fact, he had helped several clients in filing their CN applications—not always getting what the client wanted. On at least one occasion a 90-bed request in Everett, Washington, was denied completely.

Jim Odin asked of the architect, "What number of beds do you believe we should ask for?" The response to this was that the nursing home be built in increments of 60 beds. That was the way staffing resident care was administered most efficiently. The administrator concurred with this based on his experience with the many-sized homes within the Good Samaritan Society.

The Home's apparent need to serve its current 139 residents and meet some of the backlog of its 84-person waiting list were the major factors in the committee's decision to seek either 180 or 240 beds. Realistically, the Home could expect to get no more than 180 beds. However, at the suggestion of the LRPC chairman, the committee agreed to ask for 210 beds in its application. This, it was thought, would permit the regulators to disallow some beds, and at the same time allow the Home what it needed to provide its program. However, the politics of the situation should be subordinated to the economics of getting an efficient-sized operation to begin with. All the executives were concerned with breaking even, particularly since the new home appeared to have substantially higher fixed plant costs.

At this point Jim Odin asked the architect what the cost of the facility might be if it was built for 180 and/or 210 beds. Preliminary figures, which the architect believed would meet the CN application needs, were

1. Construction costs would be $8200 a bed if 210 beds were planned.
2. Construction costs would be $9000 a bed if 180 beds were planned.
3. $1000 per bed for drapery, furniture, and so forth.
4. Laundry and kitchen equipment would cost $50,000.
5. Land improvements, $100,000.

Conservative estimates of depreciation were 3¹/₃ percent on the building, 10 percent on furnishings and equipment, and 5 percent on land improvements.

"Well, Don," concluded the president, "What else do we need to agree on to provide realistic data for determining financial feasibility?" The administrator (with the architect agreeing on manpower needs) said that he would draw up expenses based on new building and equipment costs, unit costs in the most recent operating statement (see Exhibit 6), and the following assumptions:

1. For a 180-bed operation he could get along with his present manpower.
2. A 210-bed facility would require more help:

   1 LPN at $3.50 per hour (rate paid in past fiscal year)

   2 aides at $2.30 per hour (rate paid in past fiscal year)
3. Under any circumstances he would need:

   An assistant administrator—$12,000 per year

An Accountant—$10,800 per year

4. Most operating expenses other than salaries and salary-related expenses would vary with bed-count.
5. Property and interest expenses were related to total cost of building, equipment, and the 80 percent loan the Home would need to finance the project. Insurance expense was based on property valued at $1 million.
6. All salaries and wages would increase 5 percent except for the new administrator and accountant.
7. In the new facility the Home expected 50 percent private-pay residents and 50 percent Medicaid (state paid).
8. As of September 1, 1975, the private-pay resident daily fee would average $21.50, and the Medicaid cost reimbursement would be approximately $16.50 per day.
9. The occupancy averages would be:

   First year: 90 percent

   Second year: 95 percent

   Future years: 97 percent
10. One-half the cost of land and land improvements would apply to the nursing home. The land contract would be paid off in 1977 and incorporated in the financing plan.
11. None of the costs or expenses would relate to the retirement apartments-cottages.

Ken Christensen added, "At least two more points need to be considered. First, we must consider the working capital position we will need to carry our expanded operations. We will use our presently idle temporary investments to help finance the new nursing home; however, some of this will be tied up in working capital. Cash in bank cannot be less than $45,000, in my opinion. We asked out 55 private-pay residents to pay a month in advance, but they have not all done so. I believe we will have to tighten our controls. Conservatively, lets plan a pro-rata increase in private-pay receivables. State reimbursement for Medicaid is slow, and getting slower. We should plan on carrying all State reimbursement residents for a full month. Other current assets and liabilities should vary with resident count. The exceptions being the liability to the State which we believe will be settled in our favor and the current portion of our new debt on land and buildings. Wages pay-

able and related accounts should not vary much.

"Second, we should realize that these pro forma statements will give us an idea of the amount of money we'll have to raise through a fund drive. I have discussed this with other members of the LRPC, and it appears that we may have to raise $150,000 more than LCS raised in 1957 to put the East Valley Hospital on a firm financial footing."

The DSHS will want a pro forma income statement for the first full year of operation and a balance sheet at start-up time. After the meeting Ken Christensen, Rich Ditterman and Don Crippen started preliminary work on the report to the DSHS.

EXHIBIT 1

The Martin Luther Home

Unrestricted Fund
Balance Sheet
December 31, 1974

Assets		Claims	
Current assets		*Current liabilities*	
Cash in bank	$ 4,252	Accounts payable	$ 17,428
Temporary investments	212,544	Salaries & wages payable	17,953
Accounts receivable—residents	8,521	Cost settlement payable—state	13,000
Accounts receivable—state	31,366	Current portion—long-term debt	9,310
Inventories	12,270		$ 57,691
Prepaid items	14,452		
	$283,405		
Other assets			
Real estate contract receivable	13,365	Long-term debt	29,680
Prepaid lease payments	89,583		
	$102,948	Fund balance	308,289
Plant and equipment			
Equipment	$ 8,170		
Leasehold improvements	1,397		
Less: accum. depreciation	260		
	$ 9,307		
Total assets	$395,660	Total claims	$395,660

EXHIBIT 2

The Martin Luther Home

Statement of Revenues and Expenses
Year ended December 31, 1974

Revenues		
Basic services to residents		$750,693
Other professional services		15,780
Interest earned		20,971
Donations		16,850
Other		4,391
	Total revenues	$808,685
Expenses		
Nursing services-resident care		$296,859
Dietary		145,184
Housekeeping-laundry		50,691
Plant operations, including utilities		33,974
Administration		54,789
Employee benefits and payroll taxes		48,612
Business operating taxes		14,975
Property rental		138,155
Insurance		2,535
Depreciation		260
Bad debts		2,980
Interest		6,557
	Total expenses	$795,571
Excess of revenues over expenses		$ 13,114

EXHIBIT 3

The Martin Luther Home

Balance Sheet
Unrestricted Fund
September 30, 1975

Assets		Claims	
Current assets		*Current liabilities*	
Cash in bank	$ 29,055	Accounts payable	$ 17,515
Temporary investments	222,366	Salaries & wages payable	44,329
Accounts receivable—residents	16,357	Cost settlement payable—state	13,000
Accounts receivable—state	26,480	Current portion—long-term debt	9,974
Inventories	11,075		$ 84,818
Prepaid items	14,452		
	$319,785		
Other assets			
Real estate contract receivable	$ 10,221	Long-term debt	22,096
Prepaid lease payments	70,833		
	$ 81,054		
Plant and equipment		Fund balance	323,792
Equipment	$ 18,474		
Leasehold improvements	1,397		
Less: accum. depreciation	2,004		
	17,867		
Deferred architect fees	12,000		
	$ 29,867		
Total assets	$430,706	Total claims	$430,706

23

EXHIBIT 4

The Martin Luther Home

Statement of Revenues and Expenses
Nine months ended September 30, 1975

Revenues		
Basic services to residents		$635,930
Other professional services		8,861
Interest earned		11,813
Donations		1,863
Refund of taxes paid in prior year		3,858
Other		3,966
	Total revenues	$666,291
Expenses		
Nursing services-resident care		$252,684
Dietary		116,386
Housekeeping-laundry		46,735
Plant operations, including utilities		34,929
Administration		44,132
Employee benefits and payroll taxes		43,472
Business operating taxes		1,142
Property rental		103,616
Insurance		1,936
Depreciation		1,743
Bad debts		483
Interest		2,423
	Total expenses	$649,681
Excess of revenues over expenses		$ 16,610

EXHIBIT 5

The Martin Luther Home

Statement of Changes in Financial Position
Unrestricted Fund

	Nine months ended 9/30/75	Year ended 12/31/74
Funds provided		
Excess of revenues over expenses	$16,610	$13,114
Add items not requiring funds:		
Depreciation expense	1,743	260
Amortization of prepaid lease	18,750	25,000
Total from operation	$37,103	$38,374
Collection on contracts	3,144	3,945
Fund balance transfers	1,107	2,100
Total funds provided	$41,354	$44,419
Funds applied		
Additions to equipment, etc.	$10,304	$ 9,566
Payments of long-term debt	7,583	6,248
Payments for architect's fees	12,000	
Other	2,214	3,339
Total funds applied	$32,101	$19,153
Increase in net working capital	$ 9,253	$25,266

EXHIBIT 6

The Martin Luther Home

Per Day—Revenues and Expenses
Nine months ended September 30, 1975

		Year-to-date	Per day per unit
Resident days		36,378	
Revenues			
Nursing service			
Self-pay residents		$251,945	$ 20.917
Medicaid—Class I (state paid)		383,985	15.761
	Subtotal	$635,930	$ 17.481
Other professional services		8,861	.244
Interest earned		11,813	.325
Donations		1,863	.051
Other		7,824	.215
	Total	$666,291	$ 18.316
Expenses			
Nursing services			
Salaries			
Nursing supervisor		$ 8,487	$ .233
R.N.s		24,913	.685
L.P.N.s		63,516	1.746
Aides & orderlies		112,885	3.103
Supplies and services		13,478	.370
Medical director and medical records		4,796	.280*
Therapy, chaplaincy, etc.		24,609	.676
	Total	$252,684	$ 7.093
Dietary			
Salaries		44,570	1.225
Food		63,177	1.737
Repairs & misc.		8,639	.237
	Total	$116,386	$ 3.199
Laundry/housekeeping			
Salary—supervisor		4,857	.134
Salaries—helpers		31,722	.872
Supplies, etc.		10,156	.279
	Total	$ 46,735	$ 1.285
Plant operation			
Salaries		$ 10,610	$ .291
Electricity including heat		11,368	.311
Water, sewer, and garbage		3,174	.087
Repairs and supplies		5,180	.142
Other		4,597	.126
	Total	$ 34,929	$ .957

EXHIBIT 6 (Continued)

	Year-to-date	Per day per unit
Administration		
Salary of administrator	$ 13,573	$ .373
Salaries—admin. personnel	13,385	.367
Communications	2,020	.056
Professional services	4,210	.116
Dues and licenses	4,140	.114
Supplies	1,300	.036
Travel	1,000	.027
Other	4,504	.124
Total	$ 44,132	$ 1.213
Employee benefits and payroll taxes	$ 43,472	$ 1.195
Property rental	103,616	2.848
Other	7,727	.212
Total expenses	$649,681	$ 18.002

*Medical director added September 1, 1975. Unit cost reflects proper per day care cost for this service.

CASE 3

Harris Paper and Wood Products Company (A)

Harris Paper and Wood Products Company was founded in the early 1900s and throughout the company's history had concentrated its efforts within its primary line of business—the manufacture and sale of paper and wood products. As of late 1979 the company's primary facilities consisted of a number of manufacturing plants in the Pacific Northwest and distributorships in the western states. Most of these facilities had been developed by the company itself; acquisitions via merger or purchase from other companies had been rare.

The firm was divided into two divisions based on the type of product manufactured, the Lumber and Plywood Division and the Paper Production Division. About one-half of the company's total sales came from the Lumber and Plywood Division. Its products were made mostly from purchased timber.

The remaining one-half of the company's sales came from the Paper Production Division. Its products were used in packaging applications (the firm did not produce writing-grade paper). Both boxboard and containerboard, the two primary types of paper products, were produced by this division. Boxboard is a light, strong cardboard used in cereal boxes, detergent containers, milk cartons, and similar applications. Containerboard is commonly called "corrugated cardboard" and consists of a zigzag layer of paper glued between two paper sheets. Containerboard is used in shipping containers, heavy appliance boxes, and so forth. The company both processed and produced these paper products

This case was prepared by and used with the permission of Professor Frederick C. Scherr, West Virginia University.

from raw materials, then manufactured the final containers. A portion of the boxboard and containerboard produced by the company was sold to other box manufacturers.

Sales for the two divisions tended to fluctuate with certain sectors of the economy. Sales of the Lumber and Plywood Division were primarily related to housing starts, while those of the Paper Products Division were more closely tied to retail sales.

The manufacturing facilities operated by the company's two divisions were much varied in age and efficiency. Some facilities were new and cost-effective to operate, while others were old and expensive. The company followed a policy of closing down the older and less efficient production lines when sales were down and demand was slack. These lines would be reopened during better economic times. This strategy gave the company considerable flexibility in its production capacity and enabled reduction of certain overheads during recessionary periods.

All this was well known to Jack Arnold, treasurer and financial vice-president of Harris Paper and Wood Products. When he had joined Harris Paper and Wood Products two years previously, he had made an analysis of the company's potential growth and stability of sales and earnings. On the basis of these and other financial factors, Mr. Arnold decided that the company's capital position was not where he wanted it. The company's total debt to total assets ratio was 0.685, which he felt was too highly levered (see Exhibits 1 and 2 for the company's financial statements for fiscal years 1977 through 1979).

In an effort to correct the situation Mr. Arnold had tried to route a substantial portion of cash flow to reduce the company's debt (cash flows from profits had been high recently). As of December 31, 1979, the Harris Paper and Wood Products had two long-term debt issues outstanding. The first was a $20-million issue of 6-percent interest mortgage bonds; the principal would be due in 1999, and interest payments were to be made quarterly. The other issue consisted of 20-year debentures carrying an interest rate of 7½ percent; this interest was also to be paid quarterly. These debentures had been issued five years previously and had a provision in their indenture that 5 percent of the original issue was to be bought up on the open market each year by the firm. Such a provision would be advantageous to the investor because the buying activity would support the price of the issue. These securities normally traded around par. Mr. Arnold planned to continue this buy-up and, in addition, call 5 percent of the mortgage bonds, which would entail paying a 2-percent call premium. Neither issue had any unamortized flotation costs on the books. Also, he planned to pay the preferred stock dividend of $1.00 per share per quarter but to hold the common dividend to $.50 per share per quarter to conserve cash.

One consequence of the company's high financial leverage was that its short-term bank credit line contained some restrictive provisions and carried a relatively high annual interest rate of 12 percent. Interest on this line was calculated monthly and was based on the end-of-month credit line balance; this interest was due at the beginning of the following month. One of the more restrictive provisions of the credit line required the company to maintain an end-of-quarter current ratio of over 1.5 to 1.

Also, maximum borrowings on the line were restricted to $17.5 million. Finally, the firm was to be out of debt on the credit line for 60 consecutive days each year (provisions of this type on such credit lines are common and are designed to show that the line of credit represents seasonal, short-term debt and not permanent capitalization). Mr. Arnold was quite worried that the firm might violate provisions of the credit line agreement during the 1980 fiscal year. The firm had violated some of the provisions in fiscal 1979, but the bank had agreed to waive these provisions for that year, provided that violations did not occur in 1980.

In examining other expected revenues and expenses for 1980, Mr. Arnold found that he was able to estimate these in the short term by using several techniques. From the marketing department he found that expected sales for the year were about $150 million. However, because of the seasonality in industries served by the firm, these sales were not expected to occur evenly throughout the year. The marketing department made the following estimates of monthly sales:

Month	Net Sales (thousands)	Month	Net Sales (thousands)
1/80	10,000	7/80	16,000
2/80	10,000	8/80	15,000
3/80	10,500	9/80	13,500
4/80	12,000	10/80	12,000
5/80	15,000	11/80	10,000
6/80	16,000	12/80	10,000

From the cost-accounting and purchasing departments, he found that direct labor and direct overhead were about 20 percent of the cost of goods sold, the remainder being raw material costs. Direct labor and overhead were payable in the month incurred, while raw materials were sold to the firm on net 30-day terms. Examination of labor contracts and projections of costs for raw materials and direct overheads enabled Mr. Arnold to estimate that total cost of goods sold would rise to about 72 percent of net sales. All components of cost of goods sold were directly variable with sales. Based on talks with several other departments, he guessed that administrative and general expenses for the fiscal year were to increase at the same compounded growth rate as they had over the last two fiscal years. These expenses were primarily fixed charges for leases and management salaries. These were payable in the month incurred, and their increase was scheduled to occur in January, after which these costs would remain almost constant for the remainder of the year. The accounting department advised that depreciation for the fiscal year 1980 would be $1,020,000. A check with the tax department disclosed that federal income taxes would be 48 percent and state and local income taxes 3 percent of income before taxes. These would be paid in equal quarterly installments based on profit estimates for the year.

Mr. Arnold's discussion with the credit manager of Harris had been most helpful. Mr. Arnold had learned that most of the firm's sales were net 30-day terms, but some slowness in payments generally occurred. As a result of this, 60 percent of sales for a month were collected within the following month, 30 percent in the second month following, and the remaining 10 percent in the third month following. Further, the credit manager advised that he had made projections regarding the collection of the $12,013,000 in receivables on the books as of December 31, 1979. These projections indicated that $8.5 million would be collected in January of 1980, $2.5 million in February, and $1,013,000 in March.

A check with the inventory control manager revealed that inventory levels would be about the same in 1980 as at year-end 1979. Cash, prepaid expenses, accruals, other assests, other current liabilities, and deferred expenses would be constant throughout 1980 at year-end 1979 levels. The company's capital budget projected spending of $2.4 million on fixed assets in 1980, these expenses to occur evenly throughout the year. Initially, the interest on the bank credit line was estimated at $2 million for the year for the purpose of computing the quarterly tax payments. Mr. Arnold did not plan to do any stock financing in 1980. Besides being concerned about the firm's credit line agreement, he wanted to check that the flows of funds within the firm were in line with his objective of reducing the firm's debt.

EXHIBIT 1

Harris Paper and Wood Products Company (A)

Balance Sheet for Fiscal Years Ending 12/31/77–12/31/79
(rounded thousands of dollars, ordered in the analyst's method)

	1977	1978	1979
Assets			
Cash	$ 1,561	$ 1,732	$ 1,680
Accounts receivable	10,623	10,971	12,013
Inventories	27,321	28,902	29,345
Prepaid expenses	5,765	6,024	6,244
Total current assets	45,270	47,629	49,282
Other assets	4,806	4,532	5,011
Gross fixed assets	113,693	115,912	118,230
Less accumulated depreciation	48,162	49,125	50,108
Net fixed assets	65,531	66,787	68,122
Total assets	115,607	118,948	122,415
Liabilities & owners' equity			
Accrued interest on bank credit line	90	91	96
Principal income on bank credit line	8,972	9,056	9,600
Accounts payable—material	8,754	9,023	9,480
Accruals	4,448	4,121	2,915
Preferred stock dividends payable	30	30	30
Other current liabilities	341	359	280
Total current liabilities	22,635	22,680	22,401
Deferred expenses	2,541	3,022	2,930
Long-term debt	54,000	52,000	50,000
Preferred stock (30,000 shares)	3,000	3,000	3,000
Common equity (52,000 shares)	33,431	38,246	44,084
Owners' equity	36,431	41,246	47,084
Total liabilities & owners' equity	$115,607	$118,948	$122,415

EXHIBIT 2

Harris Paper and Wood Products Company (A)

*Statements of Income and Retained Earnings for
Fiscal Years Ending 12/31/77–12/31/79
(rounded thousands of dollars, ordered in the analyst's method)*

	1977	1978	1979
Net sales	$125,208	$132,721	$140,684
Cost of goods sold	91,989	92,801	98,903
Gross margin on sales	33,219	39,920	41,781
Administrative and general expense	21,167	22,437	23,783
Depreciation	925	963	983
Interest expense	6,405	6,257	4,644
Net other income or (expenses)	0	0	0
Income before tax	4,722	10,263	12,371
Federal income tax	2,267	4,926	5,938
State and local income tax	141	308	371
Earnings after tax	2,314	5,029	6,062
Common and preferred stock dividend	203	214	224
Increase (or decrease) in retained earnings	2,111	4,815	5,838
Retained earnings, beginning of year	34,320	36,431	41,246
Retained earnings, end of year	$ 36,431	$ 41,246	$ 47,084

CASE 4

Contemporary Furniture

As owner and general manager of "Contemporary Furniture," Robert Gruenwald was proud that opening his third retail outlet was accomplished in late October 1977 for only $11,000 cash. This amount included all deposits, furnishings, and inventory. This third store was in a shopping center in Grandview, a suburb of Kansas City, Missouri. The other two stores were in Kansas City, Kansas, and in Merriam, Kansas. Since most purchasers of the chrome furniture and furnishings products come from younger, affluent buyers, per capita income for the areas surrounding the various stores would be important. Exhibit 1 shows per capita income for various areas in the Kansas City Metropolitan Area.

"Contemporary Furniture" manufactures and retails chrome furniture in addition to selling furnishings purchased from other suppliers. The manufacturing and storage areas for items not on retail display are located in an 1800 square foot facility in an industrial area of Kansas City, Kansas. Manufacturing involves sizing, cutting, and assembling parts into finished products. Certain components are purchased ready-to-assemble, such as molded plastic or leather seats. Other parts are produced from standard-sized chrome or plastic bars. Most significant furniture pieces are delivered to customers where glass components, if any, are put in place. Normal manufacturing time runs 2 to 3 hours for a $300 standard-design table and somewhat longer for customer-designed furniture. The flexibility of modern chrome furniture permits the customer to design pieces for specific locations, functions, and so forth.

Operating results had been erratic

This case was prepared by and used with the permission of Professor Brian Belt of the University of Missouri-Kansas City and Professor Frank Keller of the University of Houston at Clear Lake City.

since the business opened in March 1974. Profits ranged from $5,000 (1976) down to large losses in 1977. Gruenwald believed that the new outlet would produce sales equal to the other two outlets in a very short period of time. Because the costs of the manufacturing facility as well as the general and administrative expenses were fixed, Gruenwald felt the additional sales would help solve the recent profit problems. Since the new store was opened in the first week of November 1977, the store should be able to participate in the heavy Christmas sales period. Exhibit 2 shows sales per store for "Contemporary Furniture" since inception. Monthly sales adjustment (MSA) values are shown to indicate the seasonal nature of sales.

Mr. Gruenwald believed that sales would be 50 percent higher in 1978 than in 1977 due primarily to the new store opening. He felt that in November and December 1977 sales would be about $51 –52,000 now that the new store was open. Gruenwald had learned of a technique called the "Percent of Sales" forecast that would help to project how much surplus would be generated for the next year. He had heard of this technique at a recent seminar for small business owners but had never attempted to use it. Exhibit 3 provides balance sheet items for the most recent period available as well as the previous two fiscal years, which end March 31; these balance sheet items can be expected to vary rather directly with sales levels. He also had heard about the use of sensitivity analysis where forecasts were made for (a) an optimistic, (b) pessimistic, and (c) average expected level of sales.

Gruenwald felt the need for some type of cash budget to indicate when the projected surpluses would be available. Mr. Gruenwald had negotiated a $55,000 note payable with Kansas City Metropolitan State Bank; the 180-day note was to mature on April 19, 1978, and Gruenwald wanted to be sure he could repay the obligation or renegotiate on a timely basis. Further, Gruenwald wanted to open a fourth "Contemporary Furniture" retail outlet in either Raytown, Missouri, or North Kansas City as soon as $15,000 was available after paying off the KC Metropolitan State Bank note. Due to the need for beginning lease negotiations as soon as possible, Gruenwald needed to know when the cash would be available.

Although the regression equation indicated a 1978 average sales-per-store of $11,400, the owner felt safer with an $11,000 average sales-per-store for calendar year 1978. For example, before applying the seasonal adjustment factor, the monthly average sales at each store were assumed to be the same and constant at $16,000. Exhibit 4 illustrates income statement accounts for the last 2½ fiscal years. Purchased goods represented essentially the cost of goods sold (COGS) and were ordered, on average, approximately one month in advance of sales and were paid two months after the purchase order. All other expenses were paid in the month of the sale. Seasonal sale factors are shown in Exhibit 1. Sales in December 1977 were expected to be $35,000 for the company. Essentially all sales were cash or credit card sales that were converted into cash within a few days.

EXHIBIT 2

Contemporary Furniture

Sales Per Store Since Inception

| | Sales per Store ($)* | | | | Monthly |
	1974	1975	1976	1977	Sales Adjustment**
Jan.	—	3,000	5,500	7,800	.75
Feb.	—	1,600	6,500	9,300	.76
Mar.	—	1,600	7,000	9,200	.76
Apr.	3,800	9,400	9,000	8,700	1.19
May	6,000	3,500	10,100	8,800	1.07
June	7,400	1,800	8,500	7,500	.97
July	4,800	7,000	8,600	10,300	1.10
Aug.	4,800	5,500	11,000	11,400	1.12
Sep.	6,400	8,500	7,700	8,700	1.13
Oct.	3,000	9,900	7,700	7,900	.96
Nov.	3,800	8,400	12,500		1.05
Dec.	3,800	9,400	12,500		1.14

Regression equation:**

$$Y = 143X + 3970$$

where: Y = monthly sales per store for any month since 3/74

X = number of months since 3/74

*Store 1 opened March, 1974; Store 2 opened May, 1975; and Store 3 opened Nov., 1977.
**Monthly Sales Adjustment (MSA) is value to multiply regression-calculated monthly sales value to obtain estimated monthly sales.

EXHIBIT 1

Contemporary Furniture

Kansas City Metropolitan Area: Population and per Capita Income by County and Selected Cities

Area	1975 Population	1974 Per Capita Income ($)
Kansas City metropolitan area	1,278,400	5,073
Leavenworth County (KS)	55,400	4,134
Johnson County (KS)	238,300	6,639
Leawood	11,400	9,844
Prairie Village	26,600	7,525
Overland Park	81,000	6,759
Merriam	11,500	6,143
Shawnee	22,700	5,376
Wyandotte County (KS)	177,600	4,221
Kansas City, Kansas	168,200	4,220
Jackson County (MO)	634,600	4,816
Raytown	33,000	5,914
Independence	111,500	4,970
Grandview	22,200	5,051
Kansas City, Missouri (part)	403,200	4,666
Clay County (MO)	133,200	4,958
North Kansas City	5,000	5,968
Kansas City, Missouri (part)	56,600	4,921
Liberty	15,000	4,738
Platte County (MO)	39,300	5,297

EXHIBIT 3

Contemporary Furniture

Selected Balance Sheet Accounts

	9/30/77	% of Sales	3/31/77	% of Sales	3/31/76	% of Sales
Assets						
Cash & Savings Acct.	$ 3,152	1.39	$ 3,547	1.54	$ 3,333	2.11
Accts. Rec.*	29,866	13.15	9,348	4.06	8,000	5.06
Inventory	14,964	6.59	23,538	10.22	20,637	13.06
Liabilities						
Accts. Payable	24,256	10.68	14,154	6.15	8,959	5.67
Accruals	2,338	1.03	2,550	1.11	2,416	1.53
Annualized Sales	227,102		230,314		157,998	
Profit Margin						
(Profit/Sales)		−14.77%		−1.25%		+2.98%

*A/R include "Layaway on Order" but exclude "Due From Officers."

EXHIBIT 4

Contemporary Furniture

*Income Statements for Fiscal Years
Ending in 1976, 1977, and First Half of
Fiscal Year to Be Ended in 1978*

	Fiscal Period Ending:		
	Mar. 31, 1976 (12 months)	Mar. 31, 1977 (12 months)	Sept. 30, 1977 (6 months)
Sales	$157,998	$230,314	$113,551
Cost of goods sold (including freight)	85,999	130,122	64,751
Delivery	1,510	2,424	2,265
Wages & wage taxes	27,349	57,645	31,123
Rent	12,191	11,616	10,137
Utilities, telephone	4,004	4,802	3,320
Insurance, licenses, other taxes	2,220	2,730	1,889
Supplies, services, miscellaneous	10,022	7,893	5,786
Advertising	7,190	10,904	7,921
Interest	2,195	4,318	2,598
Depreciation	630	749	434
Net profit*	$ 4,708	$ −2,889	$ −16,773

*Contemporary Furniture is taxed as a "Sub-Chapter S." Corporation and tax liabilities are not shown here.

C_ASE_ 5

Spring Thing

INTRODUCTION

In October 1976 Layton Chambers originated the idea of holding a rock concert, the Spring Thing, and began promoting and organizing the event. In February 1977 he arranged financing for the venture through a wealthy businessman, Dave Ralston. Relying on Chambers' original November 15 budget (Exhibit 1), Ralston committed $220,000 to back the concert. There were a variety of financial and operating uncertainties associated with the Spring Thing, and while the financier would manage the major economic and financial risks, Chambers was responsible for managing the concert's internal uncertainties.

MANAGEMENT AND CONTROL OF OPERATING RISKS

In the first week of March, two months prior to the event, Chambers began considering ways of controlling the operating risks of the concert and deciding which areas should receive the highest priority in terms of time and money. He and his staff identified promotion and admissions, advance and on-site ticket sales, and concession sales as the factors that would most affect revenues. Similarly, they determined that the major cost uncertainties would revolve around budget control over artist bookings and spectator services and the prevention of medical and security incidents that

---

This case was prepared by and used with the permission of Dr. Bruce H. Fairchild of Financial Concepts and Applications, Inc., Austin, Texas, and Professor Mike E. Miles of the University of North Carolina at Chapel Hill.

would result in postconcert litigation. Although each of these areas involved considerable uncertainty, their management would be critical to the concert's ultimate profitability. While some of these operating risks could be markedly reduced by establishing strict internal controls, there would be substantial costs, both real and opportunity, associated with their institution. Consequently, Chambers was unsure how to best evaluate specific actions in a risk-return framework.

As contract negotiations progressed and costs became more firm, the original budget proved to be less and less reliable. Although the November 15 budget had called for $30,000 in advertising, the public relations firm Chambers had contacted indicated that the promotion effort should be substantially more extensive. In order to be relatively assured of drawing up to 75,000 spectators, the agency suggested that $72,500 be spent for promotion and submitted a proposed advertising campaign for Chambers' review (Exhibit 2). They maintained that this amount was consistent with the industry rule of thumb requiring a dollar of advertising per spectator. Chambers questioned whether the additional expense would be necessary but realized that greater advertising expenditures would better serve his personal goal of self-promotion.

Twelve outlets had been selected to sell advance tickets at $10: three in both St. Louis and Springfield and two each in Kansas City, Tulsa, and Little Rock. The outlets in Kansas City, St. Louis, and Tulsa would be major department stores and ticket agencies that would receive a 5-percent commission on sales and would deposit all receipts in an escrow account until after the concert. The other advance ticket sales were to be handled gratis through record stores and "head shops" with the money they collected periodically remitted directly to Chambers. Although a ticket monitoring system was to be established, Chambers had no idea of how many tickets would be sold in advance. The public relations agency projected that 30,000 to 50,000 tickets would be sold prior to the concert and that approximately 60 to 70 percent of these would be through the major outlets with the remainder being sold through the local shops.

It was anticipated that one-third of total sales would be made well in advance of the concert, another one-third in the three days preceding the event, and the remaining one-third on-site at $12 each. These on-site sales would create a special problem due to the limited physical facilities available and the rowdiness of the crowd. Not only was there uncertainty as to the number of tickets that would be sold on the day of the concert, and therefore the number of ticket sellers needed, but there was a chance that employee theft or an actual robbery might occur. Since Chambers felt that a "hassle-free" atmosphere would be imperative to attract spectators, blatant security measures could not be taken. However, he was still concerned because from $125,000 to $250,000 cash in small bills would be involved with the on-site ticket sales and some controls would be mandatory.

In conjunction with ticket sales Chambers wanted to minimize the number of spectators getting into the concert or viewing the performance without purchasing a ticket. As illustrated in Exhibit 3, the concert area was to be located in the middle of the land tract and would be surrounded by the parking and camping areas. Nonpaying admissions could be gained either by unauthorized entrance through the gates or by spectators climbing over, under, or through restrictive barriers. Several alternatives were available to control this situation, the simplest being to construct a chain-link fence topped with barbed wire strands. The cost of such a fence would be $10,800 and although it would be reasonably effective, some 4000 to 6000 spectators would probably still be able to circumvent this barrier. Another possibility, in addition to fencing, would be to hire security personnel to constantly patrol the perimeter. It was estimated that this would result in increased wages of $4500 while reducing nonpaying entries to between 2000 and 3000. A final alternative would be to install a double ring of perimeter fences with a "no man's land" between them to be patrolled by a few security guards and possibly watch dogs. Although the second fence would cost an additional $11,000 and the personnel and dogs $1000, it would virtually eliminate any gate crashing.

Under either of these options Chambers still had to determine the number of entrance gates to install. Although a greater number of gates would reduce the probability of an enthusiastic and impatient crowd from stampeding the fence, it would also require more facilities and personnel. This would result in increased fencing costs, additional wages of $200 per gate, and would permit more ticket takers' "friends" to enter without paying. Similarly, an exit and entrance procedure would have to be established so that spectators could leave the concert and return later without being able to transfer their passes to others who had not purchased tickets.

Again Chambers was unsure of how

to assess the costs and benefits of these various alternatives. All of the projections had been based on an attendance estimate of 75,000, and the actual costs could be expected to vary, although not proportionately, with the size of the crowd. Also, while Chambers was convinced that a relaxed and unstructured environment would be necessary to attract large crowds, the financial impact of losing up to 6000 ticket sales due to lax controls was quite disconcerting.

The sale of concessions was the other area that would significantly affect the concert's total revenues. Although the landowner, Mark Stafford, had been granted the food and beverage concessions, Chambers had retained a 25 percent override on gross sales. In addition, he had contracted with independent non-food and beverage concessionaires for a fee of 30 percent of their net income (Exhibit 4). Chambers did not know what to expect from concession sales as this would largely be a function of the crowd turnout, but he felt that total receipts could range anywhere from $50,000 to $250,000. With this much cash involved, Chambers identified three areas which might influence his percentage of the concession take: (1) skimming by the concessionaires, (2) accounting practices used, and (3) robberies. Since many of the concessionaires appeared to be of rather questionable character, it was estimated that up to 25 percent of receipts might not be reported. Furthermore, procedures had not been established to control the flow of inventory into and out of the concert area or for recording sales. Finally, the heavy traffic around the concession booths would make it relatively easy for a spectator to rob a concessionaire and disappear into the crowd.

Because these potentialities contributed additional uncertainty to the concession sales, Chambers was considering various methods of controlling them. Although the least expensive approach for determining concession sales would be to accept vendors' figures, auditors could be hired for $1500 to spot-check sales and inventories. Alternatively, a required accounting system for the concessionaires could be set up to record merchandise flows and cash receipts, but this system would be dependent upon vendor compliance, and some on-site auditing would still be required. A final possibility would be for Chambers' people to take over part of the money collecting function. Although this would cost around $3000 and encounter some vendor opposition, it would eliminate the majority of the concessionaire skimming.

Chambers was also concerned about the safety of the cash that would be collected from both concessions and ticket sales. An on-site armored car, into which receipts could be periodically deposited, could be hired for $500, and armed security personnel were available for $200 apiece. However, the presence of too many of these uniformed security guards might give the adverse impression that the concert was a "rip-off" and being held solely for the financial benefit of the promoters. The only alternative to an armored car would be to make deposits directly to the Springfield National Bank by private car. This would be complicated by traffic congestion both on and off the concert site, the one to two hours it would take to make the deposits, and the lack of security during the trip.

Besides these problems affecting expected revenues, Chambers was experiencing difficulties keeping some costs in line with his original projections. Specifically, he was having trouble negotiating contracts with the artists. Although he could engage New York talent agents, he was reluctant to pay their fee of 10 percent of the cost of the musicians. In order to sign those groups that he felt would draw crowds of 60,000 to 70,000, he would have to offer them $165,000. Although this was substantially above the $100,000 budgeted on November 15, if he were forced to stay within this original amount, it was doubtful that the concert would attract more than 30,000 people. Most of the other concert costs had been fairly well budgeted, and while some were underestimated, others had been overestimated.

Chambers' final decision was to determine the precautions that should be taken to limit the possibility of sizable losses due to postconcert legal suits arising from medical incidents, personal injuries, and/or property damage. Basically, this involved deciding on the extent of medical facilities to supply, the amount of security to provide for spectators, artists, and adjacent property owners, the extent of parking and traffic control, and the amount of liability insurance to purchase. An agreement had been made with a community counseling and medical aid group to be at the concert to handle drug and minor injury problems. Chambers was uncertain, though, as to how much professional help would be needed to take care of the more serious cases. Five doctors, ten nurses, and two ambulances would cost approximately $5000 for the day.

It was estimated that a complete security program capable of controlling most possible occurrences would cost $15,000 above the necessary minimum of $6695. This would include $2000 for off-duty policemen to direct traffic, $5000 for a group of professional bouncers to guard the artists and stage area, $5000 for untrained "field hippies" to handle parking, prevent vandalism, and aid spectators, and $3000 for special agents to mingle with the crowd looking for weapons and to prevent fights or riots. While some of these security personnel were essential, others were less crucial and might not be needed.

The cost of liability insurance varied, although not proportionately, with the amount of coverage. Contact with a local insurance broker indicated that a $1 million policy could be purchased for $7000, while $5 and $10 million coverage would cost $12,000 and $18,000 respectively.

FINALIZING OPERATING RISK DECISIONS

Faced with these potential sources of uncertainty and the alternative actions by which they could be moderated, Chambers realized that numerous risk-return trade-offs would soon have to be made. The strain of preparing for the concert was beginning to show on the staff, and Chambers had developed an ulcer. To complicate matters, a local citizens group had just announced their intention to seek a court injunction to halt the concert. With only four weeks remaining

until the concert was to be held, it became apparent that the original budget of November 15 was no longer valid. On April 1 a revised estimate of expenses was prepared under the assumption that only minimal steps would be taken to reduce the various operating risks (Exhibit 5). This new budget revealed that the concert would require at a minimum $370,000 front-end financing, $100,000 more than orginally anticipated.

Armed with this revised cost estimate, Chambers contacted Ralston to discuss the additional capital requirements and ascertain his ability to provide the necessary funds. Ralston indicated that he would have extreme difficulty arranging for the extra cash, and that it would seriously threaten his personal solvency. Furthermore, he was becoming very uncomfortable over the uncertainty associated with the project and was questioning whether the potential returns were adequate compensation for the risks he was taking. Ralston wanted Chambers to make those key decisions that would affect the risk of the concert and reflect them in the budget so that he could gain a more complete grasp of the project's final risk-return construction. Only then would he consider committing any additional funds to finance the Spring Thing.

EXHIBIT 1

Spring Thing

Anticipated Expense Budget
November 15, 1975

Talent		
Artists' fees	$100,000	
Limousines	2,880	
Catered food and drinks	1,100	$103,980
Admission tickets		943
Advertising (including production)		30,000
On-site preparation		
Mowing	5,000	
Stage and platform construction	6,300	
Fencing	28,102	
Portable toilets (including servicing)	7,000	
Barricades and construction materials	1,250	
Electrical labor and equipment	3,000	
Earth moving and grading	200	
Cleanup	650	51,502
Security (including armored car)		15,976
Stagehands		2,745
Sound system rental and setup		15,000
Liability insurance		7,000
Administrative office expense		
Staff salaries	13,300	
Office rent	1,000	
Telephone and supplies	500	14,800
Tent and tarpaulin rental		1,000
Legal fees		500
Miscellaneous		1,565
Contingency surplus (10% of above total)		24,501
Total Anticipated Expenses		$269,512

EXHIBIT 2

Spring Thing

Proposed Advertising Campaign

Agency fee		$10,000
Media expenses		
Print media	$17,200	
Broadcast media	30,000	
Broadcast production	750	
Radio dubs	7,500	
Printing releases	100	55,550
Artwork and photography		
Artwork	1,000	
Posters, flyers, press kits	4,300	
Productions, stats, velox	450	
Photo reprints	150	5,900
Miscellaneous		
Mailing service	100	
Bus	50	
Telephone expense	125	
Deliveries	100	
Travel	150	
Postage	125	650
Miscellaneous		400
Total Advertising Campaign Expenses		$72,500

EXHIBIT 3
Spring Thing
Site Diagram

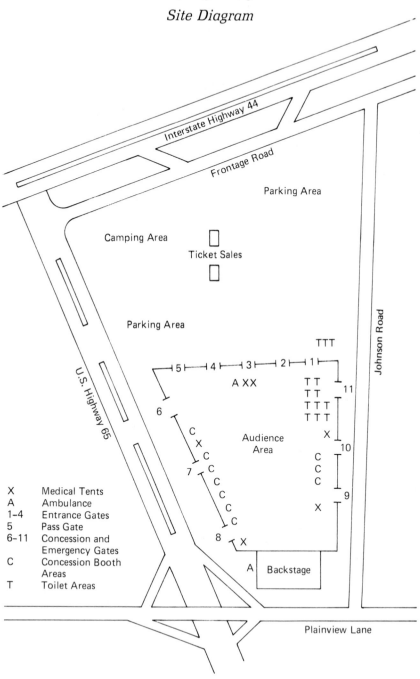

X Medical Tents
A Ambulance
1–4 Entrance Gates
5 Pass Gate
6–11 Concession and
Emergency Gates
C Concession Booth
Areas
T Toilet Areas

EXHIBIT 4

Spring Thing

On-site Concessionaires

Food and beverage concessions
    Beer and wine — Ron's Liquor Stores
    Soft drinks — M and B Catering
    BBQ beef, hamburgers, hotdogs, etc. — M and B Catering
    BBQ chicken, nachos, corn on the cob, etc. — Carol Warren
    Ice cream — Joan Marlin
    Fruits and health foods — Good Eats, Inc.
    Watermelons — Red's Fruit Stand

Clothing and apparel
    Blouses, shirts, and jackets — Exotic Imports
    Al's cutoff jeans — Al Davis
    Belt buckles and jewelry — The Posse
    "Spring Thing" blankets — Sam Johnson

Miscellaneous
    Suntan oil and jewelry — Bob Conroe
    Cigarettes — The Tobacco Shoppes
    Herbs and spices — Living Good Together, Inc.

EXHIBIT 5

Spring Thing

Revised Expense Budget
April 1, 1976

Talent		
Artists' fees	$165,000	
Limousines	2,400	
Catered food and drink	1,100	$168,500
Admission tickets		762
Advertising (including production)		72,500
On-site preparation		
Phone connections	11,484	
Stage and platform construction	5,300	
Fencing	10,800	
Portable toilets (including servicing)	7,000	
Barricades and construction materials	750	
Electrical labor and equipment	12,050	
Earth moving and grading	1,700	
Cleanup	650	49,734
Basic security		6,695
Stagehands		3,696
Sound system rental and setup		15,000
Liability insurance		7,000
Administrative office expense		
Staff salaries	15,346	
Office rent	10,000	
Telephone and supplies	1,500	26,846
Tent and tarpaulin rental		125
Legal fees		5,000
Miscellaneous		12,814
Total Revised Expenses		$368,672

CASE 6

The Cash Crisis at the Children's Treatment Center

Loan payments, government contracts, United Way money—sometimes running the not-for-profit Honolulu Children's Treatment Center was nothing but one big headache, thought Ron Williams, executive director of the center. So many children needed help, and yet more and more of his time seemed to be spent on a growing number of financial problems.

Ron saw that there wasn't enough cash to pay for the services provided by the parent agency, and payments were several years overdue. The temporary bank loan of $100,000 would need renewal soon and interest rates were moving up rapidly. The bank was unhappy that a so-called temporary loan had to be refinanced again. The United Way would reduce its support, dollar for dollar, if the center had an operating surplus of more than $5000, but without an operating surplus it might not be possible to take care of the overdue payables and

the bank loan. Actually, an operating surplus was unlikely to occur—the forecast for 1980 was a deficit of $30,000. And if that wasn't enough, today's mail brought yet another letter from the board of directors in California that said if he just managed things properly, he should be able to pay off the bank loan, eliminate the operating deficit, and get current on payables. The letter ended with the request: "Please explain." The March 1980 annual meeting with the board of directors was coming up soon and they would be expecting some answers.

THE HONOLULU CHILDREN'S TREATMENT CENTER

The center is a not-for-profit organization founded in the 1920s to provide a home for dependent and neglected children. Over the years it had evolved into

The case was written by and used with the permission of Professor Steve Dawson of the University of Hawaii and W. R. Cozens of the Honolulu Children's Treatment Center.

a fully accredited residential psychiatric facility with a complete range of professional staff providing care to over 50 emotionally disturbed children. As the only fully accredited and licensed residential setting for the treatment of children with psychiatric disabilities in the Hawaiian Islands, children were received for care from throughout the entire state. Their length of stay, depending upon the severity of their problems, ranged from 5 to 24 months with the average being 16 months. During this time, in addition to treatment for their emotional problems, they received a full range of supportive services including special education, medical care, social services, recreation, room and board, and structured leisure time activities.

The center is a subsidiary of a California-based not-for-profit corporation and operates with its own board of directors that is responsible for reviewing the budget and setting general policy. The directors meet quarterly in California and hold a meeting each March in Hawaii to review the budget for the fiscal year beginning on July 1.

As a not-for-profit organization, its basic objective is to render services. Success was measured by how much service was provided and by how well available resources were used. The Honolulu Children's Treatment Center thus differed markedly from a profit-oriented organization where decisions were intended to increase, or at least maintain, profits or to maximize the value of the firm. This was not to say that not-for-profit organizations did not report profits —there were years when reported revenues exceeded expenses. If this happened over several years, however, it was not a sign of good management but rather a warning signal that the organi-

was not accomplishing its objective of providing as much service as possible with available resources. Either it should cut the price charged for services or it should provide more services. A not-for-profit organization's usual policy should be to break even in the long run. The equity interests involved would have little incentive to build up an operating surplus since they could not sell or trade their ownership to others and no part of the assets, income, or profit would be distributed to them.

In financial reports for a not-for-profit organization, a clear distinction is made between capital costs and operating costs. Capital costs refer to the acquisition of fixed assets, equipment, and real property from which benefits will accrue over a long period of time. Operating costs include labor costs, materials consumed, and services purchased as part of operating an organization for a given period of time. The two types of costs are handled separately, as are the revenues associated with them. Depreciation is not a part of operating expenses.

SOURCES OF REVENUES

The center's operating income would be close to $1.8 million in 1980. Income was expected to come from two primary sources, government agencies and charitable groups. Both of these sources set strict limitations, typically of a line-item nature, for the use of the funds they provided. One of the most stringently enforced rules was the prohibition against the accumulation of an operating surplus. The intent was to have as much as possible of the funds go to the ultimate beneficiary. The income received each fiscal year for funding operations should be to equal the allowable operating expenses incurred in providing services. Increases in working capital were not an allowable expense. If income was greater than operating expenses, the center would run into considerable difficulty with its funding agencies. If income was less, the center would soon find its ability to continue operating impaired.

During 1980, payments from the federal government would constitute by far the largest single source of operating income, as shown in the following table:

Expected
Distribution of 1980
Operating Revenues by Source

	(%)
Federal government	65.5
Aloha United Way	14.1
State government	13.7
Contributions	3.6
Parents	1.2
Other	1.9
	100.0

Payment was usually received one to three months after billing. At the end of the federal fiscal year, federal regulations required an end-of-contract accounting. Payment for the last month was usually delayed an additional one or two months. The state government was a smaller, but still important, source of income. It, as well as parents who paid a portion of their children's expenses, was billed at the end of the month in which the service was provided, and payment was generally received within the next 30 days.

Aloha United Way was the largest nongovernment source of funds. The Children's Treatment Center was one of many local organizations receiving funds; in 1980 the United Way was expected to provide over 14 percent of the center's total revenues. United Way funds were allocated annually and distributed at the start of each month in 12 equal payments. Although the center had to apply for funds each year, experience had shown that these funds could be counted on in the future as long as the center did not make an operating surplus. The United Way reduced its payments, dollar for dollar, for any not-for-profit agency with an operating surplus of more than $5000 at the end of each year. They reasoned that funds were provided to pay for services, and if any recipient did not need them for that purpose, there were many other recipients who could use them for worthwhile purposes.

Over the years the center's sources of income had changed dramatically. Payments, for the most part, had always come from a third-party source, but there had been a long-term increase in the share provided by government, with the federal government taking an increasingly important position.

Starting in the 1950s, payments from the State of Hawaii for children placed at the Center began a slow but steady

			Sources of Income (%)					
	1972	1973	1974	1975	1976	1977	1978	1979
State of Hawaii	58	21	18	18	15	14	11	14
U.S. Government	0	45	47	53	56	58	60	65
United Way	32	25	21	18	15	15	12	14
Other*	10	9	14	11	14	13	17	7
	100	100	100	100	100	100	100	100

*Local foundations, parents, and other sources.

rise. By 1972, the year after Ron Williams became executive director, state payments were 58 percent of total income with no income at all coming from the federal government.

Without federal dollars, the center was locked into trying to maintain a semblance of quality care for a very small portion of the total number of children needing help. Thus it was with great excitement that Ron and his co-workers viewed the availability of federal funds beginning in 1973. This new source of funds allowed the center to expand rapidly and to more adequately service the pressing needs of the community. A further advantage of federal funds was that they came in the form of signed contracts, negotiated each year, which provided a guaranteed source of funding for a specific number of children. A lot of forms and government red tape were involved, but Ron and his staff had learned how to handle the administration of the contracts.

From zero in 1972 the federal funds soared to 45 percent of revenues in 1973 and 65 percent in 1979. This pattern of rapid influx of government contract payments for services had occurred in similar agencies throughout the country. The growth of federal money, however, was not matched by a similar rise in funds from other sources. Most of the growth in the center's budget—$680,000 in 1972 to $1.7 million in 1979—came from the buildup of federal contract dollars. State payments, fairly level in recent years, were well below 1972, even before adjustment for inflation. The United Way share also had been in a down trend.

EXPENSES

In simplest terms the center collected funds from its various sources and used them to pay for the services it provided for the children in its care. In the projected 1980 operating budget (see Exhibit 1), approximately 66 percent of all outlays would go for payroll expenses. The remaining 34 percent would be allocated to other operating expenses, such as supplies, travel, occupancy, and equipment. Like many service-oriented businesses, the center was labor intensive. Payroll outlays were made in the month the services were provided and the other operating expenses typically were paid later—60 percent in the month following purchase and 40 percent the month after that.

The parent agency provided many direct and indirect support services to the Honolulu Child Treatment Center, and the center in turn paid 10 percent of its total gross income to the parent agency. These payments, called the "centage" fee, were due the month following billing for the services provided. The centage fee was a major source of operating funds for the parent agency. Principal among the services it provided the center were program consultation, employee retirement and health plan provision and administration, a full range of insurance coverage, auditing services, legal services, public relations, federal-level governmental contract negotiations, fund raising for major capital expenditures, long-range fiscal and program planning, and centralized purchasing.

THE BANK LOAN

The first signs of impending financial problems came in 1977, with the situation becoming critical a year and one-half later. In July 1978 there wasn't enough cash available to meet the payroll. The center took out a bank loan of $75,000 for three months at 13 percent interest secured by federal government receivables. Everyone, including Ron, thought it was just a temporary problem. As soon as the delayed end-of-fiscal-year payments were received, the loan could be paid back. This was done, but to everyone's dismay a similar cash shortage almost immediately reappeared, necessitating another loan. This time the loan was for $100,000 at 14 percent interest and a term of six months with similar collateral. This loan was still outstanding, and it was only with some effort that the monthly interest payments had been made.

The size and cause of the loan had been a major source of concern to Ron. The center was not against borrowing for short-term needs but it was against having a loan that never seemed to get repaid. Although it had been renewed several times, the bank might decide not to renew it again since it had now become obvious this was not just a temporary need for funds. In any case bank loan interest rates had soared in recent months with the prime reaching 18 percent–double its level when the loan was first taken out and up 6 percent in the last six months.

To compound the problem, state and federal contract negotiators would not accept interest charges on the loan as a reimbursable expense. Nongovernment sources expected that their contributions would go toward providing services, not to pay loan costs. The United Way was of no help either. Since the center was funded as a not-for-profit organization, it would drop its support, dollar for dollar, for any agency that showed more than a $5000 operating surplus at the end of the fiscal year. Interest payments were not an allowable operation expense. To date, about half the interest expense had been met by income received from nongovern-

mental sources and the remainder had shown up as an increase in the operational deficit, which was projected to reach close to $30,000 for 1980. Although, in terms of the projected 1980 budget of $1.8 million, this was not high, it was still unacceptable to Ron as well as to his board of directors.

Of even greater concern to Ron and the board was the rise in payables, particularly to the parent agency. The unpaid centage fee was over $400,000 at the end of 1979. There was no penalty for late payment to the parent agency but most of the other creditors had a discount for early payment, a 1½ percent per month charge on overdue bills, or both. In 1979 no discounts were taken and late payment penalties were over $1000.

These overdue payments had become an increasing source of friction with the parent agency and were the cause of a series of letters of concern from the board of directors requesting more information and early repayment of the bank loan and the payables. In their latest letter the board pointed out that they knew the collections were now coming in at the rate of 15 percent during the month service was provided, 60 percent the month after, 20 percent the third month, and 5 percent the fourth month. "Agreeably, this should have some effect," they admitted, "but surely if you manage things properly you should be able to catch up after four months, and then you can pay the loan and begin to reduce your payables."

Before preparing a response to the board, Ron decided to go over once again the budget for 1980 (see Exhibit 1) and the 1979 financial statement (see Exhibit 2), both previously submitted to the parent agency and the United Way. The formats were consistent with the generally accepted standards of accounting as applied to not-for-profit agencies. Since there were no substantive changes in services provided or purchases forecasted for 1980, aside from cost increases due to inflation, the projections were believed to be reasonably accurate.

As Ron Williams thought about the center's financial problems and the request from the parent agency, he realized the irony of it all. Ten years ago when a lower level of services was being provided, there were few financial problems. Now that he had successfully increased the center's funding, the financial situation seemed to be falling apart. Perhaps in coming up with a response to the parent agency's "please explain" request, he would be able to find a way to resolve the potentially crippling financial situation. There was at least one consoling aspect to all this: with federal funding many more children were receiving much better care than was previously possible. The governmental third-party payments at 60 to 75 percent of total income were, from all expectations, here to stay.

EXHIBIT 1

The Cash Crisis at the Children's Treatment Center

Projected Statement of Expected Operating Expenses and Income Honolulu Children's Treatment Center—1980

Revenues	
Aloha United Way	$ 252,000
Contributions	64,000
Federal	1,171,097
Parents' payments	21,400
State	245,600
Other	34,600
Total revenues	$1,788,697
Expenses	
Personnel	$1,207,500
Field service ("centage")	178,870
Professional consultation	45,500
Supplies	90,300
Occupancy	86,000
Awards and grants	54,500
Travel	44,200
Equipment	30,000
Other*	80,905
	$1,817,775
Total expenses	
Surplus/(deficit)	($29,078)

*Includes $35,000 for payment of interest and principal on the $100,000 bank loan.

EXHIBIT 2

The Cash Crisis at the Children's Treatment Center

Honolulu Children's Treatment Center
Balance Sheets: 1972, 1976, 1979

	12/31/72	12/31/76	6/30/79
Assets			
Cash	$ 5,067	$ 24,221	$ 20,521
Accounts receivable	22,204	81,036	266,267
Prepaid expenses	—	6,840	11,850
Reserves held by headquarters*	46,649	164,260	116,890
Total assets	$ 73,920	$ 276,357	$ 415,528
Liabilities			
Accounts payable—trade	$ 17,484	$ 137,971	$ 117,322
Accounts payable—headquarters	39,752	32,619	396,896
Bank loan	—	—	100,000
Accrued expenses and payables	—	21,726	22,033
Payable to State of Hawaii	—	69,355	69,355
Loan from headquarters	—	15,000	15,000
Total liabilities	$ 57,236	$ 276,671	$ 720,606
Fund balance	16,684	(314)	(305,078)
Total claims	$ 73,920	$ 276,357	$ 415,528
Total revenues	$682,090	$1,439,651	$1,566,602

*These reserves are restricted for capital improvements and are not available to the center for operations.

PART TWO

Working Capital Management

CASE 7

The Friendly Florist

The Friendly Florist was a retail floral and gift shop located in Northwest Florida, with over 90 percent of the sales volume from the floral end of the business. It opened for business on March 31, 1979, on a very limited budget of $4000. Mr. Tim Venable, father of Sharon, who was manager of the Friendly Florist, paid the initial investment of $4000. Over the past year and a half, the business had grown as a result of hard work and an earnest desire to succeed on the part of the owners. Sharon did all the floral design work and made all the gift items that the business sold. Debbie Venable, Sharon's mother, worked at the flower shop-volunteering her time to assist wherever possible.

Neither Sharon nor her mother had any past managerial experience. Upon graduation from high school, where Sharon learned macrame, sand art, and many other crafts, she worked for one year at

Florida Floral Shop in Ft. Walton Beach, Florida: there, she obtained her experience in floral design.

The firm needed a loan to expand the business and consolidate all of its outstanding debts. Sharon went through the Small Business Administration in hopes of obtaining a loan of $20,000. After several months of deliberation, Sharon Venable received her loan on April 25, 1980. The loan was serviced by Okaloosa County Bank with a 10-percent interest rate. The date of maturity on the $20,000 note was May 1987, with payments to begin one month after the date it was issued. After they had received the loan, Sharon thought that all her financial troubles were resolved.

The Friendly Florist desperately needed a large van, as they had no delivery vehicle of their own. The maintenance and servicing of the van were insignificant factors to Sharon since the

This case was prepared by Stanley L. Blankenship under the supervision of Professor Ira W. Pyron of Troy State University, and is used with permission.

addition of delivery service would increase sales. The van was serviced at a local filling station with maintenance costs varying, depending upon the type of repair needed. Approximately $28 a week was spent on gasoline. After receiving the loan, they were able to buy a used van at a reasonably low cost. Friendly did not plan to charge their customers a delivery fee.

The Friendly Florist was experiencing cash-flow problems resulting from credit sales collections. Over three-fourths of their sales were transacted through credit that they extended themselves. This practice resulted in Friendly having virtually no cash on hand and made it very difficult for them to pay off their own debts. Both Sharon and Debbie found it hard to reject a customer because he could not pay cash for his purchase. Friendly maintained this policy in sales from the smallest floral arrangement to their most elaborate wedding displays. Although it might take more than three months, most of these customers would eventually pay off their debts.

Mr. Terry Lucas, the Friendly Florist's banker and a friend of the family, realized that the business had credit collection problems. Sharon and her mother inquired about a service charge for outstanding accounts of more than 90 days. According to Mr. Lucas, this was not a desirable plan of action. He felt that if a person was going to delay payments up to three months in the first place, the service charge would not be an incentive.

Ninety percent of the flower shop's business was completed by telephone, which was a relatively high percentage in comparison to other florists in the area. They did not inform their customers that they were willing to accept

MasterCard or Visa in payment for any purchase. This information was available only to the walk-in customers by means of a sign on the flower shop's front door.

Sharon met with Mr. Lucas in his office during the fall of 1980. Realizing the florist's collection problems, he presented Sharon with a handful of manila folders with dates at the top of each. These file folders were to be used for keeping records of customers to aid the shop in determining who had outstanding debts. Both Sharon and Mrs. Venable were excited about Mr. Lucas' suggestion and planned to implement it at once.

It was the Friendly Florist's policy that those who still had credit outstanding after 90 days, and were not given an extension agreement to pay off their debt, would have their cases turned over to a collection agency. The agency, located in Pensacola, Florida, received a percentage of the collected debts, ranging from 20 to 65 percent. Since most sales involved only small payments of money, it was of little value to turn these cases over to the agency. Friendly was debating whether to begin accepting composition arrangements, so that they would receive at least partial payment of the outstanding debts.

As mentioned above, the firm had very little walk-in business. The shop was somewhat isolated, as it was located to the rear of a small shopping complex. Sharon realized that most people did not even know that the shop existed. A small sign for the florist shop hung among other signs in front of the suites. In March of 1979, when Friendly Florist opened, Mr. Venable rented a sign for his daughter's business. The flashing neon sign was banned from the area three months after its installation.

The Venables planned to post signs

inside two of the businesses in the shopping complex. They felt that this would increase the number of walk-in customers or at least cause the residents in the Ft. Walton shopping area to become aware of the business. If location continued to be a problem, Sharon and Debbie would consider moving when their present lease was ready to expire. Friendly had 18 months left on this lease.

This problem led to another area of concern for Friendly: their advertising policies. Since this was the first business venture for the Venables, they had no knowledge regarding the best media vehicle to use for their specific needs. During the first nine months of operation, promotion people from every medium continually approached Sharon and Debbie. These advertising agents contacted them as often as five times a week. Both Sharon and her mother had difficulty turning them down, since they were so convincing in their assertion that Friendly could not exist without their help. As a result, the Venables found that they were spending many more dollars for advertising than they had allotted in their budget for this aspect of the business.

In January 1980 Mr. Gary Livers, an employee at a local advertising agency and a friend of the family, approached Sharon Venable. He sat down with Sharon and explained the advantages of utilizing his firm for all their promotional needs. Convincing Sharon that his services were vital for Friendly's future, and promising her a slight discount because of their friendship, she agreed to employ the Harvard Advertising Agency for the next two years. Costs were not expected to exceed $3400 each year. As time passed, Sharon was pleased with both the performance of Harvard and the peace of mind that she received as a result of doing business with the agency. Since that time, the advertising agents had occasionally approached Sharon and Debbie. Now, they both found it easier to resist these salesmen.

Harvard ran three spot advertisements on Saturdays and Sundays on a local television station. The spots ran for five seconds, and cost $15 apiece. Radio ads were utilized during the holidays, when flower sales increased. These were among the services that Harvard performed for the Friendly Florist.

Sharon, with the help of a local printing shop, produced a small publication with gift and decorating ideas. This booklet was distributed to hospitals, local stores, and various businesses throughout the Ft. Walton Beach area. The booklet was basically an ordering guide for flowers and plants from the Friendly Florist. It gave helpful hints for floral arrangements and upkeep of house plants.

It had been the policy of Friendly Florist to watch for engagement announcements in the local newspapers. This had allowed the flower shop to increase its wedding sales somewhat. The Friendly Florist held an open house twice during the Christmas season, in conjunction with the other stores in their shopping complex. Sharon believed it would be profitable to advertise these open houses by distributing flyers offering a 10-percent discount on all floral arrangements; gift items were not subject to this discount.

Mrs. Venable felt that Friendly should run monthly specials on different flowers, since most of their competition in the Florida panhandle area followed this policy. Presently, Friendly ran specials on two occasions only: Easter and Mother's Day. Sharon liked her mother's suggestion; monthly specials were expected to begin in January of the coming year. Both women expected this new plan to boost sales in the near future.

Since Sharon used her automobile for numerous business trips, she wondered if it would be possible to advertise the Florist shop on the sides of her car. She had no knowledge of the legal regulations governing this form of advertising and did not know where to acquire this information. The delivery van had small signs on both sides, and Sharon planned to paint larger ones on it. She realized that these steps would also benefit their advertising.

Friendly Florist had a policy of keeping prices relatively low. Compared to other flower shops within a 50-mile radius, Friendly's prices were either equal to or lower than their competition. Neither Sharon nor Debbie planned to change this policy. The Friendly Florist had attempted to have the same markup percent on all items sold. The majority of sales were small items. Wedding and funeral arrangements were considered to be important in the operation of the firm. As mentioned previously, Friendly required no delivery charge.

With net income reporting a loss through the first eight months of 1980 (see Exhibits 1 and 2), Mr. Lucas felt that Friendly needed either to increase volume or charge higher prices; but with Mrs. Venable and Sharon already set in their ways, it would be difficult to change their existing policy. Sharon was afraid that if she increased her prices, many of her present customers, whom she considered to be her most valuable assets, would shop elsewhere for their floral needs. Mr. Lucas planned a meeting with the Venable family to discuss this matter. He wanted this problem

solved very soon, as Friendly still had six and a half years left to repay their loan to Okaloosa County Bank.

Because of Sharon's talent in floral arrangement, her father suggested the possibility of starting a class in which she would instruct people in the art of arranging flowers properly. He felt this would help bring the business from a loss to a gain over a short period of time. This was only a suggestion; Sharon was presently inquiring about the fees charged by local junior colleges and arts and crafts clubs to get a "ball park" figure as to the price she would charge. Debbie insisted that this would also improve sales as more people found out about Friendly's location, their beautiful and inexpensive flowers, and their extensive service to the Ft. Walton Beach area.

As with many businesses, Friendly's sales were not always level throughout the year, although Sharon's macrame items and most of her plants sold year round. During the spring, hanging baskets seemed to be most popular; and cut flowers sold well in the winter months. Roses were always in demand and, according to Sharon, they helped absorb monthly loss Friendly incurred on their other flower lines. A large flower wholesaler, located in Pensacola, supplied Friendly with many of their fresh flowers. Roses, for example, cost between $25 and $45 per 100 from the wholesaler. Other flowers, as well as plants, were purchased at reasonable discounts.

Because of her present financial situation, Sharon had to take a part-time job at a restaurant in Ft. Walton. She worked at Friendly from 8:30 AM to 5:00 PM Monday through Saturday, and week nights from 7:00 PM to 11:00 PM at her new part-time job. Although this had improved her financial status, Sharon was considering quitting her new job because of her rigorous schedule; her parents felt this would be in Sharon's best interest as well. These financial problems had caused Mr. Venable concern since the opening of the Friendly Florist. Two options had been brought to his attention about the future of the shop, and he was seriously considering them both.

The first of these decisions involved selling the business. Mr. Brian Schmitt, the principal of a larger floral operation located in Pensacola, had expressed interest in buying out Friendly for a reasonable price. However, he planned to talk with both Debbie and Sharon about the situation before meeting Mr. Schmitt. If the family decided to sell out, Mr. Venable planned to meet with Mr. Rob Gibson, the firm's CPA, to determine a fair value for the Friendly Florist.

Friendly's banker, Mr. Lucas, would also be called on to express his opinion about the firm's value.

The other option available to Mr. Venable was to apply for counseling from the Small Business Administration; both Sharon and Debbie appeared enthusiastic about this alternative. Mr. Venable realized that the assistance provided by the SBA was free of charge. Their suggestions and recommendations could be accepted or rejected as desired.

After evaluating these options, and after consulting Mr. Gibson and Mr. Lucas, Mr. Venable decided that his business would receive assistance from the Small Business Administration. After completing some of the necessary paperwork, the Venables anxiously awaited their initial meeting with the SBA representatives.

EXHIBIT 1

The Friendly Florist

Balance Sheet
August 31, 1980
(all figures in dollars)

Assets

Current assets

Cash in bank OCB		(160.53)	
Cash in bank OCB P/R		4.87	
Accounts receivable		3,613.00	
Inventory		10,250.02	
Total current assets			13,707.36

Property & equipment

Office equipment	69.57		
Allow. for depr. office/E	25.09	44.48	
Store equipment	3,924.65		
Allow. for depr. store/E	788.92	3,135.73	
Auto & trucks	3,325.50		
Allow. for depr. A&T	249.42	3,076.08	
Total property & equipment			6,256.29

Other assets

Utility deposits		475.00	
Total other assets			475.00
Total assets			20,438.65

Liabilities & Equity

Current liabilities

Accounts payable trade	1,377.00	
Note payable OCB	20,613.24	
Note payable Coca-Cola	(34.00)	
Note payable cash register	(185.16)	
Note payable cooler	(21.01)	
FICA W/H & accrued	56.84	
Federal withholding	18.10	
State withholding	7.95	
Fla. U/C withholding	1.15	
Sales tax payable	103.21	
Total current liabilities		21,937.32
Long-term liabilities		———
Total liabilities		21,937.32

Owners' equity

Venable equity	(1,131.09)	
Equity Tim Venable	2,717.82	
Equity Sharon Venable	(1,373.24)	
Equity Debbie Venable	612.84	
Drawing Tim Venable	(2,325.00)	
Total owners' equity		(1,498.67)
Total liabilities & owners' equity		$20,438.65

EXHIBIT 2

The Friendly Florist

Income Statement
For the Eight-Month Period Ending August 31, 1980

	Year-to-date Amount ($)	(%)	Prior Fiscal Year (%)
Sales	$20,832.51	100.00	100.00
Cost of sales			
Purchases	8,003.33	38.42	64.13
Gross profit	12,829.18	61.58	35.87
Selling expenses			
Salesmen salaries	1,503.05	7.21	4.63
Advertising	2,268.56	10.89	4.94
Total selling expenses	3,771.61	18.10	9.57
Operating expenses			
Auto & truck	419.25	2.01	.78
Bank charges	101.25	.49	.54
Depreciation	794.79	3.82	1.50
Insurance—general	247.00	1.19	2.04
Interest	1,295.09	6.22	3.31
Legal & accounting	275.00	1.32	3.45
Office expense	770.66	3.70	3.88
Rent	4,373.36	20.99	27.39
Repairs & maintenance	76.94	.37	.04
Taxes & licenses	124.21	.60	.45
Taxes payroll	29.47	.14	.79
Telephone	828.03	3.97	2.65
Utilities	771.46	3.70	3.84
Total operating expenses	10,106.51	48.52	52.15
Net operating income or (loss)	($1,048.94)	(5.04)	(25.85)

CASE 8

Orleans Tubular Supply Company

In the spring of 1980 Mr. Jack Rogers, vice-president of the Bayou National Bank, was reviewing a request from Orleans Tubular Supply Company to increase its line of credit. The company's president, Mr. Mike Caldwell, had asked that the credit line be raised from $150,000 to $250,000 in order to help finance Orleans' rapidly increasing sales. Mr. Rogers had asked one of his staff members to prepare a financial analysis of Orleans' position and outline its past payment patterns. (See Exhibits 1 and 2 for Orleans' financial statements.)

Orleans had been founded in 1965 by two lifelong friends, Mr. Mike Caldwell and Mr. Steven Springer. During the first ten years, the company had experienced slow but steady growth as it established itself as a supplier of drilling pipe and casings to oil drilling companies located within a 150-mile radius of its warehouse. The partnership had been dissolved in 1975 when Mr. Caldwell bought out Mr. Springer's interest in the company for $65,000. Mr. Springer had accepted a note for the entire amount, which Mr. Caldwell paid off the following year. In order to come up with the $65,000, Mr. Caldwell had used $25,000 of his personal assets and had obtained a $40,000 ten-year loan from the Bayou National Bank. The terms of the mortgage loan had required annual payments of $4000 plus 10 percent interest on the outstanding principal.

In the past approximately two-thirds of Orleans' sales had come from small drilling companies who purchased most of their pipe and casings from small suppliers on an as-needed basis. The remaining one-third had come from large drilling companies who purchased from small suppliers only when their own stocks unexpectedly ran out or when an unusual size or grade of pipe or casing

This case was written by Charles E. Curtis under the supervision of Professor M. Edgar Barrett, Southern Methodist University, and is used with permission.

had been required. Mostly, the large drilling companies had bought their large quantities of pipes and casings directly from the manufacturers.

The demand for Orleans' products had increased rapidly since 1975. As a consequence of the Arab oil embargo, oil shortages, and increasing gasoline prices, many companies increased oil drilling activities in domestic oil fields. One of the areas that had a major increase in drilling activities was in the Orleans' locale. The company's sales had risen from $1,143,000 in 1977 to $1,756,000 in 1979. Sales would probably hit the $2 million level by 1980. By most forecasts, the level of drilling activity in the Orleans' market area should continue to increase for several years into the future.

Mr. Rogers had been favorably impressed by the manner in which Mr. Caldwell had managed the operation of his business. He had built his company's reputation with customers as a dependable supplier. He had established good relationships with his suppliers and employees. He had been viewed by the business community as a hard working and honest young businessman. Orleans had depended heavily upon its reputation to generate sales. Although the company occasionally had advertised in oil industry trade publications, most of its sales had been the result of word-of-mouth advertising. Most orders had been received over the telephone and had been shipped the same or the next business day. On occasion, a driller had come to the warehouse to pick up a rush order. The company's ability to carry a broad inventory and to respond quickly to customer needs had been a primary reason for its success and good reputation.

Orleans had carried a wide range of drilling pipes and well casings in its inventory. Drilling pipes are used to transmit the turning motion of drilling motors directly to the drill bits. Pipes are manufactured in standard 30-foot lengths with diameters ranging between $2^{3}/_{8}$ and $8^{5}/_{8}$ inches. These pipes are also produced in several different grades of steel hardness. The hardness of the steel pipes used by drillers depends upon well depths and drilling pressure. These pipes are often reused by the drillers when they move on to a new site. On the average, after about three years the pipes are discarded. Well casings are used to line well shafts in order to prevent cave-ins of the surrounding earth. Casings are usually left in the well shafts and are not reclaimed. To service these varied needs of the drillers, Orleans had stocked a large number of different types of pipes and casings. New drilling procedures and deeper wells had changed the types of pipes and casings required by drillers in recent years and had increased the variety of products that Orleans had to stock to service its customers. As a consequence of the increased product variety and increased number of customers, Orleans had increased its investment in inventory substantially from $101,000 in 1977 to $387,000 in March 1980.

THE LOAN REVIEW

After receiving the report from his staff member, Mr. Rogers reviewed Orleans' financial statements and payment history on outstanding loans. In early 1977 the company had paid down the loan balance on its credit line to zero. Again in February of 1978, the loan balance was reduced to zero. This time, however, Mr. Rogers observed, by inspecting the financial statements, that the company had been able to reduce the bank loan only after increasing its other liabilities and after Mr. Caldwell delayed taking his personal drawings. Since 1978, the loan had not been paid down. Payments on the mortgage stemming from the buy-out of Mr. Springer's interest in the company had been made on schedule in each year.

One concern that Mr. Rogers had from his inspection of Orleans' financial statements was with the steady increase in accounts receivable that had occurred over the previous three-year period. As is standard practice in the industry, Orleans had extended credit to its customers on a net 30-day basis. Mr. Caldwell had told the bank's staff member that most customers had paid on time, with only a few delaying payments for up to 90 days. Mr. Rogers was well aware of practices by many small drilling companies, especially during periods of tight money and high interest rates, to lean on the trade. As a banker, Mr. Rogers naturally was questioning whether the quality of Orleans' accounts receivable might be deteriorating and the company might have troubles with its collections in the near future.

Another concern that Mr. Rogers had was that, although the growing profits of the company was a positive sign, the cash shortage the company was experiencing could get much worse in the future and not better. As a result of Orleans' rapid increase in sales, earnings had risen steadily since 1977—almost tripling over the last three years. With the prospect of sales reaching $2 million, another record earnings year could be anticipated for 1980. He could see that the company's financing needs would easily surpass the $150,000 credit line with the Bayou National Bank if additional sources were not found. Increased inven-

tory levels would be needed to support the expected sales level. Furthermore, Mr. Rogers was aware that Mr. Caldwell would have to draw funds from the business in order to cover personal expenses and to pay income taxes. Since the company had been organized as a proprietorship for tax purposes and Mr. Caldwell had no other sources of income, he would have to pay personal income taxes on the company's profits with his drawings from company revenues. (See Exhibit 3 for a statement of changes in proprietorship for the first quarter of 1980.)

Mr. Caldwell had willingly furnished the bank staff member with all requested financial statements and information. Although Mr. Caldwell had stated to the staff member his deep concern about his company's cash shortage, he felt that the problem would work itself out as new, higher profits would be realized in 1980. He did not have a cash budget prepared to support his outlook but expressed optimism to the staff member that the firm would continue to perform successfully.

THE DECISION

After much deliberation, Mr. Rogers decided to extend an additional $100,000 credit to Orleans, with a stipulation that a fixed schedule of repayment be made before any additional borrowing could be extended. He called Mr. Caldwell to come to the bank and explained the terms of the increased line of credit. The terms were

1. $100,000 would be loaned at an interest rate 3 percent above the prime rate (the prime rate was 13 percent).

2. Twenty percent of the principal balance would be due on October 1 of

each year; interest payments would be semiannual, due on January 1 and July 1.

3. Orleans could not take on additional short-term debt from *any* other financial institution until the loan was paid off.

4. The bank could limit Mr. Caldwell's personal withdrawals of funds from the business to a maximum of $100,000 in any one year.

5. Orleans would have to maintain a minimum level of net working capital of at least $300,000.

Mr. Caldwell's reaction to the loan proposal was one of disappointment. He felt that the terms of the loan were too restrictive and that it might not allow the company to continue growing at the pace he wanted. The high interest rates on the loan would reduce his net profit margin, and he worried about what effect increasing prices to cover his financing costs might have on sales. Mr. Rogers was sympathetic to Mr. Caldwell's views and suggested that he try to find financing somewhere else to fund his increasing needs if he could not live with the terms of the proposed loan.

EXHIBIT 1

Orleans Tubular Supply Company

Comparative Balance Sheets
(dollar figures in thousands)

as of:	December 31			March 31
	1977 ($)	1978 ($)	1979 ($)	1980 ($)
Assets				
Cash	$ 99	$ 44	$ 18	$ 17
Accounts receivable (net)	121	166	227	248
Inventory	101	237	331	387
Total current assets	$ 321	$ 447	$ 576	$ 652
Property (net)	81	84	93	107
Total assets	$ 402	$ 531	$ 669	$ 759
Claims				
Notes payable–bank	96	116	146	147
Notes payable–trade	0	0	0	88
Accounts payable	82	142	188	154
Accrued expenses	2	12	39	41
Long-term debt (current)	4	4	4	4
Total current liabilities	$ 184	$ 274	$ 377	$ 434
Long-term debt	36	32	28	24
Total liabilities	$ 220	$ 306	$ 405	$ 458
Net worth	182	225	264	301
Total claims	$ 402	$ 531	$ 669	$ 759

EXHIBIT 2

Orleans Tubular Supply Company

Operating Statements
(dollar figures in thousands)

	Year Ending December 31			First Qtr.
	1977 ($)	1978 ($)	1979 ($)	1980 ($)
Net sales	$1143	$1451	$1756	$ 496*
Cost of goods sold:				
Beginning inventory	79	101	237	331
Purchases	861	1143	1330	382
Goods available for sale	940	1244	1567	713
Less ending inventory	101	237	331	387
Cost of goods sold	839	1007	1236	326
Gross profit	$ 304	$ 444	$ 520	$ 170
Operating expenses**	253	326	374	112
Net profit before taxes	$ 51	$ 118	$ 146	$ 58
Drawings by proprietor	62	75	107	21

*In the first quarter of 1979, net sales were $414,000 and net profit before taxes was $36,000.
**No allowance for a salary for Mr. Caldwell is included in either of these items as the firm was viewed as a sole proprietorship for income tax purposes.

EXHIBIT 3

Orleans Tubular Supply Company

Change in Proprietorship,
First Quarter, 1980
(dollar figures in thousands)

Proprietorship, December 31, 1979		$ 264
Net profit, first quarter	58	
Drawings by proprietor*	21	
Balance		37
Proprietorship (net worth), March 31, 1980		$ 301

*Drawings to cover living expenses and provision for payment of income tax.

CASE 9

Wall Sealants, Inc.

Bob Heath was a new employee of Klixon Incorporated, a giant multinational corporation, and was finding the firm's credit systems a bit bewildering. He had previously worked in the credit department of a much smaller and less sophisticated firm (Coombs Manufacturing) and had taken his present position as credit analyst with Klixon two months previously. He found that Klixon's method of analyzing the credit worthiness of customers and deciding to whom to grant credit was entirely different from that of Coombs Manufacturing.

Though Bob had no experience with the system used by Klixon (see Appendix A of this case for an outline of this system), he knew that there were many different approaches to the credit-granting decision. He was familiar with four such approaches.

1. Traditional Analysis Method—The

focus here is primarily on ratio analysis, with ratios measuring the credit applicant's liquidity and debt positions holding the most weight. Ratios and other data of interest concerning the credit applicant were analyzed across time (trend analysis) and with respect to industry averages. This was the system Bob Heath had used at Coombs Manufacturing. Credit analysis systems of this type, however, have several serious problems. The biggest one is how to weight the data so that a decision can be made. The analyst has a great deal of data to consider: numerous ratios computed for the applicant, their trends and levels relative to the industry, the applicant's management's experience, years in business, history of payments to suppliers, and so forth. If these factors present a mixed picture, it is not clear how they should be

---

This case was prepared by and used with the permission of Professor Frederick C. Scherr, West Virginia University.

weighted so as to give an optimum decision. Different credit analysts considering the same applicant can draw different conclusions, and this can lead to conflict. Such disagreements were one of the reasons Bob Heath had left Coombs Manufacturing.

2. *Marginal Analysis*—Whereas traditional analysis methods emphasize the credit worthiness of the credit applicant to be analyzed, marginal analysis methods also take into consideration some factors regarding the selling firm. These factors include the profitability of products to be sold, the correlations of sales of various divisions, and so forth. These factors are compared with the relative costs of a credit applicant or group of applicants: expected bad-debt costs, receivables carrying costs, costs of account administration, and so forth. This analysis method was based on the idea that when marginal revenues of an account and marginal costs of an account are equated, the profits of the firm are maximized. The major problems with this system involve the quantification of costs and revenues. It is necessary to obtain good estimates of the firm's default probabilities and payment times. This is complicated by statistical problems (see analysis method 4 below).

3. *Judgmental Weighting System*—This was the system used by Klixon Incorporated. In this system weights are attached to various factors associated with the credit applicant: various ratios, the applicant's history of payments to suppliers, marketing fac-

tors, and so forth. These weights could be derived in various ways: the credit manager's best judgment, a consensus of the credit analysts, and so forth. Based on the credit applicant's total weighted "score," credit decisions could be made. Specifically, most analysis methods of this type yield a "credit line," that is, the maximum amount of credit that the firm should extend to a credit applicant.

Though this analysis method avoids much of the ambiguity inherent in traditional methods, it still has problems. The chief of these is that there is no way to tie judgmentally derived weights back to an optimality model. Since the weights are based on the judgment of one or more persons, they are subject to the biases of those persons. Two groups developing weighting systems for similar firms might decide on different weights, and the superior decision might not be apparent.

4. *Statistical Method*—In this analysis method the idea is to predict slowness in payment or default of a credit applicant based on statistical analysis of past data for other customers. Such analysis points out what factors have been important in the past and the relative contribution of these factors to problems with customers and, therefore, credit-related costs. Any possible personal biases are eliminated since the technique considers only statistical significance. Unfortunately, there are technical statistical problems that make the technique difficult to apply. Klixon Incorporated was doing preliminary work in this area, but this

work was still considered experimental.

With all this in mind, Bob Heath wanted to analyze a new credit applicant, Wall Sealants, Inc. He had already decided to try both the traditional analysis method, which he had used at Coombs (see Exhibit 1), and Klixon's judgmental weighting system.

Exhibit 2 presents a balance sheet and income statement for Wall Sealants, Inc., for the fiscal year ending December 31, 1977. The firm had been started in the 1930s and was privately owned. The firm's managers were relatives of the founder, who had retired to live in Florida some years ago. All present officers had been with the firm all their working careers. Wall Sealants, Inc., manufactured coatings for cinder block walls. These coatings were used for waterproofing and scuff resistance and had to be applied to newly constructed walls. Sales were generally made to contractors of food processing facilities such as canneries, food packers, and breweries but were also made to hospitals, colleges, schools, and restaurants. The firm's sales were generally to companies within the continental United States. Wall Sealants maintained a modern plant and office building in a far western state. The buildings were leased, but the office furniture and production machinery were owned by the firm. The firm's long-term debt was owed to an insurance company and consisted of a long-term loan. The firm had dealt with the same bank for a number of years and maintained a satisfactory relationship. The firm had no subsidiaries or affiliates.

Wall Sealants' relationships with trade suppliers were sometimes strained. Bob Heath's file contained a "trade clearance" (a report made by creditors of Wall Sealants' payment to them). The report showed substantial slowness in payments to major suppliers. Bob had called many of the suppliers listed on the report and found the information presented to be an accurate picture of Wall Sealants' payment patterns to suppliers. This report is presented in Exhibit 3.

Bob Heath had consulted with the marketing and sales department of Klixon regarding Wall Sealants and found that expected sales were to be $15,000 per month. The marketing staff of Klixon claimed that Wall Sealants was a fairly desirable account for them since this was their first penetration into this market area. These expected sales to Wall Sealants would supplant sales to that firm by other suppliers.

EXHIBIT 1

Wall Sealants, Inc.

New Account Analysis Sheet
Used by Coombs Manufacturing

Date_____   New Account Name_____
                                             Address_____

Business Form: Corporation   Partnership   Proprietorship
Analysis based on statement dated_____
Audited   Unaudited   Audited with disclaimer

	Firm—Prior Year (if available)	Firm—Current Year	Industry
Current Ratio	_____	_____	_____
Quick Ratio	_____	_____	_____
Total Debt/Net Worth	_____	_____	_____
Accts. Rec. Turnover	_____	_____	_____
Inv. Turnover	_____	_____	_____
Profit Margin on Sales	_____	_____	_____
Years in Business	_____	_____	_____

Marketing Factors_____
_____
_____

Applicant Management Factors_____
_____
_____

                                             Analyst_____

EXHIBIT 2

Wall Sealants, Inc.

Balance Sheet and Income Statement
*For Fiscal Year Ending 12/31/77**

Cash	$ 54,750	Accounts payable	$ 511,000
Accounts receivable	659,027	Short-term notes	182,500
Inventory	638,750	Current portion, L.T.D.	18,250
Prepaid expenses	43,800	Taxes payable	109,500
Other current assets	11,113	Accruals	180,310
Total current assets	1,407,440	Total current liabilities	1,001,560
Net fixed assets	688,390	Long-term debt	173,740
Total assets	$2,095,830		
		Capital stock	100,000
		Retained earnings	820,530
		Total Lia. & Owners' Eq.	$2,095,830

Income Statement

Sales	$3,649,635
Cost of goods sold	2,554,745
Gross margin	1,094,890
Selling & other expenses	764,964
Earnings before taxes	329,926
Taxes	158,364
Earnings after taxes	$ 171,562

*(Audited by a major accounting firm; accountant's opinion contains no disclaimer)

EXHIBIT 3

Wall Sealants, Inc.

Trade Clearance for December 1977

Supplier Code No.	Most Owed ($)	Now Owing ($)	Past Due ($)	Invoice Terms Of Sale	Payment History
1	350	0	0	Net 30 days	Slow 20 days
2	100	0	0	Net 30 days	Slow 90 days
12	1,200	0	0	Net 30 days	Slow 90 days
22	54,700	37,200	18,200	Net 30 days	Slow 50 days
94	1,500	1,500	1,500	Net 30 days	Slow 15 days
42	1,200	0	0	Net 30 days	Slow 60 days
72	3,200	2,500	0	Net 30 days	Slow 45 days
74	22,600	7,300	5,100	Net 30 days	Slow 40 days
92	6,500	6,500	6,500	Net 30 days	Slow 45 days

APPENDIX A

Wall Sealants, Inc.

*Klixon Incorporated's Credit Analysis System**

The Klixon system considers 13 dimensions of credit worthiness. Scoring is based on percents of tangible net worth. To get the total credit line allowed to the credit applicant, one sums the contribution from each of the 13 dimensions and multiplies it by the tangible net worth. Should the contributions sum to a negative percent or should tangible net worth be negative or both, the customer receives no credit.

Contribution to Credit Line

1. *Initial Contribution* +10% of tangible net worth
2. *Percent of applicant's cost of sales furnished by Klixon*

under 25%	No contribution
25% to 50%	+5% of tangible net worth
over 50%	+10% of tangible net worth

3. *Applicant Payments to Trade*

Pay promptly	+10% of tangible net worth
Slowness to some suppliers only	+5% of tangible net worth
Generally slow 10–30 days	No contribution
Generally slow 31–60 days	−2.5% of tangible worth
Slowness beyond 60 days, C.O.D. or suits	−5% of tangible worth

4. *Years in Business*

less than 3	No contribution
3 to 10	+2.5% of tangible net worth
over 10	+5% of tangible net worth

5. *Profitability*
   Plus or minus .2% of tangible net worth
   for each 1% pretax profit or loss
   $$\frac{EBT}{Sales}$$

6. *Current Ratio*

2.00 and over	+10% of tangible net worth
1.25 to 1.99	+5% of tangible net worth
.75 to 1.24	No contribution
less than .75	−5% of tangible net worth

7. *Quick Ratio Restrictively Defined*
   (numerator is cash plus marketable
   securities plus accounts receivable)

2.00 and over	+15% of tangible net worth
1.00 to 1.99	+10% of tangible net worth
.80 to .99	+5% of tangible net worth
.50 to .79	No contribution
less than .50	−5% of tangible net worth

8. *Trade Payables—Inventory Relationship*
   (current liabilities divided by inventory)

less than .65	+10% of tangible net worth
.65 to .99	No contribution
1.00 and over	−5% of tangible net worth

9. *Inventory—Working Capital Relationship*
   (inventory divided by net working capital;
      an optimal range is assumed)

more than .99	−5% of tangible net worth
.50 to .99	+5% of tangible net worth
.25 to .49	No contribution
less than .25	−5% of tangible net worth

10. *Debt Position* (Tangible net worth plus
    subordinated debt divided by
    unsubordinate debt)

2.00 and over	+10% of tangible net worth
1.00 to 1.99	+5% of tangible net worth
below 1.00	−5% of tangible net worth

11. *Receivables Quality*
    .1% of tangible net worth contribution for each day that applicant's days sales outstanding is less than his terms of sale plus 30 days; −1% for each day it exceeds terms of sales plus 30 days.

12. *Inventory Management* (C.G.S. divided by
    inventory; an optimal range is assumed)

30.00 and over	No contribution
10.00 to 30.00	+10% of tangible net worth
5.00 to 9.99	+5% of tangible net worth
less than 5.00	No contribution

13. *Other Adjustments*
    (This allows the credit analyst to bring in factors not included in the other 12 dimensions. All such adjustments must be justified.)   Maximum adjustment ±10% of tangible net worth

*This system is adapted from the one presented in "Credit Limits Established by Formula and Computer," an Occasional Paper published by the Credit Research Foundation, September 1970, pages 8–13.

CASE 10

Midland Oil & Gas Company

Midland Oil and Gas Company was founded in 1932 by M. T. McCurdy. The depression of the 1930s had driven McCurdy, formerly a geologist with a major steel company in Pennsylvania, to seek his fortune in "black gold" in the plains of Texas. His first big strike had been in Midland, Texas, for which he named the company.

Over the next 40 years the company experienced a relatively high rate of growth and by the mid-1970s was regarded as one of the leading domestic companies in the exploration, development, and operation of oil and gas wells. Recently, however, McCurdy had observed that the company was requiring larger and larger quantities of cash just to maintain current reserve and production levels.

McCurdy felt that his company's current cash problems were attributable to several factors. First, the Tax Reform Act

of 1975 had eliminated the use of the percentage depletion allowance method for purposes of computing taxable income. This tax change had substantially increased the company's tax bill. Second, the increasing worldwide demand for oil had resulted in a shortage of exploration and extraction equipment. This shortage was accompanied by substantial price increases in the cost of drilling and lifting equipment. And finally, McCurdy noted that the cost of replacing the company's existing reserves through secondary and tertiary extraction methods was considerably greater than the original cost of the reserves.

McCurdy had become quite familiar with the company's recent cash-flow situation because, as chairman of the board of directors, he played a central role in the formulation and review of corporate plans. During 1978, he had reviewed a corporate proposal calling for

---

This case was prepared by and used with the permission of Professor Kenneth R. Ferris of Southern Methodist University.

an investment of approximately $200 million for 1979. The funds were to be used to replace worn-out equipment and to obtain new equipment for secondary and tertiary hydrocarbon recovery.

The proposal had assumed that 40 percent of the necessary funds could be internally generated from operations. McCurdy now questioned the validity of that assumption.

McCurdy was also concerned about how the remaining funds could be obtained. He was aware that the company had retired its preferred stock during 1978 but had also partially replaced this capital with a small public offering of common stock and the sale of $100 million of convertible debentures. McCurdy felt that another public offering of bonds or stock so soon after the previous offerings would not be well received by the market. He was also opposed to the reissuance of the preferred stock for tax reasons.

As McCurdy looked over the company's recent financial statements, he wondered whether the necessary financing might be arranged through a consortium of banks. (See Exhibits 1, 2, and 3 for financial statements.)

EXHIBIT 1

Midland Oil & Gas Company

Consolidated Balance Sheet

	12/31/78	12/31/77
Assets		
Current assets		
Cash (including certificates of deposit of $8 million)	$ 200,133,000	$ 220,500,000
Accounts receivables (net)—trade	138,200,000	106,400,000
Inventories (note 2)	117,900,000	93,600,000
Prepaid expenses	22,217,000	27,700,000
Total current assets	$ 478,450,000	$ 448,200,000
Investments		
In affiliated companies (note 1)	$ 318,000,000	$ 302,000,000
Sinking fund (note 3)	5,000,000	—
Long-term assets		
Undeveloped properties (note 4)	$ 32,700,000	$ 18,800,000
Oil and gas properties, and equipment (note 5)	670,000,000	675,000,000
Less: accumulated depreciation and depletion	(227,000,000)	(200,000,000)
Unamortized Goodwill	13,500,000	15,000,000
Total assets	$1,290,650,000	$1,259,000,000
Liabilities and Shareholders' Equity		
Current liabilities		
Accounts payables—trade	$ 10,800,000	$ 23,500,000
Federal income taxes payable	5,500,000	6,500,000
Dividends payable	4,000,000	—
Total current liabilities	$ 20,300,000	$ 30,000,000
Long-term liabilities		
10% convertible debentures	$ 100,000,000	—
Premium on debentures	7,200,000	—
Deferred income taxes (note 1)	92,000,000	80,000,000
Unfunded pension costs	125,000,000	120,000,000
Total liabilities	$ 344,500,000	230,000,000
Shareholders' equity		
Common stock, $10 par; authorized shares, 50,000,000 (note 6)	$ 206,000,000	$ 150,000,000
Preferred stock, $50 par; authorized shares, 1,000,000 (note 6)	—	25,000,000
Capital in excess of par value:		
Common	$ 315,000,000	$ 300,000,000
Preferred	—	175,000,000
Retained earnings	425,150,000	379,000,000
Total liabilities and shareholders' equity	$1,290,650,000	$1,259,000,000

EXHIBIT 2

Midland Oil & Gas Company

Consolidated Statement of Income
For the Year Ended 12/31/78

Revenues		
Oil sales	$630,970,000	
Gas sales	335,300,000	
		$966,270,000
Cost and expenses		
Cost of operations and products sold	$741,440,000	
Selling, general, and administrative	108,430,000	
Interest	9,700,000	
Amortization of Goodwill	1,500,000	
		$861,070,000
		$105,200,000
Other Sources of Income		
Income from unconsolidated subsidiaries		$ 73,300,000
Gain on sale of undeveloped properties		2,000,000
Earnings before income taxes		180,500,000
Federal income taxes (note 1)		88,350,000
Net earnings		$ 92,150,000

EXHIBIT 3

Midland Oil & Gas Company

Notes to Consolidated Financial Statements

1. Summary of Significant Accounting Policies

Principles of Consolidation

The consolidated financial statements include the accounts of Midland Oil and Gas Company and all significant subsidiaries, after elimination of intercompany transactions and balances. Income from subsidiaries in which ownership is 20 to 50 percent is recognized on an equity basis. All affiliated companies are engaged in the extraction industry.

Depreciation and Amortization

Depreciation has been provided using the straight-line method, except for depreciation of oil and gas production equipment, which is determined using the unit-of-production method.

Goodwill, obtained in conjunction with the acquisition of Northwest Drilling, Inc., on December 31, 1977, is being amortized on a straight-line basis over a ten-year period.

Exploration and Development Costs

All intangible drilling and development costs are accounted for under the "successful efforts" method of accounting as defined by Financial Accounting Standards (FAS) No. 19, entitled "Financial Accounting and Reporting by Oil and Gas Producing Companies." Geological and geophysical expenses are charged against income as incurred.

Income Taxes

The company and its subsidiaries file consolidated federal income tax returns.

Deferred federal income taxes arise principally from the use of straight-line depreciation for statement purposes and accelerated methods used in computing deductions for current income taxes. The investment tax credit is taken into income currently as a reduction of the provision for income taxes.

2. Inventories

Inventories of crude oil and unrefined products are valued at lower of cost or market, using the first-in, first-out method. The inventory amounts used in the computation of cost of sales were $120,220,000 and $95,300,000 for the years ended December 31, 1978 and 1977, respectively.

3. Sinking Fund

The 10-percent convertible debentures issued on January 1, 1978, are payable December 31, 1987. Under the terms of the bond indenture, a sinking fund was established during 1978. The cash fund will be administered by the First State Bank of Lake Highlands, Texas.

4. Undeveloped Properties

The company follows a policy of both purchasing and leasing undeveloped oil and gas properties. Consistent with FAS No. 19, leasehold costs are initially capitalized. Subsequent accounting treatment of these costs depends upon the size and cost of extraction of discovered reserves. All undeveloped properties acquired during 1977 were found to be economically productive.

During 1978, undeveloped oil and gas properties were acquired from a major shareholder in exchange for 1 million shares of the company's common stock. These properties were recorded at the par value of the issued shares.

During 1978, certain undeveloped properties located in Oklahoma were sold to the Unit Drilling and Exploration Company. The properties were sold for $9 million and had a book value of $7 million.

5. Oil and Gas Properties and Equipment

Depreciation and depletion taken during 1978 totalled $49.6 million. During 1977 the company began a program of replacing certain out-dated extraction equipment. New acquisitions in 1978 amounted to $24,650,000. The company plans to acquire approximately $200 million in new equipment during 1979.

6. Shareholders' Equity

The authorized and issued shares of capital stock at December 31, 1977 and 1978, are summarized as follows:

	Authorized Shares	Issued Shares 1977	Issued Shares 1978
Preferred stock, $50 par	1,000,000	500,000	—
Common stock, $10 par	50,000,000	15,000,000	20,600,000

During the month of January, 1978, 1 million shares of common stock were issued in exchange for undeveloped oil and gas properties (see note 4). In June 1978, a 25-percent common stock dividend was declared and distributed. A public offering of 600,000 common shares, was held in December 1978; the offering was fully subscribed.

As of December 31, 1977, 500,000 shares of $50 par preferred stock was outstanding. The entire amount was redeemed during 1978 for $202 million.

CASE 11

Woodside Sport Center, Inc.

In early May 1976 Mark Ellis, president of Woodside Sport Center, was in the process of forecasting financial requirements for the firm. For the past several years the average annual growth rate in sales had been approximately 22 percent, and according to Mr. Ellis, there was no reason to expect a decline in this growth rate over the next five-year period.[1]

HISTORY

Woodside Sport Center was founded by Mark Ellis in March 1966 in a major city in Northern California. The size of the initial store was only 300 square feet, and the company specialized in tennis equipment. Shortly thereafter, seasonal considerations caused Mr. Ellis to add ski equipment to his line of products.

During its first few months of existence, the firm was forced to move to a larger facility with 3000 square feet in order to satisfy rapidly increasing demand for its products. Furthermore, as sales continued to grow, new lines of sporting goods (e.g., backpacking, track, baseball, and kayaking) were added, and by July 1974 three retail outlets were in operation. In 1975 sales of ski equipment provided the "lion's share" of the firm's revenue. Financial statements are provided in Exhibits 1 through 4.

THE MARKET

In the market area for Woodside Sport Center, a large number of establishments sold sporting goods. Only a fraction of these were true competitors, however, since many of the stores specialized in

---

This case was prepared by and used with the permission of Professor Burton F. Schaffer, California State University, Sacramento.

[1] All names, facts, and figures have been disguised to assure anonymity.

fishing equipment or other lines that Woodside either did not carry or carried only in small quantities.

Moreover, in large part, Woodside carried major quality brands and did not compete with retailers of low-priced sporting equipment. As Mr. Ellis stated: "Most of the people who enter one of our stores know in advance that our prices tend to be higher than average because we sell quality merchandise."

Although no market penetration study had been conducted, Mr. Ellis believed that Woodside had managed to capture a "respectable" share of the market for ski equipment. In addition, he stated that most of the sales effort in the future would be aimed at increasing Woodside's share of the skiing market.

MANAGEMENT

Woodside Sport Center, Inc., was organized in a highly centralized fashion with Mark Ellis, the president and principal owner, making almost all major policy decisions. While each retail outlet had an individual with the title of manager, the authority of each manager was limited to making day-to-day operating decisions. Mr. Ellis believed that a centralized organization was justified by both his academic background and practical experience. Concerning academics, Mr. Ellis received a bachelor's degree in accounting from a major university in June 1965. Furthermore, his experience in the sports field was quite extensive in that he had been a member of a university tennis team, a tennis pro at two tennis clubs, and a teacher in a tennis clinic. In addition, he was regarded as an extremely proficient skier by those who knew him.

SALES

Although Mr. Ellis recognized the underlying assumptions of using the past to predict the future, he believed that trend analysis was adequate for forecasting sales. With respect to using past trends, Mr. Ellis stated: "Forecasting future sales with the use of past trends has always worked for me in the past, and I see no reason to change methods at this time. Of course, my predictions in the short run have tended to be much more accurate than my long-run predictions; however, from my viewpoint, forecasting errors during the operating cycle are much more costly than long-range forecasting errors. I can always change my long-run forecasts as more data becomes available, whereas I have to live with my mistakes in the short run."

Forecasted sales figures were also being used as target goals. If actual sales were falling below predicted amounts, Mr. Ellis would attempt to correct these deviations by experimenting until successful changes were found. For example, at one point in time, a line of golf equipment was introduced; however, it proved to be a slow-moving line and was deleted from the shelves.

In another instance Woodside was experiencing a decline in night patronage. To overcome this decline, evening training sessions in the use of tennis and ski equipment were offered free to the public at each store. This experiment proved to be quite successful in terms of increasing night patronage.

Advertising

As Woodside grew in sales volume over the years, advertising expenditures became increasingly important in terms of maintaining Woodside's target growth rate. Initially, advertising was basically limited to local newspaper ads; however, by 1975 expenditures were being made for direct mail and radio advertising.

Pricing

Prices on most of the merchandise were usually set in accordance with the manufacturer's suggested retail price with mark-ups averaging about 42 percent. On occasion Woodside gave team discounts with mark-ups on team purchases averaging about 33 percent. Items experiencing extended shelf-lives were marked down periodically.

FINANCIAL PLANNING

Mr. Ellis maintained full responsibility for forecasting the financial requirements of Woodside Sport Center. According to Mr. Ellis, financial planning was vitally important in an industry that relies heavily on short-term debt as a source of funds. In addition to being important, he believed that this aspect of his job was the most difficult to perform. As Mr. Ellis stated: "The most important variable used in forecasting financial requirements is projected sales volume. Currently, we are looking at an expected annual growth rate of 22 percent. This means, of course, that Woodside will have to double in size over the next five years. Therefore, we will have to expand our existing stores or possibly open a couple of new ones. Regardless of which way we go it is going to take money, and we must make plans for it now."

EXHIBIT 1

Woodside Sport Center, Inc.

Comparative Balance Sheets
(dollar figures in thousands)

	1975	1974	1973	1972	1971	1970	1969
Current assets							
Cash	$ 18	$ 33	$ 34	$ 38	$ 23	$ 38	$ 39
Accounts receivable (net)	25	27	26	25	24	29	20
Inventory	366	330	282	256	247	207	180
Other	84	42	32	25	16	6	0
Total current assets	493	432	374	344	310	280	239
Fixed assets (net)	77	64	45	23	19	11	11
Total assets	$570	$496	$419	$367	$329	$291	$250
Current liabilities							
Accounts payable	300	268	236	219	198	180	161
Other	104	88	57	46	40	26	23
Total current liabilities	404	356	293	265	238	206	184
Long-term liabilities	88	63	54	32	22	18	3
Capital stock	35	35	35	35	35	35	35
Retained earnings	43	42	37	35	34	32	28
Total liabilities and capital	$570	$496	$419	$367	$329	$291	$250

EXHIBIT 2

Woodside Sport Center, Inc.

Common Size Balance Sheets
(percent)

	1975	1974	1973	1972	1971	1970	1969
Current assets							
Cash	3.2	6.7	8.1	10.3	7.0	13.0	15.6
Accounts receivable (net)	4.4	5.4	6.2	6.9	7.3	9.8	8.0
Inventory	64.2	66.5	67.3	69.8	75.0	71.2	72.0
Other	14.7	8.5	7.6	6.7	4.8	2.0	0.0
Total current assets	86.5	87.1	89.2	93.7	94.1	96.0	95.6
Fixed assets (net)	13.5	12.9	10.8	6.3	5.9	4.0	4.4
Total assets	100.0	100.0	100.0	100.0	100.0	100.0	100.0
Current liabilities							
Accounts payable	52.6	54.1	56.3	59.8	60.2	62.0	64.4
Other	18.3	17.7	13.5	12.5	12.3	9.0	9.2
Total current liabilities	70.9	71.8	69.8	72.3	72.5	71.0	73.6
Long-term liabilities	15.4	12.8	12.9	8.6	6.5	6.2	1.2
Capital stock	6.1	7.1	8.4	9.5	10.6	12.0	14.0
Retained earnings	7.6	8.3	8.9	9.6	10.4	10.8	11.2
Total liabilities and capital	100.0	100.0	100.0	100.0	100.0	100.0	100.0

EXHIBIT 3

Woodside Sport Center, Inc.

Comparative Income Statements
(dollar figures in thousands)

	1975	1974	1973	1972	1971	1970	1969
Net sales	$1,303	$1,089	$934	$661	$584	$467	$389
Cost of sales	806	699	610	428	390	324	278
Gross profit	497	390	324	233	194	143	111
Operating and adm. expenses							
Salaries and wages	169	138	116	78	65	50	40
Rent	46	36	30	19	17	13	10
Advertising	78	59	39	25	18	14	10
Depreciation	24	17	11	5	5	3	2
Other	99	58	53	51	36	19	8
Total operating and adm. expenses	416	308	249	178	141	99	70
Net income before taxes	81	82	75	55	53	44	41

EXHIBIT 4

Woodside Sport Center, Inc.

Common Size Income Statements
(percent)

	1975	1974	1973	1972	1971	1970	1969
Net sales	100.0	100.0	100.0	100.0	100.0	100.0	100.0
Cost of sales	61.9	64.2	65.3	64.8	66.7	69.4	71.5
Gross profit	38.1	35.8	34.7	35.2	33.3	30.6	28.5
Operating and adm. expenses							
Salaries and wages	13.0	12.7	12.4	11.8	11.2	10.8	10.3
Rent	3.5	3.3	3.2	2.9	2.9	2.7	2.6
Advertising	6.0	5.4	4.2	3.8	3.1	2.9	2.6
Depreciation	1.8	1.6	1.2	.8	.8	.7	.5
Other	7.6	5.3	5.7	7.6	6.2	4.1	2.0
Total operating and adm. expenses	31.9	28.3	26.7	26.9	24.2	21.2	18.0
Net income before taxes	6.2	7.5	8.0	8.3	9.1	9.4	10.5

CASE 12

Home Health Care, Inc.

CREATION

Home Health Care, Inc., was formed as a nonprofit tax-exempt agency in late 1977. It was organized to fill what its founder felt was an unmet need for health care of home-bound patients in their residences. Since it was a health delivery agency, approval for its formation was needed from the Regional Health Planning Commission and the State Department of Health. Opposition to the agency's formation was expressed by county health departments, which had existing home health care programs. These departments felt that the new agency would compete with their programs and reduce their patient loads. These health departments were operating at budget deficits and were very concerned about any further loss of revenues through reduced patient loads. They contended that approval of this agency would result in a duplication of services and a resultant increase in service costs.

The agency's founder, Jane Fletcher, presented some very good arguments to the Regional Health Planning Commission when seeking approval of the agency.

1. Unlike the county health departments, which provided services only within their own county, this agency would provide services in three contiguous counties. There would be one centrally located office with health care delivery teams in each of the counties. This would minimize the fixed overhead and administrative costs.

2. Services would be provided by part-time employees of the agency or through contracts with other agencies providing specialized services,

---

This case was prepared by and used with the permission of Professor Paul A. Mueller of Bowling Green State University.

such as physical therapy. This would reduce wage costs to those incurred only when services were provided. The health departments operated with salaried employees, which did not allow for reduced labor costs when patient loads decreased.

3. The age demographics of the three counties demonstrated that there was a very large number of elderly and that the health departments were not capable of providing health services to all of them that may be home bound. There was a very large market that was unserviced. Through public service advertising, information dissemination by hospitals, doctors, and churches, and referrals of patients, the public awareness of the available services could be raised and better health care could be provided without any necessary reduction of patient loads for the health departments. In fact, the health departments' patient loads would benefit by more public awareness of available health care services.

4. While all counties had health departments, one county did not provide home health care.

This one county's health commissioner recommended that the regional planning commission approve formation of Home Health Care, Inc. He felt that his health department could not provide these services economically because his county was sparsely populated and very large geographically. Also, he was aware of the budget deficits of the other two county health departments. These deficits were caused in large part by their home health care services. Even with this recommendation, the regional planning commission could recommend approval of the agency in only this county and disapprove recommendation in the other two counties.

The Regional Health Planning Commission approved the agency for operation in all three counties. The State Health Department concurred, and the agency began to take form. Part-time employees were hired and contracts signed with agencies to provide specialized services. However, Ms. Fletcher knew that for success of the agency, Medicare certification was necessary. The certification evaluation was oriented not toward the need for the health services the agency provided but toward the quality and breadth of services. The qualifications of the personnel were reviewed, and the types of services provided by the agency's personnel and through contract services were identified. Because the design of the agency was to treat home-bound patients, the vast majority of the agency's patients would be the Medicare eligible elderly. The Medicare certification was received in the spring of 1978. While the agency had been treating patients between the time of state approval and Medicare certification, this certification was the life blood of the agency.

DEVELOPMENT

Since its beginning, the agency had been very successful. This success is reflected in Exhibit 1, which shows, by month, the number of visits the agency made in its three-year history. The continued success of the agency seemed assured because

1. Increased emphasis on early hospital discharge by insurance carriers

would increase the need for home health care. Patients who continued to need skilled medical care, but not on a 24-hour basis, could be discharged from the hospital to receive care in their homes. The cost would be far less than the daily cost for a hospital room.

2. Also, with the increasing number of elderly and their need for medical treatment on an out-patient basis, the home health agency could provide service for those who could not travel.

3. With the current budget constraints of federal and local governments, there would be increased emphasis on cost containment programs for health care delivery. The care of patients in their homes was by far the cheapest method of providing health care to those who were unable to travel.

Throughout its history the agency had expanded the services it provided. Currently, it offered a complete range of medical care services. It employed registered and licensed practical nurses who provided skilled nursing care. Physical, speech, and occupational therapy were provided through a contract arrangement with other agencies specializing in these services. Medical social services and nutritional counseling were also available. In late 1978 a home health aide service was initiated to provide custodial care for patients. The agency had developed a complete range of services for the homebound patient.

The operation and staffing of the agency was unique. Unlike other home health agencies within the state, which operated in only one county, this agency provided services in three counties. The agency was investigating the possibility of crossing state lines to provide services in a contiguous state. The cross-county operation reduced the administrative costs by requiring only one central office. The administrator, Ms. Fletcher, and her clerical staff worked at this office. In each county there was a team of nurses and aides that provided services within its county. The team supervisor functioned directly out of her home so there was no need for county offices. The members of the team traveled directly from their homes to the patients' and then reported the patients' conditions to their supervisor. The members of the nursing teams were all part-time employees. The nurses and home health aides were paid a fixed fee per visit, plus a mileage reimbursement. This operation and staffing of the agency allowed it to service over a wide geographical area with a minimum of fixed costs.

Physical therapy, speech therapy, and occupational therapy were provided to patients through a contract arrangement. These types of therapy were very specialized. There were other private organizations within the area that provide only these services. Through contracts, these organizations provided services to Home Health Care, Inc. These contract service organizations billed the agency, on a per visit basis, for reimbursement, at a fee with no mileage compensation.

The above operation and staffing of the agency was what made it so successful. Complete cost flexibility was built in, with little exception. Labor costs and contract service costs were totally dependent upon the patient load. The only costs that were presently fixed were the office rent and utilities, depreciation, and debt service costs. As a part of the total budget, these fixed costs were small. At the agency's beginning, these fixed costs did not exist because the central office was located in the administrator's home. Through this flexibility, the agency had survived its infancy and had grown to be an organization that would provide over 10,000 visits in 1981.

FUNDING

Ms. Fletcher, in addition to developing the conceptual need for the agency and its subsequent physical organization, supplied a large part of the financial funding. The state provided some initial seed money, but it was insufficient to meet the initial start-up costs. Many of these start-up costs were administrative and thus, not offset by patient care reimbursements. Though she drew payment for her services to the agency during its infancy, she allowed the agency to retain a portion of it to meet operating and wage expenses.

Over the three-year life of the agency, approximately 85 percent of the home visits were reimbursed through Medicare. The remaining 15 percent were reimbursed through private insurance, individual payment, or charity such as the Cancer Society. Reimbursement by Medicare was made through a set procedure. When a patient was admitted through a physician's referral, a form HCFA-1487 was submitted to the Medicare intermediary for determination of Medicare eligibility. In addition, determination had to be made as to whether payment would be made through Medicare A (posthospital plan) or Medicare B (medical plan). No billing could be submitted until the HCFA-1487 was returned by the intermediary. Eligibility determination required two to three weeks. Billing was then submitted by the agency bimonthly. Exhibit 2 presents a schedule of Medicare billings and payment receipts for the years 1978 and 1979. The payment schedule for 1980 was similar to that for late 1979, though the amounts had increased because of increased patient loads.

Time sheets for hourly employees, visitation slips for nurses and aides, and billings from contract agencies were required in the central office by the fifth of each month. The agency then paid its employees and the agencies providing contract services on the fifteenth of that month. The visitation slips and contract billings were used for billings to Medicare and to other payees. Medicare was billed twice monthly. Medicare patients whose last names began with A through M were billed the first half of the month. The remainder were billed the second half of the month. The reason behind this was that Medicare did reimbursements on a batch basis. If one single batch was submitted, it would take longer to process than if two smaller batches were submitted. All other payees were billed in the early part of the month.

At the end of each year Medicare required the submission of the "calculation of reimbursable cost of home health services" form. On this form the total costs of the home health agency had to be submitted on an accrual basis for each calendar year. These costs had to be further broken down to those attributable to Medicare. This was done on the basis of proportion of total visits that were made to Medicare patients. If the Medicare costs exceeded reimbursement by Medicare, Medicare would disburse an amount equal to the deficit. If reimbursement by Medicare exceeded the costs, the agency had to refund the excess to Medicare. With private insurance, private pay, or charitable reimbursement, there was no such required adjustment at the end of each year when actual costs were determined.

The fee structure for the agency was simple. Regardless of the service provided or the distance the agency's representative had to travel, there was one flat fee. For 1978 the fee was $20.00 per visit and during 1979 it was raised to $30.00. Currently, the agency's board was considering raising the fee once more. However, before the fee could be adjusted, it had to be justified by the agency and approved by Medicare. Justification for Medicare was a demonstrated higher cost per visit than the current reimbursement rate. Because of the agency's centralized administrative structure and employee compensation per visit, the costs per visit were lower for this agency than for other home health agencies. The cost for other agencies was in excess of

$35.00 per visit and in some cases higher than $40.00.

Presently, the agency was just able to meet its operating expenses. However, depending on the number of visits, it has had to delay wage payments to the administrator or make late payments to the contract agencies. Consequently, the administrator had not been able to draw down her note payable to the agency or to withdraw her salary retained by the agency. In fact, because of her position with the agency, while she could earn interest on her note payable, this interest expense could not be entered into the cost calculation for Medicare reimbursement. The advisory board was meeting and was considering additional bank borrowing or the establishment of a line of credit to allow Ms. Fletcher to withdraw her retained salary and eliminate or draw down her note payable. However, they were highly concerned about the 20-percent interest rate the agency had to pay for borrowed funds. Financial statements are provided in Exhibits 3 and 4.

EXHIBIT 1

Home Health Care, Inc.

Number of Visits by Month

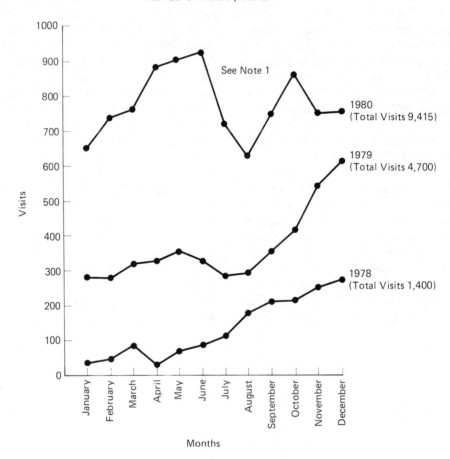

HOME HEALTH CARE, INC.
Number of Visits by Month

Note 1. Decline in visits was a result of cutback in Title XX funding for Home Health Aides.

EXHIBIT 2

Home Health Care, Inc.

Medicare Schedule of Payments
Total Medicare Billing by Month for 1978 and 1979

Total Payment Receipt by Month

1978	May ($)	June ($)	July ($)	August ($)	September ($)	October ($)	November ($)	December ($)
Sept	40	240	1460	1100	120			
Oct	720	240	360	660	1600	440		
Nov			140		1300		2860	
Dec			20					

Total Payment Receipt by Month

1979	Oct ($)	Nov ($)	Dec ($)	Jan ($)	Feb ($)	Mar ($)	Apr ($)	May ($)	Jun ($)	Jul ($)	Aug ($)	Sep ($)	Oct ($)	Nov ($)	Dec ($)
Jan	2060	1580	1080	4920											
Feb		700	3280	780	4110										
Mar		20	1120		3570	2100									
Apr					150	5550	5460								
May						480	2100	1770							
Jun						1740	30	3480	5520						
Jul						120	150	570	6810	3930					
Aug							360	810	630	1800	1230				
Sep										510	3840	2130			
Oct										60	150	720	3660		
Nov													2520	120	
Dec															

93

EXHIBIT 3

Home Health Care, Inc.

Balance Sheets as of December 31, 1978–80

Years	1978		1979		1980
Assets					
Cash		$ 2,977		$ 2,398		$13,720
Accounts receivable					
Private	$ 1,097		$ 11		$ 1,629	
Medicare	10,480		26,610		36,240	
Other reimbursement					
plans	1,600	13,177	7,661	34,282	10,912	48,781
Deposit—industrial					
insurance		42		26		63
Total current assets		$16,196		$36,706		$62,564
Equipment (net)		2,375		3,209		4,270
Total assets		$18,571		$39,915		$66,834
Liabilities and Fund Balance					
Notes payable					
Bank, unsecured		$ 4,000		—		$12,000
Administrator		—		$10,772		10,772
Accounts payable		6,253		4,341		1,761
Due to administrator		17,228		6,457		6,457
Advances		1,980		799		500
Due to Medicare					
reimbursement		—		—		2,992
Accrued liabilities					
Payroll taxes					
withheld	$ 250		$ 707		$ 3,794	
Accrued payroll	3,121		11,061		16,223	
Accrued insurance	270		458		956	
Accrued interest	111	3,752	1,206	13,432	2,412	23,385
Total current					
liabilities		$33,213		$35,801		$57,867
Fund balance (deficit)		(14,642)		4,114		8,967
Total liabilities and					
fund balance		$18,571		$39,915		$66,834

EXHIBIT 4

Home Health Care, Inc.

Income Statements for Years Ending December 31, 1978–80

	1978		1979		1980	
Revenue						
Program service fees						
Medicare	$22,087		$104,227		$185,212	
Title XX	—		9,698		23,587	
Private	1,532		2,931		7,460	
Other reimbursement plans	4,380	$27,999	17,208	$134,064	36,306	$252,565
Grants and donations		9,780		5,894		3,283
Other		—		56		59
Total revenue		$37,779		$140,014		$255,907
Operating costs and expenses						
Salaries	$28,606		$ 63,652		$126,517	
Contract service fees	5,972		26,928		68,898	
Travel	5,112		10,676		23,062	
Medical and nursing supplies	1,665		1,815		2,345	
Depreciation	353		557		796	
Administrative expenses	10,654		15,173		27,794	
Bad debts	60		2,456		1,642	
Total operating costs and expenses		52,422		121,257		251,054
Net income (loss)		($14,643)		$ 18,757		$ 4,853
Fund balance (deficit) at beginning of year		—		(14,643)		4,114
Fund balance (deficit) at end of year		($14,643)		$ 4,114		$ 8,967

PART THREE

Management of Fixed Resources

CASE 13

Computerized Time Reporting

Segment 1

In May 1978 the top management of BNP Company, a regulated monopoly in California, was faced with the decision whether or not to implement a new computerized time-reporting system in the payroll data processing group, a part of the Data Services Division, which was in the Finance and Comptroller Department. The new system of entering time into the payroll system was to replace the existing time-posting system, which had been implemented early in 1976. Computerized time posting was carried out in the headquarters Payroll Office in San Francisco; it involved 20 data entry clerks inputting daily and biweekly time to a centralized data base using on-line keyboards and CRT display stations. Computerized time posting (CTP) provided Payroll Office personnel with on-line error detection and correction procedures. Thus, time posting was completely computerized. Time reporting, however, was still a mixture of manual and computerized processes. These included:

1. Manual preparation of 3500 daily time sheets.

2. Manual delivery by mail, taxi, or hand of 3500 daily time sheets to the San Francisco Payroll Office.

3. Additional telephone reporting of time and material data for 2000 repair and maintenance personnel around the state to the San Francisco Repair and Maintenance Editing Unit.

4. Hand carrying of time sheets manually prepared in Repair and Maintenance Editing to the Payroll Office.

5. Daily telephone reporting of time data for 500 Network employees to the Network Center.

This case was prepared by Mr. James A. Wilbur under the supervision of Professor William L. Weis, Seattle University, and used with the permission of the authors.

6. Computerized teletype distribution of time sheets from the Network Center to the Payroll Office.

7. Manual preparation of 750 time sheets for biweekly time data, with subsequent delivery to the Payroll Office in San Francisco.

In February of 1978 Mike Muncy, an alert staff manager with a recent MBA in Finance, had been put in charge of the first phase of the decision process regarding computerizing these reporting procedures—a feasibility study. Upper management was now faced with evaluating his results and arriving at a decision on whether to implement the project during the next two years. Mike, along with various other first- and second-level managers in the Finance and Comptroller Department, had taken three months to assemble the following document, which on May 28 was placed on the desk of Larry Roberts, BNP's vice-president of finance and comptroller.

CTR

COMPUTERIZED TIME REPORTING

FEASIBILITY STUDY*

MAY 1978

Review of Current Problems

Computerized Time Posting (CTP) was implemented in 1976 as a Payroll Office procedure in order to solve a number of problems in that office: manual cross-adding, posting, keypunching, error analysis, and error correction. CTP did not, nor was it conceived to, address the many time-reporting problems in the field. The computerized Network system produces time sheets for the Payroll Office. There is no parallel to its management reporting system, but the Network Center, the Repair and Maintenance Editing Unit, and the biweekly reporting unit have common problems in reporting time to the payroll system. These problems include:

1. Different types of time sheets are used although oftentimes they report the same data.

2. Different methods are used for reporting time.

3. Different intervals are used for reporting time.

4. Requirements for advancing time are imposed just before closing the payroll.

5. Error-correction procedures are too complicated and time consuming.

6. Reports are late getting out.

7. Daily access to overtime or premium data does not exist.

8. Mail service is unreliable, taxi/hand-carry too expensive.

---

*Presented here in condensed form

These qualitative problems must be weighed in light of the number of employees involved: 6750 in the company's workforce. A time study conducted by the company indicates that supervisors and clerical personnel spend six minutes per day per employee recording time data alone. Thus, hundreds of hours each day are spent on time-reporting procedures that can be simplified by computerization. Computerization will provide management with more time for supervisory activities, provide more useful report data, and cut expenses.

Review of Anticipated Problems

Two known major systems will have dramatic affects on time-reporting procedures in 1979:

Functional accounting will require a variety of codes to be reported with payroll and labor by July 1, 1979. In addition to these codes, service order reporting requirements of functional accounting will represent a tenfold increase in the amount of data to be reported for repair and maintenance forces to CTP. An additional 30 clerks will be required to key this data into CTP.

Cost accounting will be implemented by year-end 1979, although no specific date has been set. It is known that productive labor hours can no longer be summarized by crew. Instead, these hours will have to be reported and entered into the CTP system at the employee (social security number) level. Because currently there is an average of eight employees per crew, this requirement will mean an increase in the amount of detail being processed. An additional ten clerks will be required to key this data into CTP.

CTR Feasibility Study Plan

In light of the current and anticipated problems just outlined, this feasibility study was undertaken to determine the economic and service advantages of a Computerized Time Reporting (CTR) system and to make appropriate recommendations.

CTR Scope Alternatives

Early in the feasibility study, two alternatives were identified as possible for the scope of the initial CTR project:

1. Convert all 6750 employees to CTR.
2. Convert only 3000 occupational employees to CTR.

CTR Scope Recommendations

Regardless of the resources made available, only so much can be accomplished by July 1, 1979, to meet the new accounting requirements on payroll and labor. To attempt only a partial conversion would greatly enhance the feasibility of implementing the system in 1979. Recommendations:

1. Initial CTR project be limited to 3000 occupational employees.

2. Network and CTP systems be modified to support functional and cost-accounting requirements of the remaining 3750 employees.

3. After the initial CTR conversion in 1979, further expansion to other groups be considered.

CTR System Alternatives

Four different configurations were identified as possible CTR system alternatives:

1. CTR on the Network time-share system.

2. CTR using P/N [BNP's shared data communications network] teleprocessing of data to current host system (CTP).

3. CTR using minicomputers as front-end processors, teleprocessing accounting data to current host system. Within this alternative three minicomputer vendor alternatives were considered: Datapoint, Four-Phase, and IBM.

4. CTR on a completely new host system using teleprocessing via P/N.

After preliminary evaluation, the first and fourth alternatives were considered unfeasible. Modifying the Network time-share system to support time-reporting requirements of the whole company was not feasible because the current computing equipment (Univac) is not capable of supporting the additional processing load. Developing a completely new CTR host system was not considered feasible because of the 12-month schedule limitation for functional accounting. Thus, the second and third alternatives remain. The CTR P/N host alternative entails modifying the existing CTP programs to support all input and output requirements of the system. CTP runs under IMS (Information Management System) on the IBM/Amdahl host system in the San Francisco Computer Center. Under a CTR configuration leased-line terminal access to the host system would be provided by P/N. The CTR minicomputer-host alternative would use minicomputers as front-end processors to support the user's input and output requirements. Dial-up access to the minicomputers would be provided. The minicomputers would in turn transmit to the existing host system (CTP) all accounting data required for subsequent processing.

Minicomputer alternatives: Costs of the three different minicomputer systems are:

	Datapoint	*Four-Phase*	*IBM*
Installed cost	$310,000	$230,000	$331,000
Annual maintenance	55,000	25,000	32,000

Minicomputer recommendation: Even though the IBM system is the most expensive, the recommendation is to go with IBM front-end processors for the following qualitative reasons:

1. IBM has a proven interface procedure with an IBM/IMS host facility.

2. IBM provides for ongoing program maintenance and testing concurrent with production processing.

3. IBM has a distinct advantage in terms of computing capacity. This extra capacity is important because it is difficult to accurately predict the future system load.

4. An IBM system will require less programming effort and has an advantage in terms of local availability of technical expertise.

5. An IBM system provides capability of printing reports in one location while key-entering time data in another.

CTR System Recommendation

Based on costs, potential savings, and all of the qualitative factors presented in this study, the recommended CTR system is the minicomputer-host alternative. Specifically, this recommendation is based on:

1. Costs. Although the capital investment requirement for the minicomputer alternative is higher, the expense during the development years (1978 and 1979) is less, and the annual recurring savings is three times that of the P/N alternative. The annual savings of the minicomputer-host system is $159,000, starting in 1980, whereas the P/N alternative shows savings of $49,000 (see Exhibits 1, 2, and 3).

2. Programming effort. Six additional programmers are required for the minicomputer-host alternative, whereas 11 are required for the P/N alternative, in 1978 (see Exhibit 4).

3. Functional accounting schedule. A CTR system should be implemented in BNP by July 1, 1979, to meet the functional accounting requirements for payroll and labor. About 12 months will be available to design, code, and test CTR. The programming complexities of the P/N host system are such that this alternative may not even be feasible, given the functional accounting schedule. The minicomputer-host alternative is the most attractive because it will enable the company to meet the functional accounting requirements.

Developmental Plan

Provided that CTR is approved as a project, the programming effort will be organized within two groups in one district of data services. A user support group will also be organized within the staff of the Finance and Comptroller Department. This support group will provide training material, methods, written procedures, and training and assistance to employees who report their time, to the clerical staff who operate the terminals, and to the managers who will use the reports. The following schedule will guide the CTR developmental activities:

Phase	Dates
Detailed definition	Jul 1 to Sep 1, 1978
Design	Sep 1 to Nov 1, 1978
Programming	Nov 1 to Apr 1, 1979
System test	Apr 1 to Jun 1, 1979
User's acceptance test	Jun 1 to Jul 1, 1979
Implementation	Jul 1, 1979

When he saw the completed feasibility study on his desk, Larry Roberts knew he was in for several rough days of conferring and decision making. Every time a system as complex as the new CTR system was being considered, upper management became nervous about the hidden costs in both capital and labor, as well as the reliability of time estimates for the project. CTR would be no exception. Larry felt uneasy about implementing a new computerized system involving both new hardware and new software in the space of one year. Moreover, the lower-level managers were recommending the most expensive system of minicomputers, saying that qualitative factors outweighed cost factors. How was a person to decide when the cost figures were at odds with other considerations?

As he left the office that May 28, Larry Roberts knew that the "clear" recommendation of Mike Muncy's feasibility study posed more questions than it answered, and that he and the other vice-presidents on the steering committee would have a dozen headaches each before the problems in authorizing the CTR project were overcome.

Later Developments

A month later the problems had still not been solved, and July 1 came and went without the CTR project formally beginning. In fact, seven months passed before the steering committee endorsed and Larry Roberts officially approved the CTR project. When the decisions had been made, Larry wondered whether they were the correct ones. Nevertheless, on February 1, 1979, the detailed definition began for a minicomputer-host CTR system. The steering committee had followed Mike Muncy's group's recommendation and purchased the IBM processors for delivery on June 1, 1979. Functional accounting requirements had been postponed for six months, until January 1, 1980. The programming groups had been staffed for the one-year project: Mike Muncy would be in charge of the minicomputer programming group, and Glen Ackley would be his counterpart in the host programming group. Roberta Norton would be the district manager over both of these groups as well as the other payroll programming staff.

Segment 2

Two and one-half years passed since Mike Muncy's group completed the feasibility study of CTR, and it appeared on Larry Roberts's desk. During the past months, as the CTR project had been converted and about one-third of the company was reporting time using the new system, some problems surfaced that threaten the success of the entire CTR project. Larry Roberts had been in constant consultation with Roberta Norton and her bosses, Division Manager Kal Wheeler and Assistant Vice-President of Data Services Bob Pinnt.

The IBM minicomputer systems used as front-end processors did not have the capacity for the volume of report processing required. Although only one-seventh of the employees had been converted to the minicomputer system, capacity had already been reached on the report-processing capability of the minicomputers. This posed a serious threat to the system configuration chosen for implementation. To make matters worse, the minicomputers had been purchased and delivered only a year earlier and now were of little use to BNP Company. IBM had been consulted recently, and it offered to take back the minicomputer system in trade for a bigger, more expensive system. Larry Roberts and his subordinates were, however, reluctant to make the same mistake twice and were reconsidering the four alternatives proposed by the initial feasibility study, two of which had been rejected early in the decision process.

In particular, the alternative of implementing CTR on the Network time-share system–an alternative that was initially rejected as not feasible owing to the incapability of the Univac equipment of supporting the additional processing load–had now become feasible. During the two and one-half years (originally intended to be one year) that CTR had been in development, the Univac equipment had been upgraded by the addition of two CPUs (central processing units). All of Larry's managers were in favor of stopping the current minicomputer development and beginning that part of the CTR system again on the Network time-share system. All of the minicomputer software would have to be rewritten and tested on the Univac system.

Roberta Norton pointed out that the costs of the minicomputer software and hardware were sunk costs and should not be considered differential to picking up a new system configuration. Larry tended to agree, but privately felt that he would look into the decision to buy the original IBM minicomputer system and find out why it had not been leased as an operating lease for a short term. Also, he wondered why the Network time-share equipment's capacity to support CTR had not been foreseen two and one-half years ago.

Uncomfortable as he was in reviewing the decisions of years past, he OK'd the reconfiguration of the CTR system using the Network time-share system and the unplugging and disposal of the IBM minicomputer system. A schedule of six months was set up to reprogram the front-end processing functions of the minicomputers to the Network time-share system. Thus, a system already delayed by one and one-half years was being delayed by another six months. His most optimistic estimate was that the CTR project would take two years longer to implement than originally planned. During those two years none of the cost savings expected by the original cost analysis had been realized, prompting Roberta Norton to write the following memo to the accounting groups who were constantly specifying requirements for changes to the new CTR system even before it was off the ground.

FUNCTIONAL AND COST ACCOUNTING GROUPS —
T. J. FLANNAGAN, MANAGER

Dear Tom,

In response to your letter of October 7, 1980, my CTR staff has reviewed the list of 14 "changes for CTR" to assess the time and costs for implementation.

The changes can't be addressed individually, since most relate to the general problem of expanding CTR to include more detailed reporting for employees. BNP is in the process of converting employees to a new CTR system, with about 14% of our 6,750 employees on the new system. Completion is scheduled for 3rd Quarter 1981, and this will satisfy all current requirements for functional and cost accounting.

Even a very gross estimate for implementation of all 14 items is a difficult task, and would require a feasibility study based on more detailed specifications than you provided in the October 7th letter.

Recognizing that you have asked for person-months and cost estimates, I am reluctant to make a wild guess in order to quantify those cost elements.

Certainly the costs would be very large—in terms of person-months for methods, training, program development, added computer capacity, and terminals and teleprocessing circuits. Ongoing costs to support expanded CTR would also be significantly large, probably not justified in terms of offsetting savings or benefits.

My observation would be that functional and cost accounting requirements already specified for CTR have caused BNP several million dollars of increased expense without any identifiable cost savings. Any future requirements must be carefully analyzed in terms of economic feasibility.

Sincerely,

ROBERTA NORTON
DISTRICT STAFF MANAGER, PAYROLL/CTR

EXHIBIT 1

Computerized Time Reporting

Gross Capital Investment ($000)[1]

				Alternative CTR Systems					
				Minicomputers and Host			P/N to Host		
Investment Type	Current System								
	1978	1979	1980	1978	1979	1980	1978	1979	1980
Furniture		28		13	4		24		
Minicomputers					331				
Terminal equipment				23	237			304	
Total	0	28	0	36	572	0	24	304	0

[1] All figures (current dollars) represent installed costs.

EXHIBIT 2

Computerized Time Reporting

Fully Allocated Departmental Expenses ($000)[1]

Expense Type	Current System			Minicomputers and Host			P/N to Host		
	1978	1979	1980	1978	1979	1980	1978	1979	1980
Comptrollers	413	442	543	413	328	177	413	328	177
Data Services	326	509	374	402	616	405	478	717	502
Department 1	12	12	12	24	117	112	24	177	112
Department 2	129	136	143	129	164	201	129	164	201
Department 3	258	269	279	258	277	284	258	275	291
Department 4	274	288	302	274	294	313	274	297	320
Department 5	0	0	0	0	17	2	0	16	1
Total Company	1412	1656	1653	1500	1813	1494	1576	1914	1604

[1] Including depreciation on a straight-line basis.

EXHIBIT 3

Computerized Time Reporting

Net Incremental Costs ($000)

	Minicomputers and Host			P/N to Host		
	1978	1979	1980	1978	1979	1980
Capital Investment						
Furniture	13	(24)		24	(28)	
Minicomputers		331				
Terminal equipment	23	237			304	
Total	36	544	0	24	276	0
Departmental Expense						
Comptrollers	0	(114)	(366)	0	(114)	(366)
Data services	76	107	31	152	208	128
Department 1	12	105	100	12	105	100
Department 2	0	28	58	0	28	58
Department 3	0	8	5	0	6	12
Department 4	0	6	11	0	9	18
Department 5	0	17	2	0	16	1
Total Company	88	157	(159)	164	258	(49)

CASE 14

The Anchorage Snack Bar and Cocktail Lounge Renovation

This certainly was not the way our capital budgeting system should work, thought Mr. Sakuda, the assistant vice-president for corporate planning at Amfac, Inc. A lot of time and effort had gone into designing the present system, but it still seemed to leave too many questions unanswered. Just today the latest problem arose during the review of the $250,000 renovation of the snack bar and lounge at the Anchorage Airport. Although the project was small relative to the expected $53 million capital budget for 1976, the issues were important. Amfac was currently using two measures of project return—the discounted cash flow (DCF) and the cash return on net assets (CRONA) invested. For both measures acceptable projects needed to exceed a 20-percent pretax hurdle rate of return. This proposal certainly looked like trouble. Its DCF was only 17 per-

cent, while its CRONA was 40 percent. If Mr. Sakuda held resolutely to the 20-percent hurdle rate, the project would get a negative recommendation. The wide separation between the DCF and the CRONA return was bound to rekindle the debate over which of these measures gives the best result.

It looked like a good time for a thorough review of the capital budgeting system. The radically different rates of return for this project were not the only problems that had arisen lately. Some of the division managers, for instance, had claimed that projects that made heavy investments in fixed assets should be viewed more favorably than projects that put funds into working capital or leasehold improvements. A hotel in Waikiki cost a lot less to build in 1960 than in 1976, for example. Another issue involved the use of CRONA to measure di-

This case was prepared by and used with the permission of Professor Steven M. Dawson of the University of Hawaii.

vision performance. If the Anchorage project with a 40-percent average CRONA was rejected, that division's manager would be complaining that he could not achieve an acceptable level of performance because all the good projects were getting sabotaged. Of course, there was that old dilemma of project risk. This was a project to expand existing facilities, and the division manager was bound to argue that the project should not receive the same risk treatment as other projects.

COMPANY BACKGROUND

Amfac is a large, diversified company whose four major divisions produced sales in 1975 of over $1 billion. The business is divided into merchandising, food processing, asset management, and hospitality divisions. As shown in Exhibit 1, merchandising was the largest division in terms of sales and assets, but it trailed food processing in its contribution to profits. Included in the merchandising division were the well-known Liberty House and Joseph Magnin store chains. Food processing ranged from Amfac's five sugar companies in Hawaii to seafoods, frozen French fries, mushrooms, and related items. The hospitality division operated Island Holidays Hotels in Hawaii and Fred Harvey Hotels and restaurants in the western United States. The asset management group provided real estate management and financial services through Amfac Mortgage Corporation and Amfac Financial, respectively.

The food-processing division, particularly the growing unit sugar cane, was the primary cause of the huge 1974 revenue and profit surge shown in Exhibit 2.

The average price of raw sugar in November 1974 was 64.5 cents a pound, far above the 10.2 cent average for 1973. This was clearly an unusual event, and it was no surprise when sugar prices fell in 1975. Ordinarily, Amfac was constructed so that some elements of the company should be strong at a time others were weak. Despite variations in individual divisions from year to year, the overall result should be a steady growth in Amfac's profitability.

CORPORATE OBJECTIVE

Amfac's corporate objective was to improve the return on total capital employed. This could be accomplished by improving the return on the existing investment base, by expanding, by entering new business areas, or by divesting unsatisfactory operations.

The return on total capital was an easily understood measure of corporate performance widely reported in the investment press. It, in essence, measures the productivity of assets under the control of management. The measure of return is not income after tax and writeoffs but before interest on long-term debt and minority interests in profits. Total capital is stockholder's equity, debt, minority interests, and deferred taxes. Looked at another way, capital equals assets less all liabilities other than debt and deferred income tax.

Systematic pursuit of this objective had slowly improved Amfac's position relative to other companies. The January 1976 *Forbes* ranking of 929 companies by their five-year return on total capital placed Amfac 405th with 9.3 percent. This compared favorably with ranks of 411 in 1975 and 434 in 1974.

CAPITAL BUDGETING SYSTEM

Projects selected by the capital budgeting process were expected to contribute to the corporate objective. At Amfac two techniques were in use:

1. *Discounted Cash Flow (DCF)*: Determines the discount rate that equates the cash investment with the future cash flow. Included in the cash outlay are expenditures for new fixed assets and necessary increases in net working capital. Trade-in or salvage values of existing assets are not considered to be a reduction of capital outlays. Instead they are included in the calculation of cash benefits. The cash benefits are project revenues minus total expenses, with depreciation added back in. Both the capital outlay and the net future benefits are on a before-tax basis. The return of working capital in the future is included with the benefits.

2. *Cash Return on Net Assets (CRONA)*: Relates the cash flows generated by the project to the capital invested. CRONA is net income before tax and financial charges, plus depreciation divided by average total assets, plus the reserve for depreciation, plus the initial present value of leases if not reported, less all liabilities except debt and deferred income taxes. CRONA is calculated for each year and for the average of five full years or the life of the project, which ever is shorter.

In the calculation of CRONA particular importance was attached to the use of cash flows in place of net income. Before CRONA was developed, RONA, or the return on net assets, had been used. It was criticized because only cash, not net income, was available for dividends or reinvestment. A second improvement contained in CRONA was its inclusion of lease commitments. Previously, when balance sheet figures were used exclusively, projects which would lease a lot of assets that were not reported on the balance sheet were able to show better performance than projects which did not lease as much. CRONA measures all projects on a comparable basis. Performance would not be affected by the financial decision to lease or purchase assets.

Minimum acceptable rates of return for DCF and CRONA were established periodically based upon the cost of capital, corporate goals, and the availability of funds. In 1976 the hurdle rate for both DCF and CRONA was 20 percent. The cost of capital, after tax, had been calculated to be about 7.2 percent, which should correspond to a before-tax cost of 14.4 percent, using a 50-percent marginal tax rate. Since Amfac was rationing capital at that time, an additional 5 percent or so had been added to bring the hurdle rate up to 20 percent.

Projects with a DCF less than 150 percent of the hurdle rate had to include a calculation of risk sensitivity. All projects requiring over $500,000 in outlays, regardless of the DCF level, also required a risk sensitivity analysis. The sensitivity analysis consisted of recomputing the DCF twice, once with the investment outlay increased 10 percent and once with revenue reduced 20 percent.

MEASUREMENT OF DIVISION PERFORMANCE

CRONA was used by Amfac as the principal measure of division performance. The calculation was similar to the calculation of CRONA in the capital budgeting system except that no forecasts were included. The figures for cash flow and capital invested were based upon the results for the current year.

THE ANCHORAGE PROJECT

In 1974 Amfac obtained the snack bar and lounge concession contract for the Anchorage International Airport. In the concession contract the State of Alaska granted the exclusive right to serve food and beverage to the general public in the present terminal. The initial contract would expire at the end of September 1980. There was a ten-year option to extend the lease period with all terms subject to renegotiation. A percentage rent was calculated at 10 percent of food sales and 15 percent of liquor sales. The present facilities produced a satisfactory CRONA in 1975.

The Alaska pipeline activity had substantially increased the domestic enplaned passenger count at the airport as the following table shows:

	Enplaned Passengers	% increase
1970	424,589	
1971	434,632	+ 2.4
1972	469,764	+ 8.1
1973	495,537	+ 5.5
1974	624,520	+26.0
1975	776,364	+24.3

In an effort to maximize sales, approval was being sought to add a snack bar in the main lobby and to redesign the cocktail lounge to increase capacity by 80 seats. Sales at the snack bar were not expected to dilute the coffee shop sales since customers would be seeking fast service or would be impulse buyers. The total project cost was estimated to be $250,000.

The projection of operating results was prepared on an incremental basis. Snack bar sales were expected to start at about $500 per day or $.20 per passenger. After 50 percent more seating was available, beverage sales were conservatively estimated to increase 12 percent in 1977 in addition to a normal 10 percent increase. The increase in 1976 sales were to offset the loss of sales during the construction period. Cost of sales were 35 percent for food and 18 percent for beverage. Employment cost projections assumed additional attendants in the snack bar and an additional bartender and two wait resses in the lounge. Operating expenses were projected at 6 percent based on previous experience. Rent was 10 percent of food sales and 15 percent of beverage sales. Property tax and insurance were based on the $250,000 investment, which was being depreciated over the basic term of the lease. The 10-year option period was not considered in the calculations, although the option would be given careful consideration. The terms of the lease could all be renegotiated then, and there was no commitment on Amfac's part to remain with the project. When the current lease expired, a new look would be taken at the opportunities to see if it would be profitable to continue.

A summary of information about the

project is presented below with the projections and calculations presented in Exhibit 3.

Capital outlay	$250,000
Discounted cash flow	17% return

Capital: 10% increase	15% return
Revenue: 20% decrease	11% return
Project's average CRONA	40.0%
Start construction	April 1976
Complete construction	June 1976
Start operations	July 1976

EXHIBIT 1

The Anchorage Snack Bar and Cocktail Lounge Renovation

Amfac Sales, Contribution and Assets by Division (1975)

Division	Sales (%)	Percent of Total Contribution[1] (%)	Assets (%)
Merchandising	63	21	42
Food processing	25	60	28
Hospitality	10	10	14
Asset management	2[2]	9[2]	16[3]
	100	100	100

[1] Income before unallocated expenses, interest, and tax.
[2] Does not include Amfac's nonconsolidated finance subsidiaries, which would increase sales about 4 percent and contribution about 9 percent.
[3] Stockholders' equity in finance subsidiaries.

EXHIBIT 2

The Anchorage Snack Bar and Cocktail Lounge Renovation

Selected Stock Price and Financial Statement Figures for Amfac

	1971	1972	1973	1974	1975
Stock price—high	$ 39⅝	$ 39¾	$ 31⅜	$ 21⅝	$ 21³/₈[b]
—low	25⅞	25	11	12⅝	13¾
Standard and Poor's 425 Index	108.35	121.79	120.44	92.91	96.15
Earnings per share[a]	1.88	2.06	2.40	5.57	3.25
Book value per share	18.60	20.36	21.96	26.16	26.42
Net income[a] (000)	19,134	24,296	26,558	56,843	37,496
Total assets (000)	451,925	559,940	659,246	749,824	738,469
Stockholder's equity (000)	212,457	240,308	259,354	306,765	321,713

[a] From continuing operations.
[b] Current price was $17.50

EXHIBIT 3

The Anchorage Snack Bar and Cocktail Lounge Renovation

Five-Year Projection of Operations—Anchorage Project

	1976 (6 mos.)	1977	1978	1979	1980 (9 mos.)
Sales (incremental)					
Snack bar food	$ 90	$180	$198	$218	$180
Beverage	—	198	218	240	198
Total	$ 90	$378	$416	$458	$378
Expenses (incremental)					
Food cost	32	63	69	76	63
Beverage	—	36	39	43	36
Employment cost	27	114	121	128	102
Operating expenses	5	23	25	27	23
Rent	9	48	53	58	48
Depreciation	30	60	60	60	40
Property tax & insurance	2	5	6	7	7
Total	$105	$349	$373	$399	$319
Contribution	(15)	29	43	59	59
Add: depreciation	30	60	60	60	40
Adjusted cash contribution	$ 15	$ 89	$103	$119	$ 99
Total capital employed— end of period	$250	$250	$250	$250	$250
Average total capital employed	$125	$250	$250	$250	$187.5
CRONA	12.0%	35.6%	41.2%	47.6%	52.8%

DCF Calculations	*Cash Flow*	*P. V. 17%*		
Year 0 (June 1976)	($250,000)	1.000		($250,000)
Year 1 (1976)	15,000	.855		12,825
Year 2 (1977)	89,000	.731		65,059
Year 3 (1978)	103,000	.624		64,272
Year 4 (1979)	119,000	.534		63,546
Year 5 (1980)	99,000	.456		45,144
				$ 846

Average CRONA

$$\frac{.5\,(12) + 35.6 + 41.2 + 47.6 + .75\,(52.8)}{.5 + 1 + 1 + 1 + .75} = 40.0\%$$

CASE 15

Texas Production, Inc.

In early 1976 Mr. John Fitzgerald, a financial analyst at Texas Production, Inc., made a proposal to his company's Planning and Evaluation Committee concerning capital budgeting procedures and evaluation. He received little acceptance for his ideas. Mr. Fitzgerald was convinced of the soundness of his recommendations and had requested a second opportunity to present his opinions concerning the investment decision process of Texas Production. The committee granted Mr. Fitzgerald a second opportunity but requested he consider the committee's reasons for not accepting his ideas before developing another presentation. Mr. Fitzgerald was now considering the reasons why his initial ideas had been rebuffed.

THE START

The president of Texas Production, Inc., Mr. Bill Lee, organized a Planning and Evaluation Committee in mid-1974. This committee was formed to insure more orderly growth and improved planning of the company's future. The members were the vice-president of finance, director of capital evaluation, and the four vice-presidents of the operating divisions. Subsequently, the committee hired Mr. John Fitzgerald, a recent MBA graduate, to help direct and to coordinate the activities of this group.

By the spring of 1975, Mr. Fitzgerald produced several special projects the committee had assigned in addition to his more routine tasks. Mr. Fitzgerald

This case was prepared by Professor David J. Springate of Southern Methodist University with the help of Mr. H. W. Tompkins, graduate student, and used with the permission of Professor Springate.

had taken a special interest in Texas Production's method for evaluating investment opportunities, and he approached the committee at this time with a proposal that he investigate this aspect of the company's financial management. After a brief review, the committee gave Mr. Fitzgerald the authority to analyze the company's investment decision process.

COMPANY BACKGROUND INFORMATION

Texas Production, Inc., was a rapidly growing domestic oil company. Operations consisting of extensive oil and gas exploration, production, and development were located in the states of Texas, Oklahoma, Ohio, Mississippi, Louisiana, Colorado, Wyoming, Kansas, and Nebraska. These states were divided into four operating divisions: Southwest, South, Mid-Continent, and West Coast.

The evolution of Texas Production had been much influenced by Mr. Lee. As president, he had carefully directed the company from a small, secondary recovery company to its later success. Mr. Lee, a petroleum engineer, initiated a course of action for building an oil company that others were to follow: finance the exploration and development of large quantities of oil and gas with the cash flow resulting from secondary recovery projects. Exhibits 1 and 2 contain recent financial statements. Exhibit 3 is a recent organization chart.

The company's first historical phase was characterized by internal growth through relatively low risk, development type, secondary recovery oil and gas endeavors. (Secondary recovery is a technique whereby water and other miscible substances are introduced into a well after the well has ceased producing oil due to the lack of reservoir pressure. The water and other substances provide pressure to the well, which allows more oil to be produced.) Investment projects were carefully selected on their ability to sustain cash flow and were low-risk opportunities.

The principal decision criterion employed in evaluating investment opportunities during this period was cash payback. Management was of the opinion that this analytical technique was sufficient for its purposes because of the almost riskless nature of investment opportunities being considered and the company's emphasis on cash flow resulting from investments.

Texas Production's second phase began in 1970 with the drilling of its first exploratory well. In the second phase, the first-phase activities were continued while higher risk exploration activities commenced. For this new segment of the company's business, Texas Production adopted a new and more sophisticated investment analysis technique, the internal rate of return method (also known in the company as the discounted cash-flow method). Wildcat wells have considerably more risk involved than secondary recovery projects, and the management believed that the internal rate of return was best suited for analyzing risky projects.

MR. FITZGERALD'S INVESTIGATION

To start his investigation, Mr. Fitzgerald explored the limitations of the internal rate of return method as it was used at Texas Production. He discovered two troublesome areas of which he felt most managers of the company were not aware. First, the difference between the calculated rate of return for a project and the company's available reinvestment opportunity rates was usually significant and, therefore, represented a potential source of error in investment analysis. Second, it seemed to him that the usual method of varying the acceptable rate of return to allow for risk in individual investment projects was not correct.

Mr. Fitzgerald knew that the internal rate of return method was a widely used analytical discounted cash-flow investment technique. The method is essentially a trial-and-error process to ·find a discount rate that equates the present value of future cash inflows with the present value of the future cash outflows.

Mr. Fitzgerald found that the internal rate of return method did not consider the time value of money to be the rate usually assumed by company managers. The implicit assumption of the method that the discount rate found to reduce the present value of project cash flows to zero is in fact equal to the investing company's stated time value of money was correct only for marginal projects. As a project's rate of return became less and approached the understood corporate rate of time value of money, the economics of a given project became relatively less attractive. For a project to be marginally acceptable, an earnings rate equal to the company's time value of money was usually required. Texas Production's required rate was 15 percent annually. The origin of this rate was the company's calculated weighted average cost of capital. In addition, management thought that this rate was an appropriate

measure of risk involved in drilling prospects.

The internal rate of return method does not allow for explicit consideration of rates at which the cash inflows from any investment can be reinvested. Instead, it assumes that the money is reinvested at the calculated internal rate of return. For a project with a high internal rate, this assumption can be very misleading. It would be a fortunate firm that had the opportunity to reinvest the cash inflow at the same high rate.

Once he understood the nature of the problem, Mr. Fitzgerald realized there was another aspect to the reinvestment rate problem. In effect, the internal rate of return method assumes that future capital to be invested is "preinvested" at the calculated internal rate of return. Mr. Fitzgerald made up an example which supposed a company to have available a waterflood, secondary project that required an initial investment of $1 million and a future investment of $.5 million in three years. The internal rate of return is 25 percent. In more detail:

The discounted cash-flow method would assume that the future investment of $500,000 "cost" the company only $256,000 (third-year present value factor for 25% × $500,000) in present-day dollars. In other words it would assume the $256,000 to be "preinvested" at a compounded rate of interest of 25 percent for three years to yield the $500,000 cash flow necessary for the investment. Mr. Fitzgerald felt this assumption could be very misleading for a company that did not generally have available projects offering high returns. In fact, the more he thought, the more he felt that since the discounted cash-flow method did not explicitly consider how cash inflows would be reinvested or how future cash out-

Year	Investment Outflow	Net Cash Inflow	Net Present Value for Rates of Return		
			20%	25%	30%
0	$1,000,000	($1,000,000)			
1	—	—			
2	—	—			
3	500,000	(500,000)		(256,000)	
4	—	776,000			
5	—	776,000			
6	—	776,000			
7	—	776,000			
8	—	776,000			
9	—	776,000			
10	—	776,000			
			+	0	—

flows would be preinvested, he felt it really did not take into account the company's time value of money.

Specifically, Mr. Fitzgerald was concerned about management's practice of establishing higher rates of return as hurdles for higher risk investment opportunities. As illustrated in the previous example, the internal rate of return method does not explicitly consider the preinvestment or reinvestment assumptions of the company's overall business. Suppose, thought Mr. Fitzgerald, management were to require a 25 percent internal rate of return for waterflood projects. The previous example of a particular investment opportunity would, apparently, meet the stated criteria. However, if the company did not have available a return on their investment of 25 percent, but had perhaps 15 percent return projects available, then the future investment of $500,000 would cost in present-day dollars considerably more, and the actual rate of return ultimately achieved would decrease to a lower level. Thus, to Mr. Fitzgerald the raising of the acceptable rate of return in the discounted cash-

flow method to account for risk in individual investment projects did not appear to be a good method to allow for risk.

As he pondered on the subject, Mr. Fitzgerald felt that the use of the discounted cash-flow method might sometimes mislead management into making an investment that was less profitable to the firm in the long run but that had a higher indicated rate of return. Adoption would actually be contrary to the long-term economic objective of maximizing shareholder's wealth over the long term.

In addition to the above procedures, Mr. Fitzgerald became aware of other methods in which risk and time value of money could be addressed. One of these methods was the net present value method, a close relative of the internal rate method. Net present value is defined as the difference between the present value of cash inflows and cash outflows, where flows are discounted at a chosen rate. Usually, a company would select for its rate either the time value of money or its cost of capital. While the net present value method is not without limitations, Mr. Fitzgerald felt it not to be encumbered with the disadvantages of the discounted cash-flow method.

The net present value method assumes all cash inflows and outflows are reinvested and preinvested at the selected discount rate. Thus, the problems centered around unrealistic investment rates would not be encountered if the net present value method were to be used with reinvestment assumed at the company's cost of capital. Use of the net present value method is structured to encourage managers to try to maximize a dollar figure rather than a percentage figure. At one point Mr. Fitzgerald wondered if the method were more oriented to the goal of maximizing shareholder's wealth over the long term than the internal rate of return method.

In his search Mr. Fitzgerald found the main disadvantage of the net present value method, as compared to the internal rate of return method, to be that the net present value figure cannot be used as a ranking or screening device because it does not permit investment comparisons. His short example illustrates his statement.

exposure. An argument could be made that the internal rate of return method would select the better investment project. In this case the internal rate of return for Project B is 78 percent as compared to only 28.6 percent for Project A.

Another method Mr. Fitzgerald encountered was the present value ratio. This tool appeared to have all the advantages of the net present value method but also had screening and ranking capabilities. The present value ratio is the present value of the expected cash inflows divided by the expected cash outflows, or simply the present value of the benefits divided by the present value of the total investment. A derivative of the net present value method, the present value ratio not only considers the time value of money but is easy to calculate.

In using the present value ratio, the present value of cash inflows is divided by the present value of cash outflows to get the present value ratio. A project with a ratio of one would be a marginal investment, expected to yield only the discount rate employed. Anything with a ratio over one would be expected to yield future profits in excess of those

Year	Project A Cash Flow	Present Value at 10%	Year	Project B Cash Flow	Present Value at 10%
0	($100,000)		0	($24,200)	
1	40,000		1	20,000	
2	40,000		2	20,000	
3	40,000		3	20,000	
4	40,000		4	20,000	
5	40,000		5	20,000	
		$51,660			$51,660

As can be seen, two projects with equal present values and equal lives have significantly different initial investments. The use of the net present value method, in this case, would lead to inconclusive results. Project B in many concerns would be considered a better investment opportunity due to less cash

yielded by a marginal investment. As a screening mechanism, projects with a present value ratio of one or greater would be accepted for further consideration. As a ranking mechanism, projects would be accepted in descending order of their respective present value ratios. In the net present value example just mentioned, Project A had a present value ratio of 1.516 while Project B had a present value ratio of 3.133.

Would the internal rate of return method have selected the correct investment opportunity? After searching, Mr. Fitzgerald found the following discussion in a finance text dealing with the energy field.

> Suppose management is confronted with the problem of two mutually exclusive waterflood or secondary recovery projects, Project A and Project B. These require the same amount of capital investment and involve the same degree of risk. The forecasted cash flow from Project A is expected to yield an internal rate of return of 22.4% while the forecasted cash flow of Project B is expected to yield an internal rate of only 16.8%. Using the internal rate of return as the main criterion for ranking projects, the decision is easy. Project A is far superior— but is it? Does Project A contribute most to the maximization of shareholder wealth over the long term? Further investigation of both projects reveals some interesting and disturbing answers to these important questions.

> Project A requires a total investment of $1.5 million, all in the first year to develop and implement the waterflood project. This particular project is characterized by a reservoir with high initial production due to flooding, a steep decline, and a relatively short project life. A tabulation of the forecasted cash inflow (excluding investment) for Project A is presented below.

Year	Cash Inflows
1	$400,000
2	800,000
3	600,000
4	300,000
5	100,000
6	0

> The internal rate of return on the investment of $1.5 million calculated in the usual manner is approximately 22.4 per-

cent. Assuming an arbitrary hurdle rate of 12 percent, the present value ratio is 1.177.

> On the other hand, Project B which also requires a total investment of $1.5 million all in the first year, is characterized by a relatively "tight" reservoir that does not flood easily. In other words, the formation the well is producing from is better suited to a long production life. The well will have very little decline once in production and a very long life. The tabular form of forecasted cash inflow (excluding investment) for Project B is as follows:

Year	Cash Inflows
1–20	$275,000/yr.

> The internal rate of return for Project B also calculated in the usual manner is approximately 16.8 percent. However, again assuming the arbitrary hurdle rate of 12 percent, the present value ratio for Project B is 1.369.

> An entirely new situation indeed has been brought to light. One project has a significantly higher rate of return than the other, yet choosing the second project is certainly the optimum decision as far as long-term stability and maximization of shareholder wealth are concerned. If Project A were chosen, management would be confronted with the problem of finding another investment in five years with at least a 16-percent rate of return. Also, it can be inferred with some valid assumptions from the cash flow forecasts that the oil reserves of Project B are more than twice the oil reserves of Project A. The implications of long-term profitability (assuming the continuation of a favorable economic environment) are fairly obvious, not only through stability but through the addition of more reserves to the current reserves.[1]

RISKS IN EXPLORATION ACTIVITIES

Mr. Fitzgerald knew that two types of risk were present in exploration activi-

[1] Source: Stanley M. Porter, *Petroleum Accounting Practices*, University of Oklahoma, 1965.

ties: (1) the presence of hydrocarbons at the site and (2) the quantities of petroleum in existence. To quantify the risk in oil endeavors, instead of merely raising the discounted cash-flow rate of return, in late 1975 he studied the possible application of simulation. Used in conjunction with expected value theory, simulation appeared to be capable of representing the risk entailed in oil and gas operations.

As Mr. Fitzgerald visualized it, simulation would involve a three-step process in implementation. First, the functional relationships present in the case under study would be defined. Second, there would be assignment of either fixed or probabilistic estimates to the independent variables. Third, values of the dependent variable—profit or cash flow—would be computed. Random sampling from the distribution of the variables would be used in this computation.

Simulation appeared to offer several advantages as a problem-solving technique for exploration activities. It provided additional insight into possible outcomes of decision alternatives; it did not require one person alone to make the input data for decisions; and it allowed a sensitivity analysis to be run on key variables. Simulation, Mr. Fitzgerald felt, allowed the possibility of a quantitative analysis of risk that could be made rigorous.

Hydrocarbon Risk

Mr. Fitzgerald found expected value theory, or mathematical expectation, to be a relatively old concept in connection with business decisions under uncertainty. The premise of expected value theory was that the expected value of a distribution of possible values would be realized by a decision maker if he accepted the alternatives over repeated trials. Thus, if a decision maker faced a probability distribution of possible profits resulting from a given decision, over the long run he would gain the "average profit."

Decision criteria that consider risk in drilling prospects could also be based on mathematical expectation. Mr. Fitzgerald thought there would be two steps in any application.

1. Finding the expected value of each outcome: This would be the product obtained by multiplying the probability of each outcome's occurrence times the associated "conditional" value of the outcome. "Conditional" means that the value of the particular outcome would only be realized if the particular outcome occurs.

2. Finding the expected value of a decision alternative: This would be the algebraic sum attained by adding the expected value of each outcome of the alternatives. [When the conditional value of each outcome is expressed as monetary profit and losses (or positive and negative cash flows), the sum would be called the "expected monetary value."]

To illustrate the above, Mr. Fitzgerald made up an example. In his example a drilling prospect existed in which the probability of a successful well was estimated to be 60 percent and the probability of a dry hole was 40 percent. There were two decision alternatives—drill the well or farm the prospect out and retain an override. If a dry hole were drilled, a loss of $200,000 would occur. If the drilling were successful, a producing well would generate a $600,000 profit. If a farm-out were to be made, the

Probability Outcome Will Occur	Outcome	Drill		Farm-Out	
		Conditional Value	Expected Value of Outcome	Conditional Value	Expected Value of Outcome
40%	Dry Hole	($200,000)	($ 80,000)	0	0
60%	Producer	$600,000	$360,000	$ 50,000	$ 30,000
			$280,000		$ 30,000

income from a producer would be $60,000. His calculations are shown above.

Using the decision rule of maximizing the expected value, Mr. Fitzgerald felt that the prospect well should be drilled. His understanding of the technique was that if he consistently accepted the drilling alternative for a large number of such investments, his average gain in profit per decision would be $280,000.

Mr. Fitzgerald was not convinced, however. Suppose he had only one such prospect to consider? It seemed to him that with only one well to drill, he was either going to make $600,000 or lose $200,000. How would he make a profit of $280,000? The answer, he concluded, was that he couldn't—the expected value did not represent one of the possible outcomes of only one trial. Mr. Fitzgerald could rationalize that the particular drilling prospect would presumably be one of many that were presented to the decision maker over a period of time. If a decision maker consistently selected the alternative having the highest positive expected value in each case, his total net gain from all decisions would be higher than his gain from any alternative decision strategy. But the implications of any single decision being made incorrectly bothered him.

Risk in Quantity of Petroleum Reserves in Existence

Mr. Fitzgerald believed that a distribution of all the possible outcomes was most useful for analyzing the risk arising from the quantity of petroleum reserves in existence. To realistically describe risk in drilling ventures, he believed that the uncertainty of each variable could best be described by a distribution.

He also knew there were many factors that might affect the ultimate return on a drilling investment. These included payments, structural position, depositional trends, drilling costs, depletion, and so forth. To properly evaluate the desirability of the investment, a numerical estimate of each variable in the return calculation could be used. In order to provide a better evaluation of an investment project, however, a probability estimate could be placed on each determining factor. That way, a joint distribution of the possible final returns could be constructed. Mr. Fitzgerald felt that an attempt to protect against uncertainty in investments by raising the required rate might be a sound theoretical position. Nevertheless, such a procedure would, in his opinion, not provide the decision maker with an explicit expression of the risk. A probability distribution would allow such risk to be assessed and would permit a better determination of risks and opportunities.

THE MEETING

After summarizing what he had found over the course of several months' work, Mr. Fitzgerald sent his analysis to the Planning and Evaluation Committee members for their review. In addition,

Mr. Fitzgerald requested the committee members to attend a meeting in January 1976 to discuss the content of his analysis. Mr. Fitzgerald was very optimistic about his findings and was convinced that the committee members would be able to see the imperfections in the present investment analysis technique. As a result, Mr. Fitzgerald did not foresee any committee resistance to his recommendations to change these techniques. Mr. Fitzgerald went into the committee meeting feeling very confident and assured of his analysis.

A considerable portion of the January 6 meeting consisted of discussing Mr. Fitzgerald's analysis. The committee members appeared impressed with Mr. Fitzgerald's work and his knowledge of the current investment analysis technique being used by Texas Production.

The vice-president of the Mid-Continent Division directed the first specific question at Mr. Fitzgerald by asking him, "Is all this technical and time consuming analysis really necessary when the individual explorationist recommending the project is apparently convinced of the attractiveness of the prospect?" Mr. Fitzgerald responded by pointing out that the most critical factor contributing to the drilling decision for the prospect well was the explorationist's recommendation. In his opinion this segment of the investment procedure was in need of examination. In expanding on his statement, Mr. Fitzgerald voiced his feelings about the individual explorationist's "commitment" to a project by saying that he visualized a typical explorationist as one who had spent a considerable amount of time and effort on a project and had become personally committed to the prospect. In other words, Mr. Fitzgerald said, if an explorationist spent

a lot of time and effort on a single prospect, he was more apt to recommend the project because of his personal feelings and would not want to reject the project because of his previous efforts. The vice-president of the Mid-Continent Division took this matter rather personally and snapped back at Mr. Fitzgerald that none of his explorationists behaved in this manner and he was appalled even at the suggestion. Mr. Fitzgerald assured the vice-president that his suggestions were not directly related to him or any other division but that he could visualize situations where the decision of individual explorationists was not as rational as it might be if the decision maker were less committed to the prospect. Mr. Fitzgerald added that, in his view, it was a rational tendency for an explorationist or any decision maker in a situation to act in this manner.

The director of capital evaluation, after this rather heated discussion, began questioning Mr. Fitzgerald about his anlaysis of the discounted cash-flow method for evaluating capital expenditures. He asked Mr. Fitzgerald if he really thought that the internal rate of return method was an inferior investment analytical tool and if his recommendations suggested a superior course that was practicable. Mr. Fitzgerald replied by asking the director of capital evaluation if he agreed with the explicit limitations of the internal rate of return method outlined in his analysis. The director replied by answering that he would have to investigate the methodology followed by Mr. Fitzgerald in order to determine the validity of his analysis. Mr. Fitzgerald, expressing his strong feelings about his method and convinced of its superiority, asked the director of capital evaluation that if he did agree with his analysis after determining its validity, would he be receptive to a change in investment analysis techniques? The director responded by saying "probably" but would not venture to say he would go through all the analysis Mr. Fitzgerald was suggesting.

The vice-president of finance decided that the meeting had progressed far enough to have Mr. Fitzgerald summarize his recommendation and asked Mr. Fitzgerald to do so.

Mr. Fitzgerald proceeded to outline his technique by recommending that Texas Production adopt the present value ratio method utilizing the company's cost of capital as the discount factor. In addition, Mr. Fitzgerald recommended Texas Production discontinue using the internal rate of return method as a tool for analyzing risk in a prospect and begin analyzing the risk involved in a particular prospect by quantitatively evaluating risk. This would be accomplished by employing simulation in conjunction with expected value calculations.

The vice-president of finance responded by saying, "While I do agree with the theory and technical segments of your analysis and recommendation, I tend to agree with the vice-president of the Mid-Continent Division that the individual explorationist promoting a given prospect would not recommend drilling the well without being convinced of the efficacy of the prospect." Mr. Fitzgerald replied by asking the vice-president that even if he did not agree with the phenomena of personal commitment, would he consider utilizing an approach to evaluating risk in exploration projects other than raising the hurdle rate for the discounted cash-flow rate of return. The vice-president answered rather briskly

that he might consider it but would be required to perform a rigorous analysis of the subject. The vice-president added, "I am convinced of the decision-making capabilities of each individual exploration manager and do not believe that a quantitatively rigorous analysis of risk would provide better information than an individual explorationist's own business experience."

The committee seemed rather upset with Mr. Fitzgerald's recommendations and proceeded to grow more skeptical as the meeting progressed. Mr. Fitzgerald, sensing this attitude, began hedging toward a recommendation that would be both less technical and better received. Specifically, he suggested that Texas Production consider employing the present value ratio as an investment analysis tool. Meanwhile, he would begin educating the committee members about his suggested procedure for analyzing risk associated with the drilling of prospect wells. Mr. Fitzgerald stated that after he had finished teaching the committee members about his suggested risk analysis techniques he was convinced that they would see the advantages in the techniques and would eventually want to employ them in all exploration decisions.

The vice-president of finance continued to question the validity of Mr. Fitzgerald's analysis and the advantages of quantitatively evaluating risk as opposed to experienced decision making. The other committee members nodded their approval of the vice-president's questioning. Finally, the vice-president stated that the committee could not make a decision on either of Mr. Fitzgerald's suggestions but would have to do some homework on the subject before a decision could be made.

After this diplomatic rejection of his

recommendation, Mr. Fitzgerald thought of attempting to suggest yet another plan. Instead, he decided to have the meeting adjourned so he could develop a better strategy for convincing the committee of the advantages of his suggested investment analysis technique. Mr. Fitzgerald requested the committee to further consider his analysis and recommendations while he, in turn, would proceed to improve his presentation so that the committee members might see the advantages in his suggested techniques.

The committee members all nodded approval but cautioned Mr. Fitzgerald that the company had received excellent results with present techniques. Accordingly, they would be hard pressed to "switch horses in the middle of the stream." However, the committee members gave Mr. Fitzgerald their approval to continue developing his proposal and said they would be happy to consider his proposal at a second meeting.

Mr. Fitzgerald, while walking to his office after the meeting, began thinking about a new and better strategy for illustrating the attractive features of his investment analysis techniques. He was convinced of the need for such techniques and felt committed to indicating its value to the committee members. Arriving at his office, Mr. Fitzgerald began in earnest to devise a new strategy directed at convincing his superiors of the advantages in his recommendations.

EXHIBIT 1

Texas Production, Inc.

Consolidated Income Statements
For the Years Ended December 31, 1974 and 1975
(thousands of dollars)

December 31	1975	1974
Operating Revenues		
Gas		
Nonaffiliated	$ 12,470	$ 9,389
Affiliated	34,567	25,944
Affiliated	901	979
Total	47,938	36,312
Other gas revenues	612	262
Total gas revenues	48,550	36,574
Oil	29,695	28,059
Natural gas liquids	9,074	7,451
Jobbing revenues	31,711	25,655
Natural gas processed by others	758	879
Other	880	
Total	120,668	98,618
Operating Expenses		
Gas purchased	77	98
Royalties on gas and natural gas		
liquids	13,010	10,668
Other operating expenses	15,804	12,667
Liquids purchased for resale	29,752	22,506
Maintenance	3,960	2,547
Nonproductive well drilling	536	39
Abandoned leases	311	1,102
Depreciation	3,446	2,705
Amortization of exploratory		
costs	10,603	6,543
Depletion	7,651	6,574
Other direct taxes	5,750	5,040
Total	90,900	70,489
Operating Income	29,768	28,129
Income Credits—Interest	41	91
Gross Income	29,809	28,220
Income Deductions—Interest	3,051	4,208
Net Income (before income taxes		
and interco. interest)	26,758	24,012
Income Taxes	3,931 cr.	10,763 cr.
Deferred Income Taxes	10,594 dr.	9,738 dr.
Investment Tax Credit	707 cr.	357 cr.
Net Income (before intercompany		
interest)	20,802	25,394
Intercompany Interest Income	25	24
Intercompany Interest Expense	6,958	7,415
Net Income	$ 13,869	$18,003

EXHIBIT 2

Texas Production, Inc.

Consolidated Balance Sheet
as of December 31, 1975 (thousands of dollars)

Assets		Claims	
Property, plant, and equipment	$319,057	Capitalization	
Less accumulated depreciation		Shareholders' equity	$ 73,404
and depletion	88,652	Long-term debt (noncurrent	
Net property, plant, and		portion)	90,035
equipment	230,405	Total capitalization	163,439
Investments		Intercompany	
Advance payments for gas—		payable/receivable—net	35,207
noncurrent miscellaneous	3,576	Current liabilities	
Total investments	3,576	Current maturities of long-	
Current assets		term debt	0
Cash	1,203	Commerical paper	0
Temporary cash investments	6	Dividends declared—	
Accounts and notes		preferred stock	0
receivable	22,231	Accounts payable	6,078
Inventories		Assignment of future gas	
Materials and supplies	7,661	purchase credits	0
Fertilizer and other		Customers' deposits	3,240
products	0	Accrued taxes	3,931
Gas stored underground	0	Accrued interest	20
Prepayments:		Accrued vacations	367
Advances and prepayments		Current portion of liability for	
for gas	0	special retirement benefits	72
Other	1,171	Total current liabilities	13,708
Total current assets	32,272	Advances for construction	1,190
Deferred debit items		Deferred income taxes	31,995
Special retirement benefits	474	Production payments	20,486
Other	(192)	Liability for special retirement	
Total deferred debit items	282	benefits (noncurrent portion)	402
Total assets	$266,535	Reserves	
		Accident and surplus	0
		Other	108
		Total reserves	108
		Total claims	$266,535

126

EXHIBIT 3

Texas Production, Inc.

Organization Chart

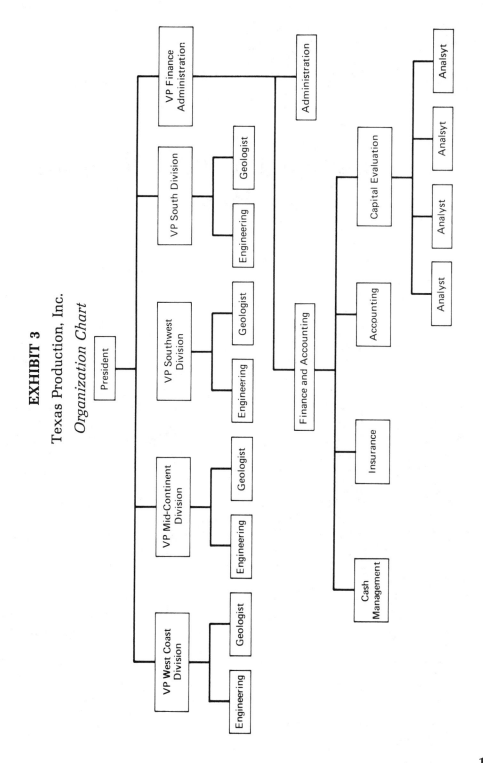

CASE 16

The Volkswagen–New Stanton Project

In the early 1970s Volkswagenwerk AG of West Germany was faced with the prospect of having to sharply raise the prices of its products in certain export markets, including the United States. The strength of the German economy had resulted in a very tight labor supply and this escalated many labor-related costs. In addition, the Deutsche mark (DM) had emerged as a currency in demand. The flight of dollars into marks had produced both dollar devaluations and mark revaluations. The net result was that the exchange rate went from DM 4.00 to the dollar in pre-1969 to DM 2.36 to the dollar by 1976 (see Exhibit 1).

The above-mentioned factors were creating a situation for Volkswagenwerk (VW) where its product prices would have to be raised sharply in the United States to merely recover costs. For ex-ample, in the pre-1969 era, to recover costs of DM 10,000 a product would have to be priced at $2500. In 1976 recovery of the same amount of DM 10,000 would require a price of $4200. Exchange rate adjustments, increasing labor and materials costs, and a maturing product—the "Beetle"—combined to affect VW's financial performance. Its sales and net income figures are summarized in Exhibit 2.

From a product marketing viewpoint, VW decided to phase out its "Beetle" model and replace it with the "Rabbit" model. The other factors mentioned above combined with the need for easier access to product markets and to skilled and semiskilled labor pools led VW to start seeking a site in the United States for establishing a manufacturing plant.

By late 1975, early 1976, VW management had narrowed its site consider-

This case was prepared by and used with the permission of Professors Ike Mathur, Southern Illinois University at Carbondale and John R. Darling, Texas Tech University. Information for this case was obtained from a variety of sources including the House Committee on Business and Commerce, Commonwealth of Pennsylvania and the Special Assistant for Government Programs, Commonwealth of Pennsylvania.

ations to two locations: one in Brook Park, Ohio, near Cleveland, and the other in New Stanton, Pennsylvania, near Pittsburgh. The New Stanton facility was a partially completed Chrysler Corporation assembly plant. If VW selected the New Stanton site it could start production of VW Rabbits by late 1977 or early 1978. Number of Rabbits produced was expected to increase from 60,000 the first year to 200,000 by the sixth year of operations. The VW plant would initially employ 3000 workers. Over a period of six years the number of workers was expected to rise to 5000. The Commonwealth of Pennsylvania estimated that direct, indirect, and induced jobs resulting from location of the VW plant in New Stanton would be 7557 in the first year of operation. These estimates implied that 4557 jobs would be indirectly related to the VW plant location. In six years total direct and indirect jobs related to the VW plant would be approximately 12,595.

FINANCING ARRANGEMENTS

VW estimated that the total cost of opening the plant in New Stanton would be $225 million. Of this amount $135 million would be made available by state agencies. The State Employees' Retirement System would provide $50 million and the Public School Employees' Retirement Fund would provide $85 million. Part of this $135 million would be made available to Greater Greensburg to purchase the Chrysler plant. Greater Greensburg would lease the plant and site to the Westmoreland County Industrial Development Authority, which in turn would lease it to VW. The lease payments would be used to amortize the loan. Part of the $135 million would be loaned to VW over a period of time as its plant and equipment needs rose. The interest rate would be 9 percent on these funds.

The Commonwealth of Pennsylvania, as an inducement for VW to locate in New Stanton, developed a substantial financing package for VW. The Pennsylvania Industrial Development Authority (PIDA) would loan $40 million to VW. Of this amount $10 million would be a special appropriation made by the Pennsylvania legislature. The amount would be loaned to VW for a 30-year period. Under normal circumstances PIDA made industrial development loans at 4 percent. However, during the first 20 years, only the interest would be payable at a 1.75 percent rate. The rate during the following ten years would be 8.5 percent on the remaining balance, and combined payments of interest and principal would be at a rate of $4 million annually. The commonwealth would also issue $20 million in 30-year serial general obligation bonds at 6.25 percent to improve the highway facilities leading to the plant site. The loan amortization schedule is shown in Exhibit 3. The commonwealth would also issue $10 million of general obligation bonds to construct a service yard and a railroad spur to link the plant with both the Baltimore and Ohio and the Norfolk and Western Railroads. These general obligation bonds would mature in 30 years and carry a coupon rate of 6.5 percent.

The Commonwealth Departments of Education and Community Affairs would commit up to $585,000 for recruitment of and training courses for potential VW employees. The Westmoreland County would forego 95 percent of local property taxes on the plant for the first three years and 50 percent for the next two years while VW moved into full production. The federal government would make a $3.2 million grant under the Federal Comprehensive Employment and Training Act to the counties of Westmoreland, Washington, Allegheny, Lawrence, and Butler for training unemployed and underemployed county residents for employment at the VW plant. This amount would not have to be repaid to the federal government.

REVENUE CONSIDERATIONS

The railroad facilities constructed by the commonwealth would be leased to Baltimore and Ohio and Norfolk and Western Railroads at a charge of $20 per loaded car. The average number of loaded cars expected to use the facility per year was 30,000.

The commonwealth estimated that the bulk of benefits would come from increased tax revenues. There would be increases in Corporate Income Tax, Sales Tax, Personal Income Tax, Realty Transfer Tax, and Liquid Fuels Tax.

It was difficult to estimate the financial performance of VW in the United States. Selected financial statistics for Chrysler, Ford, and General Motors are shown in Exhibit 4. With a U.S. scale of operations considerably smaller than the "Big Three," VW was expected to generate a return on assets that would be less than the average return on assets for the "Big Three." It was assumed that VW would generate profits of 7 percent on total New Stanton plant assets of $225 million. Pennsylvania would be able to tax 70 percent of the amount reported as net income at a corporate tax rate of 9.5 percent. For the first year of operation, under the 7-percent return on assets as-

sumption, this tax was estimated to be $225 \times .07 \times .7 \times .095 = \$1.047$ million. This amount was expected to grow at a 10-percent annual rate for six years and, for estimation purposes, was assumed to stabilize for the remaining years. A summary of the estimated corporate income taxes based on these assumptions is shown in Exhibit 5.

The Commonwealth of Pennsylvania assessed a capital stock and franchise tax annually. The revenues this tax would generate are shown in Exhibit 5.

The Foreign Corporation Excise Tax was a one-time tax and amounted to $1/3$ percent of total assets. Another one-time tax was the Realty Transfer Tax. It was 1 percent and was applicable to the purchase price of land and building. The VW land and building cost was $75 million.

VW was expected to spend $1 million for electricity, $2 million for gas, and $100,000 for phone service the first year. The Utility Gross Receipts Tax was 4.5 percent of the total utility payments. This revenue base was expected to grow at a 10-percent rate for the first six years, after which it would become stable.

It was estimated that each of the 3000 employees in the first year would pay $166 in sales tax. Each of the 3000 employees would receive an average wage of $13,574 the first year and pay personal income taxes of 2 percent on their wages. Both of these revenue sources on a *per employee* basis were expected to grow at a 10-percent rate for the first six years of operation and then stabilize.

Based on 225 work days per year, the commonwealth estimated that fuel consumption by VW plant workers would increase by 1.1 million gallons in the first year. At a liquid fuel tax rate of $0.09 per gallon the commonwealth expected to generate $99,000 in revenue from this tax. This amount was expected to grow at a rate of 4 percent per worker for the first six years of the VW plant operation, after which it was expected to stabilize.

The commonwealth had to decide if the magnitude of subsidies or incentives offered to VW were justified on a cost-benefit basis. In addition, they had to determine what was the appropriate treatment for the $40 million PIDA loan to VW. Since PIDA usually lent these funds at 4 percent, the "true" cost of the loan to VW was not clear. Some neutral observers felt that it was proper to charge interest at 4 percent on $40 million for the first 20 years and on the declining balance for years 21 to 30. The cash inflows implied by this repayment schedule would then be discounted at 6.25 percent. The net present value derived this way would constitute the cost of the VW loan. The calculations are summarized in Exhibit 6.

Still other observers reasoned that PIDA had only $30 million to lend and that the $10 million special appropriation by the Pennsylvania legislature was cost-free. They felt this $30 million amount should be considered as loaned at 4 percent with 30 annual payments of $1 million each needed to repay the loan. The implied cash inflows discounted at 6.25 percent would provide a basis for determining the cost of the VW loan. The cash inflows and present values are shown in Exhibit 7. A third group of observers had a different perspective on the cost of the loan. They contended that cash inflows and outflows needed to be adjusted for the time value of money by considering a weighted average cost of capital, which was higher than 6.25 percent.

EXHIBIT 1

The Volkswagen–New Stanton Project

Exchange Rates for Deutsche Marks and Dollars

Year	DM Exchanged for $1	$ Exchanged for DM 1
pre-1969	4.00	0.25
1969–70	3.66	0.27
1971	3.22	0.31
1972	3.12	0.32
1973	2.70	0.37
1974	2.41	0.41
1975	2.62	0.38
1976	2.36	0.42

EXHIBIT 2

The Volkswagen–New Stanton Project

Summary of VW's Sales and Net Income*
(in millions of Deutsche marks)

Year	Sales	Net Income
1967	6,935.4	121.3
1968	8,888.1	209.1
1969	10,755.4	165.9
1970	11,915.9	151.2
1971	13,338.7	70.1
1972	15,996.0	81.5
1973	16,982.0	78.5
1974	16,966.3	d 553.1
1975	18,857.3	d 142.6
1976	21,422.5	786.3

* *d* denotes a loss.

EXHIBIT 3

The Volkswagen–New Stanton Project

Loan Amortization Schedule for General Obligation Serial Bonds*

Year	Principal Remaining	Amount Retired	Interest Payment
1	$20,000,000	$666,667	$1,250,000
2	19,333,333	666,667	1,208,333
3	18,666,666	666,667	1,166,667
4	17,999,999	666,667	1,125,000
5	17,333,333	666,667	1,083,333
6	16,666,665	666,667	1,041,667
7	15,999,998	666,667	1,000,000
8	15,333,331	666,667	958,333
9	14,666,664	666,667	916,666
10	13,999,997	666,667	875,000
11	13,333,330	666,667	833,333
12	12,666,663	666,667	791,666
13	11,999,996	666,667	750,000
14	11,333,329	666,667	708,333
15	10,666,662	666,667	666,666
16	9,999,995	666,667	625,000
17	9,333,328	666,667	583,333
18	8,666,661	666,667	541,666
19	7,999,994	666,667	500,000

EXHIBIT 3 *(Continued)*

Year	Principal Remaining	Amount Retired	Interest Payment
20	7,333,327	666,667	458,333
21	6,666,660	666,667	416,666
22	5,999,993	666,667	375,000
23	5,333,326	666,667	333,333
24	4,666,659	666,667	291,666
25	3,999,992	666,667	250,000
26	3,333,325	666,667	208,333
27	2,666,658	666,667	166,666
28	1,999,991	666,667	125,000
29	1,333,324	666,667	83,333
30	666,667	666,667	41,666

*The principal remaining is at the beginning of the year, the amount retired is at year-end and the interest payment is at 6.25 percent on the principal remaining at the beginning of the year.

EXHIBIT 4

The Volkswagen–New Stanton Project

Selected Financial Statistics for U.S. Automobile Manufacturers*
(in billions of dollars)

	Chrysler		Ford		General Motors	
	1975	1976	1975	1976	1975	1976
Sales	11.598	15.538	24.001	28.840	35.725	47.181
Net income	d 0.282	0.328	0.228	0.983	1.253	2.903
Total assets	6.267	7.074	14.020	15.768	21.557	24.442
Mkt share %	13.4	15.6	26.9	24.0	54.8	57.9

*d denotes a loss. Market share is based on sales of domestic manufacturers only.

EXHIBIT 5

The Volkswagen–New Stanton Project

Summary of Estimates of Selected Tax Revenues (in millions of dollars)

Year	Corporate I.T.	Capital Stock Tax
1	$1.047	$1.436
2	1.152	1.103
3	1.267	1.159
4	1.394	1.216
5	1.533	1.278
6–on	1.686	1.342

EXHIBIT 6

The Volkswagen–New Stanton Project

Cost of $40 Million VW Loan—Alternative 1*

Year	4% Interest	Remaining Principal (000,000)	4% Interest	Present Value	Repaid Principal
1–20	$1,600,000				
21		40	$1,600,000	$449,584	$4,000,000
22		36	1,440,000	380,952	4,000,000
23		32	1,280,000	318,835	4,000,000
24		28	1,120,000	262,662	4,000,000
25		24	960,000	211,977	4,000,000
26		20	800,000	167,496	4,000,000
27		16	640,000	125,920	4,000,000
28		12	480,000	89,280	4,000,000
29		8	320,000	56,080	4,000,000
30		4	160,000	26,339	4,000,000
	ΣPV = $18,021,600			$2,089,125	ΣPV = $8,752,400

ΣPresent Values = $28,863,125
Net Present Value = ($11,136,875)

*The discount rate used is 6.25 percent. The net present value is viewed as the cost of the $40 million loan.

EXHIBIT 7

The Volkswagen–New Stanton Project

Cost of $40 Million VW Loan—Alternative 2*

Year	Principal Remaining (000,000)	Amount Retired	Interest (000,000)	Present Value
1	30	$1,000,000	$1.20	$1,129,440
2	29	1,000,000	1.16	1,027,598
3	28	1,000,000	1.12	933,845
4	27	1,000,000	1.08	847,584
5	26	1,000,000	1.04	768,238
6	25	1,000,000	1.00	695,300
7	24	1,000,000	.96	628,301
8	23	1,000,000	.92	566,775
9	22	1,000,000	.88	510,312
10	21	1,000,000	.84	458,539
11	20	1,000,000	.80	411,088
12	19	1,000,000	.76	367,635
13	18	1,000,000	.72	327,866
14	17	1,000,000	.68	291,502
15	16	1,000,000	.64	258,278
16	15	1,000,000	.60	227,952
17	14	1,000,000	.56	200,290
18	13	1,000,000	.52	175,094
19	12	1,000,000	.48	152,165
20	11	1,000,000	.44	131,318
21	10	1,000,000	.40	112,396
22	9	1,000,000	.36	95,238
23	8	1,000,000	.32	79,709
24	7	1,000,000	.28	65,666
25	6	1,000,000	.24	52,994
26	5	1,000,000	.20	41,874
27	4	1,000,000	.16	31,480
28	3	1,000,000	.12	22,320
29	2	1,000,000	.08	14,020
30	1	1,000,000	.04	1,600

$$\Sigma PV = \$13,451,600 \qquad \$10,626,417$$

$$\Sigma \text{ Present Values} = \$24,078,017$$

$$\text{Net Present Value} = (\$5,921,983)$$

*This alternative assumes that only $30 million of the loan had a cost associated with it. The interest rate is 4 percent. All cash inflows are discounted at 6.25 percent. The net present value is the cost of the $40 million loan.

CASE 17

Green Valley Hospital

Green Valley Hospital was in the process of preparing its proposed budget for calendar year 1979. This process included the development of both the operating budget and the capital budget. The entire package, once completed, would then be presented to the board of trustees at their November meeting for final approval.

At that time Mr. Rollie, the hospital's controller and budget officer, was briefing those hospital personnel concerned with the preparation of the budgets. In attendance at this meeting was the hospital administrator, the chief of the medical staff, the director of nursing, the assistant administrators, and the members of the medical staff executive committee. Each hospital service area was required to prepare its operating and capital equipment budgets. When prepared, they were submitted to the next level in the chain of supervision for re-

view and approval (Exhibit 1). Mr. Rollie had made some specific remarks regarding the preparation of the requests for capital equipment. He had concluded these remarks by stating that, in his preliminary analysis, the capital equipment budget would be at least as large as it was last year and would more than likely be increased by 5 percent to 8 percent. At the end of the meeting the hospital administrator, Mr. Rish, stated that he would like to have his administrative staff submit their budgets to him by October 15.

As Mr. Rish began preparing for the meeting with his staff, for the purpose of evaluating the capital equipment requests, he was reminded of last year's experience. During those meetings, more than 100 requests ranging from $100 to $75,000 were reviewed. In many cases the requests not only involved the department head but also the service or ac-

This case was prepared by and used with the permission of Mr. H. James Graham, Montgomery County Hospital, Blacksburg, Virginia.

tivity supervisor who actually wanted the item. It was a very tedious process. Even so, Mr. Rish questioned the quality of the decisions and the ranking of the requests that resulted. Much of the information presented with a request was of a subjective nature, except for item cost and quantity desired. When estimates concerning revenues or cost savings were presented, they were unreliable. The decision process usually resulted in a set of compromises designed to assure each department that its priority item would be high on the consolidated ranking of requests.

In addition to these problems Mr. Rish recognized another difficulty that arose when medical equipment was competing with administrative equipment. Due to the more subjective benefits associated with the medical items and the greater pressure the medical staff was able to exert on the evaluation process, these items were usually given priority over the administrative requests. He wondered if a more objective means for evaluating these equipment requests might exist.

After mulling over these problems, he discussed them with Mr. Rollie. Mr. Rollie commented that when he was working for General Mining Equipment before coming to the hospital, he occasionally assisted the finance officer in collecting and organizing data used to determine the value of a proposed project. The project's return could then be compared to the return from other proposed projects, and the one with the largest return would receive the highest ranking. Mr. Rish was encouraged to hear this and wondered if a similar process could be developed for the hospital. Mr. Rollie was not sure. He wondered if the returns on hospital equipment could

be quantified totally in dollars as were the returns of the for-profit firm where these techniques were applied. Mr. Rollie agreed to look into the matter and determine if the project analysis method he used could apply, with some modification, to the hospital's capital equipment budgeting process. Mr. Rish knew that Mr. Rollie would be busy with the new budget, so he asked him to have his recommendation on the capital budgeting process submitted to him by the end of January 1979.

HOSPITAL BACKGROUND

Green Valley Hospital was organized as a nonprofit community hospital. It was constructed in 1950 with a grant from the federal government, a local fund raising drive, and a loan from a local bank. The facility was established as a short-term, general care institution with 200 beds. The facility was expanded in 1969 to provide more space for the outpatient clinics and physicians' offices. It was registered with the A.H.A. On the 1978 J.C.A.H. inspection, it was given a one-year accreditation, with a reinspection at the end of 1979, instead of the three-year accreditation.

The hospital provided patient care in the areas of obstetrics/gynecology, pediatrics, medicine, and surgery. The hospital had an 85-percent occupancy rate, which had been about the same for the last two years. The average length of stay is 7.5 days.

Green Valley was one of two hospitals serving a population of 85,000 persons. With both hospitals, there was a total of 350 hospital beds in the community. It had been rumored that one of the national proprietary hospital chains was going to build a 100- to 150-bed facility in the community. Community growth was expected to be at approximately 1 to 2 percent for the next few years.

ADMINISTRATOR'S BACKGROUND

Mr. Rish was promoted to the administrator's position in June 1977 when the incumbent administrator resigned. His resignation was submitted to allow him to accept the administrator's position for a larger hospital in a neighboring community. At that time Mr. Rish had been the assistant administrator for Support Services at Green Valley. He assumed the assistant administrator's position in 1972 after separating from the United States Army where he had served for six years as a medical supply officer. He completed his Bachelor's degree in business prior to entering the service.

PRESENT CAPITAL BUDGETING PROCESS FOR EQUIPMENT

The hospital maintained an equipment purchase program in which the items required were ranked according to need (Exhibit 2). Items were purchased during the operating year from the list up to the limit of available funds. The program was reviewed each year prior to the beginning of the fiscal year. It was updated with additions, deletions, and revised priorities. The updated program was presented to the board of trustees for their review and approval. This presentation indicated the size of the capital budget for the coming year and those items that would probably be purchased.

The review of the equipment purchase program began at the section or service level. There, the old program was reviewed for items that had been previously programmed by that activity. Those items were then added, deleted, and ranked according to the needs of the activity at that time. When a new item was requested for inclusion in the program, the form shown in Exhibit 3 was used. Once the activity had completed the ranking of its equipment, the list was forwarded to the next level of supervision for review. The listings were then consolidated at the department level, then the administrator-chief of the medical staff level, then the board level. In the ranking process, at all levels some consideration was given for the length of time an item had been on the program, but present need usually took precedence.

Items costing less than $100 were to be purchased out of the operating budget for the section or department. All other items had to be requested and placed in the equipment purchase program for procurement.

CAPITAL BUDGETING AND EVALUATION PROCEDURES IN 1979

After his discussion with Mr. Rish, Mr. Rollie wanted to know what methods the financial experts were proposing for evaluating capital equipment requests. This would be necessary since neither he nor Mr. Rish were sure whether the for-profit methods could be adopted by the hospital. So, while preparing the 1979 budget, he began to search through some of the hospital literature available to him with regards to capital budgeting principles and techniques.

He found an abundance of information on the subject. The authors were also concerned with the budgeting problem the hospital administrator, hospital board, and medical director faced each year as they were presented a broad range of clinical and nonclinical capital requests. Usually these requests exceeded the resources available to support them. To deal with this problem, many techniques were being proposed that presented the requests and their returns in explicit terms. This allowed management to review and rank them in accordance with some specified criterion. Mr. Rollie felt that these techniques, if applied correctly, might solve many of the problems that concerned Mr. Rish.

After some additional work, Mr. Rollie came to the conclusion that a capital evaluation process should guide the acceptance of requests that are consistent with the objectives of the hospital. In order to assure this consistency, the evaluation process should include certain principles that would permit an efficient allocation of resources. Mr. Neal Gilbert, a management consultant for Coopers and Lybrand of Philadelphia, identified these principles as:

a. Cost Containment—. . . justify capital demands in terms of improving the health of the community. . . .

b. Planning—. . . the ideal capital budgeting system is an integrated planning process which should be used for both long and short range (annual) capital investments. . . .

c. Coordination—. . . coordinates the capital requests of all departments with one another and with the availability of capital funds. . . .

d. Control—. . . controls investment activity by assuring that capital funds flow only to those expenditures which will contribute the most to the fulfillment of institutional goals. . . .

e. Assessment of future financial support requirements—. . . assess the impact of the capital budget on present and future operating budgets. . . .

f. Communication—. . . encourages a better understanding of goals and objectives. . . .

g. Acceptability—. . . an ideal budgeting system is logical, systematic, objective, manageable, and flexible. . . .[1]

Mr. Rollie's readings revealed that many hospitals were using valuation methods similar to those he had used prior to coming to the hospital. These methods included the payback period, average rate of return, internal rate of return, and net present value. The payback period method was used more frequently than the others. He was surprised to find that many hospitals were not using any of these approaches for evaluating capital requests. Green Valley was not alone in the industry with its cost-need approach to capital budgeting.

Even though his hospital was not in a minority in its approach to capital budgeting, Mr. Rollie concluded that the present system was inefficient because of its unsystematic approach to decision making. There should be a proper balance between a quantitative and qualitative analysis of the investment. Also, it seemed inappropriate to be evaluating all demands as a homogeneous group. He concluded that a revision of the hospital's capital budgeting process was required to correct these shortcomings.

---

[1] Neal Gilbert, "Hospital Capital Budgeting Principles and Techniques," *Hospital Progress,* June 1975, pp. 56-57.

Mr. Rollie believed any such revision should begin with a categorization of the demands into more homogeneous groupings. This process would make it easier for the reviewers to compare requests since each group would contain projects of a similar nature and cost. A system, developed elsewhere, provided for four major categories:

Category I   Essential items to maintain operations.
Category II   Revenue-producing or cost-saving equipment.
Category III   Optional items for improvements.
Category IV   Miscellaneous items.

Within each major category, the requests could be further categorized by cost groupings.

Using this categorization system would provide the hospital's management with a technique for organizing the requests for evaluation but would not provide a means for determining the priority of the request. Mr. Rollie found two techniques for evaluating the requests, that he felt could be used at Green Valley. Both techniques allowed for quantitative and qualitative evaluations. Using these techniques would establish the balance of information he believed was necessary as a prerequisite to at least achieving some degree of consistency in the decision-making process. The first technique required four steps in evaluating a request for capital funds: (1) description of the item, (2) verification of information, (3) evaluation of the request, and (4) decision. This method used the net present value as the quantitative evaluator and a review by the medical staff as the qualitative evaluator (Exhibit 4). The second technique also made quantitative and qualitative evaluations. It too used a net present value approach in its quantitative analysis. It

further required an investment to produce sufficient positive cash flows, during a specified period, to pay back the original capital expenditure, plus provide a return on investment at a specified rate during the period (Exhibit 5). This method utilized a formal scoring sheet for ranking the investments according to the economic and subjective evaluations. This scoring lent more consistency to the evaluation process (Exhibit 6).

Mr. Rollie preferred the net present value method as opposed to any of the other evaluation techniques because it was more sophisticated and permitted an analysis of future cash flows at their discounted value. This seemed to be the more realistic approach, but he recognized that a major problem with an economic analysis of this type was deciding on the magnitude of the discount rate. This problem was actually an extension of the difficulty in determining the cost of capital for the hospital. Current practice in the hospital industry had been to use a subjective estimate that was somewhere between the unsecured borrowing rate and the rate of the return on endowment funds.

Mr. Rollie was not totally satisfied with this subjective evaluation but was encouraged to find that some research was being done to arrive at a more objective estimate. Suver and Neumann developed a model to assist hospitals in determining their cost of capital. The first step was to identify the hospital's sources of capital and the proportion of each source to the total.

Source of Capital	Contribution to Total Capital Structure (%)
1. Debt	50
2. Fund balances	
Retained earnings	30
Donations	10
Grants	10

The second step was to estimate the cost of each capital source. The cost of debt could be set at the current interest rate, but estimates of future interest rates would be better. The cost of donations and grants could be estimated by taking the average yield on tax-free municipal bonds and adding 1 or 2 percent for administrative costs in obtaining these funds. The cost of retained earnings or surplus funds could be set at the opportunity cost of investing internally. This internal rate of return from hospital projects was estimated to be between 20 and 30 percent. The hospital would have to measure the return on its assets to arrive at an exact rate for that hospital. The third step was to determine the weighted cost of each source and the average cost of capital for the hospital. This procedure was as shown below[2].

If this model were followed, a cost of capital could be determined for the hospital. This figure could then be used to determine the net present value of investment alternatives.

Another problem that Mr. Rollie discovered in using the net present value approach in the nonprofit hospital context was that the objective the net present value method sought to achieve was wealth maximization. He was certain that "stockholders' wealth" was an irrelevant issue for a nonprofit firm, but he was reluctant to discard the methodology.

Mr. Rollie was very much encouraged at the prospect of developing a capital budgeting system for Green Valley Hospital. He felt it was possible to develop a more rationale, systematic approach for evaluating capital requests. By including a subjective analysis of an investment's nonquantifiable returns, the for-profit techniques for evaluating capital investments could be adopted by the hospital. He felt that this was a reasonable modification since many of the returns on hospital investments could not be reduced to dollars. But before he made his recommendation to Mr. Rish, he wanted to discuss his ideas with some of his colleagues. Since the A.H.A. regional meeting was January 17, he could talk to some of his friends at the convention and still meet Mr. Rish's deadline for his recommendation.

Source of Capital	Percentage of Total (%)	× Cost of Source (%)	= Weighed Cost (%)
1. Debt	50	8.0	4.0
2. Fund balances:			
Retained earnings	30	30.0	9.0
Donations	10	10.0	1.0
Grants	10	10.0	1.0
	Average cost of capital		15.0

[2] The formats for presenting the sources of capital and the computation for the cost of capital were adopted, with the permission of James D. Suver and Bruce R. Neumann from their article "Cost of Capital," *Hospital Financial Management*, February 1978, p. 22.

EXHIBIT 1

Green Valley Hospital

Organizational Chart

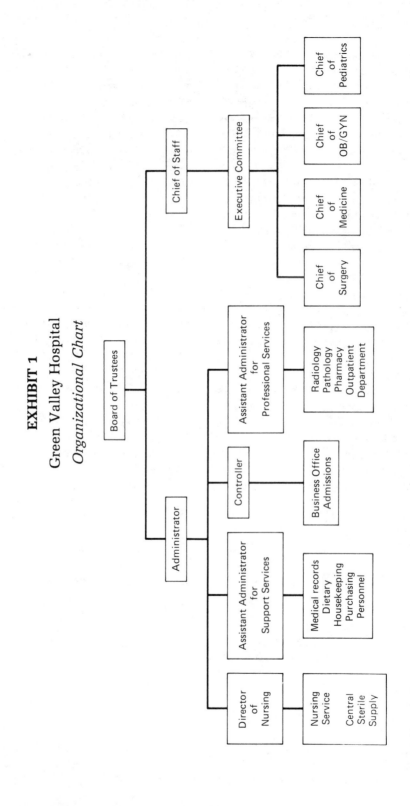

EXHIBIT 2

Green Valley Hospital

Hospital Equipment Purchase Program

Priority of Ordering	Description of Item: Nomenclature and Supply	Item Cost	Qty	Date Programmed	Requestor

EXHIBIT 3

Green Valley Hospital

Present Hospital Form for Requesting Equipment

Subject: *Request for Capital Equipment* Purchase Order # _____

Requestor: _____ Date: _____

Name of Item: _____

Cost of Item: _____

Quantity of Item(s) Required: _____

Reason for Requesting Item: _____

_____

_____

Signature of Requestor: _____

Telephone No. _____

Department Review _____

Request Approval ☐ Disapproved ☐ Date: _____

State Reason for Disapproval: _____

_____

Signature of Department Head: _____

Telephone No. _____

EXHIBIT 4

Green Valley Hospital

Capital Asset Planning Form *TECHNIQUE # 1*

1. date:
A. of request
B. when item is needed _____

2. department/division _____

3. cost center _____

4. Briefly describe item, desired location, and how its funding would be consistent with the stated goals of the department and the hospital.

(Continued on column 1, next page)

8. service availability
Will the proposed investment provide a service to the hospital's patients which is presently not available or not available in sufficient quantity?
A. service presently available *yes*_____ *no*_____
B. service presently available in sufficient quantity (if "No" give support, e.g., delays,

(Continued on column 2, next page)

144

EXHIBIT 4 (Continued)

5. classification (check only one)

A. Necessary to maintain present level of services including legally necessary items and new equipment and space to meet volume growth. _____

B. Results in a direct cost savings and/or additional revenue without reduction (or with improvement) in the quality of present services offered. _____

C. Improves the quality of present services (no material cost savings or additional revenue). _____

D. Expands the scope of present services (new programs). _____

6. cost

	cost:	verified by:
A. purchase cost	_____	_____
B. lease/rent cost	_____	_____
C. installation cost	_____	_____
D. annual operating and support costs		
1. Manpower costs	_____	_____
2. Supplies and maintenance costs	_____	_____

E. interest expense (to be completed by the budget officer) _____ _____

F. disposal cost of equipment to be replaced (less salvage value if any) _____ _____

G. Can any necessary installation not included in the purchase price be performed by the physical facilities department? yes_____ no_____

H. Can maintenance be performed by the physical facilities department? yes_____ no_____

I. Can construction be performed by the physical facilities department? yes_____ no_____

7. utilization

A. expected hours of use per day _____

B. expected days of use per week _____

C. estimated % utilization (assume 100% utilization is equal to 24 hours per day, 7 days per week) _____

comments of other departments, etc.) yes_____ no_____

9. qualitative benefit

A. Number of patients benefiting (select either #1 or #2):

   1. Number of patients *directly* benefiting from this investment per year, if any (for investments which are used directly in patient care).

      A. maximum _____

      B. most likely _____

      C. minimum _____

   2. Number of patients *indirectly* benefiting from this investment per year, if any (for investments which are not used directly in patient care).

      % of Average Daily Inpatient Census _____

      % of Average Daily Outpatient Visits _____

B. Number of other departments which will directly benefit from this investment. _____
Briefly describe how these departments will make use of the proposed investment.

C. Primary contribution to patient welfare (check one or give approximate percentage of the number of patients in each group).

   1. lifesaving or life-extending therapy _____

   2. restorative benefits or rehabilitation therapy _____

   3. preventive _____

   4. diagnostic _____

   5. patient service or convenience _____

D. Nature of other contribution (check one or more).

   1. staff and employee service or convenience _____

   2. research _____

   3. education _____

   4. other (describe briefly) _____

E. expected useful life of the service or program _____

F. Briefly describe the consequences if this investment is not made this year.

10. quantitative benefit	department estimate	financial analysis estimate
A. number of years that economic benefits will be received	_____	_____
B. expected annual cost savings (explain briefly)	_____	_____
C. annual revenue resulting from this investment (explain briefly)	_____	_____

11. comments (add any information that may be useful in the decision-making process)

12. Net Present Value (to be completed by the financial analysis department) _____

13. medical review committee ranking (to be completed by the medical review committee)

Reprinted from the article "4-Step Capital Budgeting," *Hospital Financial Management*, June 1976, p. 51, at the permission of the author R. Neal Gilbert.

EXHIBIT 5

Green Valley Hospital

*The Development Model: A Standard Summary
and Analysis of Development Expenditures**   *TECHNIQUE #2*

PURPOSE: To summarize the essential information required to evaluate the relative contribution to hospital operation of any addition to patient services or adjustment or extension of any support or administrative department.

SECTION I: Background

A. Describe the proposed development expenditures.

B. Does this development expenditure duplicate a patient service provided by another hospital in the area? Yes___ No___
If yes, what hospital(s)?

C. Does this proposed development expenditure require approval by comprehensive health planning?
Yes___ No___
If no, explain why not.

D. Is there evidence to believe that the development expenditure will favorably affect any hospital service or department other than that most directly affected?
Yes___ No___
If yes, explain.

SECTION II: Incremental Economic Analysis

Purpose: To provide the information required to determine the economic benefits of the development expenditure in relation to other proposed expenditures.

A. Required Initial Investment

	Cost	Depreciable Life (years)	Annual Depreciation
Capital expenditures — attach support including installation cost			
Special training cost	___		
Initial expenditure			

B. Expected Additional (Incremental) Revenue

Unit of Service	Projected Annual Volume Inpatient	Outpatient	Suggested Patient Charge
a.			
b.			
c.			
d.			

D. Incremental Financial Analysis (to be completed by treasurer)

Let X = Total annual revenue   = _____(B)
    X_1 = Annual inpatient revenue   = _____(B)
    X_2 = Annual outpatient revenue   = _____(B)
    Y = Total operating cost   = _____(C)
    Z = Allowable depreciation   = _____(A)

$$\frac{X_1}{X} \times (Y+Z) = Y_1 = \text{Inpatient operating cost*} \quad = \quad \underline{\quad}$$

$$\frac{X_2}{X} \times (Y+Z) = Y_2 = \text{Outpatient operating cost**} \quad = \quad \underline{\quad}$$

E = Total initial expenditure   = ___
Present value
  = Present value of $1 received each year for 5 years @ 6% interest**   = 4.212

68.5 = % cost reimbursers inpatient
.03 = % bad debts inpatient
.20 = % contractual allowances & bad debts outpatient
(Continued)

EXHIBIT 5 (Continued)

Annual Incremental Revenue

Inpatient	Outpatient	Total

C. Expected Annual Incremental Operating Cost Increases (Decreases)—attach detail in support of each factor

	Incremental Annual Cost
Personnel	$
Employee benefits @ 12%	
Physician cost	
Materials and supplies	
Maintenance contracts	
Insurance	
Other	
Total incremental annual cost	$

Formulation:

Gross revenue	X
Less	
Contractual allowances inpatient	$-.685 X_1 + .685 Y_1$
Bad debts inpatient	$-.03 X_1$
Contractual allowances and bad debts outpatient	$-.20 X_2$
Net patient revenue	$X -.715 X_1 - .20 X_2 + .685 Y_1$
Operating cost	$-Y$
Net incremental revenue (NIR) =	$X -.715 X_1 - .20 X_2 + .685 Y_1 - Y$

Net present value of project:
4.212 (NIR) − E = net present value = $ (attach calculations)

*If the project or expenditure does not result in new revenue but does affect operating cost, use 12 percent as outpatient and 88 percent as inpatient cost.

**In order to properly analyze the return from investment, it is important to realize that the hospital could invest its funds in other investments and make a return. Here six percent is an acceptable return. That being the case, a dollar received one year from now is worth only 94¢ as compared to a dollar received now. An initial expenditure made now would be made in current dollars while the payback will be in dollars which, when compared to current dollars, are worth less. Five years is used as a standard payback period.

SECTION III: Subjective Evaluations

A. Physician Impact

1. Will this expenditure or project result in a change in physician attitude toward the hospital? Yes___ No___
   If no, ignore the remainder of A and proceed to B.
2. What is the scope of the physician attitude change? (Check one)
   ___a. One or two physicians will be affected.
   ___b. The majority of the physicians in a hospital service will be affected.
   ___c. A substantial portion of the medical staff will be affected.
   Explain your answer. (Attach memorandum).
3. What is the intensity of the effect on physician attitude? (Check two answers — one for acceptance and one for nonacceptance).

Not Accepted

☐ −4 The physicians affected will move their practices to other hospitals.

☐ −3 The physicians affected will tend to reduce their practices at the hospital.

2. If yes, check the answers below which best describe the expected community impact. (Check one for acceptance and one for nonacceptance).

Not Accepted

☐ −4 Intense and widespread negative reaction in the community will result in a severe blow to the hospital's image.

☐ −3 A widespread negative effect on the hospital's general image and reputation will result.

☐ −2 The hospital's image will be damaged among certain groups in the community.

☐ −1 The attitudes of a relatively few people will be negatively affected.

   0 No effect

Accepted

☐ 1 Relatively few people will be positively affected.

☐ 2 Certain groups in the community will be favorably impressed.

☐ 3 A widespread positive effect on the

(Continued)

EXHIBIT 5 (Continued)

☐ −2 The physicians affected, at the very least, will be disgruntled and will tend to discuss the lack of the expenditure or project in the community and with other physicians.

☐ −1 The physicians will be aware of the lack of support for the project and expenditure and will be less likely to believe that the hospital is maintaining a proper level of patient care.

☐ 0 No effect.

Accepted

☐ 1 The physicians affected will be aware of the expenditure or project and will be satisfied that the hospital is maintaining a high level of patient care.

☐ 2 The physicians affected will be very impressed and will tend to discuss the expenditure or project favorably in the community and with other physicians.

☐ 3 The physicians affected will tend to moderately increase their practices at the hospital.

☐ 4 The physicians affected will move their practices to the hospital.

Explain these answers.

B. Community Impact

1. Will this expenditure or project have an effect on community attitude toward this hospital? Yes___ No___
   If no, proceed to C.

hospital's image and reputation will result.

☐ 4 Significant and widespread positive community reaction will contribute significantly to the hospital's general image and reputation.

Explain the answers.

C. Employee Impact

1. Will this expenditure or project have an effect on the attitude of the hospital's personnel? Yes___ No___

2. If yes, check the answers which best describe the expected employee impact. (Check one for acceptance and one for nonacceptance).

Not Accepted

☐ −4 Major and widespread negative impact on employee morale and attitude toward the hospital will result.

☐ −3 Widespread disappointment with the hospital and some general negative effect on the hospital's image among employees will result.

☐ −2 A limited group of employees (one or two departments) will react negatively.

☐ −1 Relatively few employees will be disturbed.

☐ 0 No effect.

Accepted

☐ 1 Relatively few employees will know about the decision, but they will be pleased.

☐ 2 A limited group (one or two departments) will be very pleased.

☐ 3 Nearly all employees will be pleased.

☐ 4 Major and widespread positive impact with long-term effect on employee attitude toward the hospital will result.

Explain these answers.

EXHIBIT 6

Green Valley Hospital

Development Analysis Score Sheet

	Item No.	Instructions	Value To be Assigned	Raw Score	Instructions	Priority Score
Economic Evaluation	Section II					
	A3	If total initial expenditure is less than $25,000	+1			
		If total intital expenditure is more than $25,000	−1			
	C4	If total annual incremental cost increase is less than $50,000	+1			
		If total annual incremental cost increase is greater than $50,000	−1			
	D	If present value is equal to or greater than zero	+2			
		If present value is less than zero	−2	____		____
		Total economic score	____		If total economic raw score is greater than zero, enter raw score in priority score column.	

(*Continued*)

EXHIBIT 6 (Continued)

Subjective Evaluation	Section III			
	A2a		1	Not applicable
	A2b		2	If A3 is greater than 4, the priority score is 1.
	A2c		3	If A3 is greater than 4, the priority score is 3.
	A3	Add positive and negative answers	1–8	If raw score exceeds 4, the excess is priority score.
	B	Add positive and negative answers	1–8	If raw score exceeds 4, the excess is priority score.
	C	Add positive and negative answers	1–8	If raw score exceeds 4, the excess is priority score.
		Total subjective score	____	____
		Total Score		

[1] The score sheet is weighted towards the small, profitable project. This concept is based on the limited resources of the hospital and the broader impact a group of smaller projects will have on the hospital and community than a single, costly project.

[2] Reprinted with permission from *The Hospital Progess*, December 1975. Copyright 1975 by The Catholic Hospital Association.

CASE 18

General Telephone Company of Florida*

In early December of 1979 Mr. George Gage, president of General Telephone Company (GTC) of Florida, requested Mr. Walter Cohen to submit a proposal that would address the practicality of expansion into the fiber optics field. Having 15 years of experience in operations research at GTC, Mr. Cohen heads the firm's analysis team. The analysis team was made up of eight GTC managers, with two managers from each of the areas of operations research, engineering, marketing, and finance. In conducting a two-year study of the fiber optics prospects in the telecommunications industry, the analysis team had gathered extensive market and cost information on the new product. The data had to be summarized, and recommendations had to be made to the board of directors at the January 15, 1980, meeting.

THE TELECOMMUNICATIONS INDUSTRY

The telecommunications industry encompasses the data communications and long-distance telephone markets. The data communications market includes networks that are capable of transmitting data (e.g., words, numbers, photographs) worldwide instantaneously. By 1985, this market was expected to quadruple in size to $20 billion in annual revenues. The long-distance telephone market was promising, with toll volume expected to grow at an 11- to 12-percent annual rate over the decade of the 1980s.

Traditionally dominant, the telephone segment of the industry operated as a monopoly within constraints set by the government. The American Telephone and Telegraph Company, which

---

*The information contained herein does not necessarily represent the views of General Telephone Company of Florida's management and its president; and further, portions of the statistics included do not represent fact, but rather theory in developing a classroom case model. This case was prepared by Jerome S. Osteryoung and John T. Lindow, Florida State University, and was used with the permission of Professor Osteryoung.

controlled the Bell System and operated about 81 percent of the telephones in service in the United States, was subject to a degree of competition from independent telephone companies. Consolidation of independent telephone companies was common; economies of scale, improvements in service, and greater management expertise resulted from such efforts. The largest of the telephone holding companies formed was General Telephone & Electronics Corporation (Exhibit 1).

Industry revenues are dictated by utility commissions. "Fair" rate increases had been allowed by the government, but problems had ensued:

1. Authorized rate increases as a percentage of the amounts requested by telephone companies had been on the decline.

2. Regulatory lag had lengthened. There is a lag between the time the request for a rate increase is submitted and the date that the regulatory body begins to consider the rate case. In 1979 this lag spanned 11 months, up from 6.8 months in 1975. In addition, there is a delay until the rate increase is granted.

Constructive influence on the regulatory commissions for the granting of reasonable rate increases is critical to the profitability of a telephone company. Costs are passed directly on to consumers through telephone rate increases; as a result, expenditures for administrative facilities are often excessive.

The telephone industry had effected cost reductions through improvements in productivity and through a greater usage of internal financing. Productivity improvements were reflected in the following measures:

1. A decline in the number of employees per 10,000 phones.

2. An increase in the volume of business per employee.

3. Lesser increases in operating costs (and telephone rates) than in the consumer price index (CPI).

Economies of scale and technological advances had contributed to the realization of higher productivity. The industry was pursuing advances in the use of fiber optics, packet switching, the picturephone, and the advanced mobile phone service (AMPS).

Internal financing accounted for two-thirds of financing needs in the telecommunications industry. For the industry capital expenditures for 1980 were projected at $22 billion, up from $19.5 billion in 1979. A great deal of the capital expenditures were for maintenance of the present level of service. The capital-intensive nature of the industry subjected individual firms to the dual effect of both higher inflation and higher interest rates. The capital projects' costs rise with inflation, which push up the financing costs of the projects (assuming constant interest rates). When interest rates are raised, higher effective project costs are compounded.

The 1980s were expected to be a period of moderate growth for the telephone industry. Competition was expected to intensify; congressional actions and court rulings had favored competition in the industry. Productivity improvements through technological advances would assume a critical role in maintaining a competitive stance in the 1980s.

GENERAL TELEPHONE COMPANY OF FLORIDA

The General Telephone Company of Florida is in the business of constructing, installing, maintaining, and operating a telephone system in Florida. GTC serves a population of 2.2 million with over 1.6 million telephones in service. More than 11.7 million miles of wire in cable form the base of the system. The major telephone exchanges of the firm are listed in Exhibit 2. Comparative income statements and balance sheets of the firm are given in Exhibit 3. GTC of Florida is a wholly-owned subsidiary of General Telephone and Electronics Corporation (GTE).

GTE, the parent corporation, is a holding company that acquires the interests of telephone and other telecommunications companies. In 1980 GTE owned telephone companies in 31 states, with over 17.3 million phones in service. The firm reported 1979 consolidated net income of $645 million on assets of $18.4 billion. GTE Laboratories, Inc., a subsidiary of GTE, is a research firm located in Waltham, Massachusetts. Research is conducted to improve existing technology and to create new methods of transmitting information more efficiently.

FIBER OPTICS

Fiber optics, or lightwave fiber communications, is the transmission of information in the form of impulses of light along very thin strands of glass. The light impulses can be turned on and off millions of times a second, allowing an optical fiber to simultaneously handle hundreds of telephone calls. Optical fiber could replace the conventional transmission of communication through electrical impulses along copper wire and coaxial cable.

Fiber optics had several advantages. First, the glass fiber cable is lighter in weight and smaller in size than traditional copper cable. This could be a critical consideration in congested urban areas. Fiber optic cable had already replaced bulky copper cable in trunk lines in Chicago and in several other cities. With 86 percent of its cable underground, GTC of Florida might benefit from such a conversion in urban areas such as Tampa, Clearwater, and St. Petersburg. Second, the optical cable is more dependable than copper cable; it is less vulnerable to moisture. Third, fiber optics is a noise-free transmission carrier because glass is undisturbed by the proximity of electrical power lines, lightning surges, and cross-talk. Fourth, economies of scale in production make fiber optics technology cost-competitive with copper. Finally, the basic ingredient of glass (i.e., sand) is in unlimited supply.

RESEARCH RESULTS

Through efforts coordinated with GTE Laboratories, GTC's analysis team conducted a study of fiber optics. On the macro level the analysis team elicited subjective probability estimates of future telephone industry demand from ten telecommunications industry experts. Using a cross-impact analysis and the facilities of a local university, the experts projected demand probabilities for the 1980s in three periods: the near-term (1980–82), the intermediate-term (1983–85), and the long-term (1986–89).[1] The experts considered three demand levels: high (a 12-percent annual demand increase), medium (a 10-percent annual demand increase), and low (a 6-percent annual demand increase). The consensus of the experts is summarized in Exhibit 4. In general, the experts believed that: high demand suggested high demand in the following period; medium demand suggested moderate-to-high demand in the following period; low demand suggested low-to-moderate growth in the following period.

On the micro level GTE Laboratories provided data regarding the costs, communication capacity, and durability of fiber optic cable. The analysis team calculated annual cost savings expected from the installation of fiber optic cable, based on the revenue (demand) and cost estimates. Cost savings resulted from lower material costs (copper prices were soaring), lower labor costs (fewer maintenance crews would be required), and lower overhead costs (e.g., fewer trucks would be needed since each truck could carry more fiber optic cable than [bulky] copper cable). Cost-savings figures are summarized in Exhibit 5. A sample calculation of an expected cost-savings figure is presented in Exhibit 6.

THE ALTERNATIVES

During 1979, GTC of Florida allocated $245.3 million for capital expenditures. Company policy required a minimum return of 15 percent on all projects undertaken. Top management indicated full support for funding of the fiber optics project if the minimum return was expected to be realized. Mr. Walter Cohen outlined two proposals for conversion to fiber optic cable. A third option available would be to conduct more extensive research in cost-savings techniques, without undertaking any conversion to fiber optic cable.[2]

Several assumptions were made:

1. The initial investment outlay, stated net of proceeds from scrap value of the cable replaced, would occur on January 15, 1980. The initial conversion to fiber optics (either full or partial) would be completed by Decem-

---

[1] Cross-impact analysis is an extension of the Delphi technique. In the Delphi technique a group of experts are administered a questionnaire in which estimates of either historic or futuristic data are elicited. A consensus is reached; anonymity of the experts is preserved. Delphi estimates of historical data (e.g., almanac data) are remarkably accurate; Delphi estimates of futuristic data are widely used.

Two general procedures describe cross-impact analysis. First, in face-to-face interaction, participants reach a consensus on the probabilities of occurrence of certain future events (e.g., telephone demand levels for several future time periods). Second, participants consider interactions among the future events and, based on the "impact" of the occurrences of other events, revise their initial probability estimates through consensus.

For example, the experts might estimate the probability of high demand in the 1986–89 period as .45. However, if high demand is assumed for both the 1981–82 and 1983–85 periods, the experts would revise their estimate upward (perhaps to .75). A summary of the "impacted" probabilities is given in Exhibit 4.

[2] The evaluation of the alternatives should be based on decision tree analysis. See Magee, "Decision Trees for Decision Making" (*Harvard Business Review,* July/August, 1964, pp. 126–38) and "How to Use Decision Trees in Capital Investment" (*Harvard Business Review,* September/October, 1964, pp. 79–96).

ber 31, 1980.[3] Costs of subsequent conversions and replacements were *not* stated net of abandonment proceeds.

2. Abandonment entailed removal of the cable from the ground. Abandonment proceeds would be realized on the date of abandonment.[4]

3. Cost savings, stated on an after-tax baris, would be realized at year-end. The cost-savings figures would be equivalent to cash flows (i.e., the effect of any additional depreciation tax shield from an investment would be included in the cost-savings figure).

4. No cost savings would be realized until the conversion process was complete.

5. Negative figures are indicated by parentheses ( ). Negative cost savings (i.e., additional costs) could arise from lower demand than expected or from start-up costs of a conversion or replacement.[5]

FULL CONVERSION

A full conversion to fiber optic cable in GTC's major exchanges would entail a cash outlay of $50 million in 1980. Annual after-tax cost savings for 1981–82 would be $12MM, $6MM, and $(3MM) for high, medium, and low demand levels, respectively. Through the 1980s management had several options available:

1. Assuming high demand for 1981–82, management could realize $18MM in annual cost savings for the 1983–85 period and $30MM in annual cost savings for the 1986–89 period. Alternatively, management could abandon the project on December 31, 1982, and realize $22MM in cash or abandon the project on December 31, 1985, and realize $15MM in cash.

2. Assuming medium demand for 1981–82, management could realize $12MM in annual cost savings for the 1983–85 period and $18MM in annual cost savings for the 1986–89 period. Alternatively, management could abandon the project on December 31, 1982, and realize $22MM in cash or abandon the project on December 31, 1985, and realize $15MM in cash.

3. Assuming low demand for 1981–82, management would not follow through with the full conversion project for the remainder of the decade.

---

[3] In subsequent decisions in which a strategy change is made and a new project (full conversion, partial conversion, or replacement with copper) is undertaken, assume that the replacement-conversion would be complete as of the decision date. Assume that the investment cost would be paid on the decision date, and cost savings would commence immediately.

[4] Abandonment values (AV) are calculated as follows:

$$AV = \frac{\text{Salvage}}{\text{proceeds}} - \frac{\text{Costs of}}{\text{removal}} - \frac{\text{Tax Shield from loss on sale of}}{\text{cable (net of ITC recapture)}}$$

[5] Replacement with copper cable always would entail negative cost savings (i.e., higher costs) because cost savings were based relative to maintaining copper cable from January 1980 to December 1989. It would be more costly (initially) to use copper cable after a fiber optics project was undertaken and subsequently disbanded than it would be to use copper cable over the entire period. For example, labor costs would rise as hiring costs increased (more maintenance crews would be required).

If the fiber optic cable was replaced with copper cable, management could minimize losses at $(2MM) and $(1MM) for the 1983–85 and 1986–89 periods, respectively. Installation and material costs of this replacement would total $12MM. Alternatively, management could abandon the full conversion project on December 31, 1982, and realize $22MM in cash or abandon the replacement project on December 31, 1985, and realize $15MM in cash.

PARTIAL CONVERSION

A second option would be the conversion of GTC's Tampa and St. Petersburg exchanges to fiber optic cable. A cash outlay of $30MM would be required in 1980. Annual after-tax cost savings for 1981–82 would be $6MM, $5MM, and $(1MM) for high, medium, and low demand levels, respectively. Management's options through the remainder of the decade would be as follows:

1. Assuming high demand for 1981–82, management could realize $9MM and $12MM in annual cost savings for the 1983–85 and 1986–89 periods, respectively. Management could abandon the partial conversion project on December 31, 1982, and realize $13MM in cash or abandon the project on December 31, 1985, and realize $8MM in cash. Alternatively, management could implement full conversion on December 31, 1982, at a cost of $40MM and realize $16MM and $30MM for the 1983–85 and 1986–89 periods, respectively. Abandonment monies of $15MM could be realized on December 31, 1985, if the

full conversion effort was deemed undesirable at that time.

2. Assuming medium demand for 1981–82, management could realize annual cost savings of $8MM for the 1983–85 period and $11MM for the 1986–89 period. Management could abandon the project on December 31, 1982, and realize $13MM in cash or abandon the project on December 31, 1985, and realize $8MM in cash.

3. Assuming low demand for 1981–82, management could realize $1MM and $2MM in annual cost savings for the 1983–85 and 1986–89 periods, respectively. Management could abandon the project on December 31, 1982, and realize 13MM in cash or abandon the project on December 31, 1985, and realize $8MM in cash. Alternatively, rather than abandoning the project in 1985, management could replace the fiber optic cable with copper cable costing $20MM. An annual cost savings of $(2MM) for the 1986–89 period would then be expected.

Another option available to management would be to replace the fiber optic cable with copper cable on December 31, 1982. The copper cable replacement would cost $12MM. The replacement option would yield annual cost savings of $(2MM) and $(1MM) for the 1983–85 and 1986–89 periods, respectively. This option could be abandoned on December 31, 1985, yielding a cash flow of $4MM.

NO CONVERSION

If neither the full nor partial conversion projects were deemed desirable, management would undertake an extensive research project that would be directed along cost-minimization lines. New labor-saving techniques would be explored and evaluated as part of the research. An initial outlay of $10MM cash would be required in 1980. Annual cost savings for 1981–82 would be $1MM, regardless of the demand level. Once again, management would be faced with several decisions across the decade:

1. Assuming high demand for 1981–82, management could shift to a full conversion project on December 31, 1982, at a cost of $70MM. Annual cost savings of $16MM and $30MM could then be realized for the 1983–85 and 1986–89 periods, respectively. Management would retain the right to abandon the full conversion project on December 31, 1985. $20MM in proceeds could be expected from abandonment at that date.

   Alternatively, management could shift to a partial conversion project on December 31, 1982, at a cost of $45MM and realize annual cost savings of $8MM and $11MM for the 1983–85 and 1986–89 periods, respectively. Management could abandon this project on December 31, 1985, netting $8MM in abandonment proceeds.

   Finally, management could abandon the research efforts on December 31, 1982. But the research "investment" would provide no abandonment value.

2. Assuming medium demand for 1981–82, management could realize annual cost savings of $3MM for the 1983–85 period and $5MM for the 1986–89 period. The research efforts could be abandoned on either December 31, 1982 or 1985, with no proceeds.

   Alternatively, management could shift to a partial conversion project on December 31, 1982, at a cost of $45MM and expect to realize annual cost savings of $6MM and $10MM for the 1983–85 and 1986–89 periods, respectively. Abandonment of this project on December 31, 1985, would yield $8MM.

3. Assuming low demand for 1981–82, management could realize annual cost savings of $3MM and $5MM for the 1983–85 and 1986–89 periods, respectively. The research efforts could be abandoned on either December 31, 1982 or 1985, with no proceeds.

THE DECISION

Mr. Cohen prepared a summary of the annual cash flows (i.e., cost savings) and abandonment proceeds (see Exhibit 5). In the summary Cohen compiled only those flows related to decisions made by management in January 1980, which would be followed through to the end of the decade. Strategy changes during the decade (at either December 31, 1982 or 1985) were not considered in Cohen's summary. For example, if management accepted the partial conversion project at the January 1980 board meeting and demand levels in 1981 and 1982 were high, annual cost savings of $6MM, $9MM, and $12MM could be expected in the near, intermediate, and long-term future, assuming that status quo was maintained at decision points December 31, 1982, or 1985. Recall, however, that other options would be available at these decision points—specifically, shifting to full conversion (and realizing higher future cash flows) or abandoning the partial conversion project (and realizing immediate cash flows).

Mr. Cohen had to incorporate all of the available options into his presentation to top management at the upcoming board meeting. To ensure funding for one of the fiber optics projects (either full or partial conversion), Cohen had to present evidence that a conversion project could achieve at least the minimum 15 percent required return. A comparison of the net present values (NPVs) of the full-conversion project, the partial-conversion project, and the no-conversion project alternative was necessary. Risk, measured in terms of variability in the expected net present values of cash flows, was an important consideration. An evaluation of the options should be conducted in which both the NPVs and the variability in the flows were considered. A comparison of the coefficients of variation under each alternative would assess the relative risk of each project.[6]

EXHIBIT 1

General Telephone Company of Florida

Major Holding Companies of Independent Telephone Firms

Holding Company	Telephones in Service at December 31, 1979 (in millions)
General Telephone & Electronics	17.3
United Telecommunications	4.5
Continental Telephone	3.1
Central Telephone & Utilities	1.9

Source: Moody's Public Utility Manual (1980).

---

[6] The coefficient of variation is defined at $T/E(X)$, where T is the standard deviation of the expected values and $E(X)$ is the expected NPV of the project.

EXHIBIT 2

General Telephone Company of Florida

Major Exchanges

Exchange	Telephones in Service at December 31, 1979
Tampa	423,161
St. Petersburg	309,601
Clearwater	225,899
Sarasota	135,824
Bradenton	89,399
Lakeland	88,781

Source: Moody's Public Utility Manual (1980).

EXHIBIT 3

General Telephone Company of Florida

Comparative Income Account, Years Ended Dec. 31
(in thousands of dollars)

	1979	1978	1977	1976	1975	1974
Operating revenues						
Local service	270,508	236,993	229,640	185,201	153,334	132,307
Toll service	327,528	293,996	246,258	215,885	174,110	157,497
Miscellaneous	13,436	12,072	10,797	10,092	8,904	7,637
Prov. for uncollective accts.	dr7,004	dr5,012	dr4,859	dr3,847	dr4,059	dr3,965
Gross operating revenues	604,468	538,049	481,836	407,331	332,290	293,476
Maintenance	150,045	124,332	104,799	84,579	71,268	66,425
Prov. for depreciation	107,046	106,332	90,380	81,042	72,051	60,494
Other operating expenses	133,365	109,888	98,231	86,375	71,015	63,874
General taxes	44,701	40,469	37,996	32,936	27,021	23,173
[1]Fed. income taxes	25,204	30,530	28,332	15,734	338	cr4,048
[1]Deferred fed. inc. taxes	24,172	20,567	21,804	19,571	17,832	16,706
Net earnings	119,935	105,835	100,294	86,094	72,765	66,852
Other income, net	dr417	dr46	dr61	dr447	dr967	146
Total income	199,518	105,835	100,233	86,647	71,798	66,998
Interest paid	52,549	45,287	44,124	42,647	45,375	44,333
Amort. of debt discount, etc.		220	222	207	207	163
Int. charged to construction	cr3,327	cr4,825	cr5,705	cr4,804	cr7,819	cr8,195
Net income	70,296	65,153	61,592	48,597	34,035	30,692

(Continued)

EXHIBIT 3 (Continued)

General Telephone Company of Florida

Comparative Balance Sheet, Years Ended Dec. 31
(in thousands of dollars)

	1979	1978	1977	1976	1975
Assets					
Telephone plant	1,863,173	1,696,866	1,583,436	1,486,255	1,383,875
Less: depreciation reserve	387,663	348,157	304,837	274,713	232,447
Net property & plant	1,475,510	1,348,709	1,278,599	1,211,542	1,151,427
Current assets:					
Cash	9,655	7,606	7,795	7,567	8,407
Receivables, (net)	73,319	54,595	51,392	43,952	36,734
Materials & supplies	37,537	27,635	21,238	29,324	29,704
Prepayments	8,653	10,301	4,435	5,578	4,465
Deferred charges	2,079	2,196	3,907	7,596	8,823
Total assets	1,606,753	1,451,042	1,367,366	1,305,559	1,239,560
Liabilities and owners' equity					
Preferred stock	92,000	92,000	92,000	92,000	92,000
Common stock (par $25)	375,000	375,000	375,000	375,000	350,000
Retained earnings	118,781	99,478	80,158	63,168	55,966
Less: cap. stock expense	....	....	....	....	....
Long-term debt	513,668	525,445	528,717	535,353	487,759
Short-term debt	134,020	79,671	53,381	50,212	96,407
Current and accrued liabilities:					
Accounts payable, etc.	18,408	15,511	31,120	15,499	14,015
Due to affiliated cos.	27,047	17,041	14,601	8,688	8,316
Customers' deposits	4,290	3,942	3,393	2,872	2,458
Advance billing & payments	9,691	8,635	8,448	6,540	6,290
Accrued federal inc. taxes	1,060	1,167	1,988	1,210	2,046
Other current liabilities	74,323	33,811	9,533	18,101	20,830
Res. for storm dam. & oth. def. credits	320	350	553	6,970	5,666
[1]Deferred investment tax credit	73,788	61,720	53,502	44,797	33,687
[1]Deferred fed. & state inc. tax	164,351	137,271	114,612	85,149	64,119
Total liabilities and owners' equity	1,606,753	1,451,042	1,367,366	1,305,559	1,239,560

EXHIBIT 4

General Telephone Company of Florida

Probabilities Elicited From Experts

x_i (demand level$_{1983-85}$)		$P(x_i\|H_1)$	$P(x_i\|M_1)$	$P(X_i\|L_1)$
High		0.70	0.40	0.20
Medium		0.20	0.45	0.40
Low		0.10	0.15	0.40

x_i	x_i^*	$P(x_i^*\|x_i \cap H_1)$	$P(x_i^*\|x_i \cap M_1)$	$P(x_i^*\|x_i \cap L_1)$
High	High	0.75	0.60	0.30
	Medium	0.20	0.35	0.40
	Low	0.05	0.05	0.30
Medium	High	0.40	0.35	0.20
	Medium	0.50	0.55	0.40
	Low	0.10	0.10	0.40
Low	High	0.20	0.15	0.10
	Medium	0.40	0.35	0.30
	Low	0.40	0.50	0.60

Legend
H_1 = high demand in 1981–82
M_1 = medium demand in 1981–82
L_1 = low demand in 1981–82
x_i = demand level "i" in 1983–85
x_i^* = demand level "i" in 1986–89

EXHIBIT 5

General Telephone Company of Florida

Option	1981–82 demand	Annual After-Tax Cost Savings[a]			Abandonment Values[b]	
		1981–82[c]	1983–85[d]	1986–89[e]	12/31/82	12/31/85
Full Conversion	High	$12MM	$18MM	$30MM	$22MM	$15MM
	Medium	6MM	12MM	18MM	22MM	15MM
	Low	(3MM)	N.A.[f]	N.A.	22MM	15MM
Partial Conversion	High	$ 6MM	$ 9MM	$12MM	$13MM	$ 8MM
	Medium	5MM	8MM	11MM	13MM	8MM
	Low	(1MM)	1MM	2MM	13MM	8MM
No Conversion	High	$ 1MM	N.A.	N.A.	0	N.A.
	Medium	1MM	3MM	5MM	0	0
	Low	1MM	3MM	5MM	0	0

[a] Assumes that the original option is followed through the decade.
[b] Abandonment values are assumed as $0 on 12/31/89. See note 4 for the calculation of an abandonment value.
[c] Based on high, medium, or low industry demand levels for 1981–82.
[d] Based on the expected cost-savings figure for 1983–85 given a high, medium, or low industry demand level in 1981–82 (see Exhibit 6).
[e] Based on the expected cost-savings figure for 1986–89 given a high, medium, or low industry demand level in 1981–82 followed by a high, medium, or low industry demand level in 1983–85 (see Exhibit 6).
[f] Not applicable.

EXHIBIT 6

General Telephone Company of Florida
Sample Calculation of an Expected Cost-Savings Figure[a]

(1) 1981–82 Demand (x_1)	(2) 1983–85 Demand (x_2)	(3) Annual Cost Savings$_{1983-85}$	(4) $P(x_2 \mid x_1)$[b]	(5) = (3) * (4) Weighted Annual Cost Savings$_{1983-85}$
High	High	$25.0MM	0.70	$17.5MM
	Medium	8.0MM	0.20	1.6MM
	Low	(10.0MM)	0.10	(1.0MM)

Expected Annual Cost Savings$_{1983-85}$ = $18.0MM[c]

(6) $x_1 \cap x_2$	(7) 1986–89 Demand (x_3)	(8) Annual Cost Savings$_{1986-89}$	(9) $P(x_3 \mid x_1 \cap x_2)$[b]	(10) = (8) * (9) Weighted Annual Cost Savings$_{1986-89}$
High ∩ High	High	$45.0MM	0.75	$33.8MM
	Medium	12.0MM	0.20	2.4MM
	Low	(15.0MM)	0.05	(.8MM)
High ∩ Medium	High	$45.0MM	0.40	$18.0MM
	Medium	12.0MM	0.50	6.0MM
	Low	(15.0MM)	0.10	(1.5MM)
High ∩ Low	High	$45.0MM	0.20	$9.0MM
	Medium	12.0MM	0.40	4.8MM
	Low	(15.0MM)	0.40	(6.0MM)

$x_1 \ x_2$	Weighted Annual Cost Savings$_{1986-89}$	$P(x_2 \mid x_1)$[b]	Expected Annual Cost Savings$_{1986-89}$
High ∩ High	$35.4MM	0.70	$24.8MM
High ∩ Medium	22.5MM	0.20	4.5MM
High ∩ Low	7.8MM	0.10	.8MM

Expected Annual Cost Savings$_{1986-89}$ = $30.0MM[c]

[a] Assuming full conversion project is undertaken in January 1980 and is maintained through the 1980s (refer to Exhibits 4 and 5).
[b] Per Exhibit 4.
[c] Sums are rounded off.

CASE 19

T. A. Atwood Company

Bill Speas looked up from the schedule he had just constructed showing deliveries of liquid asphalt to construction projects. "Well I guess I have all the data put together now. Let's see if the return really is as good as Jon thinks it is."

Bill Speas was an MBA student at the Babcock School, a graduate school of management at Wake Forest University. As part of his studies, he was required to undertake a project with some outside organization. The project he selected was a study of an investment in hauling equipment by a Winston-Salem construction company, T. A. Atwood Company.

BACKGROUND ON THE COMPANY

T. A. Atwood was founded in 1947 by two brothers. Over a period of years the company became one of the leading contractors in North Carolina, specializing in highway construction, paving, and landscaping. One of their larger projects was

the construction of a section of Interstate 40.

In the early seventies the recession in the construction industry and some ventures into real estate projects had caused substantial cash-flow problems for the company. Because of this shortage of capital, in 1973 controlling interest in the company was sold to a large construction firm located in Charlotte, North Carolina. Operating responsibility was assumed by Jon Atwood, son of one of the founders. The acquiring company had its own difficulties in 1974, however, and was not able to provide the financial support that was envisioned.

In 1975 Jon Atwood arranged financing with a large North Carolina bank (First Citizens Bank & Trust Company) to reacquire 100-percent ownership of the company. At that point in its history, the company had grown to a medium-sized construction firm, with billings in the $9- to $10-million range and employees numbering over 250. The growth had been financed principally through debt. Exhibits

This case was prepared by and used with the permission of Jack D. Ferner, Lecturer in Management, Babcock Graduate School of Management, Wake Forest University.

1 and 2 contain summary balance sheets and income statements for years 1975 and 1976. When Bill undertook the project early in 1977, cash was tight, and the large bank loan imposed a number of restrictive covenants on further borrowing and acquisition of equipment and other fixed assets.

THE INVESTMENT BEING CONSIDERED

The investment analyzed by Bill Speas involved the transportation of liquid asphalt used in paving projects. The liquid asphalt was supplied by American Oil Company's facility in Wilmington, North Carolina. Arrangements were made with a contract carrier, E. C. Whitfield, to pick up the liquid asphalt from American Oil in Wilmington and deliver it to Atwood's storage facilities near Winston-Salem. The procedure was to mix hot asphalt with crushed stone to produce the blacktop material used on road surfaces. This was done in the general locality of the paving project to minimize transportation costs. In this instance the liquid asphalt was hauled approximately 210 miles. E. C. Whitfield provided this hauling service for a number of contractors and had a fleet of specialty tractors and trailers. The trailers were heated to keep the asphalt from solidifying and had a capacity of 6000 gallons. A rig (tractor and trailer) could make two hauls in a day. The service was excellent and required only a 12-hour notice by Atwood.

Jon Atwood was considering an investment in equipment that would enable the company to do the hauling inhouse and eliminate the outside carrier. T. A. Atwood had paid E. C. Whitfield almost $88,000 the previous year. Whether this would justify the sizable investment involved was the question. To decide this he asked Bill Speas to make a determination of (1) the number of rigs that would be required to service the needs in the Winston-Salem–Forsyth County area and (2) whether such an investment could be economically justified. The company had two other similar operations in Pitt and Guilford Counties, but these operations were somewhat smaller. Jon Atwood preferred to consider only the Winston-Salem–Forsyth County operation initially.

EQUIPMENT SCHEDULING

The first problem faced by Bill Speas in undertaking the project was to develop a schedule of the hauls of liquid asphalt to meet the company's needs in Forsyth County in 1977 and beyond. In talking with the management of the company, Bill learned the difficulties of predicting new business in the construction industry. He was told that the intricacies of the bidding process (particularly municipal government bids) and the uncertain economic conditions, made forecasting for a small firm tenuous. It was finally decided to use 1976 as a model. This was a good year for the company. Overall, work had been steady and profits were reasonably high. The projects being bid in 1977 would produce the same approximate results if a sufficient number could be closed on a timely basis. Significant growth was not possible with the present financial constraints. Thus, management decided to base the justification for the investment on 1976 volume of operations.

The company kept records of all materials requisitioned on projects. Thus,

Bill was able to determine the truckloads (6000 gallons) of liquid asphalt used each day during 1976. He also found that the company had facilities (heated storage) for six truckloads in Forsyth County. Bill thought about the possibility of adding to this storage, but found that, aside from the cost, there was not adequate space.

From this information Bill constructed the delivery schedule mentioned earlier. Inventories would be kept at a maximum except during slack periods when they would be reduced to economize on storage costs. He explained this schedule to company personnel as follows: "If the company purchases one rig with the capacity to make two hauls per day, on a seven-day basis, that equipment would have met most of the liquid asphalt needs during 1976. Stockouts would have occurred four times during the year for a total of five truckloads. During peak periods (April–November) there would be a good deal of weekend and overtime work."

For example, let's look at an eight-day period in September:

and equipment utilization, and sometimes penalties. It was agreed, however, that E. C. Whitfield could be counted on to haul the few makeup loads necessary to prevent stockouts, even though there was a question of whether they would provide the same reliability on this reduced basis. It was decided to proceed with the analysis based on the use of one company-owned rig.

INVESTIGATION OF EQUIPMENT NEEDS

Bill proceeded to talk with equipment companies about the type of equipment best suited for this job and the associated operating costs. Cummins Corporation supplied detailed information about the performance of their engine. Data on the actual run, which included road and traffic conditions, were obtained and fed into a computer program. Time and fuel consumption information was produced. Specifications on the tractor, trailer, tires, and maintenance procedures were developed.

	Mon Sep 20	Tues 21	Wed 22	Thurs 23	Fri 24	Sat 25	Sun 26	Mon 27
Beginning inventory (max. 6)	6	4	4	2	0	0	2	4
Usage	4	2	4	4	4	0	0	0
Deliveries (max. 2)	2	2	2	2	2	2	2	2
Ending inventory	4	4	2	0	(−2)	2	4	6

As can be seen, demand was heavy during the first five days, a stockout would have occurred on Friday, and weekend work would have been required to rebuild the inventory.

Company personnel pointed out that stockouts were very serious and could cause expensive delays, lost manpower

The net price of the equipment was determined to be:

Tractor		$31,540
Trailer		21,136
	Total	$52,676

The tractor was estimated to have a seven-year life with a 10-percent salvage value and the trailer a ten-year life with 10 percent salvage. In addition, $6725 in maintenance equipment would have to be purchased. This would have a life of seven years with no salvage value.

OPERATING COSTS

Bill collected information on operating costs from company personnel as well as the equipment manufacturers. Since the company did not have extensive experience in the use of long-haul equipment, additional data were obtained from the local operations of Pilot Freight and Roadway Express. Details on Bill's cost estimates are shown below:

1. *Hauling Costs (E. C. Whitfield)*
   During 1976 T. A. Atwood paid E. C. Whitfield $87,922 to haul liquid asphalt to their Forsyth County plant. This amounted to about $240 per truckload. This represented the major cost savings available to the company if it were to use its own equipment, less any loads that would have to be contracted to avoid stockouts.

2. *Drivers' Wages*
   Drivers had to be paid for the entire year. Overtime would be paid for hours worked beyond the normal eight hours. Runs on weekends had to be paid at overtime rates (time and one-half). Trip time was based upon Cummins Corporation's study of their engine over the route. Thus, a normal day would cost $57.12 per man, but a trip day $83.90 because the work time amounted to 10.5 hours. Two men would be required year-round.

By combining the trip schedule derived from 1976 data with the Cummins estimates of trip time and the company's wage rates, Bill was able to determine the monthly labor costs.

Example: Month of April 1976

Work days (2 men)	44		
Trips scheduled	31		
Normal pay ($57.12)	13 days	$ 743	
Trip pay ($83.90)	31 days	2,601	

Total wage cost for April	$3,344

Yearly projection based on 1976 requirements

Jan	$ 2,620
Feb	2,419
Mar	3,003
Apr	3,344
May	3,859
Jun	3,236
Jul	4,615
Aug	3,943
Sep	4,279
Oct	4,027
Nov	3,638
Dec	2,708
	$41,691

3. *Maintenance*
   Bill found that maintenance would be a major cost of operating hauling equipment. A cost of $3525 was estimated from information obtained from Roadway Express' and Pilot Freight's historical averages for comparable equipment. This figure included both scheduled and unscheduled maintenance and replacement tires.

   Because of the need to maximize reliability of the T. A. Atwood hauling operation, however, it was decided that a preventive maintenance program should be adopted. Spills were a major concern and a breakdown of the heating equipment would cause the liquid asphalt to solidify in the tanktruck. The equipment supervisor estimated costs based on scheduled maintenance involving oil changes, lubrication, filters, annual tuneups, and once-a-year tire changes:

	Yr 1	Yr 2 and Beyond
Oil changes, lubrication, filters	$ 847	$1017
Tuneups	300	300
Tires	1280	1280
Total	$2427/yr	$2597/yr

Bill summarized the maintenance costs as follows:

	Total Maintenance	— Preventive Maintenance	= Unscheduled Maintenance
1977	$3525	$2427	$1098
Subsequent years	$3695	$2597	$1098

Bill realized that T. A. Atwood was not experienced at maintaining this type equipment. There could also be some unusual costs arising from the special problems of asphalt spills and breakdowns in the heating equipment. He wasn't sure how to reflect these factors in his analysis.

4. *Insurance*

The annual insurance premium of $2000 was estimated by C. C. Insurance Agency. Bill included in the cost estimate $1000 for the deductible portion every second year for expected accidents. According to the equipment supervisor, Mike Beauchamp, this insurance would cover the tractor-trailer, driver, cargo, spills, and other such liabilities and damages.

5. *Fuel*

Cost per annum was based upon the Cummins test run, which indicated a consumption of 6.14 miles per gallon. A safety factor of 5 percent was incorporated by Bill. A cost of $.45 per gallon was used and included road tax. The fuel cost, therefore, was $32.40 per trip times 373 trips per year for a total annual cost of $12,085.

METHOD OF FINANCING

Jon Atwood told Bill he would prefer to purchase the rig through an equipment loan. He pointed out that the construction industry financed much of its equipment needs this way. Because the equipment represented more or less adequate security for such a loan, it would have little or no effect on the company's existing loans and would not affect its ability to finance other projects.

Bill found a 100-percent loan on the tractor, trailer, and maintenance equipment could be obtained from Ford Motor Credit on the following terms:

a. Four-year installment loan with 48 equal monthly payments

b. Interest at 6 percent per year add-on (6%/yr. × initial loan)

c. Collateral interest in the equipment

OTHER CONSIDERATIONS

Bill found that the company's policy was to depreciate equipment of this type on a straight-line basis for both tax and reporting purposes. IRS would allow a seven-year life on the tractor and ten years on the trailer. On this basis the full 10 percent investment tax credit could be taken. The market value of the equipment at any point in time was estimated to be approximately the book value net of depreciation. The company's marginal tax rate was approximately 50 percent.

Bill also discussed the firm's cost of capital with Jon Atwood. Atwood told Bill to use 10 percent as an average cost of capital, a number he and the treasurer had worked out. When Bill studied the financial statements (see Exhibits 1 and 2), however, he questioned that figure. The company had a great deal of debt which was largely secured by the fixed assets. The availability of additional funds seemed to be dependent on this type of security, plus personal signatures. Jon Atwood stated that he felt he should earn a high return on his investment because of the risks involved.

Jon Atwood brought up the matter of inflation. Since costs had risen so rapidly in the construction industry, he felt inflationary factors should be brought into the analysis. After referring to industry sources Bill "guess-timated" inflation would occur at the following rates for various costs:

General price-level inflation in the construction industry	6%
Specific cost elements in the construction industry	
Wages, fuel, insurance, and hauling costs	5%
Maintenance	7%
Licenses	2%
General price-level inflation in the trucking and hauling industry	5%

In reflecting on the inflation rates, Atwood commented that he felt that energy shortages could cause a much more rapid rise in fuel costs then the 5 percent projection. He also pointed out that his labor was nonunion and drawn largely from rural areas. As the local economy developed, he felt his labor rates could escalate more rapidly than the national average.

He concluded that "inflation is awfully hard to figure. I wonder what the analysis would look like if the inflation were twice what's being predicted."

In the course of considering the possibility of doing the hauling inhouse, Jon Atwood discussed the matter with Ed Whitfield, the president of E. C. Whitfield. Whitfield expressed concern over the prospect of losing all or most of the business since it represented substantial volume and profits. A few days later he called Atwood and asked whether a three-year fixed price contract would dissuade Atwood from doing the hauling inhouse. This would mean that the current price would hold firm for three years with the one stipulation that if fuel costs increased more than 15 percent, an adjustment would be made.

THE FINAL RECOMMENDATION

Bill pulled together the figures in a present value analysis (see Exhibit 3). He noted with enthusiasm that the net present value was a positive $20,000.

"Before I show this to Jon I had better be able to defend the assumptions. Did I handle the inflation issue correctly? What was its impact? What about the uncertanties in the assumptions? What impact will they have?"

Also, in examining data from prior years and observing the sharp economic cycles in the construction industry, Bill was concerned whether the use of 1976 figures was presenting an optimistic picture. There were times when volume slumped badly and when the requirements for liquid asphalt fluctuated greatly.

Finally, Bill remembered a recent conversation with his faculty advisor who asked some tough questions: Why wasn't this investment analyzed like any other investment the firm would make? Why did this investment and the financing stand on its own? Would it affect the cost of capital or not? What was the marginal cost of capital? What would it do to the company's ability to raise capital for other purposes?

EXHIBIT 1

T. A. Atwood Company

Balance Sheet
December 31, 1976 and 1975
(in thousands of dollars)

	1976	1975
Assets		
Current assets		
Cash	$ 271	$ 35
Accounts receivable	1,094	1,361
Costs and estimated earnings on uncompleted contracts in excess of billings	84	95
Inventories	177	196
Land held for resale	154	153
Prepaid expenses	67	20
Total current assets	$1,847	$1,860
Property and equipment		
Land	86	120
Buildings	52	34
Construction equipment	3,358	3,114
Other	75	80
Total	3,571	3,348
Less: accumulated depreciation	(2,341)	(2,079)
Net property and equipment	1,230	1,269
Other assets	283	248
Total	$3,360	$3,377
Liabilities and Shareholders' Equity		
Current liabilities		
Current maturities of long-term debt	$ 595	$ 603
Accounts payable	719	966
Customer advances	107	152
Estimated warranty losses	38	15
Accrued liabilities	113	62
Total current liabilities	1,572	1,798
Deferred items	131	102
Long-term debt	1,175	1,258
Shareholders' equity		
Common stock	258	258
Retained earnings	226	(37)
Less treasury stock	(2)	(2)
Shareholders' equity	$ 482	$ 219
Total	$3,360	$3,377

EXHIBIT 2

T. A. Atwood Company

Income Statement
For Years Ending Dec. 31, 1976 and 1975
(in thousands of dollars)

	1976	1975
Revenues	$9,943	$9,068
Cost of revenues	8,813	8,488
Gross profit	1,130	580
Selling, general and administrative expense	707	575
Interest expense	208	196
Other income	(116)	(107)
Income (loss) before taxes and extraordinary credit	331	(84)
Income taxes (credit)	116	(16)
Income (loss) before extraordinary credit	215	(68)
Extraordinary credit	47	74
Net income	$ 262	$ 6

Notes to Financial Statements

1. The company recognizes revenues on long-term contracts on the percentage completion method.
2. Long-term debt is comprised of demand notes and installment notes. The average interest rate is approximately 10.5 percent. The notes are secured by construction equipment and personal signatures of the owners.
3. The construction equipment has been appraised and the estimated "sales value" is $2.1 million and the "going concern" value $3.5 million.
4. Minimum lease commitments are $182,218 for 1977.

EXHIBIT 3

T. A. Atwood Company

Cash-Flow Analysis—Financing the Purchase via the Equipment Loan
(showing proceeds of the loan, the interest and principal repayments)

	Annual Inflation Rate	0	1	2	3	4	5	6	7	Total
A. Present hauling cost—E. C. Whitfield	5%		87922	87922	87922	92318	96934	101780	106869	661667
B. Initial investment—January 1977										
Tractor/trailer		(52676)								(52676)
Special maintenance equipment		(6725)								(6725)
Proceeds from loan		59401								59401
Principal repayment			(12232)	(13977)	(15723)	(17469)				(59401)
Investment tax credit			5940							5940
Salvage value									10975	10975
C. Less operating expenses										
Outside loads (5 per year)	5%		1200	1260	1323	1389	1459	1532	1608	9771
Drivers' wages	5%		41691	43776	45964	48263	50676	53209	55870	339449
Preventive maintenance	7%		2427	2779	2973	3181	3404	3642	3897	22473
Unscheduled maintenance	7%		1098	1175	1257	1345	1439	1540	1648	9332
Insurance	5%		2000	3000	2100	3150	2205	3308	2315	18078
License fees	2%		808	824	841	857	875	892	910	6007
Fuel	5%		12085	12689	13324	13990	14689	15424	16195	98396
Interest payments			6183	4437	2691	945				14256
Total operating expense			67492	69940	70473	73120	74747	79547	82443	517762
D. Net cash flows before taxes (A+B−C)			14138	4005	1726	1729	22187	22233	35401	101419
E. Taxes: Subtract investment tax credit			(5940)							(5940)
Add back principal repayment			12232	13977	15723	17469				59401
Subtract depreciation expense			(6918)	(6918)	(6918)	(6918)	(6918)	(6918)	(6918)	(48426)
Taxable income			13512	11064	10531	12280	15269	15315	28483	106454
Income tax			6756	5532	5265	6140	7635	7657	14242	53227
F. Net cash flows after taxes (D−E)			7382	(1527)	(3539)	(4411)	14552	14576	21159	48192
G. Inflation adjustment—6% const. industry			.94340	.89000	.83962	.79209	.74726	.70496	.66506	
Inflation adjusted cash flows			6964	(1359)	(2971)	(3494)	10874	10275	14072	34361
H. Cost of capital discount (10%)			.90909	.82645	.75131	.68301	.62092	.56447	.51316	
Discounted cash flows			6331	(1123)	(2232)	(2386)	6752	5800	7221	20363
Net present value		$20363								

CASE 20

Elkem-Spigerverket A/S

In January 1977 Mr. Kjell Karlsen, the administrative director of Elkem-Spigerverket A/S (ES), a diversified industrial firm headquartered in Oslo, Norway, was preparing for a meeting of the firm's investment committee to consider two very large capital budgeting projects: the Ceiling Tile Plant and the Special Iron Ore Refining Plant. As both projects were very large and as they were quite different in character, acceptance of either one would involve not only large capital requirements but, in effect, a change of emphasis in the corporation's strategy. The Special Iron Ore Plant was proposed by the Iron Refining Division and was very much along the lines of the firm's traditional business of metal refining. The Ceiling Tile Plant, on the other hand, was proposed by the firm's new Finished Product Division, which, at the time of the case, was a smaller part of ES's overall operations.

ES had been formed in 1972 by the merger of two very large Norwegian companies. Total revenues in 1976 were about 2.45 billion kroner or roughly $460 million at the prevailing exchange rate of 5.3 kr./$. The two firms, which merged in 1972, had both acquired a number of smaller firms before that date, and the new company had also acquired a few smaller firms since. As a result, ES's operations were wide ranging, both by location and in product lines. About 60 percent of ES's total sales came from outside Norway. About 70 percent of total sales were made by the three metal divisions: Iron Refining, Steel, and Aluminum (the Iron Refining Division produced alloys used in the production of various specialty steels). Only 14.5 percent of total revenue came from the Finished Product Division, which produced a variety of branded products such as chain saws, hardware, insulation, pack-

*This case was prepared by and used with the permission of William O. Cain, Jr., DBA, of Execucom while he was Visiting Professor at the North European Management Institute.

aging material, and fiberglass products. (Financial statements for 1974–76 are found in Exhibits 1 and 2.)

As the income statements show, ES's profit picture had deteriorated in recent years. The Iron Refining Division had 12-percent lower sales in 1976 than in 1975 because of less tonnage and lower prices. It had lost about 20 million kroner before taxes in 1976. The Finished Products Division had 15-percent greater sales in 1976 than 1975. It showed a profit of 6 million kroner before taxes in 1976. These results were contrary to previous trends in that, historically, the Iron Refining Division had been the most profitable one in the country. The Finished Products Division had operated at a loss in most previous years.

The company had a decentralized management philosophy, and line managers were given very high degrees of autonomy with respect to virtually all phases of plant and division operations. In general, they were not required to use headquarters-provided staff services but could instead purchase them elsewhere or do without them altogether. Thus, it was necessary for headquarters staff people to "sell" their services to the division and plant managers. The major exception to this decentralized philosophy was capital expenditures. As described below, large capital requests were subject to thorough review and approval at the headquarters level.

BUSINESS CONDITIONS

In 1973–74 the so-called energy crisis disrupted the world economy and brought on a recession that lasted into 1975. The recovery from the recession was somewhat weak, and the general level of demand from most products that ES made increased only slightly in the past year. The Norwegian economy, in particular, however, had shown quite remarkable growth in certain sectors. The overall rate of real growth in gross national product had been 7 percent in 1976, despite an inflation rate of roughly 10 percent. It was true, however, that the shipbuilding yards, which formed a major component of Norwegian industry and used a lot of steel, were suffering very severely as a result of the over capacity in the tanker market which had developed in the wake of the energy crisis.

One bright spot in the long-term prospects of the Norwegian economy was the oil that had been discovered recently in the North Sea. Very substantial oil revenues were expected to begin in the 1980s. According to a survey done by the British magazine, *The Economist*, Norway would have the highest per capita income in the world at that time.

The Norwegian Government was dominated by the Labour Party, and it regulated business operations in Norway quite strictly. There were very strict environmental laws that had recently been passed requiring large expenditures by ES and other manufacturing industries. It was believed that these amounts would decrease gradually in the next ten years. The trend towards so-called democratization meant that one-third of the representatives in the corporate board of representatives were elected by the employees. Financing in the domestic debt market was very strictly regulated, requiring applications explaining in great detail the use to which the money was going to be put. Further, electric power was allotted by the government to various industries. Therefore, it was necessary for ES to convince the authorities of the value of granting ES electric power allotments. Perhaps the governmental policy most significant to business was the commitment to full employment. Even though unemployment rates were high in Europe and the United States, Norway had only 1 to 2 percent unemployment. Given the many regulations with which individual businesses were faced, they ran a severe risk if they attracted unfavorable attention by laying off workers except when absolutely necessary.

CAPITAL BUDGETING PROCEDURE

There were two different approaches taken to capital project approval at ES, depending on the size of the project involved. In keeping with the firm's decentralization philosophy, relatively small projects requiring up to 500,000 kroner (roughly $100,000) could be approved by the division manager personally. Further, he/she was free to delegate authority to approve projects up to this limit to the plant managers within the division. Each year each division was assigned its annual "investment allotment" which the division manager could use for all projects falling under his/her 500,000-kr. appropriation authority. Further, the division manager could also divide up his/her own investment allotment to the various plants in the division. There were three categories of projects: required-by-law, necessary, and desirable. Required-by-law meant that the project had to be undertaken in order to bring the plant involved into compliance with government regulations. Necessary meant that the project was necessary in order for the firm to continue to compete at the same

level as before within its present line of business. Desirable projects were those that improved working conditions or else involved a cost reduction, additional capacity, or expansion into new business. When possible, desirable projects were justified on the basis of a financial criterion.

The divisional investment allotments were set in the following manner: In the fall each division submitted its proposed list for the following year of all projects under 500,000 kroner categorized as required-by-law, necessary, or desirable. The basis for the assignment of the investment allotments was the total of the required-by-law and necessary projects for each division. In 1975 proposed projects in these two categories alone totaled 125 percent of the amount of money available for capital budgeting projects from all three categories. Therefore, each division's investment allotment was 80 percent of the total of required-by-law and necessary projects it had submitted in the budgeting process. In 1976 the combined total of required-by-law and necessary proposed projects was again 125 percent of the money available.

Of course, various individuals, both in the different divisions and on the corporate staff, had different ideas about what "necessary" really meant. Therefore, in 1976 the corporate risk manager (who helped make decisions with respect to insurance coverage for the company) reviewed the list of required-by-law and necessary projects submitted by each division and passed on the merits of them case by case. Therefore, each division was assigned a total investment allotment adjusted to reflect the categorization made by the risk manager. The division personnel were still free to substitute other projects which the risk manager had considered not really necessary; but, of course, in order to do so they had to eliminate projects the risk manager had classified as necessary.

As the amounts for environmental expenditures required by law declined and as the company's results improved with the world economy generally, it was expected that it would be possible to accept desirable projects in 1977. The figures in Exhibit 3 show the estimates made by the Long-Term Planning Department of the likely levels of future capital expenditures.

For small projects the usual criterion used was the internal rate of return, and the basic hurdle rate of the corporation was 20 percent. Small projects were analyzed on a before-tax basis, and, in general, uncertainty was not explicitly considered in performing analyses. However, division personnel could either do such an analysis themselves or have it done by headquarters staff personnel by paying for this analysis from their own budgets.

Large projects (such as those described in the following sections) could not be approved by individual division chiefs but instead had to be referred to the administrative director (Mr. Karlsen) or to the board of directors if they exceeded one million kroner. Such projects as these were considered by the firm's investment committee. They were analyzed more thoroughly than the small projects. Uncertainty was treated by the use of available computer models and simulation techniques which required an assessment of probability distributions for relevant variables. Inflation was handled either by applying an estimated general price index to all items or by estimating the rate of inflation for each of the different components of the cash-flow streams associated with investment projects. The possibility of specific kinds of financing being available for certain projects was dealt with by calculating a return on equity figure, assuming that 35 percent of the project was financed by equity and the remainder with debt using the most favorable rates available for debt for that specific project. Further, the net present value, using a 20 percent discount rate, and the excess present value index were calculated for all such large projects. (A more detailed explanation of the capital budgeting procedure is given in Appendix A.)

THE CEILING TILE PLANT

One of ES's wholly-owned subsidiaries, Takstein A/S, produced a special kind of acoustical ceiling tile from wood and other raw materials found in abundance in Norway. It was superior to other ceiling materials. The overall demand for ceiling tile had increased greatly over the past several years and was anticipated to show steady growth over the coming decade. Ceiling tile, however, was a bulky product, and thus, it was necessary for plants to be in the vicinity of the market being served. At present Takstein had four plants located in Norway. The oldest one was in the Oslo area, while the other three were in the west and north. The Finished Product Division, of which Takstein was a part, proposed to establish a new plant about 50 kilometers from Oslo. This new plant would completely replace the old Oslo plant. At the time of the case, all four existing plants were operating at full capacity.

Takstein competed with two other Norwegian producers of about the same size as Takstein itself. One of these competitors had recently begun using a new technology for producing acoustical ceiling tile, which gave the competitor a very significant cost advantage over Takstein. The new technology was more capital intensive and also required more space. It could not be installed in the present plant near Oslo because not enough room was available. The new plant would have about twice the capacity of the one it was replacing, and its installation would increase Takstein's overall production capacity by about 30 percent. The plant was expected to cost about 50 million kroner (see Exhibit 4 for detailed calculations). Demand was expected to continue to increase so that the new plant would operate at full capacity by 1981. As shown in Exhibit 4, the expected rate of return for the project was 14 percent.

If the plant was not constructed, Takstein would most likely end up as a high-cost producer in the Oslo area and eventually be forced to close its present plant and lay off the 70 workers employed there. The plants outside the Oslo area were expected to continue to be viable because none was located in an area where the market was large enough to justify the cost of constructing a plant using the new technology.

THE SPECIAL IRON ORE REFINING PLANT

This was an extremely large project involving construction of a new plant, conversion of an old furnace, and expansion of mining operations which was estimated to cost 660 million kroner (about $125 million), an amount about three times the total of the company's capital expenditures in 1976. Due to the nature of the refining process, it could not easily be scaled down. The rate of return on the entire project was 13 percent. (See calculations in Exhibit 5.)

ES owned an iron mine whose ore contained a special metal that was a valuable alloying element for specialty steels. This ore could be separated by refining into the special metal itself, for which there was a good market, and a very pure pig iron alloy that had a higher market value than ordinary pig iron because it could be used in making so-called ductile cast iron.

The division chief, Mr. Sydvar, estimated that worldwide demand for this special pig iron would increase by approximately 10 percent per year for the next several years. All the principal resources required by the plants—iron ore, coal, coke, and electric power—were found in Norway. Were the plant constructed, it would increase ES's refining capacity of the special ore from 90,000 tons per year to 250,000 tons per year.

The ore came from a mine 200 kilometers further north than the present plant. It was expected to operate at a loss of 2.5 million kroner in 1977. The present refining plant, which purchased all of the ore from the mine, was expected to operate at a profit of 4 million kroner in 1977. As wage levels increased, however, Mr. Sydvar forecasted that the mine and plant together would operate at a combined loss in three to four years' time. Since this loss would only widen over time, the mine would eventually be closed.

If the proposed new refining plant were built, however, economies of scale would make the existing mine profitable.

It had proven reserves sufficient to last for ten more years. Another mine a few kilometers away had recently been discovered with proven reserves of the same kind of ore, which would also last for ten years. Other amounts were also thought to lie in the area sufficient for an additional 30 years.

The present refining plant could be converted into a furnace for an ordinary alloy through an investment of 60 million kroner. (This amount was included in the 660 million kroner required to undertake the entire project.) ES had use for the additional capacity, and a bargain furnace built "from scratch" would cost about 160 million kroner. Therefore, the present plant would definitely be converted if the special iron ore mine were closed.

One of the major questions posed by the consideration of the special iron ore project was the electric power it would require. One of Norway's most valuable resources was the large amount of hydroelectric power generated from its waterfalls and dammed reservoirs. There had been, however, no increase in the corporation's allotment of guaranteed power (which cost at the time 40,000 kroner per million kWh) for the past five years. Therefore, ES had been forced to purchase additional power ("random" power) at generally higher costs (as much as 120,000 kroner more per million kWh in the winter) in greater and greater amounts each year. Since this random power might not be available at all at certain unpredictable times, the government would not allow construction of the plant unless sufficient guaranteed power were available. The company had requested an increase in its allotment of guaranteed power and hoped that the government would soon approve this. If

an additional allotment could be obtained, it would not necessarily influence the allocation of power to other divisions. The primary basis for the government's power allocation decisions was the effect approving the specific request would have on the local and national economy and environment, rather than on the basis of the company making the request. (To put it another way, individual *plants* were allotted power, rather than whole companies getting it.) It was not really feasible for ES to transfer an allotment of power granted for use at one location to some other plant.

The present plant used about 200 million kWh per year. It would require about 260 million kWh per year when converted to a furnace for the ordinary alloy.

The proposed plan for the new special iron ore refining plant called for the construction of a completely new facility on a "greenfield" site nearby. The process that would be used in the new plant would involve preheating the ore before it went into the electric furnace. This would reduce the electric requirement per ton by half. Therefore, it would require only 80 million more kWh per year to process the 250,000 tons of ore that could be handled by the new plant. ES was seeking an allotment for 340 million additional kWh to enable it to operate both the proposed new special iron ore refining plant and the converted furnace to produce the ordinary alloy.

The Iron Refining Division had prepared a report for the Department of Industry entitled "Power-Consuming Industries in Norway." This reviewed the potential demands for power by the steel and aluminum industries, as well as by the fertilizer and petrochemical industries. To support the case for the Special Iron Refining Plant allotment, the report pointed out that it would be located in a less-industrialized part of Norway, that much of its production would be exported, that it would use Norwegian raw materials (making it independent of developments in other countries), and that, in addition to the jobs provided by the plant itself, several ancillary service businesses would benefit if the plant were established.

Mr. Sydvar hoped that the principal factor, that is, the number of people the new plant and expanded mine would employ, would help influence the authorities to approve the request. At the time of the case the mine and plant employed a total of 380 people. If the mine were forced to close and the plant converted to an ordinary furnace, only 70 people would be employed. On the other hand, if the new plant were built and the mine operations expanded, 540 people would be employed, in addition to the 70 working on the furnace. Dividing 540 jobs into the 340 million kWh allotment sought, Mr. Sydvar argued that each additional job required only 600,000 kWh per year. Roughly three to four times this amount of power would be required to provide the same number of jobs in the more power-intensive aluminum industry, for example.

The local authorities in the areas where the plant and mine were located supported the proposed project wholeheartedly. Several of them had gone to the Storting (Norway's Parliament) in Oslo to testify in favor of it in hearings of the Committee on Industry.

The project would be built in one of the outlying districts of Norway and thus would be eligible for the special "DU-finansiering" described below. Mr. Sydvar felt that with this financial incentive, the project would definitely be worth undertaking.

DEBT FINANCING OPPORTUNITIES

Many of the debt financing opportunities ES had were tied to the specific project being financed. The most favorable form of financing was "DU-finansiering," money supplied by the National District Development Agency which was responsible for increasing the amount of industry in certain less-industrialized parts of Norway. Under this program up to 35 percent of the cost of a project could be financed from this source, and up to half of that amount could be in the form of a pure grant. Such financing would not be available for the proposed ceiling tile plant but might be available for the special iron ore plant. Neither the total amount of financing nor the fraction that would be a pure grant was known in January 1977. However, Mr. D. T. Halvorssen, the manager of the finance department, estimated that 10 percent of the cost of the plant could be obtained as a grant and an additional 15 percent as a loan. Such loans would carry an interest rate of 6½ pecent, they would have a 10- to 15-year term, and they would be paid in equal semiannual installments beginning two years from the date of the loan. An additional advantage of this kind of financing was that if the plant were later expanded, the National District Development Agency would agree to take a subordinated position to the lenders supplying the funds for expansion.

Another very substantial source of

funds, which would be available for the special iron ore refining plant, were the so-called participatory bonds. All commercial banks and insurance companies in Norway were required by the government to participate in a program of lending money to corporations and other large users of capital at an attractive rate for certain kinds of projects. The loans carried a fixed interest rate of 7½ percent and a term of either 17 or 18 years. The typical minimum amount for such a loan was about 15 million kroner. They were to be repaid in equal installments beginning two years from the date of the loan. The decision to approve a participatory bond was made by the Norwegian Ministry of Finance. A first mortgage was usually required for projects financed in this way. The most ES ever got in any one year from this source had been 75 million kroner. They once obtained 100 million kroner on a single project, but the amount was spread out over a three-year period. For the special iron ore refining plant, it was expected about 180 million kroner could be obtained this way, but that it would have to be taken down over a three-year period in installments of 60 million each.

Takstein could not borrow directly in the participatory market. Its most attractive source of funds would be Dennorske Industribank (DnI), 51 percent of which was owned by the government. DnI could borrow on the international market by issuing government-guaranteed bonds. It would then relend the money to smaller Norwegian companies who assumed the currency risk involved themselves. Takstein could probably obtain, at the time of the case, either dollar loans at 8½ percent or Swiss franc loans at 5½ percent in this way. Repayment terms would be from 10 to 15 years. A first mortgage would be required. In general, ES preferred to borrow in Swiss francs because the company had large sales in Germany, for which it received German marks, a strong currency that tended to fluctuate with the Swiss franc. The equivalent of about 25 million kroner could be obtained by Takstein in this way.

Two other possible sources of financing were quasigovernmental institutions that raised their own capital by issuing participatory bonds and then lent the money to other firms. They lent money at an 8½-percent rate for five to ten years and usually required a first or second mortgage with a limit on total project mortgages of about 60 percent of the total investment. About 20 million kroner of such financing would be used for the ceiling tile plant.

Exhibit 6 summarizes the debt financing plans that would be used.

EQUITY FINANCING AND DIVIDEND POLICY

In the near future ES was planning to make a rights offering for 48 million kroner of new stock which would be sold at par. Under the terms of the offering each holder of four shares of the presently outstanding common stock would receive the right to buy one share of new stock at par value—or 50 kroner. (There were 3.9 million shares outstanding). In January 1977 the stock was trading on the Oslo Stock Exchange at from 150–155 kroner per share. The rights themselves would be traded on the Oslo Stock Exchange prior to the actual issuance of the new stock.

In addition, the company planned to issue one new share of stock at no charge to every holder of six shares of its outstanding common stock. This was in effect a 16²/₃ percent stock dividend. To see the effect the two actions would have on typical shareholders, consider one who owned 12 shares of ES stock in January 1977. At prevailing market prices these were worth about 1800 kroner. After the rights offering and stock split the shareholder would have to pay 150 kroner for the three shares of stock he/she bought under the rights offering and would receive an additional two shares of stock as part of the stock dividend. Thus, the stockholder would end up with 17 shares of stock.

Convertible debentures had recently been made legal in Norway, but management did not consider using them in 1977.

As can be seen from the balance sheet in Exhibit 1, the firm's equity to long-term capitalization ratio was 33 percent. Management felt that this ratio should be increased during the coming years to 35 or 40 percent, and the stock issue described above was a step in this direction. Some of the convenants in the company's existing loan agreements specified that the firm had to maintain at least 1 kroner of equity for every 2.5 kroner of total debt, so the new equity capital also increased the debt levels allowed by these convenants.

In 1974 and 1975 ES paid out 6 kroner per share in dividends on its common stock. Earnings per share in 1976 were only 2.90 kroner. Accordingly, the board of directors reconsidered the dividend to be declared. The employees introduced a resolution in the corporate general assembly to reduce the dividend substantially. This was voted down. The board felt that the company's cash flow was sufficient to allow the dividend to be maintained and that it ought to be increased because results were expected to improve in 1977. Finally, the decision was reached to declare a dividend for 1976 of 5 kroner per share, or a total of 19.5 million kroner.

TAX CONSIDERATIONS

One significant feature of Norwegian tax laws was that dividends were only taxed once. The national income tax rate for corporations was 27.8 percent. The municipal tax rate was 23 percent for all municipalities. At the national level dividends were tax deductible for the corporation but taxable to the individual receiving them, while at the municipal level the opposite was true. The typical shareholder had a marginal income tax rate (to the national government) of about 45 percent on dividends.

Another feature of Norwegian tax laws was that corporations were allowed a deduction of 50 percent of their net income before taxes for any money earmarked for investment in certain less-industrialized regions, most of which were found in north Norway. This was part of a government program to encourage investment in such areas. Such funds actually had to be invested within five years of the time they were deducted for tax purposes. To the extent that ES was able to find good uses for these reserves in district development projects, it was thereby able to reduce its tax bill significantly.

In a typical situation up to 35 percent of the cost of a new asset would be transferred from the district development fund reserve directly to the equity account. The remaining 65 percent would be subtracted from the district development fund reserve and from the book value of the asset, leaving only 35 percent of the initial cost to be depreciated. Thus, using the district development fund money allowed the firm to write off 135 percent of the cost of the asset and to accelerate the write-off of the cost of the asset to the time that the money is actually earned, which may be as long as five years before the asset is purchased.

At the end of 1976 ES had 183 million kroner of district development fund reserves. The special iron ore plant would qualify as a valid use of such funds, but the ceiling tile plant would not. It was expected that all of these reserves would be used before the five-year expiration period even if the special iron ore plant were not built.

Finally, ES was allowed to deduct 25 percent of the depreciable amount of an investment as first-year depreciation. In analyzing the special iron ore plant, it was assumed that this would be done since the district development fund reserves would be used up regardless of whether this project was taken.

STRATEGIC CONSIDERATIONS

Because of the size of the ceiling tile plant and the special iron ore plant investments, if one were accepted and the other not, it would be a major strategic decision for the company. Mr. Hansen, the director of the Finished Product Division, who had requested the ceiling tile plant, argued that it made sense for the company to build it as a step towards diversifying away from highly cyclical commodity-like businesses such as met-

als refining. He felt there was less risk of price swings in branded products, that they would use less energy per dollar of sales and profit as well as per employee, and that they represented better use of Norwegian skilled labor. The Norwegian labor force was highly educated and, in Mr. Hansen's opinion, was better employed making products requiring a high degree of technical know-how. On the other hand the head of the Iron Refining Division, Mr. Sydvar, argued that it would be better for ES to concentrate on the business they knew best and that had produced greatest profitability in the past. Further, he argued that the scale of the company's metal refining businesses were so much greater in proportion to the differing lines of businesses in the product division that those smaller businesses demanded a disproportionately large share of top management time.

The kind of project ES might be called upon to undertake in the future was the conversion of one of the existing aluminum plants from Soderberg anodes to prebaked anodes in connection with its modernization and expansion. While such a project was not considered to be necessary for another five years, when undertaken it would require 800 million kroner and would also require a very large increase in electric power to run it.

Mr. Karlsen realized that as the investment committee deliberated the immediate decision at hand, these large strategic considerations would really be the deciding factors in choice of projects. He knew also that the decision made would affect the direction of ES's operations for many years to come.

EXHIBIT 1

Elkem-Spigerverket A/S

Consolidated Balance Sheets as of December 31, 1974–76

	Amounts in 1000 kroner		
	1974	*1975*	*1976*
Assets			
Cash	201,923	172,658	204,797
Receivables	527,933	455,193	574,420
Inventories	423,922	513,873	589,138
Investments and long-term receivables	313,961	367,878	415,203
Property, plant, and equipment	728,634	925,209	1,058,408
Total Assets	2,196,373	2,434,811	2,841,966
Liabilities and shareholders' equity			
Current liabilities	618,491	650,874	725,041
Long-term debt	798,005	864,880	1,131,893
Other liabilities	68,923	68,544	63,422
District Development Fund	136,810	188,430	182,855
Initial depreciation	68,047	62,945	36,575
Other investment funds	22,282	13,806	6,568
Investment funds	227,139	265,181	225,998
Shareholders' equity	481,463	581,209	692,490
Under par value consolidated subsidiaries	2,352	4,123	3,122
Total Liabilities	2,196,373	2,434,811	2,841,966

EXHIBIT 2

Elkem-Spigerverket A/S

Income Statements for the Years 1974–76

	Amounts in 1000 kroner		
	1974	*1975*	*1976*
Net sales	2,124,108	2,060,672	2,447,974
Cost of goods sold	1,704,584	1,780,147	2,211,623
Depreciation	114,714	114,421	128,991
Operating margin	304,810	166,104	107,360
Income from investments	28,506	36,240	38,870
Interest and other financial expenses	88,208	82,745	107,142
Other income	23,924	26,148	33,090
Other expenses	54,325	28,157	17,796
Share of result, companies with limited liabilities	(1,450)	(11,320)	(14,126)
Net income	213,257	106,270	40,246
Minority interests	(1,896)	3,818	(8,300)
Net income before taxes	211,361	110,088	31,946
Provision for taxes	35,081	41,397	20,606
Net income after taxes	176,280	68,691	11,340

EXHIBIT 3

Elkem-Spigerverket A/S

*Estimates of Probable Future Capital
Expenditures (not including either the
Special Iron Ore Plant or the
Ceiling Tile Plant)
(all figures in millions of
Norwegian kroner)*

	1977	1978	1979	1980	1981
Required-by-law	70	60	50	30	30
Necessary	120	120	130	130	140
Desirable	50	75	85	120	120
Total	240	255	265	280	290

EXHIBIT 4

Elkem-Spigerverket A/S

*Estimated Present Value at 14% (after taxes) of Takstein Plant
(all figures in millions of kroner)*

Estimated initial cost (1977)		
Construction	40.4	
13% Norwegian Investment Tax	5.2	(not depreciable)
10% Allowance for Contingencies	4.6	
Total Estimated Cost	50.2	

Estimated cash inflows in nominal amounts including an 8 percent estimated annual inflation rate

Year	(1) Profit Before Taxes	(2) Depreciation	(3) Profit After Taxes	(4) Net Cash Flow	(5) Present Value at 14%
			50% (1–2)	(2) + (3)	
1978	6.25	11.25	−2.5	8.75	7.67
1979	8.08	1.78	3.15	4.93	3.79
1980	10.10	1.78	4.16	5.94	4.01
1981	12.32	1.78	5.27	7.05	4.17
1982–87 (yearly)	13.38	1.78	5.8	7.58	17.45*
1988–97 (yearly)	17.50	1.78	7.86	9.64	13.56*

Present value at 14 percent of cash inflows = 50.65

*Present values of several years of equal amounts.

EXHIBIT 5

Elkem-Spigerverket A/S

Estimated Present Values at 13% (after taxes) of Special Iron Ore Refining Plant Project
(all figures in millions of kroner)

Estimated initial cost (to be incurred in 1978) (expressed in 1977 kroner)

	Conversion of Old Plant Only	Conversion, New Plant, and Mine Expansion
Construction	53.0	584.0
13% Norwegian Investment Tax (not depreciable)	7.0	76.0
Total Estimated Cost	60.0	660.0

Estimated cash inflows in nominal amounts including an 8 percent estimated annual inflation rate

	Conversion of Old Plant Only				
	(1)	*(2)*	*(3)*	*(4)*	*(5)*
	Profit		*Profit*	*Net Cash*	*Present*
Year	*Before Taxes*	*Depreciation*	*After Taxes*	*Flow*	*Value at 13%*
			50% (1–2)	(2) + (3)	
1979	16.52	13.25	1.64	14.89	11.66
1980	20.16	2.44	8.86	11.30	7.83
1981	22.78	2.44	10.17	12.61	7.73
1982	28.5	2.44	13.03	15.47	8.40
1983–98 (yearly)	40.7	2.44	19.13	21.57	75.67*

1977 present value at 13 percent of cash inflows = 111.29

	Conversion, New Plant, and Mine Expansion				
	(1)	*(2)*	*(3)*	*(4)*	*(5)*
	Profit		*Profit*	*Net Cash*	*Present*
Year	*Before Taxes*	*Depreciation*	*After Taxes*	*Flow*	*Value at 13%*
			50% (1–2)	(2) + (3)	
1979	82.6	146	−31.7	114.30	89.5
1980	100.8	23	38.9	61.9	42.9
1981	123.3	23	50.1	73.1	44.8
1982	159	23	68	91	49.4
1983–98	229.4	23	103.2	126.2	442.7*

1977 present value at 13 percent of cash inflows = 669.3

*Present value of several years of equal amounts.

EXHIBIT 6

Elkem-Spigerverket A/S

Proposed Debt Financing Plans

Project	Sources	Rates	Maturity (in years)	Millions of Kroner	Percent of Total Financing
I. Takstein	DnI	8%	10–15	20	40
	quasigovernmental	8½%	5–10	12.5	25
Total debt				32.5	65
II. Conversion of old	"participatory"	7½%	17–18	15	25
refining plant only	unsecured	8%	20	24	40
Total debt				39	65
III. Conversion, new	"DU-finansiering"	6½%	10–15	90	13.6
plant, and mine	"participatory"	7½%	17–18	180	27.2
expansion	unsecured		20	159	24.2
Total debt				429	65

In addition, it was expected that a pure grant could be obtained from the National District Development Agency for 66 million kroner (10 percent of the total cost) for the third project—converting the old plant, building a new one, and expanding the mine.

APPENDIX

Elkem-Spigerveket A/S

Excerpts from Elkem-Spigerverket's Capital Budgeting Manual

Introduction

Here follows a short introduction to investment analysis: This is meant to be an aid for the plants as well as a listing of simple guidelines which investment analyses should generally follow.

General

It is the difference between what must be paid out and what is received back which decides a project's profitability.

It is the cash flow which is the basis for the profitability calculation. Therefore, it is also important that the data which form the basis for the cash flow estimates be well founded. For the purposes of calculation, we assume that the inflows and outflows happen at the end of the year. The size of the cash flow depends on whether we consider the project before or after taxes. For most projects it will only be necessary to look at the cash flow before taxes. With the larger projects where the financing form is also made clear, it can, however, also be necessary for an after-tax calculation to be made. If this is done, it will be communicated back to the plant.

The approach used here will apply only to investment analyses before taxes, and the usual requirement for the analysis of projects will also be a before-tax analysis.

The important cash inflows in a cash flow stream are:

sales income
cost savings

Appendix (continued)

rationalization profits (e.g., from consolidation of operations)
scrap value when discarding
recovery of working capital at the end of the analysis period

The most important disbursement elements are:

fixed assets cost (including start-up cost)
working capital requirements
variable production costs
   raw materials
   component parts
   supplies
   energy
   payroll
fixed cost (exclusive of depreciation)
maintenance cost

We should note especially that costs that do not entail actual cash pay-out (for example, depreciation) shall not be included. Similarly, at the end of the analysis period we will take the required working capital as an inflow with appropriate deduction for expected loss and obsolescence.

Generally, it is easier to establish the elements of a cash-flow stream for the first year in an analysis period. For the development of the receipts and disbursements during the analysis period we shall, however, consider the expected price and cost changes. In making estimates in this connection it is recommended that the plant use as a basis the same assumptions used in the latest long-term plan. To the extent the conditions have changed since this point in time the original assumptions should be adjusted.

Inflows that occur early during the analysis period are more valuable than inflows that come in later years. It is therefore necessary to correct the raw cash-flow stream so that the amounts in the different years become comparable. This we do by discounting the amounts. All three profitability goals we shall present here have such a comparison. The reason we have chosen to use several criteria is because there is no objectively correct way to compare amounts from different years in the period. The three return criteria are:

internal rate of return (which is normally used)
present value (which is recommended in special cases)
excess present value index (which is recommended for ranking different projects)

Choice Among Investment Projects
The firm has developed a computer model—INVESTOPT—to help with ranking large projects. All projects with a required investment that exceeds the division chief's appropriation authority will be evaluated centrally.

Projects which lie within the plant manager's or the division's appropriation authority should be ranked by the plant or the division. To the extent that one wishes to rank according to return criteria, it is recommended that one rank by using the excess present value index. This is because of the assumption about reinvestment of cash inflows being preferable to that used in ranking by the internal rate of return.

Uncertainty
It is apparent that many of the estimates that we use in our investment analyses are uncertain. For projects with small capital requirements uncertainty plays, however, only a minor role. For larger projects it is necessary to consider uncertainty seriously.

Appendix (Continued)

We wish to be able to answer questions of how certain we are that we will be able to reach at least the required rate of return. The firm has worked out a computer model—INVESTRISK—which takes account of uncertainty per se in the investment analysis.

For all projects that are justified by return criteria and that must be handled by the board of directors, an uncertainty analysis will be done with the help of INVESTRISK. For other projects it is up to the plants themselves to decide how they will consider uncertainty in the project analysis.

PART FOUR

Acquisitions, Bankruptcy, Reorganization

CASE 21

The Coca-Cola Company®

Shortly after taking over as chairman of the board at The Coca-Cola Company in 1981, Mr. Roberto C. Goizueta stated that the company was going to pursue a more aggressive investment strategy. One of the areas he targeted for acquisition possibilities was the entertainment business. Mr. Goizueta was quoted as saying that ". . . the entertainment business provides an opportunity for high growth potential without requiring two things that The Coca-Cola Company isn't good at: high technology and investment in hardware." Furthermore, he continued, ". . . the growth of the new media—cable television and pay television . . . will foster overall growth in sales and profitability in the whole entertainment field." In late 1981 merger negotiations had begun in New York between Mr. Goizueta and two Columbia Pictures Incorporated ex-

ecutives, Chairman Herbert A. Allen and President Francis T. Vincent, Jr.

THE COCA-COLA COMPANY®

The Coca-Cola Company (hereafter, Coca-Cola) had its origin in Atlanta, Georgia, in 1886. Over the next century the company established itself as the largest manufacturer and distributor of soft drink concentrates and syrups in the world. Its major product, Coca-Cola, had sales in over 145 foreign countries. In addition to soft drink products, Coca-Cola manufactured, produced, distributed, and sold citrus, coffee, tea, wine, and plastic products (see Exhibits 1, 2, and 3 for Coca-Cola's financial statements and business data).

Coca-Cola had been the dominant force in the soft drink industry for sever-

This case was prepared by and used with the permission of Linda M. Roush and David Loy.

al decades. The company's primary activities were the manufacture of soft drink concentrates and syrups which it sold to independently owned bottling and canning operations and to approved fountain wholesalers. Besides supplying syrups and concentrates to bottlers, Coca-Cola gave strong promotional and marketing support as well.

The soft drink industry had been highly competitive throughout its history, with competitors including producers of nationally and internationally advertised brands, as well as regional producers and private label suppliers. Important competitive factors in the industry were major advertising and sales promotion programs and the frequent introduction of new packaging and new products. Three-fourths of all soft drink sales in the United States in the 1981–82 period were accounted for by the four leading companies. Coca-Cola had the largest market share with 34.5 percent.

Company	Market Share (%)
Coca-Cola	34.5
Pepsico, Inc.	24.1
Dr. Pepper	6.7
Seven-Up Co.	6.3

The soft drink industry grew rapidly during the 1960–1980 period. Advertising expenditures by most companies in the industry were aimed at the youthful consumer, representing the "baby boom" market. By 1980, these consumers had matured and the companies shifted some of their marketing programs to appeal to a broader market. By 1982, articles in soft drink industry trade journals proclaimed the industry to have entered the maturity stage of its life cycle.

Forecasts of sales growth for the industry in the decade of the 1980s had been a modest 3 to 4 percent per annum.

COLUMBIA PICTURES INCORPORATED

Columbia Pictures Incorporated (hereafter, Columbia) began in 1920 when two brothers, Harry and Jack Cohn, formed the C.B.C. Sales Company. From its start as a "shoestring" operation, the company grew over the decades to become one of the leading movie production companies in the world. Through its Columbia Pictures Division, Columbia engaged in the production and worldwide distribution of motion pictures for exhibition initially in theaters. Generally, Columbia produced or arranged with independent production companies for the making of most of the films it distributed. Oftentimes, the company arranged with third parties for the financing of its motion pictures.

Columbia arranged for the distribution of motion pictures through its worldwide distribution organization. Motion pictures were licensed for exhibition in theaters on percentage, modified percentage, or flat rental bases or on variations thereof. Most of the motion pictures distributed by Columbia for theatrical showings also were made available through licensing arrangements for exhibition on pay television and, thereafter, for exhibition on one of the three U.S. television networks and on local U.S. television stations and foreign television stations. In 1982 Columbia's film library contained over 1800 theatrical motion pictures that could be available for theatrical re-release and distribution to pay and free television and other home entertainment markets. The success of a motion picture depended largely on public taste, which was both unpredictable and susceptible to change. The success or failure of any single film was difficult to predict before release. The production of a motion picture required expenditures of substantial funds that were committed mainly on the basis of Columbia's evaluation of the commercial potential for the proposed project. The success of a motion picture was also significantly affected by the popularity of other motion pictures that were being distributed by other companies in the same season. Moreover, in recent years, while box office receipts were relatively stable, the costs of producing and distributing motion pictures had increased substantially and participations payable to creative and artistic personnel had increased in many instances. For the entire industry a combination of these cost and revenue factors brought about an increase in the percentage of unprofitable films.

The availability of alternative forms of leisure-time entertainment, including expanded pay and cable television, caused major changes in the entertainment industry in the 1980s. Revenues from licensing of motion pictures to network television decreased since 1979 while revenues from pay television, video discs, and cassettes increased. A critical factor determining the revenues derived from the re-release of motion pictures to these markets had been the original success of the movie at the box office.

In addition to motion pictures Columbia had operations in other areas of the leisure-time entertainment industry. It engaged in the production and distribution of television series and features;

the design, manufacture, and sales of pinball machines; the production of commercials; the publication and distribution of sheet music and song books; merchandising; out-of-home advertising; and operation of radio stations (see Exhibits 3, 4, and 5 for Columbia's financial statements and business data). In 1981 Columbia entered into an agreement and plan to merge with The Outlet Company, a Rhode Island broadcasting concern. Columbia's proposed offer to Outlet shareholders was a package of Columbia preferred stock, valued at approximately $45 per share of Outlet stock. At the time of the Coca-Cola–Columbia merger negotiations, the Columbia-Outlet merger had not been completed.

Columbia's Recent History

The decade of the 1970s was a volatile period for Columbia. A $50 million loss in 1973 left the future of the company uncertain. As a result of the loss, new management was brought in to turn the company around, and by 1978, record high earnings were recorded in the amount of $68.8 million. However, in 1978, one of Columbia's top officials was forced to resign after being accused of check forgery. In the midst of this controversy a group of stockholders, led by Herbert A. Allen, took over control of Columbia and installed new management. In 1979 Mr. Allen, owning 6.2 percent of Columbia's common stock, became chairman of the board.

Mr. Allen was president of an investment banking firm, Allen and Company. He built a reputation for insightful financial decisions and ability to attract superb managers. As chairman of Columbia, Mr. Allen installed as president of the company, Francis T. Vincent, Jr., and as president of the motion picture subsidiary, Frank Price. Both men had outstanding management records in non-show business related companies. Although there were reservations about whether conflicts between fiscally oriented managers and "creative" movie producers could be avoided, Mr. Vincent and Mr. Price were able to reestablish Columbia's image in the industry and maintain its profitability. Mr. Price imposed tight controls over film budgets and was successful in keeping movie production cost under control, even though other movie companies frequently experienced major cost overruns. Under the new management, Columbia improved its distribution network and marketing operations.

In 1980 financier Kirk Kerkorian attempted to acquire Columbia at a price of $50 per share. Mr. Allen and other Columbia shareholders fought off the takeover bid.

REASONS FOR THE MERGER

The joint proxy statement dated April 5, 1982, stated several reasons for the proposed merger between Coca-Cola and Columbia. From the viewpoint stated by the Coca-Cola management, the major reason for the merger with Columbia was to gain diversification into new consumer-oriented markets with growth potential. Coca-Cola's management believed that the entertainment–leisure-time markets had the growth potential they desired. They claimed that the entertainment business would benefit from the growth of media, such as cable television, other home-paid television and home video. Also, they believed Columbia's entertainment business would be compatible with Coca-Cola's existing soft drink business. For one reason they held that both entertainment and soft drink industries depended on marketing skills and mass consumer demand for their products. For another reason they argued that both industries operated in a similar manner; for example, their principal products were sold to ultimate consumers through distribution systems primarily owned by third parties, who had substantial investment in fixed assets. Additional reasons raised by the Coca-Cola management were:

1. The size of the Columbia operations were small relative to that of Coca-Cola such that the essential nature of Coca-Cola would not be changed.

2. The value of Columbia's film library was understated on its financial statements and contained hundreds of titles available for exploitation in markets, including the home video and cable television segments.

3. The management of Columbia earned a reputation as being strong and fiscally conservative.

4. Poor performance by the Gottlieb subsidiary of Columbia would be overcome in the future as operations shifted from pinball products to video games.

5. Columbia's management developed and implemented strategies that reduce the earnings volatility experienced by Columbia in the past.

6. Each company should benefit from the other's strengths in marketing, advertising, and merchandising.

From the viewpoint stated by Columbia's management, Coca-Cola was considered an attractive merger partner because they felt both companies shared common interests and abilities. For example, they believed that both companies had strong marketing skills and extensive international operations. They felt that with Coca-Cola's vast financial resources, needed financing would be available for expanding their future motion picture operations and other products. Furthermore, Columbia's management held that their recent stock price had not reflected accurately their company's earnings growth potential in the future. Whereas future price levels of Columbia common stock might reflect that earnings growth potential, the management proposed current stockholders should be able to realize the present value of that potential through the merger.

TERMS OF THE MERGER AGREEMENT

The formal agreement between Coca-Cola and Columbia, dated March 17, 1982, stated the terms of the merger. At the option of Columbia stockholders, they could exchange their stock for either Coca-Cola common stock or cash. Coca-Cola placed a 12.4 million limit on the total number of its shares that would be exchanged for Columbia common stock and a $336.7 million limit on the total amount of cash that would be paid. As long as neither limit was exceeded, Columbia shareholders could freely elect to receive either Coca-Cola common stock or cash. If either limit was exceeded, Coca-Cola would specify pro rata amounts of cash and/or common

stock to distribute to Columbia shareholders tendering their stock. The effective time of the merger was specified as the date upon which a filing of a Certificate of Merger had been made with the Secretary of State of the State of Delaware.

For Columbia shareholders who elected to receive Coca-Cola common stock, each share of Columbia common stock issued and outstanding immediately prior to the effective time of the merger should be converted into 1.2 fully paid and nonassessable shares of Coca-Cola common stock plus an additional number of shares equal to the quotient obtained by dividing $32.625 by the average market price of Coca-Cola common stock for 15 consecutive days before the effective time of the merger. The average market price should be determined as the average of the high and low sales prices and the closing prices of Coca-Cola common stock as reported on the New York Stock Exchange Composite Tape. For Columbia shareholders who chose to receive cash, each share of Columbia common stock would be converted into rights to receive cash in the amount of $32.625 plus an additional amount equal to the product of 1.2 times the average market price of Coca-Cola common stock for 15 consecutive days before the effective time of the merger. The merger agreement would be effective only as long as the average market price of Coca-Cola common stock on the effective date of the merger was not less than $27.25.

For certain major shareholders of Columbia common stock, Coca-Cola reached separate agreements that no Columbia shareholder should receive more than 500,000 shares of Coca-Cola common stock after the merger was completed. Major shareholders of Columbia owned approximately 1.2 million shares of Columbia common stock.

As a further development in the merger, Coca-Cola agreed to take Columbia's place in the proposed merger between Columbia and The Outlet Company. Outlet shareholders were offered $24 cash and 0.89 share of Coca-Cola common stock for each share of Outlet common stock.

The proxy statement reported that Coca-Cola planned to fund the cash amounts involved in the merger from internal sources, and issuance of short-term and long-term debt. A Coca-Cola subsidiary arranged standby financing with three banks in the amount of $300,000 for a period of two years. The company had not ruled out the possibility of arranging a longer-term debt arrangement for the required funds. Interest rates on the longer-term debt were projected at approximately 14 percent per annum.

Certain other expenses were incurred in the merger arrangement that had to be paid by Coca-Cola and Columbia. Allen and Company acted as financial advisor to Columbia and received $4 million plus expenses for its services. Morgan Stanley Company would receive $750,000 for its services should the merger be completed. (Consolidated financial statements are shown in Exhibits 6 and 7.)

STOCK MARKET REACTION TO THE MERGER ANNOUNCEMENT

On January 15, 1982, the last day of trading prior to the agreement in principle between Coca-Cola and Columbia with respect to the merger, the closing prices of Coca-Cola and Columbia common stock was $34.375 and $41.75, respectively. On January 18, 1982, the first day of trading after the merger announcement, Coca-Cola's stock price dropped $2.25 per share to close at $32.125. On the other hand Columbia's common stock rose by $20.75 to close at $62.50.

On March 2, 1982, the day before the approval of the terms of the merger was announced, the closing prices were $30.25 and $61.50 for Coca-Cola and Columbia, respectively. On April 1, 1982, the closing prices were $33.125 and $67. Based on the average market prices of Coca-Cola common stock for 15 consecutive trading days before April 1, 1982, the cash amount for the merger would have been $71.66 per share of Columbia common stock.

Reaction by stock market analysts to the Coca-Cola offer to acquire Columbia was mainly critical. One comment was that the merger would cause an immediate dilution in Coca-Cola 1982 earnings per share of approximately 8 percent. Another comment was that the earnings of Columbia in the past had been taxed at an effective rate of 24 percent, while as a part of Coca-Cola's earnings, they would be taxed at a higher effective rate of 44 percent. Further comments reflected that Coca-Cola offered to pay five times Columbia's book value per share, while the average figure for 1981 recent takeovers was 3.5 times book value per share. Also, analysts found little possibility for significant synergies to develop from the combined operations of the two companies. Finally, the analysts found it difficult to assess the value of Columbia's film library without actually looking at the individual films. They seriously doubted that the premium Coca-Cola had offered for Columbia common stock would be realized from exploiting the film library. (Price, earnings, and dividends data are provided in Exhibits 8 and 9.)

Analysts who took a positive view of the merger stressed the long-term potential of the Columbia business. They felt that Coca-Cola had to offer a substantial premium for Columbia common stock in order to head off rival bids for the company. The analysts stated that Columbia's strong management had the ability to make the company a highly profitable operation.

To comments that Coca-Cola made an "overly generous" offer to Columbia, Mr. Goizueta responded that "An acquisition is like a marriage . . . You look at the bride and you like her. She's beautiful. She comes from a good family. You think you're going to be happy with her, so the last thing you talk about is the dowry."

EXHIBIT 1

The Coca-Cola Company

Consolidated Balance Sheets
(dollar figures in thousands except share data)

DECEMBER 31	1980	1981
ASSETS		
CURRENT ASSETS		
CASH	$ 129685	$ 120908
MARKETABLE SECURITIES, AT COST		
(APPROXIMATES MARKETS)	101401	218634
TRADE ACCOUNTS RECEIVABLE, LESS ALLOWANCES		
OF $8579 IN 1981 AND $8594 IN 1980	523123	483491
INVENTORIES	810235	750719
PREPAID EXPENSES	57809	62494
TOTAL CURRENT ASSETS	$ 1622253	$ 1636246
INVESTMENTS AND OTHER ASSETS	302184	387418
PROPERTY, PLANT, AND EQUIPMENT		
LAND AND IMPROVEMENTS	96567	96468
BUILDINGS	537235	570356
MACHINERY AND EQUIPMENT	1183438	1271065
CONTAINERS	314349	306243
	2131589	2244132
LESS ALLOWANCES FOR DEPRECIATION	790749	834676
NET PROPERTY, PLANT, AND EQUIPMENT	1340840	1409456
FORMULAE, TRADEMARKS, GOODWILL, AND CONTRACT RIGHTS	140681	131661
TOTAL ASSETS	$ 3405958	$ 3564781

EXHIBIT 1 (Continued)

DECEMBER 31	1980	1981
LIABILITIES & STOCKHOLDERS' EQUITY		
CURRENT LIABILITIES		
NOTES PAYABLE	$ 87587	$ 89647
CURRENT MATURITIES OF LONG-TERM DEBT	7528	5515
ACCOUNTS PAYABLE AND ACCRUED EXPENSES	733023	672049
ACCRUED TAXES-INCLUDING INCOME TAXES	233442	239114
TOTAL CURRENT LIABILITIES	$ 1061580	$ 1006325
LONG-TERM DEBT	133221	137278
DEFERRED INCOME TAXES	136419	150406
STOCKHOLDERS'EQUITY		
COMMON STOCK, NO PAR VALUE-		
AUTHORIZED-140,000,000 SHARES;		
ISSUED-124,024,735 SHARES IN 1981		
AND 123,989,854 SHARES IN 1980	62372	62389
CAPITAL SURPLUS	113172	114194
RETAINED EARNINGS	1914547	2109542
	2090091	2286125
IN TREASURY, AT COST	15353	15353
TOTAL STOCKHOLDERS' EQUITY	$ 2074738	$ 2270772
TOTAL LIABILITIES & STOCKHOLDERS' EQUITY	$ 3405958	$ 3564781

SEE NOTES TO CONSOLIDATED FINANCIAL STATEMENTS

EXHIBIT 2

The Coca-Cola Company

Consolidated Income Statements
(dollar figures in thousands except per share data)

YEAR ENDED DECEMBER 31	1979	1980	1981
NET SALES	$ 4688739	$ 5620749	$ 5889035
COST OF GOODS SOLD	2583210	3197733	3307574
GROSS PROFIT	2105529	2423016	2581461
SELLING, ADMINISTRATIVE, AND GENERAL EXPENSES	1414858	1681861	1782875
OPERATING INCOME	690671	741155	798586
OTHER INCOME (EXPENSES)			
INTEREST INCOME	36304	40099	70632
INTEREST EXPENSE	10602	35102	38349
OTHER DEDUCTIONS—NET	2783	9425	23615
INCOME FROM CONTINUING OPERATIONS BEFORE INCOME TAXES	713590	736727	807254
INCOME TAXES	318443	330409	360184
INCOME FROM CONTINUING OPERATIONS	395147	406318	447070
DISCONTINUED OPERATIONS			
INCOME FROM DISCONTINUED OPERATIONS (NOTE A)	24973	15790	5641
GAIN ON DISPOSAL OF DISCONTINUED OPERATIONS (NOTE B)	0	0	29071
NET INCOME	$ 420120	$ 422108	$ 481782
PER SHARE			
CONTINUING OPERATIONS	3.20	3.29	3.62
DISCONTINUING OPERATIONS	0.20	.13	.28
NET INCOME	$ 3.40	$ 3.42	$ 3.90

SEE NOTES TO CONSOLIDATED FINANCIAL STATEMENTS

The Coca-Cola Company

Notes to Exhibits 1 and 2
Consolidated Financial Statements

NOTE A ACCOUNTING POLICIES: THE MAJOR ACCOUNTING POLICIES AND PRACTICES OF COCA COLA ARE AS FOLLOWS:

INVENTORIES ARE VALUED AT THE LOWER OF COST OR MARKET. THE LAST-IN, FIRST-OUT METHOD IS USED FOR SUGAR AND OTHER SWEETNERS USED IN DOMESTIC BEVERAGES, FOR CERTAIN CITRUS CONCENTRATE PRODUCTS, AND FOR SUBSTANTIALLY ALL INVENTORIES. ALL OTHER INVENTORIES ARE VALUED ON THE AVERAGE OR FIRST-IN, FIRST-OUT METHOD. THE EXCESS OF CURRENT COSTS OVER LIFO STATED VALUES AMOUNTED TO APPROXIMATELY $76,000,000 AND $109,000,000 AT DECEMBER 31, 1981 AND 1980, RESPECTIVELY.

PROPERTY,PLANT AND EQUIPMENT IS STATED AT COST, LESS ALLOWANCE FOR DEPRECIATION, EXCEPT THAT FOREIGN SUBSIDARIES CARRY BOTTLES AND SHELLS IN SERVICE AT AMOUNTS (LESS THAN COST) WHICH, IN GENERAL, CORRESPOND WITH DEPOSIT PRICES OBTAINED FROM CUSTOMERS. APPROXIMATELY 87% OF THE DEPRECIATION EXPENSE WAS DETERMINED BY THE STRAIGHT-LINE METHOD. A PORTION OF THE DEPRECIATION DETERMINED BY THE STRAIGHT-LINE METHOD FOR FINANCIAL STATEMENT PURPOSES IS CALCULATED ON ACCELERATED METHODS FOR INCOME TAX PURPOSES. DEFERRED INCOME TAXES ARE PROVIDED TO RECOGNIZE TIMING DIFFERENCES IN REPORTING DEPRECIATION FOR ACCOUNTING AND TAX PURPOSES. INVESTMENT TAX CREDITS ARE ACCOUNTED FOR BY THE FLOW-THROUGH METHOD.

FORMULAE, TRADEMARKS, GOODWILL AND CONTRACT RIGHTS ARE STATED ON THE BASIS OF COST AND, IF PURCHASED SUBSEQUENT TO OCTOBER 31, 1970, ARE BEING AMORTIZED, PRINCIPALLY ON A STRAIGHT-LINE BASIS, OVER THE ESTIMATED FUTURE PERIODS TO BE BENEFITED (NOT EXCEEDING 40 YEARS). ACCUMULATED AMORTIZATION AMOUNTED TO $16,168,000 AND $12,189,000 AT DECEMBER 31, 1981 AND 1980, RESPECTIVELY.

AT JANUARY 1, 1980, COCA-COLA BEGAN CAPITALIZING INTEREST COST AS PART OF THE COST OF ACQUISITION OR CONSTRUCTION OF MAJOR ASSETS AS REQUIRED BY STATEMENT OF FINANCIAL ACCOUNTING STANDARDS NO. 34. INTEREST CAPITALIZED WAS $7,893,000 IN 1981 AND $5,674,000 IN 1980.

THE FINANCIAL STATEMENTS OF FOREIGN OPERATIONS ARE TRANSLATED TO UNITED STATES DOLLARS IN ACCORDANCE WITH PROVISIONS OF STATEMENT OF FINANCIAL ACCOUNTING STANDARDS NO. 8.

NOTE B ACQUISITIONS: IN 1979 COCA-COLA ACQUIRED THE ATLANTA COCA-COLA BOTTLING COMPANY FOR APPROXIMATELY $65,000,000 IN CASH. SEVERAL OTHER COMPANIES, PRIMARILY BOTTLING OPERATIONS, WERE ACQUIRED IN EXCHANGE FOR CASH AND NOTES IN 1979 AND 1980 AND HAVE BEEN INCLUDED IN THE INCOME STATEMENT FROM THE DATE OF PURCHASE. THE PURCHASED COMPANIES HAD NO SIGNIFICANT EFFECT ON OPERATING RESULTS IN 1979 OR 1980.

NOTE C DISCONTINUED OPERATIONS: IN SEPTEMBER 1981 COCA-COLA SOLD AQUA-CHEM, INC., A WHOLLY-OWNED SUBSIDIARY WHICH PRODUCED STEAM GENERATORS, INDUSTRIAL BOILERS, AND WATER TREATMENT EQUIPMENT. ON FEBRUARY 4, 1982, COCA-COLA SOLD ITS TENCO DIVISION, A PRODUCER OF INSTANT COFFEES AND TEAS, FOR APPROXIMATELY BOOK VALUE.

NET SALES OF DISCONTINUED OPERATIONS WERE $240,216,000, $291,846,000 AND $272,663,000 IN 1981, 1980, AND 1979, RESPECTIVELY. AT DECEMBER 31, 1981, ASSETS OF $60,967,000 AND LIABILITIES OF $16,308,000 APPLICABLE TO DISCONTINUED OPERATIONS ARE INCLUDED IN THE BALANCE SHEET.

EXHIBIT 3

The Coca-Cola Company

1981 Business Segment Data For
Coca-Cola Company and Columbia Pictures Incorporated
(dollar figures in thousands)

THE COCA-COLA COMPANY

NET SALES		
SOFT DRINKS	$ 5889035	
OTHER INDUSTRIES	4683467	79.53 %
	1205568	20.47 %
NET SALES BY GEOGRAPHICAL AREAS		
UNITED STATES AND PUERTO RICO	3238673	54.99 %
LATIN AMERICAN	608110	10.33 %
EUROPE AND AFRICA	1096257	18.62 %
CANADA AND PACIFIC	945995	16.06 %

COLUMBIA PICTURES INDUSTRIES

REVENUES	$ 686600	
FILMED ENTERTAINMENT		
FEATURE FILMS		
THEATRICAL	327200	47.66 %
TELEVISION	54000	7.86 %
TELEVISION PROGRAMS	165800	24.15 %
OTHER	75500	11.00 %
AMUSEMENT GAMES	39700	5.78 %
MEDIA AND OTHER	24400	3.55 %
NET SALES BY GEOGRAPHICAL AREAS		
UNITED STATES	481500	70.13 %
EUROPE	104600	15.23 %
FAR EAST	35600	5.18 %
NORTH AMERICA (EXCEPT U.S.)	38900	5.67 %
LATIN AMERICA	26000	3.79 %

EXHIBIT 4

The Coca-Cola Company

Columbia Pictures Industries, Inc.
Consolidated Balance Sheets
(dollar figures in thousands)

	JUNE 28, 1980	JUNE 27, 1981	DEC. 26 1981*
ASSETS			
CURRENT ASSETS			
CASH	$ 31801	$ 9852	$ 13396
RECEIVABLES, LESS ALLOWANCE OF $5625, $5870, AND $5851, RESEPECTIVELY	157062	170962	172027
INVENTORIES (NOTE D)	82130	81593	103339
PREPAID EXPENSES AND OTHER CURRENT ASSETS	4521	3744	3305
TOTAL CURRENT ASSETS	$ 275514	$ 266151	$ 292067
LONG-TERM RECEIVABLES	28953	60156	92442
INVENTORIES (NOTE D)	117378	178914	230515
FIXED ASSETS, AT COST, LESS ACCUMULATED DEPRECIATION AND AMORTIZATION OF $27,256, $32,658, AND 22,320, RESPECTIVELY	31496	42193	30225
FRANCHISE RIGHTS AND BROADCASTING LICENSES	3160	12414	10157
EXCESS OF COST OVER NET ASSETS OF ACQUIRED COMPANIES	19456	19813	19173
OTHER ASSETS AND DEFERRED CHARGES	12547	11489	32908
TOTAL ASSETS	$ 488504	$ 591130	$ 707487

(Continued)

205

EXHIBIT 4 (Continued)

	JUNE 28 1980	JUNE 27 1981	DEC. 26 1981
LIABILITIES AND STOCKHOLDERS' EQUITY			
CURRENT LIABILITIES			
LOANS PAYABLE	$ 468	$ 2403	$ 20191
ACCOUNTS PAYABLE AND ACCRUED EXPENSES	46087	61789	67698
CONTRACTUAL OBLIGATIONS AND PARTICIPANTS' SHARES	92703	77509	98459
ACCRUED INCOME TAXES	11217	12436	14776
TOTAL CURRENT LIABILITIES	$ 150475	$ 154137	$ 201124
ADVANCE COLLECTIONS ON CONTRACTS	16705	23912	61372
CONTRACTUAL OBLIGATIONS AND PARTICIPANTS' SHARES	37836	62387	76579
LOANS PAYABLE	33627	99395	90572
SUBORDINATED DEBT	21725	103630	104313
STOCKHOLDERS' EQUITY			
COMMON STOCK-$.10 PAR VALUE; AUTHORIZED 20,000,000 SHARES; ISSUED 10,072,273, 10,422,936, AND 10,537,008, RESPECTIVELY	1007	1042	1054
DEFERRED COMPENSATION UNDER RESTRICTED STOCK AWARDS	0	0	-9824
CAPITAL IN EXCESS OF PAR VALUE	101715	110356	111368
RETAINED EARNINGS	125505	164264	184764
	228227	275662	287362
LESS TREASURY SHARES (16,791, 2,455,491, AND 2,170,491, RESPECTIVELY) AT COST (NOTE C)	91	127993	113835
TOTAL STOCKHOLDERS' EQUITY	$ 228136	$ 147669	$ 173527
TOTAL LIABILITIES AND STOCKHOLDERS' EQUITY	$ 488504	$ 591130	$ 707487

SEE NOTES TO COLUMBIA PICTURES FINANCIAL STATEMENTS

*UNAUDITED.

206

EXHIBIT 5

The Coca-Cola Company

Columbia Pictures Industries, Inc.
Consolidated Income Statement
(dollar figures in thousands, except per share data)

	FISCAL YEAR ENDED			SIX MONTHS ENDED	
	JUNE 30, 1979	JUNE 28, 1980	JUNE 27, 1981	DEC. 27, 1980	DEC. 26, 1981*
REVENUES	$ 544872	$ 691814	$ 686611	$ 329433	$ 377562
COSTS AND EXPENSES					
COSTS RELATING TO REVENUES	$ 408093	$ 548458	$ 537744	$ 254184	$ 290235
SELLING, GENERAL, AND ADMINISTRATIVE EXPENSES	69322	79309	88924	43254	48395
INTEREST EXPENSE, NET (NOTE F)	11448	1740	1411	-3269	7680
TOTAL COSTS AND EXPENSES	$ 488863	$ 629507	$ 628079	$ 294169	$ 346310
INCOME FROM CONTINUING OPERATIONS BEFORE INCOME TAXES	56009	62307	58532	35264	31252
INCOME TAXES	16383	17400	14250	8900	8300
INCOME FROM CONTINUING OPERATIONS	39626	44907	44282	26364	22952
DISCONTINUED OPERATION, NET OF TAX BENEFITS OF $262 (NOTE B)	-638	0	0	0	0
NET INCOME	$ 38988	$ 44907	$ 44282	$ 26364	$ 22952

(Continued)

207

EXHIBIT 5 (Continued)

| | FISCAL YEAR ENDED | | | SIX MONTHS ENDED | |
	JUNE 30, 1979	JUNE 28, 1980	JUNE 27, 1981	DEC. 27, 1980	DEC. 26 1981*
PER SHARE OF COMMON STOCK (NOTE A)					
INCOME FROM CONTINUING OPERATIONS	$ 4.07	$ 4.50	$ 4.66	$ 2.58	$ 2.79
DICONTINUED OPERATION	-.06	0	0	0	0
NET INCOME	$ 4.01	$ 4.50	$ 4.66	$ 2.58	$ 2.79
NET INCOME, ASSUMING FULL DILUTION	$ 3.87	$ 4.37	$ 4.43	$ 2.45	$ 2.62

SEE NOTES TO COLUMBIA PICTURES FINANCIAL STATEMENTS

* UNAUDITED

The Coca-Cola Company

Notes to Exhibits 4 and 5
Columbia Pictures Industries Financial Statements

NOTE A SUMMARY OF SIGNIFICANT ACCOUNTING POLICIES:

FOREIGN CURRENCY: FOREIGN ASSETS AND LIABILITIES ARE TRANSLATED TO THEIR U.S. DOLLAR EQUIVALENTS BASED ON RATES OF EXCHANGE PREVAILING AT THE END OF EACH RESPECTIVE PERIOD EXCEPT FOR FILM INVENTORIES AND FIXED ASSETS, WHICH ARE TRANSLATED AT RATES PREVAILING AT ACQUISITION. REVENUE AND EXPENSE ACCOUNTS ARE TRANSLATED AT WEIGHTED AVERAGE EXCHANGE RATES DURING THE PERIODS EXCEPT FOR AMORTIZATION OF FILM INVENTORY AND DEPRECIATION OF FIXED ASSETS, WHICH ARE BASED ON THE HISTORICAL DOLLAR EQUIVALENT OF RALTED ASSETS. AGGREGATE EXCHANGE GAINS AND LOSSES ARE INCLUDED IN NET INCOME.

RECOGNITION OF REVENUES: REVENUES FROM THEATRICAL EXHIBITION OF FEATURE FILMS ARE RECOGNIZED ON THE DATES OF EXHIBITION. REVENUES FROM TELEVISION LICENSING IS RECOGNIZED WHEN EACH FILM IS AVAILABLE FOR TELECASTING. LONG-TERM RECEIVABLES AND RELATED LIABILITIES TO PARTICIPANTS ARISING THROUGH SUCH TELEVISION LICENSING ARE RECORDED AT THEIR PRESENT VALUES.

INVENTORIES: FILM COSTS FOR PRODUCTION, PRINT, PRE-RELEASE AND NATIONAL ADVERTISING AND RELATED INTEREST ARE CAPITALIZED AS INCURRED. THE INDIVIDUAL FILM FORECAST METHOD IS USED TO AMORTIZE THESE COSTS BASED ON REVENUES RECOGNIZED PROPORTIONAL TO MANAGEMENT'S ESTIMATE OF ULTIMATE REVENUES TO BE RECEIVED. THE COSTS OF COOPERATIVE AND OTHER FORMS OF LOCAL ADVERTISING ARE CHARGED TO EXPENSE AS INCURRED.

THE COSTS OF FEATURE FILMS IN RELEASE, FEATURE FILMS COMPLETED BUT NOT RELEASED, AND TELEVISION FILMS ARE CLASSIFIED AS CURRENT ASSETS TO THE EXTENT THESE COSTS ARE TO BE RECOVERED THROUGH THE RESPECTIVE PRIMARY MARKETS. ALL OTHER COSTS RELATING TO FILM PRODUCTION ARE CLASSIFIED AS NON-CURRENT ASSETS.

DEPRECIATION AND AMORTIZATION OF FIXED ASSETS: THESE AMOUNTS ARE BASED ON THE STRAIGHT-LINE METHOD AT VARIOUS RATES RELATED TO THE USEFUL LIVES, OR, FOR LEASEHOLD IMPROVEMENTS, OVER THE TERM OF THE LEASE, IF SHORTER.

INTANGIBLES: THE EXCESS OF COST OVER NET ASSETS OF ACQUIRED COMPANIES AND THE BROADCASTING LICENSES OF THREE RADIO STATIONS ARE BEING AMORTIZED ON A STRAIGHT-LINE BASIS OVER 40 YEARS. FRANCHISE RIGHTS ARE BEING AMORTIZED OVER THEIR ESTIMATED RESPECTIVE LIVES, WHICH RANGE FROM 1 TO 12 YEARS.

INCOME TAXES: INCOME TAXES ARE COMPUTED ON FINANCIAL STATEMENT INCOME WITH DEFERRED TAXES BEING RECOGNIZED ON ITEMS OF INCOME OR EXPENSE WHICH ENTER INTO DIFFERENT FISCAL PERIODS ON A TAX RETURN BASIS. INVESTMENT TAX CREDITS ARE ACCOUNTED FOR UNDER THE FLOW-THROUGH METHOD. THE STATUTORY FEDERAL INCOME TAX RATES ARE RECONCILED TO COLUMBIA'S EFFECTIVE INCOME TAX RATES AS FOLLOWS:

IN 1981, STATUTORY FEDERAL INCOME TAX RATE	46.0 %
INVESTMENT TAX CREDITS	-24.4 %
STATE TAXES	2.7 %
EFFECTIVE INCOME TAX RATE	24.3 %

INVESTMENT TAX CREDIT CARRYFORWARDS FOR FINANCIAL STATEMENT PURPOSES AGGREGATED APPROXIMATELY $22,200,000 AT JUNE 27, 1981. CARRYFORWARDS ON A TAX RETURN BASIS AGGREGATE APPROXIMATELY $35,200,000 AT JUNE 27, 1981 AND EXPIRE BETWEEN 1993 AND 1996.

NOTE B BUSINESS CHANGES:

IN JANUARY 1981, COLUMBIA ACQUIRED NEW YORK SUBWAYS ADVERTISING FOR $10,000,000 IN CASH AND 50,000 SHARES OF COMMON STOCK. THE ACQUISITION WAS ACCOUNTED FOR AS A PURCHASE. ON SEPTEMBER 28,1979, COLUMBIA SOLD "ARISTA", A RECORD COMPANY, FOR ABOUT $50,000,000. THE NET GAIN ON THE SALE OF $4,017,000 WAS LATER REVERSED DUE TO FUTURE POSSIBLE EFFECTS OF VARIOUS UNDERTAKINGS MADE TO THE PURCHASER.

(Continued)

Notes (Continued)

NOTE C PURCHASE OF TREASURY STOCK:

ON FEBRUARY 25, 1981, COLUMBIA PURCHASED 2,438,700 SHARES OF COLUMBIA COMMON STOCK HELD BY CERTAIN STOCKHOLDERS FOR $91,451,250 ($37.50 PER SHARE) IN CASH AND $42,677,250 ($17.50 PER SHARE) PRINCIPAL AMOUNT OF 6% SUBORDINATED PROMISSORY NOTES, DUE FEBRUARY 2, 1983. THE 6% SUBORDINATED PROMISSORY NOTES WERE RECORDED NET AMORTIZED DEBT DISCOUNT OF $6,856,000 ($5,664,000 FOR JUNE 27, 1981).

NOTE D INVENTORIES:

INVENTORIES FOR JUNE 27, 1981 ARE COMPRISED OF THE FOLLOWING: (DOLLAR FIGURES IN THOUSANDS)

CURRENT UNAMORTIZED FILM COSTS		
RELEASED	$	38881
COMPLETED, NOT RELEASED		7754
IN PROCESS		16381
TOTAL CURRENT UNAMORTIZED FILM	$	63016
AMUSEMENT GAMES		8257
OTHER		10320
	$	81593
NON-CURRENT UNAMORTIZED FILM COSTS		
RELEASED	$	70543
COMPLETED, NOT RELEASED		1502
IN PROCESS		106869
TOTAL NON-CURRENT UNAMORTIZED FILM	$	178914

EXHIBIT 6

The Coca-Cola Company

Columbia Pictures Industries, Inc.
Pro Forma Combined Statement of Financial Position
(dollar figures in thousands, except per share data)

THE FOLLOWING PRO FORMA COMBINED STATEMENT OF FINANCIAL POSITION COMBINES THE CONSOLIDATED BALANCE SHEET OF THE COCA-COLA COMPANY AS AT DECEMBER 31, 1981 AND THE UNAUDITED CONSOLIDATED CONDENSED STATEMENT OF FINANCIAL POSITION OF COLUMBIA AS AT DECEMBER 26, 1981, GIVING EFFECT TO THE MERGER UNDER THE PURCHASE METHOD OF ACCOUNTING.

| | HISTORICAL | | PRO FORMA | |
	THE COCA-COLA COMPANY	COLUMBIA*	ADJUSTMENTS (NOTE A)*	COMBINED FOR MERGER*
ASSETS				
CURRENT ASSETS	$ 1636246	$ 292067	$ 0	$ 1928313
LONG-TERM INVENTORIES	0	230515	0	230515
LONG-TERM RECEIVABLES AND OTHER NON-CURRENT ASSETS	387418	125350	-1302 (B)	511466
FIXED ASSETS, NET	1409456	30225	0	1439681
FORMULAE, TRADEMARKS, GOODWILL, CONTRACT RIGHTS AND OTHER INTANGIBLE ASSETS	131661	29330	-19173 (B)	141818
EXCESS OF COST OVER NET ASSETS ACQUIRED IN MERGER	0	0	544681 (B)	544681
TOTAL ASSETS	$ 3564781	$ 707487	$ 524206	$ 4796474
LIABILITIES AND STOCKHOLDERS' EQUITY				
CURRENT LIABILITIES	$ 1006325	$ 201124	$ 1365 (B)	1208814
DEFERRED INCOME TAXES AND OTHER LIABILITIES	150406	137951	0	288357
LOANS, MORTGAGES AND NOTES PAYABLE	137278	90572	328836 (B)	556686
SUBORDINATED DEBT	0	104313	-53402 (B)	50911
TOTAL LIABILITIES	$ 1294009	$ 533960	$ 276799	$ 2104768
STOCKHOLDERS' EQUITY				
COMMON STOCK	62389	1054	6122	68511
DEFERRED COMPENSATION UNDER RESTRICTED STOCK AWARDS	0	-9824	9824	0
CAPITAL SURPLUS	114194	111368	414812	529006
RETAINED EARNINGS	2109542	184764	-184764	2109542
	2286125	287362	245994	2707059
LESS TREASURY SHARES	15353	113835	-113835	15353
TOTAL STOCKHOLDERS' EQUITY	$ 2270772	$ 173527	$ 359829	$ 2691706
TOTAL LIABILITIES AND STOCKHOLDERS' EQUITY	$ 3564781	$ 707487	$ 636628	$ 4796474
BOOK VALUE PER SHARE OF COMMON STOCK	$ 18.37	$ 20.72	$ 0	$ 19.81

*UNAUDITED

SEE NOTES TO PRO FORMA COMBINED FINANCIAL STATEMENTS

EXHIBIT 7

The Coca-Cola Company

Columbia Pictures Industries, Inc.
Pro Forma Combined Statement of Income
(dollar figures in thousands, except per share data)

THE FOLLOWING PRO FORMA UNAUDITED COMBINED STATEMENT OF INCOME COMBINES THE CONSOLIDATED STATEMENT OF INCOME OF THE COCA-COLA COMPANY FOR THE YEAR ENDED DECEMBER 31, 1981 AND THE UNAUDITED CONSOLIDATED CONDENSED STATEMENT OF INCOME OF COLUMBIA FOR THE TWELVE MONTHS ENDED DECEMBER 26, 1981, GIVING EFFECT TO THE MERGER, UNDER THE PURCHASE METHOD OF ACCOUNTING, AS IF IT HAD OCCURRED AT THE BEGINNINGS OF SUCH PERIODS.

	THE COCA-COLA COMPANY (HISTORICAL)	COLUMBIA (HISTORICAL)*	PRO FORMA ADJUSTMENTS TO COLUMBIA (NOTE C)*	COLUMBIA AS ADJUSTED*	ADJUSTMENTS TO COMBINED (NOTE A)*	COMBINED FOR MERGER*
REVENUES	$ 5889035	$ 734740	$ 0	$ 734740	$ 0	$ 6623775
COSTS RELATING TO REVENUES	3307574	573795	0	573795	0	3881369
SELLING, GENERAL AND ADMINISTRATIVE EXPENSES	1782875	94065	-1575	92490	-548 (B)	1874817
OPERATING INCOME	798586	66880	1575	68455	548	867589
INTEREST INCOME/EXPENSE, NET	32283	-12360	-4446	-16806	-41041 (B)	-25564
OTHER DEDUCTIONS, NET	23615	0	0	0	21787 (B)	45402
INCOME FROM CONTINUING OPERATIONS BEFORE INCOME TAXES	807254	54520	-2871	51649	-62280	796623
INCOME TAXES	360184	13650	-491	13159	-18879	354464
INCOME FROM CONTINUING OPERATIONS	447070	40870	-2380	38490	-43401	442159
INCOME FROM DISCONTINUED OPERATIONS	34712	0	0	0	0	34712
NET INCOME	$ 481782	$ 40870	$ -2380	$ 38490	$ -43401	$ 476871
PER SHARE OF COMMON STOCK						
INCOME FROM CONTINUING OPERATIONS	$ 3.62	$ 4.81		$ 4.76		$ 3.25
INCOME FROM DISCONTINUED OPERATIONS	.28	0		0		.26
NET INCOME	$ 3.62	$ 4.81		$ 4.76		$ 3.25
NET INCOME, ASSUMING FULL DILUTION	$ 3.90	$ 4.45		$ 4.48		$ 3.51
WEIGHTED AVERAGE NUMBER OF COMMON AND COMMON SHARE EQUIVALENTS (IN THOUSANDS)						
PRIMARY	123610	8489		8094		135856
FULLY DILUTED	123610	9980		9585		135856

SEE NOTES TO PRO FORMA COMBINED FINANCIAL STATEMENTS

The Coca-Cola Company

Notes to Exhibits 6 and 7
Pro Forma Combined Financial Statement

NOTE A   ACCOUNTING FOR THE MERGER:

THE MERGER WILL BE ACCOUNTED FOR AS A PURCHASE OF COLUMBIA BY COCA COLA AND IN ACCORDANCE WITH GENERALLY ACCEPTED ACCOUNTING PRINCIPLES, THE PURCHASE PRICE WILL BE ALLOCATED TO COLUMBIA'S CONSOLIDATED ASSETS AND LIABILITIES BASED UPON THEIR FAIR VALUES, AS DETERMINED BY STUDIES TO BE UNDERTAKEN, AS OF THE EFFECTIVE TIME OF THE MERGER.   FOR PRO FORMA PURPOSES, IT IS ASSUMED THAT THE COST TO COCA COLA FOR COLUMBIA WILL EXCEED THE NET BOOK VALUE OF COLUMBIA'S CONSOLIDATED ASSETS AND LIABILITIES.   THIS ASSUMED EXCESS WILL RESULT IN FUTURE CHARGES TO THE COMBINED RESULTS OF OPERATIONS OF THE TWO COMPANIES IN AN AMOUNT WHICH DEPENDS UPON THE PARTICULAR ALLOCATIONS MADE TO THE VARIOUS ASSETS AND LIABILITIES OF COLUMBIA.   THESE CHARGES ARE NOT DEDUCTIBLE FOR INCOME TAX PURPOSES.   ALLOCATION OF THIS EXCESS IS NOT PRESENTLY PRACTICABLE AND IS PRESENTED IN THE PRO FORMA COMBINED FINANCIAL STATEMENTS AS "EXCESS OF COST OVER NET ASSETS ACQUIRED IN MERGER."

NOTE B   PURCHASE PRICE:

THE ESTIMATED VALUE OF THE AGGREGATE PURCHASE PRICE IS APPROXIMATELY $753,855,000 BASED UPON THE PER SHARE CLOSING PRICE ($34,375) OF COCA COLA COMMON STOCK ON JANUARY 15, 1982.   AT DECEMBER 26, 1981, THERE WERE 10,204,470 SHARES OF COLUMBIA COMMON STOCK ISSUED AND OUTSTANDING, ASSUMING THE CONVERSION OF COLUMBIA'S CONVERTIBLE DEBENTURES AND THE EXERCISE OF ALL STOCK OPTIONS.   HAD THE MERGER BEEN CONSUMMATED ON DECEMBER 26, 1981, COCA COLA WOULD HAVE EXCHANGED 12,245,365 SHARES OF ITS STOCK PLUS $332,921,000 FOR ALL 10,204,470 SHARES OF COLUMBIA COMMON STOCK.

THE PRO FORMA ADJUSTMENT FOR THE PURCHASE PRICE ASSUMES THAT THE CASH PORTION IS FINANCED BY COCA COLA WITH LONG-TERM DEBT, IN THE PRINCIPAL AMOUNT OF $328,836,000 BEARING INTEREST AT AN ANNUAL RATE OF 14% AND WITH THE ESTIMATED NET PROCEEDS FROM THE EXERCISE OF COLUMBIA STOCK OPTIONS OF APPROXIMATELY $4,085,000.

THE EXCESS OF COST OVER THE NET BOOK VALUE OF THE CONSOLIDATED ASSETS AND LIABILITIES ACQUIRED IN THE MERGER (ESTIMATED TO BE $544,681,000, AFTER THE ELIMINATION OF AMOUNTS FOR DEFERRED INCOME TAXES AND THE EXCESS OF COST OVER NET ASSETS ACQUIRED PREVIOUSLY RECORDED BY COLUMBIA OF APPROXIMATELY $1,365,000 AND $19,173,000, RESPECTIVELY) IS BEING AMORTIZED ON A STRAIGHT-LINE BASIS OVER 25 YEARS AT THE RATE OF APPROXIMATELY $21,787,000 PER YEAR.   "SELLING, GENERAL, AND ADMINISTRATIVE EXPENSES" HAVE BEEN REDUCED BY $548,000 IN THE PRO FORMA COMBINED STATEMENT OF INCOME TO ELIMINATE AMORTIZATION OF THE EXCESS OF COST OVER NET ASSETS PREVIOUSLY RECOGNIZED BY COLUMBIA.

NOTE C   COLUMBIA COMMON STOCK REPURCHASE:

ON FEBRUARY 25, 1981, COLUMBIA REPURCHASED 2,438,000 SHARES OF COLUMBIA COMMON STOCK HELD BY CERTAIN STOCKHOLDERS.   SEE NOTES TO EXHIBITS 3 AND 4: NOTE C.

EXHIBIT 8

The Coca-Cola Company

Common Stock Prices and Dividends
The Coca-Cola Company and Columbia Pictures Incorporated

| YEAR | THE COCA-COLA COMPANY COMMON STOCK PRICE | | | | COLUMBIA PICTURES INCORPORATED COMMON STOCK PRICE | | | |
	HIGH	LOW	CLOSE	DIVIDEND	HIGH	LOW	CLOSE	DIVIDEN
1979								
QUARTER 1	46.125	39.75	43.25	0.49	25.375	18.25	21.375	0.10
QUARTER 2	42.125	36.625	41.25	0.49	26.375	20.125	22.00	0.10
QUARTER 3	40.875	36.375	39.25	0.49	26.25	21.375	23.125	0.00
QUARTER 4	36.75	31.50	34.50	0.49	37.25	22.50	34.125	.125
1980								
QUARTER 1	38.875	28.875	31.50	0.54	36.75	27.00	30.25	.125
QUARTER 2	35.875	29.75	33.00	0.54	32.00	27.00	29.25	.125
QUARTER 3	38.875	32.00	32.25	0.54	37.00	28.50	33.75	.125
QUARTER 4	34.125	29.125	33.375	0.54	44.50	32.00	43.375	0.15
1981								
QUARTER 1	37.875	28.875	31.50	0.58	44.50	35.00	44.25	0.15
QUARTER 2	40.25	33.75	34.75	0.58	45.375	35.75	36.25	0.15
QUARTER 3	34.75	30.50	33.75	0.58	39.125	31.50	34.00	0.15
QUARTER 4	37.00	33.00	34.75	0.58	47.50	33.875	44.375	0.15
1982								
QUARTER 1	36.875	29.75	32.75	0.58	68.875	41.625	67.25	0.15

EXHIBIT 8 (Continued)

COMMON STOCK PRICES, DIVIDENDS, AND PRICE/EARNINGS
THE DOW JONES INDUSTRIAL AVERAGE

CALENDAR YEAR	CLOSING PRICE	COMPANY DIVIDENDS	PRICE/EARNINGS
1979			
QUARTER 1	838.74	12.11	6.9
QUARTER 2	841.98	12.49	6.5
QUARTER 3	878.67	12.51	6.4
QUARTER 4	838.74	13.87	6.7
1980			
QUARTER 1	785.75	13.23	6.5
QUARTER 2	867.92	13.20	7.5
QUARTER 3	932.42	13.53	8.4
QUARTER 4	963.99	14.40	7.9
1981			
QUARTER 1	1003.9	13.86	8.1
QUARTER 2	976.88	14.19	7.6
QUARTER 3	849.98	13.73	6.9
QUARTER 4	875.00	14.44	7.7
1982			
QUARTER 1	822.77	13.92	8.5

EXHIBIT 9

The Coca-Cola Company

Earnings Per Share

YEAR	COCA–COLA WITHOUT MERGER EARNINGS (IN MILLIONS)	EARNINGS PER SHARE	COCA–COLA WITH COLUMBIA EARNINGS (IN MILLIONS)	EARNINGS PER SHARE *
1977	$ 331.2	2.68		
1978	374.7	3.03		
1979	420.1	3.40		
1980	422.1	3.42		
1981	481.8	3.90		
1982 EST. *	481.0	3.90	$ 512.0 EST.	$ 3.77
1983 EST.	529.0	4.28		
1984 EST.	555.0	4.49		
1985 EST.	583.0	4.72		
1986 EST.	612.0	4.95		

YEAR	COLUMBIA EARNINGS (IN MILLIONS)	EARNINGS PER SHARE
1977	$ 34.6	$ 4.04
1978	68.8	7.40
1979	39.1	4.01
1980	44.9	4.50
1981	44.3	4.66
1982 EST.	31.1	3.26
1983 EST.		
1984 EST.		
1985 EST.		
1986 EST.		

*
ESTIMATED FIGURES ARE BASED ON CASEWRITER'S FORECASTS.
EARNINGS PER SHARE FOR COMBINED COMPANIES IS BASED ON THE ASSUMPTION THAT THE
MAXIMUM NUMBER OF SHARES PERMITTED TO BE ISSUED BY COCA–COLA, 12,245,365, WOULD,
IN FACT, BE ISSUED.

CASE 22

Holiday Inns, Incorporated

During late October of 1979, representatives of the boards of directors of Holiday Inns, Inc., and Harrah's sat down to discuss a new set of merger terms for the two companies. A merger agreement had been executed on September 24, 1979, where Holiday Inns was obligated to issue not more than 1.775 shares of Holiday Inns' common stock for each share of Harrah's common stock. If the market price of Holiday Inn stock was below $20 per share during the months prior to the actual merger date, Harrah's could terminate the transaction.

On September 28, 1979, the price of Holiday Inns' common stock declined below $20 per share for the first time since the terms of the merger were negotiated. By October 26, 1979, the price had declined to $16.75 and the managements of Harrah's and Holiday Inns decided that it was no longer practical to proceed with the original merger agreement.

BACKGROUND OF HOLIDAY INNS, INC.

Holiday Inns was incorporated in 1954 in Tennessee by Kemmons Wilson, a Memphis real estate developer who built his first motel shortly after a miserable family vacation in "cramped and costly" hotels. By the late 1960s, the company was building a new inn somewhere in the world every 2½ days. As of August 31, 1979, there were 1736 Holiday Inns facilities located in 55 countries, making Holiday Inns the world's largest hotel chain. (Financial statements for Holiday Inns are provided in Exhibits 1 and 2.)

Holiday Inns growth came to an abrupt halt with the 1973–74 Arab oil embargo. As travel declined, occupancy rates and operating profits fell; in just the first quarter of 1974, profits plunged by 64 percent from the previous year level. Alarmed, the company brought in Mr.

This case was prepared by and used with the permission of professor Richard E. White of the University of North Florida.

Roy E. Winegardner as vice-chairman and heir apparent to Mr. Wilson. His job was to restore the company to profitability in a time of rapid change and increasing competition.

The new management team decided to confine the company's business to hotels and restaurants, and it set about selling off diverse operations acquired during the years of rapid growth. The plan worked. Holiday Inns' net income soared over the next five years to a record $62.8 million in 1978—up from $26.9 million in 1974.

Wall Street was not impressed with the results. Holiday Inns' price-earnings ratio was 8 versus Hilton's price-earnings ratio of 12. "We gave them an A-plus for their efforts, but they still were not in the same league as, say, a Hilton," said Joseph Doyle, a vice-president and analyst at Smith Barney, Harris and Upham. "The reason for the difference is gambling. With only two casinos, both in Las Vegas, Hilton earned a 26.4% return on equity in 1978 compared with Holiday Inns' 11.9% return. Hilton's casinos consistently earn between 35% and 40% return on investment, compared with a 15% return for the Holiday Inn in Las Vegas, one of the company's best properties."

It became painfully clear to Mr. Winegardner that the company must abandon its opposition to gambling. It was not going to be an easy task to accomplish. Holiday Inns was known as the company that opened management meetings with a prayer, provided chaplains on call for its guests, and did not allow bars in its inns until the early 1960s. Finally, in March, 1977, after the retirement of several directors opposed to gambling, the board of directors voted unanimously to permit casino-hotels.

The company began to move rapidly into the gambling business after the dis-senting directors retired. In September 1978, Holiday Inns announced a joint venture with L & M Walter Company for a $75 million hotel-casino complex in the marina area of Atlantic City and a wholly owned hotel-casino in the Boardwalk area for $175 million, also in Atlantic City. On August 31, 1979, Holiday Inns acquired, for $17 million, a 40 percent interest in River Boat Casino, Inc., which operated contiguous to the Holiday Inn-Center Strip in Las Vegas. The company's biggest star was to be Harrah's, the nation's oldest and largest gambling concern with hotels and casinos in Reno and Lake Tahoe, Nevada.

BACKGROUND OF HARRAH'S

Harrah's was founded by William F. Harrah in 1937 and was continuously operated under Mr. Harrah's control from that time until his death on June 30, 1978. Presently, Mr. Harrah's estate, for which Mr. Mead Dixon, chairman of the board of Harrah's, was the sole executor, owned 5,930,301 shares (approximately 70.1 percent) of the outstanding Harrah's common stock. No other stockholder controlled over 5 percent of the outstanding common stock. (Financial statements for Harrah's are provided in Exhibits 3 and 4.)

Harrah's was engaged in the operation of two luxury hotel-casino facilities, two theater-restaurants, two show lounges, a variety of restaurants and cocktail bars, and the world's largest collection of antique, classic, and special-interest automobiles. The hotel-casinos were among the largest in the Reno and Lake Tahoe area. However, in Reno, three Las Vegas hotel-casino operators had commenced operations of hotel-casinos since May 1978, and other existing casinos had expanded their facilities. Harrah's credited the continuing upgrading and expansion of its facilities and expanding customer base as factors primary to its continuing ability to compete successfully and to its financial growth.

Harrah's had increased its earnings at a compounded growth rate of 19 percent per year for the past 27 years. Gross revenues for 1979 were up 6.7 percent. The decline in earnings for 1979 was due to the intense competition for labor in the Reno-Lake Tahoe area causing labor costs to accelerate rapidly. Labor costs, which comprised over 40 percent of the total operating costs, rose $7.2 million (11.2 percent) in 1979, although the number of employees did not change significantly. The other factor affecting earnings was the increased promotional expense due to new hotel-casino openings in the area. Promotional expenses were up $6.1 million (14.7 percent) to $47.8 million in 1979. Harrah's anticipated that employee and promotional expenses may continue to have an adverse effect on its earnings for 1980. Although the opening of new hotels and casinos decreased the company's market share and earnings, Harrah's believed such developments would ultimately favorably affect its revenues and earnings due to the increased number of tourists and gambling customers that would be attracted to the Reno-Lake Tahoe area.

BACKGROUND AND REASONS FOR THE MERGER

Prior to 1977, the management of Holiday Inns closely examined the potential of its existing and possibly new lines of business and determined that there was limited growth opportunity in the transportation business. A decision was made

to concentrate the assets of Holiday Inns in the hospitality business, focusing on hotels and two new areas, free-standing restaurants and casino gambling. During 1977 and 1978, the board of directors endorsed entry into casino gambling. In 1979 Holiday Inns entered into the family restaurant business by acquiring Perkins Cake & Steak, Inc. Similarly, Holiday Inns believed that the most desirable way to enter the casino gambling business was through acquisition of a company with a proven record of operating results and an established capability in the management and control of casinos. An in-depth review by Holiday Inns of possible candidates for acquisition identified Harrah's as the most desirable choice.

Considerable discussions were held between the managements of Harrah's and Holiday Inns, but no firm acquisition offers were made because it appeared to be premature to find a common ground for a merger. As a result of the discussions, in July 1979 the managements of the two companies decided upon the joint-venture form as a means for developing their respective plans to expand in the casino gambling business. In September 1979 the joint venture acquired a 4.5-acre parcel of real estate on the Boardwalk in Atlantic City for approximately $27 million for the purpose of building a 500-room hotel and a 60,000-square-foot casino.

The effective working relationship established between the managements of Harrah's and Holiday Inns during the formation and early phases of the joint venture provided a basis for talks regarding the possible acquisition of Harrah's by Holiday Inns. When the discussions commenced, Harrah's management expressed the view that it may be desirable for Harrah's stockholders to continue to own an equity interest in the combined company and that an acquisition in a tax-free reorganization would be preferable.

Holiday Inns with their investment banker, Solomon Brothers, analyzed the possibility of a transaction in which all of Harrah's common stock would be converted into Holiday Inns common stock and determined that such a transaction would not be in the best interests of Holiday Inns or its stockholders. As a result of its evaluations, Holiday Inns determined that, assuming the price and terms of a transaction could be agreed to, it could partially accommodate Harrah's desires as to continuing equity participation and tax-free treatment, while at the same time avoiding an all-stock transaction, by structuring a transaction in which 51 percent of Harrah's common stock would be converted into Holiday Inns common stock in a tax-free reorganization, and 49 percent of Harrah's common stock would be exchanged for cash. All of the cash would have to be paid to the estate with Harrah's other shareholders receiving stock in a tax-free transaction. On September 24, 1979, the merger agreement between Holiday Inns and Harrah's was executed.

As a consequence of the estate's ownership of Harrah's stock, any cash it received on a merger of Harrah's could be treated for federal income tax purposes as a dividend unless the number of shares for which cash was received equaled at least approximately 40 percent of the total outstanding stock. Moreover, any merger would accelerate the federal estate tax on the estate, which could otherwise be payable over a 15-year period, and the estate would require substantial cash to pay such tax. Approximately 51 percent of the out-

standing shares of Harrah's common stock would be converted into shares of Holiday Inns common stock having a value of $35.50 per share of Harrah's common stock determined pursuant to a specified formula, and approximately 49 percent of the outstanding shares of Harrah's common stock owned by the estate would be converted into the right to receive $35.50 cash per share. Holiday Inns was not obligated to issue more than 1.775 shares of Holiday Inns common stock for each share of Harrah's common stock. If the market of Holiday Inns common dropped below $20 per share prior to the merger date, Harrah's could terminate the transaction.

On September 28, 1979, the price of Holiday Inns common stock declined below $20 per share. By October 26, 1979, the price had declined to 16¾ and Harrah's canceled the merger agreement.

NEGOTIATIONS REENTERED— OCTOBER 30, 1979

Holiday Inns was concerned that weakness in the price of their common stock might make any future agreement impossible. The price of the common stock had declined from 22⅞ to 16¼ in the six-week period, ending October 30, 1979. It was felt that the drop in the stock price was due to the decline in the stock market rather than a negative reaction to the proposed merger. The Dow Jones Industrial Average had dropped to 792 from 900 in the same six-week period.

Holiday Inns began to consider whether a convertible debenture might be used instead of a direct exchange of shares. In this way they could exchange shares at a higher price in the future and the convertible debenture would also avoid immediate dilution of the earnings per share. It appeared long-term debt could be raised for about 12 percent. Convertible debentures might be issued in the 10 percent range, depending on the conversion price set by the negotiators. It was difficult to determine how long these rates would apply. The prime rate, which had been stable all summer, rose to 12.90 percent in September and was at 14.39 percent by late October. The company felt that it was only a matter of time before long-term rates began to rise more sharply.

The success or failure of the merger would depend on whether Holiday Inns negotiators could offer a satisfactory price to Harrah's stockholders as well as meeting the needs of the Harrah estate. Holiday Inns also had to determine the form in which the exchange would be made. (Data related to market prices, earnings and dividends, earnings forecasts, and price-earnings ratios are provided in Exhibits 5 to 8.)

EXHIBIT 1

Balance Sheets for Holiday Inns, Inc.

	Dec. 31, 1978	Aug. 24, 1979
Assets		
Current assets		
Cash	$ 18,366	$ 23,283
Temporary cash investments	138,105	191,133
Accounts and notes receivable	120,294	131,669
Inventories	19,237	19,248
Prepayment and other current assets	8,028	8,750
Total current assets	$ 304,030	$ 374,083
Capital construction fund	4,070	4,640
Investments and long-term receivables	60,323	74,202
Net property and equipment	651,461	720,469
Deferred charges and other assets	15,016	54,469
Net assets of discontinued operations	99,489	—
Total assets	$1,134,389	$1,227,863
Current liabilities		
Accounts payable	$ 52,241	$ 54,416
Accrued expenses	123,944	122,674
Other current liabilities	20,712	15,540
Current portion of long-term debt	25,568	22,829
Total current liabilities	$ 222,465	$ 215,459
Long-term debt		
5–12¾% mortgages, due in 1998	124,540	119,560
5–9¼% U.S. government Merchant Marine Bonds, due in 1998	72,645	69,588
5–15¾% notes payable, maturities to 1998	43,957	75,850
8% debentures, maturities to 1985	16,826	8,380
6–16⅓% capital lease obligations, maturities to 2003	43,208	54,997
Deferred credits	40,920	47,650
Deferred income taxes	17,440	17,779
Total long-term debt	$ 359,536	$ 393,804
Stockholders' equity		
Series A common, $1.125 par; authorized 5,000,000, issued 704,961 and 714,036 shares	$ 803	$ 793
Common, $1.50 par, authorized 60,000,000 shares; issued 32,340,679 and 30,289,895 shares	45,435	48,511
Capital surplus	118,648	153,877
Retained earnings	395,982	423,261
Capital stock treasury at cost (common 341,634 and 368,869; Series A 72,192 shares)	(8,480)	(7,842)
Total stockholders' equity	$ 552,388	$ 618,600
Total liabilities and stockholders' equity	$1,134,389	$1,227,863

EXHIBIT 2

Income Statements for Holiday Inns, Inc.
(dollar figures in thousands)

	Years Ended December 31			Eight Months Ended August 24 (Unaudited)	
	1976	1977	1978	1978	1979
Net revenues	$ 736,366	$ 791,430	$ 935,823	$ 592,284	$ 720,664
Costs and expenses					
Operating costs	611,437	642,406	736,093	466,817	575,861
Depreciation and amortization	44,312	46,558	49,911	32,200	35,786
Interest	25,938	23,814	27,581	18,033	17,380
Foreign currency translation loss (gain)	3,076	1,009	717	625	(19)
Income from continuing operations before income taxes	$ 51,603	$ 77,643	$ 94,521	$ 74,609	$ 91,656
Provision for income taxes	18,893	32,713	42,016	31,930	39,412
Income from continuing operations	32,710	44,930	52,505	42,679	52,244
Discontinued operations, less applicable income taxes*	6,139	7,726	10,287	9,311	(14,527)
Net income	$ 38,849	$ 52,656	$ 62,792	$ 51,990	$ 37,717
Income per common share	$ 1.27	$ 1.71	$ 2.04	$ 1.69	$ 1.20
Average number of common shares outstanding	30,657	30,762	30,854	30,846	31,351

*On August 21, 1979, the company sold its Trailways, Inc., bus subsidiary and ertain related operations for a loss. The loss from discontinued operations equals a loss of $.46 per share.

EXHIBIT 3

Holiday Inns, Inc.

*Balance Sheets for Harrah's for June 30, 1979
(in thousands of dollars)*

	June 30, 1979
Current assets	
Cash	$ 10,587
Short-term investments	14,000
Receivables	6,658
Inventories	4,891
Prepaid expenses	2,999
Total current assets	$ 39,135
Unexpended mortgage bond proceeds	18,000
Property, plant, and equipment	201,974
Less: accumulated depreciation & amortization	54,568
Net property, plant, and equipment	$ 147,406
Leasehold improvements	3,019
Unamortized lease acquisition cost	1,077
Notes receivable	1,106
Deferred charges and other assets	2,545
Total assets	$ 212,288
Current liabilities	
Notes payable	$ 621
Accounts payable	2,861
Accrued expenses	5,437
Retentions	2,605
Federal income taxes	1,750
Dividends payable	1,057
Total current liabilities	$ 14,331
Long-term debt	
9½% first mortgage bonds due in 1996	$ 50,000
Notes payable	1,628
Total long-term debt	$ 51,628
Other liabilities	$ 2,162
Deferred federal income taxes	5,250
Shareholders' equity	
Common, $.50 par; authorized 25 million shares; issued and outstanding 8,459,019 shares	4,230
Additional paid-in capital	26,656
Retained earnings	110,819
Less: deferred compensation under restricted stock plan	2,788
Total stockholders' equity	$ 138,917
Total liabilities & stockholders' equity	$ 212,288

EXHIBIT 4

Holiday Inns, Inc.

Income Statements for Harrah's
(dollar figures in thousands)

	Years Ended June 30			Eight Months Ended August 31 (unaudited)	
	1977	1978	1979	1978	1979
Net revenues	$161,591	$185,011	$195,558	$129,262	$140,495
Costs and expenses					
Operating costs	123,180	139,696	153,313	99,319	107,005
Depreciation and amortization	6,599	7,599	8,246	5,051	5,691
Interest	4,691	6,534	4,691	3,688	3,368
Income from operations before income taxes	27,121	31,182	29,308	21,204	24,431
Provisions for income taxes	12,475	14,300	13,400	9,611	11,156
Net income	$ 14,646	$ 16,882	$ 15,908	$ 11,593	$ 13,275
Income per common share	$ 2.08	$ 2.36	$ 1.92	$ 1.57	$ 1.57
Number of common shares outstanding	7,055	7,155	8,299	7,384	8,455

EXHIBIT 5

Holiday Inns, Inc.

Market Prices of Common Stock of Holiday Inns, Inc.
and Harrah's for 1975–1979

	Holiday Inns, Inc.		Harrah's	
Year	High	Low	High	Low
1975	$16.50	$ 5.125	$10.625	$ 8.00
1976	20.00	10.625	14.875	12.00
1977	16.125	11.125	18.125	13.375
1978				
First quarter	16.875	14.125	19.50	16.125
Second quarter	19.375	15.875	30.875	18.25
Third quarter	32.75	17.00	40.50	21.25
Fourth quarter	28.25	15.50	40.50	21.25
1979				
First quarter	20.375	15.25	27.25	17.00
Second quarter	21.50	16.00	25.875	18.125
Third quarter	22.875	16.875	32.750	19.125
Closing prices for Nov. 1, 1979	$16.25		$30.25	

EXHIBIT 6

Holiday Inns, Inc.

Earnings Per Share, Dividends Per Share, and Book Value for Holiday Inns, Inc. and Harrah's

Fiscal Year	I. Holiday Inns, Inc.		
	Earnings Per Share	Dividends Per Share	Book Value
1975	$ 1.35	$ .350	
1976	1.27	.400	
1977	1.71	.465	
1978	2.04	.560	
1979	2.25 (est)	.66 (est)	
1978, August 24, (8 mo.)	1.69	.280	
1979, August 24, (8 mo.)	1.21	.330	$18.77

Fiscal Year	II. Harrah's		
	Earnings Per Share	Dividends Per Share	Book Value
1975	$ 1.50	$ .260	
1976	1.67	.300	
1977	2.08	.350	
1978	2.36	.425	
1979	1.92	.500	
1978, August 31, (8 mo.)	1.57	.225	
1979, August 31, (8 mo.)	1.57	.250	$16.42

EXHIBIT 7

Five-Year Forecast of Earnings for Holiday Inns, Inc.;
Excluding Harrah's

	1980	1981	1982	1983	1984
Net Income Available to Common Stockholders (in millions)	74.5	78.7	83.3	88.2	93.4
Number of Shares Outstanding (in millions)	32.667	32.667	32.667	32.667	32.667
Primary Earnings Per Share	2.28	2.41	2.55	2.70	2.86

*Casewriter's estimate.

EXHIBIT 8

Holiday Inns, Inc.

Price-Earnings Ratios of Selected
Companies in the Casino-Hotel Business

Company	Price-Earnings Ratio
Bally Manufacturing	21
Caesar's World	26
Hilton	10
Holiday Inns	8

CASE 23

W.T. Grant Company

On October 2, 1975, W.T. Grant filed for protection under Chapter XI of the National Bankruptcy Act. This action followed suspension of trading in Grant's stock on the New York Stock Exchange on Monday, September 30, 1975, and brought to a head the financial problems of Grant that had begun to surface in recent years. For the fiscal year ended January 31, 1975, Grant was the nation's seventeenth largest retailer with almost 1200 stores, a payroll of over 82,000 employees, and sales of $1.7 billion. Financial data for W.T. Grant is provided in Exhibits 1 through 7.

Chapter XI of the National Bankruptcy Act provides opportunities for a business in financial difficulty to seek the

protection of the courts while it attempts to recover going concern status. Various arrangements are possible under Chapter XI but, in general, management of the debtor company continues to control the assets and operations of the company while a plan for the payment of its debts is developed and implemented. A committee of the company's creditors is normally elected to work with management of the troubled concern.

In contrast, Chapter X of the Act, when invoked by either the debtor firm or its creditors, generally provides for a court-appointed trustee to assume control of the company's assets and operations. All classes of creditors, as well as shareholders, have a stronger voice and,

---

This case was prepared by and used with the permission of Professors James A. Largay III and Clyde P. Stickney, Jr. of The Amos Tuck School of Business Administration, Dartmouth College.

consequently, more protection as rehabilitation of the company is planned and implemented.

GRANT'S LAST DECADE

The Marketing of Grant

During 1963–1973, W.T. Grant opened 612 new stores and expanded 91 others. Much of that expansion was concentrated in the 1969–1973 period when 369 new stores were opened, 15 on one particularly busy day. Louis C. Lustenberger, president of Grant from 1959–1968, started the expansion program although later, as a director, he became concerned over dimensions of the growth and the problems it generated. After Mr. Lustenberger stepped down, the pace of expansion was stepped up under the leadership of Chairman Edward Staley and President Richard W. Mayer.

Historically, Grant's reputation was built on low-priced soft goods; its clientele tended to be lower-income consumers, with its major competition being growing discount chains like K-Mart. As the expansion program developed, however, Grant began to alter its marketing strategy to compete also with established private-brand retailers such as Montgomery Ward and J.C. Penney. Furniture and private-brand major appliances were added to the product line.

To help customers finance purchases of furniture, appliances, and other items, a credit card system was implemented. Each store administered its own credit department and had authority to accept or reject credit applications and establish credit terms. At most stores customers were allowed 36 months to pay for their purchases; the minimum monthly payment was $1. Consistent with this decentralization of credit administration, inventory and pricing decisions were also made by local store managers. Compensation of store managers included salary plus stated percentages of the store's sales and profits.

Financing the Expansion

Grant leased most of its store space: in 1974–75, Grant was leasing approximately 52 million square feet of space in 1070 stores around the country. Since Grant was gone by the time the Financial Accounting Standards Board issued Statement of Financial Accounting Standard No. 13, its long-term leasing arrangements were not reported on its balance sheet. Plant assets consisted mostly of store fixtures. Grant's recorded long-term debt consisted primarily of two $100 million issues in 1971 and 1973.

Banks entered the picture in a big way in 1974. In the spring of that year, both Moody's and Standard & Poors eliminated their credit rating for Grant's commercial paper. To provide financing, a group of 143 banks agreed to offer lines of credit totaling $525 million. A short-term loan of $600 million was obtained in September 1974 with three banks—Morgan Guaranty, Chase Manhattan, and First National City—absorbing about $230 million of the total. These same three banks also loaned $50 million out of a total of $100 million provided to Grant's finance subsidiary.

Dividends had been paid consistently from 1906 until August 27, 1974, when they were passed for the first time in the company's history. Treasury stock costing almost $50 million was acquired during 1969–1972.

Grant's financial reports were affected by changes in accounting policies. In fiscal year 1970 the company began consolidating its wholly owned finance subsidiary. Through fiscal year 1974 Grant recorded the total finance charge on credit sales as income in the year of the sale. Beginning in fiscal year 1975, finance charges on credit sales were recognized as income over the life of the installment contract.

Advance and Retreat—The Attempt to Save Grant

Support of the banks during the summer of 1974 was accompanied by a top management change. Messrs. Staley and Mayer had stepped down in the spring and were replaced in August 1974 by James G. Kendrick, brought in from Zeller's Ltd., Grant's Canadian subsidiary. As chief executive officer, Mr. Kendrick moved to cut Grant's losses. Payroll was slashed significantly, 126 unprofitable stores were closed, and the big-ticket furniture and appliance lines were phased out. New store space brought on-line in 1975 was 75 percent less than in 1974.

The positive effects of these moves could not overcome the disastrous events of early 1975. In January Grant defaulted on about $75 million in interest payments, and in February results of operations for the year ended January 31, 1975, were released. Grant reported a loss of $177 million with substantial losses from credit operations accounting for 60 percent of the total.

The banks now assumed a more active role in what was becoming a struggle to save Grant. Robert H. Anderson, a vice-president of Sears, was offered a lucrative $2.5 million contract, decided to accept the challenge to turn the company around, and joined Grant as its new president in April 1975. Mr. Kendrick remained as chairman of the board. The banks holding 90 percent of Grant's debt extended their loans from June 2, 1975, to March 31, 1976. The balance of about $56 million was repaid on June 2. A major problem confronting Mr. Anderson was to maintain the continued flow of merchandise into Grant stores. Suppliers had become skeptical of Grant's ability to pay for merchandise and, in August, the banks agreed to subordinate $300 million of debt to the suppliers' claims for merchandise shipped. With the approach of the Christmas shopping season, the need for merchandise had become critical. Despite the bank's subordination of their claims to those of suppliers and the intensive cultivation of suppliers by Mr. Anderson, sufficient quantities of merchandise were not being received in the stores.

During this period, Grant reported a $111.3 million net loss for the six months just ended on July 31, 1975. Sales had declined 15 percent from the comparable period in 1974. Mr. Kendrick observed that a return to profitability before the fourth quarter was unlikely.

On October 2, 1975, the Chapter XI bankruptcy petition was filed by the company. The rehabilitation effort was formally under way, and the protection provided by Chapter XI permitted a continuation of the reorganization and rehabilitation activities for the next four months. On February 6, 1976, after store closings and liquidations of inventories had generated $320 million in cash, the creditors committee voted for liquidation and W.T. Grant ceased to exist.

EXHIBIT 1

W.T. Grant Company

Comparative Balance Sheets
(as originally reported)

January 31:	1966	1967	1968	1969	1970[a]	1971	1972	1973	1974	1975[b]
Assets										
Cash and marketable securities	$ 22,559	$ 37,507	$ 25,047	$ 28,460	$ 32,977	$ 34,009	$ 49,851	$ 30,943	$ 45,951	$ 79,642
Accounts receivable[c]	110,943	110,305	133,406	154,829	368,267	419,731	477,324	542,751	598,799	431,201
Inventories	151,365	174,631	183,721	208,483	222,128	260,492	298,676	399,533	450,637	407,357
Other current assets	—	—	—	—	5,037	5,246	5,378	6,649	7,299	6,581
Total current assets	$284,867	$322,443	$342,174	$391,772	$628,409	$719,478	$831,229	$979,876	$1,102,686	$924,781
Investments	38,419	40,800	56,609	62,854	20,694	23,936	32,367	35,581	45,451	49,764
Property, plant, and equipment (net)	40,367	48,071	47,572	49,213	55,311	61,832	77,173	91,420	100,984	101,932
Other assets	5,231	5,704	8,737	6,744	2,381	2,382	3,901	3,821	3,862	5,790
Total assets	$368,884	$417,018	$455,092	$510,583	$706,795	$807,628	$944,670	$1,110,698	$1,252,983	$1,082,267
Equities										
Short-term debt	$ —	$ —	$ 300	$ 180	$182,132	$246,420	$237,741	$390,034	$453,097	$600,695
Accounts payable	64,813	80,802	91,108	109,792	104,144	118,091	124,990	112,896	103,910	147,211
Current deferred taxes	35,038	46,371	52,839	60,848	80,443	94,489	112,846	130,137	133,057	2,000
Total current liabilities	$ 99,851	$127,173	$144,247	$170,820	$366,719	$459,000	$475,577	$633,067	$690,064	$749,906
Long-term debt	70,000	70,000	62,622	43,251	35,402	32,301	128,432	126,672	220,336	216,341
Noncurrent deferred taxes	6,269	7,034	7,551	7,941	8,286	8,518	9,664	11,926	14,649	—
Other long-term liabilities	4,784	4,949	4,858	5,519	5,700	5,773	5,252	4,694	4,195	2,183
Total liabilities	$180,904	$209,156	$219,278	$227,531	$416,107	$505,592	$618,925	$776,359	$929,244	$968,430
Prefered stock	$ 15,000	$ 15,000	$ 14,750	$ 13,250	$ 11,450	$ 9,600	$ 9,053	$ 8,600	$ 7,465	$ 7,465
Common stock	15,375	15,636	16,191	17,318	17,883	18,180	18,529	18,588	18,599	18,599
Additional paid-in capital	25,543	27,977	37,428	59,945	71,555	78,116	85,195	86,146	85,910	83,914
Retained earnings	132,062	149,249	167,445	192,539	211,679	230,435	244,508	261,154	248,461	37,674
Total	$187,980	$207,862	$235,814	$283,052	$312,567	$336,331	$357,285	$374,488	$360,435	$147,652
Less cost of treasury stock	—	—	—	—	(21,879)	(34,295)	(31,540)	(40,149)	(36,696)	(33,815)

(Continued)

231

EXHIBIT 1 (Continued)

January 31:	1966	1967	1968	1969	1970ᵃ	1971	1972	1973	1974	1975ᵇ
Total stockholders' equity	$187,980	$207,862	$235,814	$283,052	$290,688	$302,036	$325,745	$334,339	$323,739	$113,837
Total equities	$368,884	$417,018	$455,092	$510,583	$706,795	$807,628	$944,670	$1,110,698	$1,252,983	$1,082,267

ᵃ In the year ending January 31, 1970, W. T. Grant changed its consolidation policy and commenced consolidating its wholly owned finance subsidiary.

ᵇ In the year ending January 31, 1975, W. T. Grant changed its method of recognizing finance income on installment sales. In prior years all finance income was recognized in the year of the sale. Beginning in the 1975 fiscal period, finance income was recognized over the time the installment receivable was outstanding.

ᶜ Accounts receivable is composed of the following:

	1966	1967	1968	1969	1970	1971	1972	1973	1974	1975
Customer installment receivables	$114,470	$114,928	$140,507	$162,219	$381,757	$433,730	$493,859	$556,091	$602,305	$518,387
Less allowances for uncollectible accounts	(7,065)	(9,383)	(11,307)	(13,074)	(15,270)	(15,527)	(15,750)	(15,770)	(18,067)	(79,510)
Unearned credit insurance	—	—	—	—	(5,774)	(9,553)	(12,413)	(8,768)	(4,923)	(1,386)
Unearned finance income	—	—	—	—	—	—	—	—	—	(37,523)
Net	$107,405	$105,545	$129,200	$149,145	$360,713	$408,650	$465,696	$531,553	$579,315	$399,968
Other receivables	3,538	4,760	4,206	5,684	7,554	11,081	11,628	11,198	19,484	31,233
Total receivables	$110,943	$110,305	$133,406	$154,829	$368,267	$419,731	$477,324	$542,751	$598,799	$431,201

EXHIBIT 2

W.T. Grant Company

Statements of Income and Retained Earnings
(as originally reported)

Year Ended January 31:	1966	1967	1968	1969	1970	1971	1972	1973	1974	1975
Sales	$839,715	$920,797	$979,458	$1,091,658	$1,210,918	$1,254,131	$1,374,811	$1,644,747	$1,849,802	$1,761,952
Concessions	1,614	2,249	2,786	3,425	3,748	4,986	3,439	3,753	3,971	4,238
Equity in earnings	1,186	2,072	2,987	3,537	2,084	2,777	2,383	5,116	4,651	3,086
Other income	999	1,049	2,010	2,205	2,864	2,874	3,102	1,188	3,063	3,376
Total revenue	$843,514	$926,167	$987,241	$1,100,825	$1,219,614	$1,264,768	$1,383,735	$1,654,804	$1,861,487	$1,772,652
Cost of goods sold	$578,072	$631,585	$669,560	$ 739,459	$ 817,671	$ 843,192	$ 931,237	$1,125,261	$1,282,945	$1,303,267
Selling, general & administration	202,008	228,433	246,653	275,668	306,629	329,768	373,816	444,377	518,280	540,953
Interest[a]	4,846	9,055	11,248	13,146	14,919	18,874	16,452	21,127	51,047	199,238
Taxes: Current	1,413	13,541	17,530	25,600	24,900	21,140	13,487	9,588	(6,021)	(19,439)
Deferred	25,487	11,659	9,120	8,400	13,100	11,660	13,013	16,162	6,807	(98,027)
Other expenses	440	616	567	657	586	557	518	502	—	24,000
Total expenses	$812,266	$894,889	$954,678	$1,062,930	$1,177,805	$1,225,191	$1,348,523	$1,617,017	$1,853,058	$1,949,992
Net income	$ 31,248	$ 31,278	$ 32,563	$ 37,895	$ 41,809	$ 39,577	$ 35,212	$ 37,787	$ 8,429	$ (177,340)
Dividends	(10,211)	(14,091)	(14,367)	(17,686)	(19,737)	(20,821)	(21,139)	(21,141)	(21,122)	(4,457)
Change in accounting principles:										
Consolidation of finance sub.	—	—	—	4,885	(2,932)	—	—	—	—	—
Recognition of financing charges	—	—	—	—	—	—	—	—	—	(28,990)
Change in retained earnings	$ 21,037	$ 17,187	$ 18,196	$ 25,094	$ 19,140	$ 18,756	$ 14,073	$ 16,646	$ (12,693)	$ (210,787)
Retained earnings—beg. of period	111,025	132,062	149,249	167,445	192,539	211,679	230,435	244,508	261,154	248,461
Retained earnings—end of period	$132,062	$149,249	$167,445	$ 192,539	$ 211,679	$ 230,435	$ 244,508	$ 261,154	$ 248,461	$ 37,674

(Continued)

EXHIBIT 2 (Continued)

[a] For fiscal years 1966 to 1973, amounts include only interest expense. The amounts for 1974 and 1975 are composed of:

	1974	1975
Interest expense	$ 78,040	$ 86,079
Estimated uncollectibles	21,198	155,691
Administration of credit activity	39,803	48,609
Less finance charges on customers' accounts	(87,994)	(91,141)
Total	$ 51,047	$199,238

EXHIBIT 3

W.T. Grant Company

Statements of Changes in Financial Position
(as originally reported)

Year Ended January 31:	1966ª	1967ª	1968ª	1969ª	1970	1971	1972	1973	1974	1975
Sources of working capital										
Operations:										
Net income	$ 31,248	$ 31,278	$ 32,563	$ 37,895	$ 41,809	$ 39,577	$ 35,212	$ 37,787	$ 8,429	$(177,340)
Plus: Depreciation	6,868	7,524	8,203	8,381	8,972	9,619	10,577	12,004	13,579	14,587
Deferred taxes	1,143	765	517	390	345	233	1,145	2,262	2,723	(14,649)
Other	378	164	130	231	180	74	(520)	(558)	(497)	(2,013)
Less: Equity in earnings	(1,172)	(1,073)	(1,503)	(1,761)	(2,084)	(2,777)	(2,383)	(3,403)	(3,570)	(331)
Total from operations	$ 38,465	$ 38,658	$ 39,910	$ 45,136	$ 49,222	$ 46,726	$ 44,031	$ 48,092	$ 20,664	$(179,746)
Sale of common: to employees	3,431	2,695	4,113	5,432	5,279	5,218	7,715	3,492	2,584	886
on open market		—	—	—	—	—	2,229	174	260	—
Issue of long-term debt	35,000	—	—	—	—	—	100,000	—	100,000	—
Other	—	30	59	523	—	—	—	2,228	(601)	—
Total sources	$ 76,896	$ 41,383	$ 44,082	$ 51,091	$ 54,501	$ 51,944	$ 153,975	$ 53,986	$ 122,907	$(178,860)
Uses of working capital										
Dividends	$ 10,211	$ 14,091	$ 14,367	$ 17,686	$ 19,737	$ 20,821	$ 21,139	$ 21,141	$ 21,122	$ 4,457
Acquisition of prop., plant, & equip.	8,008	15,257	7,763	10,544	14,352	16,141	25,918	26,250	23,143	15,535
Acquisition of treasury stock	186	441	316	178	22,102	13,224	—	11,466	133	—
Reacquisition of preferred stock		—	155	923	1,037	948	308	252	618	—
Retirement of long-term debt		—	1,500	1,500	1,687	1,538	5,143	1,760	6,336	3,995
Investment in securities	128	269	418	35	—	436	5,951	2,040	5,700	5,182
Other	548	72	202	735	58	47	46	(79)	41	727
Total uses	$ 19,081	$ 30,130	$ 24,721	$ 31,601	$ 58,973	$ 53,155	$ 58,505	$ 62,830	$ 57,093	$ 29,896
Net change in working captial	$ 57,815	$ 11,253	$ 19,361	$ 19,490	$ (4,472)	$ (1,211)	$ 95,470	$ (8,844)	$ 65,814	$(208,756)

(Continued)

EXHIBIT 3 (Continued)

Year Ended January 31:	1966ᵃ	1967ᵃ	1968ᵃ	1969ᵃ	1970	1971	1972	1973	1974	1975
Analysis of inc. (dec.) in work. cap.										
Cash and short-term securities					$ 7,338	$ 1,032	$ 15,842	$ (18,908)	$ 15,008	$ 33,691
Accounts receivable					55,491	51,464	57,593	65,427	56,047	(121,351)
Merchandise inventories	Not disclosed on				13,504	38,365	38,184	100,857	51,104	(43,280)
Prepayments	a comparable basis ⟶				635	209	428	1,271	651	11,032
Short-term debt	with above sources and uses				(64,005)	(64,288)	8,680	(152,293)	(63,063)	(147,898)
Accounts payable					(2,064)	(13,947)	(6,900)	12,093	8,987	(42,028)
Deferred taxes (installment sales)					(15,371)	(14,046)	(18,357)	(17,291)	(2,920)	101,078
Net change in working capital	$ 57,815	$ 11,253	$ 19,361	$ 19,490	$ (4,472)	$ (1,211)	$ 95,470	$ 8,844	$ 65,814	$ (208,756)

ᵃ Amounts reported each year in the Statement of Changes in Financial Position were based on the assumption that W.T. Grant Financial Corporation, an unconsolidated subsidiary, had been consolidated.

EXHIBIT 4

W.T. Grant Company

Comparative Balance Sheets

(as retroactively reported for changes in accounting principles)

January 31:	1966	1967	1968	1969	1970[b]	1971	1972	1973	1974	1975[b]
Assets										
Cash and marketable securities	$ 22,638	$ 39,040	$ 25,141	$ 25,639	$ 32,977	$ 34,009	$ 49,851	$ 30,943	$ 45,951	$ 79,642
Accounts receivable[c]	172,706	230,427	272,450	312,776	368,267	358,428	408,301	468,582	540,802	431,201
Inventories	151,365	174,631	183,722	208,623	222,128	260,492	298,676	399,533	450,637	407,357
Other current assets	3,630	4,079	3,982	4,402	5,037	5,246	5,378	6,649	7,299	6,581
Total current assets	$ 350,339	$ 448,177	$ 485,295	$ 551,440	$ 628,409	$ 658,175	$ 762,206	$ 905,707	$ 1,044,689	$ 924,781
Investments	13,405	14,791	16,754	18,581	20,694	23,936	32,367	35,581	44,251	49,764
Property, plant and equipment (net)	40,372	48,076	47,578	49,931	55,311	61,832	77,173	91,420	100,984	101,932
Other assets	1,222	1,664	1,980	2,157	2,381	2,678	3,901	3,821	5,063	5,790
Total assets	$ 405,338	$ 512,708	$ 551,607	$ 622,109	$ 706,795	$ 746,621	$ 875,647	$1,036,529	$1,194,987	$1,082,267
Equities										
Short-term debt	$ 37,314	$ 97,647	$ 99,230	$ 118,125	$ 182,132	$ 246,420	$ 237,741	$ 390,034	$ 453,097	$ 600,695
Accounts payable	58,252	75,885	79,673	102,080	104,144	118,091	124,990	112,896	104,883	147,211
Current deferred taxes	36,574	44,667	56,545	65,073	80,443	58,536	72,464	87,431	103,078	2,000
Total current liabilities	$ 132,140	$ 218,199	$ 235,448	$ 285,278	$ 366,719	$ 423,047	$ 435,195	$ 590,361	$ 661,058	$ 749,906
Long-term debt	70,000	70,000	62,622	43,251	35,402	32,301	128,432	126,672	220,336	216,341
Noncurrent deferred taxes	6,269	7,034	7,551	7,941	8,286	8,518	9,664	11,926	14,649	—
Other long-term liabilities	4,785	5,159	5,288	5,519	5,700	5,773	5,252	4,694	4,196	2,183
Total liabilities	$ 213,194	$ 300,392	$ 310,909	$ 341,989	$ 416,107	$ 469,639	$ 578,543	$ 733,653	$ 900,239	$ 968,430
Preferred stock	15,000	15,000	14,750	13,250	11,450	9,600	9,053	8,600	7,465	7,465
Common stock	15,375	15,636	16,191	17,318	17,883	18,180	18,529	18,588	18,599	18,599
Additional paid-in capital	25,543	27,977	37,428	59,945	71,555	78,116	85,195	86,146	85,909	83,914
Retained earnings	136,226	153,703	172,329	189,607	211,679	205,381	215,867	229,691	219,471	37,674
Total	$ 192,144	$ 212,316	$ 240,698	$ 280,120	$ 312,567	$ 311,277	$ 328,644	$ 343,025	$ 331,444	$ 147,652
Less: cost of treasury stock	—	—	—	—	(21,879)	(34,295)	(31,540)	(40,149)	(36,696)	(33,815)
Total stockholders' equity	$ 192,144	$ 212,316	$ 240,698	$ 280,120	$ 290,688	$ 276,982	$ 297,104	$ 302,876	$ 294,748	$ 113,837
Total equities	$ 405,338	$ 512,708	$ 551,607	$ 622,109	$ 706,795	$ 746,621	$ 875,647	$1,036,529	$1,194,987	$1,082,267

(Continued)

EXHIBIT 4 (Continued)

[a] See note a to Exhibit 1.
[b] See note b to Exhibit 1.

[c] Accounts receivable is composed of the following:

	1966	1967	1968	1969	1970	1971	1972	1973	1974	1975
Installment receivables					$ 381,757	$ 433,730	$ 493,859	$ 556,091	$ 602,305	$ 518,387
Less:										
Allowance for uncollectible accounts		Not disclosed on a fully			(15,270)	(15,527)	(15,750)	(15,770)	(16,315)	(79,510)
Unearned credit insurance		← consolidated basis →			(5,774)	(9,553)	(12,413)	(8,768)	(4,923)	(1,386)
Unearned finance income		with finance subsidiary			—	(61,303)	(69,023)	(74,169)	(59,748)	(37,523)
Net					$ 360,713	$ 347,347	$ 396,673	$ 457,384	$ 521,319	$ 399,968
Other receivables					7,554	11,081	11,628	11,198	19,483	31,233
Total receivables	$ 172,706	$ 230,427	$ 272,450	$ 312,776	$ 368,267	$ 358,428	$ 408,301	$ 468,582	$ 540,802	$ 431,201

238

EXHIBIT 5

W.T. Grant Company

Statement of Income and Retained Earnings

(as retroactively revised for changes in accounting principles)

Year Ended January 31:	1966	1967	1968	1969	1970	1971	1972	1973	1974	1975
Sales	$839,715	$920,797	$979,458	$1,096,152	$1,210,918	$1,254,131	$1,374,812	$1,644,747	$1,849,802	$1,761,952
Concessions	1,614	2,250	2,786	2,873	3,748	4,986	3,439	3,753	3,971	4,238
Equity in earnings	1,172	1,073	1,503	1,761	2,084	4,175	3,951	5,116	4,651	3,086
Other income	998	1,314	2,038	2,525	2,864	1,214	1,270	918	2,996	3,376
Total revenues	$843,499	$925,434	$985,785	$1,103,311	$1,219,614	$1,264,506	$1,383,472	$1,654,534	$1,861,420	$1,772,652
Cost of goods sold	$578,072	$631,585	$669,560	$741,181	$817,671	$843,192	$931,238	$1,125,261	$1,282,945	$1,303,267
Selling, general, & administration	202,011	228,514	246,527	277,366	306,629	363,854	411,225	476,280	540,230	540,953
Interest[a]	4,814	7,319	8,549	9,636	14,919	(11,559)	(16,361)	(7,636)	24,054	199,238
Taxes: Current	1,126	14,463	18,470	27,880	24,900	22,866	13,579	11,256	(6,021)	(19,439)
Deferred	25,487	11,369	9,120	8,400	13,100	9,738	12,166	14,408	9,310	(98,027)
Other expenses	441	616	566	665	586	—	—	—	—	24,000
Total expenses	$811,951	$893,866	$952,792	$1,065,128	$1,177,805	$1,228,091	$1,351,847	$1,619,569	$1,850,518	$1,949,992
Net income	$ 31,548	$ 31,568	$ 32,993	$ 38,183	$ 41,809	$ 36,415	$ 31,625	$ 34,965	$ 10,902	$ (177,340)
Dividends	(10,211)	(14,091)	(14,367)	(17,686)	(19,737)	(20,821)	(21,139)	(21,141)	(21,122)	(4,457)
Changes in accounting principles:										
Consolidation of finance subsidiary	—	—	—	(3,219)	—	—	—	—	—	—
Recognition of financing charges	—	—	—	—	—	(21,892)	—	—	—	—
Changes in retained earnings	$ 21,337	$ 17,477	$ 18,626	$ 17,278	$ 22,072	$ (6,298)	$ 10,486	$ 13,824	$ (10,220)	$ (181,797)
Retained earnings—beginning of period	114,889	136,226	153,703	172,329	189,607	211,679	205,381	215,867	229,691	219,471

(Continued)

239

EXHIBIT 5 (Continued)

Year Ended January 31:	1966	1967	1968	1969	1970	1971	1972	1973	1974	1975
Retained earnings—end of period	$136,226	$153,703	$172,329	$189,607	$211,679	$205,381	$215,867	$229,691	219,471	$ 37,674

a For fiscal years 1966 to 1970, amounts include only interest expense. The amounts for fiscal years 1971 to 1975 are composed of the following:

	1971	1972	1973	1974	1975
Interest expense	$ 18,874	$ 16,452	$21,127	$ 78,040	$ 86,079
Estimated uncollectibles	257	222	20,049	21,198	155,691
Administration of credit activity				39,803	48,609
Less finance charge on customers accounts	(30,690)	(33,035)	(48,812)	(114,987)	(91,141)
Total	$(11,559)	$(16,361)	$(7,636)	$24,054	$199,238

EXHIBIT 6

W.T. Grant Company

Statement of Changes in Financial Position
(as retroactively revised for changes in accounting principles)

Year Ending January 31:	1966a	1967	1968	1969	1970	1971	1972	1973	1974	1975
Sources of working capital										
Operations										
Net income		$ 31,568	$ 32,993	$ 38,183	$ 41,809	$ 36,415	$ 31,625	$ 34,965	$ 10,902	$(177,340)
Plus: Depreciation		7,524	8,203	8,388	8,972	9,619	10,577	12,004	13,579	14,587
Deferred taxes		765	517	390	345	233	1,145	2,262	2,723	(14,649)
Other		374	130	231	180	74	(520)	(558)	(498)	(2,013)
Less: Equity in earnings		(1,073)	(1,503)	(1,761)	(2,084)	(2,777)	(2,383)	(3,403)	(3,570)	(331)
Total from operations		$ 39,158	$ 40,340	$ 45,431	$ 49,222	$ 43,564	$ 40,444	$ 45,270	$ 23,136	$(179,746)
Sale of common to employees		2,695	4,113	5,432	5,279	5,218	7,715	3,491	2,584	886
Issue of long-term debt		—	—	—	—	—	100,000	—	100,000	—
Other		30	59	523	—	1,544	2,229	2,484	259	—
Total sources		$ 41,883	$ 44,512	$ 51,386	$ 54,501	$ 50,326	$150,388	$ 51,245	$125,979	$(178,860)
Uses of working capital										
Dividends		$ 14,091	$ 14,367	$ 17,686	$ 19,737	$ 20,821	$ 21,139	$ 21,141	$ 21,122	$ 4,457
Acquisition of prop., plant, & equip.		15,257	7,763	10,626	14,352	16,141	25,918	26,251	23,143	15,535
Acquisition of treasury stock		—	—	3,665	22,102	13,224	—	11,466	133	—
Reacquisition of preferred stock		—	155	923	1,037	948	308	252	618	—
Retirement of long-term debt		—	1,500	1,500	1,687	1,538	1,615	1,584	6,074	3,995
Investment in securities		269	418	35	—	436	5,951	2,216	5,700	5,282
Other		487	440	636	58	1,960	3,574	—	904	627

(Continued)

EXHIBIT 6 (Cont.)

Year Ending January 31:	1966[a]	1967	1968	1969	1970	1971	1972	1973	1974	1975
Amount due to change in acct. prin.						21,820				
Total uses		$ 30,104	$ 24,643	$ 35,071	$ 58,973	$ 76,888	$ 58,505	$ 62,910	$ 57,694	$ 29,896
Net change in working capital		$ 11,779	$ 19,869	$ 16,315	$ (4,472)	$(26,562)	$ 91,883	$(11,665)	$ 68,285	$(208,756)
Analysis of inc. (dec.) in working cap.										
Cash and short-term securities		$ 16,402	(13,899)	$ 498	$ 7,338	$ 1,032	$ 15,842	$(18,908)	$ 15,008	$ 33,691
Accounts receivable		57,721	42,023	40,326	55,491	(9,839)	49,873	60,281	72,220	(109,601)
Inventories		23,266	9,091	24,901	13,505	38,364	38,184	100,857	51,104	(43,280)
Prepayments		449	(97)	420	635	209	132	1,271	650	(718)
Short-term debt		(60,333)	(1,583)	(18,895)	(64,007)	(64,288)	8,679	(152,293)	(63,063)	(147,598)
Accounts payable		(17,633)	(3,788)	(22,407)	(2,064)	(13,947)	(6,899)	12,094	8,013	(42,328)
Deferred taxes		(8,093)	(11,878)	(8,528)	(15,370)	21,907	(13,928)	(14,967)	(15,647)	101,078
Net change in working capital		$ 11,779	$ 19,869	$ 16,315	$ (4,472)	$(26,562)	$ 91,883	$(11,665)	$ 68,285	$(208,756)

[a] Not reported on a retroactively revised basis.

EXHIBIT 7

W.T. Grant Company

Other Data

December 31	1965	1966	1967	1968	1969	1970	1971	1972	1973	1974
W.T. Grant Co.										
Sales (millions of dollars)[a]	$ 839.7	$ 920.8	$ 979.5	$1,096.1	$1,210.9	$1,254.1	$1,374.8	$1,644.7	$1,849.8	$1,762.0
Number of stores	1,088	1,104	1,086	1,092	1,095	1,116	1,168	1,208	1,189	1,152
Store area (thousands of square feet)[a]	⟶ Data not available ⟶					38,157	44,718	50,619	53,719	54,770
Dividends per share[a]	.80	1.10	1.10	1.30	1.40	1.40	1.50	1.50	1.50	.30
Stock price—high	31⅛	35⅛	37⅜	45⅛	59	52	70⅝	48¾	44⅜	12
low	18	20½	20¾	30	39¼	26⅞	41⅞	38¾	9⅞	1½
close (12/31)	31⅛	20¾	34⅜	42⅝	47	47⅛	47¾	43⅞	10⅞	1⅞
Variety store industry										
Sales (millions of dollars)[a]	5,320	5,727	6,078	6,152	6,426	6,959	6,972	7,498	8,212	8,714
Standard & Poors										
Variety Chain—high	31.0	31.2	38.4	53.6	66.1	61.4	92.2	107.4	107.3	73.7
Stock price—low	24.3	22.4	22.3	34.7	48.8	40.9	60.2	82.1	60.0	39.0
Index: close (12/31)	31.0	22.4	37.8	50.5	59.6	60.4	88.0	106.8	66.2	41.9
Aggregate economy										
Gross National Product (billions of dollars)	684.9	747.6	789.7	865.7	932.1	1,075.3	1,107.5	1,171.1	1,233.4	1,210.0
Average bank short-term lending rate	4.99%	5.69%	5.99%	6.68%	8.21%	8.48%	6.32%	5.82%	8.30%	11.28%
Standard & Poors 500 Stock										
Price Index: high	92.6	94.1	97.6	108.4	106.2	93.5	104.8	119.1	120.2	99.8
low	81.6	73.2	80.4	87.7	89.2	69.3	90.2	101.7	92.2	62.3
close (12/31)	92.4	80.3	96.5	103.9	92.1	92.2	102.1	118.1	97.6	68.6

[a] These amounts are for the fiscal year ending January 31 of year after the year indicated in the column. For example, sales for W.T. Grant of $839.7 in the 1965 column are for the fiscal year ending January 31, 1966.

243

CASE 24

Varo, Inc.

"We have come a long way from the dark days just a few years ago when in 1971, for instance, Varo reported a net loss of about $14.6 million . . . ," stated Don Guth, the present chief financial officer of the company.

Varo had become a major manufacturer of military night-viewing systems and believed it was the nation's largest manufacturer of image-intensifier tubes used in these systems. Varo was also the nation's largest producer of semiconductor high-voltage rectifiers and multipliers used in consumer and industrial electronic products. Rectifiers convert alternating current into direct current, a form required by most electronic devices. Multipliers increase the voltage of a power source and act as rectifiers.

Varo designed, developed, and was a principal supplier of high-voltage rectifiers and multipliers sold to U.S. color television manufacturers. The company produced power conversion equipment, primarily for military applications, and the LAU 7/A airborne missile launcher, along with other weapons delivery systems.

Exhibit 1 shows an annual total dollar breakdown of the gross profit and operating revenues from sales by its major product lines from 1971 through 1976. During the three fiscal years and nine months ended January 31, 1976, the percentages of Varo's operating revenues from sales to the U.S. government were approximately 30, 35, 38, and 28 percent, respectively. Operating revenues from foreign government sales were approximately 4 percent in 1973, 4 percent in 1974, 13 percent in 1975, and 26 percent in the first nine months of 1976. It was expected that a significant portion of Varo's future revenues would be subject

This case was prepared by and used with the permission of Professors George W. Trivoli, Nova University, Fort Lauderdale, and John D. Williams, University of Akron.

to U.S. and foreign government military spending and U.S. policies regarding foreign military sales.

Mr. Guth was discussing the most recent issue of 1,245,180 common shares in May 1976 worth about $12.7 million with a friend visiting his office at the Garland, Texas, headquarters of Varo. Mr. Guth had joined the company in 1971 at the depths of their financial difficulties as vice-president, chief financial officer. A complete description of Varo's economic history follows.

The Rapidly Deteriorating Situation in 1971–72

During the last quarter of Varo's fiscal year ended April 30, 1971, management concluded that major revaluations and write-offs of assets should be made for the year. As a result, Varo reported a net loss of approximately $14.6 million, including approximately $5.5 million from operations and approximately $9.1 million from extraordinary charges. As at April 30, 1971, Varo's trade accounts payable were approximately $4.9 million, including $2 million in excess of 60 days.

Beginning in December 1970, management took major steps to reduce costs and cash requirements, including reduction of employees and sales of unprofitable divisions and product lines. The compensation of all salaried personnel was reduced by 10 percent in December 1970 in an effort to reduce cash requirements (2 percent of which was restored in May, 3 percent in July, and the remaining 5 percent in November 1971). The number of employees was reduced to 1731 at May 1, 1971, from approximately 2500 at the same date the previous year.

Management initiated efforts (subsequently concluded) to sell or discontinue unprofitable divisions and product lines in order to reduce cash requirements and, in some instances, to obtain working capital. PEK, Inc., a wholly-owned subsidiary of Varo engaged in the business of specialized light sources and associated equipment was sold. After Varo's Transportation Division failed to receive a contract for a mass transportation system from the Dallas-Fort Worth Regional Airport, management in April directed that this division be sold or discontinued within two months in view of its cash requirements, and the division was thereafter sold to Rohr Corporation. (Mr. William J. Holt, a vice-president and director of Varo at the time of the sale, continued to manage the transportation business as a vice-president of a subsidiary of Rohr.) Efforts initiated during this period also resulted in the disposition of the assets of Varo Optical, Inc. (Texas), a wholly-owned subsidiary of Varo located in Puerto Rico engaged in the manufacture of ophthalmic lenses, and disposition of the assets of Varo Inertial Products, Inc., a wholly-owned subsidiary of Varo engaged in the manufacture of gyroscopes, accelerometers, and other inertial products. Varo also discontinued its efforts in connection with the design and manufacture of automatic vending machines. All divisions or product lines sold or discontinued (except Varo Gyrex product line, which was engaged in the design and manufacture of machines to apply liquid coatings to panels for photo-resist purposes) were unprofitable. The banks released their related security interest in order to permit Varo to use the proceeds of such sales and dispositions for working capital and the payment of trade creditors. Such cash proceeds received from the disposition of various divisions and product lines totaled approximately $1.8

million through October 31, 1971. Varo consolidated its remaining operations into five divisions or operating units in an attempt to improve operating efficiency and reduce expenses by consolidating functions such as marketing, industrial relations, accounting, engineering, and facilities.

Capital Reorganization of 1971

The losses experienced in the years ending April 30, 1971 and 1972 (see consolidated statements, Appendix A) were the result of both operating losses and major revaluations and write-offs. By the end of fiscal 1972, nearly all divisions and product lines that had contributed heavily to the losses of prior years had been either sold or discontinued. By consolidation of its remaining operations, coupled with a sharp increase in semiconductor product sales, Varo returned to profitability in the year ended April 30, 1973.

On March 4, 1971, the company requested extraordinary contractual relief from the government in the amount of $6.7 million and requested partial payments of an additional $4.8 million on outstanding claims of $7.4 million, under the provisions of Public Law 85-804 in order to continue operations and performance of its government contracts, but such relief was denied by the government on April 12, 1971. The government also delayed, and threatened to discontinue, progress payments under government contracts because of Varo's financial condition. In addition to the reported losses, Varo had contingent liabilities as a result of a total of approximately $4.7 million claimed under various lawsuits pending against Varo at the close of fiscal year 1971.

Substantial additional financing was necessary immediately for the company to continue operations. Varo requested its line of credit with the banks be increased by $1 million and that the government increase progress payments to 95 percent of cost incurred under Varo's government contracts. The government replied that the request for increased progress payments would be considered only if the banks loaned the additional $1 million to Varo.

In an attempt to secure the additional $1 million, Varo instituted a recapitalization in April 1971 with Republic National Bank of Dallas, Irving Trust Company, Union Bank, and First National Bank of Garland.

April Refinancing. On April 14, 1971, Varo entered into a new loan agreement under which the banks agreed to increase Varo's line of credit by $1 million, subject to certain conditions precedent, including:

1. The board of directors be unchanged, Mr. Erickson be the chief executive officer, and a chief financial officer acceptable to the banks be elected.

2. Varo organize a new subsidiary to acquire all the assets of Varo's Semiconductor Division (discussed hereafter).

3. Varo enter into a new security agreement giving the banks security interests in virtually all unpledged assets, including equipment, general intangibles, stock and other securities of subsidiaries, and the right to require additional collateral (the banks already had security interests in Varo's accounts receivable, inventory, and contract rights under the prior loan agreement).

4. The appropriate government agencies be committed to provide for progress payments under Varo's existing government contracts computed on the basis of 95 percent of the costs incurred under such contracts.

5. Irrevocable proxies be delivered for at least 25 percent of the outstanding stock of Varo permitting the banks to vote for any three of the persons nominated to be directors of the company (proxies subsequently were delivered representing approximately 22.4 percent of the outstanding stock).

The total line of credit under the new agreement was $14,749,200 (an increase of $1 million over the prior loan agreement) to be represented by a promissory note payable upon demand by the banks, and the banks had the right to reduce such line of credit from time to time. The loan agreement contained highly restrictive affirmative and negative covenants affecting the business and operations of Varo; however, management deemed virtually all action of the company to be subject to the banks' approval in view of the demand note and the banks' right to reduce the line of credit. All conditions of the loan agreement were met to the satisfaction of the banks, and the additional $1 million was made available to the company on May 19, 1971. The government thereafter increased Varo's progress payments, which resulted in an additional $2.2 million made available to the company.

Varo-Semiconductor, Inc. In accordance with the condition in the April loan agreement, Varo organized a new subsidiary, Varo-Semiconductor, Inc., ("Semiconductor") in May 1971, which acquired all the assets and assumed related liabilities of Varo's semiconductor division. The original semiconductor division was engaged in the manufacture of high-voltage rectifiers and similar devices primarily for the commercial market and was Varo's only operation that had been consistently and substantially profitable. Semiconductor assumed all trade payables and $2.6 million in debt to the banks and issued Varo its note for $1 million for the assets of the original division. The additional $1 million made available by the banks under the April loan agreement was loaned directly to Semiconductor, which used such funds to discharge the note to Varo given in connection with the acquisition of assets. All of the common stock of Semiconductor (at that time constituting the only class of capital stock) was delivered to the banks as collateral under the April loan agreement (together with the stock of all of Varo's other subsidiaries). Semiconductor had its own separate and independent board of directors elected by Varo, and its business and affairs were managed independently of the management of Varo.

Added Difficulties in 1971

Notwithstanding the additional $1 million made available under the April loan agreement, substantial additional corporate action was required in view of the $14.6 million of losses incurred during Varo's fiscal year ended April 30, 1971, resulting in a negative net worth of approximately $5.1 million. Management considered and explored various alternative actions to permit the company to continue its business and operations, including merger or consolidation with another business, sale of Semiconductor, and reorganization of its debt under the bankruptcy law. Management concluded, however, that such alternatives as were available were not in the best interest of Varo's stockholders and creditors. Varo proposed to the banks a substantial recapitalization of the company involving the conversion of approximately $7 million in debt to equity, and tentative acceptance of such proposal by the banks was announced on July 2, 1971.

Negotiations with the banks continued throughout the summer as to the specific terms and conditions of the recapitalization plan. Additional delay in consummation of the plan was caused by the banks' requirement that Varo satisfactorily conclude negotiations with certain other major creditors. Such delay unfavorably affected the company's obtaining new business, particularly from the government. In addition, Varo received notice on August 10, 1971, that the American Stock Exchange was considering delisting Varo's shares in view of the company's financial condition.

In view of the company's financial condition and the other circumstances discussed above, management concluded that the recapitalization plan, discussed below, was the best alternative available to the company, it offered an opportunity to continue business and operations and ultimately recover from the financial reverses previously experienced.

OCTOBER 1971 RECAPITALIZATION PLAN

On October 18, 1971, Varo consummated a plan of recapitalization with the banks, resulting in the conversion of $14 million of Varo's $14.7 million current bank debt into stock of Varo and Semiconductor

long-term debt. Although each of the transactions described below was an integral part, and required for the closing, of the recapitalization plan, the conversion of current bank debt can be summarized as follows:

Varo Common Stock	$ 2,699,999
Semiconductor Preferred Stock	5,000,000
Varo Note	2,049,201
Semiconductor Note	5,000,000
	$14,749,200

Conditions of Loan Agreement

Varo Common Stock. Varo issued 1,914,893 shares of its common stock, without par value, to the banks in consideration for the cancellation of $2,699,999 of Varo indebtedness to them the effective purchase price of $1.41 per share (the market price was Varo's stock on October 18, 1971, was $1.75 per share). As part of the transaction, Varo agreed to register such shares for sale under the Securities Act of 1933 if the banks wanted to sell not less than 50 percent of such shares. The issuance of such common stock also caused an upward adjustment of 15,180 shares issuable upon the exercise of 30,000 previously outstanding stock purchase warrants and a downward adjustment of the exercise price of the resulting 45,180 shares to $3.34 per share.

Semiconductor Preferred Stock. Semiconductor issued 1 million shares of its newly created class of preferred stock, $5.00 par value, in consideration for the cancellation of $5 million indebtedness to the banks. The preferred stock provided for cumulative annual dividends, out of earned surplus available therefor, of 22.5¢ per share in each fiscal year after April 30, 1971, payable in quarterly installments. Voluntary redemption at $5.00 per share plus unpaid cumulative dividends was permitted, and mandatory total redemption on the same terms was required on May 1, 1981. The preferred stock also carried mandatory partial redemption provisions after April 30, 1974, out of sinking funds based on (i) 25 percent of net profits (profits after federal income tax and before extraordinary items) for fiscal years 1974 and thereafter; and (ii) proceeds from the sale of assets securing indebtedness to the banks.

Varo Redemption of Semiconductor Preferred Stock. Varo was obligated on or after October 31, 1976 (or earlier if Semiconductor defaulted or was bankrupt) to purchase the Semiconductor preferred stock upon demand of the banks for $5.00 per share plus unpaid cumulative dividends. The banks' right to require such purchase continued until Semiconductor redeemed such preferred stock. Varo was not obligated to purchase such preferred stock, however, unless Varo had "surplus" available in an amount equal to the purchase price.

Semiconductor Common Stock. In addition to the banks' security interest in the outstanding common stock of Semiconductor, the banks had the option to purchase all of the outstanding common stock of Semiconductor from Varo. The basic purchase price was $500,000, but such price would be increased (not to exceed $2 million) by (i) the amount by which $5 million exceeded Semiconductor's indebtedness to the banks on the date of purchase plus (ii) all amounts paid to the banks in redemption of Semiconductor's preferred stock by Varo or Semiconductor. Such purchase price

could be paid by the cancellation of indebtedness or by the return of Varo's common stock at the then market value (provided Varo could legally acquire its own shares at such time). The banks' option to purchase such shares was exercisable until May 1, 1981 (unless at an earlier time Varo had discharged its obligations to the banks and the banks owned no common stock of Varo). If, however, the banks exercised options and thereafter sold Semiconductor's common stock for an amount exceeding the banks' purchase price (plus expenses associated with the option and sale), then all excess amounts were to be credited against all debts or other obligations of Varo to the banks.

Varo Loan Agreement. Varo entered into a new loan agreement with the banks covering a continuation of $2,049,201 of indebtedness to the banks. Such indebtedness was represented by a note bearing interest, payable monthly, at the rate of 1 percent over the prime rate of Republic National Bank of Dallas. This (resulted in an actual rate of 6 percent at January 31, 1972, and an average effective rate of approximately 6.8 percent considering average cash balances with the banks from October 18, 1971, through January 31, 1972. The principal was payable in quarterly installments of $250,000 commencing November 1, 1972. The agreement contained numerous negative covenants precluding the payment of dividends, pledging assets, incurring liabilities, merger or consolidation, investments, sale or repurchase of securities, and other matters. In addition, there were limitations upon the purchase and disposal of assets and lease and rental commitments. The agreement contained extensive reporting requirements, and

Varo was required to maintain consolidated net working capital of at least $5 million. The indebtedness was secured by all previous collateral given to the banks as well as a new security agreement giving the banks interests in chattel paper, leases, instruments of indebtedness, stock of subsidiaries, existing and future equipment and tools, intangible property (e.g., patents, drawings, trade secrets, know-how, etc.), inventory and contract rights, and all proceeds of the foregoing. Four subsidiaries of Varo were also jointly and severally liable to the banks under the loan agreement.

Semiconductor Loan Agreement. A separate loan agreement was entered into with the banks by Semiconductor, with Varo and certain of its subsidiaries signing as accommodation parties. Such agreement covered $5 million of Semiconductor's indebtedness to the banks represented by a promissory note bearing interest, payable monthly, at the rate of 1 percent over the prime rate of Republic National Bank of Dallas. Principal payments in the amount of $250,000 were to be made quarterly commencing February 1, 1972. The agreement contained provisions similar to Varo's loan agreement (a default under Varo's loan agreement was also a default under Semiconductor's agreement). It contained additional provisions authorizing the banks to require, after April 30, 1974, redemption of Semiconductor's preferred stock in lieu of principal payments (in which event such principal payments would be deferred until after November 1, 1976). Semiconductor's advances of cash to Varo or its other subsidiaries also had been restricted. Semiconductor's indebtedness to the banks was secured by a security agreement giving the banks a security interest in substantially all tangible and intangible assets of Semiconductor.

Debt Assumption Agreement. In consideration of Semiconductor's assuming the additional primary obligation to the bank for $6,336,000 of Varo's $14.7 million total indebtedness, Varo issued two promissory notes to Semiconductor. A $2,835,000 note was to bear interest from October 18, 1971, at 7 percent per annum payable annually beginning November 1, 1973, and the principal was due on November 1, 1976. The second note, in the principal amount of $3 million, was to bear interest from October 18, 1971, at 7 percent annum payable beginning November 1, 1972, and the principal was due on November 1, 1976. However, the interest and principal indebtedness under the note were to be credited with all federal income tax savings accruing to Semiconductor. Semiconductor was part of the consolidated group of Varo and its subsidiaries for tax purposes (such credits being in lieu of any other obligation of Semiconductor to Varo on account of the benefits received from any such tax savings).

Bank Relationship. In addition to Varo's detailed reporting requirements to the banks for financial and other information, Varo had worked closely with the banks' representatives in its business and financial planning for the last year. Management believed the recapitalization plan represented the first time any major bank in the Southwest had taken such a substantial equity position in a financially distressed company in an attempt to assist and permit the company to work out of its difficulties.

Consummation of the recapitalization plan was, in management's opinion, essential for the company's survival, but additional problems remained unsolved. New business did not develop at the rate anticipated by management, particularly in view of two substantial contracts Varo was seeking but failed to receive in the fall of 1971. On January 31, 1972, Varo's net consolidated working capital was approximately $4.7 million (Varo's loan agreement required $5 million), which was an event of default if not cured within 30 days after receipt of written notice from the banks. Such notice was not received, and the banks advised Varo that, as of March 3, 1972, no decision had been made with respect to whether such notice would be given. Although Varo's most significant unprofitable contracts were scheduled to be completed shortly thereafter, further substantial cost reductions were necessary to keep the company's available financing. It was necessary for Varo to obtain additional working capital.

OUTSTANDING STOCK— PRINCIPAL STOCKHOLDERS

The sole voting securities of Varo on January 31, 1972, were its common stock, without par value, and no other class of Varo stock was outstanding. At the record date there were 4,099,732 of these shares.

Turnaround after 1974

Operating revenues increased $22.2 million (66 percent) in 1974 over 1973 due mainly to increased sales volume of semiconductor products resulting from increased demand in the television receiver market. Also contributing to the increase in operating revenues in 1974 was an increased sales volume of electronic bomb fuses to the U.S. Navy.

Indebtedness to Banks. In connection with the recapitalization of Varo in 1971, Varo and its subsidiaries entered into certain term-loan agreements with its primary lending banks. Under these term-loan agreements, Varo granted to the banks an option to purchase all of the outstanding common stock of Semiconductor for a maximum price of $2.5 million (see the Varo Consolidated Financial Statements). Shortly thereafter, Varo entered into a line of credit agreement with Republic National Bank of Dallas (RNB). Various amendments were effected in each of these agreements between 1971 and 1975.

In November 1974 Varo repaid the remaining balance of the line of credit, and the line of credit agreement expired under its terms. In April 1975 Varo repaid the remaining balance of Varo's term note to the banks. However, Varo's term-loan agreement also covered its guaranty obligations under Semiconductor's term-loan agreement (as well as other obligations). Since a balance remained under Semiconductor's loan agreement, Varo's term-loan agreement and the option to purchase the Semiconductor common stock did not expire. Consequently, Varo and each of its subsidiaries remained subject to the numerous restrictive covenants contained in the Varo term-loan agreement.

On April 30, 1975, Varo's Consolidated Balance Sheet reflected a current cash balance of approximately $6,158,000, of which $2,476,000 was attributed to Varo and its subsidiaries excluding Semiconductor. Varo was prohibited under its term-loan agreement from utilizing any of Semiconductor's cash. Varo anticipated that it would be able to generate sufficient cash from operations to meet its cash requirements. However, in the event that cash requirements increased or cash shortages were experienced, Varo, because it was prohibited under its term-loan agreement from granting security for loans to lending institutions other than the banks, would be required to seek additional cash from the banks.

Also in April 1975, an amendment to Semiconductor's term-loan agreement was consummated to effect the redemption of $1 million of preferred stock of Semiconductor pursuant to Varo's commitment to do so in connection with a 1974 amendment to Varo's term-loan agreement. To effect such redemption, the banks provided Semiconductor with an additional $1 million, pursuant to their prior agreement to do so, to provide funds for the redemption of $1 million of Semiconductor preferred stock held by the banks. That amount of stock was redeemed (200,000 shares) and Semiconductor issued an additional note to the banks in the amount of $1 million. Such additional note provided for interest, payable monthly, at the prime rate of RNB, and included provisions for installments, each in the principal amount of $250,000 payable on February 1, May 1, August 1, and November 1, 1977. The amendment to Semiconductor's term-loan agreement also gave the banks the right to apply any portion or all of any principal payment from time to time coming due or made (including prepayments) under the term-loan agreement to the redemption of shares of the remaining preferred stock of Semiconductor held by the banks. Each such redemption should operate to defer the payment of

an equal amount of principal under the Semiconductor term-loan agreement to quarterly payments after November 1, 1977. As of July 15, 1975, Semiconductor's term indebtedness under the aforementioned loan agreement with the banks was $3 million (including the additional $1 million to effect the redemption of shares described above). The banks held $3,250,000 par value of Semiconductor's preferred stock.

Varo's Status in 1976

In the 1975 Annual Report to Stockholders, the president and chief executive officer stated the following:

> Those who have followed the history of Varo over the past several years will readily appreciate the fact that its financial problems, while receiving most of the attention, were only one side of the coin. On the other side of the coin and vital to the recovery of the company, have been changes in management, organization and corporate philosophy; and, most important, in the nature of the business activities which make up the company as it is constituted today.
>
> During the past few years, Varo has greatly simplified its structure. The extent of its activities—particularly those of a marginal, speculative or experimental character—has been drastically curtailed. Its corporate staff has been pared to the bare essentials. It is a far easier overall organization to understand, explain and control from day to day.
>
> Varo is now focused on two principal product categories: Night Vision and Defense Products, originally domestic but increasingly international, and Semiconductor Products for U.S. and foreign commercial uses. In both categories, Varo has capabilities for research, design and development, as well as manufacturing and marketing. These two principal classifications reflect product groups based

largely on similarities in complexity and in techniques of development, manufacturing, and marketing of the products within each group and in the organizational structure of Varo.

The operating revenues in fiscal 1976 increased $25.1 million (51 percent) over fiscal 1975 while cost of sales and contracts increased $14.6 million (42 percent). The increase in operating revenues was due principally to increased sales of night-vision and defense products to foreign governments. During fiscal 1976, sales to foreign governments increased 164 percent compared to 1975. Semiconductor products' revenues increased 35 percent due to increased demand in the television market and an expansion of product lines using semiconductors.

BUSINESS SUMMARY

Contributions of Major Product Groups

Exhibit 2 sets forth contributions of Varo's major product groups to consolidated operating revenues for the last five fiscal years.

Contributions of Product Lines*

Exhibit 3 sets forth contributions of Varo's product lines to gross profits for the five years, 1972 through 1976.

CAPITALIZATION IN 1976

Exhibit 4 sets forth the capitalization of Varo at April 9, 1976, and is adjusted to give effect to the purchase of 557,393

shares of Varo's common stock by an Emloyee Stock Ownership Trust for Varo employees (the "ESOT") and Varo's $3,659,000 obligation resulting therefrom, the exercise of 45,180 warrants at $3.34 per share and a $416,000 reduction in retained earnings resulting from Varo's $800,000 pretax contribution to the ESOT on April 29, 1976.

VARO'S OPERATIONS IN 1976

Backlog

Many of Varo's military products were manufactured under long-term contracts, and backlog for these products represented future revenues to be recognized as costs were incurred and profits were recorded. The semiconductor product backlog represented orders for three to six months of shipments and was taken into revenue at the time of shipping.

The following table sets forth the approximate backlog of Varo as of April 30, 1975 and 1976. Of the total backlog at April 30, 1976, approximately 35 percent was represented by contracts with the U.S. government and 38 percent by contracts with foreign governments. All such U.S. government contracts had been funded. It was estimated that approximately 95 percent ($31 million) of the backlog in April 1976 had been funded for payment by April 1977. As sales to U.S. and foreign governments were usually under large, long-term contracts, the backlog was subject to fluctuations and could at any particular time consist of contracts from a limited number of customers.

---

*Contributions to Varo's business by product lines are shown only as to gross profit due to the disposition of several major product lines and subsidiaries since 1971.

| Revenue backlog | At April 30, | |
(millions)	1975	1976
Night-vision products	$19.3	20.4
Semiconductor products	7.9	6.7
Power conversion products	3.5	.3
Other products	4.4	5.1
Total	$35.1	32.5

Materials

Materials used in the manufacture and assembly of Varo's products, with the exception of certain components, were generally available from numerous sources. Certain components of night-vision devices were available from only one or a limited number of sources, and Varo was experiencing, and could continue to experience, delays in obtaining micro-channel plate amplifiers, a key component for its second-generation image-intensifier tubes. Varo was developing two additional sources for this component; however, each of these sources had to be qualified as "approved sources" by the U.S. government before supplying the component for use in tubes delivered to the government. Also, Varo had been unable to obtain an adequate supply of a component used in the LAU 7/A airborne missile launcher.

Because of price and performance advantages, Varo had increased its foreign purchases of some materials used in night-vision devices. In addition, increased sales to foreign governments had led to commitments to purchase materials and components from suppliers domiciled in the purchasing country. Approximately $250,000 (4 percent) and $2,056,000 (15 percent) of Varo's purchases of material for night-vision devices during the years ended April 30,

1975 and 1976, respectively, were from foreign sources.

Foreign Sales

Foreign sales were made both through manufacturers' representatives and directly to customers. Manufacturers' representatives were responsible for approximately 40 and 17 percent of Varo's foreign sales in the fiscal years ended April 30, 1975 and 1976 respectively. Varo was entitled to receive $3.5 million in 1976 on contracts which representatives' commissions of $295,000 might be payable. Such commissions were payable only as Varo received payment for the products delivered under these contracts. Representatives with which Varo worked usually represented numerous other manufacturers with the particular country involved.

Varo's total foreign sales represented approximately 18 and 35 percent of its total revenues for the fiscal years ended April 30, 1975 and 1976, respectively, and approximately 15 and 41 percent of its gross profits for those periods. Foreign military sales accounted for 13 and 30 percent of the company's revenues in the 1975 and 1976 fiscal years. The overall profitability of Varo's foreign-government sales was substantially greater than that of its other foreign sales.

Most of Varo's exports, exclusive of semiconductor products, were contained in the Department of State's Munitions List. Consequently, approval of and licenses for the export of these products had to be obtained from the Department of State. Licenses were granted for individual shipments. While no substantial difficulties had been experienced in the past in obtaining the requisite licenses, frequent changes in government policies with respect to various foreign nations made it difficult to be assured that future licenses could be obtained.

Legislation was being considered by Congress that, if enacted, might establish a more restrictive policy towards foreign military sales. Varo was unable to predict what effect, if any, such legislation would have on its operations.

United States Government Contracts

During the four fiscal years ended April 30, 1976, the percentages of Varo's operating revenues from sales to the U.S. government were approximately 30, 35, 38, and 27 percent, respectively.

Substantially all Varo's contracts with the U.S. government provided for progress payments. When progress payments were received, title to all inventory produced or acquired under the contract was vested in the government.

All Varo's U.S. government contracts could be terminated at the convenience of the government, in which event Varo was entitled to receive payment at the contract price for completed items accepted by the government and to be reimbursed for costs incurred in the performance of the work terminated, together with a reasonable profit on the completed work.

Varo's government contracts, both as prime contractor and as subcontractor for other prime contractors, were subject to the Renegotiation Act of 1951, under which "excess profits" had to be refunded to the government. Clearances under the Renegotiation Act had been secured by Varo through April 1974 and no refund claims were pending.

Varo's government contracts contained standard clauses included for the government's protection. Many of these clauses permitted adjustments in the contract price. Price adjustments generally related to Varo's "cost of performance" determined under government regulations (which contained restrictive definitions of costs). Some standard contract clauses permitted retroactive downward price adjustments even after contract completion. In addition, dispute procedures under government contracts required the contractor to proceed with performance as directed by the government pending an administrative appeal. These procedures could result in substantial delays in obtaining upward price adjustments.

Completion

Although competitive conditions varied with each of Varo's product lines, the markets for substantially all of the products manufactured by Varo were competitive. Price was the principal competitive factor in most of Varo's sales, although product performance was equally significant for high-technology products. In each of its sales areas, Varo competed with a number of other companies, many of which had substantially greater financial and other resources. Moreover, Varo's ability to compete effectively in these areas depended on the continuing improvement of existing products and the development of new products to meet changing customer requirements.

Employees

On April 30, 1976, Varo employed 1805 persons. 114 were involved in administrative and executive activities, 53 in marketing, 175 in engineering and product development, and 1463 in manufacturing, testing, and assembly. Varo considered its employee relations to be good. None of Varo's employees were covered by a collective bargaining agreement.

The highly technical nature of Varo's business required the employment of qualified engineering and technical personnel. Attracting and retaining such personnel was difficult and costly.

Finally, in the Annual Report to Stockholders of 1976, the chairman of the board and chief executive officer summarized the accomplishments of Varo as follows:

> It gives us great pleasure to report to you that in our thirtieth year we accomplished many of the goals set forth in the annual report just two years ago.
>
> > This was the best year in our history for revenues, earnings, return on investment, and growth of stockholders' equity.
> >
> > Varo product lines achieved excellent increases through expanded sales to foreign customers and by increases in consumer spending due to a recovery of the economy.
> >
> > Record revenues were received from international markets.
> >
> > Varo retired all of its debt to both foreign and domestic banks.
> >
> > Varo terminated the option held by its lending banks to acquire all of the common stock of its subsidiary, Varo Semiconductor.
> >
> > Varo Semiconductor redeemed the remainder of its preferred stock held by the lending banks.
> >
> > A new, unsecured line of credit for four million dollars was established.
> >
> > An Employee Stock Ownership Plan (ESOP) was established to make it possible for each employee to participate as a stockholder and to provide increased motivation for performance.
> >
> > Finally, with the election of S. T. Yanagisawa, Chief Executive Officer, as Chairman of the Board, and J. J. Collmer as President, the management

> organization of Varo was consolidated and strengthened.
>
> In addition, we made further progress in our longer term objectives in the First Quarter of Fiscal 1977.
>
> > 1,245,180 shares of Varo common stock owned by Varo's lending banks were widely redistributed in a secondary public offering to many new stockholders, whom we proudly welcome to Varo.
> >
> > Varo's listing application for its common stock on the New York Stock Exchange was approved on July 7, 1976.
> >
> > A patent and know-how agreement was made between Varo and Hitachi Ltd. Japan, to enable Varo to manufacture an improved type of glass-passivated high-voltage diode.
> >
> > A much needed retirement plan was established for Varo employees.
>
> The operating philosophy that enabled us to meet and overcome the challenges of the past years and led us to four consecutive years of profitability will be continued. We are confident that emphasis on quality in our products and dedication to the motivation, participation and reward of our employees will sustain long-term customer and investor confidence in our performance. These policies form the real strength of Varo and have led to consistently profitable operations in recent years.
>
> Now that we have established a solid financial base, we can concentrate our efforts on the development of new quality products in closely related markets to ensure the solid future growth of Varo.

PRICE RANGE OF COMMON STOCK

The following table shows the reported high and low sales prices for Varo's common stock on the American Stock Exchange as reported by National Quotation Bureau, Inc., for the calendar periods indicated:

Period	1974		1975		1976	
	High	*Low*	*High*	*Low*	*High*	*Low*
First quarter	3⅛	2¼	2¼	1⅛	12½	4¾
Second quarter	2½	2	5⅞	1¾	11*	8¼ *
Third quarter	2⅜	1½	7¼	4¼		
Fourth quarter	1⅞	⅞	5⅜	4⅛		

*Through May 13, 1976.

On May 17, 1976, the reported last sale price on the American Stock Exchange for Varo's common stock was $10.25. This became the offering price for the 1,245,180 shares formerly owned by Varo's lending banks, netting those banks $11,891,469.

The Wall Street Journal, August 4, 1976, printed a news story under the title "Varo Consents to Dual Listing on Amex, Big Board as Mart Move to Lift Bar," portions of which are quoted below.

> Varo Inc. disclosed that its board effectively has consented to permit trading in its stock to continue on the American Stock Exchange after Varo shares also become listed on the New York Stock Exchange Aug. 23.
>
> The decision makes the Garland, Texas, electronics company the first to consent to dual Amex-Big Board trading of its stock in light of previously reported impending major policy switches at the two exchanges. Both the Big Board and Amex are preparing to lift barriers that had prevented them from trading each other's listed issues.
>
> Varo has been one of the Amex's most briskly traded stocks in recent months. From a 1974 ranking of 333rd most active, among about 1,300 issues, the company rose to 89th last year on total volume of 1.2 million shares.[1]

---

[1] Rustin, Richard E., Staff Reporter, *Wall Street Journal,* Vol. LVIII, No. 4, Aug. 4, 1976, p. 6.

EXHIBIT 1

Varo, Inc.

Operating Revenues and Gross Profit by Divisions (in millions)

	Years ended April 30,					Nine months ended January 31,	
	1971	1972	1973	1974	1975	1975	1976
Operating Revenues							
Night-vision products	$ 8.0	6.9	4.4	7.1	14.1	8.3	23.2
Semiconductor products	6.9	12.7	21.3	32.2	22.1	17.8	21.6
Power conversion products	12.2	8.3	4.0	4.9	7.6	5.1	5.8
Other products	5.1	3.5	4.1	11.8	5.4	4.7	2.4
Total	$32.2	31.4	33.8	56.0	49.2	35.9	53.0
Gross Profit							
Night-vision products	$ 0.2	1.0	0.2	2.1	4.7	3.0	8.5
Semiconductor products	2.4	3.7	7.3	10.7	5.9	4.8	5.9
Power conversion products	1.8	1.9	1.0	1.0	2.5	1.6	2.1
Other products	(3.1)	(2.5)	—	1.4	1.1	1.0	0.9
Total	$ 1.3	4.1	8.5	15.2	14.2	10.4	17.4

EXHIBIT 2

Varo, Inc.

Contributions of Major Product Groups to Operating Revenues (in millions)

	Years ended April 30,				
	1972	1973	1974	1975	1976
Night-vision products					
Night-viewing systems	$ 3.5	1.3	2.3	5.6	17.0
Image-intensifier tubes	3.4	3.1	4.8	8.5	16.3
	6.9	4.4	7.1	14.1	33.3
Semiconductor products					
High-voltage products					
Rectifiers	5.1	5.4	9.5	6.2	6.8
Multipliers	5.5	13.0	18.3	12.9	19.0
Medium & low voltage					
rectifiers	2.1	2.9	4.4	3.0	4.1
	12.7	21.3	32.2	22.1	29.9
Power conversion products	8.3	4.0	4.9	7.6	7.5
Other products	3.5	4.1	11.8	5.4	3.6
TOTAL	$31.4	33.8	56.0	49.2	74.3

EXHIBIT 3

Varo, Inc.

Contributions of Product Lines to Gross Profits (in millions)

	Years ended April 30,				
	1972	1973	1974	1975	1976
Night-vision products	$1.0	0.2	2.1	4.7	13.0
Semiconductor products	3.7	7.3	10.7	5.9	7.9
Power conversion products	1.9	1.0	1.0	2.5	2.8
Other products	(2.5)	—	1.4	1.1	1.0
Total	$4.1	8.5	15.2	14.2	24.7

EXHIBIT 4

Varo, Inc.

Capitalization at April 9, 1976

	Outstanding	As Adjusted
	(thousands of dollars)	
Long-term debt[1]		
6 to 7¾% mortgage notes and other	$ 1,146	1,146
ESOT notes[2]	—	2,700
Total long-term debt	$ 1,146	3,846
Stockholders' equity		
Common stock ($.10 par value) 10 million shares authorized, and 4,116,382 issued[3]	412	416
Additional capital	8,264	8,411
Retained earnings[4]	5,745	5,329
	14,421	14,156
Adjustment reflecting ESOT obligation[5]	—	(3,659)
Total stockholders' equity	14,421	10,497
Total capitalization	$15,567	14,343

[1] Excludes current portion of $324,000 on mortgage notes and other and $500,000 on ESOT notes.

[2] Will bear interest at 2 percent over the prime rate of Republic National Bank of Dallas, whose prime rate on April 9, 1976 was 6¾ percent.

[3] Excludes 403,050 shares reserved for issuance under stock option plans.

[4] Does not include earnings since January 31, 1976.

[5] Reflects $3.2 million in ESOT notes payable to banks and $459,000 cash payment to be made to banks in the first quarter of fiscal 1977.

APPENDIX A

Varo, Inc.

Consolidated Statements of Operations
Six years ended April 30, 1976
(not covered by accountants' report)

	1971	1972	1973	1974	1975	1976
	Years ended April 30					
	(thousands of dollars)					
Operating revenues	$32,155	$31,444	$33,832	$56,040	$49,224	$74,335
Cost of sales and contracts[a]	30,849	27,322	25,362	40,883	34,986	49,611
Gross profit	1,306	4,122	8,470	15,157	14,238	24,724
Selling and administrative expenses[a]	5,053	4,019	5,049	5,734	5,945	7,817
Operating income (loss)	(3,747)	103	3,421	9,423	8,293	16,907
Other expense (income):						
Interest expense:						
Long-term debt	473	741	740	970	669	378
Other	1,193	353	62	168	244	143
Sundry—net[b]	(216)	(4)	167	1,508	(17)	669
Minority interest[c]	—	121	225	225	203	73
	1,450	1,211	1,194	2,871	1,099	1,263
Earnings (loss) from continuing operations before federal income taxes and other items	(5,197)	(1,108)	2,227	6,552	7,194	15,644
Federal income taxes (credits):						
Current	—	—	—	—	2,113	5,865
Deferred	(1,221)	(127)	—	—	140	1,753
Provision offset by extraordinary credits	—	—	1,154	3,201	1,027	—
	(1,221)	(127)	1,154	3,201	3,280	7,618
Earnings (loss) before discontinued operations and extraordinary items	(3,976)	(981)	1,073	3,351	3,914	8,026
Discontinued operations, net of income taxes[d]						
Earnings (loss) from operations	(1,990)	(37)	88	(120)	(192)	—
Loss on disposition	(938)	(199)	—	—	(156)	—
Earnings (loss) from discontinued operations	(2,928)	(236)	88	(120)	(348)	—
Earnings (loss) before extraordinary items	(6,904)	(1,217)	1,161	3,231	3,566	8,026
Extraordinary credits (charges)—net[e]	(7,663)	(573)	1,016	3,201	1,027	—
Net earnings (loss)	($14,567)	($1,790)	$ 2,177	$ 6,432	$ 4,593	$ 8,026

	1971	1972	1973	1974	1975	1976
			Years ended April 30			
			(thousands of dollars)			
Earnings (loss) per share[f]						
Before discontinued operations and extraordinary items	$(1.82)	(.31)	.26	.82	.95	1.84
From discontinued operations	(1.34)	(.07)	.02	(.03)	(.08)	—
Extraordinary credits (charges)—net	(3.51)	(.18)	.25	.78	.25	—
Net earnings (loss)	$(6.67)	(.56)	.53	1.57	1.12	1.84
Fully diluted						$1.82

[a] Depreciation expense for the six years ended April 30, 1976, was $926,000, $755,000, $701,000, $737,000, $867,000, and $1,014,000, respectively.

[b] Sundry—net for the three years ended April 30, 1976, is summarized as follows:

	1974	1975	1976
		Years ended April 30	
		(thousands of dollars)	
Cost incurred in connection with proposed sale of Semiconductor (1)	$ 450	—	—
Equity in net loss of Micropac to the date of sale, net of $18,000 gain on sale (2)	201	—	—
Write-off of estimated royalty (3)	596	—	—
Termination of option of creditor banks to purchase Semiconductor (4)	—	—	500
Loss on sale of Varo Inc. Electro-kinetics Div., a wholly-owned subsidiary	—	—	315
Other—net	261	(17)	(146)
	$1,508	(17)	669

(1) During 1974 the company and Semiconductor incurred costs amounting to $450,000 related to a proposed underwritten public offering of up to 60 percent of the company's ownership of Semiconductor. In February 1974 the company postponed the sale of Semiconductor indefinitely due to unfavorable market conditions and accordingly, the deferred costs related thereto were charged to expense. In August 1974 the company officially withdrew the offering.

(2) In February 1974 the company sold its 64.7-percent interest in the outstanding common stock of Micropac Industries, Inc. (Micropac) along with certain other related receivables and warrants to purchase additional Micropac common shares for $600,000. Prior to the date of sale, the company recorded its investment in Micropac at equity. The 1974 net loss on Micropac was $201,000 which is comprised of a $219,000 equity adjustment for the company's share of the net loss of Micropac to the date of sale reduced by an $18,000 gain on sale.

(3) In July 1971 the company sold all of its rights in a horizontal transportation system for cash and retained a royalty payable out of the purchaser's sales of the system within a specified period. To date the company has not received any proceeds from the royalty agreement. During the year ended April 30, 1974, the company's management concluded that the ultimate realization of this asset was unlikely and accordingly the estimated royalty was written off at that time.

(4) In connection with a 1971 recapitalization plan the company issued to the company's major creditor banks an option to purchase the common stock of Semiconductor from the company. During 1976 the company negotiated the termination of the option and execution of the mutual releases with the banks.

[c] Minority interest represents dividends on the preferred stock of Varo Semiconductor, Inc. (Semiconductor), a subsidiary of Varo, Inc.

(Continued)

d The revenues and expenses of discontinued operations have been excluded form the various captions in the consolidated statements of operations and the net results are shown an earnings (loss) from discontinued operations. The losses and anticipated losses from the sale of discontinued operations are shown as loss on disposition of discontinued operations.

The results of discontinued operations and losses incurred on their disposition are summarized as follows:

	Years ended April 30					
	1971	*1972*	*1973*	*1974*	*1975*	*1976*
	(thousands of dollars)					
Earnings (loss) from operations						
Operating revenues	$ 5,906	4,226	2,785	2,316	229	—
Costs and expenses—net	7,563	4,263	2,565	2,425	421	—
Write-off of assets and preoperating costs	490	—	—	—	—	—
	8,053	4,263	2,565	2,425	421	—
Earnings (loss) before income taxes	(2,147)	(37)	220	(109)	(192)	—
Less income tax credits (expense)	157	—	(132)	(11)	—	—
Earnings (loss) from operations	(1,990)	(37)	88	(120)	(192)	—
Loss on disposition of discontinued operations	(938)	(199)	—	—	(301)	—
Less income tax credit	—	—	—	—	145	—
Loss on disposition	(938)	(199)	—	—	(156)	—
Earnings (loss) from discontinued operations	$(2,928)	(236)	88	(120)	(348)	—

e Extraordinary credits charges are summarized as follows:

	Years ended April 30					
	1971	*1972*	*1973*	*1974*	*1975*	*1976*
	(thousands of dollars)					
(Write-off) recovery of product development and preoperating costs	$(4,643)	141	—	—	—	—
Reduction of carrying value of assets and investments	(2,719)	(62)	—	—	—	—
Provision for settlement of costs in connection with lawsuits, net of income tax benefit of $130,000 in 1973	—	(506)	(140)	—	—	—
Tax benefit from use of loss carryforward	—	—	1,156	3,201	1,027	—
Other—net	(301)	(146)	—	—	—	—
Extraordinary credits (charges)—net	$(7,663)	(573)	1,016	3,201	1,027	—

PART FIVE

Management of Financial Structure

CASE 25

Green Meadows Project

On a rainy day in August 1973 Roger Lund sat at his desk trying to analyze the data he had gathered to make an initial recommendation concerning financial compensation to a private contractor. His aim was to recommend a maximum allowable rate of return figure that would ultimately be incorporated in a contract between the Lightning Aircraft Corporation (LAC) and the Central Region Development Agency (CRDA).

Mr. Lund was a recently graduated MBA from a major southeastern university. As his first task on joining the staff of the development agency some three months earlier, he had been assigned to work on financial aspects of the preliminary contract negotiations currently under way with LAC. These negotiations concerned Green Meadows, a proposed community for which the aircraft company might become the prime private developer in partnership with CRDA.

EARLY HISTORY OF THE PROJECT

The Central Region Development Agency, headquartered near the Ozark Mountains, had considerable experience in various aspects of regional economic development and was considered by many as a model for such a government agency. Certainly it was one of the earliest, having been established in the late 1930s. The agency's development activities had grown and now encompassed a wide front. For example, infrastructure activities included dam building and maintenance, power generation, recreation area and waterfront management and forestry activities. The agency also attempted to aid local economic development more directly through such means as identification of target industries, promotion to assist local industrial development activities, and economic planning for urban re-

This case was prepared by and used with the permission of Professor David J. Springate, Southern Methodist University.

newal. These economic and development activities were carried out for an area of approximately 35,000 square miles encompassing six midwestern states. Total staff numbered about 18,000. CRDA was funded by annual government appropriations passed by Congress and by individual state legislatures. To partially repay past government appropriations, CRDA made annual payments to its sponsoring organizations amounting to millions of dollars. Although a government agency, CRDA had considerable freedom and autonomy from sister governmental organizations and from its sponsors in pursuing its activities.

The idea of Green Meadows itself had arisen some ten years earlier when plans for damming the Kokomo River were first formulated. The site of the dam and subsequent lake on the Kokomo seemed to Mr. Jim Colbeck, then a regional planner, to be a logical spot for a new town—one where CRDA could profitably use its expertise gained in past development and also develop additional expertise in an area new to the agency, that of planning and development for a completely new community.

The idea lay dormant for several years at CRDA but was revived in 1970 after Mr. Colbeck became head regional planner. As the idea became accepted and somewhat modified at the higher levels of CRDA management, the Green Meadows project seemed to offer the chance to reach previously identified economic and social objectives relating to better job opportunities and to provide a wider range of housing for area residents. It also allowed the attainment of additional objectives relating to the private sector. Specifically, if a private concern was made a partner or major contractor in developing the new town, it was hoped

that new, useful concepts in joint management of residential and industrial development would evolve. It was held by some professionals at CRDA that as land became scarcer near other metropolitan centers and as government entered the planning and regulating frameworks in increasing intensity, the apparent need for closer collaboration and for new, proven modes of joint public-private action would increase. In this sense CRDA could make a contribution to national development and growth.

In 1971 LAC contacted CRDA and asked if the latter might be interested in exploring the possibility of LAC's participation in developing the new town. LAC was a giant in the aerospace industry, being active in military and civilian aircraft and advanced space vehicles. Lately, the company had become more active in its attempts to diversify. These attempts had taken LAC into alternate forms of ground transportation, electronic services, and systems management. It was the combination of a desire to diversify and to use its corporate system's management skills that led LAC to consider working with CRDA in new town development.

After a preliminary examination of CRDA's ideas, lasting several months, LAC decided to try to continue developing the Green Meadows concept. At the same time CRDA had, by open contest, determined that there were no other suitable private partners seriously interested in exploring the possibility of joining CRDA in developing Green Meadows.

During the last half of 1972 and the early part of 1973, the two parties worked together to collect basic economic, financial, and physical data on which to base preliminary plans for the possible new town. The planning framework

visioned a 20-year town development period once all plans were finalized. Not
only did the basic physical conceptual-
ization of the town and its waterfront
have to be carried out but coordination
and exploratory work were entailed with
various state agencies and local governments and some federal agencies. Additionally, the economics behind the new
town, its likely population and attraction
for industry, a "time line" for its possible
development, a tentative financing plan,
and a tentative development plan, all
had to be determined if the potential
partners were to make an intelligent individual investment decision.

THE PROBLEM AT HAND

By the summer of 1973, the two organizations were approaching the point where
formalization of a planning and development contract between them was becoming appealing to both parties. A split of
project management, planning, and financial responsibility, at least on major
points, was required. One unresolved
area that remained, blocking the execution of a preliminary agreement which
would assign major responsibilities and
allow teams to proceed with more detailed contract drafting for subsequent
adoption, was the lack of agreement
over appropriate compensation for LAC.
It was at this point that Mr. Ben Harris,
who headed CRDA's ad hoc Green
Meadows investigation team under Mr.
Colbeck, added Roger Lund to his staff.
The latter's first task would be to advise
Mr. Harris and his superiors on some of
the financial arrangments between the
two prospective parties to the Green
Meadows agreement.

The specific task that confronted Mr.

Lund was to recommend a maximum
rate of return that LAC might earn on
the funds it committed to the Green
Meadows project. It was anticipated that
LAC would make investments to develop
some of the residential properties in the
new town and prepare them for sale to
subdevelopers. These sales would provide project revenues. Delayed reimbursement to LAC would prove necessary since revenues in the initial years
would not match anticipated outlays. Exhibit 1 provides a summary of one early
projection of the anticipated cash flows
for LAC under certain assumptions relating to town development costs, revenues,
and effective tax rate.

Earlier in 1973 it had been agreed
that LAC's maximum earnings rate
would be limited in return for its first
call on project revenues. Further, LAC
would be reimbursed on the basis of an
allowed percent annual return, after tax,
on each dollar invested. Thus, as Roger
Lund began his task, he knew that LAC
might earn up to X percent, after tax, a
year on each dollar the corporation had
remaining invested in Green Meadows.
However, the question of how large X
was to be was still open to question. It
was anticipated that returns above the
set X percent would go to CRDA or be
held in public trust for eventual return to
the new community.

If agreement on certain major items,
including return, was reached between
the negotiators for CRDA and LAC, a
20-page preliminary agreement would be
reviewed and ultimately signed by the respective top managements. Work would
then start on a larger, much more detailed, contract and on further joint planning for the town of Green Meadows.
LAC expected to use basically the small
team of negotiators and analysts it had

supported at CRDA headquarters for the past 18 months.

COST OF CAPITAL APPROACH

Mr. Lund's first thought was to find what past achieved rates of return on individual investment projects in LAC had been. This did not prove practical, however, for two reasons. First, LAC did not have much information readily available. Second, LAC would naturally prefer a relatively high limit to be set, so Mr. Lund felt that any information obtained on past achieved rates of return might be slanted in favor of projects that had proved successful.

Mr. Lund next turned to a consideration of cost of capital. He had available to him past balance sheets and income statements for LAC for the years 1968–72 (see Exhibits 2 and 3). Further, he had compiled a matrix of annual rates of return actually achieved by stockholders of Lightning Aircraft in the past (Exhibit 4). For assumed holding periods of differing lengths with starting years and ending years between 1958 and 1972, he had computed the annual realized rates of return taking into account starting stock prices, ending stock prices, and interim dividends. The mean figure was 8.1 percent, which Mr. Lund proposed to use as his basic cost of equity. To be conservative he adjusted this cost up to 9 percent. This last refinement allowed for underpricing of 10 percent should LAC decide to provide new equity investment through stock flotation.

Knowing that long-term debt for a company with LAC's current bond rating was priced in the market to yield 7.6 percent, Mr. Lund wondered if he could reasonably measure the cost of capital for LAC using the information he had at hand and what the relevance of the resulting calculation would be. His thoughts were that he could take the cost of equity as 9 percent (the average of the entries in the matrix of rates of return achieved by shareholders, modified for underpricing as above), that 7.6 percent could be taken as a measure of the cost of debt, and that the current proportions of debt and equity in the LAC corporate capital structure could be used to compute a weighted cost of capital.

If he did proceed in this manner, Mr. Lund was unsure how taxes should be taken into account. His inclination was to use the average of percentage figures over 15 previous years for income taxes as a percent of reported net earnings before taxes. However, considering income taxes as a percent of operating income reported in past years or looking at taxes actually payable "in cash" in any year as a percent of earnings before tax in that year gave substantially different figures as seen in the following table.

Most of the negative entries in the table were due to tax credits.

As a partial check on the applicability of the calculations he might make, Mr. Lund thought he should be able to use returns attained by a sample of firms in the real estate industry and reported in *Moody's Handbook for Investors*. Using industry data provided on average share prices and dividends for a representative sample of firms, he was able to compute annual rates of return in a manner similar to Exhibit 4. The results of his computations are given in Exhibit 5. A cost of capital figure of about 11 percent was calculated.

	Tax Rates for Previous 15 Years		Tax Rates for Previous 5 Years		1972 Tax Rate
	Average	Standard Deviation	Average	Standard Deviation	
Income tax as a percent of year's operating income	.20	.21	−.35	.64	−.04
Income tax as a percent of net earnings before tax (extraordinary items not considered)	.29	.51	−.26	.96	−.22
Tax currently payable as a percent of current earnings before tax in any year	.47	.29	.58	.35	.40

OTHER CONSIDERATIONS

As stated, Mr. Lund was not sure that the cost of capital approach was the correct one to use. Some other information he had assembled included:

1. Data from the Federal Trade Commission and Securities Exchange Commission: Using the FTC-SEC Quarterly Financial Reports for Manufacturing Companies, Mr. Lund determined that for aircraft manufacturers the average for 1965–72 of achieved quarterly rates of profit after tax as a percent of total equity was 11.6. Over the same period the average return on fixed assets and inventory before taxes for six durable-goods industries was 20.5 percent.

2. First National City Bank data: The monthly letter of April 1973 showed a 1972 average rate of return on net worth of 12.1 percent for 2414 diversified manufacturing concerns. The average reported rate of return on net worth over the last 25 years averaged 11.3 percent. For 44 aerospace companies, the 1972 industrial average was 8.8 percent.

3. A Report in the May 1973 issue of Fortune: About one-third of the largest 500 domestic corporations earned more than 12 percent on the book value of corporate equity in 1972. The median realized return was 10.3 percent.

As a final consideration, Mr. Lund was mulling over the use of the so-called Capital Asset Pricing Model, a one-period model developed using assumptions of perfect capital markets. One expression of the model held that the expected return of any security above a "riskless" rate of interest (a hypothetical construct) is related to the volatility of the security (a measure of the tendency of any security to vary compared to swings in some overall market index) and expected market rates of return in the following manner:

$$E(R_i) - R_f = \beta_i \left(E(R_M) - R_f \right)$$

where,

$E(R_i)$ = expected return on the security being considered;

R_f = riskless rate of return;

β_i = index of volatility for the security, that is, the ratio of its change in value for a given change in the value of the market index;

$E(R_M)$ = expected rate of return for the market index, commonly the 425 industrial stocks used as an index by Standard and Poors.

If he used this concept, Mr. Lund intended to use the following facts:

1. A leading stock analyst's handbook had recently judged LAC to have a β of 1.45.

2. Current long-term government debt was selling for 7.2 percent.

3. A study by Fisher and Lorie had shown that over the years 1926–60 the average annual rate of return of stock listed on the New York Stock Exchange assuming the investment of dividends and tax exemptions was 9.0 percent.[1]

4. The average β of four real estate companies in the business of assembling undeveloped real estate and providing for some development figures to 1.58 using data from the stock analyst's handbook.

In talking with Mr. Albert Fry, a member of the local LAC analysis and negotiating team, Mr. Lund learned that in LAC's opinion a 15 percent return on capital employed represented the lowest figure for which the company should settle with CRDA. Apparently aircraft manufacturing returned "about 30 percent" per year and new town development was felt to be "half as risky." At the same time Mr. Fry showed Roger Lund some literature relating to one British new town and one in the United States. In these cases rates of return on equity between 10 and 20 percent had been achieved by the private developers. In Mr. Lund's view, however, this latter data had limited direct application to his current problem. The literature referred to towns where a developer had carried out all development functions and been responsible for complete development. In the present case CRDA would provide financing for nearly $30 million of infrastructure to be ultimately installed. Furthermore, at a cost of about $5 million, CRDA had already assembled the land that would ultimately be used for the Green Meadows project. LAC's anticipated cumulative investment was $58.2 million (see Exhibit 6). At any moment its investment exposure would be less than this due to the generation of ongoing project returns for LAC.

---

[1] Lawrence Fisher and James Lorie, "Rates of Return on Investments in Common Stock," *Journal of Business*, January, 1964.

EXHIBIT 1

Green Meadows Project

A Projected LAC Cash Flow for Green Meadows Project
(dollars in thousands)

Project Year	Cash Flows From Revenues Before Tax	Cash Flows For Taxes	Cash Flows to Cover Expenditures	Total Incremental Net Cash Flows Due to Project
(Col. 1)	(Col. 2)	(Col. 3)	(Col. 4)	(Col. 5 = 2 + 3 + 4)*
1 (1972)	$ —	$ 115	$ (231)	$ (115)
2	—	104	(209)	(105)
3	—	104	(209)	(105)
4	—	213	(426)	(213)
5	744	(53)	(2641)	(1950)
6	1767	(291)	(2533)	(1057)
7	2555	(208)	(2652)	(306)
8	2969	(279)	(2094)	595
9	2969	(293)	(1937)	738
10	2839	(178)	(2330)	332
11	3107	(233)	(2653)	221
12	3581	(368)	(2500)	713
13	3581	(368)	(3107)	106
14	3940	(364)	(2404)	1173
15	3813	(367)	(3410)	36
16	3834	(377)	(2774)	684
17	4112	(509)	(3007)	596
18	4112	(509)	(2744)	859
19	4260	(517)	(3093)	650
20	4112	(525)	(2734)	852
21	4113	(526)	(3514)	73
22	5026	(725)	(3000)	1300
23	5026	(725)	(3000)	1300
24	5026	(742)	(2886)	1398
25	5026	(742)	(2863)	1421
26	5175	(935)	107	4347

*Numbers may not add due to rounding.

EXHIBIT 2

Green Meadows Project

Balance Sheets of Lightning Aircraft Corporation
(dollars in thousands)

	1972	1971	1970	1969	1968
Cash	$ 39,742	$ 68,844	$ 49,346	$ 63,340	$ 45,515
Notes and accounts receivable	112,728	115,920	79,923	82,161	47,659
Receivables under federal government contracts	99,632	86,912	79,231	67,712	77,725
Refundable income taxes	—	1,760	3,488	7,525	—
Inventories	884,071	1,068,850	1,162,640	1,088,541	798,833
Prepayments	5,320	4,998	5,385	9,333	10,048
Total current assets	1,141,493	1,347,284	1,380,013	1,318,612	979,780
Long-term notes receivable	195,933	193,296	201,952	177,492	161,875
Leased aircraft	20,250	28,177	44,685	55,303	70,457
Property, plant, and equip,	826,211	840,261	861,469	862,371	804,773
Less: Depreciation reserve	527,936	490,085	446,367	387,182	315,218
Net property account	298,275	350,176	415,102	475,189	489,555
Other assets	3,418	3,318	3,267	3,310	3,506
Total assets	$1,659,369	$1,922,251	$2,045,019	$2,029,906	$1,705,173
Notes payable to banks	$ 83,499	$ 196,322	$ 89,661	$ 115,637	$ —
Notes & accts. payable	253,709	410,926	592,695	574,197	463,330
Accrued wages, taxes, etc.	116,067	101,537	104,706	121,451	133,501
Provision for income taxes	959	—	—	—	7,230
Current portion/long-term debt	111,140	96,562	80,790	31,163	11,458
Total current liabilities	565,374	805,347	867,852	842,448	615,519
Deferred income taxes	1,560	13,260	13,416	19,578	37,392
Deferred investment credit	25,818	34,632	45,864	53,664	53,196
Long-term debt	392,058	411,495	486,530	493,324	366,984
Capital stock (par $5)	348,783	348,692	348,690	348,691	347,582
Retained earnings	325,776	308,825	282,667	272,201	284,500
Total stockholders' equity	674,559	657,517	631,357	620,892	632,082
Total claims	$1,659,369	$1,922,251	$2,045,019	$2,029,906	$1,705,173
Equity market value (in thousands) on December 31	422,276	314,995	240,971	475,760	909,409

EXHIBIT 3

Green Meadows Project

Income Statements of Lightning Aircraft Corporation
(dollars in thousands)

	1972	1971	1970	1969	1968
Sales, less discounts, returns, and allowances	$1,848,272	$2,371,056	$2,868,117	$2,210,976	$2,553,704
Less: Cost of goods sold, selling and admin. expenses	1,743,824	2,268,515	2,743,419	2,116,728	2,350,795
Depreciation and amortization	59,217	69,895	76,730	82,154	73,192
Operating profit	45,231	32,646	47,968	12,094	129,717
Other income	18,132	20,920	19,118	14,797	13,041
Total income	63,363	53,566	67,086	26,891	142,758
Interest & debt expense	44,015	44,072	59,762	38,022	26,092
Balance	19,348	9,494	7,324	d 11,131	116,666
Federal income tax	Cr 4,368	Cr 8,001	Cr 9,907	Cr 19,110	51,948
Net income before extraordinary items	23,716	17,495	17,231	7,979	64,718
Extraordinary items	—	Cr 15,428	—	—	—
Net income	23,716	32,923	17,231	7,979	64,718
Retained earnings, beginning	308,825	282,667	272,201	284,500	240,032
Dividends	6,765	6,765	6,765	20,278	20,250
Retained earnings, end	$ 325,776	$ 308,825	$ 282,667	$ 272,201	$ 284,500

EXHIBIT 4

Green Meadows Project

Percent Annual Return on Equity Purchase of Lightning Aircraft Corporation Stock for Holding Period of Various Lengths

Starting Year	*Ending Year* 1959	1960	1961	1962	1963	1964	1965	1966	1967	1968	1969	1970	1971	1972
1958	−31	−10	6	−6	−7	10	20	16	19	12	6	1	3	4
1959		23	32	12	9	22	31	27	28	19	11	6	8	9
1960			42	6	5	21	33	27	29	19	10	4	6	7
1961				−24	−15	4	30	24	27	16	6	−9	7	−4
1962					2	41	56	41	41	24	11	11	6	8
1963						98	95	58	54	30	13	−8	6	8
1964							94	41	41	16	−6	16	−12	−7
1965								2	19	−5	−20	−27	−21	−15
1966									40	−7	−25	−32	−24	−16
1967										−36	−44	−46	−34	−24
1968											−48	−49	−32	−20
1969												−45	−20	−5
1970													34	35
1971														36

Notes: Average Annual Return = 8.1%
      Adjustments made for stock dividends and stock splits
Example: Adjusted stock price Dec. 31, 1958 = $23.04
      Adjusted stock price Dec. 31, 1960 = $18.38
      Dividend per share in 1959 = $ .49
      Dividend per share in 1960 = $ .58

$$\text{Solution to } (18.38 + .58) = \frac{\$.49}{(1+x)} + \frac{\$23.04}{(1+x)^2}$$

$$\text{is } x = -10\%$$

EXHIBIT 5

Green Meadows Project

Computed Cost of Capital for Representative Sample of Firms in Real Estate Industry

I. *Computed Recent Annual Return on Equity Purchases of Firms for Varying Holding Period Lengths*

Starting Year	Ending Year					
	1966	*1967*	*1968*	*1969*	*1970*	*1971*
1965	9	33	51	47	30	27
1966		64	79	64	37	32
1967			95	64	28	24
1968				37	3	7
1969					−22	−8
1970						13

Average of above entries = 33.6%

II.

Capital Component	Assumed Proportion of Capital Structure	After Tax Cost (Percent)	Weighted Average Cost (Percent)
Debt	.8	5*	4
Equity	.2	33.6	6.8
			10.8

Source: *Moody's Handbook for Investors.*
*Reflects the fact that long-term business loans from banks in August 1973 were being charged an average of 9.5% before tax in 35 financial centers.

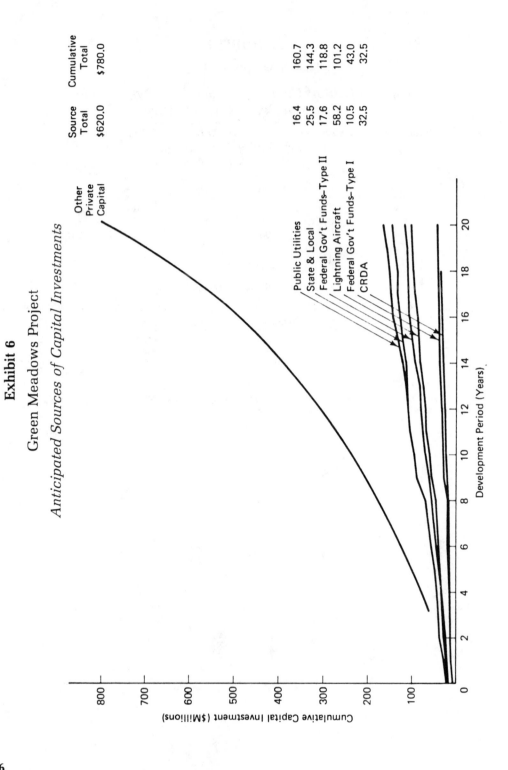

Exhibit 6

Green Meadows Project

Anticipated Sources of Capital Investments

	Source Total	Cumulative Total
Other Private Capital	$620.0	$780.0
Public Utilities	16.4	160.7
State & Local	25.5	144.3
Federal Gov't Funds–Type II	17.6	118.8
Lightning Aircraft	58.2	101.2
Federal Gov't Funds–Type I	10.5	43.0
CRDA	32.5	32.5

CASE 26

Quinsy & Juster Manufacturing Co., Inc.

In April 1979 Jonas Quinsy, senior vice-president of finance for Quinsy & Juster Manufacturing Co., Inc., met with Rebecca Yeung, one of his staff assistants in the capital budgeting division.

Mr. Quinsy stated, "Well, Becky, the reason I called this meeting is to review the preliminary capital expenditures requests received from the various divisions of Q & J. As you can see, we have a substantial number of requests to consider [see Exhibit 1]. As it turns out, the budget is rather established. We will go with our traditional 10-percent internal rate of return benchmark. Using this standard, the IM division will be allocated $6 million, the MH division will get $7.2 million. I really feel sorry for the SM folks. They do a nice job of producing steady earnings year in and year out. But I just cannot justify approving a project for them which has a 9-percent IRR. I

guess they will have to make do with $20 million.

"Now, if the PC division numbers are correct, we will let them have $8 million. Since its last request appears to return just 10 percent, we'll scrub it—No pun intended. Let's see, that makes a $41.2 million budget. I believe that that is the budget the Executive Committee will support.

"Becky, I would like for you to go over the projections made by the various divisions. See what revenue forecasting procedure they are using. See if appropriate adjustments have been made to the initial forecasts. For example, if a division is using the composite sales force method of forecasting, see if the forecasts have been properly adjusted downwards—those sales personnel are perpetual optimists.

"Also, check to see that costs have

This case was written by and used with the permission of Ike Mathur.

been forecasted properly. For example, do the projections allow for hiring additional sales personnel as needed? Also spot check on the equipment needs and delivery dates. Some of these divisional managers will sit down and forecast $10 million in new sales for next year. Then you start checking on their equipment needs and find out that the machines they plan to utilize in one year have an 18-month lead time to delivery.

"Finally, check to see that the depreciation methods are consistent. Some of the managers have figured out that a barely acceptable project begins to look good if they can super-depreciate new assets. You may find a case or two where the equipment's economic life is 10 years while its accounting life is two years. In these situations it would not be inappropriate to rework the IRR calculations. Do you have any questions?"

"Well, I am sure I will have a number of questions as I begin to evaluate the requests," replied Ms. Yeung, "but right now I have just one question and it really does not have much to do directly with my assignment. Why do we use 10 percent as the hurdle to accept or reject projects? It must have some rationale behind it."

"Of course it does," said Mr. Quinsy. "As grandpa—God bless his soul—always used to say, to succeed in business you have to make consistently good decisions. I really, truly subscribe to that philosophy. We have used 10 percent in the past and have come up with some darn good projects. To make current projects meet the same standards as the ones in the past, we continue to use the 10-percent rate. I guess you could say that using 10-percent as the hurdle rate for new projects accomplishes two objectives: (a) it forces us to accept new projects that are at least as good as the ones already on our books; (b) it makes our decision-making consistent over time."

"Thank you for your explanation. I will work on these requests and get my report to you by the end of the week," Ms. Yeung stated as she left Mr. Quinsy's office.

COMPANY BACKGROUND

In 1889 Amos Quinsy, who had a brilliant mechanical mind but a very poor sense of customer relations, met Yertram Juster, who was seeking employment. It became apparent to both men that their talents complemented each other's. While Quinsy handled the technical aspects of the business, Juster handled distribution and selling. In 1897 the name of the company was expanded to give Juster his due recognition.

Until the mid-1950s the company's product line had remained in two areas, industrial machinery and specialty machinery. The company had made a number of acquisitions starting in 1958 and by late 1978 was manufacturing products in two other areas as well—material handling and pollution control.

In 1978 the company generated sales of over $576 million on total assets of $516.8 million. Net income of $37.5 million was realized in 1978 for a profit margin of 6.5 percent. Income statements and balance sheets for Quinsy & Juster are given in Exhibits 2 and 3.

Industrial Machinery Division

The Industrial Machinery Division produced a variety of numerically controlled machine tools; expendable tools such as drills, jigs, taps, and dies; hand tools such as socket and wrench sets, pliers, and shears; and portable pneumatic hand tools such as drills, and sanders. These products were typically purchased as cost-saving devices. Occasionally, buyers would acquire these products to improve the quality of their own products. The market for these products was reasonably mature. Most sales were to replace existing units that had either become obsolete or worn out.

Sales of these products were greatly affected by fluctuations in the economy. During good economic times, demand for these products increased dramatically. Since fixed costs in manufacturing these products tended to be high, the impact of improved sales on profits was very strong. The reverse also held true. Profits declined very sharply when the economy became sluggish. The overall growth rate for this division was expected to average around 4 to 6 percent per annum. In 1978 the division accounted for 28 percent of total sales and 23.5 percent of total net income (see Exhibit 4).

Material-Handling Division

The Material-Handling Division made both fixed and mobile material-handling equipment. Fixed material-handling products included conveyor belt systems and hoists, while the mobile products included gasoline and electric-powered fork-lift trucks, and special truck attachments for lumber handling.

Sales for material-handling equipment were greatly affected by corporate spending on equipment. Generally speaking, when the economic environment was good, capital equipment spending increased and sales and profits of the division increased. The reverse was true during recessionary periods. Sales were also affected by plant capacity utilization. When plants were operating at high utilization rates, generally around 85 percent, firms had a higher propensity to buy material-handling equipment.

The division accounted for 30 percent of sales and 41.5 percent of corporate profits in 1978.

Specialty Machinery Division

The primary thrust of the Specialty Machinery Division was to make plastics and textile machinery. In the plastics machinery area the division made a variety of extrusion and injection-molding machines. Sales from the automotive and housewares industries had been coming in at a steady pace until 1973. The OPEC oil embargo severely affected the production of petrochemical firms. With the uncertainty regarding plastics resins, demand for plastics machinery fell dramatically. More recently, sales had picked up and prospects for the future looked very good.

In the textile area the division manufactured a number of machines that were utilized to convert raw fibers into yarn and fabrics. Recently, the division had been putting more emphasis on selling highly automated looms. Foreign manufacturers were an important competitive factor in this area. However, with the recent decline of the dollar against the leading European and Asian currencies, this competitive pressure had been somewhat eased. Most observers viewed the industry to be in a declining stage.

The Specialty Machinery Division accounted for 30 percent of sales and 13.8 of profits in 1978.

Pollution Control Division

The Pollution Control Division was a relatively new one that was started to capitalize on the firm's existing technological know-how. The division made electrostatic precipitators that were used to remove granular pollutants from smokestack emissions. The division also made a sulphur dioxide scrubber. Sulphur dioxide is a by-product of burning coal with some sulphur content. EPA requirements called for compliance with sulphur dioxide emission standards. The division's scrubber was purchased by small power plants.

Starting with the oil embargo in 1973, oil prices had been in a steady upward spiral. As a result, many oil- and gas-fired power plants were converting to coal as a fuel supply. Burning coal produces particulate pollutants as well as gaseous pollutants. Controlling these pollutants requires precipitators, scrubbers, filters, and centrifugal or gravitational collectors. It was felt that pollution control equipment of the type manufactured by this division would remain in high demand for many years.

The Pollution Control Division produced 21.2 percent of profits on 12 percent of sales in 1979.

CURRENT SITUATION

As Ms. Yeung started work on her assignment, she felt somewhat puzzled by Mr. Quinsy's response to her questions. She was not sure that 10 percent was in fact the company's cost of capital. She felt that a more precise estimation of the company's cost of capital might yield different answers. Also, she wondered whether the same hurdle rate should be applied to the projects from the different divisions.

The recent price of Quinsy & Juster common stock was around $21.75—about the same as the price prevailing in December 1978. The 1979 dividends per share were expected to be $0.10 higher than the $1.10 paid out in 1978.

The preferred stock had been issued in the midsixties. It paid an annual dividend of $7 on each $100 par value preferred stock. The recent price of its preferred stock was $73.50 a share.

The firm had issued some bonds seven years earlier. These bonds paid interest at an annual rate of 8 percent on a face value of $1000 each. The bonds, which were currently selling for $847.88, were to mature in 15 years. These bonds were noncallable. Any callable bonds issued currently would carry an interest premium of 0.5 percent over the interest paid on noncallable bonds. Selected ratios from four industries are provided in Exhibit 5.

EXHIBIT 1

Quinsy & Juster Manufacturing Co., Inc.

Preliminary Capital Expenditure Requests

Division and Project	Amount ($)	IRR (%)
Industrial Machinery Division		
NC project	3,000,000	28
Retooling (expendible tools)	3,000,000	17
Hand tools	2,800,000	9
Material-Handling Division		
Conveyer R&D	1,000,000	40
Fork-lift power conversion	1,200,000	21
Timber handling	5,000,000	12
Hoisting	800,000	0
Specialty Machinery Division		
Plastics forming	20,000,000	12
Textile machinery	15,000,000	9
Pollution Control Division		
Precipitator R&D	5,000,000	20
Solid wastes R&D	3,000,000	30
Scrubber R&D	4,000,000	10
Total Requests	63,800,000	

EXHIBIT 2

Quinsy & Juster Manufacturing Co., Inc.

Income Statements for Years Ending December 31
(in thousands of dollars)

	1978	1977	1976	1975	1974
Sales	$576,100	$512,700	$427,200	$313,400	$262,200
Cost of goods sold*	410,000	352,900	289,100	210,100	173,400
Administrative expenses	94,100	84,700	70,900	53,700	47,300
Earnings before taxes	$ 72,000	$ 75,100	$ 67,200	$ 49,600	$41,500
Taxes	34,500	36,000	32,900	23,300	19,900
Net income	$ 37,500	$ 39,100	$ 34,300	$ 26,300	$21,600

*Includes a depreciation charge of $10 million for 1978.

EXHIBIT 3

Quinsy & Juster Manufacturing Co., Inc.

Balance Sheets, December 31
(in thousands of dollars)

	1978	1977	1976	1975	1974
Cash equivalents	$ 22,500	$ 28,800	$ 20,700	$15,300	$ 12,600
Accounts receivable	128,300	128,100	100,800	75,900	63,900
Inventories	219,000	210,300	188,100	135,300	103,200
Prepaid expenses	3,600	2,700	2,100	1,100	900
Total current assets	$373,400	$369,900	$311,700	$227,600	$180,600
Buildings	72,000	63,000	50,900	38,600	35,500
Machinery, equipment	147,000	126,900	100,800	75,500	71,500
Accumulated depreciation	82,500	73,500	63,100	49,700	43,900
Land	6,900	5,400	4,300	4,100	3,700
Total assets	$516,800	$491,700	$404,600	$296,100	$247,400
Accounts payable	65,400	63,600	59,200	41,300	26,500
Notes payable	104,200	105,500	81,300	56,700	36,800
Taxes payable	11,400	10,500	10,800	7,100	4,800
Total current liabilities	$181,000	$179,600	$151,300	$105,100	$ 68,100
Long-term debt	92,400	96,000	66,000	26,400	33,000
Deferred taxes	7,500	4,600	3,200	2,900	2,500
Other debt	1,500	1,300	900	700	600
Total debt	$282,400	$281,500	$221,400	$135,100	$104,200
Preferred stock	2,300	2,300	2,300	2,300	2,300
Common stock ($1 par)	12,100	12,100	12,100	12,100	12,100
Surplus capital	43,000	43,000	43,000	43,000	43,000
Retained earnings	177,000	152,800	125,800	103,600	85,800
Total claims	$516,800	$491,700	$404,600	$296,100	$247,400

EXHIBIT 4

Quinsy & Juster Manufacturing Co., Inc.

Sales and Profit Contributions by Division

Division	% of sales	% of profits
Industrial machinery	28.0	23.5
Material handling	30.0	41.5
Specialty machinery	30.0	13.8
Pollution control	12.0	21.2

EXHIBIT 5

Quinsy & Juster Manufacturing Co., Inc.

Selected Statistics from Four Industries

Industry	TD/TA Ratio (%)	Profit Margin (%)	Price/ EPS	Dividend Yield (%)
Industrial machinery	46	12.0	8	5.3
Material handling	50	10.0	9	4.5
Specialty machinery	42	8.0	5	8.8
Pollution control	39	9.0	10	3.0

$C\underline{ASE}$ 27

Alpha Omega Electronics (A)

INTRODUCTION

In mid-September 1974 James Van Dell, a director and financial consultant of Alpha Omega Electronics (AOE), was considering the development of this start-up electronics company. In addition to his reflection upon what happened over the past year compared to what was planned, he also was speculating on the future of this young struggling firm. Exhibits 1 and 2 provide the financial results for the first fiscal year of operations ending August 31, 1974. Although an operating loss for the first 12 months was anticipated, the firm had expected to have initial sales by March 1974 and cash receipts from operations by either April or May of 1974. As of August 1974, no sales or cash receipts from operations had been realized. Consequently, the firm was faced with the need to raise additional capital to carry

on. AOE's difficulties appeared to be the result of the time spent in product design and development, which was longer than originally planned. However, Van Dell was not altogether certain of the validity of this conclusion because it was possible that the original schedule for completion of product development was unrealistic. Furthermore, he realized a number of other strategic decisions had been made over the past year that clearly affected the firm's commitment to expenditures and their current financial condition. Each of these decisions, such as the extent of product development, the marketing effort, and the manufacturing commitments, all had alternatives that could have altered the present condition of the firm. Looking to the future, Van Dell remained optimistic. In spite of not yet having firm sales, AOE had generated substantial interest by industry in their products, and it would not take

This case was prepared by and used with the permission of Professor James A. Hoeven, Colorado State University.

much in monthly sales in order to generate a positive cash flow from operations.

ORGANIZATION PRODUCT AND MARKET

AOE was the dream come true for its founder and president, John Atkins. Upon release from the Navy in 1957, Atkins worked as a design engineer in electronics for seven years for two different research and development companies. In 1964 he joined Bell and Howell and within several years headed up their electronics design department. During his five years with Bell and Howell, he completed a Master's degree in electrical engineering and also became intrigued with the possibilities of solid-state electronics to provide automated control of production for industry. As a result of this intrigue, he began, during his own free time, the preliminary design of a prototype electronic controller, which was later to be the product base for the formation of AOE. In 1969 Atkins began a Ph.D. program in electronic engineering at Midwestern University. While completing his degree at MU, he acted as a consultant in computer technology for a locally based firm and also served on the staff of the University Computer-Managed Learning Laboratory. Becoming deeply involved with computer technology only further reinforced his belief of the industrial need for automated electronic controls, yet a control system that did not require the complexity of computer technology. Having completed his Ph.D. program, Atkins and a university associate began building a prototype of the Production Control Center (PCC) and laying down plans for the formation of Alpha Omega Electronics.

Shortly thereafter, Atkins met a local businessman, David McDonnel, and James Van Dell, an assistant professor of finance at Midwestern University, and together these individuals acted as the founders and organizers of AOE. Exhibits 3 and 4 provide summary data as envisioned by Atkins relating to the goals and philosophy of the firm and some basic information on the Production Control Center. Prior to any direct contact with the market, the founders of AOE believed there was a tremendous untapped market for solid-state programmable controllers for industry. The principal means of automated control for machines and production processes at that time was relay logic that, in simple terms, consisted of cabinets full of complex latter-networks of electrical wiring and relay switches. These systems were clearly outmoded; first, due to their relative unreliability compared to solid-state electronics; and, second, because of their inflexibility in terms of programming changes in the sequence of events on machines or change in the production process. While full-fledged computer systems and minicomputers had made a slight penetration of the industrial market by 1973, their application to most industrial needs was a matter of "over kill," with far more sophistication and expense than required. Other programmable controllers, similar to the Production Control Center, had been introduced to industry. However, none had the uniqueness of programming with a standard tabulator card in terms of the production operation desired. Typically, they required the use of "programming language." Furthermore, the PCC required no peripheral equipment in order to interface with the production process other than direct wires to the controller itself. Finally, the market in 1973 for such controllers was still very new, with the first sales being made to the auto industry in 1970. Total sales of all programmable controllers in that year were $2 million. However, by 1973 industrial surveys were estimating total sales of programmable controllers of $75 to $100 million per year.

PRODUCTION AND MARKETING

In early May 1973 Van Dell, who was acting as a financial advisor to Atkins, indicated that some critical decisions had to be made with regard to plans for product development, production, and marketing before a financial plan could be developed to support these activities. He suggested that one alternative was to turn the product over completely, when fully developed and tested, to some interested firm. Remuneration for AOE would be in the form of an initial licensing fee and a provision for royalties on each system that was sold for some contracted period of time. While there was only limited discussion given to this alternative, Van Dell believed it did fit into the original goals and objectives of the firm as envisioned by Atkins. A second alternative would be to retain all rights to the product but to have all production done by contracting with outside firms. The third alternative was for AOE to undertake, itself, all development and manufacture of its product. The criteria involved in this decision included the dollar investment of initial equity capital in fixed assets for production, control considerations in terms of the quality and reliability of the finished product as well as proprietary interest in the product, and finally, the probability of ongoing product development that would require at least some form of pilot production. Atkins decided that the control criterion was critical and that there was certain to be ongoing product development that would require at least limited production capability. Although Van Dell realized the initial equity capital raised would be very dear capital if the firm was truly successful, he thought there was a possibility to lease a majority of the fixed assets. Therefore, the decision was made to include production facilities in the financial plan for the manufacture of AOE products.

The alternatives in marketing the product included a direct sales force, the use of national or regional distributors, or the commission of manufacturer's representatives (reps). It was obvious that the dollar cost and the amount of equity investment involved in creating and maintaining a direct sales force for this new start-up company was prohibitive. Although the industrial market or segments within this total industrial market that AOE would penetrate had not yet been defined, it was clear that potential users would be located throughout the entire nation. Given the newness of programmable controllers in general and AOE's product in particular, it was also apparent that national or regional distributors were not the answer either. While the heavy emphasis of a systems approach, such as required in marketing computers, was not necessary, application engineering to some degree was anticipated. This meant that sales to either end users or to original equipment manufactures (OEM) would require direct sales contact that would include an understanding and definition of the operation of a machine or a production process to be automated with AOE's controller. With these considerations in mind the decision was made to establish a network of manufacturers' representatives, recognizing, however, that in the early stages these representatives would require substantial support from AOE. In terms of pull strategy it would mean product releases and advertising layouts in appropriate trade journals—with a follow-up direct mail campaign to those indicating an interest from these product releases or ads. It also meant missionary sales calls be made along with the manufacturers' reps calls to those potential customers who indicated sufficient interest in the product.

FIRST FINANCIAL PLAN—JULY 1973

Exhibit 5 is a memorandum prepared by Van Dell for Atkins in June 1973. The purpose of this memorandum was to provide a basis upon which a strategy could be developed for the financing of the new enterprise. The essence of this memorandum was: one, a new enterprise goes through three distinct stages of development; two, the types of capital available and their cost differ for each stage, primarily due to the degree of risk associated with the particular stage of development; and three, the timing and amount of capital to be raised depends upon decisions involving the timing and amount of investment, which in turn has impact upon the cost of capital to the firm and the amount of wealth accruing to the founders and original investors. For example, the memo indicated that normally only equity capital was available in stage I and that the amount of capital raised in this stage should be re-

stricted to the absolute essentials to be accomplished in this stage. This capital is always the most expensive capital ever raised by a new firm that is successful and continues to grow in terms of sales and profitability. The high cost is due to the high degree of risk and uncertainty of this stage, which is a pre-operations and preearnings period of development. Another crucial consideration discussed in the memo was the length of the gestation period or time required to reach break-even in operating revenues and operating costs. The real question, however, is whether the length of this period can be planned, realizing it is also, in part, a function of the type of enterprise.

By July 1973 Atkins and a technical associate, who later became a vice-president of the firm, had completed the following tasks:

1. A prototype of the PCC controller was completed along with a suitcase demonstration kit that could be used to demonstrate changes implemented into a hypothetical production process by inserting different cards with different programs into the PCC. The demonstration kit was simply a series of electronic lights that were turned on or off at different frequencies or intervals. Demonstrations were intended for both investment promotion and sales effort.[1]

2. A final draft of the patent application covering the PCC was forwarded to the Federal Patent Office.

3. A preliminary market estimate based upon Dun & Bradstreet "1971 Million

---

[1] Actually little or no use was made of this demonstration kit for sales effort. Potential buyers were interested in the solution to their problems and not this general application demonstration.

Dollar Directory" and selected standard industrial classifications (SIC) numbers indicated that 4700 U.S. industrial firms that presumably could use the PCC had $304 billion in annual sales. Atkins conservatively estimated that, in the near future, these firms would be spending 0.1 percent of their annual sales for automation control systems, which meant a market size of $304 million.

4. A list of capital requirements totaling $457,000 had been prepared by Atkins for one year's operating expenses and other capital acquisitions that included (see Exhibit 6):
   personnel
   physical plant and equipment
   (plant to be rented and
   equipment purchased)
   indirect materials and supplies
   promotional and marketing
   production materials (based upon
   100 units for the 12-month period).

From the information on capital requirements, Van Dell determined that $300,000 of paid-in capital should be sufficient to launch the new firm. His basic assumption, in addition to Exhibit 5 supplied by Atkins, included occupancy of a leased plant in November 1973; equipment rental of approximately $1400 per month and equipment purchases of $10,000 in November 1973 and another $30,000 in February 1974; production expenses of direct labor, material, and subcontracting to begin in January 1974; purchases of development parts of $800 per month beginning in January 1974; marketing expenses of $3000 per month beginning in September 1973 and rising to $4000 in November; sales of five units at $3360 per unit per month beginning in

March, April, and May 1974 and rising to ten units in June through August 1974; and finally, a 30-day collection period. He forecasted that the company would first achieve a positive cash flow from operations in July when collection of sales receipts would total $33,600.

The next problem to resolve was who to seek for the capital investment required and how the ownership should be structured among the founders (Atkins and two technical associates), the organizers (McDonnel and Van Dell), and other new investors. There was special interest on the part of McDonnel to contact local investors, in part because they could identify closely with the new firm, and also because he believed the firm would be successful and promotion of local investments was his business. The positive arguments supporting the backing by professional venture capital, however, were also considered. It was decided, however, to raise the initial capital on a private placement basis and not to register with the SEC or the State of Colorado for a public offering. The principal reasons for this decision were the time involved in such a registration and the belief that a public offering should be deferred for the future, after the firm had demonstrated that it was profitable and had a strong potential for growth in sales and earnings.

Exhibit 7 reflects the proposed structure of ownership and the initial offering to new investors that was finally resolved in late July 1973. New investors were offered a package of common stock at $10 per share along with $1000 convertible debentures with a 7 percent coupon and a conversion ratio into common stock of 40 shares per debenture. The positive arguments for the convertible debentures were the likelihood that a somewhat higher price could be obtained for this initial capital and the fact that definite control would remain with the founders and organizers prior to any conversion of the debentures, and especially in the event that all or a large majority of the debenture issue went to one single investor such as a venture capital firm. Furthermore, the option arrangement, after earnings permitted, would provide a vehicle to once again restore ownership control even after the conversion of debentures. The negative aspect of the debentures was clearly the fixed interest obligation for a new start-up firm that could become a distinct cash-flow burden unless the firm was as successful as expected. As indicated in the proposal, the founders received 8000 shares of stock at $1 per share in exchange for their contribution of concepts and development; each of the two organizers received 2500 shares in exchange for $20,000 cash. The weighted average cost per share of new investors, upon conversion of their debentures, was just in excess of $18 per share.

Although the positive advantages of securing funds from a financially sound venture capital firm were considered, the enthusiasm of the founders and organizers naturally led to rather immediate demonstrations and investment by local investors. This enthusiasm also overcame any possibly conservative, yet rationale, consideration to have the entire $300,000 of capital in hand before committing funds that had already been raised to start up the new enterprise. Atkins argued vehemently that time was of essence and that AOE must move immediately to secure its place in the potentially explosive market it intended to enter.

Early interest by investors in AOE was developed through direct contact by Atkins, McDonnel, and Van Dell or by word of mouth from those who had invested. In nearly all cases a demonstration of the prototype PCC was made, and investors were given an investment brochure to examine. The brochure contained the aforementioned exhibit on goals and philosophy and the proposal for investment, resumes of the founders, product literature, the preliminary market estimate, and certain projected financial data. In addition to Exhibit 7, potential investors were given pro forma income statements, balance sheets, and Exhibits 8 and 9. Exhibit 8 is a break-even analysis and Exhibit 9 was included in the investment brochure to indicate to investors the potential earnings per share of their investment at different levels of annual sales, although no specific timing was given as to when the upper sales levels would be reached. This exhibit indicated a tremendous potential for earnings and a subsequent appreciation in the value of an investment in AOE.

By mid-October 1973, approximately $90,000 had been raised from ten investors including McDonnel and Van Dell who by this time had each anteed up an additional $10,400. However, the feeling was that valuable time was being spent by Atkins in demonstrations and that AOE should seek a financial agent who had the sort of contacts necessary to raise the balance of the funds required in a more expeditious and professional manner. It was assumed they would have contact with larger investors. Between mid-October and the beginning of March, three such agents were contacted. The first, although very interested in the potential for the firm, finally refused to proceed further until such time as a

PCC, the prototype or otherwise, was installed and operating in an industrial environment that had a reasonably broad market application. The second agent made a sincere attempt, but was unsuccessful in interesting his investment contacts in AOE. The third presented a proposal to AOE in which the terms and conditions, including a substantial number of warrants, were totally unacceptable to AOE principals. Throughout this entire period, however, effort continued to interest small investors, and by the end of May, AOE had raised the entire $300,000 from a total of 52 investors.

JULY, 1974—PROBLEMS AND A NEW PLAN

While everyone was pleased with having raised $300,000 from small investors without paying a penny's worth of commission, and under the conditions of a deteriorating equity market, it became evident by the end of May that additional capital would be required. Atkins was in part correct when he stated at the first annual stockholders' meeting in mid-June that management had lived within the original operating budget. It had in terms of the disbursements side of the budget, but it certainly had not in terms of meeting the schedules for development, manufacturing, and sales that were equally necessary if the objectives of the financial operating plan were to be realized. Although Atkins admitted that AOE was behind in its schedule for development of the production model of the PCC, he argued that the additional savings in manufacturing and the additional capabilities and features of the production model justified the delay in the sched-

ules. He also noted that AOE was well development of two additional products. The prototypes of the Operational Control System (OCS) and a Tennis Control Center (TCC) were both scheduled for completion in August 1974. The latter had been sold to a local indoor tennis center.

This appraisal by Atkins, however, did not alter the fact that the delays in meeting schedules, beginning with development, created a chain reaction of delays in manufacturing and sales. The manufacturing representatives had been promised demonstration units in March which Allan Robinson, the marketing vice-president, felt were very important to obtain orders. He also believed that failure to complete development and to produce units could create a credibility problem with the manufacturer's reps. All of this, of course, had its impact upon the financial condition of the firm and the feasibility of this initial capital raised to carry the firm to the point in time when cash flow from operations was positive. With the advantage of hindsight, Van Dell and Robinson both wondered whether there was an alternative to the extensive product development that was performed on the PCC and whether the right product had received the company's initial attention since feedback from the market indicated that the strongest interest in controllers was coming from the machine tool industry, whose applications were more suitable to the second product in the product line, the Operational Control System (OCS). Finally, if all the product development performed by AOE was necessary, then what else could have been done to stretch the life of the initial $300,000 of capital? What were the alternatives to the strategic decisions made by the firm, and what different impact would they have had upon the present situation?

In spite of these developments, enthusiasm for the future of AOE remained strong. Robinson, the vice-president for marketing, had established a network of ten domestic representatives. As a result of a U.S. Department of Commerce subsidized trip to a Paris trade show, AOE was also being solicited by representatives in France and Switzerland. Department of Commerce figures indicated an annual market potential of $30 million in France alone. Hundreds of inquiries had been received from domestic industrial firms resulting from product releases in trade journals. AOE had followed up each of these inquiries with direct mail and had already made a number of direct calls on firms with particular interest in order to perform whatever application engineering was required. The first completed PCC was already scheduled to be shipped to one of the nation's largest chemical companies (DuPont) by July 15, 1974, to be tested in their laboratory.

Upon successful tests there was an excellent possibility of an order for 30 controllers from this one firm.

Immediately following the stockholders' meeting, the board of directors met and adopted the second financial plan that called for an additional $175,000 through the sale of 7000 shares of authorized, but unissued, common stock at $25 per share. It was also agreed that all existing shareholders should have a 30-day "first right of refusal," even though the articles of the corporation did not provide for preemptive rights. In order to increase the opportunity for investment in AOE, a line of credit of up to $100,000 was arranged with a local bank for the specific purpose of selling stock. Interested investors were permitted to purchase stock by signing notes payable to AOE with a term of no more than six months and with interest at 11 percent. The stock would not be issued until payment of the note, but in the meantime AOE could borrow on its line of credit by pledging the personal notes to the bank.

EXHIBIT 1

Alpha Omega Electronics (A)

Balance Sheet

	August 31, 1974	
Current Assets		
Cash	$ 1,675	
Accounts receivables	945	
Subscription receivables	51,250	
Inventories:		
Raw material	42,708	
In process	15,410	
Finished goods	19,500	
Prepaid expense	6,648	
Total current assets		$138,136
Fixed Assets		
Leasehold imp.	4,957	
Equipment	22,075	
Less depreciation	2,256	
Total fixed assets		24,776
Other Assets		
Deposits	6,736	
Organization expense	254	
Total other assets		6,990
Total assets		$169,902
Current Liabilities		
Notes—bank	20,000	
Notes—other	0	
Accounts payable	41,044	
Payroll tax	4,692	
Interest	2,512	
Property tax	722	
Total current liabilities		68,970
Convertible Debt.		204,000
Stockholders' Equity		
Common stock	137,966	
Common stock subscribed	52,325	
Retained earnings	(293,359)	
Total stockholders' equity		(103,068)
Total liabilities and stockholders' equity		$169,902

EXHIBIT 2

Alpha Omega Electronics (A)

Operating Statement

		12 mo.—8/31/74
Income		
Sales	$ —	
Interest	417	
Total		$ 417
Sales Expense		
Salaries	25,132	
Advert. and shows	19,188	
Travel	16,489	
Brochures & aids	8,755	
Telephone & other	3,696	
Total		73,260
Development Expense		
Salary—parts		25,189
Production Expense		
Salary	55,178	
Labor and parts	22,061	
Subcontract	10,744	
Equipment rent	5,768	
Other mfg. expense	759	
Freight	1,402	
Total		95,912
General and Admin. Expense		
Salaries	34,764	
Clerical salaries	7,632	
Rent—Equipment, building	7,770	
Utilities	5,594	
Insurance	5,890	
Depreciation & amortization	2,331	
Recruiting	3,553	
Professional service	5,998	
Office expense	2,534	
Payroll taxes	10,065	
Miscellaneous	5,943	
Interest	7,341	
Total general and admin. expense		99,415
Total expenses		$293,776
Net loss		(293,359)

EXHIBIT 3

Alpha Omega Electronics (A)

Goals and Philosophy

AOE is to be Product Development "Breeder."

AOE is to be a technologically concentrated organization composed of a relatively small group of highly competent specialists. The internal organization and administration will be based on the avoidance of "Peter's Principle."

The "breeder" philosophy of AOE permits unlimited growth—without undermining the basis for the growth.

Simply stated this philosophy centers on development of products that can be the basis for the new production firms or even new industries. For large volume production AOE would have the option of contracting, selling on a royalty basis, or acquiring appropriate firms having the necessary production facilities. The competence, talents, and skills of AOE would not be diluted by assigning creative individuals to routine production and administration. The AOE nucleus remains intact to develop new products.

The products to be considered are to be conducive to production technique, i.e., "One-of-a-kind" products are to be given very low priority except under special circumstances.

Initial product line will be aimed towards industrial control and production applications.

Conception rather than direction, will be the prime determination of product lines.

EXHIBIT 4

Alpha Omega Electronics (A)

Production Control Center (PCC)

The only digital process controller requiring *no* external input/output or interface equipment and *no* knowledge of computer programming.

The Production Control Center (PCC) is delivered *complete* ready to function right out of the carton.

The PCC is an advanced concept in control systems. The goal of the PCC design is to achieve a system of great flexibility and versatility having a uniquely simplified operating method.

While the PCC is in essence a compact special-purpose electronic digital control system, using computer circuits and principles, the system concept eliminates the complexity involved in programming and connecting external equipment to a general-purpose computer. In fact, the PCC requires no peripheral or interface equipment. The PCC provides direct outputs in the form of standard control signals or through its internal relays. The control functions are changed merely by inserting a new Program Card. The Program Card is a standard tabulator or "computer" card. The cards can be punched on any keypunch machine or on a simple hand punch. The simple punching directions are in terms of the production operation desired, not in a programming language. Therefore, we may summarize as follows:

To use and operate the PCC simply

1. Determine what operations and/or equipment are to be controlled.
2. Punch a Program Card. This serves as the means of connecting the desired control functions. *No* knowledge of programming is required; the hole location is easily determined by reference to only one diagram.
3. Connect the PCC inputs and outputs to the appropriate equipment.
4. Insert the Program Card. Start the operation.

EXHIBIT 5

Alpha Omega Electronics (A)

Memorandum on Financing the New Product or New Enterprise

A. The evolution of the new enterprise with respect to financing could be characterized as going through three distinct *stages of development.*[a]

  Stage I *Preoperation stage* sf,1 : Informality exists with respect to the business organization of the new enterprise.

  1. The stage begins with the conception of an idea or an idea for a product that has some marketable use.
  2. The product idea may be converted into a working prototype model that may be tested and used for demonstration purposes.
  3. Patent application typically is involved in this stage of development when patentable rights are believed to exist with the idea or product.
  4. Market analysis of the saleability of the idea or product is also involved in the preoperation stage of development.

  Stage II *Premature operation stage*: Structure and formality is introduced into the business organization with the beginning or business operations.

  1. The enterprise locates itself with a place of business with the beginning of operations.
  2. Operations include: the efforts of the enterprise to secure revenue from the sale of product or service; the acquisition of personnel and assets that are necessary to support the sales; and finally, the provision for sources of funds to support the investment in assets.
  3. This stage of development is characterized by revenue growth. It is also a profit gestation period whose length of time depends upon the growth rate of revenues and/or the absolute investment in fixed assets and the presence of fixed expenses.

  Stage III *Mature operation stage*: The enterprise matures and becomes seasoned with a *history* of revenues, expenses, and earnings.

  1. Growth in revenue and further expansion in assets may continue, but the ability to provide a return on investment has been established.
  2. Further sales growth may result from a larger market or the introduction of other new products; however, the firm must continue to add to its asset base and provide new sources of funds to support the increased level of assets. The revealing characteristic of this stage of development in terms of finance is the ability of the enterprise to generate retained earnings.

B. Sources of Finance Available in the Different Stages of Development

  Stage I

  1. Stage I does not provide the possibility of debt financing unless the loan is secured by personal collateral or the personal ability to repay by the entrepreneur. The new enterprise has neither collateral or the ability to repay in Stage I.
  2. Formal equity markets involving public issue through investment brokerage houses are not a "typical" source of finance in this stage of development.
  3. Personal savings and borrowing by the entrepreneur are a common source of finance in Stage I development.
  4. Should personal savings and borrowing prove inadequate, private investors can prove to be an important source of early risk capital. The "apparent" risk may be reduced for such investors due to greater familiarity with the entreprenuer and the new enterprise; therefore, the price paid may be correspondingly higher.

(Continued)

EXHIBIT 5 (Continued)

Stage II

1. The options or possible sources of financing are increased measurably over those in Stage I.
2. Retained earnings can become a source of funds in this stage.
    a. How soon retained earnings will become a source of finance depends upon the gestation period for profits. The gestation period, in turn, depends upon decisions relating to pricing and investment in fixed assets. For example, Polaroid decided to introduce the Land Camera at a high price and to subcontract much of its production. The combination of these decisions not only meant a lower breakeven point in terms of sales volume but also a *shorter period of time* when retained earnings could become a source of finance.
    b. The emergence of retained earnings is not only a source of funds, in and of itself, it also increases the availability of other sources since the enterprise now demonstrates an ability to pay (i.e., dividends and/or interest and other fixed finance charges).
3. Debt financing may be available under special conditions even at the beginning of Stage II.
    a. Normal debt financing would be available on a self-liquidating basis. The best example is seasonal requirements for working capital. However, this source does not provide for expansion or growth in assets.
    b. Certain types of fixed assets have a marketable or liquidation value in alternative uses; therefore, they may serve as sufficient collateral even in the absence of a proven ability to repay.
    c. The presence of bona fide contracts, in hand, from customers with strong credit ratings can also serve as collateral for debt finance, providing the lender has confidence in the enterprise being able to deliver an acceptable product or service. The estimated profit portion of the contract is in addition to the collateral value of the contract and could be viewed as ability to pay and a source of expansion capital. Sales contracts could actually be secured in Stage I, thus available at the beginning of Stage II.
    d. Normal debt financing may even be available on a term-loan basis depending upon the thoroughness and outcome of steps taken in Stage I, that is, testing prototype, patent rights granted (patent pending), optimistic market analysis, and sound financial planning that is reflected in forecasted operating budgets and pro forma financial statements.
    e. Debt financing may also be available via government-insured loans such as those backed by the SBA.
4. No cost sources of funds.
    a. Once operations begin, sources of funds are made available by trade creditors, accrued payrolls, income tax accruals, and other miscellaneous accruals which bear no financial charges provided they are paid back in terms.
    b. Another possible "free" source of funds may come from customer advances. The possibility of this source of funds depends upon the desirability of the product and the urgency of need by the customer. Once again, this source could actually be generated in Stage I.
5. Semi debt-equity sources of finance.
    a. This type of debt financing may be available early in Stage II because it offers the investor the advantage of participating in the results of earnings in addition to the security of his fixed interest and fixed obligation.

EXHIBIT 5 (Continued)

    b. This source of funds possesses convertible features that permit conversion into equity ownership at some prescribed ratio between the face value of the debt investment and a number of unissued shares of common stock. The emergence and growth of retained earnings increases the value of each share of common stock and at some point will become attractive enough for the debt holder to convert.

Stage III

    1. Enterprises in this stage of development, depending upon size, have virtually all sources of finance available because of their seasoned record of profitability, ability to service debt, and dividend payments. However, their cost of obtaining these services, that is, their cost of capital, still may vary depending upon their growth in earnings and dividends, the proportion of debt in their capital structure and the regularity of dividend payments.

C. Maximizing the Original Shareholders' Wealth

    1. Ultimately shareholders' wealth will depend upon the "trade-off" between risk and profitability.

        a. All steps taken to reduce risk early in the development of the firm will enhance his wealth since the price other investors are willing to pay for ownership increases as the probability of future earnings becomes more certain.

        b. All steps taken to enhance profitability and earnings will also enhance his wealth through the multiple that is reflected in the price-earnings ratio.

    2. The *timing* and the *amount* of finance to be raised, which is caused by decisions involving the timing and amount of investment, also affect the shareholders' wealth due to their impact upon the cost of capital to be acquired.

        a. The amount of equity capital raised in Stage I should be restricted to the absolute essentials to be accomplished in this stage. At this stage the risk or uncertainty of future earnings for the new enterprise is high; therefore, the cost of this risk capital is also high and unnecessarily dilutes the entrepreneur's ownership.

        b. Since available capital is still relatively scarce at the beginning of Stage II, the priorities for investment of capital must be examined carefully. The return on investment of capital must clearly be greater than the relatively high cost of capital or otherwise dilution will result.

        c. The length of the gestation period before earnings emerge in Stage II affects the availability of capital and its cost. The presence of earnings increases the availability of debt financing whose lower explicit cost reduces the overall cost of capital to the new enterprise. However, the rate of growth in earnings once they emerge is equally important, for it influences price-earnings ratios and the cost of equity capital. Careful analysis is required to determine the proper trade-off between these two factors that involve the timing and amount of capital to be raised.

[a] Identification of these stages of development appears in *New Enterprises and Small Business Management*. Donham and Day, Richard D. Irwin, Inc. 1959, pp. 473.

EXHIBIT 6

Alpha Omega Electronics (A)

Capital Requirements

I. Personnel
    A.   Interim Salaries of Officers   64,000

        1. President, Director, and Manager of Operations (1)*
        2. Vice-President, Director, and Manager of Technical Services (1)
        3. Director and Manager of Product Development (partial availability basis) (1)
        4. Vice-President and Financial Manager (partial availability basis) (1)
        5. Vice-President and Sales and Marketing Manager (1)
        6. Other Directors—compensation on stock basis only.

    B.   Professional Personnel   38,000

        1. Production Engineer/Manager of Production (1)
        2. Mechanical Engineer/Designer (1)

    C.   Support Personnel—Skilled   38,000

        1. Model Maker/Machinist (2)
        2. Electronic Technician (2)
        3. Draftsman (1)
        4. Secretary/Receptionist/Bookkeeper (1)

    D.   Support Personnel—Semiskilled   6,000

        1. Maintenance/Shipping-receiving/stock (2)

    E.   Production Personnel—Un- to Semiskilled   32,000

        1. 10 required, averaging 6 full-time (2–3)

Total, direct remuneration	178,000
FICA, FUT	16,000
Medical Plans	3,000
Margin, 20%	39,000
Total remuneration	236,000

    F.   Recruiting Expenses (1–2)   4,000

        1. Ads
        2. Travel reimbursement
        3. Fees

    G.   Professional Services   6,000

        1. Accounting
        2. Legal
        Total, category I, Personnel   246,000

II. Facilities
    A.   Physical Plant (1)   13,400

        1. Rent
        2. Utilities
        3. Telephone
        4. Insurance

EXHIBIT 6 (Continued)

B.	Equipment		72,500
	1. Machinery & Instruments (1–3)		
	2. Installed Equipment (1–2)		
	3. Test & Development Processor (3)		
	4. Design/Drafting Equipment (1–2)		
	5. Office Equipment (1–3)		
	Total, physical plant & equipment	85,900	
	Margin, 20%	17,200	
	Total, category II, Facilities		103,100

III. Indirect Material & Supplies

A.	General and Administrative		4,000
	1. Office Supplies (1–3)		
	2. Facility Supplies (1–3)		
	3. Sales (2–3)		
B.	Development		10,000
	1. Design Supplies (1–3)		
	2. Components/Small Parts (1–3)		
	Total, gen., admin., & devel.	14,000	
	Margin, 25%	3,500	
	Total, category III, Indir. Material		17,500

IV. Promotional & Marketing 20,000

A.	Brochures (1–2)		
B.	Advertisements (2–3)		
C.	Travel Expenses (1–3)		
	Total, broch., adv., & travel	20,000	
	Margin, 25%	5,000	
	Total, category IV, Promotion		25,000

V. Production Materials
(Based upon 100 units out of 150 units projected for initial 12-month period.)

A.	Direct Material (2–3)		32,400
B.	Sub-contracting (2–3)		20,000

(*Continued*)

EXHIBIT 6 (Continued)

Total, direct mat., subcontract.	52,400
Margin, 25%	13,100

Total, category V, Production Mat.	65,500

Total categories I through V, Phase 2+	457,100

*Numbers in parenthesis indicate time-based priorities.

EXHIBIT 7

Alpha Omega Electronics (A)

Proposal For Investment in Alpha Omega Electronics

A.   To be issued:
1.   200 convertible debentures par value $1000, 7% coupon due July 1, 1978 (5 year). Each debenture convertible into 40 shares of common stock (no par) (conversion price $25 per share for common stock). Debentures callable at $1060 per debenture any time subsequent to July 1, 1975.
2.   6000 shares of common stock (no par) at $10 per share.
The above debentures and common stock are to be sold together as a unit. A unit includes one convertible debenture and 30 shares of common stock for a total of $1300. The minimum number of units to be sold to an investor is 8 units or $10,400.

B.   Issued:
1.   8000 shares of common stock to founders in exchange for their development of the Production Control Center including prototype, patent application, etc.
2.   5000 shares of common stock to organizers and promoters in exchange for $40,000 in cash.
Total capitalization will be $308,000, $200,000—convertible debentures and $108,000—common stock. The initial capitalization will be reflected in assets of $300,000 of cash and $8000 of development for the Production Control Center.

C.   Stock options:
1.   8000 shares of common stock (no par) to be reserved for later issue to management and directors at $10 per share. Stock may not be issued until such time as earnings per share exceed $10 per share on a post conversion of debenture basis.

EXHIBIT 8

Alpha Omega Electronics (A)
Break-Even Analysis

1973–1975 Level of Fixed Costs		($)	(%)
Selling price net of distribution discount		3360	100
Direct—variable costs per unit			
Direct labor	320		
Direct materials	324		
Sub-contract	200		
Total		844	25
Contribution per unit P-V		2516	75
Fixed costs	yearly	month	
Manufacture burden	78000	6500	
Selling & promotion	69000	5750	
General & admin.	80395	6700	
Total	227395	18950	

$$\text{Break-Even Sales} = \frac{\text{Fixed Cost \$}}{1 - \dfrac{V}{P}}$$

	yearly	month
=	$227,395	$18,950
	.75	.75
=	303,193	25,267
Break-Even Units =	303,193	25,267
	3,360	3,360
=	90 units	7.5 units

EXHIBIT 9

Alpha Omega Electronics (A)

Relationship of Sales to Earnings Per Share (EPS) and Future Market Value of Common Stock

Sales					Earnings		Earnings Per Share $	Return on Stockholders' Equity
Units		$		Fixed Cost	Before Tax	After Tax		
Mo	Yr	Mo	Yr					
10	120	33,600	403,200	230,000	72,400	37,648	1.98*	21%*
15	180	50,400	604,800	230,000	223,600	116,272	6.12*	64%*
20	240	67,200	806,400	230,000	374,800	194,896	10.25*	108%*
30	360	100,800	1,209,600	350,000	557,200	289,744	10.73**	76%**
40	480	134,400	1,612,800	350,000	859,600	446,992	16.55**	117%**
50	600	168,000	2,016,000	500,000	1,012,000	526,240	15.04***	114%**

*Without conversion of convertible stock, 20,000 shares common stock.
**After conversion, $200,000 convertible debentures into 8000 additional shares C.S.
***After conversion of convertible debentures *and* exercise of all options on 8000 shares to management and directors.

CASE 28

Wells Fargo & Company

Here was an opportunity to apply what he had learned in the classroom, thought Stan Wong, a second year student at the Pacific Coast Banking School. For two weeks each year a select group of bankers took courses and listened to outside speakers at the school held on the University of Washington campus. One of the speakers, Mr. Cooley, described in his talk what appeared to Stan Wong to be a very complicated situation.

As president and chief executive officer of Wells Fargo & Company, the holding company for Wells Fargo Bank, Mr. Cooley needed to make a crucial recommendation regarding the upcoming dividend declaration. Earlier in the summer BankAmerica Corp., the world's biggest bank holding company, was refused permission to acquire 50 percent of the voting shares of Allstate International S.A. of Zurich, Switzerland, by the Fed's

Board of Governors. A major reason for the refusal was the applicant's inadequate capital base. Citicorp, Bankers Trust, and First Chicago, each among the nation's ten biggest banking operations, also had planned acquisitions turned down by the Fed in recent months. Just last week Wells Fargo also encountered problems with capital inadequacy. After consultation with the Fed, the bank's holding company withdrew its application for acquisition of Atlantic Pacific Leasing, Inc., an auto leasing firm. The action was consistent with recently announced policies of the Fed discouraging proposals that would entail the use of funds for further nonbank expansion by bank holding companies.

The Fed's message seemed clear. Before certain bank holding companies could get approval to continue their aggressive expansion programs their capi-

---

This case was prepared from publicly available sources by and used with the permission of Professor Steve Dawson of the University of Hawaii.

tal base needed improvement. Whatever the merits of the Fed's view of capital adequacy, its permission was required before acquisitions could be made.

A recommendation regarding the next dividend payment was needed for the upcoming meeting of the board of directors. Undoubtedly there would be considerable interest at the meeting in finding a way to improve the level of capital. Certainly one option was to raise new equity funds in the stock market, although bank stock prices were currently well below their recent highs. A dividend increase might boost the stock's price and allow new capital to be raised with fewer shares. On the other hand a higher dividend would increase the amount of external funds needed. A dividend cut instead would reduce the need for external capital.

Recalling Mr. Cooley's challenge that the school's students climb down from their ivory towers and face a business world problem, Stan Wong returned home planning to research Wells Fargo's dividend situation and to prepare a recommendation of his own.

WELLS FARGO BANK

Wells Fargo Bank, N.A., traces its origin to the express and banking firm founded in 1852 by Henry Wells and William Fargo. The original company operated the westernmost leg of the pony express and ran several stagecoach lines. Even today the stagecoach remains a prominent symbol of the company. The bank now provides a full range of consumer and corporate banking services through its branch network in California.

Since 1967, several significant changes were made at Wells Fargo. The bank used to be particularly strong in North-

ern California but was virtually absent in Southern California. In 1967 the decision was made to challenge the competition in the south and a rapid buildup of branches began. By the end of 1974 the projection was for 62 branches in Southern California out of a total of 313 offices. The Southern California expansion had been associated with a rapid buildup of both deposits and loans.

The second important development at Wells Fargo was the 1969 reorganization with the bank becoming a wholly owned subsidiary of a bank holding company. Bank holding companies offered many significant advantages for aggressive, innovative bank management and most large banks and many smaller banks became part of a holding company. Wells Fargo & Company owned all the capital stock of Wells Fargo Bank. The holding company also owned subsidiaries operating in several areas closely related to banking, but the bank remained the dominant part of the holding company's activities and the source of most of its income. At the end of 1973 total assets for the bank were $11.59 billion as compared with $11.77 billion for the consolidated holding company.

BANK HOLDING COMPANIES

A formerly independent bank could become part of a bank holding company through a simple exchange of stock. The bank's shareholders exchanged their shares of bank stock for shares of stock in the newly created bank holding company whose primary asset was its ownership of the bank. The beauty of the holding company form of organization was that the holding company might engage in activities that were forbidden to the bank. The ability to offer new and diversified services became important for banks when they outgrew their public service image in the early 1960s and became energetic profit-seeking organizations.

The ability of bank holding companies to engage in activities unrelated to banking had caused concern among bank regulators responsible for the safe operation of the bank. The result was a series of legislative restrictions that were intended to protect bank depositors and to preserve public confidence in the banking system. The 1956 Bank Holding Company Act gave the Federal Reserve Board the power to regulate bank holding companies that controlled two or more banks. The act limited nonbanking activities to the performance of services that were "a proper incident to" banking and, in addition, were "of a financial, fiduciary, or insurance nature."

One-bank holding companies were deliberately excluded since many organizations such as the Goodyear Tire and Rubber Company, Hershey Foods, and the United Mine Workers owned small banks. In 1967, however, the one-bank holding company loophole was discovered and numerous banks quickly reorganized and began to expand into nonbanking areas. The 1970 Amendments to the Bank Holding Company Act extended the Fed's supervision to one-bank holding companies and limited their expansion to activities "so closely related to banking or managing or controlling banks as to be a proper incident thereto."

Bank regulators believed that to assure the solvency of bank subsidiaries and to protect bank depositors, the banking subsidiaries had to be insulated from the business risk associated with the operations of the parent holding com-

pany and nonbank subsidiaries. Accordingly, there were regulations that limited the amount of dividends a bank subsidiary could pay to the parent holding company. The National Bank Act, as amended, required a national bank to obtain approval from the Comptroller before paying dividends in any year which exceeded net profits for that year plus retained net profits for the preceding two years. The Federal Reserve Act imposed identical restrictions on state member banks with approval to be obtained from the board of governors. State banking laws generally restricted payment of dividends out of capital. There were also important limitations on the ability of the bank to loan funds to the parent company or to other parts of the holding company.

CAPITAL ADEQUACY IN BANK HOLDING COMPANIES

Before bank holding companies became widespread, bank regulators needed only to look at the bank when determining capital adequacy. Bank holding companies had severely complicated the situation, and there were two basic alternatives available to bank regulators. First, since the bank subsidiary was essentially separate from the rest of the holding company, it was possible to restrict capital adequacy to the bank as was done previously. The second approach was to consider the holding company as a single entity.

It appeared the Fed had decided to follow the second approach and to consider the capital adequacy of the whole organization. The plain fact was that troubles in the parent company or the other subsidiaries could lead to a loss of confidence in the bank. In a strictly legal sense losses in another subsidiary or the parent company should have no direct effect on the bank. However, depositors and borrowers could associate the bank with other parts of the organization and past experience had shown that only in very unusual cases had bank holding companies chosen to abandon a failing subsidiary.

WELLS FARGO & COMPANY: RELATIVE PERFORMANCE

As of June 30, 1974, Wells Fargo & Company ranked fourteenth in the United States in deposits and fourth on the West Coast. The data in Exhibit 1 are for bank holding companies. Figures for individual banks were difficult to obtain since most banks were part of bank holding companies. Wells Fargo was an aggressive practitioner of liability management, the use of short-term purchased funds to meet loan commitments. The use of purchased funds permitted loans to grow faster than regular demand and savings deposits. Over the previous ten years the common equity accounts at Wells Fargo had grown more slowly than for most other big bank holding companies.

EVENTS IN 1974

When 1974 started, the outlook was fairly bright for banks and bank holding companies. New areas were being opened for further holding company expansion and the prospect was for interest rates to decline somewhat from their recent historically high levels. Banks are essentially financial intermediaries, obtaining funds from depositors and other sources and lending them to borrowers.

The banks' profit comes from the spread between the cost of obtaining funds and the return on loans and investments. The high interest rates in 1973 were associated with a contraction in the spread for Wells Fargo as is shown in Exhibit 2. Unfortunately, the bright hopes for 1974 soon began to turn sour. Interest rates went up, not down, and purchased funds became increasingly expensive. The controversy about Franklin National Bank added to an increasingly negative regulatory environment. Franklin had too many risky loans financed by high cost purchased funds and a staggering loss in foreign exchange trading that forced it deeply in debt to the Fed. By August, 1974, it was struggling to survive and to avoid being merged into another bank. Within a short period of time an unusual number of banks appeared to be overloaned, overborrowed, overdiversified, and undercapitalized.

The Fed and other regulators attempted to bring things back under control by slowing the growth of bank holding companies until their financial base could be reestablished. On June 19, 1974, the board of governors surprised the banking community and denied BankAmerica Corporation's application to obtain 50 percent of Allstate International S.A., a foreign insurance company. The order denying the application contained the following statement:

> The Board also noted its general concern with the tendency of many U.S. banking organizations to pursue a policy of rapid expansion in domestic and foreign markets. Such expansion can expose the organizations to potential liabilities and risks disproportionate to the stated size of their investment in any particular venture. Such expansion should therefore be premised on a strong capital base. While the Board recognizes the quality and ex-

perience of the Applicant's management, the present capital position of the Applicant is somewhat lower than what the Board would consider appropriate in light of its recent asset growth. In such circumstances, the Board would prefer to see funds first used to enlarge the capital position of such organization.

Responding to the Fed's denial, a spokesman for BankAmerica was quick to respond that

our capital position is strong and fully capable of building dividend growth. Liquidity management is a key element in the evaluation of capital adequacy. BankAmerica has a reputation of superior performance in this area. Capital adequacy is a complex subject, and a whole host of management relationships must be taken into consideration. Capital ratio analysis, taken by itself, doesn't do justice to the subject.

WELLS FARGO: THE CAPITAL BASE

The capital base could be examined both for the bank subsidiary and for the bank holding company as a consolidated unit. In this section the bank's capital will be examined first, followed by the holding company.

Like most banks, Wells Fargo Bank had seen its capital base decline when measured by the traditional relationship to bank assets. As is shown in Exhibit 3, Wells Fargo's capital ratio had declined from 6.7 percent in 1969 to 4.3 percent in 1973. Wells Fargo was above the 3.7 percent figure for Bank of America but well below the 5.3 percent level for the ten largest U.S. banks. In 1972, the only year in which Wells Fargo did not show a decline, there was a large issue of common stock. In November 1972 the holding

company for Wells Fargo issued 910,000 common stock shares at $27 to provide additional capital funds for Wells Fargo Bank. At the end of August 1974, there were about 19.7 million shares outstanding.

Exhibit 4 gives a further breakdown of the capital level of Wells Fargo Bank. From 1969 through 1973 total assets more than doubled but total capital, which includes long-term debt capital, only increased by 32 percent.

The 1973 increase in total capital was the result of several conflicting forces. Long-term debt capital increased by $25 million and net income for the bank was $44,293,000. Offsetting these increases in capital were several capital reductions. A $24,176,000 dividend was paid to the parent company. There was also a $15,880,000 charge against the bank's undivided profits for a transfer to the reserve for loan losses. This charge was in addition to the $11,034,000 charged against income. There was a related increase in deferred taxes of $9,720,000. In 1973 there was also a charge of $12,220,000 to undivided profits, which represented the excess of purchase price over the value of assets purchased in a German bank. This entry was made in accordance with the requirements of the U.S. Comptroller of the Currency. The Comptroller's ruling conflicted with generally accepted accounting principles and it was expected that the entry would be reversed in 1974 and the resulting "goodwill" would be written-off over a 40-year period.

Ordinarily, all expenses such as bad loan losses and the reserves created to absorb them should flow through the income statement. Banks, however, were able to take part of the reserve directly from retained earnings. Bank regulators said that for financial statement purposes banks should use a five-year average loan-loss experience to determine the minimum reserve. The Internal Revenue Service, in contrast, allowed banks to show a tax-free reserve for loan losses equal to a 20-year average loss rate applied to eligible existing loans. Generally, the 20-year average loss rate was higher than the five-year formula figure. Only the five-year formula reserve had to come out of reported earnings. The rest was debited directly to earned surplus.

Banks were still the major component of consolidated bank holding companies. The equity capital to asset ratios in Exhibit 5 are for consolidated bank holding companies. Wells Fargo had a capital ratio of 3.9 percent, which just exceeded the 3.8 percent for BankAmerica. The average capital ratio for the 14 largest bank holding companies in the United States was 4.7 percent.

HOLDING COMPANY EARNINGS AND DIVIDENDS

The exceptional asset increases achieved by Wells Fargo Bank (Exhibit 4) were matched by the increases in consolidated net income (Exhibit 6) reported by the holding company. As operating income, or net income before security gains and losses, increased, dividends paid to stockholders also increased, but at a slightly slower rate. In the last quarter of 1973 the dividend was raised from $0.215 to $0.24 per share. At an annual dividend rate of $0.96 per share, the payout on 1973 net income would have been 42.7 percent. The $0.24 quarterly dividend was maintained during the first half of 1974. About 19.7 million shares were outstanding.

Past Dividend Increases: Stock Market Response

When reported earnings increased in 1972 and 1973, Wells Fargo & Company increased the dividend payment. Exhibit 7 shows the resulting market price action for Wells Fargo Stock relative to the New York Stock Exchange financial index with the date of the dividend announcement equal to an index of 1.000.

Stock Price

Investors appeared to have reached the same conclusion as the bank regulators about the outlook for bank holding companies, and many bank holding company stocks were selling below their recent highs. Wells Fargo was no exception. The price now was around $16, but earlier in 1974 it had been $27. In contrast, the book value per share was a little over $21.

For purposes of comparison Stan Wong assembled Exhibit 8 to show price earnings ratios and dividend payouts for the other large bank holding companies in the country. The earnings and dividends were for 1973 and the stock prices rounded to the nearest dollar were as of August 1, 1974.

Debt as Capital

In recent years some banks, including Wells Fargo, had been able to count long-term debt as part of their capital base. In recent months, however, the Fed had become distinctly cool toward this approach to capital acquisition. By various means the Fed had conveyed the message that it was equity capital, not borrowed debt capital, which had to be built up.

DIVIDEND RECOMMENDATION

At this point Stan Wong realized there were three distinct alternatives for the dividend payment, none of which could be ruled out yet. First, the dividend could be raised in hopes that the stock price would then recover some of its recent decline. Second, the dividend could be reduced or eliminated altogether so as to increase capital retention. Finally,

of course, there was the traditional way around hard decisions—make no change in the present policy. For purposes of his analysis, Stan Wong decided an adequate level of capital might exist if the holding company raised enough equity funds to raise the bank's capital ratio to 5.3 percent, the average for the ten largest U.S. banks. No new debt would be included but the existing capital debt would still be counted.

EXHIBIT 1

Wells Fargo & Company

Measures of Bank Holding Company Performance
June 30, 1974

Bank Holding Companies	Total Deposits ($millions)	Loans as a % of Deposits	Net Fed. Funds Borrowed as a % of Loans	10-Year Growth Common Equity (%)
1. BankAmerica	$46,862	61	4	6.7
2. Citicorp	41,468	77	8	6.1
3. Chase Manhattan	35,266	72	8	5.0
4. Manufacturers Hanover	21,986	73	7	5.1
5. J. P. Morgan	18,302	66	9	4.3
6. Bankers Trust New York	17,939	65	6	4.6
7. Chemical New York	16,693	71	8	3.6
8. Western Bankcorp.	14,740	72	8	6.5
9. First Chicago	14,403	82	8	5.6
10. Continental Illinois	13,957	86	(17)	5.7
11. Security Pacific	12,571	70	10	6.3
12. Marine Midland Banks	11,793	59	7	6.1
13. Charter New York	9,786	51	1	6.1
14. Wells Fargo	8,880	82	20	4.8

Source: "Annual Survey of Bank Performance," *Business Week*, September 21, 1974. Data are from Investor's Management Sciences, Inc.

EXHIBIT 2

Wells Fargo & Company

Yield Spread for Wells Fargo Bank: 1969–1973

Year	Gross Yield on Earning Assets (%)	Pooled Cost of Invested Funds (%)	Net Spread (%)
1969	7.41	3.70	3.71
1970	7.98	4.17	3.81
1971	7.18	3.76	3.42
1972	6.88	3.60	3.28
1973	8.21	5.45	2.76

Source: Wells Fargo & Company Annual Report.

EXHIBIT 3

Wells Fargo & Company

Ratio of Bank Capital[1] to Total Assets
1969–1973

Banks	Year (%)				
	1969	1970	1971	1972	1973
Wells Fargo Bank, N.A.	6.7	6.4	5.1	5.5	4.3
Bank of America	4.1	4.2	4.1	4.0	3.7
10 largest U.S. banks: (domestic and foreign offices)	7.3	6.7	6.6	6.0	5.3
326 weekly reporting large commercial banks	8.0	8.4	8.3	8.2	7.9
All 14,228 insured commercial banks	8.6	8.5	8.3	8.0	7.9

[1] Includes debt capital.

Sources: *Moody's Bank and Finance Manual* and M.A. Schapiro & Co., Inc., *Bank Stock Quarterly.*

EXHIBIT 4

Wells Fargo & Company

Asset and Capital Accounts: Wells Fargo Bank, N.A.
1969–1973 ($millions)

Year	Assets	Debt Capital	Equity Capital	Total Capital	Total Capital To Assets (%)
1969	$ 5,700.8	$50.0	$331.0	$381.0	6.7
1970	6,209.4	50.0	349.3	399.3	6.4
1971	7,785.7	50.0	348.9	398.9	5.1
1972	8,924.7	50.0	436.4	486.4	5.5
1973	11,590.1	75.0	427.2	502.2	4.3

Source: *Moody's Bank and Finance Manual.*

EXHIBIT 5

Wells Fargo & Company

Ratio of Bank Holding Company
Capital To Total Assets: 1973

Bank Holding Company	Capital to Assets[1] (%)
BankAmerica	3.8
Citicorp	5.4
Chase Manhattan	5.0
Manufacturers Hanover	4.5
J. P. Morgan	6.7
Bankers Trust N.Y.	3.6
Chemical New York	5.6
Western Bankcorp	4.9
First Chicago	4.5
Continental Illinois	4.6
Security Pacific	4.2
Marine Midland Banks	4.6
Charter New York	4.9
Wells Fargo & Company	3.9

[1] Includes debt capital.

Source: *Moody's Bank and Finance Manual.*

EXHIBIT 6

Wells Fargo & Company

Operating Earnings and Dividends:
Wells Fargo & Company
1969–1973

Year	Net Income Before Security Gains and Losses		Dividends Paid per Share	Dividend Payout (%)
	Total ($Thousand)	Per Share		
1969	$32,047	$1.75	$0.80	45.7
1970	32,584	1.77	0.80	45.2
1971	34,352	1.85	0.80	43.2
1972	39,094	2.10	0.86	41.0
1973	44,119	2.25	0.885	39.3

Source: *Moody's Bank and Finance Manual.*

EXHIBIT 7

Wells Fargo & Company

Stock Price Behavior Relative to the NYSE
Financial Index At Date of
Dividend Increase Announcement

Days Before and After Dividend Announcement	Stock Price Index[a]	
	May 17, 1972[b] *Dividend Increase*	*August 21, 1973*[c] *Dividend Increase*
−10	.997	1.037
−5	1.026	1.009
−4	1.026	1.008
−3	1.008	1.012
−2	.998	.997
−1	1.009	1.015
0	1.000	1.000
+1	.990	.976
+2	.981	.965
+3	.979	.972
+4	.989	.950
+5	.985	.956
+6	.980	.937
+7	.992	.920
+8	.984	.901
+9	.990	.903
+10	.989	.904

[a] $\dfrac{\text{Wells Fargo Market Price}}{\text{NYSE Financial Index}}$ = 1.000 at time of dividend announcement.

[b] On May 17, 1972, the dividend was raised from $.20 to $.215 per share.

[c] On August 21, 1973, the dividend was raised from $.215 to $0.24 per share.

Sources: *Wall Street Journal* and *Barrons*.

EXHIBIT 8

Wells Fargo & Company

Stock Prices, Price Earnings Ratios, and Dividend Payouts
14 Largest U.S. Bank Holding Companies
August, 1974

	Current Market Price	1974 Price Range	Price Earnings Ratio	Dividend Payout (%)
1. BankAmerica	$30	$48–$27	9.7	40.4
2. Citicorp	30	46–28	14.6	34.8
3. Chase Manhattan	33	56–32	6.7	40.6
4. Manufacturers Hanover	30	40–25	7.5	43.9
5. J. P. Morgan	49	69–47	10.2	38.2
6. Bankers Trust New York	37	57–31	5.8	47.5
7. Chemical New York	33	47–31	6.6	57.4
8. Western Bankcorp	17	30–16	4.8	39.4
9. First Chicago	21	37–16	8.7	33.7
10. Continental Illinois	33	59–28	6.0	35.2
11. Security Pacific	17	25–14	5.9	44.8
12. Marine Midland Banks	17	25–16	4.9	51.4
13. Charter New York	22	30–20	5.7	51.5
14. Wells Fargo	16	27–13	7.1	40.4

CASE 29

Aloha Airlines

On a bright sunny day in late December 1972, Kenneth F. C. Char, president of Aloha Airlines, sat thoughtfully in his office at Hawaii International Airport reviewing the 1972 financial results. It had been a banner year. The company had made an unprecedented financial turnaround with a solid net profit after several successive years of losses. Passenger traffic was up, the load factor was impressive, and Aloha's share of the interisland market had increased significantly over its arch rival and sole competitor, Hawaiian Airlines. However, Char realized his company was in dire need of long-term funds. He wondered whether a "reverse stock split" might facilitate the sale of additional stock.

Aloha recorded a net profit of $1,417,000 during 1972, compared to a loss of $825,000 in 1971. Operating revenues were up 35.5 percent. The passenger load factor rose seven points to a respectable 57.4 percent, and Aloha's share of the interisland market increased to 40.8 percent from 36.8 percent.

The outlook for 1973 was most encouraging. Gross national product was advancing at an annual rate of 12 percent. Economists for the First Hawaiian Bank and the Bank of Hawaii were predicting even greater increases for Hawaii. Aloha had just achieved greatly improved operating efficiency through the introduction of a computerized crew record keeping system and the installation of reduced thrust take-off techniques. New and increased promotional activities were reflected in a 33.5-percent increase in traffic for a total of 1,496,558 passengers carried in 1972. The company joined with United Air Lines, Avis, and Sheraton in a huge Waikiki '73 promotion; and to meet expanded demand Aloha increased its offerings of one-day, two-island, and other packaged tours. As

This case was prepared by and used with the permission of Professor Russell A. Taussig of the University of Hawaii.

a result of these marketing and operating improvements, along with a rapid increase in the Japanese visitors to Hawaii, management expected the company to show a net profit of over $1.5 million for the first half of 1973 compared to a net loss of about $500,000 for the same period in 1972. Advance reservations for 1973 were well ahead of those of the previous year.

However, along with generally favorable prospects, President Char recognized he faced several life-or-death problems. He needed more aircraft. He was confronted with a sizable amount of overdue short-term debt. He required equity financing.

Bulls on Aloha credited the 1972 turnaround in financial performance to the improved national economy, greater operating efficiency, new and enhanced promotional activities, as well as the rapid increase in Japanese visitors to Hawaii. On the other hand bears noted that a major, and transitory, factor was the scheduling agreement between Aloha and Hawaiian, which virtually guaranteed Aloha a "fair share" of the interisland market. The scheduling agreement by its terms was soon to expire, and Aloha then faced the dismal prospect of a substantial loss of market share. The expiration of the scheduling agreement was viewed by some of Aloha's financial analysts as a life-or-death problem. After an aborted Hawaii-Aloha merger, the parties concluded a scheduling agreement approved by the Civil Aeronautics Board (CAB) that limited the number of flight frequencies for the industry. The agreement would expire on July 15, 1973. The CAB had denied Aloha's petition for extension.

In July 1973 Aloha filed an antitrust suit against Hawaiian Airlines in U.S. District Court, alleging Hawaiian attempted to monopolize interisland air transportation in Hawaii in violation of federal and state antitrust laws. Aloha sued for $7.7 million which, if sustained, would be subject to triple damages. This lawsuit was unsettled at the time these facts were written. Hawaiian had filed cross complaints. Informed legal sources were of the opinion that acrimonious forensic skirmishes would be in the courts for many years. More than anything else, this litigation evidenced the mortal combat between Hawaiian Airlines and Aloha for the interisland market.

Now that he had turned Aloha around, Kenneth Char was confident he could quickly take the company up to new and greater heights. But to do so he felt he would need to incur major capital expenditures. He thought the company would have to acquire two additional Boeing 737s, raising the company's passenger fleet to six 737s. The two additional aircraft necessitated 1973 capital expenditures of about $1 million for down payments, according to Char's reckoning. Although Kenneth Char felt two more 737s were necessary, his views on capacity expansion were questioned by some critics of Aloha's management. At issue was the sizable capital budget for Aloha in 1973. In addition to the proposed appropriations for new aircraft, the company needed approximately $1,750,000 to repay loans and past due obligations.

When Kenneth Char was asked why equity was being used to replace loans and past due obligations, he simply replied that a sizable portion of the past due obligations consisted of back taxes due to the state, which the state was not legally authorized to roll-over or defer. Moreover, additional debt financing, he felt, was an impossibility—the company, in his opinion, had exceeded its debt capacity and had no collateral to offer as security for a loan.

Kenneth Char discussed the financial problems with John H. Sakamoto, treasurer. After considering several approaches to raising the needed $2,750,000 in long-term funds, Char and Sakamoto agreed that one alternative was the sale of additional stock. However, the market price of the company's shares had been under $1.00 for a considerable period of time. To raise that price, so as to sell common stock on terms most advantageous to the corporation, Sakamoto explained it would be necessary to effect a "reverse stock split"; that is, combine some number of outstanding shares into one share, creating a common stock with a higher pro forma market price per share. Sakamoto went on to explain that what he meant by selling the stock on terms most advantageous to the company was simply getting the most money out of the proposed stock offering by adjusting the price per share so that it would be removed from the catty and doggy class. Char was impressed. Yet with the best interest of the stockholders in mind, he asked Sakamoto to prepare within the week a study of the strengths and weaknesses of the reverse stock split. The study was to include a review of the journal literature, a statistical analysis of reverse splits, an in-depth review of the effects for companies that recently had reverse splits, and an evaluation by the investment bankers for the company. Char also asked that the study include a careful analysis of the peculiar circumstances of Aloha that would require any special variants to the usual procedures that otherwise would be followed with

the proposed reverse split. Sakamoto instructed his assistant, Leslie Lee, a recent MBA graduate, to prepare the requested memorandum.

HISTORY OF ALOHA AIRLINES AND FINANCIAL STATUS

Aloha Airlines, Inc., was incorporated in 1946 as a competitor to Hawaiian Airlines, which, until then, held a monopoly on interisland traffic. Public passenger travel in 1973 among the islands was exclusively by air and was provided almost entirely by Aloha and Hawaiian.

Aloha provided regularly scheduled service among Honolulu and five airports on the four largest neighbor islands, Kauai, Maui, Molokai and Hawaii (see Exhibit 1 "Route Map"). The majority of the company's passengers were visitors to Hawaii. The Hawaii Visitors Bureau reported that the number of tourist visits to the neighbor islands increased from 953,000 in 1968 to 1,893,000 in 1972. The number of hotel rooms on the neighbor islands increased from 5,500 to 11,200 in the same period. Between 1968 and 1972 the number of revenue passengers carried by Aloha increased from 825,000 to 1,497,000, and the load factor increased from 50.8 to 57.4 percent, although seating capacity almost doubled. Hawaiian's load factor in 1972 was 60.4 percent. Average fare per passenger increased from $11.87 in 1968 to $15.22 in 1972. Hawaiian's average fare in 1972 was $15.48.

Fares were of two basic types—regular air fares and "common fares" received in connection with a passenger's travel from the mainland. Regular air fares were those charged to persons not eligible for common fares. In 1972 approximately 44 percent of the passengers paid regular fares. The remainder, who paid common fares, were passengers from the mainland who traveled to the outlying islands at a charge of $9.00 per stopover. Aloha received from the mainland carriers 80 percent of the standard adult fare plus $5.50 of the stopover fees charged at intermediate points and $1.50 of the stopover fee at the points of entry and exit to Hawaii. The yield on common fares compared favorably with the yield on regular fares.

Aloha carried 1,496,558 passengers during 1972, a 33.5 percent increase over 1971. These passengers accounted for

1971. There had been no fare increase since a 2-percent raise in 1970.

3. Substantial additional expenses associated with the introduction of the new Boeing 737 in 1969.

4. Substantial decline in Aloha's share of interisland traffic from 42.3 percent in 1967 to 36.8 percent in 1971, primarily as a result of over scheduling by Hawaiian.

Passengers carried by Aloha and Hawaiian for the five years ending in 1972 were as indicated in the following table:

| | Revenue Passenger Miles (000) | | | | |
	1968	1969	1970	1971	1972
Aloha Airlines	110,303	130,669	130,940	147,367	206,111
Hawaiian Airlines	191,212	196,548	224,140	253,099	298,736
	Percentage of Revenue Passenger Miles				
	1968	1969	1970	1971	1972
Aloha Airlines	36.6	39.9	36.9	36.8	40.8
Hawaiian Airlines	63.4	60.1	63.1	63.2	59.2

40.8 percent of the interisland air traffic in 1972, compared with 36.8 percent in 1971. In 1971 its load factor was 50.5 percent, and its 1972 load factor was 57.4 percent. The break-even load was 52.0 percent in 1971.

Throughout the five years ending in 1972, Aloha sustained losses averaging approximately $2 million annually except for the last year when it reported a profit of about $1.5 million (see Exhibit 2). The principal reasons for the losses were:

1. Extraordinary charge of $1,367,045 in 1970 as a result of cancellation of an aircraft purchasing agreement.

2. Substantial increases in the costs of labor, fuel, landing fees, and maintenance during the years 1968 through

As a result of the operating losses sustained from 1967 to 1971, Aloha's liabilities of $10,958,000 at December 31, 1972, exceeded its assets by $1,137,000. However, this stockholders' deficiency of 10.3 percent on liabilities represented a gain in stockholders' equity of $1,117,000 compared to the prior year. (Details of financial condition are shown in Exhibits 3 and 4.)

The financial statements for Hawaiian Airlines reflect a similar improvement in operating results for 1972 and a more solvent financial position (see Exhibits 5 and 6).

In summarizing the history of Aloha and its financial status, it can be seen that after a series of operating losses from 1967 to 1971, the company apparently had turned the corner in 1972. However, the market price of its common stock had not reflected the turnaround. Following are the closing bid prices on the Honolulu Stock Exchange for the period from January 1, 1968, to May 7, 1973:

tween $20 to $40 for stocks in the United States. This buying-range argument supports reverse splits as well as regular splits—the company just comes into the buying range from a different direction.

One of the few studies on companies executing reverse splits showed that on

Year	High	Low	Year	High	Low
1968	$4½	$2¹⁵/₁₆	1972		
1969	5½	1¾	First quarter	$1⅛	$ .75
1970	3⅛	.65	Second quarter	1¼	1.00
1971	1¼	.50	Third quarter	1.00	.90
			Fourth quarter	1.00	.80
			1973		
			First quarter	1.00	.70
			Second quarter		
			(through May 7, 1973)	.75	.65

Regular and Reverse Stock Splits

Empirical studies, though by no means uncontroversial, tended to show that stock splits generally enhanced the aggregate market value of a company's stock. Researchers have argued that stock splits increase market values because

1. they reduce the price of a 100-share round lot, thereby making the stock attractive to a greater number of potential investors;

2. they are psychologically associated in the minds of investors with good fortunes for the investors;

3. they generally are the harbinger of an increase in cash dividends.

If stock splits produce higher aggregate stock values, do reverse splits depress them? Some knowledgeable financial experts point out that splits—reverse or otherwise—signal management activity and are attention getters. They argue that an optimum price per share is be-

the average 54 percent declined in total market value, 46 percent increased; but the size of the declines exceeded the advances, resulting in a mean decline of 28 percent.[1] West/Brouilette listed the advantages and disadvantages of reverse splits:

Advantages:

1. Higher per share prices enhance the prestige of a company and facilitate issuance of new shares.

2. Lenders often refuse to take very low priced shares as collateral for loans; thus, reverse splits increase loan values.

3. Reverse splits may improve a company's credit ratings.

4. Higher per share prices can reduce trading charges.

5. Reducing the number of shares in the hands of odd lotters may cause them to sell, thus reducing the cost of keeping stockholder records.

---

[1] Richard E. West and Alan E. Brouilette, "Reverse Stock Splits," *Financial Executive* (Jan. 1970), pp. 12–17.

6. Earnings per share will increase, thereby influencing perception of a company's size and importance.

7. Higher price per share allows for less violent percentage fluctuations in market price.

Disadvantages:

1. A reverse split is generally not regarded by the investment community as a harbinger of good times; the reverse split firm finds itself associated in the minds of investors with hardship cases.

2. The reverse split requires a special vote by stockholders, generally with two-thirds approval.

3. The mailing of proxies, and related costs, constitutes a drain on the treasury many companies can ill afford to pay.

4. The reverse split is no guarantee that the price will remain up; with little or no earnings the stock may drift back to its old price.

5. The reverse split encourages small holders to sell, thereby depressing the price of the stock.

6. Stocks of small- and medium-sized companies are ailing partly because they don't have large "floats"—that is, enough shares to attract institutional buyers who want to take big positions, or retail brokers who want stocks that can be merchandised in volume through their branch networks. The trouble with a reverse split is that it reduces a company's float even more.

Discussions with Investment Bankers

Management recognized the pitfalls of the proposed reverse split; nevertheless, they faced grave financial problems. With the background of the study in mind, they arranged a consultation with Dominick and Dominick, their investment bankers.

The investment bankers pointed out that because brokers consider small trades unprofitable, they won't solicit orders or extend margin credit for shares selling below $5. "Thus," they said, "ironically, companies find their shares unmarketable as the price becomes more of a bargain." In late December 1972, the stocks of 303 Amex companies, and 47 Big-Board companies, were "untouchables" selling below $5.

The investment bankers suggested a reverse split of 1 for 5 for Aloha and indicated that after the reverse split, they would consider an underwriting for 600,000 of the new Aloha shares (or a lesser number of shares if deemed appropriate at the time of underwriting). They also agreed to take as part of their compensation for the sale of the new stock warrants for 30,000.

Silence fell over the group at the close of the conference with the investment bankers.

Char's Dilemma

On December 26, 1972, Kenneth Char found himself in the happy position of gaining on his arch rival John Magoon of Hawaiian Airlines. But he had problems. He was in dire need of cash.

He was unclear about the size of the reverse split, timing, and alternatives. It was an uncommonly beautiful December day—even for Hawaii. Char climbed aboard the noon Aloha flight for Kauai. He knew just the spot where he could reflect peacefully on the problems of Aloha. Some companies who had gone through a reverse stock split are listed in Exhibit 7.

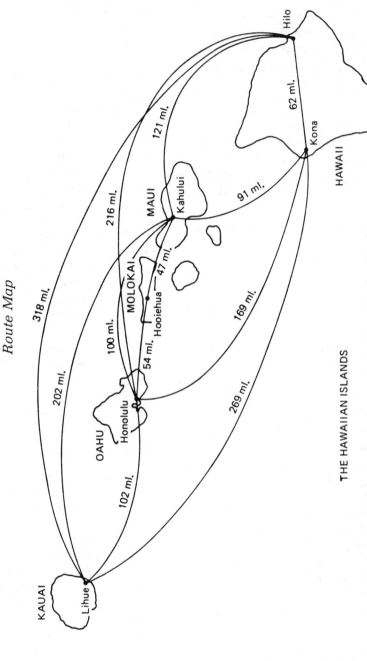

EXHIBIT 1

Aloha Airlines

Route Map

THE HAWAIIAN ISLANDS

Note — The Company's Certificate of Public Convenience and Necessity allows the Company to provide service between any two points within the State of Hawaii.

EXHIBIT 2

Aloha Airlines

Income Statement

	Year ended December 31,					Three months ended March 31, 1973 (unaudited)	
	1968	1969	1970	1971	1972	1972	1973
Operating revenues							
Passenger	$ 9,792,467	$12,972,048	$14,651,669	$16,550,736	$22,775,952	$5,266,287	$6,730,115
United States mail	118,534	126,592	143,464	137,133	122,628	28,494	32,157
Freight and excess baggage	97,266	180,768	322,119	390,625	447,865	135,263	130,983
Incidental revenue, net, primarily service contracts	148,030	16,550	317,517	492,723	321,704	22,730	70,643
Total operating revenues	10,156,297	13,295,958	15,434,769	17,571,217	23,668,149	5,452,774	6,963,898
Operating expenses							
Flying operations	3,581,521	6,231,152	5,401,703	5,456,986	6,895,847	1,624,966	1,863,216
Maintenance	2,612,309	2,714,612	2,662,989	3,081,300	3,192,978	948,494	714,707
Passenger service	389,819	624,398	626,976	721,417	946,580	199,662	273,940
Aircraft and traffic servicing	2,046,561	2,407,131	3,091,484	3,547,858	4,259,678	1,017,921	1,292,657
Promotion and sales	1,656,831	1,951,940	2,279,005	2,840,044	4,070,573	937,430	1,157,128
General and administrative	771,004	934,461	1,206,510	1,070,133	1,262,998	316,255	358,444
Taxes, other than income and payroll not included elsewhere	193,419	204,043	481,481	510,076	547,583	147,543	170,486
Depreciation not included elsewhere	669,774	607,351	536,095	274,034	149,683	34,595	36,741
Amortization of deferred charges and provision for inventory obsolescence not included elsewhere	138,520	273,729	416,497	348,922	236,933	84,436	59,383
Total operating expenses	12,059,758	15,948,817	16,702,740	17,850,770	21,562,853	5,311,302	5,926,702
Operating earnings (loss) before federal subsidy	(1,903,461)	(2,652,859)	(1,267,971)	(279,553)	2,105,296	141,472	1,037,196
Federal subsidy	—	—	789,000	—	—	—	—
Operating earnings (loss)	(1,903,461)	(2,652,859)	(478,971)	(279,553)	2,105,296	141,472	1,037,196

(Continued)

EXHIBIT 2 (Continued)

Nonoperating income and (expenses)							
Interest expense (primarily on long-term debt)	(256,940)	(357,664)	(501,528)	(573,829)	(507,789)	(119,702)	(120,982)
Amortization of debt discount and expense	(17,247)	(32,903)	—	—	—	—	—
Equipment rental income, net of depreciation	—	38,457	45,934	63,712	64,379	15,649	15,649
Sundry, net	83,909	(121,248)	(101,010)	(91,980)	(244,880)	4,430	6,121
Net nonoperating income and (expenses)	(190,278)	(473,358)	(556,604)	(602,097)	(688,290)	(99,623)	(99,212)
Earnings (loss) before income taxes and extraordinary items	(2,093,739)	(3,126,217)	(1,035,575)	(881,650)	1,417,006	41,849	937,984
Provision for (refund of) income taxes							
Federal	(710,682)	—	—	—	629,000	14,764	418,903
State	(19,416)	—	—	—	85,000	1,834	56,013
	(730,098)	—	—	—	714,000	16,598	474,916
Earnings (loss) before extraordinary items	(1,363,641)	(3,126,217)	(1,035,575)	(881,650)	703,006	25,251	463,068
Extraordinary items							
Tax benefit arising from utilization of net operating loss carryforwards	—	—	—	—	714,000	16,598	474,916
Gains (losses) from disposition of flight equipment	—	(194,126)	(27,896)	193,405	—	—	—
Terminated merger negotiation costs	—	—	—	(137,712)	—	—	—
Charges related to the cancellation of aircraft purchase agreements	—	—	(1,367,045)	—	—	—	—
	—	(194,126)	(1,394,941)	55,693	714,000	16,598	474,916
Net earnings (loss)	$(1,363,641)	$(3,320,343)	$(2,430,516)	$ (825,957)	$ 1,417,006	$ 41,849	$ 937,984
Net earnings (loss) per share	$(.19)	$(.39)	$(.28)	$(.10)	$.16	$.00	$.11

EXHIBIT 3

Aloha Airlines

Balance Sheet

December 31, 1972 with comparative figures for 1971

Assets	1972	1971
Current assets		
Cash	$ 335,150	$ 203,458
Accounts and notes receivable		
Traffic and service, net	3,045,963	2,378,092
Lease rent	—	360,083
Other	442,148	195,042
Net accounts and notes receivable	3,488,111	2,933,217
Expendable parts and supplies, at average cost less allowance for obsolescence	550,945	550,940
Prepaid expenses and other current assets	757,965	489,554
Total current assets	5,132,171	4,177,169
Property and equipment, at cost less accumulated depreciation and maintenance reserves (notes 1, 2, and 3)		
Operating	1,065,101	1,159,596
Nonoperating	2,136,914	2,392,262
Total property and equipment	3,202,015	3,551,858
Deferred charges and other assets, at cost (note 1)		
Leased aircraft rentals and sundry	1,223,700	1,174,729
Unamortized developmental and preoperating costs	263,315	710,916

Liabilities and Stockholders' Deficiency	1972	1971
Current liabilities		
Current installments of long-term debt (note 3)	$ 998,236	$ 1,001,286
Unsecured demand notes payable (note 3)	300,000	1,450,000
Accounts payable—general	1,938,276	2,404,147
Collections as agent—traffic and other	699,999	538,147
Accrued taxes, other than income	1,046,648	850,305
Accrued salaries, wages and vacation allowance	1,336,829	1,314,233
Other, including accrued pension liability	826,673	655,529
Unearned transportation revenue (note 1)	148,452	174,002
Total current liabilities	7,295,113	8,387,649
Long-term debt, excluding current installments (note 3)	2,973,634	2,706,119
Maintenance liability reserves for leased flight equipment (note 1)	580,565	953,894
Sundry deferred credits	109,134	121,261
Total liabilities	10,958,446	12,168,923
Stockholders' deficiency		
6% convertible preferred stock, noncumulative, with voting rights; $.25 par and liquidating value per share.		

(Continued)

EXHIBIT 3 (Continued)

Assets	1972	1971
Total deferred charges and other assets	1,487,015	1,885,645
Total assets	$9,821,201	$9,614,672

Liabilities and Stockholders' Deficiency	1972	1971
Authorized 11,300,000 shares; outstanding 266,410 shares (271,490 shares in 1971)	66,603	67,873
Common stock of $.25 par value per share. Authorized 16,000,000 shares; issued 8,617,445 shares (8,612,365 shares in 1971)	2,154,362	2,153,092
Total capital stock	2,220,965	2,220,965
Paid-in capital	3,006,210	3,006,210
Deficit	(6,364,420)	(7,781,426)
Net stockholders' deficiency	(1,137,245)	(2,554,251)
Contingent liabilities and commitments	$ 9,821,201	$ 9,614,672

EXHIBIT 4

Aloha Airlines

Notes to Financial Statements
December 31, 1972

(1) Summary of Significant Accounting Policies

Depreciation of Property and Equipment

Depreciation is provided on the "straight-line" basis over the estimated useful lives of the assets. In depreciating its owned flight equipment, the "built-in overhaul" method is use d for airframes and engines. Under this method, the estimated cost of one overhaul is deducted from the depreciable base. This amount is then amortized to expense over the FAA prescribed "time between overhaul" interval of hours flown.

Repairs, Maintenance, and Replacements

The company provides maintenance liability reserves on its leased aircraft for estimated airframe and engine overhaul costs. Accordingly, costs for major airframe and engine overhauls are provided by charges to maintenance expense and credits to the maintenance liability reserves for leased flight equipment on the basis of hours flown. Actual overhaul costs are then charged directly to the reserve account.

Routine maintenance, repairs, and minor renewals are charged to operations in the period in which incurred while replacements and betterments are capitalized by charges to the appropriate accounts. The cost and accumulated depreciation in respect to assets sold or otherwise disposed of or replaced are eliminated from the asset and accumulated depreciation accounts. Any gain or loss from the disposition of such assets is treated as nonoperating income (expense) except that major disposals of flight equipment are treated as extraordinary items.

Developmental and Preoperating Costs

During 1969 the company converted its jet fleet operations from BAC 1-11 to Boeing 737-200 aircraft. In connection therewith, lease and other termination costs were incurred and deferred to be amortized. In 1972, by directive of the Civil Aeronautics Board, the unamortized balance of such costs, $219,437, was charged to nonoperating expense. Amortization charges for 1971 have been reclassified accordingly. All other preoperating costs connected with the Boeing 737-200 aircraft are being amortized over a five-year period from March 1969.

Inventories

Inventories of flight equipment expendable parts and materials and supplies are priced at average cost. A reserve for obsolescence is provided for flight equipment expendable parts on a straight-line method over the estimated useful lives of the related aircraft and engines.

Revenue

Revenue is not recognized until flight tickets are used by passengers. Unearned transportation revenue shown on the balance sheet represents tickets sold but unused.

Lease Rent

Rental payments on leased flight equipment are charged to operations on a straight-line basis over the terms of the applicable leases. Under its lease agreement for the rental of three of the Boeing 737-200 aircraft, inclusive of spare parts (see note 2), the company has paid approximately $1,131,000 to December 31, 1972, in lease rental in excess of straight-line rental amortization. This amount was classified at December 31, 1972, as a deferred charge. In 1971 a corresponding amount, $748,426, was classified among current assets as prepaid expenses. The

(Continued)

EXHIBIT 4 (Continued)

balance sheet and statement of changes in financial position for 1971 have been restated accordingly.

(2) Property and Equipment

At December 31, 1972, the company operated five Boeing 737-200 aircraft under leases expiring in 1973 (one aircraft), 1976 (one aircraft), and 1982 (three aircraft). Lease rental payments on this equipment including spare parts will amount to approximately $2,275,000 in 1973, $2,000,000 in 1974 and 1975, $1,775,000 in 1976, and $1,525,000 in 1977 and thereafter. Under the lease expiring in 1976 the company holds an option to purchase the aircraft at $2,935,000 less $17,374 for each month that rent payments are made to the lessor. It is intended that the aircraft under lease expiring in 1973 will be returned in March 1973.

On January 5, 1973, the company entered into an agreement to acquire two used Boeing 737-100 aircraft at an aggregate price of approximately $5,600,000, including spare equipment, for delivery in March and April 1973. Financing arrangements are presently under negotiation.

One BAC 1-11 aircraft is owned by the company and leased to another carrier under a one-year lease beginning in April 1969, with nine consecutive one-year renewal periods. Failure to renew the lease during this period requires the payment by the lessee of termination fees ranging from $150,000 to $75,000. Under the lease agreement, the lessee also has the option to purchase the aircraft at its fair market value at any time after the end of the sixth year. Depreciation and interest charges on this aircraft exceed rental income by approximately $75,000 annually (see note 3).

The balance of major classes of depreciable assets at December 31, 1972, and the estimated useful lives of such assets are summarized as follows:

	Operating	Nonoperating
Airframes, engines and other flight equipment (estimated useful life, 7 to 12 years)	$ 384,147	$3,507,477
Ground equipment (estimated useful life, 5 to 10 years)	1,134,450	—
Buildings and leasehold improvements (amortization period, 20 years, life of lease)	$ 670,513	—
Furniture, fixtures and office equipment (estimated useful life, 10 years)	226,471	—
	2,415,581	3,507,477
Less accumulated depreciation and maintenance reserves	1,363,093	1,370,563
	1,052,488	2,136,914
Work in progress	12,613	—
	$1,065,101	$2,136,914

(3) Long-Term Debt

Long-term debt at December 31, 1972, is summarized as follows:

Aircraft manufacturers:
  Purchase mortgage agreement, in
    1967 for $2,871,349, interest
    6¼%; maturity, June 1, 1977,
    payable in quarterly

EXHIBIT 4 (Continued)

installments of $97,079 including interest	$1,512,992
Unsecured note in 1970 for $1,463,000, interest 1½% above prime rate; maturity December 15, 1975; payable in monthly installments of $40,639 plus interest (plus one payment of $81,278 on May 31, 1973) payments to begin March 15, 1973	1,463,000
Bank:	
Loan agreement in 1972 for $950,000, interest 8%; maturity August 7, 1977; payable in quarterly installments of $50,000 plus accrued interest. Payment guaranteed by the endorsement of an officer and stockholder	900,000
Insurance companies:	
Mortgage loans in 1962 for $150,000, interest 6%; maturity June 1, 1977; payable $12,896 each year for principal and interest	$ 93,510
Equipment purchase agreements:	
Installment contracts in 1968 for $180,551 and in 1969 for $42,614, interest from 6½% to 12.83%; payable $402 a month, including interest	2,368
	3,971,870
Less amounts due within one year	998,236
Long-term debt, excluding current installments	$2,973,634

The BAC 1-11 aircraft (included in nonoperating property), related equipment, and rental proceeds are pledged to secure the mortgage note payable to the manufacturer.

The company has also pledged its leasehold interest in the Administration Building at Honolulu International Airport as collateral for the insurance company mortgage loans, and certain equipment is serving as collateral under the equipment purchase agreements.

Current notes payable at December 31, 1972, were:

Note payable to banks, 7½% interest, unsecured, due on demand. Payment guaranteed by the endorsement of an officer and stockholder	$ 100,000

(Continued)

EXHIBIT 4 (Continued)

Note payable to stockholder, 7½% interest, unsecured, due on demand	200,000
	$ 300,000
Bank:	
Loan agreement in 1972 for $950,000, interest 8%; maturity August 7, 1977; payable in quarterly installments of $50,000 plus accrued interest. Payment guaranteed by the endorsement of an officer and stockholder	900,000
Insurance companies:	
Mortgage loans in 1962 for $150,000, interest 6%; maturity June 1, 1977; payable $12,896 each year for principal and interest	93,510
Equipment purchase agreements:	
Installment contracts in 1968 for $180,551 and in 1969 for $42,614, interest from 6½% to 12.83%; payable $402 a month, including interest	2,368
	3,971,870
Less amounts due within one year	998,236
Long-term debt, excluding current installments	$2,973,634

EXHIBIT 5

Aloha Airlines

Balance Sheet for Hawaiian Airlines

December 31	1972	1971
Current assets		
Cash	$ 1,052,275	$ 1,832,294
Certificates of deposit	1,910,000	—
Accounts receivable—less allowance for doubtful accounts: 1972, $150,000; 1971, $50,000	4,798,914	3,416,384
Expendable parts, materials, and supplies—at average cost—less allowance for obsolescence: 1972, $100,250; 1971, $87,122	828,748	716,910
Prepaid expenses	286,976	402,219
Total current assets	8,876,913	6,367,807

EXHIBIT 5 (Continued)

	1972	1971
Property and equipment—at cost		
Flight equipment (pledged as collateral to mortgage notes)	22,690,288	28,807,787
Ground equipment, buildings, and leasehold improvements	4,796,891	4,634,962
Total operating property and equipment	27,487,179	33,442,749
Less accumulated depreciation (and airworthiness reserve in 1971)	11,020,299	13,766,828
Operating property and equipment—net	16,466,880	19,675,921
Non-operating property and equipment, less accumulated depreciation	2,927,821	—
Property and equipment—net	19,394,701	19,675,921
Other assets		
Costs of introducing new types of equipment—less amortization	553,048	699,786
Debt expense—less amortization	153,792	206,971
Noncurrent receivable	70,000	360,000
Long-term prepayments and other	358,203	405,457
Total other assets	1,135,043	1,672,214
Total assets	$29,406,657	$27,715,942
Current Liabilities		
Current portion of long-term debt	$ 2,225,478	$ 2,550,506
Accounts payable and accrued liabilities	5,222,480	3,245,295
Current portion of accrued vacation liability	765,000	658,000
Taxes other than income taxes	417,224	400,600
Unearned transportation revenue	285,000	225,000
Total current liabilities	8,915,182	7,079,401
Long-term debt		
Mortgage notes	6,931,651	8,957,132
6% senior subordinated notes	1,600,000	1,800,000
8½% convertible junior subordinated debentures	2,774,200	2,775,500
Total long-term debt	11,305,851	13,532,632
Other liabilities and deferred credits		
Noncurrent portion of accrued vacation liability	703,584	618,827
Deferred credits (principally pension fund credits)	506,257	621,899
Total other liabilities and deferred credits	1,209,841	1,240,726
Stockholders' equity		
Capital stock—authorized shares of $3 par value each: 1972, 6,000,000 shares; 1971, 3,500,000 shares; outstanding: 1972, 1,371,906 shares; 1971, 1,371,690 shares	4,115,718	4,115,070
Capital in excess of par value	3,587,387	3,586,744
Retained earnings (deficit)	272,678	(1,838,631)
Stockholders' equity	7,975,783	5,863,183
Total liabilities and stockholders' equity	$29,406,657	$27,715,942

EXHIBIT 6

Aloha Airlines

Income Statement for Hawaiian Airlines
For the Years Ended December 31, 1972 and 1971

	1972	1971
Operating revenues		
Passenger	$33,753,291	$28,779,141
Freight, mail, and excess baggage	2,646,961	2,290,066
Ground servicing contracts and other—net	1,145,422	626,795
Total	37,545,674	31,696,002
Operating expenses		
Flying operations	9,798,058	8,518,122
Maintenance	5,290,399	4,392,830
Passenger service	1,851,644	1,533,562
Aircraft and traffic servicing	7,372,173	6,226,027
Promotion and sales	5,703,724	4,275,813
General and administrative	2,629,586	2,344,672
Depreciation and amortization	2,154,820	2,640,257
Total	34,800,404	29,931,283
Operating income	2,745,270	1,764,719
Nonoperating expense		
Interest on long-term debt	1,065,168	1,217,467
Other—net	38,297	31,124
Total	1,103,465	1,248,591
Income before charge equivalent to income taxes	1,641,805	516,128
Charge equivalent to income taxes	833,112	263,968
Income before extraordinary items and cumulative effect on prior years of a change in accounting principle	808,693	252,160
Extraordinary items		
Offsetting credit to charge equivalent to income taxes arising from carryforward of prior years' operating losses	1,073,234	216,183
Write-off of unsuccessful merger negotiation costs less credit equivalent to income taxes of $47,785	—	(45,648)
Cumulative effect on prior years of a change in accounting principle—less charge equivalent to income taxes of $240,122	229,382	—
Total	1,302,616	170,535
Net income	2,111,309	422,695
Retained earnings (deficit), beginning of year	(1,838,631)	(2,261,326)
Retained earnings (deficit), end of year	$ 272,678	$(1,838,631)
Primary earnings per share		
Income before extraordinary items and cumulative effect on prior years of a change in accounting principle	$ .59	$ .18
Extraordinary items	.78	.13
Cumulative effect on prior years of a change in accounting principle	.17	—
Net income	$1.54	$ .31

EXHIBIT 6 (Continued)

Fully diluted earnings per share		
Income before extraordinary items and cumulative effect on prior years of a change in accounting principle	$ .50	$ .18
Extraordinary items	.65	.13
Cumulative effect on prior years of a change in accounting principle	.12	—
Net income	$1.27	$ .31
Pro forma amounts—assuming the new accounting principle is applied retroactively:		
Income before extraordinary items	$ 808,693	$ 299,665
Primary earnings per share	$ .59	$ .22
Fully diluted earnings per share	$ .50	$ .22
Net income	$ 1,641,805	$ 520,338
Primary earnings per share	$1.20	$ .38
Fully diluted earnings per share	$1.02	$ .38

EXHIBIT 7

Aloha Airlines

Some Reverse Splits, 1968–1972

Firm	Exchange	Year	Ratio	Business
American Motor Inns	American	1968	1–2	Motor inns
Canadian Merrill Ltd.	American	1971	1–5	Contract copper mining
C. L. Financial	American	1972	1–5	Hldg. Co., ins., linen supply
Danmont Corp.	OTC	1972	1–2	Hvy. equip., electr., aerosp., med.
Entron, Inc.	American	1970	1–3	Electronic equip. for military
First S&L Shares	American	1971	1–5	Hldg., sav & loan, Colo., Kansas
Great Basins Petroleum	American	1968	1–2	Oil/gas leases, const., drill
Marinduqne Mining & Industrial	American	1971	1–4	Copper mining, cement
Marion Corp.	OTC	1969	1–4	Oil/gas. crude process.
Meridian Industries	American	1971	1–3	Metal/plastic prod/elec sup.
Nucor Corp.	New York	1972	1–4	Fabricator of steel joints
Omega-Alpha Inc.	OTC	12/72	1–10	Floor covering, wire/cable
Royal American Industries	American	1971	1–10	Fla. land, radio & T.V. bdcsts
Supercrete Ltd.	American	1969	1–3	Concrets blocks, pipe, etc.
Surveyor Fund	NYS	1972	1–4	Closed-end investment trust
Triangle Corp.	OTC	1970	1–5	Tools/hand special: contr's
Wheelabrator-Frye	NYS	1972	1–3	Mtl, clean, air pol, ind., eng.
Bunker-Ramo Corp.	NYS	1973	1–3	Producer electrical components

CASE 30

Advanced Computer Systems, Inc. (B)

Late in the afternoon of February 22, 1977, Mr. John Fitzpatrick sat at his desk pouring over the audited financial statements which had just arrived from the accountants (see Exhibits 1 to 3). Results for the year had not turned out nearly as well as planned. Fitzpatrick riffled through the five-year corporate plan and prior statements and jotted down a few summary figures.

	Sales	Profit or (Loss)
	(thousands of dollars)	
Actual results (audited)		
1974	$1548.5	$ 177.1
1975	1804.1	100.9
1976	1910.2	49.1
1976 Interim Statements (unaudited)		
3-months	$ 160.6	$(80.1)
6-months	439.6	(129.3)
9-months	992.9	(133.0)
11-months	1401.3	(68.6)
Five-Year Plan (beginning of 1976)		
1976	$2700.0	$ 190.0
1977	3500.0	225.0
1978	4500.0	300.0
1979	5500.0	350.0
1980	6500.0	425.0

Fitzpatrick reflected on the situation, "the opportunities for this company look just great. On the other hand the needs are also great in terms of capital, and especially management to do the necessary planning, controling and marketing. Shall I hang on or sell out?"

Advanced Computer Systems, Inc. (Adcomp) was a technology-based company specializing in the design and manufacture of minicomputer systems and related peripheral equipment which had applications in industry, medicine, and

---

This case was prepared by and used with the permission of Jack D. Ferner, Lecturer in Management, Babcock Graduate School of Management, Wake Forest University.

scientific research. For background information on the company, its products and financial condition refer to Advanced Computer Systems, Inc. (A).

EVENTS IN 1976

In May 1976 (time of the Adcomp (A) case), the officers of Adcomp were faced with a number of difficult commitments, problems, and decisions:

1. A commitment to a five-year corporate plan which reflected a continued high rate of growth of about 30 percent per year.

2. Diversification into what they considered a number of sophisticated product lines to be marketed in a variety of industries. These included:

   Nuclear Systems—the main product being the TP-5000 pulse height analysis system.

   Peripheral products including a magnetic tape unit which sold for approximately $3000 per unit (see Exhibit 4).

   Special systems such as a large reactor safety control system for the TVA ($1.3 million contract).

   Environmental systems including an isotope identification system.

   Medical systems—body fluids analysis.

   Fiber optics—computer signal transmission.

3. The building of a 15,000 square foot office, laboratory, and assembly facility at a cost of $310,000.

4. Strains on the working capital position as a result of a substantial backlog of large systems contracts and the resultant investment in personnel

and other development costs.

5. An opportunity to sell $500,000 in debentures through Chadwick Associates.

As 1976 progressed, the problems of producing the large systems contracts and the obsolescence of one of the company's commercial products caused financial strains on the company (see the interim financial statements in Exhibits 4 and 5). The magnetic tape unit, which the company had counted on for several hundred thousand dollars in sales, had provided for barely $100,000 as a result of the introduction of the floppy disc by IBM. Additional difficulties were experienced because of the expense and delays of moving into the new facility. Although the employees considered the building a great improvement in working conditions, there were a number of initial dislocations.

As a result of these events, Fitzpatrick had decided not to attempt to conclude the financing of the debenture issue. The risks involved in taking on more debt appeared too great to him.

In addition he was becoming increasingly concerned over the time and other commitments the company required of him. Much of the burden of financial and general management decision making fell on him since the full-time management was technically oriented and experienced. Fitzpatrick's principal job as chief executive officer of another completely separate company was putting increased demands on his energies. His very heavy business schedule infringed heavily on his family life.

For these reasons, Fitzpatrick continued to ponder the best course for Adcomp. He had sought advice from various sources and pursued financing alternatives and possible opportunities to sell the company.

A PROSPECTIVE BUYER EMERGES

Early in 1977 the Edison Engineering division of Commonwealth Corporation large multinational company approached Fitzpatrick concerning the acquisition of Adcomp. Commonwealth Corporation was an engineering, manufacturing, and construction organization serving power and process industries throughout the world. The Edison Engineering Company was a leader in the design and manufacture of combustion equipment and related controls used in power generation.

The president of Edison explained his interest in acquiring Adcomp were synergetic in nature. Edison's control systems were basically of conventional design and utilized standard electrical and mechanical components. Because of the increasing scope and complexity of turbine generation installations, however, more sophisticated, computerized control systems were becoming necessary. Thus, the Edison division was seeking a way to rapidly acquire technical know-how in the computer systems field, expertise which they presently did not have. They stated that they felt Adcomp possessed this technology and would like to discuss terms of a merger.

Fitzpatrick encouraged Edison's interest, and they proceeded to make a thorough investigation of the personnel, facilities, technology, and financial condition of Adcomp. In the course of this the Adcomp management was assured that the company would not be moved, the incumbent management would stay, and the company would have autonomy to pursue its products and markets ex-

cept for a commitment to develop combustion control systems for Edison.

FITZPATRICK'S DECISION

In February, as Fitzpatrick pondered the audited figures for 1976, it appeared certain some kind of a deal could be made to sell Adcomp to Edison. While Edison was waiting for the audit before entering into final negotiations, they were aware of the approximate results and there would be no big surprises.

In Fitzpatrick's mind the Commonwealth group of companies had the financial resources to adequately develop and market Adcomp's diverse product lines. It would also relieve him of his commitments (including loan guarantees), and he felt he would realize an attractive profit on his investment (Fitzpatrick paid $80,000 in cash and short-term notes). Commonwealth had said they would pay cash on an installment purchase to stretch over four fiscal years to relieve the tax burden on the Adcomp owners. Fitzpatrick would sever most of his involvement with Adcomp.

On the other hand profits had declined for two years. Fitzpatrick thought it probably wasn't the opportune time to get the best price. In another year or two profits likely would improve. Perhaps, he reasoned, the equity market for new issues would turn favorable and Adcomp could be taken public. While the stock of the company was not presently publicly traded, small amounts had recently sold at prices as high as $10 per share (there were 253,155 shares outstanding on December 31, 1976).

Fitzpatrick knew that within a few hours he would have to answer two questions: first, would he sell the company; secondly, at what price?

EXHIBIT 1

Advanced Computer Systems, Inc. (B)

Balance Sheet
December 31, 1976 and 1975

Assets	1976	1975
Current assets		
Cash—including certificates of deposit of $29,608 ($10,999 in 1975) (note 4)	$ 149,556	$ 385,324
Receivables—trade, less provision for doubtful accounts of $2000 (note 4)	632,717	373,802
Refundable income taxes (note 1)	126,482	45,479
Inventories (notes 1, 2, and 4)	211,530	205,190
Costs and estimated earnings in excess of billings on incompleted contracts (note 1)	383,130	420,510
Total current assets	$1,503,415	$1,430,305
Other asset—investment (note 3)	7,770	—
Property, plant, and equipment (notes 1 and 4):		
Land	38,350	38,350
Equipment, less accumulated depreciation of $38,981; 1975—$35,665	66,858	52,193
Construction in progress	235,227	—
	$ 340,435	$ 90,543
Total assets	$1,851,620	$1,520,848

Liabilities and Stockholders' Equity	1976	1975
Current liabilities		
Note payable—bank	$ —	$ 122,876
Current maturities of long-term debt (note 4)	50,285	108,842
Accounts payable—trade	355,177	338,718
Accrued liabilities	40,018	23,389
Deferred income taxes (note 1)	291,424	141,402
Total current liabilities	$ 736,904	$ 735,227
Long-term debt (note 4)	598,738	320,620
Stockholders' equity		
Common—no par value: (note 5) Authorized 300,000 shares; 1975 outstanding 253,155 shares; 1975 252,968 shares	157,057	155,187
Paid-in capital	12,034	12,034
Retained earnings	346,887	297,780
	515,978	465,001
Total liabilities and stockholders' equity	$1,851,620	$1,520,848

See notes to financial statements.

EXHIBIT 2

Advanced Computer Systems, Inc. (B)

Statement of Income
Years Ended December 31, 1976 and 1975

	1976	1975
Sales—net	$1,910,248	$1,804,097
Cost of products sold	1,199,072	1,054,893
Gross profit on sales	$ 711,176	$ 749,204
Other expenses		
Systems development expenses	$ 112,391	$ 126,963
Marketing	282,924	239,046
General and administrative including interest of $30,618; 1975—$12,289	243,074	197,932
Total other expenses	$ 638,389	$ 563,941
Income before income taxes	$ 72,787	$ 185,263
Provision for income taxes	23,680	84,357
Net income	$ 49,107	$ 100,906
Earnings per share	$ .19	$ .40

See Notes to Financial Statements.

EXHIBIT 3

Advanced Computer Systems, Inc. (B)

Notes to Financial Statements
December 31, 1976

1. Summary of Accounting Policies and Practices

(a) Income from incompleted contracts is accounted for using the percentage of completion method. Accordingly, revenues are included in sales in the amount of $1,360,212 for 1976 ($1,088,045 for 1975) and related costs in the amount of $829,829 for 1976 ($576,407 for 1975) are included in cost of sales which are applicable to incompleted contracts. For income tax purposes income is accounted for using the completed contract method. Deferred income taxes are provided for the timing difference.

(b) Inventories (see note 2) are stated at the lower of cost or market. Cost of raw materials used in systems development is determined by the first-in, first-out method. Cost of finished goods and work in process is determined by the standard cost method and is substantially actual cost.

EXHIBIT 3 (Continued)

(c) Property, plant, and equipment are stated at cost and include expenditures for new equipment and major betterments and renewals. Depreciation is determined using the straight-line method and is based on the following estimated useful lives: equipment 5 to 10 years.

(d) Research and development costs are expensed in the year incurred. In 1976 these costs amounted to $45,533 ($88,172 in 1975) (see note 6).

(e) Investment tax credits are taken as reductions in the current provision for federal income taxes in the year in which the related assets were placed into use.

2. Inventories

Inventories, priced on the basis described in note 1, are summarized as follows:

	1976	1975
Finished goods	$ 49,284	$ 69,023
Work in process	85,995	47,672
Raw materials	76,251	88,495
	$211,530	$205,190

3. Investment

The investment, stated at cost, consists of 1,554 shares of local development company purchased for the purpose of enabling the development company to participate in a SBA Section 502 loan.

4. Long-Term Debt.

Long-term debt consists of the following:

	1976	1975
10% SBA guaranteed bank loan due in monthly installments of $6,143 including interest through July 1982	$338,229	$429,462
5½ to 10% SBA Section 502 building lease purchase obligation due in monthly installments aggregating $2,309 including interest through September 1996	260,794	—
5½ to 10% SBA Section 502 equipment lease purchase obligation due in monthly installments aggregating $717 including interest through September 1984	50,000	—
	$649,023	$429,462
Less: Current maturities	50,285	108,842
	$598,738	$320,620

All of the company's receivables, inventories and property, plant and equipment as well as certificates of deposit in the amount of $19,409 are pledged as collateral.

(Continued)

EXHIBIT 3 (Continued)

5. Common stock and stock options

The company has a stock option plan under which options to purchase shares of the company's stock may be granted to certain officers and key employees at a price not less than the market value at the date of the grant and at times which expire no later than the five years after the grant. A total of 18,750 shares have been reserved for this plan. Outstanding options at December 31, 1976, totaled 8300 shares (3900 in 1975). The option price is $10.00 per share to certain key employees. Such options, if not exercised, expire at various dates through 1981.

There is a stock bonus plan for certain officers and key employees. Shares of the company's common stock are issuable under the plan over a four-year period subsequent to the date of grant, subject to the grantee's continued employment. The number of shares reserved for the stock bonus plan is unspecified. During 1976, awards totaling 187 shares (399 in 1975) were issued having a market value of $1870 ($3990 in 1975). No further compensation has been accrued under this plan.

There is also a stock purchase plan for all eligible employees of the company. Shares of the company's common stock are issuable under the plan over a five-year period commencing July 1, 1971. A total of 10,000 shares have been reserved for this plan. No shares were issued during the current year while 20 shares were issued in 1975 at a price of $8.50 per share, which, as authorized under the plan, is 85 percent of fair market value.

6. Change in accounting for research and development costs

In years prior to 1975, the company's policy was to capitalize research and development costs which were deemed to have continuing value and amortize such costs to income of subsequent years. As required by Statement No. 2 of the Financial Accounting Standards Board, the company has changed its accounting to expense such costs as incurred and the financial statements of prior years have been restated to apply the new method retroactively. The effect of the accounting change was to reduce net income for 1975 by $26,772 ($.10 per share).

Retained earnings for 1975 have been adjusted for the effect (net of income taxes) of applying retroactively the new method of accounting.

EXHIBIT 4

Advanced Computer systems, Inc. (B)

Interim 1976 Balance Sheets (unaudited)

(in thousands of dollars)	3/31/76	6/30/76	9/30/76	11/30/76
Current assets				
Cash and certificates of deposit	14.6	6.8	57.9	27.0
Accounts receivable—net	704.4	721.1	698.9	480.8
Inventory—net	270.5	362.8	344.9	664.8
Total current assets	989.5	1090.7	1101.7	1172.6
Other assets—net		7.7	7.7	9.2
Equipment and leasehold improvements				
Manufacturing and test	75.1	75.0	88.9	92.1
Office furniture and fixtures	14.0	14.8	16.1	16.1
Land	38.4	38.4	38.4	38.4
Less: Accumulated depreciation	37.8	40	42.2	43.7
Total equipment & leasehold improvements	89.7	88.2	101.2	102.9
Total assets	1079.2	1186.6	1210.6	1284.7
Current liabilities				
Notes payable—current	38.0	38.0	38.0	—
Current maturities of long-term debt	52.9	52.9	52.9	52.9
Accounts payable	172.4	255.6	293.6	306.4
Advance customer payments	22.0	—	—	—
Accrued expense	—	.2	—	—
Sales commissions payable	5.6	19.0	18.0	23.4
Income taxes payable	(45.5)	(.1)	(.1)	(.1)
Deferred income taxes	141.4	141.4	141.4	141.4
Short-term debt—equipment	—	39.3	39.5	—
Total current liabilities	386.8	546.3	583.3	524.0
Long-term debt				
SBA guarantee loan	307.9	304.7	295.2	288.7
Land and equipment loan	—	—	—	77.5
Stockholders' equity				
Common stock	167.2	167.2	167.2	167.2
Retained earnings—prior periods	297.8	297.8	297.8	297.8
Net income (loss)	(80.5)	(129.4)	(132.9)	(70.5)
Total liabilities and stockholders' equity	1079.2	1186.6	1210.6	1284.7

EXHIBIT 5

Advanced Computer Systems, Inc. (B)

Interim 1976 Income Statements (unaudited)

(in thousands of dollars)	3 Mos. ending 3/31/76	6 Mos. ending 6/30/76	9 Mos. ending 9/30/76	11 Mos. ending 11/30/76
Revenues				
Sales				
Systems	150.5	411.7	922.5	1310.6
Peripherals	10.1	42.6	85.4	106.0
Less: Discounts and allowances		14.7	15.0	15.2
Net sales	160.6	439.6	992.9	1401.4
Other income	1.4	3.0	3.2	3.4
Total	162.0	442.6	996.1	1404.8
Cost of sales				
Systems				
Materials	51.5	145.0	400.2	586.6
Production labor	11.1	24.9	43.8	52.4
Engineering labor	13.6	32.5	83.4	102.6
Other direct costs	5.7	19.6	40.0	43.9
Overhead	10.9	25.0	52.3	64.8
Total	92.8	247.0	619.7	850.3
Peripherals				
Materials	2.3	10.6	21.8	27.3
Direct labor	1.5	3.6	7.5	9.9
Other direct cost	—	—	—	—
Overhead	.6	1.4	3.0	4.0
Total	4.4	15.6	32.3	41.2
Other costs and expenses				
Manufacturing				
Indirect and nonchargeable labor	9.6	21.0	36.1	43.2
Fringes	2.8	5.2	9.5	13.2
Rent	2.0	3.0	5.0	6.0
Supplies and expense	2.5	6.8	9.5	10.8
Freight in	1.3	2.2	4.2	6
Product support	.8	1.8	3.2	4.7
Depreciation & amortization	1.9	3.8	5.7	6.9
Under (over) absorbed labor	(1.2)	(1.8)	(2.3)	.8
Overhead applied	(19.9)	(40.3)	(67.8)	(81.0)
Total	(.2)	1.7	3.1	10.6
Total costs	97.0	264.3	655.1	902.1
Gross profits on sales	65.0	178.3	341.0	502.7
Other expenses:				
Research and development	26.3	42.8	74.9	99.7
Marketing expense	60.8	144.3	215.4	255.6
General and administrative	58.4	120.6	183.6	217.9
Total	145.5	307.7	473.9	573.2
Net income (loss) before income taxes	(80.5)	(129.4)	(132.9)	(70.5)
Income tax expense	—	—	—	—
Net income (loss)	(80.5)	(129.4)	(132.9)	(70.5)

CASE 31

Dalton House, Inc.

In January 1980 Mr. Donald Arnot, chief executive officer and majority stockholder of a leading publishing firm, Dalton House, Inc., was considering the acquisition of a local, professional major league baseball team. Although Dalton House had no experience in the management of a professional sports franchise, Mr. Arnot was a "star" athlete in college and had once considered playing professional baseball. Now in his midforties Arnot still maintained an inner craving for the sport, a craving, he thought, that could be satisfied by owning his own team.

As one of the leaders in the book publishing industry, Dalton House was considered by industry analysts to have a highly competent management team. The company had, in the past, made corporate acquisitions solely within its field of expertise, book publishing. The corporation generated all of its sales revenue from the printing of textbooks, paperback books, professional books, hard cover books, and book-of-the-month clubs. The finance department of Dalton House was responsible for locating companies that could be acquired. The acquisitions were required to remain within the guidelines set forth by the board of directors of privately held Dalton House. The acquisition strategy of the company was conservative, and potential purchases had to meet growth and profitability objectives.

Dalton House believed its sales growth had kept pace with growth in industry sales during the 1970s (Exhibit 1) and maintained that its conservative acquisition strategy was a cornerstone in this achievement. The value of annual shipments in the book printing industry (Exhibit 2) had shown a stable increase in the latter half of the 1970s and was expected to continue this growth trend over the next decade.

This case was prepared by and used with the permission of Mr. John R. Grady of the Public Service Commission of Maryland.

THE INDUSTRY

The book printing industry could be characterized as having a labor-intensive production process. Labor costs accounted for 35 to 60 percent of the total cost of the product. The industry depended on skilled laboreres, requiring higher wage rates than normal assembly line or production process laborers earned in other industries. Apprentice programs were also necessary for proper training of skilled laborers. Management had to thus make a substantial investment in each employee, and employees, in turn, did not drift in and out of jobs as was common in other assembly line processes. However, publishing firms were susceptable to the demands of a highly unionized labor force, particularly since labor played such a significant role in the overall production process.

In light of the large increases in labor wage rates and employee benefits during the decade of the seventies, the book printing industry was seeking to control costs through productivity gains. Growth rates in productivity were being achieved through increased investment in technologically superior equipment. The costs for capital investment were high, new equipment typically reached into the hundreds of thousands of dollars; but the new machines decreased a firm's reliance on labor while increasing productivity. Industry analysts believed that the completely automated printing process might be possible by 1990, which would require vast financial resources for the firms that automated in hope of remaining cost competitive.

Availability of paper supplies, a crucial input into the production process, was also a source of concern within the printing industry. Shortages of 5 percent

and more had been common throughout the industry, and this trend was expected to continue in the foreseeable future. The shortfall in supply was presently being compensated for by the use of more expensive imported paper.

Being the fourth largest energy user among all U.S. manufacturing industries and the largest single user of fuel oil made the printing industry highly reliant upon available energy supplies. In order to decrease this reliance, especially with spiraling energy costs, the trend in the industry was towards energy conservation, which necessitated capital expenditures for energy saving equipment and materials.

Anticipating the Future

Management of Dalton House felt it was important that the company keep up with the technological advances in the industry. The company had spent $5,250,000 on equipment acquisitions during 1979, $2 million in 1978, and $2 million in 1977 (Exhibit 3). Recognizing the trends in the industry, management felt increased capital investment would be necessary for the next five to ten years if Dalton House was to remain competitive with the rest of the industry.

Unit sales in the publishing industry were not growing, as the number of copies printed annually had not increased since 1974. Dalton House management believed that this situation would continue for the next five years and possibly longer. Current growth in demand was primarily in short-term trade and professional books rather than longer-run textbooks.

Dalton House sought to achieve its growth-in-earnings objectives by regularly adding new subsidiaries, all within their area of publishing expertise. Acquisition focus was placed on those companies that were capturing a growing segment of their own market. Acquisition by Dalton House of 14 book clubs in the past decade had meant that 34 percent of pretax earnings originated from this source.

Industry analysts believed that the larger publishers would expand their shares of the book printing business. Many smaller publishers would be unable to secure the financial resources needed to fully automate their processes and the more profitable ones would be acquired by the large publishing houses.

THE LAKELAND THRILLS

Mr. Arnot was interested in an investment that was not closely related to Dalton House's area of expertise, The Lakeland Thrills. Lakeland is a large city on the eastern coast of the United States. The Great Lakeland metropolitan area had a population of 11,528,649. The Thrills were one of two major league baseball teams in Lakeland. Each team was in a different league. The Thrills generated their income primarily from paid admissions to their baseball games and from related activities such as television and radio fees, concession sales, and parking income. In addition, the Thrills received 20 percent of gross receipts from paid admissions to baseball games that they played while visitors to another team. The Thrills also had to pay the visiting team to their home games the same 20 percent of admission receipts. Home attendance figures and gross ticket receipts are listed in Exhibit 4. Attendance figures and gross income from away games is also shown in this exhibit.

Related Revenues and Expenses

The Thrills played all of their home games at Mackey Stadium, which was owned by the city of Lakeland. The Thrills had signed a 20-year lease with the city which was to expire after the 1981 baseball season. The baseball club paid an annual rent of $50,000, the most favorable lease agreement at that time in the 12-team Northern League. According to the lease agreement, the Thrills could operate the stadium parking lots but had to pay the city 20 percent of gross receipts from operating the lots. Exhibit 5 shows gross receipts from the parking lots for the years 1975–1979. The Thrills paid the city of Lakeland $29,867 for use of the lots in 1979.

The baseball club had an agreement with the city of Lakeland and Ace Services, as concessionaire, for the sale of concessions at each of the Thrills' home games. The agreement with the city and the concessionaire was updated and renewed annually. The baseball club received various percentages of the gross receipts on items sold by Ace Services during home games. The Thrills were obligated, through the lease agreement, to pay the city a share of their concession income. Exhibit 6 shows the annual net share of concession income received by the baseball team.

The Media

Major League Baseball had signed television agreements with two national networks, North American Broadcasting Company and International Broadcasting Company. The agreements stated that each of the 26 major league baseball teams received an equal share of the total revenue provided by the contracts. Each team was to receive approximately

$1,715,330 for each of the years 1980 through 1983. Teams that participated in post-season play received additional revenue determined by the number of games they played. Each team had to pay a portion of these revenues into the Major League Baseball Players Pension Plan and into a fund to cover the cost of operating the Office of the Commissioner of Baseball.

The Thrills had sold local television rights to their games to WWRO-TV for the 1979 through 1982 baseball seasons. The Thrills had also sold local radio rights to WSEV for the 1979 through 1982 baseball seasons. Actual revenues generated from these sources for the years 1975 through 1979 are presented in Exhibit 7.

An agreement with the Pastaid Printing Company allowed that company to print and sell scorebooks at each of the Thrills' games. The baseball team received the greater of $28,000 or 27 percent of the profits from the sale of scorebooks. Revenues received in 1979 as a result of the agreement were $28,671 (Exhibit 8).

THE BASEBALL ENVIRONMENT

Each of the 26 major league teams had voted to accept a financial assistance fund designed to meet contingencies that might arise during negotiations of the basic agreement between the Major Leagues and the Major League Baseball Players Association. The Major League Baseball Players Association was recognized by the Major Leagues as the sole and exclusive bargaining agent for Major League players with regard to all terms and conditions of employment except individual salaries. Each team would contribute to the fund 2 percent of its gross

home ticket revenue for the 1979 and 1980 baseball seasons. The assets of each team's fund were invested in government securities and were currently carried as an asset of The Lakewood Thrills (Exhibit 9). The current agreement expired December 31, 1979, and the Major League Baseball Players Association had the option of going on strike if a new agreement was not reached by the owners of the teams and representatives from the Players Association. In the past, for example, a players' strike delayed the opening of the 1972 baseball season by two weeks. The games originally scheduled to be played during this period were not made up.

THE PLAYERS

During the baseball season each club could retain up to 25 players on its team roster (40 players after September 1). Each player signed a contract with the parent club according to the rules of baseball. The minimum salary any player could earn for a full season in the major leagues was $28,000. There was no maximum salary limiting the earnings of a player. Many players hired a professional agent to negotiate the players' contracts with the parent club. As of December 31, 1979, the aggregate annual salaries for the players on the Lakeland Thrills' active and disabled roster was $2,447,685, one of the smallest payrolls of the 26 professional baseball teams.

Under the terms of the basic agreement signed between the Major Leagues and the Major League Baseball Players Association, all players signing Major League contracts after August 9, 1976, were obligated to one club for six years of service. After serving six years in the major leagues, a player could become a free agent, offering his playing services to any of the 26 teams that were interested in bidding for him. This clause in the basic agreement was viewed by most people associated with the sport of baseball as the primary reason that the average player's salary had risen from $47,000 in August 1976 to $123,000 in December 1979. At the end of the 1980 playing season, three players on the Thrills' major league active and disabled roster would be eligible to become free agents. Players eligible to become free agents at the end of the 1981 and 1982 seasons numbered six and eight, respectively.

Sixty percent of the players on the Thrills' active roster were brought up to the team through the Lakeland player development program. The Thrills operated four minor league baseball teams. The Thrills provided players to each of the different skill-level teams and bore the cost of player salaries, training, and other expenses incurred in operating the teams. Costs of this player development program amounted to $1,867,527 in 1979, $1,775,528 in 1978, and $1,663,903 for 1977. These expenses were slightly lower than the average amount spent on player development programs by the 26 major league teams.

THE NEW GAME OF BASEBALL

With the arrival of the free agent system at the end of the 1976 season, baseball had changed considerably. As average player salaries rose rapidly, so did team operating expenses (Exhibit 10). Although each of the 26 major league teams was allowed to sign free agents, not all teams participated in the drafting and signing of these players. Many teams felt that the signing of a few highly talented and productive free agents

would provide the impetus needed to make that club a championship team. Other teams argued that the salaries given to free agents were too high and these players were not worth that much money to the ball club. Players becoming free agents after the 1979 season and before the start of the 1980 season agreed to contracts worth $150,000 to $1 million annually per player. The medium salary was $322,000.

The Thrills and Free Agents

The Thrills had chosen not to take a very active part in the bidding and signing of free agents. While the Thrills had signed only two free agents, both at the lower end of the skill and salary scale, other teams had signed as many as six players. Peter David, general manager of the Thrills' maintained that investment in a player development program was more important to the Thrills' future than investment in highly priced free agents.

The Thrills were one of six teams in the Sunrise Division of the Northern League. In the past three baseball seasons the Thrills had finished sixth in their division. Players on the Thrills had criticized the team management for not signing some free agents that could improve the quality of the team. Team players had also criticized management for not paying salaries that were competitive with the overall major league salary structure. Additionally, management had been criticized for trading, to other teams, many of their "star" players who had sought large salary increases.

Lakeland area fans had also criticized the ownership and management of the Thrills. During the early 1970s the Thrills were near the top of their division in the won-lost standings. During this time the Thrills were attracting large home game crowds, 2,746,034 fans in the 1970 season and 2,307,480 in 1971. The team was highly profitable and was recognized as having one of the best player development systems in the major leagues. While baseball attendance in the Northern League had steadily increased since 1975, attendance at the Thrills' home games had decreased during the same period (Exhibit 11).

The Aftereffects

With the decline in fan attendance and support, combined with three consecutive years of last place finishes, team morale had declined. The stigma of a loser was being attached to the Thrills' organization. Trades for quality players with other major league teams, formerly a method used to help improve a team's field performance, was a limited tool in the hands of the Thrills. Free agency had decreased the number of players available to be traded. Many contracts gave the player the right to refuse a trade and many of these players were unwilling to be traded to a losing team. Finally, the Thrills had so little sought after talent in their organization that other teams were unwilling to trade quality players because the Thrills could not offer comparable talent in exchange.

SALE OF THE TEAM

The owners of the Thrills had decided to sell the team. The team had lost money during the past two seasons (Exhibit 10) and under the thrift policies advocated by the owners, a reversal in the bottom line did not appear promising. Offers to purchase the team would be accepted through a bidding process. Individuals or organizations participating in the bidding process would be informed if another group had "topped" their offer. A new round of bidding would then begin, and this process would continue until all final bids had been received with the highest one being accepted as the purchase price of the team. Acceptance of the terms of the sale and of the new owners had to be given by a majority of the 12 owners of the Northern League teams.

The purchase of two teams, one in each of the Northern and Southern Leagues, had been approved and finalized during 1979. The cost of these purchases were reported to be $12 million to $13 million each. Both teams had lost money during the 1977 and 1978 seasons; however, their losses were only half as great as those of the 1979 Thrills. The two teams, the Appolos and the Skyers, were highly competitive teams. The Appolos finished first in their division while the Skyers finished second in theirs during the 1979 season. Both teams earned a profit in 1979. The Thrills, although currently inferior to these two teams in player talent and on-the-field performance, had a much larger population from which to attract fans.

THE DECISION

Mr. Arnot could remember the days, as late as 1975, when the Thrills were the pride of Lakeland. The Thrills were a fun team to watch; they had winning seasons. The fans flocked to see the Thrills play. Each year in the past the team ranked in the top 25 percent of professional baseball teams in annual attendance. In 1979 they ranked in the bottom 25 percent. The Thrills in the past outdrew, in average attendance, their crosstown rivals, the Dynamos. In 1979 the

Dynamos attendance was over three times as great as that of the Thrills.

Turning a Team Around

With a new owner the Dynamos attempted to create a new image in 1975. The new owner and his management team promised to give the city a team Lakeland could be proud of. The Dynamos had consistently fielded losing teams in the previous ten years. The Dynamos proceeded to make successful trades and signed top name free agents. The Dynamos sought players that were highly talented and colorful, on and off the field. The players created controversy, the news media loved it and publicized it, and the fans flocked to see the new champions of the city, all at the expense of the Thrills.

The owner of the Dynamos, once a star athlete in college, was of a new breed of owners in baseball. He took an active interest in the ballclub, invested heavily in the team, and created a new concept for his baseball team. He marketed his team as a form of active entertainment rather than as the old passive concept of baseball, "America's favorite pastime."

Mr. Arnot remembered the old "subway series" when two teams from Lakeland would play in the World Series for the championship of baseball. Lakeland, during the 1940s and 1950s, was the baseball capital of the world. Mr. Arnot envisioned what it would be like for two Lakeland teams to once again compete for the World Championship of Baseball. The Dynamos were already competing for the top baseball crown in the late 1970s; all that was needed to complete the dream was for the Thrills to improve and win their league.

CONCLUSION

The Thrills needed new ownership–one that was responsive to the needs and wants of its fans. Baseball analysts believed that in addition to the purchase price, $10 million would be needed to strengthen the Thrills' management, playing team, and player development program. Players' salaries were also expected to continue their upward climb, and a new agreement had to be negotiated between the Major Leagues and the Major League Baseball Players Association.

All bids had to be received by the present owners of the Thrills within the next week. Mr. Arnot needed to decide how much to bid for the team. The excitement of the subway series that he witnessed as a child and the thrill of playing ball at the major college level had resurfaced within Donald Arnot. The deadline for the initial round of bidding was only seven days away.

EXHIBIT 1

Dalton House, Inc.

Statements of Consolidated Income and Retained Earnings
(in thousands of dollars, except per share data)

| | Year Ended December 31 | | |
	1979	1978	1977
Sales and other revenue	$259,500	$234,788	$211,959
Cost of operations	206,646	187,615	171,626
Write-down of investment in Hoco Systems Inc.	—	—	3,191
Interest and other income—net	823	335	497
Income before income taxes	53,677	47,508	37,639
Income taxes	26,468	23,363	18,579
Net income	$ 27,209	$ 24,145	$ 19,060
Retained earnings at beginning of year	104,719	98,057	89,571
Cash dividends	12,880	17,483	10,574
Retained earnings at end of year	$119,048	$104,719	$ 98,057
Net income per share of common stock	$2.73	$2.42	$1.91

EXHIBIT 2

Dalton House, Inc.

Value of Shipments in Book Printing Industry
(in billions of dollars)

1977	1978	1979	(estimated) 1980
$1.72	$1.95	$2.14	$2.37

EXHIBIT 3

Dalton House, Inc.

Consolidated Balance Sheets
(in thousands of dollars)

December 31	1979	1978	1977
Current assets			
Cash	$ 2,175	$ 3,486	$ 4,638
Marketable securities	4,785	13,966	2,621
Receivables	65,593	54,404	63,773
Inventories, at cost			
Finished goods	40,108	33,605	35,010
Paper, supplies, other	6,008	5,012	5,168
Prepaid expenses	10,448	8,698	8,355
Deferred income tax benefits	8,167	7,277	—
Total current assets	$137,284	$126,448	$119,565
Property and equipment—less			
accumulated depreciation	51,838	43,419	38,138
Other assets			
Advances to authors	7,056	6,431	7,557
Excess of cost over net value			
of assets acquired	2,408	2,084	2,123
Investments in and notes			
receivable from other			
companies	1,425	1,631	1,391
Cash value of life insurance	1,147	1,051	999
Total other assets	12,036	11,197	12,075
Total assets	$201,158	$181,064	$169,778
Current liabilities			
Accounts payable	$ 9,922	$ 9,499	$ 7,916
Accrued royalties	13,918	13,049	12,384
Other accrued expenses	13,619	10,732	10,171
Federal & foreign income tax	8,128	7,539	7,088
Unexpired subscriptions	6,858	7,088	6,186
Advance subscription			
payments	13,901	12,190	12,017
Total current liabilities	66,346	60,097	55,762
Deferred income taxes	1,766	2,074	1,781
Stockholders' equity			
Common stock	3,539	3,539	3,539
Capital surplus	21,803	21,759	21,760
Retained earnings	119,048	104,719	98,057
Less treasury stock	11,344	11,124	11,124
Stockholders' equity	133,046	118,893	112,232
Total claims	$201,158	$181,064	$169,778

EXHIBIT 4

Dalton House, Inc.

Lakeland Thrills' Home and Away Attendance and Receipts

Season	Home Attendance	Gross Ticket Receipts $	Away Attendance	Away Gross Income $
1979	803,105	3,694,283	1,584,753	1,457,973
1978	1,025,460	4,204,386	1,465,060	1,201,349
1977	1,086,028	4,452,715	1,497,439	1,227,890
1976	1,495,192	5,457,451	1,417,660	1,034,892
1975	1,761,716	6,342,178	1,313,357	945,617

EXHIBIT 5

Dalton House, Inc.

Mackey Stadium Gross Parking Lot Receipts

Season	Receipts
1979	$149,334
1978	$190,680
1977	$201,942
1976	$278,024
1975	$327,584

EXHIBIT 6

Dalton House, Inc.

Lakeland Thrills Net Concession Income

Season	Receipts
1979	$ 511,578
1978	$ 653,218
1977	$ 691,800
1976	$ 952,437
1975	$1,122,213

EXHIBIT 7

Dalton House, Inc.

Lakeland Thrills Local Television and Radio Rights

Season	Revenue
1979	$2,500,000
1978	$2,200,000
1977	$2,075,000
1976	$1,890,000
1975	$1,760,000

EXHIBIT 8

Dalton House, Inc.

Revenues Received From Scorecard Agreement with Pastaid Printing Co.

Season	Revenue
1979	$28,671
1978	$36,609
1977	$38,772
1976	$53,378
1975	$62,893

EXHIBIT 9

Dalton House, Inc.

Balance Sheet, Lakeland Thrills

	November 30		
	1979	1978	1977
Current assets			
Cash	$ 81,276	$ 123,842	$ 127,651
Certificates of deposit and commercial notes	2,695,963	2,839,198	2,992,762
Accounts receivable	93,405	152,205	167,367
Notes receivable	45,290	64,900	53,450
Total current assets	$2,915,934	$3,180,145	$3,341,230
Property and equipment— less accumulated depreciation	65,037	65,801	70,054
Franchise	1,555,750	1,555,750	1,555,750
Other assets	413,668	484,763	536,290
Total assets	$4,950,389	$5,286,459	$5,503,324
Current liabilities			
Accounts payable	$ 298,804	$ 214,041	$ 228,405
Accrued expenses	435,274	342,258	345,763
Total current liabilities	734,078	556,299	574,168
Other liabilities	324,000	138,000	131,000
Stockholders' equity			
Common stock, par value $1 per share; authorized 1,000,000 shares, issued 1,000 shares	1,000,000	1,000,000	1,000,000
Retained earnings	2,892,311	3,592,160	3,798,156
Stockholders' equity	3,892,311	4,592,160	4,798,156
Total claims	$4,950,389	$5,286,459	$5,503,324

EXHIBIT 10

Dalton House, Inc.

Income Statement, Lakeland Thrills

	Year Ended November 30				
	1975	*1976*	*1977*	*1978*	*1979*
Operating revenues					
Game receipts	$6,514,016	$5,798,109	$5,067,545	$4,820,162	$4,592,030
Television and radio	2,000,000	2,170,000	2,768,205	2,961,510	3,351,710
Concessions	1,285,106	1,105,815	830,572	789,827	640,249
Other	133,890	103,168	53,215	114,851	62,642
Total operating revenues	9,933,012	9,177,092	8,719,537	8,686,350	8,646,631
Operating expense	5,772,501	6,214,078	8,228,077	8,976,453	9,753,297
Income (loss) from operations	4,160,511	2,963,014	491,460	(290,103)	(1,106,666)
Other income					
Interest	87,229	64,840	14,421	8,459	4,443
Income (loss) before income taxes	4,247,740	3,027,854	505,881	(281,644)	(1,102,223)
Income tax provision	1,588,618	1,151,757	185,622	(75,648)	(402,374)
Net income (loss)	$2,659,122	$1,876,097	$ 320,259	($ 205,996)	($ 699,849)

EXHIBIT 11

Dalton House, Inc.

Annual Attendance

Season	Northern League	Lakeland Thrills
1975	16,899,300	1,761,716
1976	16,960,419	1,495,192
1977	19,413,492	1,086,028
1978	20,468,846	1,025,460
1979	21,559,631	803,105

PART SIX

Management of Term Financing

CASE 32

Harris Paper and Wood Products Company (B)

Mr. Jack Arnold had joined Harris Paper and Wood Products Company in late 1977 as treasurer and financial vice-president. His initial analysis had indicated that the company's capital structure was not optimal; it contained too much debt. He felt that the company's capital structure had too high a cost of capital as a result of this highly leveraged position. (See Exhibits 1 and 2 for Harris Paper's financial statements for fiscal year 1977 through 1979).

COMPANY HISTORY AND BACKGROUND

Harris Paper and Wood Products Company was founded in the early 1900s as a manufacturer and marketer of paper and wood products. By 1980 the company had a number of manufacturing plants located in the Pacific Northwest

and distributorships throughout the western states. The company's sales were divided equally between its two major divisions, the Lumber and Plywood Division and the Paper Production Division. Harris Paper's major product lines included plywood and lumber, boxboard, and containerboard.

Sales for the two divisions fluctuated with different sectors of the economy. Lumber and plywood sales were strongly related to new housing starts. Paper products and cardboard were in demand when retail sales were booming.

Manufacturing facilities operated by the company were highly variable in age and efficiency. The company had constructed some new, cost-efficient plants. However, they continued to use many others that were very old and expensive to operate. The company followed a policy of closing the older and less efficient lines when sales were down and de-

This case was prepared by and used with the permission of Professor Frederick C. Scherr, West Virginia University.

mand slackened. In the event of an economic resurgence, the older plants were reopened.

THE PROBLEM BANK LOAN

Before Mr. Arnold had joined Harris Paper, the company had negotiated a line of credit with a bank, calling for an interest rate of 12 percent per year. The loan agreement had provisions and restrictions that were interfering with Harris Paper's ability to carry on its operating and financial activities. The company found it could not meet several of the restrictive provisions of the agreement; however, the bank was very resistant to attempts at revising the agreement to give the company greater financing flexibility. Because of the problems with the bank and because Harris Paper's president did not want to change banks, Mr. Arnold decided to seek a term loan for $16 million to replace the company's bank credit line. This amount was determined by projections of the financial needs of the firm for 1980 (the firm's business was quite seasonal, the year-end credit line balance representing a low point in the required line). This would be used to completely pay off the bank credit line as of year-end 1979 and create a permanent marketable securities account with the remaining portion of the term loan. These marketable securities would be short-term government treasury bills and would be liquidated when the firm needed cash, then later replenished. If cash needs were greater than could be provided by this source, the bank credit line would be utilized. It was expected, however, based on the seasonality of the firm's business, that

this line of credit would have a zero balance as of the end of the fiscal period.

In checking with other financial officers of the firm, Mr. Arnold found that Harris had a fairly reliable system of projecting the values of certain financial statement accounts in the intermediate term based on percent of sales (see Exhibit 3). This system had recently been revised to take into account future costs, demand, and other economic factors. The marketing department had also provided sales estimates, based on multiple regression analysis and projected economic variables, for the fiscal years 1980 –1985 (see Exhibit 4). He was also able to make an approximate forecast of expected capital expenditures and depreciation for these periods (see Exhibit 5). Mr. Arnold intended to honor the provisions of the indenture on one of the long-term debt issues, which called for the buy-up of $2 million (market value) of these securities each year. For 1979 Mr. Arnold intended to pay cash dividends to common shareholders in the amount of $2 per share. He expected that this dividend would be growing at about 10 percent per year. (Harris' dividend payout ratio was traditionally very low.) The firm's preferred stock also paid $4/share cash dividends each year.

Mr. Arnold had contacted several institutional investors regarding the possibility of a term loan. The conversation with John Lyons had been typical. "Jack, we are perfectly willing to consider making an amortized intermediate-term loan to Harris Paper. I think that an interest rate of 9 to 10 percent might be an appropriate range, and we are willing to fit the amortization schedule to your expected cash flows. However, in situations of this sort, I think it is appropriate to ask several questions. One area of concern is the term of the loan; you're going to have to be a lot more specific there. Another question we usually ask is, how are you going to pay the loan back? Where will the cash come from? It's my understanding that you don't intend to refund the term loan with debt and that your board of directors has ruled out stock financing in the fore-seeable future. Finally, most lenders are going to want to see some evidence that your forecasts of future financial positions are reasonable."

Prior to contacting lenders on a formal basis, Mr. Arnold wanted to be sure that he could satisfy these inquiries. One of his steps was to collect data from the financial statements of several firms similar to Harris (see Exhibit 6).

EXHIBIT 1

Harris Paper and Wood Products Company (B)

Balance Sheet for Fiscal Years Ending 12/31/77– 12/31/79
(rounded thousands of dollars; ordered in the analyst's method)

	1977	1978	1979
Assets			
Cash	1,561	1,732	1,680
Accounts Receivable	10,623	10,971	12,013
Inventories	27,321	28,902	29,345
Prepaid Expenses	5,765	6,024	6,244
Total Current Assets	45,270	47,629	49,282
Other Assets	4,806	4,532	5,011
Gross Fixed Assets	113,693	115,912	118,230
Less Accumulated Depreciation	48,162	49,125	50,108
Net Fixed Assets	65,531	66,787	68,122
Total Assets	115,607	118,948	122,415
Liabilities & Owners' Equity			
Accrued Interest on Bank Credit Line	90	91	96
Principal Income on Bank Credit Line	8,972	9,056	9,600
Accounts Payable–Material	8,754	9,023	9,480
Accruals	4,448	4,121	2,915
Preferred Stock Dividends Payable	30	30	30
Other Current Liabilities	341	359	280
Total Current Liabilities	22,635	22,680	22,401
Deferred Expenses	2,541	3,022	2,930
Long-Term Debt	54,000	52,000	50,000
Preferred Stock (30,000 shares)	3,000	3,000	3,000
Common Equity (52,000 shares)	33,431	38,246	44,084
Owners' Equity	36,431	41,246	47,084
Total Liabilities & Owners' Equity	115,607	118,948	122,415

EXHIBIT 2

Harris Paper and Wood Products Company (B)

*Statements of Income and Retained Earnings for
Fiscal Years Ending 12/31/77–12/31/79
(rounded thousands of dollars; ordered in the analyst's
method)*

	1977	1978	1979
Net Sales	$125,208	$132,721	$140,684
Cost of Goods Sold	91,989	92,801	98,903
Gross Margin on Sales	33,219	39,920	41,781
Administrative and General Expense	21,167	22,437	23,783
Depreciation	925	963	983
Interest Expense	6,405	6,257	4,644
Net Other Income or (expenses)	0	0	0
Income Before Tax	4,722	10,263	12,371
Federal Income Tax	2,267	4,926	5,938
State and Local Income Tax	141	308	371
Earnings After Tax	2,314	5,029	6,062
Common and Preferred Stock Dividend	203	214	224
Increase (or Decrease) in Retained Earnings	2,111	4,815	5,838
Retained Earnings, Beginning of Year	34,320	36,431	41,246
Retained Earnings, End of Year	$ 36,431	$ 41,246	$ 47,084

EXHIBIT 3

HARRIS PAPER AND WOOD PRODUCTS COMPANY (B)

Harris' System of Intermediate-Term Financial Forcasting

Financial Statement Entry	Forcasting Method
Sales	Multiple regression analysis from mrktg dept.
Earnings after taxes	5.5% of sales
Cash	1.5% of sales
Accounts receivable	10% of sales
Inventory	20% of sales
Prepaid expenses	3% of sales
Other assets	3% of sales
Accounts payable–raw materials	4% of sales
Accruals	2% of sales
Other current liabilities	0.2% of sales
Gross fixed assets & depreciation	Based on capital budget
Deferred expenses	2% of sales
Long–term debt	Based on long–term financing plans and repayment schedules

EXHIBIT 4

Harris Paper and Wood Products Company (B)

Marketing Department's Multiple Regression Estimate of Yearly Sales, 1980–1985

Fiscal Years	Projected Sales
1980	150,000,000
1981	162,000,000
1982	176,580,000
1983	194,238,000
1984	198,123,000
1985	204,067,000

EXHIBIT 5

Harris Paper and Wood Products Company (B)

Schedule of Estimated Future Capital Expenditures and Yearly Depreciation (Generated 12/31/79)

Fiscal Year	Projected Capital Budget	Yearly Depreciation
1980	2,400,000	1,020,000
1981	3,000,000	2,000,000
1982	3,500,000	3,000,000
1983	4,500,000	3,500,000
1984	5,500,000	4,000,000
1985	6,500,000	5,000,000

EXHIBIT 6

Harris Paper and Wood Products Company (B)

Financial Statement Data for Several Firms Similar to Harris as of 12/31/79

(Entries expressed as percent of total assets)

	Firm A	Firm B	Firm C	Firm D	Firm E	Firm F
Cash and mar. sec.	8.4	6.3	9.1	6.9	5.1	11.4
Accts. rsv.	23.6	17.9	16.4	25.6	21.7	15.2
Inventory	12.7	18.2	16.7	13.8	15.2	15.2
All other CA	1.4	2.0	1.2	0.9	3.9	0.4
Other assets	6.9	1.3	0.0	3.6	5.8	2.5
Net fixed assets	47.0	54.3	56.6	49.2	48.3	55.3
Total assets	100.0	100.0	100.0	100.0	100.0	100.0
Due to banks—short term	2.5	1.1	3.2	1.5	0.0	3.8
Due to trade	11.8	14.3	16.9	15.6	10.8	10.0
All other C.L.	8.1	11.6	15.6	8.7	6.7	6.9
Long-term debt	40.7	28.3	26.1	31.0	40.0	32.3
Total debt	63.1	55.3	61.8	56.8	57.5	53.0
OE	36.9	44.7	38.2	43.2	42.5	47.0
Total liabilities & OE	100.0	100.0	100.0	100.0	100.0	100.0

CASE 33

Baker Bros., Inc.

Early in September 1974, Jack Faulkner was starting his second week as secretary-treasurer of Baker Bros., Inc. An experienced financial manager, Mr. Faulkner was well aware that Paul Stewart, president of Baker Bros., had hired him to "put the company's financial house in order." However, despite a week of nonstop discussions with other company executives, all he had found out about Baker Bros.' financial situation was that suppliers were clamoring for payment and that cash was available to satisfy only the most pressing needs.

To help him understand Baker Bros.' financial situation, Mr. Faulkner had collected the summary financial information shown in Exhibits 1, 2, 3, and 4. As he was looking through some of the recent financial statements, the accounts payable clerk dropped a stack of overdue invoices on his desk. A note attached stated that cash was not available to pay the suppliers.

COMPANY ORGANIZATION AND HISTORY

Baker Bros., Inc., was organized as a Florida corporation in 1944 with its headquarters in Jacksonville. Since that time, the company has become a major southeastern distributor of heating, air conditioning, and refrigeration equipment, parts, and supplies with 45 outlets in Florida, Georgia, Alabama, North Carolina, South Carolina, and Mississippi. Through the addition of sales outlets to expand its market area and broadening of its product line, Baker Bros. increased sales from $7.7 million in 1968 to $36 million in its fiscal year ended January 31, 1974.

Each sales outlet or "store" operated by Baker Bros. serves as a sales and distribution point for the full line of aproximately 20,000 climate control and refrigeration products carried by the

This case was prepared by and used with the permission of Professor Charles W. Young, University of North Florida.

company. Each store is run by a manager who is responsible for the hiring and supervision of personnel and for sales, credit, purchasing, inventory, and cost control at the store level. Management feels that this delegation of authority and responsibility is a major contributor to the company's success, and managers are paid on the basis of the net profit generated by their stores. Decisions affecting company policy, selection of senior management, capital expenditures, and addition of product lines are reviewed by corporate management.

SUPPLIERS

Products sold by the company are purchased on a regular basis from approximately 250 manufacturers and suppliers.

tion contractors, institutions, governmental units, and a variety of commercial users such as supermarket chains. Substantially all sales to customers are on open account, and no single customer accounts for as much as 1½ percent of total sales during any one year. Terms typically are 2/10, net 30, but extended terms are sometimes offered to gain a competitive advantage.

The company solicits sales from customers in both the new construction and the replacement and repair markets. New equipment sales provide relatively lower gross margins than sales of replacement parts. It is difficult for the company to monitor sales by market category; however, estimates of total sales contributed by products sold in the two markets during each of the past four fiscal years are as follows:

	1974	1973	1972	1971
New construction	35%	20%	15%	9%
Replacement and repair	65%	80%	85%	91%

Special-order items are purchased occasionally from an additional 400 vendors. The largest single supplier of new air conditioning equipment and parts to the company provides approximately 15 percent of total purchases each year. The company has nonexclusive wholesale distributorship agreements with many of its suppliers. These agreements are generally informal and are subject to termination by either party on short notice. Most purchases are made on open account with terms of 2/10, net 30.

CUSTOMERS

Sales are made to approximately 8000 customers consisting of mechanical, heating, air-conditioning and refrigera-

FINANCIAL HISTORY

In 1964 the Allied Chemical Company acquired a 57-percent interest in Baker Bros., Inc., through purchase of common stock at an aggregate cash price of $302,550. Allied's ownership was increased to 80.7 percent in 1967 when the company purchased a substantial block of common stock from another shareholder. On June 10, 1971, in an underwritten public offering, Allied sold 358,092 shares of common stock, and the company sold 51,908 shares at $18.00 per share. This sale plus a private sale to Baker Bros.' management personnel liquidated Allied's holdings in the company. In mid-1974, after a 100-percent stock dividend in May 1972, the company had

1,109,574 shares of common stock issued and outstanding distributed among 588 holders of record. Selected high and low common stock prices are shown in Exhibit 5.

Long-term debt outstanding on January 31, 1974, was as follows:

Bank loan—7¾%	$ 810,000
Insurance Co., loan—8½%	2,000,000
Mortgage notes—5¾% to 8%	101,719
Other notes—8%	110,000
	3,021,719
Less: Current maturities	203,785
Remainder	$2,817,934

The insurance company loan was closed on July 13, 1973, with part of the proceeds of $2 million applied to reduce the long-term bank loan from its previous high of $1.7 million. Principal payments on the insurance company loan are deferred until December 1, 1978, at which time payments of $100,000 will be due on each of the June 1 and December 1 interest payment dates until the note is paid in full on June 1, 1988. Covenants in the loan agreement require Baker Bros. to maintain consolidated net working capital of not less than $7 million and a consolidated current ratio of at least 2 to 1. Further, the company is precluded from incurring any funded or current debt except that short-term bank borrowing, not to exceed $1 million, is permitted providing that the company is out of the bank for 60 consecutive days in each fiscal year. A number of other negative covenants are also imposed by the loan agreement but none of them appear to materially constrain the company's ability to operate as it has in the past. However, violation of any of the negative covenants, in addition to failure to make payments of principal and interest when due, gives the insurance company the option to declare the loan immediately due and payable.

CURRENT SITUATION

While looking through the stack of reports and statements he had gathered on his desk, Mr. Faulkner noted that during the three years of public ownership the management of Baker Bros. has devoted most of its attention to promoting growth in both sales and earnings per share. In fact, growth was the major topic discussed by the president in his letter to shareholders in the fiscal year 1973 annual report. In this letter the 33-percent increase in sales and 23-percent growth in earnings per share were highlighted, and continued growth was predicted for 1974.

Emphasis on growth was also apparent in the 1974 annual report. For example, the president's letter predicted:

"The Southeast, as a whole and Florida in particular, continues to be the nation's premier growth area. Management believes that exploitation of the market coverage we have achieved and continued efforts to control costs should result in another excellent year for the company."

This letter also mentioned the energy crisis that hit the country in late 1973; shortages, rising costs, and declining home construction as problems plaguing the industry in early 1974. The impact of these factors was predicted to be less severe in Florida because of the strength of the state's residential construction industry and because many expected construction to rise during the second half of 1974. (Data on building permits issued in the United States and the company's major market areas during 1972, 1973, and 1974 are shown in Exhibit 6.)

As Mr. Faulkner dug deeper into the financial information he had collected, he was surprised to find that the outstanding short-term loan was $700,000 over the limit imposed by the term-loan debt covenant. Although a quick check provided information that the insurance company had agreed to the additional bank debt, their agreement had been obtained with the understanding that the loan would be reduced to $1 million by January 31, 1975. However, the insurance company had waived the requirement that Baker Bros. be out of the bank for 60 days during fiscal year 1975.

Analysis of the July 31, 1974, accounts receivable balance provided the aging schedule shown in Exhibit 7. When questioned about the overdue amounts, the accounts receivable clerk reported that most accounts overdue in excess of 180 days represented sales of new equipment to construction contractors.

Investigation of the inventory balance disclosed that the company had adopted a policy in 1974 to build inventory as a hedge against future shortages. About $1.6 million was added to inventory during fiscal year 1974 for this purpose, and the buildup had continued into 1975. Further, it was found that there had been no significant inventory revaluations during the last several years to reflect obsolescence, deterioration, or reductions of cost to market. Because purchases were initiated by store managers and all inventory was located at one of the 45 stores, there was little information available at the Jacksonville headquarters to identify either the unit composition of the inventory or its marketability.

As Mr. Faulkner continued to peruse the information he had accumulated, he knew that Mr. Stewart expected him to convert his impressions of Baker Bros.' financial situation into an analysis that would clearly identify the magnitude and urgency of the company's problems and to propose a plan for their solution.

EXHIBIT 1

Baker Bros., Inc.

*Statements of Consolidated Income
for the Years Ended January 31
(dollar figures in thousands)*

	1971	1972	1973	1974
Net sales	$15,284	$21,445	$28,454	$36,085
Cost of merchandise sold	11,542	16,289	21,544	27,737
Gross profit on sales	3,742	5,156	6,910	8,348
Operating expense*	2,427	3,415	4,548	5,786
Profit from operations	1,315	1,741	2,362	2,562
Other income	9	41	65	200
Interest expense	51	101	158	300
Income before income taxes	1,273	1,681	2,269	2,462
Provision for income taxes	606	812	1,158	1,239
Net income	$ 667	$ 869	$ 1,111	$ 1,223
Earnings per share	$ .67	$ .81	$ 1.00	$ 1.10
*Includes:				
Provision for doubtful acc.	NA	NA	NA	$ 225
Depreciation and				
amortization	NA	NA	NA	$ 72

EXHIBIT 2

Baker Bros., Inc.

Consolidated Balance Sheets
January 31
(dollar figures in thousands)

	1971	1972	1973	1974
Assets				
Current assets				
Cash	$ 315	$ 585	$ 559	$ 320
Accounts & notes rec. (net)	2,005	2,679	3,919	5,418
Inventories	3,913	4,325	6,711	8,336
Other current assets	21	5	19	101
Total current assets	6,254	7,594	11,208	14,175
Property, plant, & equip. (net)	419	422	676	759
Goodwill	181	169	378	354
Other assets	19	22	23	8
Total assets	$6,873	$8,207	$12,285	$15,296
Liabilities and Stockholders' Equity				
Current liabilities				
Notes payable to banks	$ 10	$ 0	$ 521	$ 800
Current portion—LTD	103	212	297	204
Trade accounts payable	1,160	1,232	2,850	3,415
Accrued liabilities	1,164	792	960	899
Total current liabilities	2,437	2,236	4,628	5,318
Long-term debt	1,360	1,192	1,720	2,818
Stockholders' equity:				
Common stock—$.10 par	50	55	111	111
Other paid-in capital	238	1,066	1,057	1,057
Retained earnings	2,788	3,658	4,769	5,992
Stockholders' equity	3,076	4,779	5,937	7,160
Total claims	$6,873	$8,207	$12,285	$15,296

EXHIBIT 3

Baker Bros., Inc.

*Quarterly Statements of Consolidated Income**

(dollar figures in thousands)

	3 Months 4-30-72	6 Months 7-31-72	9 Months 10-31-72	12 Months 1-31-73	3 Months 4-30-73	6 Months 7-31-73	9 Months 10-31-73	12 Months 1-31-74	3 Months 4-30-74	6 Months 7-31-74
Net sales	$ 5,754	$13,687	$21,552	$28,454	$ 7,649	$18,062	$27,625	$36,085	$ 7,981	$19,049
Cost of goods sold	4,378	10,422	16,455	21,544	5,870	13,905	21,301	27,737	6,178	14,584
Gross profit	1,376	3,265	5,097	6,910	1,779	4,157	6,324	8,348	1,803	4,465
Operating expenses	947	2,070	3,268	4,548	1,271	2,723	4,258	5,786	1,427	3,059
Profit from operations	429	1,195	1,829	2,362	508	1,434	2,066	2,562	376	1,406
Other income	11	24	36	65	12	73	136	200	89	150
Interest expense	36	79	108	158	44	97	162	300	81	176
Income before taxes	404	1,140	1,757	2,269	476	1,410	2,040	2,462	384	1,380
Income taxes	201	568	875	1,158	242	719	1,040	1,239	195	704
Net income	$ 203	$ 572	$ 882	$ 1,111	$ 234	$ 691	$ 1,000	$ 1,223	$ 189	$ 676
Earnings per share	$ .18	$ .52	$ .80	$ 1.00	$ .21	$ .62	$ .90	$ 1.10	$ .17	$ .61

*Unaudited

EXHIBIT 4

Baker Bros., Inc.

Quarterly Consolidated Balance Sheets for 1972, 1973 and 1974*
(dollar figures in thousands)

	4-30-72	7-31-72	10-31-72	1-31-73	4-30-73	7-31-73	10-31-73	1-31-74	4-30-74	7-31-74
Assets										
Current assets										
Cash	$ 661	$ 496	$ 451	$ 559	$ 677	$ 598	$ 399	$ 320	$ 564	$ 416
Accounts & notes rec.	3,452	4,285	4,266	4,095	4,752	5,930	5,636	5,629	5,605	6,712
Allow for bad debts	158	230	301	177	243	313	413	211	233	276
Inventory	6,055	6,368	6,312	6,711	8,642	9,773	8,762	8,336	10,655	10,132
Prepaid and other	8	17	29	20	8	17	30	102	21	34
Total current assets	10,018	10,936	10,757	11,208	13,836	16,005	14,414	14,176	16,612	17,018
Property, plant & equip.	834	939	967	953	1,006	1,051	1,077	1,103	1,131	1,154
Accumulated depr.	289	302	316	277	291	306	324	343	362	376
Net	545	637	651	676	715	745	753	760	769	778
Goodwill	395	394	383	377	372	366	360	354	348	342
Other assets	29	22	18	24	41	24	25	6	31	22
Total assets	$10,987	$11,989	$11,809	$12,285	$14,964	$17,140	$15,552	$15,296	$17,760	$18,160
Liabilities and Stockholders' Equity										
Current liabilities										
Notes payable—bank	$ 334	$ 778	$ 547	$ 521	$ 800	$ 1,000	$ 900	$ 800	$ 800	$ 1,400
Trade accounts payable	2,867	3,222	2,883	2,850	4,909	5,726	3,768	3,415	5,657	5,379
Current portion—LTD	213	223	294	297	318	206	206	204	204	202
Accrued taxes	299	194	304	392	461	284	257	230	313	165
Other	371	341	376	569	472	370	560	669	622	453
Total current liab.	4,084	4,758	4,404	4,629	6,960	7,586	5,691	5,318	7,596	7,599
Long-term debt	1,877	1,833	1,697	1,719	1,833	2,926	2,923	2,818	2,815	2,725
Stockholders' equity:										
Common stock	111	111	111	111	111	111	111	111	111	111
Paid-in capital	1,055	1,057	1,057	1,057	1,057	1,057	1,057	1,057	1,057	1,057
Retained earnings	3,860	4,230	4,540	4,769	5,003	5,460	5,770	5,992	6,181	6,668
Stockholders' equity	5,026	5,398	5,708	5,937	6,171	6,628	6,938	7,160	7,349	7,836
Total claims	$10,987	$11,989	$11,809	$12,285	$14,964	$17,140	$15,552	$15,296	$17,760	$18,160

*Unaudited

371

EXHIBIT 5

Baker Bros., Inc.

Common Stock Prices
(Traded Over the Counter)

	High	Low
1972		
Quarter Ended:	27¼	15¼
4-30-73	21¼	15
7-31-73	20	15½
10-31-73	21	16¾
1-31-74	19½	6
4-30-74	6¾	4⅞
7-31-74	4⅞	3⅛

EXHIBIT 6

Baker Bros., Inc.

Private Residential Construction
Authorized (14,000 Places) [1]

	Number of Housing Units			
	United States	South	Florida	Alabama
1972	2,218,922	905,426	278,145*	28,323*
1973	1,819,535	763,166	266,982	20,390
1972				
Jan	137,324	61,526	18,900	1,687
Feb	148,069	63,682	17,454	1,610
Mar	191,071	80,669	22,586	2,285
Apr	191,792	74,066	18,425	2,704
May	206,919	78,770	21,237	2,242
Jun	214,598	84,039	22,906	2,270
Jul	179,637	72,317	21,050	2,094
Aug	206,424	81,461	22,356	2,942
Sep	190,570	82,793	34,602	2,895
Oct	201,110	82,885	29,442	2,691
Nov	176,842	69,791	22,617	3,272
Dec	174,566	73,427	25,068	2,484
1973				
Jan	152,077	72,688	21,882	2,605
Feb	145,696	70,066	22,564	1,970
Mar	184,402	75,445	23,284	1,849
Apr	185,386	74,923	26,230	2,077
May	191,707	78,943	26,756	1,976

EXHIBIT 6 (Continued)

Jun	193,719	87,309	41,409	1,348
Jul	157,326	60,286	21,435	1,405
Aug	162,855	62,194	21,380	1,440
Sep	125,190	50,274	14,376	2,424
Oct	122,948	48,976	15,617	1,476
Nov	107,160	44,377	13,069	873
Dec	91,069	37,685	14,694	1,260
1974				
Jan	85,937	41,698	16,572	1,293
Feb	85,528	41,262	15,171	1,120
Mar	117,988	47,081	15,181	2,158
Apr	128,084	47,717	13,778	1,278
May	114,043	39,994	11,180	984
Jun	99,878	34,245	11,856	1,057
Jul	93,606	32,850	8,279	842

[1] Source: U.S. Dept. of Commerce, "Construction Review," various issues.

*(13,000 places)

EXHIBIT 7

Baker Bros., Inc.

Aging of Accounts Receivable
July 31, 1974
(dollar figures in thousands)

	AMOUNT	%
Current		
Overdue:	$2,685	40
31–60	805	12
61–90	671	10
91–120	470	7
121–150	403	6
151–180	336	5
Over 180	1,342	20
Total	$6,712	100
July sales	$3,443	

CASE 34

The Quality Foods Company

In July 1980 Lynn Davis, executive vice-president of finance at the Quality Foods Company, was asked to submit a proposal to the executive committee concerning whether the company should lease or purchase its automobile fleet. At that time Jo Evans was participating in Quality Foods' summer internship program. Jointly, Ms. Davis and Ms. Evans began developing a car-leasing proposal to be presented to the executive committee. Excerpts from their preliminary proposal are given below.

CAR-LEASING PROPOSAL

We presently own 100 automobiles. The mileage on these vehicles varies from approximately 15,000 to 30,000 miles per year. Our policy is to replace each vehicle at the earlier of 60,000 miles or three years. As a result of this policy, we buy in the neighborhood of 45 new automobiles each year.

The following three alternative courses of action are to be discussed:

1. We continue to purchase our automobiles from the automobile dealers who submit the lowest bids. Oftentimes, the cars provided by the lowest bidders do not correspond to our specifications.

2. We have a third party purchase our new automobiles for us. Whereas leasing companies represent a significant buying power in the marketplace, they can acquire new automobiles at a cost that is about $800 below our lowest bids from automobile dealers. The leasing companies charge $250 per car for their purchasing services. With the leasing company procuring our automobiles, delivery of the new car is made to an automobile dealership that is convenient to the plant or salesman. The

---

This case was prepared by and used with the permission of David Loy.

leasing company delivers automobiles that are equipped exactly as we specify. Finally, the leasing company disposes of the used vehicle so as to maximize the value to us by either (1) selling the car to our employee, (2) selling it to the dealer who delivers the new vehicle, or (3) wholesaling it in the auto auction.

3. We enter into an open-end lease agreement. The lease is satisfied by quarterly payments (made in advance) based on the cost of the automobile plus interest (13 percent) and a small quarterly management fee (.0012 × base price). Our best leasing deal is to obtain a 16-quarter lease that we would terminate at the end of three years (12 quarters). At the end of three years the resale value of the used vehicle is compared to the remaining book value of the vehicle according to the leasing company's records. The difference, if positive, we receive from the leasing company. If the difference is negative, we pay the amount to the leasing company. Typically, open-end leases are categorized as capital leases in accordance with the requirements of Financial Accounting Standards Board Statement 13. The investment tax credit ($3^{1}/_3$ percent of the purchase price of the new automobile) is passed through to our company in the form of lower lease payments.

COMPARISON OF ORDERING PROCEDURES

Present Procedures: The fleet manager is responsible for obtaining new cars or granting permission to obtain new cars to salesmen who live outside the Danville area (the company headquarters). If the salesman lives outside the Danville area, he is responsible for obtaining estimates from three separate automobile dealers. The automobile dealer is requested to give an estimate on the car, equipped, if possible, as company policy dictates; and he is asked to determine the trade-in value of the used car. The fleet manager is required to issue a purchase order either to the dealer in Danville with the lowest bid price or the external dealer with the lowest bid price. Titles and licenses are handled either by the fleet manager or the company salesmen. Delivery time on new cars is normally six to eight weeks.

In a number of instances we have been paying up to $800 over dealer cost. Forty-five vehicles were purchased in the last few years from outside the Danville area that cost approximately $40,497 more than they would have if they were purchased in Danville. Danville-purchased vehicles, in the majority of instances, approximated dealer costs. The trade-in values offered in Danville could not be judged as to whether they were at, above, or below fair-market value.

Procedures Under a Leasing Company: The salesman or plant manager calls the company fleet manager and indicates his color preference and car model preference. If the salesman has a dealer preference where his car is to be delivered, he indicates that preference at the time his order is placed. The fleet manager calls the leasing company and places the order for the new car. In six to eight weeks the salesman is advised to go to the dealership and pick up the new car. The leasing company disposes of the used cars, then they title and license the new cars. A summary of owning versus leasing considerations is presented in Exhibit 1.

TELEPHONE SURVEY OF LEASING COMPANY CLIENTS

On August 12 and 13, Ms. Davis and Ms. Evans called several clients of three regional leasing companies. In most cases the list of clients was obtained from the leasing companies' sales representatives. From these telephone conversations, information was obtained about the quality of leasing services and about the performance of regional leasing companies. Ms. Davis concluded that the ZZZ Leasing Company had fewer complaints than the other two companies in the region and that their clients were well satisfied. With the survey completed, Ms. Davis was ready to give her preliminary findings to the executive committee.

CASH-FLOW ANALYSIS

After hearing Ms. Davis give her preliminary report, one of the elder members of the executive committee requested that a cash-flow analysis of the lease-versus-buy alternatives for the automobile fleet be conducted. He observed that Alternative 1—the company purchasing its own fleet—was clearly inferior to both Alternatives 2 and 3. He suggested that the issue be tabled until the next committee meeting at which time Ms. Davis could bring her final report to them. The next day Ms. Davis and Ms. Evans collected the following information about Alternatives 2 and 3.

1. Automobile prices are $9,330 per car.
2. Automobiles are to be retained and used by the company for three years.
3. Automobiles are to be sold after three years for approximately $4000. The tax for the gain on the sale is estimated to be $1534.
4. Automobiles are depreciated for tax purposes over a four-year period using the sum-of-the-years'-digits method. The salvage value is estimated to be zero.
5. The investment tax credit ($3\frac{1}{3}$ percent) equals $310.69. This amount reduces the net outlay per car to $9,019.31.
6. Quarterly lease payments for the first, second, and third years are $1146; $790; and $505, respectively. (See the Lease Schedule below.)
7. First lease payment due when the car is delivered; last lease payment due at the beginning of the twelfth quarter.
8. Investment tax credit is passed through to our company as the leasing company lowered its rate schedule to compensate us for the investment tax credit.
9. Resale value of the car at the end of three-year lease period is estimated to be $4000, which would result in a before-tax gain to us of $3067.

After collecting the data, Ms. Davis and Ms. Evans discussed how they were going to analyze it and make their presentation to the committee. Both Ms. Davis and Ms. Evans did some background reading and asked friends who worked for other companies to find the best method of comparing the leasing and buying alternatives. A number of different methods were suggested, and the more they got into the analysis, the more complicated the problem became. Ms.

Davis noted that the various models and procedures recommended to her were alike in that they all focused on the pattern of cash outflows for the buying and leasing alternatives and the discount factor or interest rate. Unfortunately, that was where the similarities stopped. Ms. Evans had found reference in which a table had been set up showing a schedule of cash flows for the lease alternative and one for the buying alternative. For the buying alternative, it was assumed that the funds to purchase the assets would be borrowed. Ms. Davis thought that the buying and borrowing alternative would be the most beneficial for Quality Foods since the company's tax bracket was around 50 percent. Because of accelerated depreciation, investment tax credits, and interest expense deductions, the company could take advantage of all the tax benefits enjoyed by the leasing companies. One of the most puzzling issues Ms. Davis found in her search for a method to analyze the data was that the various models used different discount factors; some used the cost of capital; some used the before-tax cost of debt; some used the after-tax cost of debt; and some used complex mathematically determined rates that she did not understand. At this point, both Ms. Davis and Ms. Evans were thoroughly confused. They collected additional data and estimated the company's cost of new debt funds to be 12 percent and the marginal cost of capital to be 20 percent. In order to get a start on the analysis, they began setting up tables to show the cash flow patterns for the leasing versus buying alternatives. For simplicity, they assumed that tax and lease payments would be made on January 1, April 1, July 1, and October 1 of each year. The quarterly lease payment schedule for a single automobile is presented below. Quality Food Company's balance sheet is presented in Exhibit 2.

16-Quarter, Open-End Lease Schedule			
Quarter (1)	Rate* (2)	Automobile Base Price (3)	Quarterly Lease Payment (2) × (3)
0–3	12.283%	$9330.00	$1146
4–7	8.467%	9330.00	790
8–11	5.413%	9330.00	505

*A $3\frac{1}{3}$-percent investment tax credit has been passed through to the firm in the calculations that were made to arrive at these rates.

EXHIBIT 1

The Quality Foods Company

Comparison of Owning Versus Leasing

Factors	Owning	Leasing
Purchase price	The acquisition price for similar type automobiles is not the same throughout the country.	The acquisition price for similar type automobiles is the same throughout the country.
Options	We frequently pay for options over and above our authorized list.	Cars will be equipped as we specify, unless the salesman wishes to pay for additional options.
Ordering procedures	Fleet manager or salesman obtains three bids for the new cars and three estimates for the used cars' trade-in value.	Fleet manager calls the leasing company and places the order for the new cars.
Titling of new vehicles	Fleet manager or salesman obtains title and license for the new car, at the company's expense.	Leasing company obtains title and license for the new car at their expense.
Out-of-pocket costs	Lower financing cost (12% for debt and 13% for leasing). Receive trade-in value of used car.	Lower purchase price, higher operating expenses (.0012 management fee). Receive or payout difference between trade-in value and guaranteed value to leasing company.
Formality		All cars will be ordered through one individual or department. This procedure provides a definite restriction on the unauthorized acquisition of new vehicles. Also, this procedure will yield listings which indicate our present position in terms of ownership and vehicle fleet at convenient time periods.

EXHIBIT 2

The Quality Foods Company

Balance Sheet
June 30, 1980

Assets	
Current assets	$65,250,000
Other assets	1,051,000
Property, plant, and equipment	24,814,000
	$91,115,000
Liabilities and Owners' Equity	
Current liabilities	$18,001,000
Long-term debt	14,034,000
Other liabilities	1,490,000
Owners' equity	57,590,000
	$91,115,000

CASE 35

The DC-9 Lease

On February 1, 1978, Ben Sharp found himself thinking about his just concluded meeting with the people from Hawaiian Airlines. As vice-president and chief administrative officer at Hawaii Bancorporation Leasing, an affiliate of the Bank of Hawaii, he was used to drawing up the lease terms for equipment used by many local businesses. Tour buses, medical equipment, bakery delivery trucks—those no longer presented much of a problem. But a DC-9-50? They cost $10 million each, and he could already imagine the reaction of people around the bank holding company if he proposed that it become the owner of one. Nevertheless, Hawaiian Air was definitely interested in adding another DC-9 to their fleet, and at the meeting they had provided him with details on the new plane.

The next step was to prepare a lease proposal for Hawaiian Air to consider. In principle this should be done the same as for any other leased asset. The bank holding company expected to earn a certain return on its funds and it was just a matter of working out the lease payment after taking into account the financials of the transaction. But this lease was something special for other reasons than the fact it was a DC-9-50. It was the largest single transaction entered into by the leasing company since its start in 1973, and it could open up an important new market. Already Hawaiian Air leased four other DC-9s from mainland institutions in addition to the four it owned directly. Entry into this market could be a real coup—one that other lessors were unlikely to sit back and watch passively. To be able to close the deal with Hawaiian Air, Mr. Sharp knew that the lease proposal should beat out the competition, appeal to Hawaiian Air, and meet the requirements of the holding company.

This case was prepared by and used with the permission of Steve Dawson of the University of Hawaii and Jim Puhl of the Bank of Hawaii.

HAWAII BANCORPORATION AND BANCORP LEASING

In 1971 Hawaii Bancorporation was organized as a one-bank holding company of the Bank of Hawaii. Its objective then, as now, was to provide varied financial services to customers in Hawaii and the South Pacific. One of the first nonbank subsidiaries formed was Hawaii Bancorporation Leasing, which had grown steadily since 1973. Responding to customer needs, Bancorp Leasing had widened the types of leases and leasing services it provided. At mid-1978 leases totaled close to $25 million with $15 million invested in leveraged leases.

In a typical lease transaction, the potential lessee determined the equipment needed, negotiated the purchase price, and then worked with Bancorp Leasing to negotiate the specific lease terms. After the lease proposal was agreed to, the bank's Credit and Loan Review Department conducted a financial analysis of the lessee. Bancorp Leasing's standards were close to those needed to qualify for a bank loan except that lessees did not need capital to pay part of the purchase price. Once the credit check was complete and the transaction was approved by the credit committee, Bancorp Leasing ordered the equipment from the seller selected by the lessee. The lease began once the equipment was inspected and accepted by the lessee.

When a bank or bank-affiliated leasing company purchased personal property as a part of a lease, the relationship between the bank and the customer was similar to a loan. Banks and their leasing affiliates were limited to financial leases that were noncancelable, full-payout leases in which the full purchase price plus carrying costs were repaid over the life of the lease. If the lease was canceled, the lessee had to compensate the lessor for costs incurred, including the unamortized cost of the leased asset. If necessary, the lessor could exercise first claim to the leased assets ahead of other creditors, subject to the discretion of the bankruptcy trustee. Most leases were also net, which meant the lessee paid taxes, maintenance, insurance, and other service costs.

Numerous restrictions established by the Federal Reserve Board, which regulates bank holding companies, made it difficult for the Bank of Hawaii to provide funds to Bancorp Leasing, so all funds came directly from or through the holding company. The bank could not, for example, lend funds greater than 10 percent of its capital and surplus to individual affiliates. Even these loans had to be secured by high quality collateral (i.e., U.S. government securities) that had a market value in excess of the loan amount. Except for an initial capital infusion, the holding company funds were treated as debt by the leasing subsidiary.

1977 Financial Structure ($000)

	Bank Holding Company Consolidated	Parent
Debt	$1,342,918	$31,071
	(93.8%)	(27.7%)
Equity	$ 83,150	$83,150
	(6.2%)	(72.3%)

To augment these resources, leveraged leasing was often used, especially for larger transactions. In a leveraged lease another lender, usually an insurance company, provided from 60 to 80 percent of the funds as a loan to Bancorp Leasing. If more than 80 percent was provided by the lender, the bank holding company did not qualify as a lessor for tax purposes under IRS rules.

Legal ownership of the asset remained with Bancorp Leasing as did the tax benefits. The lender did not have recourse to Bancorp Leasing if a problem developed, but it did have first claim to the leased asset. The principal advantage of a leveraged lease was that it allowed Bancorp Leasing to leverage itself into greater returns on funds invested due to the substantial tax savings that resulted during the early years of the lease from accelerated depreciation, interest on the loan, and the investment tax credit.

Bancorp Leasing was expected to contribute to the financial objectives established by its parent. One of the most important objectives was to maintain, and preferably increase, the return on assets invested. At present, Bancorp Leasing expected to earn a 10-percent average annual return (after tax) on funds it invested in leveraged leases. This was higher than the 7-percent return expected by the bank on leveraged leases, but the extra return was explained by (1) the higher credit risk believed to be associated with leasing, (2) the relatively long maturity of leveraged leases that resulted in an interest-rate risk, and (3) the fact that the 10- and 7-percent figures (roughly 20 and 14 percent, respectively on a pretax basis) were calculated before subtracting the cost of invested funds.

The 10-percent return target for Bancorp Leasing was arrived at by a combination of a survey of mainland leasing companies and a feeling among executive management that new activities should increase the overall return on stockholders' equity.

Competition from other leasing companies sometimes made it difficult for Bancorp Leasing to hold to the 10-percent return target. As a result, certain top quality leases had been placed with the bank since the bank had the advantage of a lower cost of funds. The lease was placed in the bank by the simple measure of naming the bank as lessor in the lease documentation. During 1978, the average cost of interest-bearing bank deposits was about 6 percent, and it would cost the holding company more if it was to borrow from the large east-coast banks which charged the prime rate plus compensating balances. Holding company borrowing was on an incremental basis to provide funds to Bancorp Leasing. If the lease went to the bank, the holding company would reduce its borrowing needs by an equivalent amount. Easier access to the lower cost bank funds was one reason many bank holding companies were now conducting their leasing transactions in the bank rather than in a leasing affiliate. Leases placed with the bank were expected to earn 7 percent after tax on the funds invested, less than the 10 percent for Bancorp Leasing.

In analyzing any potential lease, Bancorp Leasing used a discounted cash-flow approach that concentrated on the amount and timing of all cash flows generated by the lease. The objective was to determine the amount of the annual lease payment that must be charged if (1) Bancorp Leasing was to earn 10 percent on its invested funds or (2) if the Bank of Hawaii was to earn 7 percent on its invested funds. It was only necessary to compute one annual lease payment depending on whether it felt Bancorp Leasing or Bank of Hawaii should make the lease.

From all reports the volume of leasing in the United States had increased steadily in recent years, and the experience at Bancorp Leasing had been no exception. There were many reasons for companies to lease assets. Based upon its experience to date, Bancorp Leasing believed most of its customers fell into one of three groups:

1. Companies that paid little or no federal income tax. The ownership of equipment created tax benefits through the investment tax credit and accelerated depreciation. These were lost by a company that did not have an income tax liability. Bancorp Leasing could use these tax shields if it owned the equipment and it could pass the benefits back to the lessee as lower lease payments.

2. Companies that were cash short. Many companies did not have the cash needed to make a down payment to purchase expensive assets. Rather than go without the asset, one solution was to lease the asset from another company with the financial means to make the purchase.

3. Companies that wanted a fixed payment. An obvious alternative to leasing an asset was to borrow the money and buy it. Because of rapid changes in the level of interest rates in recent years, however, many loans had a floating interest rate that was tied to the prime rate of interest. The uncertainty related to interest rate changes had led some bank customers to turn to leasing with its fixed payments over the life of the lease.

There were, of course, companies that for a variety of other reasons either could not buy equipment or would be better off financially to lease than to purchase. To reach its potential customers, Bancorp Leasing had an extensive

marketing program. Several of the advertisements that appeared in the press are contained in Exhibit 1.

HAWAIIAN AIR

Hawaiian Air had come a long way since its first flight almost 50 years ago inaugurating Hawaii's commercial air service. Now Hawaiian Air provided regularly scheduled flights between the six major islands, and more passengers were often carried in a single day than were carried in the whole first year of operation. Its major competitor was Aloha Airlines, and in recent years Hawaiian had controlled between 55 and 58 percent of the passenger market. Following partial deregulation by the Civil Aeronautics Board, Hawaiian Air acquired an air cargo division based in Macon, Georgia. The company also had pending several new route applications which, if successful, would open up routes to the U.S. mainland and to Samoa and Fiji. Aside from some military charter business about 20 years ago, Hawaiian's regular service had been confined to the islands of Hawaii.

Profits in recent years had been erratic, as shown below. Early forecasts for 1978 were that another loss would be reported, perhaps larger than in 1975.

Financial Statement Reported Net Income ($000)	
1973	$1,312
1974	2,339
1975	(444)
1976	782
1977	634

Because of differences between taxable income reported to the Internal Revenue Service and reported net income for financial statement purposes, little or no tax had been actually paid for several years. At the present time Hawaiian had significant unused investment tax credits of which $138,000 would expire in 1978, $549,000 in 1979, and $2,932,000 in 1983.

THE DC-9 PROPOSAL

Many of the terms for the DC-9-50 lease had already been determined. The basic provisions were:

1. The lease would be for 15 years.

2. The purchase price of the new DC-9-50 was $10 million.

3. The investment tax credit was 10 percent and it would be amortized for reporting purposes over the life of the lease. For tax and cash-flow purposes it was recognized in the first year.

4. Double declining balance depreciation switching to straight line would be used for a ten-year life and zero salvage value. The actual economic life was estimated to be 18 to 21 years. Recent IRS guidelines required that for leveraged leasing the estimated residual value should be at least 20 percent of the original cost of the asset. In this case, however, the plane could be depreciated to a zero salvage value because the asset depreciation range method was used by the lessor, and the lessor was fairly certain it would retain ownership of the plane over the aircraft's entire useful life. (See Exhibit 2.)

5. The gross excise tax was 4 percent of the lease payment if the lease was placed in Bancorp Leasing. The bank, however, was not subject to gross excise taxes, and if the lease was

placed in the bank the lessee would pay the tax only if it was imposed at a later date by state authorities.

6. The expected residual salvage value was 20 percent of the purchase price, but it could actually be either higher or lower. This amount was subject to tax at ordinary rates since the asset was being depreciated to a zero residual value.

7. The average combined federal and state corporate income tax rate for Hawaii Bancorporation was 28 percent. The combined marginal rate was 50.982 percent, assuming sufficient taxable income available to take advantage of all deductions and credits. The possibility existed that the federal tax rate would be lowered in the future.

8. The lease would be leveraged with a mainland insurance company providing $6 million in a 13-year loan at 9.5 percent interest on the outstanding balance. The loan was repayable in equal annual installments.

9. The sinking fund rate would be 0-percent. Bancorp Leasing preferred to look at the transaction on a clean, conservative basis. The reason for the 0 percent rate was that the bank had assets in excess of $1.7 billion, and at any time it would have $150 to $170 million in nonearning reserve assets. Therefore, it was quite likely the funds would not be reinvested. Occasionally, for competitive purposes, it would use a 3- or 4-percent sinking fund rate since that was the approximate after-tax cost of certain bank debt. The rationale for using the after-tax cost of debt was that the funds could be used to retire debt even if the company could not,

or did not, reinvest the funds. The sinking fund was formed only after the $4 million of original investment plus the desired gross margin (after tax but before cost of funds) of either 7 or 10 percent had been repaid.

10. To accommodate the lessee, lease payments would be made at the end of each year.

The terms of the lease proposal would need to meet Internal Revenue Service requirements for leases. The principal points were:

1. The lessor retained the risks of ownership, including the possibility the residual value would be less than expected.

2. The useful life of the asset had to be at least 20 percent longer than the lease term. Lease rentals had to be large enough to cover the cost of the asset and provide a return on the lessor's investment.

3. The lessee did not have the right to buy the property at the end of the lease for less than its fair-market value.

PRESENTING THE LEASE PROPOSAL

The people at Hawaiian Air were familiar with leasing since they were already leasing four DC-9s from mainland institutions as well as large amounts of other equipment. Nevertheless, since competition for this lease was likely to be spirited, Mr. Sharp sensed that he should be ready to handle inquiries in at least three areas. First of all, what would be the net cost of the lease to Hawaiian Air so that they could compare the offer with others? Second, would the lease affect Hawaiian Air's cost of capital or its debt capacity? Third, the company would likely ask why the leasing subsidiary (or bank) was proposing a lease rather than a bank loan. Was it because the lease would earn a higher return than the loan and, thus, be more costly to Hawaiian Air?

In reference to the second area, Mr. Sharp checked with the accountants to see how the DC-9 lease would be reported in Hawaiian Air's financial statements. Hawaiian Air, of course, preferred that it be treated as an operating lease, which would not be treated as a liability on its balance sheet. The relevant parts of FASB 13 dealing with lease accounting are attached as Exhibit 3. Mr. Sharp knew it would make the lease proposal more attractive to Hawaiian Air if the lease could be treated as an operating lease.

Hawaiian Air had invited other lessors to submit bids for this lease. The DC-9-50 was well regarded within the leasing industry and generally attracted considerable attention for bidding purposes. Consequently, Mr. Sharp expected Hawaiian Air would receive several proposals.

EXHIBIT 1

The DC-9 Lease

Bancorp Leasing Advertisements

At Bancorp Leasing, we specialize in TRUE LEASES. This means that we own the equipment and absorb the resulting tax benefits, which we then pass back to you in the form of lower lease rates. These rates, along with the advantages of 100-percent financing and the tax deductibility of the level lease payments, help maximize your cash flow and reserve your present capital for other more profitable investments.

Since you make your lease payments with tomorrow's less valuable dollars, you also gain a hedge that helps protect your firm from the eroding effects of inflation. In addition, you avoid the market risk inherent in obsolescent-prone equipment that depreciates with each passing day.

TRUE LEASES are worth looking into. If you need $25,000 or more of equipment, give us a call and we'll talk about TRUE LEASING. We just might be good for each other.

Sometimes ownership of equipment in your business makes a lot of sense. And sometimes it costs you hard-earned capital. Tax deductible payments on a TRUE LEASE from Bancorp Leasing often make much more sense than a string of monthly loan payments that lead to ownership of obsolete equipment.

There are plenty of other advantages to our TRUE LEASE you should know about too. For example, TRUE LEASE can improve your cash flow because you don't need a down payment. And you can often get lower rates than with conventional financing. We also make sure you get the best possible lease tailored to your particular business needs.

At Bancorp Leasing, leasing is all we do. So why not fill out the coupon below and send it back to us for more information? Or give us a call and let's talk. We just might be good for each other.

Have you ever tried to get a loan for some expensive new equipment for your business— without a down payment? You don't have to guess what a big problem that might be.

But with a TRUE LEASE from Bancorp Leasing, you don't need a down payment. Just tell us what you want, and we'll buy it for you. It can be as easy as that.

There are plenty of other TRUE LEASE advantages you should know about too. Like longer terms than a loan, a good hedge against inflation, and tax deductible payments to name just a few.

If you don't know much about TRUE LEASES, you ought to. And at Bancorp Leasing, that's all we do. So why not fill out this coupon and send it back to us for more information? Or just give us a call and let's talk. We just might be good for each other.

EXHIBIT 2

The DC-9 Lease

Annual Depreciation and Loan Repayment

Year	Depreciation Reported Depreciation	Remaining Book Value	Loan Repayment ($822,912 annual) Interest	Principal	Remaining Balance
1	$2,000,000	$8,000,000	$570,000	$252,912	$5,747,088
2	1,600,000	6,400,000	545,973	276,939	5,470,149
3	1,280,000	5,120,000	519,664	303,248	5,166,901
4	1,024,000	4,096,000	490,856	332,056	4,834,845
5	819,200	3,276,800	459,310	363,602	4,471,243
6	655,360	2,621,440	424,768	398,144	4,073,099
7	655,360	1,966,080	386,944	435,968	3,637,131
8	655,360	1,310,720	345,527	477,385	3,159,746
9	655,360	655,360	300,176	522,736	2,637,010
10	655,360	-0-	250,516	572,396	2,064,614
11	—	—	196,138	626,774	1,437,840
12	—	—	136,595	686,317	751,523
13	—	—	71,395	751,523	-0-
14	—	—	—	—	—
15	—	—	—	—	—
	$10,000,000	—	$4,697,862	$6,000,000	—

EXHIBIT 3

The DC-9 Lease

Criteria for Classifying Leases: FASB 13

If at its inception, a lease meets one or more of the following four criteria, the lease shall be classified as a capital lease by the lessee. Otherwise, it shall be classified as an operating lease.

1. The lease transfers ownership of the property to the lessee by the end of the lease term.
b. The lease contains a bargain purchase option.
c. The lease term is equal to 75 percent or more of the estimated economic life of the leased property.
d. The present value at the beginning of the lease term of the minimum lease payments, excluding that portion of the payments representing executory costs such as insurance, maintenance, and taxes to be paid by the lessor, including any profit thereon, equals or exceeds 90 percent of the excess of the fair value of the leased property to the lessor at the inception of the lease over any related investment tax credit retained by the lessor and expected to be realized by him. A lessor shall compute the present value of the minimum lease payments using the interest rate implicit in the lease. A lessee shall compute the present value of the minimum lease payments using his incremental borrowing rate, unless (i) it is practicable for him to learn the implicit rate computed by the lessor and (ii) the implicit rate computed by the lessor is less than the lessee's incremental borrowing rate. If both of those conditions are met, the lessee shall use the implicit rate.

Hawaiian Air's incremental borrowing rate is 10 percent.

PART SEVEN

Management of Long-Term Financing

CASE 36

Advanced Computer Systems, Inc. (A)

In May 1976 Messrs. John Fitzpatrick, Walter Bernstein, and William Gibbons were reviewing the current status of Advanced Computer Systems, Inc., (Adcomp) in contemplation of an important new financing step. The three men were the principal officers and owners of Adcomp. They had before them the latest financial statements and a commitment letter outlining the terms of the financing proposal.

Fitzpatrick finally put the papers aside, gazed at the pictures of various computer-related products that adorned his well-appointed office, and remarked, "With a two-million-dollar order backlog —more than the $1.8 million sales all of last year—this should be the best year in our history, although you sure can't tell it from the latest financials. The way our orders have been bunched, shipments have been slow, and cash is awfully

tight again. Lots of hard work has been done on the large contracts we closed earlier in the year, but it's been mostly engineering. We haven't built much of the hardware yet where the big dollars are in terms of billings.

"In addition, we agreed to the five-year plan, involving diversification into several sophisticated product lines. We're adding expensive people, facilities and overhead."

Bernstein chimed in, "Yes, and if we are to achieve that plan, we must commit more dollars to the development work. There are a couple of good technical people available if we have the money to hire them."

Gibbons interrupted with, "I don't see how we can hire more high-priced engineers when I'm having all I can do to meet the payroll now. We've got our suppliers all stretched out, and they're

---

This case was prepared by and used with the permission of Jack D. Ferner, Lecturer in Management, Babcock Graduate School of Management, Wake Forest University.

screaming for payment. Pretty soon they'll stop shipping and then see what happens to the five-year plan. John, we really need that financing."

Fitzpatrick fidgeted for a moment before replying, "I agree we need the cash from the financing, but we already have a lot of debt to service, and I'm nervous about taking on more. Do you think we can—safely?"

Advanced Computer Systems, Inc., is a high-technology company engaged in the design and manufacture of minicomputer systems and related peripheral products for sale to industry, science, and medicine.

COMPANY HISTORY

Adcomp was founded in October 1967 as an 80-percent owned subsidiary of Tennessee Electronic Corporation, a nuclear instrumentation company in Oak Ridge, Tennessee. There were four other founding stockholders of the company: John Fitzpatrick; Dr. Walter Bernstein, who became president and technical director; Dr. William Gibbons, vice-president and general manager; and Mr. Norman Hall, another scientist who never took an active role.

For several years prior to the formation of the company, Drs. Bernstein and Gibbons had worked with nuclear instrumentation systems at the Oak Ridge National Laboratory where they were experimental physicists. They participated in the rapid growth of small computer systems in scientific instrumentation. It was evident to the founders that the rapidly falling price and versatility of the storage program logic of the small computer made it ideally suited to many applications. At the time of Adcomp's founding there was no commercial

source for a complete computer-oriented analytical instrumentation system, although an increasing number of such systems were being constructed on a "do it yourself" basis. The founders thought that the time was ripe for offering a modular system that would take advantage of their accumulated experience. With this background Adcomp was formed in 1967.

The company's first product was a nuclear pulse height analysis system used in nuclear research and industrial applications. Most of the company's first year was spent designing and testing the company's first minicomputer system, the TP-1000, and associated peripheral devices and software to support the system.

The peripheral components that were developed included a small cartridge-type magnetic tape recorder, an operator-oriented control panel, an automatic loading and starting device, a light pen, several display systems and interfaces with various other instrumentation. The company's first sales were to universities and governmental agencies.

In 1968–69 the Vietnam buildup had depressed nuclear research. As a result, Tennessee Electronics began to experience falling sales and mounting operating losses. Thus, the parent company could not supply Adcomp with the management time, sales support, and services that were originally envisioned. Divestment was agreed to by all parties, and as a result, Mr. Fitzpatrick's offer to buy out Tennessee Electronic's 80-percent interest in Adcomp for $80,000 in installment notes was accepted.

Free of Tennessee Electronic's marketing organization, which was entirely in the nuclear field, Adcomp was able to seek wider markets. Rapid growth followed as industrial and medical markets were opened up until these segments of the business became 75 to 80 percent of total sales. The company had seen rising sales and profits in all years except one. In 1972 the electronics industry in general, and computer firms specifically, suffered a recession, and there was a drastic shake-out of marginal firms. (See Exhibits 1, 2 and 3 for historical financial statements.)

INVESTMENT AND GROWTH PHILOSOPHY

The company's 1976 "Corporate Mission" was stated:

> To invest in any area of suitable profit and growth potential in which Adcomp Systems has or can acquire the technical and marketing capabilities and which involves customers solving problems through the use of dedicated minicomputers and related peripheral equipment.

The owners of Adcomp believed strongly in the potential that existed for their product line as well as their technical abilities. In approaching the market they chose a strategy of diversification rather than specialization. This strategy was intended to protect against over-reliance on a single customer, changing economic conditions and government priorities, and product obsolescence.

In carrying out this mission, the owners tended to avoid issuing large amounts of equity funds and suffering substantial dilution. Their opinion was that reckless growth and investment could be risky and was what produced the inevitable disaster in 1972 when hundreds of electronics and computer-related firms failed or were assimilated by other companies.

Nonetheless, at the end of 1975 management viewed the prospects for the company to be excellent. After a careful evaluation of their technical capabilities, the needs in the marketplace, and the competitive factors, they adopted an ambitious five-year plan that would require additional financing. Exhibit 4 is a summary of this plan showing sales and profit projections.

COMPANY'S PRODUCT LINES

1. Nuclear Systems: Management stated that Adcomp was recognized as a pioneer in this field and enjoyed a growing position of leadership as physicists became aware of the advanced system hardware and software programming the company offered.

2. Peripheral Products: Adcomp developed a line of low-cost peripheral devices to support its original TP-1000 system, and these products represented a significant portion of the company's total sales. The most widely sold item in this line had been a magnetic tape unit used for data input-output and data storage.

3. Special Systems: These systems were designed to fit a customer's specific data-handling problems. The design and manufacture of these systems represented a substantial part of the company's business volume, and although this product line involved committing resources to "one of a kind" efforts, it could lead to solutions of more universal problems and was looked upon as a feeder in establishing "standard systems" for much wider markets. The most recent example was a $732,000 sale to

TVA for a reactor safety control system, which could ultimately become a standard system for sale to the entire utility industry.

4. Medical Systems: Adcomp designed and constructed the first data acquisition-analysis systems for the Body Fluids Analysis System developed at Oak Ridge National Laboratory. Adcomp was approached by most of the large pharmaceutical and instrument manufacturing firms interested in this field and ultimately signed a long-term manufacturing agreement with American Instrument Company. Adcomp delivered over 75 of these "Rotochem" systems that were marketed throughout the world by AMINCO.

5. Environmental Systems: Monitoring air and water quality on a continuous basis had become a required activity in many industries. The most stringent quality requirements related to the nuclear power industry. Adcomp developed an Isotopic Identification System and supporting software programs. Important sales had been made to Radiation Management, Inc., Utah State Division of Health, and Allied General Nuclear Services.

6. Fiber Optics System: This system employed glass fibers developed by Corning Glass to communicate mass amounts of computer data optically rather than by present conductive wire transmissions. Adcomp had developed a pilot system that communicated 500 feet over a varied environment. This had already led to two contracts to develop larger systems, one with Arnold Research Center for

a 7000-foot underground data link between two computer facilities.

OPERATIONS

Adcomp's operations included engineering capabilities and a development laboratory containing a sizable amount of electronic and computer gear. R & D was budgeted for $150,000 in 1976.

In addition, there were facilities for light fabrication and assembly of components. Much of the work, however, was subcontracted. Buyouts (the company's term for purchased components) were estimated to account for 60 percent of the cost of goods sold.

The company had historically grown in a series of leased quarters and occupied space in two buildings approximately one-half mile apart, both in Oak Ridge, Tennessee. Recognizing the inefficiency of cramped and spread out quarters, the board decided to construct a new building that would provide for more orderly expansion and bring all employees under one roof.

Sales of standardized products were made through an international network of manufacturers' representatives, who were paid on a commission basis. The company's product managers, however, dealt extensively with customers when custom designs or special problems were involved.

MANAGEMENT

The company had grown for seven years with its original management, although introduction of a new professional manager-chief executive had been under consideration for some time by the board. Dr. Bernstein served as president since the founding of the company and managed its day-to-day affairs until 1972. At that time Dr. Gibbons, the vice-president, was given the additional duties of general manager, responsible for day-to-day operations, in order to free Dr. Bernstein for product development and sale of special systems. In May 1969 when Mr. Fitzpatrick acquired the Adcomp major interest, he became chairman of the board and treasurer. Mr. Fitzpatrick's role was only part-time, his main occupation being president of another corporation in Oak Ridge. Nevertheless, he spent many evening and weekend hours on Adcomp business. Together Messrs. Bernstein, Gibbons, and Fitzpatrick owned over 90 percent of the outstanding stock in the company.

Adcomp management prided itself in discriminating selection of technically qualified people. The company presently employed 50 people, half of whom held college degrees; four were Ph.D.s and five held Master's degrees in technical or business fields.

FINANCIAL PERFORMANCE

The company's audited balance sheets and income statements for the past seven years are summarized in Exhibits 1, 2, and 3. Pro forma financial statements for the next five years (1976–1980) are summarized in Exhibit 4. Internal, unaudited statements for the four months ending April 30 are shown in Exhibits 5 and 6.

With the exception of 1972, the performance trends were upward. Net worth advanced from $50,000 to $465,000 by December 31, 1975. The company's return on net worth ranged between 20 and 40 percent, and return on sale had been between 5 and 10 percent. The current ra-

tio had been between 1.35 and 2.64 over five years and was 1.95 at December 31, 1975.

The company's growth had been financed principally from retention of earnings, short-term bank loans, SBA-guaranteed term loans, a mortgage loan, and progress payments from customers:

1. Equity: The company was originally financed through a $100,000 issue of common capital stock. Subsequent additions to common stock and paid-in capital accounts total $67,000.

    Early development costs resulted in a retained earnings deficit that was not erased until 1971. The recession and resulting loss in 1972 pushed the retained earnings into a deficit position again. Recent profits had been retained in the business, and the stockholders' equity had grown to approximately $465,000.

2. Short-Term Loans: The company borrowed short-term funds from banks to finance temporary working capital needs. For example, in the spring of 1976 the company was enjoying a backlog of about $2 million. Most of the initial work, however, was engineering with little equipment being shipped. Thus, revenue recognized was low (the company recognized revenue on large contracts on a percentage completion method), and an interim loss occurred. The company currently had $38,000 in notes payable to a local bank.

3. SBA Guaranteed Loans: In 1971 the company secured a $260,000 five-year, 7-percent term loan from a local participating bank with a 90-percent guarantee by the U. S. Small Business Administration (SBA). Pay-

ments of $5149 per month would continue until November 1976, when the loan would be retired. In December 1975 a new loan was negotiated in the principal amount of $370,000; interest 10 percent, terms seven years, equal monthly installments of $6143 beginning January 31, 1976. The note was secured by the accounts receivable, inventories, and equipment that existed on December 31, 1975, plus the personal guarantees of the officers and their wives.

4. Mortgage Loan: Early in May 1976 an arrangement was finalized with a bank and a local development company, Ridge Development Corporation, for the financing of a 15,000

velopment. The average interest rate on the loans was 8¾ percent, and the monthly payment $3100. Other than the land, which had been previously acquired, this project and the financing were not reflected on the current financial statements. The design had been completed and foundations started. The company expected to move into the new premises and begin mortgage payments shortly after the first of 1977.

5. Proposed Debentures: In his search for additional financing Fitzpatrick approached Chadwick Associates, financial consultants, and subsequently, the following agreement was entered into:

Dear Mr. Fitzpatrick:

This letter is to set forth our understanding whereby Chadwick Associates is authorized to act as Adcomp Systems, Inc.'s nonexclusive agent in approaching venture capital firms, investment bankers, and other sophisticated investors for the purpose of securing capital for Adcomp Systems, Inc., along the following lines:

A 7-year, $500,000 subordinated debenture; interest only payable quarterly for the first 2 years at 8%; interest at 10% on the unpaid balance and principal repayments in 20 equal quarterly installments for the next five years. The debenture will have warrants to purchase from 15% to 25% of the Company's stock at a nominal cost (15% with $200,000 of after tax profits in 1976 and 25% with $50,000 of after tax profits).

square foot building. This move would consolidate operations and provide much needed space for development.

The total cost of the project was estimated at $310,000; the term was for 20 years. The financing was done under the 503 SBA program, which involved 50 percent bank participation on a first mortgage, 40-percent SBA participation (second mortgage), and 10-percent participation by Ridge De-

In conversation with the principal, Mr. Cecil Chadwick, Fitzpatrick had been assured that Chadwick had commitments for the funds as outlined. Also, when asked about the possibility of a straight equity issue, Chadwick responded, "possible, but harder to do in today's market, and if we did you would have to take a lot more dilution, maybe 50%." Fitzpatrick had been unable to secure a firm commitment for straight equity, although he had talked to several parties.

JOHN FITZPATRICK'S BACKGROUND

Fitzpatrick was in his mid-forties. He had been raised in a middle-class family in a small industrial town in Massachusetts. After college he entered an MBA program. His schooling was interrupted by a two-year stint in the Air Force where he served as a procurement officer. After receiving his MBA, Fitzpatrick joined a three-man consulting firm that became heavily involved with the shoe industry. He participated in the development of a patented shoe manufacturing system, which was marketed in Europe as well as the United States.

He stated that he left this job mostly because his employer refused to let him participate in the ownership of the new process. He then accepted a position as president of a small company in the irradiation business in Oak Ridge, Tennessee. He became active in the community being appointed director of the Chamber of Commerce, director of a venture capital group, and director of companies in the electronics and chemical process industries. He was elected "Young Man of the Year" in Oak Ridge and the State of Tennessee. He participated in a small group of businessmen that acquired and then expanded a local bank. Later, the bank was sought after by a large bank in the area, and the group sold out for a handsome profit.

In 1968 Fitzpatrick changed jobs moving to another company in Oak Ridge. He became president of the company in 1971, and the company prospered under his direction. He invested $50,000 in stock in that company, borrowing the funds. Fitzpatrick acquired his 80-percent ownership in Adcomp during this period through an installment purchase.

The Fitzpatrick family had expanded to five children, a dog, a couple of resort properties, a country club membership, a Winnebago, and an antique fire truck. Fitzpatrick was intent on achieving business and financial success. Further, he expressed willingness to assume personal risks and make sacrifices as necessary.

EXHIBIT 1

Advanced Computer Systems, Inc. (A)

Comparative Balance Sheets (Audited)

	Nov 30 1969	Nov 30 1970	Dec 31 1971	Dec 31 1972	Dec 31 1973	Dec 31 1974	Dec 31 1975
Assets							
Current assets							
Cash	$ 17,509	$ 52,590	$ 225,452	$ 122,143	$ 78,877	$ 88,266	$ 385,323
Accounts receivable—net	14,200	68,127	68,784	134,536	337,931	420,583	373,802
Inventories (note a)	26,006	34,365	46,359	60,387	109,787	153,470	205,190
Prepaid expenses/tax refunds	573	937	—	—	—	—	45,479
Revenues in excess of billings on incompleted contracts (b)	—	42,648	83,708	11,667	115,128	167,462	420,510
Total current assets	58,288	198,667	424,303	328,733	641,723	829,781	1,430,304
Equipment/leaseholds—net (c)	3,340	9,178	21,342	20,652	18,269	34,677	52,193
Land	—	—	—	—	—	—	38,350
Deferred charges							
Systems development costs (d)	35,486	76,091	124,795	124,452	106,262	—	—
Organizational expense	4,315	2,744	1,043	79	—	—	—
Total Assets	101,429	286,680	571,483	473,916	766,254	864,458	1,520,847
Liabilities and Stockholders' Equity							
Current liabilities							
Notes payable—current (e)	14,135	73,157	45,277	48,550	56,236	55,823	231,717
Accounts payable	9,448	25,746	38,713	77,434	241,654	226,003	338,718
Advance customer payments	—	—	30,475	—	—	—	—
Accrued expense	11,474	38,714	27,541	15,836	9,623	28,821	23,389
Income taxes payable	—	250	13,200	—	69,470	125,402	—
Deferred income taxes (b)	—	9,700	5,800	—	1,090	15,815	141,402
Total current liabilities	35,057	147,567	161,006	141,820	378,073	451,864	735,226
Long-term debt (f)	—	—	211,091	162,542	110,482	54,659	320,620
Deferred income taxes	15,810	39,760	53,460	53,760	53,760	—	—
Stockholders' equity							
Common capital stock	119,602	120,802	128,312	147,176	151,616	161,061	167,221
Retained earnings (deficit) (g)	(69,040)	(21,449)	17,614	(31,382)	72,323	196,874	297,780
Total stockholders' equity	50,562	99,353	145,926	115,794	223,939	357,935	465,001
Total claims	$ 101,429	$ 286,680	$ 571,483	$ 473,916	$ 766,254	$ 864,458	$1,520,847

See accompanying notes in Exhibit 3.

EXHIBIT 2

Advanced Computer Systems, Inc. (A)

Comparative Income Statements (Audited)

	8 Mos. Ending 11/30/69	12 Mos. Ending 11/30/70	13 Mos. Ending 12/31/71	12 Mos. Ending 12/31/72	12 Mos. Ending 12/31/73	12 Mos. Ending 12/31/74	12 Mos. Ending 12/31/75
Sales—net (note a)	$ 73,791	$ 407,701	$ 712,361	$ 531,465	1,025,248	$1,548,527	$1,804,097
Cost of goods sold	19,613	188,323	347,542	199,983	537,562	831,385	1,054,893
Gross profit	54,178	219,378	364,819	331,482	487,686	717,142	749,204
Systems development expense	—	16,159	66,731	104,365	72,348	62,387	126,963
Marketing expense	18,589	61,738	118,128	137,014	122,765	162,403	239,046
Gen. & admin. expense	28,419	59,990	117,897	143,318	118,308	147,350	197,932
Total expense	47,008	137,887	302,756	384,697	313,421	372,140	563,941
Income before tax & extraordinary items	7,170	81,491	62,063	(53,215)	174,265	345,002	185,263
Provision for income tax	3,786	40,200	24,300	(15,258)	81,870	167,949	84,357
Income before extraordinary items	3,384	41,291	37,763	(37,957)	92,395	177,053	100,906
Extraordinary items	—	6,300	1,300	—	11,310	—	—
Net income (loss)	$ 3,384	$ 47,591	$ 39,063	$ (37,957)	$ 103,705	$ 177,053	$ 100,906

See accompanying notes in Exhibit 3.

399

EXHIBIT 3

Advanced Computer Systems, Inc. (A)

Notes to Financial Statements

(a) Inventories

Inventories are stated at the lower of cost or market. Cost of raw materials used in systems development is determined by the first-in, first-out method. Cost of finished goods and work in process is determined by the standard cost method and is substantially actual cost.

Inventories, priced on the basis described above, are summarized as follows:

	1975	1974
Finished goods	$ 69,023	$ 34,707
Work in process	47,672	67,311
Raw materials	88,495	51,452
	$205,190	$153,470

(b) Incompleted Contracts

Income from incompleted contracts is accounted for using the percentage of completion method. Accordingly, revenues are included in sales in the amount of $420,510 for 1975 ($167,462 for 1974) and related costs in the amount of $224,434 for 1975 ($90,642 for 1974) are included in cost of sales which are applicable to incompleted contracts. For income tax purposes income is accounted for using the completed contract method. Deferred income taxes (those contained in current liabilities) are provided for the timing difference.

(c) Equipment and Leaseholds

Depreciation and amortization is determined principally using the straight-line method and is based on the following estimated useful lives: equipment 3 to 10 years, leasehold improvements 2 years.

(d) Research and Development Costs

Research and development costs are expensed in the year incurred. In 1975 these costs amounted to $88,172 ($35,005 in 1974).

In prior years the company's policy was to capitalize research and development costs which were deemed to have continuing value and amortize such costs to income of subsequent years. As required by Statement No. 2 of the Financial Accounting Standards Board, the company has changed its accounting to expense such costs as incurred and the financial statements of prior years have been restated to apply the new method retroactively. The effect of the accounting change was to reduce net income for 1975 by $26,772 ($.10 per share) and to increase net income for 1974 by $15,499 ($.06 per share).

The balances of retained earnings for 1974 and 1975 have been adjusted for the effect (net of income taxes) of applying retroactively the new method of accounting.

The deferred income taxes in the long-term liability account prior to 1974 account for the timing differences between reporting income incorporating the deferred systems development cost method and tax reporting which does not allow the deferment of such costs (must be expensed in the current year).

EXHIBIT 3 (Continued)

(e) Notes Payable—Current

	1975	1974
Short-term bank loans	$122,875	$ —
Current maturities of long-term debt	108,842	55,823

(f) Long-term Debt

Long-term debt consists of the following:

	1975	1974
7 and 10% SBA guaranteed bank loans, due in monthly installments of $5149 and $6143, respectively, including interest, through May 1976 and July 1982, collateralized by pledge of accounts receivable, inventories, and equipment having a net cost of $631,185 at June 30 1975.	$429,462	$110,482
Less: Current maturities	108,842	55,823
	$320,620	$54,659

(g) Retained Earnings

Retained earnings were adjusted in 1972 and 1974 by decreases of $11,039 and $52,502, respectively.

EXHIBIT 4

Advanced Computer Systems, Inc. (A)

Five-Year Corporate Plan
Summary of Sales and Net Income

	Pro Forma Income Statements *(000 Omitted)* Year Ending December 31					
	Actual	*Projections*				
	1975	*1976*	*1977*	*1978*	*1979*	*1980*
	($)	*($)*	*($)*	*($)*	*($)*	*($)*
Sales						
Systems	1,709	2,340	3,040	3,990	4,940	5,890
Peripherals	90	350	450	500	550	600
Other	5	10	10	10	10	10
Total sales	1,804	2,700	3,500	4,500	5,500	6,500
Cost of goods sold						
Systems	1,005	1,440	1,850	2,410	2,970	3,530
Peripherals	50	135	180	200	220	240
Total COGS	1,055	1,575	2,030	2,610	3,190	3,770
Gross margin	749	1,125	1,470	1,890	2,310	2,730
Expenses						
Systems development expense	127	150	175	200	225	250
Marketing	239	330	450	630	825	975
G & A	198	300	400	500	600	700
Total expenses	564	780	1,025	1,330	1,650	1,925
Income before taxes	185	345	445	560	660	805
Taxes	84	155	220	260	310	380
Income after taxes	101	190	225	300	350	425

The complete Five-Year Corporate Plan included a detailed analysis of technical capabilities of Adcomp, the market needs, competition factors and sales forecasts, and cost estimates by product line.

EXHIBIT 5

Advanced Computer Systems, Inc. (A)

Balance Sheet
(Unaudited)
April 30, 1976

Assets

Current assets

Cash		$ 19,293
Accounts receivable–net		309,513
Inventories		
Parts and materials	$116,093	
Work in progress—systems	49,196	
Work in progress—peripherals	41,384	
Completed systems for resale	69,046	$ 275,719
Prepaid expenses/tax refunds		—
Revenues in excess of billings on		
incompleted contracts		340,672
Total current assets		$ 945,197
Equipment and leasehold		
Improvements		
Manufacturing and test	$ 75,087	
Office furniture and fixtures	14,834	
Less: accumulated depreciation and		
amortization	38,571	$ 51,350
Land		$ 38,350
Deferred charges		—
Total assets		$1,034,897

Liabilities and Stockholders' Equity

Current liabilities

Notes payable—current	$ 38,000	
Current maturities of long-term debt	52,857	
Accounts payable	161,123	
Advance customer payments	—	
Accrued expense	(5)	
Sales commissions payable	13,479	
Income taxes payable	(45,479)	
Deferred income taxes	141,402	
Total current liabilities		$ 361,377
Long-term debt		307,887
Deferred income taxes		—
Stockholders' equity		
Common capital stock	$167,221	
Retained earnings—prior years	297,780	
—current year		
(loss)	(99,368)	$ 365,633
Total claims		$1,034,897

EXHIBIT 6

Advanced Computer Systems, Inc. (A)

Statement of Income
(Unaudited)
4 Months Ending April 30, 1976

Revenues			
Sales			
Systems	$264,084		
Peripherals	20,518		
Less: discounts and allowances	(13,943)		
Net sales	$270,659		
Other income	1,402		$272,061
Cost of sales			
Systems			
Materials	$ 93,644		
Production labor	16,721		
Engineering labor	21,172		
Quality control	4,271		
Other direct costs	8,438		
Direct overhead	16,498	$160,744	
Peripherals			
Materials	$ 5,228		
Direct labor	2,311		
Other direct costs	—		
Direct overhead	920	$ 8,459	
Other costs and expenses			
Manufacturing			
Indirect & nonchargeable labor	$ 12,119		
Consultants	—		
Payroll taxes	2,667		
Group insurance	1,072		
Travel	—		
Rent	2,517		
Instruction manuals	—		
Equipment lease & rental	—		
Expendable tools & equipment	388		
Supplies & expense	3,544		
Freight in	1,632		
Product support	1,146		
Depreciation & amortization	2,525		
Under (over) absorbed labor	134		
Overhead applied	(26,635)	$ 1,109	$170,312

EXHIBIT 6 (Continued)

Gross profit on sales		$101,749
Other expenses		
Research and development	$ 32,470	
Marketing expense	92,424	
General and administrative	76,223	$201,117
Net income (loss) before		
income taxes		$(99,368)
Income tax expense		—
Net income (loss)		$(99,368)

CASE 37

Alpha Omega Electronics (B)

INTRODUCTION

Late in June 1975 James Van Dell, a director and financial consultant of Alpha Omega Electronics (AOE), was speculating on the future of this start-up electronics company whose past 23 months had been full of both optimistic developments and disappointments. As a result of new firm orders that developed in late May and June, it appeared that this struggling young firm might be experiencing a new breath of life. AOE, which began its formal business activities in September 1973, had disbursed over $600,000 to date and had realized, prior to the new orders in May and June, less than $50,000 in sales scattered between October 1974 and March 1975.

In general, over the past 23 months, the firm had failed to meet its time schedules with respect to product development, sales projections, and manufac-turing capabilities, all of which showed up in the deteriorated financial condition of the company (see Exhibits 1 and 2). Late in June 1975, however, new orders totaled nearly $140,000, not to mention other very exciting potential sales that could evolve out of these new orders. While the timing of the recovery of capital expenditures by industry was still uncertain, basic economic indicators revealed that there was a strong probability that the current business recession had reached a cyclical bottom with the prospects of an economic recovery in the second half of 1975. Specifically, Van Dell was considering the feasibility of survival and success for AOE with the firm's present backlog of orders and the injection of an additional $200,000 of capital. There was a strong probability that $50,000 of this capital would be committed soon by a new investor who would also take over as the new presi-

This case was prepared by and used with the permission of Professor James A. Hoeven, Colorado State University.

dent of AOE early in July. He had been offered the vacant position of chief executive officer of the company along with 5000 shares of common stock at a price of $10 per share. The balance of the funds were to be secured through the sale of 5000 additional shares of common stock at the same $10 price, and hopefully, the last $100,000 would be raised by an SBA loan.

SECOND FINANCIAL PLAN— JULY 1974

Back in the previous July, AOE learned that the initial $300,000 of capital raised in its first financial plan had proved to be inadequate [see Alpha Omega Electronics (A)]. Consequently, the board of directors adopted a second financial plan that called for an additional $175,000 of equity capital through the sale of 7000 new shares of common stock at a price of $25 per share. The directors chose to raise the price per share because they believed that certain elements of risk had been lessened with respect to an investment in AOE.

The basis for arriving at a need of $175,000 additional capital were new assumptions for production and sales. Five PCCs were scheduled for completion in June and ten each in July, August, and September. Since marketing had made some selected offers for limited trial periods on new installations, no receipts from sales were planned before November. However, the new forecast assumed a cash break-even could be reached by January 1975. Monthly disbursements were not expected to increase with production, since adequate inventory was already on hand.

Significant developments between August 1974 and January 1975 could be summarized as follows. The PCC sent to DuPont did not do well in its tests. It was clear later on that the design still contained bugs that had to be removed. It was not until late September that the first ten units of the PCC were completed, and final tests indicated that all of these units had flaws. On the other hand, the OCS prototype was completed in August under the project leadership of an engineer hired early in February. In demonstrations with potential users, it generated significant enthusiasm, and within a short period of time, AOE had secured single orders for this controller from the following companies and for the following applications:

1. Lester Engineering, an original equipment manufacturer (OEM) of die casting machines;

2. Dana Corporation, a manufacturer of auto parts using the OCS on a friction welding machine;

3. Cherry Rivet, a West Coast subsidiary of a large U.S. conglomerate involving the control of a vacuum furnace;

4. General Electric, one of the nation's largest appliance manufacturers in which the OCS operated testing procedures on an assembly line; and

5. Spraymation, an original equipment manufacturer of a newly designed system of die dispensing pumps.

General Electric drafted their purchase order for one OCS controller but with a retroactive reduction in price on the first, when and if they ordered ten more—which they actually required. The order placed by Spraymation involved additional development, for it required some

modifications of the original design of
the PCC. However, this customer later
provided AOE with a very loose but significant letter of intent that indicated
their customer, one of the largest textile
manufacturing firms in the United States,
United Merchants, would require 66 such
systems and the price quotation for each
of AOE's controllers was approximately
$12,000.

After $90,000 of capital was raised,
all from existing stockholders, AOE experienced great difficulty in raising the
balance of the funds required. Furthermore, since the firm had slipped again in
terms of production and sales, it was obvious that more than $175,000 of equity
capital would be required unless bank
debt could be arranged on the strength
of collateral created from sales and accounts receivable. As early as September, AOE began in earnest to solicit
interest from venture capital firms located virtually all over the United States.
Within several months of continuous
search, it became apparent that such
capital for a start-up firm without proven
sales and earnings, like AOE, was nonexistent. The equity market had deteriorated to such an extent that many brokerage houses had literally closed up
their equity underwriting departments.
The NYSE Industrial Index had fallen
from a level of over 70 in January 1973 to
approximately 38 by December 1974.
Whatever liquidity these venture capital
firms possessed was being held in high
grade, high interest earning fixed income
securities or being reserved for the additional needs of other enterprises they
had invested in earlier. The situation
was in striking contrast to the 1965–69
period in which venture capital was
knocking on the doors of firms such as
AOE. Realizing the futility of this effort,

a parallel attempt was initiated to interest a compatible industrial firm in some
sort of association with AOE. While total acquisition could be considered, the
principals of AOE were looking for an
injection of new equity or a combination
of equity and debt capital in exchange
for AOE common stock. It was hoped
that this different approach, direct to industrial firms, might turn up a special
compatibility in terms of market, products, or technology that would be attractive enough to secure the capital that
AOE required. While this effort did develop some interest, the interest did not
materialize in the period now being discussed. Therefore, more will be said
about it later. However, before moving
on, a definite problem that would have
had to be faced with the sale of stock to
some large and sophisticated investor
should be mentioned. The problem
would have been the price of the stock,
for it most certainly would have been
significantly lower than the price of $25
paid by the last individual investors.

By early December 1974, all equity
capital had been disbursed, and the
company had begun to borrow small
amounts against its first line of credit
with the bank on the strength of good investor prospects (still in the category of
small investors.) However, this required
the personal endorsements of up to
$35,000 by nine of AOE's board mem-
bers. Also, due to the strained cash position by this time, Van Dell found it
necessary to talk almost daily to trade
creditors because of delinquent bills.
Other than the tennis control center that
had been installed locally in late September 1974, AOE had shipped only one
controller, an OCS to Lester Engineering,
the die casting manufacturer, in late November 1974. A second OCS was

shipped in late December to General Electric, and two more units were shipped in January to Dana Corporation and Cherry Rivet. The die dispensing controller was scheduled to be shipped in January but did not go out until February 15, 1975. Together these invoices totaled about $30,000.

BANK FINANCING—JANUARY 1975

Anticipating these shipments, Van Dell went to the local bank in late December and requested a second $100,000 line of credit to be supported by accounts receivable and raw parts inventory. The line of credit was approved after the corporation agreed to pledge all accounts receivables, raw parts inventory, all fixed assets that had not been leased, and additional personal endorsements by McDonnel, Van Dell, and three other board members who were also principal investors in AOE. Although the total line was $100,000, drawings were to be limited to 80 percent of accounts receivable and 75 percent of raw parts inventory. Disbursements for the first three months of the year were budgeted at $30,000 per month or a total of $90,000. Robinson and Atkins provided a sales forecast through the first six months of the year that included only identified names of firms they believed would place orders with AOE. In the case of each identified firm, personal contact had been made, application engineering had been completed, and positive feedback with regard to placing an order with AOE had been received. This forecast, which was considered conservative, totaled approximately $250,000 by the end of June, although sales for the second quarter were somewhat larger than the first. In spite of this forecast and the bank loan ar-

rangement, Van Dell told the board of directors in January that additional equity capital had to be pursued. The balance of funds to be raised to complete the second financial plan at this time was about $70,000. Van Dell suggested the corporation set up an escrow fund to receive and hold cash commitments for equity investments with a provision that these funds not be released to AOE until a minimum of $50,000 was raised and, with a deadline of March 15, 1975. The directors agreed that such an arrangement would make it easier for them to talk to prospective investors; consequently, this plan was adopted by the board. While these equity funds were considered very important to the future of AOE, efforts also continued to pursue some form of affiliation with another industrial firm.

ATTEMPTS TO SECURE CAPITAL FROM INDUSTRY

Before March 15, 1975, $67,000 of new equity from small investors was received; so, the escrow account was released to AOE. In addition, contact was made with several interested industrial firms. The first resulted in a mutual rejection due to lack of a strong product and market compatibility and also because the other firm was already straddled with an immense amount of debt. It was questionable in the minds of AOE's principals whether this other firm would be able to provide the funds required by AOE for future growth. The second firm was a relatively large, financially sound, and very profitable company that had established a venture capital subsidiary to make minority investments in other firms that showed potential for transferable technology to the parent company as well as being profitable. AOE placed great hopes on an affiliation with this company but was rejected on several points. The first was the absence of proven management; the second was their belief that AOE's marketing was not well focused and was too much of a shotgun approach; and third there was an uncertainty of transferable technology.

The third industrial company that investigated AOE was a Chicago firm, and their interest developed out of an old personal acquaintanceship between that company's president and Atkins. There was no question about product and market compatibility. This firm possessed an electronic division that was already marketing a process controller in the area of scales and weights, but their controller was much more sophisticated and expensive than AOE's product line. They were very interested in the technology and market potential of AOE's less expensive programmable controllers. It was not until late April, however, before members of their board of directors made a final visit to AOE to make a financial offer. By this time, AOE was in serious financial difficulty. Not a single new order had been consummated since the previous November. All of the new equity funds had been disbursed, in addition to nearly $80,000 on the bank line of credit, and the note endorsers had refused temporarily to permit AOE to draw further on its line of credit. There had been a cut in AOE's personnel, and those that remained on the payroll were accepting only 75 percent of their normal salary. In addition, the accounts payable, most of which were delinquent, had reached approximately $60,000. The offer made to AOE by the Chicago firm was indeed stingy and clearly reflected an awareness of these developments. Their

offer consisted of an option, to be exercised within three years by them, to buy 100 percent, or as near to 100 percent as possible, of AOE's outstanding stock for $250,000. In the meantime sufficient new stock would be issued to them for a nominal price in order to give them majority voting control. They would agree to inject a minimum of $200,000 of capital into AOE in the form of a loan.

On May 3, 1975, the board of directors met to make a decision upon the offer which didn't appear to have much success of being accepted, even if the alternative was to close the doors. Before any discussion of the offer took place, Atkins announced his resignation as president of AOE and as a member of the board of directors. His reasons were that he was physically and mentally exhausted and that the company was in such a demoralized state that he personally could do nothing more to lead it out of this condition. He would not even consider several weeks away from the job before making his final decision; therefore, the board had no other alternative but to reluctantly accept his resignation.

If it were not for two other possibilities to raise additional equity capital, the board might have decided that day to close the doors for AOE. The first was an investment interest shown by the president and sole owner of the die dispensing manufacturer. This company was not large, and it had a tremendous stake in the promotion of its newly developed system of pumps that permitted great accuracy in the dispensing of fluids. An electronic control system was an absolute necessity to provide the accuracy that was made possible by their pumps, and AOE's controller had been specifically designed for their system.

Further, they were very intrigued with AOE's concept of explicitly programming with a card and simplicity of interface with their pumps. This company anticipated installing 66 such systems, at $100,000 each, for one large customer alone. This customer manufactured textiles in 11 different U.S. plants.

A second possibility was generated through a relative of an executive officer of an Arab venture capital firm. The amount of capital that AOE required was of no consequence to this firm, and they possessed a reputation for their willingness to assume risk and the quickness in which they moved. With these possibilities in mind, the endorsers of the bank note approved a further draw of $20,000 which would carry the firm another 30 days on the reduced employee payroll.

The board took over the management of the firm with McDonnel assuming the primary interim management responsibilities. The board decided to not accept the Chicago-based firm's offer and instead counter-offered with an $850,000 option that had to be exercised by them in two years or AOE could buy back all stock issued to them for $200,000. The board did not expect this counteroffer to be accepted.

During the month of May, an order was finalized with Uniroyal, a major U.S. tire manufacturer. AOE's controller was to automate one of their Banbury processes, a universal process employed by all firms that produced synthetic rubber. This order was considered to have a great future potential. In addition, Dana Corporation, who had purchased an OCS controller to operate their friction welder, gave verbal approval to AOE to build an auxillary quality assurance system to operate in conjunction with the control-

ler. Together, these orders totaled nearly $20,000. Finally, verbal assurance was received from a manufacturer's representative that within a short time AOE would receive a purchase order for $50,000 from Bechtel, one of the largest engineering firms in the world, for a system to control the cooling ponds for a nuclear energy plant.

Although the directors of AOE were encouraged by the new orders, further disappointment resulted when both the pump manufacturer and the Arab venture capital firm decided against an equity investment in AOE. Due to the desperate need for capital, yet the positive development of new orders, McDonnel decided to try to reopen acquisition negotiations with the Chicago-based firm and was successful. By this time, Atkins had begun doing consulting work for the firm. However, after another four-week delay, the Chicago-based firm's directors decided they were no longer interested in AOE on any basis.

Early in June, Van Dell stepped in to relieve McDonnel of primary management responsibilities, and very soon the purchase order was received for the nuclear energy control system. Following this, a reorder for nine additional OCS controllers was received from General Electric as well as an identical unit for Ocean Spray, a large manufacturer and national distributor of fruit juices. This meant that AOE had a total backlog of slightly over $100,000 and was very optimistic about $40,000 more before long from Spraymation, the pump manufacturer, since their first system was being installed with AOE's controller in a textile plant in South Carolina. There were four additional systems required in this one plant.

By mid-June, AOE was totally out of

cash, but the only absolutely necessary cash disbursements required in the balance of the month were the payroll, C.O.D. payments on parts, and utilities. Suppliers had been threatening to bring suit for some time. However, AOE's relationship with the bank cast a rather strange protective umbrella over the firm. Every single asset of the firm had been pledged to the bank, and given the size of the bank loan at $170,000, there was virtually no possibility of a supplier realizing anything should their suit bring about involuntary bankruptcy. Although the bank was not pleased with their loan to AOE, they did have personal endorsements to cover deficiencies in the liquidation of assets. They also were unusually sympathetic about repayment of principal and did not want to be the party that closed the doors.

In mid-June and prior to the final rejection of some form of acquisition by the Chicago-based firm, Van Dell and two other directors and note endorsers discussed the situation of AOE with the bank's loan officers. In this meeting the advisability of making all disbursements that were absolutely necessary until a decision had been reached regarding the acquisition was discussed. In addition to waiting for the acquisition decision, discussion was also given to the strategy of going through a staged rather than an immediate liquidation. AOE had virtually all the inventory necessary to complete certain of its orders. Therefore, it made sense to spend a limited amount of dollars to convert raw materials into much more valuable accounts receivable or even finished goods. The other benefit from such a strategy was the extension

of time that might bring about another favorable development. From its inception, the management, the stockholders, and, most certainly, the note endorsers of AOE had been buying time.

JULY 1975

In considering the future of AOE in July 1975 and whether $200,000 would be sufficient capital, Van Dell realized that a great deal depended upon the turn around of the economy and capital expenditures by industry. He knew that AOE had thousands of dollars of potential business in its files that had gone dormant earlier in the year only because of the economic recession. He wondered how successful AOE might be in rejuvenating that business in the coming months. In this context, he was also reviewing in his mind all of the past struggle and disappointments experienced by AOE. He was questioning what part was due to fortuitous events, such as an extremely depressed equity market in 1973–1974 followed by the recession in 1975, and what part was contributed by errors in judgment. Since he had been responsible as the financial officer of the firm and was a university professor instructing courses in finance, he was particularly concerned with decisions made regarding the financial support of the enterprise. Finally, he wondered about his own investment rationale that resulted in repeated personal investments in AOE, and in addition, his co-endorsement of a large corporate debt to the bank.

EXHIBIT 1

Alpha Omega Electronics (B)

Balance Sheet

		May 31, 1975
Current assets		
Cash	$ 5,738	
Accounts receivables	20,231	
Subscription receivables	10,000	
Inventories		
Raw material	43,570	
In process	19,555	
Finished goods	25,000	
Prepaid expense	1,219	
Total current assets		$125,313
Fixed assets		
Leasehold imp.	5,738	
Equipment	25,372	
Less: Depreciation	4,866	
Total fixed assets		26,244
Other assets		
Deposits	7,300	
Organization expense	172	
Total other assets		7,472
Total assets		$159,029
Current liabilities		
Notes—bank	140,063	
Notes—other	29,960	
Accrued P.R.	12,894	
Accounts payable	76,652	
Payroll tax	11,872	
Interest	15,124	
Property tax	500	
Total current liabilities		287,065
Convertible debt		72,000
Stockholders' equity	425,291	
Common stock subscribed	10,000	
Retained earnings	(635,327)	
Total stockholder equity		(200,036)
Total liabilities and stockholders' equity		$159,029

EXHIBIT 2

Alpha Omega Electronics (B)

Operating Statement

	9 mo.—5/31/75
Income	
Sales	$46,210
Interest	2,208
Other	1,001
Total	$ 49,419
Sales expense	
Commissions	893
Salaries	20,059
Advert. & shows	6,293
Travel	23,939
Brochures & aids	11,277
Telephone & other	2,373
Total	64,834
Development expense	
Salary and parts	33,176
Production expense	
Salary	42,608
Labor and parts	83,211
Subcontract	8,527
Equipment rent	11,616
Other mfg. expense	6,021
Freight	2,432
Total	154,415
General and admin. expense	
Salaries	46,632
Clerical salaries	6,081
Rent—equipment, building	8,671
Utilities	14,868
Insurance	10,137
Depreciation & amortization	2,692
Recruiting	2,448
Professional service	8,760
Office expense	2,151
Payroll taxes	10,346
Miscellaneous	7,154
Interest	19,022
Total general and admin. expense	138,962
Total expenses	391,387
Net loss	(341,968)

CASE 38

Delta Steel Corporation

In July 1983 Mr. James Drummond, vice-president of finance for Delta Steel Corporation (hereafter referred to as Delta), was looking forward to meeting Mr. Allan Solomon, representing Farmer, Hutton and Barron, an investment banking firm. The purpose of the meeting was to evaluate alternative methods for financing capital equipment needs at Delta, and to prepare a recommendation for consideration by Delta's Board of Directors.

BACKGROUND

Delta is a medium-sized steel manufacturing firm located in a Midwestern state. Originally incorporated in 1907, it was reincorporated in Delaware in 1964. It has four major operating divisions. The steel division produces and markets various grades of carbon steel, stainless steel, and specialty steels. Its steel is

sold in ingots, bars, hot and cold rolled steel, pipe, tubing, and galvanized sheets. The division is also engaged in mining iron ore and coal which are consumed in the division's steel-making plants. As Exhibit 1 shows, the steel division has accounted for the majority of the company's revenues and operating income.

The manufacturing and engineering division produces and sells equipment for use in oil and gas drilling. Additionally, the division constructs buildings, bridges, and transmission towers and is an active bidder on jobs requiring large amounts of steel. A small but growing segment of the division provides construction and engineering consulting services. The division is the second largest in the firm in terms of sales.

The petrochemicals division produces and markets various types of chemicals, plastic resins, fertilizers, and

---

This case was prepared by and used with the permission of Ike Mathur.

herbicides. The division's profitability lagged in recent years due to severe competition in the industrial and agricultural chemicals industries.

The mining division mines iron ore, coal, uranium, and other minerals for sale to non-Delta businesses. The division is actively involved in exploration and development, and while the smallest in terms of sales, generated the highest profit margins in the firm.

In recent years Delta made an effort to diversify into nonsteel related areas, without noticeable success. Its consolidated balance sheets and income statements are shown in Exhibits 2 and 3.

INDUSTRY BACKGROUND

The steel industry in the United States experienced major problems for many years. Many of the companies utilized obsolete production facilities. Troublesome government regulations and relatively high labor costs plagued the industry. Domestic raw steel production declined steadily from 150,800 tons in 1973 to 113,00 tons in 1982. In the meantime, imported steel appeared to have a firm grip on about 18 percent of the U.S. domestic steel market. These problems were further compounded by the increased use of steel-substitute products in manufactured goods, resulting in a decline in domestic steel consumption.

Tough government regulations related to pollution control dampened industry profits. On the bright side, the Economic Recovery Tax Act (ERTA) of 1981 allowed for more liberal depreciation of fixed assets. These liberalized depreciation rules, as well as new investment tax credits, could very well allow the capital-intensive steel industry to show marginally adequate profits in the future.

The U.S. Commerce Department estimated that the U.S. steel industry spent about $3.1 billion in 1981 and about $3.8 billion in 1982 on capital expenditures. The majority of capital expenditures were going towards improving operating efficiency.

Many industry observers felt that the fortunes of the steel industry would decline before showing any improvement. Nevertheless, the industry might be able to negotiate wage concessions from its labor unions. Also, firms might attempt to improve their profitability by diversifying into nonsteel areas.

DELTA'S FINANCING NEEDS

Based on assessment of divisional capital expenditure needs, Mr. Drummond concluded that Delta needed $40 million in external financing in the next six to ten months. The majority of funds were going to be used to upgrade equipment and incorporate new technology into the existing manufacturing processes. Some of the funds were designated for installation of state-mandated pollution control equipment. Mr. Drummond also felt that more than $40 million needed to be raised externally, with the funds in excess of $40 million being added to the firm's working capital.

At the present time Delta had 19 million of its 30 million authorized shares outstanding. They were currently trading at $11 a share. Per share financial and stock price data are provided in Exhibit 4.

In Mr. Drummond's earlier conversations with members of the board of directors, it became apparent to him that the board preferred to raise funds through either issuing new common stock or selling bonds. Given current market conditions, the bonds would probably carry a coupon rate of about 13 percent. The existing long-term debt was rated A2 and was scheduled to mature between 1987 and 2002. The debt was callable and had sinking fund requirements.

As Mr. Drummond waited for Mr. Solomon's arrival, he went over a mental checklist of questions that he specifically wanted to ask Mr. Solomon. Chief among these were the potential impact of the new financing on Delta's earnings and price per share and the flotation costs involved in selling the stocks or bonds.

Mr. Drummond also tried to anticipate the questions that Mr. Solomon might ask. He felt that Mr. Solomon would probably ask questions related to Delta's dividend policy and to the need for any possible improvement in the firm's measures of liquidity. In preparation for the meeting, Mr. Drummond compiled some information on the steel industry, and on selected firms in the industry (see Exhibits 5 and 6).

EXHIBIT 1

Delta Steel Corporation

Divisional Sales and Operating Income *

Division	Sales %	Operating Income %
Steel	65	63
Manf. and Engrg.	16	15
Petrochemicals	11	7
Mining	8	15

*Divisional sales and operating income figures are expressed as a percentage of the corresponding figures for Delta and are representative of an average in recent years, rather than reflective of figures for the latest operating period.

EXHIBIT 2

Delta Steel Corporation

Consolidated Balance Sheet, December 31
(in thousands of dollars)

	1980	1981	1982
Current assets			
Cash	$ 49,100	$ 55,200	$ 47,100
Mkt. securities	43,700	98,500	14,000
Receivables	193,100	194,200	190,100
Inventories	115,200	115,600	117,700
Total current assets	$ 401,100	$ 463,500	$ 368,900
Land	31,100	31,100	31,100
Plant, equipment	1,341,700	1,421,100	1,453,300
Acc. depreciation	799,900	825,600	836,100
Net plant, equipment	541,800	595,500	617,200
Investments	52,400	47,900	33,100
Other assets	60,600	60,200	58,500
Total assets	$1,087,000	$1,198,200	$1,108,800
Current liabilities			
Accts. payable	107,300	109,700	113,500
Notes payable	14,200	19,100	22,100
Accrued taxes	44,400	54,200	48,400
Employee costs	76,700	92,500	97,100
Other liabilities	15,500	5,700	6,900
Total current liabilities	$ 258,100	$ 281,200	$ 288,000
Long-term debt	240,300	230,700	220,600
Def. taxes, credits	50,100	89,400	78,300
Other liabilities	42,400	27,900	25,600
Total liabilities	$ 590,900	$ 629,200	$ 612,500
Common stock	169,700	175,600	175,600
Earned surplus	40,000	40,000	40,000
Retained earnings	286,400	353,400	280,700
Total claims	$1,087,000	$1,198,200	$1,108,800

EXHIBIT 3

Delta Steel Corporation

*Consolidated Income Statement, Year Ending December 31
(in thousands of dollars)*

	1980	1981	1982
Sales	$1,251,300	$1,412,000	$1,127,000
Cost of goods sold	1,011,200	1,112,100	991,000
Selling expenses	43,700	47,600	49,900
Other expenses	149,400	164,200	174,000
Operating income	$ 47,000	$ 88,100	$ (87,900)
Interest, dividend income	33,200	47,900	33,100
Interest expense	20,900	22,300	22,900
Income taxes	19,400	28,400	(23,300)
Net income	$ 39,900	$ 85,300	$ (54,400)
Common dividends	14,200	18,300	18,300
Addition to ret. earnings	$ 25,700	$ 67,000	$ (72,700)

EXHIBIT 4

Delta Steel Corporation

Per Share Financial Data

	1977	1978	1979	1980	1981	1982
Earnings	$ 0.44	$ 1.14	($ 1.70)	$ 2.10	$ 4.49	($ 2.86)
Dividends	0.80	0.75	0.75	0.75	0.96	0.96
Sales	50.00	57.89	68.01	65.85	74.32	59.32
Price						
High	13	13	11	11	14	13
Low	7	6	5	5	6	5

EXHIBIT 5

Delta Steel Corporation

Selected Steel Industry Statistics*

				Year			
	1976	1977	1978	1979	1980	1981	1982
Net income/sales (%)	3.53	0.68	3.12	1.46	2.72	1.57	Def
Dividends/net income (%)	45.61	210.32	36.66	74.59	42.19	32.87	Def
Dividends/price (%)	4.67	6.14	6.54	7.45	6.88	6.58	6.67
Price/earnings per share	9.93	36.56	5.69	10.15	6.28	4.81	Def

*Price is the average for the high and low for the year. Def. means deficit.

EXHIBIT 6

Delta Steel Corporation

*Comparative Financial Data on Selected Competitors**

	1977	1978	1979	1980	1981	1982
Net income/sales (%)						
Inland Steel Corp.	3.3	4.9	3.6	0.9	1.5	Def
Interlake, Inc.	2.4	1.1	3.6	1.3	4.8	0.75
Kaiser Steel Corp.	0.7	1.8	5.0	17.8	Def	Def
NVF Corporation	4.0	6.3	9.1	1.6	2.1	Def
Republic Steel Corp.	1.4	3.2	3.0	1.4	4.4	Def
Dividend payout ratio (%)						
Inland Steel Corp.	49	62	37	45	175	Def
Interlake, Inc.	33	70	125	33	97	282
Kaiser Steel Corp.	25	292	86	17	0	0
NVF Corporation	0	0	0	0	0	0
Republic Steel Corp.	30	63	32	30	63	Def
Dividend yield (%)**						
Inland Steel Corp.	6.4	7.5	8.5	8.3	7.2	5.1
Interlake, Inc.	7.0	8.9	8.7	8.2	7.0	9.0
Kaiser Steel Corp.	5.9	6.7	4.2	0.0	0.0	0.0
NVF Corporation	0.0	0.0	0.0	0.0	0.0	0.0
Republic Steel Corp.	6.0	9.2	8.7	8.3	8.5	5.7
Price/earnings (high-low)						
Inland Steel Corp.	12-8	6-4	6-5	24-19	13-8	Def
Interlake, Inc.	12-8	17-12	4-3	15-10	4-3	35-22
Kaiser Steel Corp.	Def	18-10	7-3	2-1	Def	Def
NVF Corporation	6-3	4-2	9-3	49-19	23-12	Def
Republic Steel Corp.	14-9	4-3	4-3	9-6	3-2	Def
Long-term debt/long-term debt + common equity%						
Inland Steel Corp.	32.3	31.5	30.1	35.5	34.3	38.8
Interlake, Inc.	20.7	29.2	27.2	27.1	25.4	25.8
Kaiser Steel Corp.	31.3	39.1	35.6	26.2	49.9	46.7
NVF Corporation	39.3	36.8	67.0	64.7	74.9	82.8
Republic Steel Corp.	22.7	21.4	20.1	27.1	18.4	37.8

Source: Standard & Poor's Reports
*Def means deficit.
**Based on average of high and low prices.

CASE 39

Bell Canada

"Wow! Bell Canada is looking for rate increases that could amount to added revenues of over one-half of a billion dollars by the end of 1979," Bill Simmons said as he looked up from his copy of *The Financial Post*.[1] This remark was made to his colleague, Jack Barlow, with whom he worked as a financial analyst in the research department of one of the largest insurance companies in Canada. "You follow Bell a lot closer than I do," continued Simmons, "so perhaps you can explain why they are looking for such a large rate increase."

"Well, yes, it is part of my job to follow Bell. And, I know that they are seriously strapped for funds right now when both inflation and demand have com-

bined to drive up their construction budget to over $1 billion a year."

Bell Canada, the largest telecommunications company in Canada,[2] was incorporated under the Federal Laws of Canada and, as such, was regulated by the Canadian Radio-Television and Telecommunications Commission. As a federally regulated, investor-owned, public utility operating throughout both the Province of Ontario and the Province of Quebec, Bell Canada was required to apply for, rather than simply announce, changes in its tariff schedule—the document which indicated the prices at which Bell Canada offered its telecommunications services to subscribers. Thus, when Bell Canada filed a rate application on

This case was prepared by Professor John D. Forsyth as a basis for class discussion rather than to illustrate either effective or ineffective handling of an administrative situation. Copyright 1978 by IMEDE (International Management Development Institute), Lausanne, Switzerland. Not to be used or reproduced without permission.

[1] Bill Simmons was reading the following article when he made his remarks: "Customers will pay the price if Bell Canada doesn't get rate increases," by Robert Jamieson, *The Financial Post* (Feb. 11, 1978), p. 5.

[2] Selected financial information on Bell Canada and the financial markets in Canada are given in Exhibits 1 through 7.

February 1, 1978, it applied for rate changes that were expected to generate additional revenues of $171 million in the second half of 1978 and $339 million in 1979.

By precedent, the Canadian Radio-Television and Telecommunications Commission could be expected to hold formal hearings during the spring of 1978, at which time, it would listen to arguments both in favor of, and against, the changes in the tariff schedule. Then the commission was empowered to accept, in whole or part, the proposed changes in either modified or unmodified form.

"Bell Canada's problem is 'textbook' in its simplicity. Given the current situation in the capital markets and the risk-return opportunities Bell Canada offers to potential investors, the company has to increase its stream of internally generated funds if it is going to continue with its present construction program," asserted Barlow.

"It may be simple to you but I don't understand," responded Simmons.

Barlow smiled. "If you run some sources and applications of funds statements out on Bell, you'll see that they obtain about one-half of their financing from external sources. This external sourcing of funds requirements is fine so long as there is an equity base—it seems that the Commission is willing to allow Bell a return on equity of 12 percent, but Bell fell short of that allowed rate of return by 3-percentage points in 1977, and look at what the shortfall has done to the price of their stock. How can they issue new common stock when the book value per share exceeds the current market value? Can you think of a better example of producing dilution from the point of the existing shareholders? I can't. Therefore, I don't see how they can touch the equity market."

"Moreover, without an adequate equity base," continued Barlow, "Bell is really limited in raising debt capital. The dilemma is straightforward. They can't issue equity without meeting the market's required rate of return. Even a company as large as Bell Canada cannot continue to issue debt capital without putting strains on the financial structure as well as their ability to service the annual financial charges. I am sure that Bell has to watch their debt-equity ratio or else they will lose all their future flexibility in financing and probably lose their double A credit rating as well. Forty-five to fifty percent debt is about all they can handle. And as I recall, the Commission tacitly agreed with Bell Canada last year that the pre-tax earnings should be sufficient to cover the interest charges by 3.5 to 4 times—so if I exam . . ."

"OK, I think I understand what you are saying," interrupted Simmons. "You are arguing that Bell cannot issue equity capital without penalizing existing shareholders, but in the absence of an increase in the equity base, the issuance of additional debt capital can only be undertaken with severe penalties."

"That's right," answered Barlow, "and just turn it around. If Bell were allowed to try to increase their revenues, and if revenues and earnings did increase, then they could simultaneously do three things. First of all, they would provide better coverage of their interest charges. Additionally, they would increase the rate of return to the equity holders and, of course, unless they changed their dividend policy their retained earnings would increase as well. Thus, an increase in revenue could be expected to both reduce the risk to the debt holders and increase the equity base. And, the issuance of debt capital would become much easier in the future."

Simmons quickly responded, "Well, I know a solution to Bell's problems."

"What's that?" said Barlow.

"Simple! All Bell has to do is to cut back on their construction budget," Simmons asserted.

"Well, I suppose you're right," reflected Barlow. "But that is the question that has to be answered by the Commission. The government takes pride in the reputation of Canada in the telecommunications field. But we can't have our cake and eat it too."

"Sorry, I don't follow you on that one," frowned Simmons.

"Well, you've got to consider how Bell plans to spend the billion dollars on construction activities this year. Probably no more than two-thirds of that sum will be used to meet increases in demand for their services. The remainder goes into modernization and replacement activities. So, what gets cut out if the construction budget has to be decreased?" questioned Barlow. After a pause, he continued with the observation "I am quite satisfied with my own telephone service. I pick up the phone—get a dial tone—push a few buttons—and I am talking to my family in Vancouver. I guess it is easy to take that kind of service for granted. But, on the other hand, when our new summer place is finished up north, I want a private line when I move in; not a week or a month later."

"OK, I see what you are driving at," Simmons interjected. "But all the same, they sure are asking for a big increase. I'll have to think that one over."

Simmons returned to his copy of *The Financial Post.*

EXHIBIT 1

Bell Canada

*Income Statement**

	Consolidated	Non-Consolidated
	(thousands of dollars)	
	Year 1977	Year 1977
Operating revenues		
Local service	$1,151,763	$1,107,640
Long-distance service	1,031,553	970,453
Miscellaneous—net	135,120	55,322
Total operating revenues	2,318,436	2,133,415
Operating expenses	1,708,534	1,572,495
Net operating revenues	609,902	560,920
Sales revenues— manufacturing & distributing	1,241,451	—
Less: Cost of sales	874,265	—
Selling, general, administrative & other expenses	229,079	—
	1,103,344	—

(Continued)

EXHIBIT 1 (Continued)

	Consolidated (thousands of dollars) Year 1977	Non-Consolidated (thousands of dollars) Year 1977
Net sales revenues	138,107	—
Total net revenues	748,009	—
Other income		
Interest charged to construction	16,193	15,683
Equity in net income of associated companies	13,094	—
Dividends—from subsidiary companies	—	19,637
—from associated companies	—	7,362
Interest charged to construction	—	15,683
Miscellaneous	13,403	10,279
Total other income	42,690	52,961
Income before underlisted items	790,699	613,881
Interest charges		
Interest on long-term debt	213,371	—
Other interest	8,454	—
Total interest charges	221,825	202,393
Income before income taxes, minority interest & extraordinary item	568,874	—
Income before income taxes	—	411,488
Income taxes	249,334	178,593
Income before minority interest & extraordinary item	319,540	—
Minority interest	33,332	—
Income before extraordinary item	286,208	—
Extraordinary item	2,367	—
Net income	288,575	232,895
Dividends on preferred shares	31,534	31,534
Net income applicable to common shares	$ 257,041	$ 201,361

*Source: *Bell Canada Annual Report, 1977*

EXHIBIT 2

Bell Canada

Balance Sheet

	Consolidated (thousands of dollars) December 31, 1977	Non-consolidated December 31, 1977
Assets		
Telecommunication property— at cost		
Buildings, plant and equipment	$8,068,746	$7,691,786
Less: accumulated depreciation	2,372,364	2,266,382
	5,696,382	5,425,404
Land, and plant under construction	269,461	254,875
Material and supplies	102,807	97,190
	6,068,650	5,777,469
Manufacturing & distributing property—at cost		
Buildings, plant, and equipment	387,506	—
Less: accumulated depreciation	209,494	—
	178,012	—
Land	11,907	—
	189,919	—
	6,258,569	—
Investments		
Associated companies—at equity	143,852	—
Other	2,346	—
	146,198	—
Investments—at cost		
Subsidiary companies	—	212,431
Associated companies	—	107,971
		320,402
Current assets	872,249	287,910
Deferred charges	53,678	37,623
Total assets	$7,330,694	$6,423,404

(Continued)

EXHIBIT 2 (Continued)

	Consolidated (thousands of dollars) December 31, 1977	Non-consolidated (thousands of dollars) December 31, 1977
Liabilities and Shareholders' Equity		
Shareholders' equity		
Capital stock		
Preferred shares	$ 356,492	$ 356,492
Common shares	1,094,008	1,094,008
Premium on capital stock	527,143	527,143
Contributed surplus	15,290	—
Retained earnings	882,537	682,748
	2,875,470	2,660,391
Minority interest in subsidiary companies		
Preferred shares	31,543	—
Common shares	163,914	—
	195,457	—
Long-term debt	2,679,867	2,497,159
Current liabilities	724,550	485,190
Deferred credits		
Income taxes	833,574	758,969
Other	21,776	21,695
	855,350	780,664
Total liabilities & shareholders' equity	$7,330,694	$6,423,404

EXHIBIT 3
Bell Canada
Extract from "Notes to Financial Statements"

The accompanying financial statements have been prepared in accordance with Canadian generally accepted accounting principles. With respect to Bell Canada and its subsidiary companies, the only important difference between Canadian and United States generally accepted accounting principles is in regard to the accounting for translation of foreign currency transactions and financial statements of foreign subsidiary companies.

Bell Canada and its telephone subsidiary and associated companies are subject to regulation, including examination of accounting practices, by their respective regulatory authorities. Bell Canada is regulated on the ba-sis of its nonconsolidated financial statements in which its investments in subsidiary and associated companies are carried at cost. The system of accounts and accounting practices are similar to those being used in the telecommunication industry.

Consolidation

The accounts of companies in which Bell Canada owns more than 50 percent of the outstanding common shares have been fully consolidated and the investments in associated companies (50 percent or less, and 20 percent or more) have been accounted for by the equity method.

EXHIBIT 4

Bell Canada

Nonconsolidated Statement of Changes in Financial Position
(thousands of dollars)

	Year ended December 31,				
	1973*	1974*	1975*	1976*	1977
Source of funds					
Operations					
Income before extraordinary items	$175,230	$185,007	$ 212,734	$ 238,493	$ 232,895
Items not affecting current funds					
Depreciation	258,560	289,824	341,396	385,410	427,853
Deferred income taxes	74,292	72,427	78,097	87,509	102,765
Interest charged to construction	(9,957)	(14,258)	(17,231)	(14,734)	(15,683)
Other—net	5,399	6,139	6,838	6,929	7,255
Total from operations	503,524	539,139	621,834	703,607	755,085
Extraordinary item	5,396	—	—	—	—
Net proceeds from the sale by Bell Canada of common shares of a subsidiary	—	—	118,112	—	—
Adjustment to deferred income taxes	22,398	—	—	—	—
Proceeds from long-term debt	153,631	245,063	220,997	251,663	255,204
Proceeds from issue of Bell Canada common shares upon exercise of warrants	—	—	—	763	118,607
Proceeds from preferred shares	49,788	91,448	123,336	68,248	—
Issue of common shares upon conversion of convertible preferred shares	—	9,456	112,258	34,655	18,952
Miscellaneous	8,118	26,466	13,544	11,608	17,356
Decrease in working capital	—	78,676	—	137,453	88,312
	$742,855	$990,248	$1,210,081	$1,207,997	$1,253,516
Disposition of funds					
Capital expenditures					
Gross capital expenditures	$554,699	$794,109	$ 815,679	$ 901,324	$ 951,079
Deduct: charges not requiring funds	(18,200)	(24,275)	(26,639)	(25,221)	(14,703)

(Continued)

EXHIBIT 4 (Continued)

	Year ended December 31,				
	1973	*1974*	*1975*	*1976*	*1977*
Increase (decrease) in material and supplies	16,588	7,985	(5,619)	27,567	(3,234)
Net expenditures	553,087	777,819	783,421	903,670	933,142
Dividends	119,288	133,534	160,263	172,816	207,160
Reduction of long-term debt	25,991	42,781	64,136	93,145	76,604
Acquisition of investments	1,475	24,145	6,088	1,670	3,545
Conversion of preferred shares	—	9,456	112,261	34,684	18,975
Miscellaneous	5,986	2,513	2,156	2,012	14,090
Increase in working capital	37,028	—	81,756	—	—
	$742,855	$990,248	$1,210,081	$1,207,997	$1,253,516
The increase (decrease) in working capital is accounted for by:					
Increase (decrease) in current assets					
Cash and temporary cash investments	$ 45,108	$(59,132)	$ 102,734	$ (43,450)	$ (84,209)
Accounts receivable	13,854	43,631	40,866	(14,466)	25,066
Other	1,217	142	3,433	(1,133)	830
(Increase) decrease in current liabilities					
Accounts payable	(12,823)	(17,331)	4,199	(71,114)	6,718
Advance billing for service	(2,257)	(3,189)	(3,408)	(4,001)	(4,757)
Dividends payable	(2,094)	(3,726)	(6,550)	(4,629)	(6,897)
Taxes accrued	(23,007)	11,011	(36,364)	36,574	4,184
Interest accrued	(2,867)	(1,508)	(4,111)	(5,780)	(10,836)
Debt due within one year	19,897	(48,574)	(19,043)	(29,454)	(18,411)
Increase (decrease) in working capital, as above	$ 37,028	$(78,676)	$ 81,756	$ (137,453)	$ (88,312)

*Restated.

EXHIBIT 5

Bell Canada

Book Value, Earnings, and Dividends

Year	Book Value per Share— Average	Earnings per share—Basic*	Common Dividends per Share**
1968	$40.14	$3.39	$2.50
1969	40.87	3.20	2.50
1970	41.64	3.52	2.50
1971	42.55	3.76	2.65
1972	43.65	4.15	2.65
1973	45.15	4.37	2.85
1974	46.86	4.52	3.12
1975	48.38	4.83	3.44
1976	51.94	5.23	3.58
1977	52.44	4.73	4.08

*Before extraordinary items.
**Declared.

EXHIBIT 6

Bell Canada

Capital Structure Ratios—Year End

Year	Debt (%)	Straight Preferred (%)	Convertible Preferred (%)	Common Equity (%)
1968	45.5	—	—	54.5
1969	47.8	—	—	52.2
1970	46.2	—	3.1	50.7
1971	46.6	—	5.9	47.5
1972	47.5	—	5.6	46.9
1973	47.5	1.4	5.3	45.8
1974	48.9	1.2	6.9	43.0
1975	48.0	1.0	6.5	44.5
1976	48.7	2.4	5.3	43.6
1977	49.8	2.1	4.6	43.5

EXHIBIT 7

Bell Canada

Market Value/Share and Toronto Stock Exchange Index of Industrials

Year	Month	Bell Canada Average Market Price*	T.S.E. Average Actual**
1972	March	45.63	200.84
	June	43.31	202.89
	September	43.19	211.82
	December	44.25	218.55
1973	March	44.25	222.00
	June	42.63	208.97
	September	40.50	219.18
	December	39.69	206.78
1974	March	44.19	222.03
	June	41.50	190.78
	September	41.81	159.11
	December	44.00	153.62
1975	March	47.56	181.23
	June	45.13	187.38
	September	42.38	182.74
	December	42.94	173.44
1976	March	45.13	191.24
	June	47.44	189.59
	September	50.50	187.22
	December	46.94	171.07
1977	March	47.88	1022.11
	June	49.75	1031.24
	September	51.19	1000.07
	December	51.50	1059.59

*Bell Canada average market price—Toronto Stock Exchange average of high and low.

**Source *T.S.E. Monthly Reviews* (1977 Figures reflect expansion of the T.S.E. Industrial Index to include a composite of 300 companies representing other areas such as Mining, Utilities, Manufacturing, etc.).

CASE 40

Ashland Oil, Inc.

"You hear a lot about making big money in oil and gas exploration, but the truth of the matter is that it's a lousy business."

So spoke Orin E. Atkins, chairman of the board and chief executive officer of Ashland Oil, Inc. The time was June 1978, and Mr. Atkins had recently announced that he was trying to sell Ashland's entire exploration and production business, including its foreign interests.

To auction away an oil firm's reserves, which many considered to be the heart of the business, was not looked upon by many with favor. One industry observer, for example, commented that it was ". . . like throwing your wife into the street."[1] Nonetheless, this was exactly what Orin E. Atkins set out to do.

COMPANY HISTORY

The corporate history of Ashland Oil, Inc., could be traced back to the Swiss Oil Corporation. The Swiss Oil Corporation was incorporated in Kentucky on June 21, 1918. In 1925 it acquired the producing properties of Union Gas and Oil Co., also located in Kentucky. The latter owned 95 percent of the capital stock of the Ashland Refining Company which had been organized in Kentucky in February of 1924. In October 1931 the Ashland Refining Company organized the Ashland Oil & Transportation Company to acquire the pipeline properties of Cumberland Pipeline Company. Soon, the little refinery was making more money than Swiss Oil. Ashland Oil and Re-

This case was prepared by Deepak Rai and Charles E. Curtis, Research Assistants, under the supervision of Professor M. Edgar Barrett of Southern Methodist University, and used with the permission of Professor M. Edgar Barrett.

[1] "Ashland Oil: Getting Out of Crude as it Sheds Lackluster Operations," *Business Week,* September 4, 1978, page 90.

fining Company was incorporated in Kentucky on October 31, 1936, as a consolidation of Swiss Oil and its subsidiary, Ashland Refining Company. Since then the company had been run with two objectives: operations and acquisitions. With acquisitions, more and more refining capacity, pipelines, and crude oil sources were added. By the 1960s, Ashland, no longer a "little guy," was widely considered as one of the larger oil companies. Its present name was adopted on February 2, 1970. (See Exhibits 1 to 4 for financial statements and Exhibits 5 and 6 for acquisitions and subsidiaries.)

While chemical interests had been added in the 1950s, it was only in the late 1960s and early 1970s that Ashland truly diversified. It acquired O. K. Tire and Rubber with over 900 franchised stores; Warren Brothers, a leading highway contractor; Catalin Corporation, a producer of synthetic resins; Fisher Chemicals; and ADM Chemicals. In 1969 Arch Mineral Corporation (a 49 percent owned affiliate of Ashland Coal) was created.

PRINCIPAL BUSINESSES IN 1979

Petroleum Division. The petroleum division had the responsibility for the supply and transportation of the crude oil requirements for Ashland's seven refineries and for marketing, transportation, and storage of refined petroleum products for sale outside the company (see Exhibit 7 for petroleum statistics).

The company's principal refineries were modern, efficient facilities. They included crude oil atmospheric and vacuum distillation units, fluid catalytic cracking units, and desulfurization units. One of the refineries, the Findlay refinery, produced largely asphalt. It operated on a seasonal basis, as the producing and marketing of asphalt were concentrated in the period from April to October. Asphalt was also produced at Ashland's other five refineries. The Catlettsburg and Buffalo refineries were also equipped to manufacture a wide range of petrochemicals (see Exhibits 8 and 9 for refinery statistics and geographic locations).

Ashland's seven refineries were concentrated around the highly industrialized Ohio Valley. As one company official put it, "They're in the market place, not in Houston."[2] Further, Ashland's refineries used almost 5 percent less energy per barrel than the average refinery. Since fuel costs were one of the highest operating costs of refining, this represented a sizable saving. Robert Yancey, Ashland's president, explained the reason for this as being "We built our refineries in a northern climate where we *had to* conserve heat—another factor was that we never had the low cost of natural gas used as fuel by the refiners in the big producing states . . . I'd spot the major oil companies 50 cents a barrel in refining and beat them at the end of the day."[3]

Ashland, in fact, had traditionally kept its refining capacity short of its total needs. To fill the gap, it bought products from other refineries for resale. Though such sales were not very profitable, Ashland rarely ever had to cut its refinery runs. For example, in 1976 Ashland sold about 100,000 barrels per day that it did not refine. As a result, it was

---

[2] "Crude Poor Ashland Oil: Prototype of the Future," *Business Week,* January 31, 1977, page 98.

[3] *Ibid.*

able to keep its refineries operating at nearly 89 percent of capacity.

Marketing of Petroleum Products

Ashland's principal marketing area for gasoline and fuel oils included the Ohio River Valley and the upper Midwest, the East Coast, and a portion of the Southeastern United States. The company marketed its petroleum products directly through 150 bulk plants and also under various brand names through approximately 2400 retail outlets (see Exhibit 10 for gasoline marketing area information).

Ashland was one of the principal marketers of residual and distillate fuel oil to commercial, utility, and industrial consumers in the Midwest and on the East Coast. Competition in these markets was provided by refiners and broker-resellers and was influenced by a combination of price and reliability of supply and service.

Products under Ashland's "Valvoline" brand name included motor oil, other automotive and industrial lubricants, automotive chemicals, and oil, air, and fuel filters. Valvoline products were sold throughout the United States through an estimated 60,000 dealers and jobbers. They were also marketed elsewhere throughout the world.

Ashland had the image of possessing a very efficient distribution system. Its heart was seen as being the network of independent jobbers and retailers. "We have never tried very hard to develop a brand program like the majors did," said Charles Luellen, group marketing vice-president. "That is a very expensive way to sell gasoline so we concentrated on sales to independent jobbers."[4] In the

opinion of an industry refinery-marketing analyst, it costs a major oil company about 15 cents to sell a gallon of gasoline in 1977 versus 3 cents for an independent retailer.[5]

Transportation

Ashland used a total of approximately 6200 miles of crude oil and refined products pipelines at the end of fiscal 1979. These pipeline facilities consisted of approximately 3100 miles of wholly owned pipelines, 1100 miles of additional facilities in which Ashland held varying percentage interests, and 2000 miles of crude oil gathering lines, truck pipelines, and accompanying facilities which Ashland operated under long-term leases with options to purchase.

The company had access to 43 product terminals during the year. These facilities consisted of 20 river terminals, 19 pipeline terminals, and four lake terminals accessible by ocean-going vessels.

Ashland's river transportation facilities, including towboats, barges, and terminals, provided low-cost transportation for both crude oil and refined products on the Ohio and Mississippi Rivers and their tributaries. The company owned or leased 22 towboats and 218 barges.

The company's fleet also included a 259,234 deadweight ton VLCC (very large crude carrier), which the company owned. In addition, six vessels totaling 998,021 deadweight tons were under long-term charters. Remaining crude transportation requirements were filled by securing tankers on a spot basis for individual voyages.

Ashland Petroleum leased 932 railroad cars at the end of fiscal 1979. The

---

[4] *Ibid.*
[5] *Ibid.*

company also owned an extensive number of tractor-trailer units, additional trailers, and a large fleet of tank trucks and general service trucks.

Chemicals

Ashland's chemical operations were conducted by the Ashland Chemical Company Division. It was primarily engaged in the manufacture, distribution, and sale of numerous chemical products. The division had manufacturing and distribution facilities in 28 states and 14 foreign nations. Revenues of the Chemical Company for fiscal 1979 were 15.1 percent of total Ashland revenues. Net income was 19.3 percent of the total net income of Ashland.

In 1974 Atkins said that, "the government is going to keep price ceilings on consumer-oriented fuel such as gasoline and homeheating oil. You will probably be able to get more money by going into higher margined petrochemicals."[6]

Consistent with this philosophy, Ashland put substantial amounts of capital into chemicals. In fact, during fiscal 1979, the chemical division was the second largest recipient of Ashland's capital expenditures (see Exhibit 11 for capital expenditures).

However, Ashland's record in the chemical business was a bit spotty. After the big expansion and acquisition program in the early 1960s, chemical profits sagged for a five-year period, despite an increase in sales. In 1974, however, Atkins was confident that the overcapacity that hit the chemical industry would not recur. "The cost of new capacity is so high that the industry won't have the

propensity to create the gluts that it had in past years."[7]

Ashland's chemical plants were constructed on existing refinery properties. This provided guaranteed access to refinery-produced feedstocks for chemical production.

Coal

Ashland was the sixth largest coal producer in the United States in 1979. Net income from coal operations in that year was 3.3 percent of the total net income of the company. According to Mr. Yancey, "We see coal as a tremendous growth area for us in the 1980s."[8]

Ashland's coal operations were conducted primarily by two separate companies: Arch Mineral Corporation (Arch) and Ashland Coal, Inc. Arch was 50 percent owned by Ashland and had been formed in 1969. It was primarily engaged in seeking out, acquiring, and developing coal reserves intended to supply the electric utility market. During fiscal 1979, Arch sold a total of 12.9 million tons of coal from six operating surface mines located in Alabama, Illinois, and Wyoming. The sale of coal from each mine had been arranged primarily under contracts with utility companies. A large portion of these sales were under long-term contracts with market reopener clauses and/or provisions for the pass-through of various elements of cost, including reclamation costs. The balance of the sales were represented by short-term contracts at prevailing spot prices.

Ashland Coal, a wholly owned subsidiary, was engaged in the production, transportation, processing, and market-

---

[6] "Chemical Change," *Forbes,* November 15, 1974, page 68.

[7] *Ibid.*

[8] "Crude Poor Ashland Oil: Prototype of the Future," *op. cit.*

ing of bituminous coal. Production was primarily from surface mines in eastern Kentucky and West Virginia. Since its inception in 1975, the primary emphasis and direction of Ashland Coal had been placed on the acquisition and development of steam coal reserves.

Construction

Ashland's construction operations were conducted by Ashland-Warren, Inc., an indirect, but wholly owned subsidiary. The company was engaged principally in the production and sale of construction materials and the performance of contract construction work. Materials produced and sold included asphalt and ready-mixed concrete, crushed stone and other aggregate, concrete blocks, and certain specialized construction materials. Areas of contract construction included the paving of highways; urban streets; roadways; bus lanes; airport, shopping center, and other commercial parking areas; and sidewalks and driveways with asphalt and portland cement concrete surfacing.

During 1979, Ashland-Warren sold the assets of its northeast regional operations. As a result, Ashland-Warren's operations were concentrated in the southern and southwestern United States.

Shipbuilding

Levingston Shipbuilding Company, an indirect, wholly owned subsidiary of Ashland, operated fabrication yards in Texas. Levingston manufactured various types of marine equipment, including semisubmersible and jack-up drilling platforms for the petroleum industry, drilling ships, pipe laying, derrick and tanker barges, and other vessels. It also performed major marine repair projects. It had eight dry docks, a marine railway, and two large machine shops. In the fall of 1978 the Federal Maritime Administration contracted with Levingston to build up to five 36,000 deadweight ton dry-bulk cargo ships, with scheduled delivery dates from December 1980 to December 1982.

Exploration

Ashland's exploration activities were conducted by Ashland Exploration, Inc., an indirect, wholly owned subsidiary. As of 1979, the company was engaged in the exploration for, and production of, oil and gas in the Eastern part of the United States and, through various subsidiaries, in Nigeria and Sharjah.

At the beginning of fiscal 1979 Ashland owned interests in producing oil and gas leases in 18 states and in the Gulf of Mexico. Between them, these lease properties contained 9034 (3990 net) producing wells. Production averaged 12,600 net barrels per day of oil and natural gas liquids and 153 million net cubic feet per day of natural gas. At year-end, after the sale of much of its properties, Ashland owned 2783 (2398 net) producing wells.

The major retained interest consisted of producing and nonproducing properties located in the central and eastern regions of the United States, primarily in the states of Illinois, Indiana, Kentucky, Ohio, Virginia, and West Virginia. The average price received during fiscal 1979 by all oil companies for a barrel of oil was $11.37. The average price received by Ashland for a barrel of oil from these remaining properties, however, was $18.93. The difference in price was due to the fact that 97 percent of Ashland's production in the remaining properties was of the "stripper" category and was thus not subject to governmental price controls.

ASHLAND WITHIN THE INDUSTRY

Within the United States oil industry Ashland maintained a steady relative position throughout the 1970s. The following data indicates Ashland's rank among all U.S. oil companies in four categories:[9]

	1978	1976	1974	1972
Operating revenues	13th	13th	14th	14th
Net income	16th	18th	19th	16th
Gasoline sales	15th	16th	15th	15th
Total assets	17th	18th	17th	18th

EXPLORATION ACTIVITIES

In the late 1960s Ashland decided to diversify into crude oil exploration and production. While Orin Atkins believed that the marketing of refined products should continue to be Ashland's primary line of business, he was apparently concerned about the "opportunity loss" of not being an active participant in the exploration and production phase of the business.

In August of 1969 Atkins discussed his strategy: "We're one of the few oil outfits that pays a real tax bill. By drilling, (we'll) get the 27.5% oil depletion allowance and what the oil companies call the intangible drilling costs for tax purposes. When you drill a well, you get immediate savings in tax of about 60% of the costs. . . . We have developed a strong enough base to afford some of the risks of exploring for oil. . . . This is a real first-class crap game."[10]

Ashland's initial exploration activities required an investment of $43 million dollars in the 1966–69 period. The massive investment reduced the firm's earnings per share from $2.48 in 1966 to $2.19 in 1969. The outcome of one of the exploratory efforts was the drilling of eight dry holes in the Santa Barbara channel and the taking of an $8 million write-off in 1969 related to those efforts.

Again in 1971 Ashland was forced to take large write-offs related to exploration in Alaska, after drilling a series of dry holes. In 1972 the company purchased from Union Carbide Corporation that firm's oil and gas properties and extended its exploration activities even further. However, the exploration arm of Ashland lost money in 1973.

Success continued to elude Ashland in its exploration activities as the 1970s wore on. In 1973 through 1975 it drilled a number of dry holes in Iran and abandoned its concession there in 1975. In 1976 it also abandoned its efforts in the Java Sea, after taking a significant write-off related to those activities. Although the company did drill some successful wells during the seventies, by 1977 it had developed only enough producing wells to supply 20 percent of the crude needed by its refineries. See Exhibit 12 for Ashland's production and reserve figures for 1969–1979.

One of the reasons was the increasing cost of finding oil. According to the American Petroleum Institute, the cost of drilling an average well rose 38 percent

---

[9] *National Petroleum News, Facts Books,* 1979, 1977, 1976, 1974.
[10] "A First Class Crap Game,"*Forbes,* August 1, 1969, page 41.

from 1974 to 1976. Later in the 1970s, as more attention was given to offshore properties, such as the Baltimore Canyon, the average price of drilling a well increased even more, as a single offshore well in such an area could cost up to $10 million. Ashland's finding costs (the financial outlay needed to find and develop reserves) was $3.75 per barrel, averaged over the 1974 to 1978 period, which was higher than the industry average over the same period of $3.09 per barrel.

There were other factors affecting the profitability of the exploration and production activities of other companies. After the 1973 oil embargo, many foreign governments, particularly in the Middle East, became increasingly hard-nosed about allowing American and European companies to make huge profits on the oil produced in their countries. Their method of preventing such large profits was to raise their interest in the wells operated by other companies or nationalize those properties entirely. Both of these tactics were used increasingly throughout the seventies, so that the profitability of overseas production for many companies declined. In addition, currency devaluations in 1976 severely crimped earnings from foreign operations for many companies.

Throughout the 1970s, as its exploration and production fortunes were rising and falling, Ashland's refining and marketing operations increased significantly. From 1972 through 1977 revenues from those activities increased from $1.3 to lion. At the same time earnings increased in all but one of those years, making Ashland one of the few U.S.

companies to earn money consistently through the 1970s on refining and marketing. Throughout the period Ashland's refineries ran at high capacity, reaching 89 percent of capacity in 1976.

In 1978 Atkins reflected on the state of Ashland's exploration and production operations:

> It's become the kind of game we can't play. We've spent almost $900 million in the last five or six years . . . my nose is just above water at that level.[11]

Mr. Atkins went on to say that the high cost of offshore properties, changed tax policies at home, and more aggressive governments abroad had eroded the profitability in exploration and production for all but the largest or luckiest oil companies. He publicly blasted Washington for creating "a hostile environment toward exploration."[12] Yet, he clearly felt that the federal government would serve an important role as a sort of insurer-of-last-resort for Ashland if crude oil shortages were to develop.

Ashland's refineries were located on strategic sites near or alongside significant industrial complexes in Kentucky, Ohio, New York, and Minnesota. Atkins observed that, "if our refineries don't have crude oil, no industry runs in those areas and no commercial enterprises operate."[13] He simply did not believe that the federal government would allow such a situation to develop.

THE DIVESTMENT DECISION

As noted earlier, Ashland decided in 1978 to divest itself of much of its oil and gas producing properties. Later the

---

[11] "Ashland Oil: Getting Out of Crude as it Sheds Lackluster Operations," *op cit.*
[12] *Ibid.*
[13] *Ibid.*

same year when this strategy was publicly announced, Atkins explained his phaseout of oil production by saying, "Right now you have a surplus of oil and we see that situation continuing two or three years at least."[14]

Atkins was the first to admit that the divestment decision was not an easy one. "I stayed awake most nights for three months thinking about this."[15] He felt the sell-off would fit in with Ashland's larger strategy of selling off businesses with low profitability and lackluster growth prospects. The total planned divestment would trim almost $1.5 billion from the $5.1 billion in revenues that Ashland had reported during fiscal 1978. The plans Atkins had for the proceeds of this unprecedented move were rather unconventional. Some of the money was to go toward retiring Ashland's debt, repurchasing shares of common stock, and making new investments. A good part of the money, however, was targeted for the shareholders in the form of higher or even special dividends. Said Atkins, "Unfortunately, the great majority of corporations in America are run for the employees but we're going to run this one for the shareholders."[16]

The divestment decision, and the logic used by Atkins to support that decision, did not generate total support within the firm. The president of Ashland Exploration, Inc., for example, was quoted as having said: "I can't understand it myself. Production and exploration operations are the best part of an oil company."[17]

Others charged Ashland with having had an erratic and irregular commitment towards finding oil. Senior Vice-President Burt E. Hamric, for example, disclosed that, "Our (Exploration and Production) budget would fluctuate wildly from year to year, or within a year."[18]

IMPLEMENTING THE DIVESTMENT DECISION

In October of 1978 Ashland sold its 79 percent interest in Ashland Oil Canada Limited. This was an oil and gas exploration and production company in Canada. The sale garnered approximately $316 million in before-tax gross cash proceeds.

In December of 1978 Ashland sold its coating resins business and its related facilities in Newark, New Jersey, Valley Park, Missouri, and Pensacola, Florida. These sales brought in approximately $20 million in cash. In January of 1979 it sold the Chemical Products Division of Ashland Chemical for approximately $60 million in cash.

In April of 1979 Ashland sold most of the Northeast Region of the Ashland-Warren construction division for approximately $42 million in cash. Ashland decided that for the then-present time it would discontinue efforts to divest any other parts of the Ashland-Warren operations, with the possible exception of Levingston Shipbuilding Company and certain road construction operations in the western United States.

In March and April of 1979 Ashland

---

[14] *Ibid.*
[15] *Ibid.*
[16] *Ibid.*
[17] *Ibid.*
[18] "Ashland Oil: Scrambling for Crude After Premature Sell-off," *Business Week,* February 4, 1980, page 111.

made the following sales of various oil and gas properties:

Oil and gas producing properties in the Rocky Mountains, southeast, and southwest regions for approximately $117 million in cash.

Oil and gas leasehold estates and other property interests in the Rocky Mountain, southeast, and southwest regions for $17 million in cash.

Mid-Continent region oil and gas properties for approximately $331 million in cash.

Oil and gas properties located offshore Louisiana and Texas and support facilities for approximately $266 million in cash.

All stock interest in Ashland Oil (GB) Limited, which held an interest in the United Kingdom North Sea production properties known as the Thistle Field, for a total consideration of $94.5 million.

The March-April 1979 sale of these oil and gas properties and operations, adjusted for other miscellaneous sales, resulted in the receipt by Ashland of before-tax net cash proceeds of approximately $826 million. In connection with the sales it was estimated that U. S. federal income taxes of $256 million would be payable by Ashland in fiscal 1980.

Two other significant events occurred during late 1979 as Ashland's management moved toward full implementation of the divestment decision. First, bids in excess of $100 million were made for Ashland's remaining domestic oil and gas properties. These properties were located in the central and eastern portions of the United States. The bids were rejected.

The second event involved the sale of the Brae Field interests. This occurred on November 13, 1979, and involved Ashland's interest in an oil and gas producing property known as the Brae Field in the United Kingdom sector of the North Sea. The sale resulted in the receipt of approximately $3.7 million in cash and the purchaser's assumption of approximately $16.9 million in indebtedness.

USE OF THE DIVESTMENT MONIES

Industry observers believed that the proceeds of the various sales of properties would provide at least $700 million for Ashland to invest elsewhere. Mr. Atkins, however, stated that the available money was of a lesser amount. The sharp increase in crude oil prices had resulted in larger investments in inventory. Changes in the terms for buying foreign crude oil —with payment required within 30 days rather than within 60 days—was said to have absorbed more than $200 million of Ashland's cash. Further, Atkins said that Ashland also had taxes to pay, probably referring to the $256 million which would be due in fiscal 1980.

Ashland was said to be interested in making acquisitions. However, Atkins observed that, "we feel that at the present juncture of the economy, there are more pitfalls in acquisition areas than opportunities."[19]

Ashland's management did make some other uses of the funds, however.

---

[19] "Ashland Oil Believes It Was Right In Sale of Most Exploration, Production Interests," *Wall Street Journal*, February 1, 1980.

Basically, they were used to (1) retire debt, (2) repurchase shares, and (3) pay additional cash dividends to the remaining shareholders. More specifically, the following events took place:

1. In November of 1978 the 10-percent sinking fund debentures due in the year 2000 were redeemed at a redemption price of $110.6 million.

2. Throughout 1978 and 1979 the firm purchased a total of 15.6 million shares of its common stock for approximately $565 million. (The 15.6 million number is after giving effect to the November 1978 three-for-two stock split.)

3. In November 1978 the quarterly cash dividend on the common stock was increased from 50 cents per share to 60 cents per share on a presplit basis (to 40 cents on a postsplit basis).

4. In March 1979 the board of directors further increased the dividend rate to 50 cents per (postsplit) share.

5. In December 1979 the dividend was further increased to 55 cents per share.

CRUDE OIL: SUPPLY, PRICE, AND GOVERNMENT INVOLVEMENT

Due to the influence of OPEC and the Arab oil embargo of 1973–74, both the price and supply of crude oil were substantially altered. All firms involved in the refining business were affected. To what extent, however, depended upon such factors as location of the refineries, amount of proved reserves, and terms of contractual obligations.

In August of 1973 the federal government, through the Federal Energy Administration (FEA), installed price controls in order to keep U.S. producers from re-

alizing "windfall profits" as a result of OPEC raising the world market price. Production at 1973 levels was classified as "old" oil. Its price was frozen at $5.25 per barrel. The price of "new," stripper, or imported oil was allowed to float with the market, up to a ceiling of $14 per barrel.

Price controls substantially affected the independent refiners. Integrated majors began canceling the contracts they had with independent refining firms because each barrel they sold at $5.25 had to be replaced by uncontrolled oil. Therefore, the independents had to rely heavily on new or imported oil in order to keep their refineries running.

In addition, retail prices were controlled by formulas based on each refiner's average cost of crude oil and refining. The majors not only had lower cost crude going into their refineries; but, as a result, they were forced to reduce their retail prices and, hence, increase their market share.

In early 1974 the FEA chose to once again intervene in the marketplace. At this time the administration's intention was to place all domestic refiners on an equal footing to weather the economic storm caused by the Arab oil embargo. The allocation program, which went into effect February 1, 1974, attempted to distribute all available oil to maintain existing refiners' operations at equal capacity utilization ratios.

The FEA estimated the national average crude oil supply-capacity ratio to be 77 percent. Refiners with ratios below 77 percent were allowed to buy oil from refiners with ratios above 77 percent. The FEA determined the amount of oil a company must buy or sell, but the refiners arranged contracts on their own. The sale price was determined by the seller's average cost of crude. The program succeeded in equalizing capacity utilization. However, since not all sellers had the same average cost of crude, industry crude costs and product prices still varied greatly.

The Entitlements Program

The entitlements program went into effect in November 1974. This new program attempted to solve the price squeeze the independents were facing by equalizing crude acquisition costs. The refiners who ran more than the industry average of old oil were required to compensate those who ran less. The amount of these payments, or "entitlements", was determined by the difference between the cost of old oil ($5.25) and the average cost of new, stripper, and foreign oil.

During 1976 Ashland paid an average of $12.46 per barrel for its crude, but because it was able to sell entitlements, its average cost was reduced to $11.52 per barrel. Ashland sold $132 million worth of entitlements during the first 14 months of the program. Amerada Hess, the biggest benefactor from the program, sold $299 million worth during the same time period. According to one industry source, "I have a lot of respect for Ashland's efficiency but they wouldn't be in business without entitlements."[20]

THE IRANIAN OIL CUTOFF

Iran was supplying 100,000 barrels per day to Ashland when the next major disruption of supply occurred on November 12, 1979. The Department of Energy's Office of Hearings and Appeals (OHA) ordered nine oil companies to supply Ashland with 80,000 barrels per day until February of 1980 to partially make up for the loss of oil from Iran. They responded to this order with a suit that sought to overturn it and harshly attacked Ashland's planning. They contended that not only did they face tight supply situations themselves but that Ashland had just recently sold off its oil and gas producing capabilities, indicating at the time that other companies would have to help it if things got tough. In addition, Marathon Oil challenged the constitutionality of the OHA action.

The outcome of the legal action was expected to go Ashland's way because federal policy had generally been drifting toward a government-controlled system of allocation of crude, regardless of its source. Beyond that, Ashland, despite its medium size, operated one of the most powerful lobbies in Washington. Because it had always been dependent on other producers for its crude oil, Ashland had been particularly vulnerable to political actions that might interfere with its supply.[21]

CRUDE OIL SUPPLY AND THE DIVESTMENT

At the time its oil and gas properties were sold, Ashland claimed that the sale would not have a material effect on its supply of crude oil since its properties

---

[20] Crude Poor Ashland Oil: Prototype of the Future," *op cit.*

[21] The lobby did cause Ashland some trouble, however. During 1973 and 1974, the company was twice convicted of violating the Federal Election Campaign Act of 1971 by making illegal political contributions in the United States. As a result, Ashland signed a consent decree promising not to make illegal political donations in the future.

Ashland was also charged with concealing payoffs to foreign officials in connection with its oil exploration and production. In response, the SEC insisted that Ashland publicly reveal the recipients of all its illegal payments. Ashland reluctantly complied.

had provided less than 10 percent of the crude oil refined by its refineries. Negotiated lease and contract purchases of U.S. crude oil accounted for approximately 95,000 barrels per day. During fiscal 1980, Ashland anticipated Canadian imports to be in the range of 10,000 to 15,000 barrels per day. The balance of Ashland's requirement of 295,000 barrels per day was expected to come from two sources. First, much of it would result from contracts with members of OPEC, including Saudi Arabia, Abu Dhabi, and Algeria. Second, the firm planned to make use of spot purchases from the North Sea, Mexico, and other miscellaneous sources.

During fiscal 1978, approximately 22 percent of Ashland's crude oil requirements had been satisfied by direct and indirect purchases from Iran. This percentage declined to about 16 percent in fiscal 1979, largely as a result of the change in the Iranian government and the cessation of purchases from Iran at the end of November 1979. On November 12, 1979, President Carter suspended imports of Iranian oil due to events in Iran involving American citizens.

During fiscal 1978 and 1979, approximately 52,000 barrels per day or 14 percent of Ashland's crude requirements were satisfied directly or indirectly by purchases from Abu Dhabi. That country advised Ashland in late 1979 that its crude shipments in 1980 would be reduced to 20,000 barrels per day.

Ashland was unable to predict the effect these actions would have on its crude oil requirements or the price that it would have to pay to obtain crude. However, Ashland's management did believe

that a government allocation program might well be needed to give it access to other sources of crude. Barring such a move, these actions by suppliers could have had a material adverse effect upon its ability to operate its refineries at near capacity.

Ashland estimated that its crude oil requirements for its refineries would average approximately 412,000 barrels per day for fiscal 1980. Most of this would be derived from negotiated lease and contract purchases. Less than 11,000 barrels per day of Ashland's crude oil requirements was expected to be satisfied in fiscal 1980 from production owned by Ashland.[22] Of this amount, 2300 barrels were to be produced in the United States, 6400 barrels in Nigeria, and 2200 in Sharjah.

THE IMPACT AND THE RETURN

The doubling in oil prices in 1979 increased the reported profits of most oil companies to politically embarrassing levels. This trend, however, was not evenly distributed throughout the industry. Ashland Oil, for example, reported a year-to-year increase of 16 percent. This contrasted sharply with firms such as Mobil, which reported an increase of 70 percent.

When Ashland decided to sell its oil and gas properties, among the first to buy was Lear Petroleum Corporation. In March of 1979 they paid $17.8 million to obtain exploratory leases on 1.1 million acres in 19 states. Two months later, with its first exploratory well on these properties, it found natural gas south of

---

[22] Ashland's fiscal year ended on September 30th.

Tyler, Texas. This discovery was large enough to guarantee a substantial drilling program. When Lear bought from Ashland, they also hired David L. Paffett who had been Ashland's exploration manager. A delighted Paffett, now Lear's vice-president of exploration, gleefully explained, "The first well has paid for the entire bid, and that ain't just blowing smoke."[23]

However, there were no loud complaints from Ashland's stockholders. The sale of its domestic and Canadian oil and gas properties—including 41 million barrels of proven oil reserves, 906.7 billion cubic feet of gas and 5.4 million acres of leases—netted Ashland over $1 billion. As noted earlier, Ashland returned some of the proceeds to stockholders in the form of higher cash dividends. The price of its common stock moved up quite significantly over roughly the same time frame. Between June 1978 and April 1979 the market price per share rose by 50 percent (see Exhibit 13).

Industry experts, however, were not so complimentary in their view of the firm's divestment actions. Many of them suspected that Ashland could have netted substantially more from the sale of its exploratory acreage if it had simply waited another year. "Most clearly, because Ashland failed to anticipate that crude prices would rise, it badly underestimated the worth of its now divested assets."[24]

Orin Atkins, however, was not contrite. Based on the technical data available to him at the time of the sales, he later calculated that the changed economics of 1980 might have resulted in a 10-percent increase in the sales prices. While admitting that oil prices had risen, he noted that Ashland's original projections had included the assumption that the windfall profits tax would eventually be based on a 50-percent tax rate. By early 1980, he noted, it looked like the tax rate was going to be 70 percent. When the tax was signed into law in April of 1980, the total tax on the estimated $1 trillion "windfall" resulting from price decontrol was expected to be $779 billion ($227 billion taxed by the federal windfall and $552 billion taxed by state and local governments).[25]

RECENT EVENTS

In late 1979 Ashland quietly began what appeared to be a reversal of its crude divestment strategy. Without the fanfare that accompanied the sell-off, Ashland financed an exploratory venture by Patrick Petroleum Company off the Texas coast. Ashland expected to spend up to $25 million for the privilege of having the first option to buy what Patrick might find. In January of 1980 Ashland tentatively agreed to search jointly for oil with Basic Resources International of Luxembourg. This exploration program was to be in Guatemala. It was expected to cost Ashland between $10 million and $20 million per year.

At the same time Ashland continued to seek higher returns from its expertise in refinery processes. In early 1980 the company planned to build a pilot plant for proving the feasibility of producing a petroleumlike fuel from coal. If success-

[23] "Ashland Oil: Scrambling for Crude After Premature Sell-off," *op cit.*
[24] *Ibid.*
[25] *Wall Street Journal,* April 1, 1980.

ful over a four- to five-year period, the small plant might lead to a commercial size installation, estimated to cost about $1.5 billion, excluding another $500 million for coal facilities. Ashland officials expected such a large plant would be built in cooperation with several other oil companies so that the financing requirement could be split up.

In April of 1980 the company announced its discovery of a new, more efficient refinery process which could improve the yield of gasoline from residual fuel. As Orin Atkins described it, "the process increases the yields of gasoline in excess of 70%" and reduces crude oil consumption 20 percent.[26] In addition to utilizing the new technology to increase its own refinery efficiency, Ashland hoped to license the technology to other major oil companies in exchange for long-term supplies of crude oil.

Ashland was also planning to spend some of its divestments-related cash proceeds to prepare its refineries to operate with the higher proportion of heavy crudes available in the international markets. Crude-starved Ashland felt that this would be to their advantage in future years.

To further alleviate this tightness in crude supplies, Ashland searched internationally for new sources. The firm was successful in increasing the size of its oil supply contract with Saudi Arabia to 28,000 barrels a day, from 23,000 barrels a day. In so doing, it became the only U.S. company to deal directly with the Saudi oil company, Petromin. Ashland also concluded a deal with the Saudis to build a $200 million lubricating oil refinery in their country in exchange for future increases in oil shipments to Ashland. It was hoped the increase would be up to 40,000 barrels a day above current contracts.

Ashland also depended on terms of the agreements under which it has sold its oil reserves and producing properties for crude oil. Those agreements in most cases gave Ashland the right to purchase crude oil from the new owners of the properties, but most of these oil rights agreements were due to expire in two to three years after the purchase. It was therefore questionable in the spring of 1980 whether Ashland could maintain the pace of refinery runs (about 85 percent of capacity) that it considered desirable for profitable operation.

---

[26] *Wall Street Journal*, April 1, 1980

EXHIBIT 1

Ashland Oil, Inc.

Statement of Consolidated Income

(In thousands) Year ended September 30	1979	1978	1977	1976	1975
Revenues					
Sales and operating revenues	$6,740,363	$5,426,167	$5,051,893	$4,406,714	$3,924,273
Equity income	16,619	13,214	12,287	13,796	16,224
Gain on sale of operations	505,714	193,094	—	—	—
Interest and other income	82,759	42,451	40,231	38,330	38,895
	7,345,455	5,674,926	5,104,411	4,458,840	3,979,392
Costs and expenses					
Operating and general					
Raw materials, products, services and supplies	5,490,000	4,118,993	3,770,293	3,243,681	2,906,710
Salaries, wages and employee benefits	512,494	526,854	463,675	409,168	363,105
Dry hole costs	6,929	8,470	14,537	11,325	19,607
Taxes other than income					
Product and property	29,119	31,248	26,782	20,924	19,409
Payroll	29,808	29,235	25,697	24,289	22,380
Excise	266,496	259,516	266,315	261,463	244,760
Noncash charges					
Depreciation, depletion and amortization	134,153	174,526	151,720	133,456	109,709
Reserve for exploration costs in foreign areas	—	—	13,921	11,744	6,911
Interest expense	75,903	82,180	69,256	59,389	54,717
	6,544,902	5,231,022	4,802,196	4,175,439	3,747,308
Income before income taxes	800,553	443,904	302,215	283,401	232,084
Income taxes					
Federal and state	76,451	97,361	83,726	87,727	60,529
United States investment tax credit	(22,094)	(14,490)	(17,970)	(13,063)	(6,879)
United States deferred	38,919	(1,908)	36,397	25,832	25,685
Foreign current	25,818	40,588	36,154	39,742	34,266
Foreign deferred	865	2,194	(357)	1,868	4,469
Tax on gain on sale of operations	154,341	75,385	—	—	—
	274,300	199,130	137,950	142,106	118,070
Net income	$526,253	$244,774	$164,265	$141,295	$114,014

445

EXHIBIT 2

Ashland Oil, Inc.

Statement of Changes in Consolidated Financial Position

(In thousands) Year ended September 30	1979	1978	1977	1976	1975
Working capital was provided from					
Operations					
Net income	$ 526,253	$244,774	$164,265	$141,295	$144,014
Add expenses (income) not affecting working capital in the current year					
Depreciation, depletion, and amortization (includes capitalized leases)	138,117	162,537	141,998	120,298	105,738
Write-off or amortization of exploration costs	(3,203)	14,630	11,442	14,493	3,698
Valuation loss on VLCC	—	31,925	—	—	—
Deferred income taxes	2,780	286	36,040	27,700	30,154
Equity income (net of dividends)	(10,384)	(8,221)	(7,974)	(11,309)	(13,166)
Working capital provided from operations	653,563	445,931	345,771	292,477	240,438
Increase in long-term debt	150,392	109,710	314,820	13,038	79,620
Other long-term liabilities	6,180	19,869	3,040	(2,315)	(16,012)
Increase in minority interests	—	6,410	1,589	1,659	520
Issuance of capital stock	—	—	65,874	—	—
Net book value of property disposals	33,031	12,858	16,141	30,299	36,330
Noncurrent net assets of operations sold	335,582	86,643	—	—	—
Total working capital provided	1,178,748	681,421	747,235	335,158	340,896
Working capital was used for					
Cash dividends	69,469	68,657	63,160	51,501	45,566
Property, plant and equipment including properties acquired from other companies	292,184	317,318	500,819	255,627	279,961
Payments and current portions of long-term debt and capitalized leases	208,772	201,952	141,972	33,104	35,004
Purchase and retirement of common stock	560,941	—	—	—	—
Redemption of preferred stock	5,000	—	—	—	—
Investments, prepaid royalties and other—net	2,062	8,639	19,923	6,822	4,171
Total working capital used	1,138,428	596,566	725,874	347,054	364,702
Increase (decrease) in working capital	$ 40,320	$ 84,855	$ 21,361	$(11,896)	$(23,806)

EXHIBIT 3

Ashland Oil, Inc.

Consolidated Balance Sheet

(In thousands) Year ended September 30	1979	1978	1977	1976	1975
Assets					
Current assets					
Cash	$ 35,681	$ 42,079	$ 55,544	$ 50,088	$ 83,271
Short-term securities	625,517	33,856	37,296	75,353	59,838
Receivable from sale of Ashland Oil Canada Limited	—	315,840	—	—	—
Accounts receivable (less reserve)	652,436	540,737	479,101	416,486	403,717
Construction completed and in progress, at contract prices	47,468	77,197	54,895	43,631	32,250
Inventories—Crude oil	141,166	131,667	165,013	111,430	84,649
Petroleum products	96,701	99,691	119,899	78,019	78,530
Chemicals and other products	101,754	105,579	109,906	95,405	98,565
Materials and supplies	23,744	30,987	35,514	39,199	41,922
Prepaid expenses	28,614	21,307	21,344	18,546	28,712
Total current assets	1,753,081	1,398,940	1,078,512	928,157	911,454
Investments and other assets					
Investments in and advances to unconsolidated subsidiaries and affiliates	108,726	97,218	81,597	81,497	73,052
Notes and other receivables	12,895	19,625	25,507	22,990	21,112
Other assets, prepaid royalties and deferred charges	58,173	56,477	49,541	29,275	27,313
	179,794	173,320	156,645	133,762	121,477
Property, plant and equipment (net)					
Petroleum	722,327	641,959	596,636	491,922	426,404
Chemical	118,627	142,918	130,971	119,479	106,737
Coal	112,965	102,586	89,093	21,338	23,758
Construction	108,265	145,465	141,435	128,984	120,992
Exploration	43,625	390,888	374,779	260,362	263,688
Canada	—	—	157,045	126,638	114,769
Other	74,530	42,241	52,403	55,262	52,828
	1,180,339	1,466,057	1,542,362	1,203,985	1,109,176
	$3,113,214	$3,038,317	$2,777,519	$2,265,904	$2,142,107

(Continued)

Exhibit 3 (Continued)

(In thousands) Year ended September 30	1975	1976	1977	1978	1979
Liabilities, redeemable preferred stock, common stock, and other stockholders' equity					
Current liabilities					
Short-term debt	$ —	$ —	$ 16,573	$ 68,036	$ 16,949
Accounts payable	444,491	438,892	544,789	549,591	858,596
Accrued taxes other than income and excise taxes	14,272	15,150	18,012	19,919	22,241
Accrued interest	6,333	6,663	11,686	14,688	12,960
Excise taxes	25,122	22,378	23,799	14,356	17,475
Income taxes	30,491	74,103	56,079	129,929	300,948
Current portion of long-term debt and capitalized leases	28,512	20,634	35,876	145,868	27,039
Total current liabilities	549,221	577,820	706,814	942,387	1,256,208
Long-term debt—less current portion					
Senior debt	452,814	449,991	612,226	512,559	391,985
Subordinated debt	60,000	52,998	72,470	59,233	26,292
Capitalized lease obligations—less current portion	512,814	502,989	684,696	571,792	418,277
Other long-term liabilities	212,113	201,450	194,105	188,075	180,746
Deferred income taxes	36,529	34,205	35,731	70,048	76,228
Minority interests in consolidated subsidiaries	102,176	129,876	169,477	116,055	118,841
Redeemable preferred stock	20,714	22,374	23,963	—	—
$2.40 convertible preferred series of 1966	23,729	8,183	—	—	—
$5.00 convertible preferred series of 1969	1,053	1,053	1,053	1,053	—
$2.40 convertible preferred series of 1970	2,127	2,059	1,234	1,219	—
$5.00 convertible preferred series of 1970	185	185	185	184	8
Cumulative preferred stock, 8.375% series of 1974	50,000	50,000	50,000	50,000	45,000
Cumulative preferred stock, 8.50% series of 1976	—	—	50,000	50,000	50,000
Stated value	77,094	61,480	102,472	102,456	95,008
Excess of redemption value over stated value	122,902	120,825	96,854	96,407	405
	199,996	182,305	199,326	198,863	95,413
Common stock and other stockholders' equity					
Common stock—par value $1 per share	25,084	25,856	27,390	27,841	30,576
Paid-in capital	117,262	128,360	148,269	148,398	105,083
Retained earnings	494,540	586,935	687,591	874,254	835,255
Shares in treasury at cost and excess of redemption value over stated value of preferred stock	(128,342)	(126,266)	(99,843)	(99,396)	(3,413)
	508,544	614,885	763,407	951,097	967,501
	$2,142,107	$2,265,904	$2,777,519	$3,038,317	$3,113,214

EXHIBIT 4

Ashland Oil, Inc.

Revenue and Income by Line of Business

(In thousands) Year ended September 30	1979	1978	1977	1976	1975
Revenues					
Sales and operating revenues					
Petroleum	$4,922,093	$3,560,788	$3,412,807	$2,867,052	$2,583,014
Chemical	1,016,510	882,940	802,316	723,708	622,825
Coal	159,147	139,711	109,180	5,839	1,022
Construction	797,879	760,291	628,812	618,155	545,267
Exploration	178,018	206,913	186,653	181,917	145,019
Canada	—	228,101	218,454	194,229	173,531
Intersegment sales	(333,284)	(352,577)	(306,329)	(184,186)	(146,405)
	6,740,363	5,426,167	5,051,893	4,406,714	3,924,273
Other					
Gain on sale of operations	505,714	193,094	—	—	—
Equity income	16,619	13,214	12,287	13,796	16,224
Other	82,759	42,451	40,231	38,330	38,895
	$7,345,455	$5,674,926	$5,104,411	$4,458,840	$3,979,392
Income before income taxes					
Operating income					
Petroleum	$ 203,710	$ 158,777	$ 223,520	$ 221,671	$ 180,776
Chemical	69,719	38,946	22,662	12,604	11,363
Coal	12,258	16,552	13,627	2,410	2,719
Construction	22,889	41,722	35,165	40,098	37,147
Exploration	56,437	71,513	51,121	39,099	35,502
Canada	—	52,808	40,989	25,951	24,076
Other	(2,856)	(29,872)	(6,842)	(5,441)	(11,731)
	362,157	350,446	380,242	336,392	279,852
Other income					
Gain on sale of operations	505,714	193,094	—	—	—
Equity income	16,619	13,214	12,287	13,796	16,224
Interest expense	(75,903)	(82,180)	(69,256)	(59,389)	(54,717)
Other (net)	(8,034)	(30,670)	(21,058)	(7,398)	(9,275)
	$ 800,553	$ 443,904	$ 302,215	$ 283,401	$ 232,084

Source: Ashland Oil, Inc., 1979 Financial and Operating Supplement.

EXHIBIT 5

Ashland Oil, Inc.

Major Acquisitions and Divestments

	Major Acquisitions	
Date	*Selling Firm*	*Business Sector*
1939	Owensboro-Ashland	Operated crude gathering lines
1948	Allied Oil Company	Production, refining, transportation and marketing
1963	Union Carbon Company	Oil and gas production
1966	O.K. Tire and Rubber Company	Marketer of tires, manufacturer of tread rubber
	Warren Brothers Co., Inc.	Paving and highway construction
	Fisher Chemical Co., Inc.	Chemical operations
	Catalin Corporation	Synthetic resins
1967	Archer-Daniels-Midland Co.	Chemical operations
1968	Wanda Petroleum Co., Inc.	Liquid petroleum gas operations
	New Haven Trap Rock Co.	Quarrier of trap rock, road construction
	F.H. Ross Co.	Chemicals
1970	Canadian Gridoil Ltd.	Oil and gas production
	Northwestern Refining Co.	Oil refining, marketing, and transportation
1971	Macasphalt Corp.	Construction
	Eastern Seaboard Petroleum Co.	Marketer of distillates and heavy fuel oils
	Union Carbide Petroleum Corp.	Domestic and foreign oil and gas properties
1972	Reno Construction	Road paving and construction materials
	Empire State Oil Co.	Oil and gas exploration and production
1975	Levingston Shipbuilding Co.	Manufactures marine equipment
1976	Coastal Chemical Co.	Chemicals
	General Oils, Inc.	Oil and gas exploration and production
1977	Fil Nutter Coal Operations	Coal
	Nielsons, Inc.	Heavy construction firm
	Chemical Supply Co.	Chemicals
1978	Maxwell Bridge Co., Inc.	Construction
	Ted Wilkerson, Inc.	Construction

EXHIBIT 5 (Continued)

Date	Major Acquisitions Selling Firm	Business Sector
	Major Divestments	
1970	American Independent Oil Co.	Oil and gas exploration and production
1972	Wanda Petroleum Co., Inc.	Liquid petroleum gas operations
1978	Ashland Oil Canada, Ltd.	Oil and gas exploration and production
	Operation of Ashland Chemical Co.	Coating resins business
1979	Chemical Products Division of Ashland Chemical Co.	Chemical products
	Majority of foreign and domestic exploration and production operations	Oil and gas exploration and production

EXHIBIT 6

Ashland Oil, Inc.

Principal Subsidiaries
September 30, 1979

Arch Mineral Corporation (50%)
Ashland Coal, Inc.
Ashland Exploration, Inc.
Ashland Indonesia Co.
Ashland Oil Enterprises, Inc.
Ashland Oil Holdings, Inc.
Ashland Oil Investments, Inc.
Ashland Oil and Refining Co.
Ashland Oil and Transportation Co.
Ashland Petroleum International, Inc.
Ashland Synthetic Fuels, Inc.
Ashland-Warren, Inc.
Levingston Shipbuilding Co.
Nielsons, Inc.
O.K. Tire and Rubber Co., Inc.
SuperAmerica Stations, Inc.
Valvoline Oil Co.
Valvoline Oil and Chemicals Ltd.

Source: Ashland Oil, Inc., Form 10-K, 1979.

EXHIBIT 7

Ashland Oil, Inc.

Petroleum Statistics

	1979	1978	1977	1976	1975
Petroleum Manufacturing					
Crude oil refining capacity					
(barrels per stream day)	475,000	395,000	395,000	395,000	395,000
Crude oil refined (barrels per day)					
(Segregated by original source of					
crude)					
United States	108,852	119,650	112,666	140,224	138,640
Canada	34,568	32,825	54,433	67,185	83,884
Foreign	224,322	200,477	191,127	140,748	108,366
Total	367,742	352,952	358,226	348,157	330,890
Average crude oil cost					
(per barrel)	$ 17.44	$ 14.04	$ 13.49	$ 12.64	$11.55
Less entitlements	(.88)	(.80)	(1.06)	(1.12)	(.58)
Net crude oil cost	$ 16.56	$13.24	$ 12.43	$ 11.52	$ 10.97
Product realization	$ 21.39	$ 16.42	$ 15.55	$ 14.01	$ 13.39
Product manufactured					
Gasoline and jet fuel	54.4%	56.8%	55.2%	54.9%	53.5%
Kerosene and distillate	24.5	23.0	24.2	24.6	25.1
Heavy fuel oil	9.0	9.4	10.1	9.7	10.5
Asphalt	8.3	7.8	6.4	6.1	6.4
Other	3.8	3.0	4.1	4.7	4.5
Total	100.0%	100.0%	100.0%	100.0%	100.0%
Petroleum marketing					
(barrels per day)					
Gasoline and jet fuel	233,344	226,655	226,433	221,208	204,945
Kerosene and distillate	95,308	96,437	97,978	93,819	84,121
Heavy fuel oil	145,930	132,866	144,785	130,386	129,571
Asphalt	30,791	29,190	25,690	24,323	22,551
Other	25,162	23,656	22,013	22,510	20,343
Total	530,535	508,804	516,899	492,246	461,531

Source: Ashland Oil, Inc. Annual Report, 1979.

EXHIBIT 8

Ashland Oil, Inc.

Domestic Refining Capacity and Utilization—1978

Capacity Rank	Company	Capacity 000b/d	Runs	Runs/Capacity
1	Exxon	1,574.0	1,426.0	90.6%
2	Standard of California	1,449.5	1,122.0	77.4
3	Standard (Indiana)	1,238.0	1,114.0	90.0
4	Shell	1,123.4	1,040.0	92.6
5	Texaco	1,059.0	997.0	94.1
6	Gulf	948.7	844.8	89.0
7	Mobil	901.0	788.0	87.5
8	Atlantic Richfield	847.0	815.0	96.2
9	Sun	569.0	551.9	97.0
10	Marathon	533.0	498.9	93.6
11	Union	490.0	430.5	87.9
12	Standard (Ohio)	452.0	423.7	93.7
13	Ashland	364.9	352.9	96.7
14	Continental	363.0	343.5	94.6
15	Phillips	302.0	440.4[1]	145.8
16	Cities Service	291.0	175.1	60.2
17	Coastal States	266.3	222.0	83.4
18	Champlin	240.3	228.3	95.0
19	Getty	220.6	235.4	106.7
20	Tosco	213.0	150.0	70.4

[1] Includes natural gas liquids.
Source: *Market Shares and Individual Company Data for U.S. Energy Markets: 1950–1978,* American Petroleum Institute, 1979.

EXHIBIT 9

Ashland Oil, Inc.

Ashland's 1979 Refining Capacity

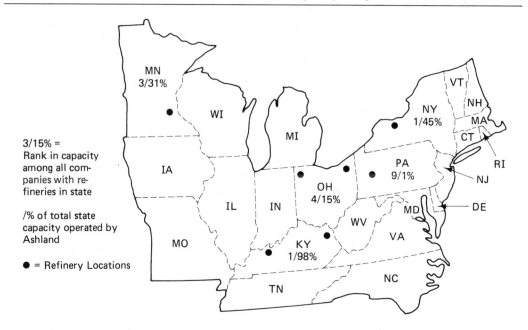

3/15% =
Rank in capacity
among all com-
panies with re-
fineries in state

/% of total state
capacity operated by
Ashland

● = Refinery Locations

Source: *Oil & Gas Journal*, March 24, 1980.

EXHIBIT 10

Ashland Oil, Inc.

Ashland's 1979 Gasoline Sales

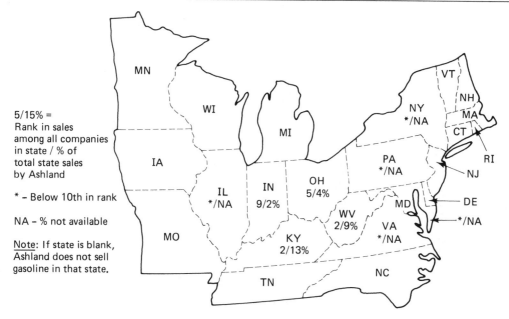

5/15% =
Rank in sales
among all companies
in state / % of
total state sales
by Ashland

* – Below 10th in rank

NA – % not available

Note: If state is blank,
Ashland does not sell
gasoline in that state.

Source: *National Petroleum News,* Mid–June, 1979.

EXHIBIT 11

Ashland Oil, Inc.

Ashland Oil's Capital Expenditures: 1969–79
(millions of dollars)

	Total	Petroleum Refining	Exploration and Production	Chemical	Coal	Construction	Canada	Other
1980 (est.)	$300	$170	$30	$30	$35	$25	$—	$10
1979	292	142	26	24	31	29	—	40
1978	317	131	59	18	25	34	42	8
1977	501	149	155	25	78	39	50	5
1976	256	105	53	26	—	34	32	6
1975	240	72	87	29	6	38	34	14
1974	188	37	51	12	—	34	29	25
1973	175	33	70	14	—	—	29	29
1972	124	35	24	23	—	—	15	27
1971	86	28	15	7	—	—	13	23
1970	82	28	18	14	—	—	9	13
1969	115	34	33	16	—	—	9	23

Sources: Ashland Oil, Inc. Annual Reports, 1979, 1978, and 1973, and *Wall Street Journal*, Feb. 1, 1980, estimated.

EXHIBIT 12

Ashland Oil, Inc.

Ashland Reserve and Production Data

| | Oil Production Barrels/Day | Gas Production MCF/Day | Proved Reserves | |
			Oil Mil. Barrels	Gas Billion C.F.
1979	28,372	176,371	15	173
1978	59,585	233,000	99	1,114
1977	59,335	215,000	101	1,082
1976	64,201	230,000	82	1,098
1975	62,498	254,000	82	1,155
1974	55,341	272,449	NA	NA
1973	50,987	312,201	167	1,362
1972	41,696	171,669	170	1,389
1971	41,192	153,772	147	1,312
1970	31,950	109,357	108	1,189
1969	32,471	105,015	104	1,178

Source: *Ashland Financial and Operating Supplements,* 1969–1979 editions.

EXHIBIT 13

Ashland Oil, Inc.

Common Stock Statistics

Year	Price Range		Annual Dividend	Earnings[1]	Book Value
1979[2]	45½	27	$1.80	$15.55	$29.33
1978	34	18	1.33	5.51	$22.76
1977	24⅞	19⅜	1.27	3.73	27.75
1976	23	12⅞	1.10	3.35	24.88
1975	16½	11	.98	2.94	21.46
1974	18¼	10¼	.92	2.96	19.56
1973	22½	14	.82	2.24	16.16
1972	23⅜	15⅝	.80	1.76	14.15
1971	20⅜	12⅝	.80	.98	13.06
1970	18⅞	11⅜	.80	1.39	13.25
1969[3]	36⅝	15	.80	1.53	13.79

[1] All earnings per share data assumes no conversion and is stated after consideration for special items.

[2] There was a 3 for 2 stock split in 1979. By November 1979, the annual dividend had been increased to $2.20.

[3] Restated for comparative purposes on a pooling of interest basis.

Sources: *Moody's Industrial Manual,* 1978 and 1972. Ashland Oil, Inc. Annual Report, 1979.

PART EIGHT

INTEGRATIVE FINANCIAL PLANNING

$C\underline{ASE}$ 41

CMC Industries

On April 15, 1980, the following conversation took place at the offices of CMC Industries:

Prescott: (President) ". . . Okay, capital expenditures for '80 are now budgeted at $52 million. Can we afford to build the new plant in San Diego that Walter Chase wants?"

Frankall: (V.P. Finance) "I don't think so, Bill. The cement plant modernization program over the past six years and the new plant in Dallas have been very costly—we have too much debt as it is."

Thompson: (Treasurer) "In addition, any debt funds we could raise would be very expensive. The bond market is in a shambles—double A bonds come with an 11¼% coupon. We would be lucky to find buyers at 13%!"

Frankall: "We might be able to swing it in early '81 if we cut our dividend to the bone and found some way to speed up the collection of the Power Equipment Division's receivables. All that capital tied up in receivables is hurting us. Even then the funds for the new plant would require a much higher debt level."

Prescott: That inflation project your staff has been working on will be ready tomorrow, right? Why don't you bring that with you when we meet with Chase then. I would like to make a decision on this as soon as the board meets next

This case was prepared by Robert Fowkes under the supervision of Associate Professor Allen Michel of Boston University, and used with the permission of Professor Michel.

week to decide on this quarter's dividend. I suspect they'll want to raise it again."

BACKGROUND

With the completion of its Dallas, Texas, plant in 1979, CMC jumped to the number two position in the cement industry, both in sales ($578 million) and annual rated capacity (7.9 million tons). CMC had eight plants located in seven states: California, Florida (2), Georgia, Oklahoma, Pennsylvania, Texas, and Virginia. Of the top ten cement producers in the United States, CMC was thought to have the most modern production facilities.

In 1969 CMC acquired a leading producer of lawn and garden power equipment. It was management's belief at the time that diversification into an unrelated but growing market would enhance CMC's growth prospects and reduce its dependence on the cyclical cement industry.

The acquisition proved to be quite a success. As shown in Exhibit 1, sales increased from $65 million in 1970 to $350 million in 1979. Operating earnings increased during the same period from $6.5 million to $34 million.

THE CEMENT INDUSTRY

Cement production was one of the most energy-intensive industries in the country, and the companies in this industry were hard hit by the oil price increases begun in 1973. The rise in costs resulted in considerably lower profit margins throughout the industry.

In the interests of energy efficiency most producers switched from high-priced petroleum fuels to powdered coal. This switch reduced energy costs and insured fuel availability but required additional capital expenditures for pollution control equipment. Eighty-five percent of domestic producers now had coal-burning capacity, although only 62 percent were using it as their fuel.

While choice of fuel was one important element in the industry's energy costs, another was manufacturing process. There were two basic processes in the production of cement: wet and dry. The dry process was much more energy efficient; with suitable technology it saved 40 percent in energy costs. While the larger companies had been relatively quick to convert to the dry process, the smaller companies, especially those in weak markets, had been unable to raise the capital to do so.

Competition in the cement industry was primarily determined by the nature of the product. Since cement was produced to universal specifications, there was very little product diversification or brand recognition. The low value-to-weight ratio made delivery to principal markets beyond a range of 200 miles rare, but delivery expenses still accounted for 20 to 25 percent of the cost to the buyer.

Because of these geographical limitations, competition in the industry was entirely regional. As one might expect, the competitive forces differed from market to market. In 1979 overcapacity and weak demand resulted in cement prices of $48 per ton in the Northeast. At the same time the price was over $70 per ton in the tight, fast-growing California markets.

Although domestic conditions of the industry had been erratic, the threat of imported cement was practically nonexistent due to the cost of transportation. All current imports were made by domestic producers in tight markets as a service to their customers (10 percent in 1979). Profit margins were narrow or nonexistent on these sales and a cutback here was likely if demand eased.

Because of the expense of energy efficient technology and the keen competition for domestic markets, the number of firms in the industry had been decreasing. This situation was likely to continue as long as the capital expenditures needed to replace and modernize facilities continued to increase faster than cement prices. Those companies able to (1) diversify into several markets and (2) afford the investment required to save on energy costs would be able to survive.

Long-term prospects for the industry depended on production capacity, ability to adopt new technology, general economic activity, and development and use of alternative production processes. As illustrated in Exhibit 2, a reasonable rate of return from additions to capacity was based on an optimistic forecast for cement prices.

CMC'S CEMENT DIVISION

Bill Prescott had been president of CMC only a year in 1974 when he made the decision to completely modernize CMC's facilities. As a result, debt as a percentage of capital rose from 35 percent in early 1974 to more than 48 percent in 1978. CMC now enjoyed the highest operating margin on its domestically produced cement and the lowest energy costs per ton in the industry, although other cement producers were also beginning to modernize. Financial statements of CMC for 1975 through 1979 are presented in Exhibits 3 and 4.

The cement division's operating results for 1975–1979 were far above the industry average (see Exhibits 5 and 6). These were achieved even with 12 percent of 1979 sales made up of low-margin imports. Cement division operating results for its domestic and imported cement can be found in Exhibit 7.

Walter Chase, the cement division manager, had always been in favor of the Texas plant and felt that it had been built largely because of his efforts in its behalf. After almost a full year in operation, the modern dry process plant was operating at a cost savings that supported his belief in the project. Even in the first year, demand was sufficient to run the plant at 93 percent of rated capacity —whereas 90 percent had been considered maximum for older CMC plants. Energy use per ton was 8 percent less than any other CMC plant, while operating margin was only slightly higher. Since energy costs were variable, the potential for continued cost savings was substantial: The higher the energy costs, the greater the savings. Only the possibility that weak demand would force the plant to operate at less than capacity threatened its profitability.

THE POWER EQUIPMENT DIVISION

CMC's Power Equipment Division (PED) was a leading producer of outdoor power equipment. Its products were marketed under a variety of trade names. Their products included consumer and institutional lawnmowers, tillers, lawn trimmers, snowthrowers, chainsaws, and irrigation equipment.

The PED's sales and earnings growth had been quite strong since the company was acquired in 1969 (Exhibit 1). Its management had aggressively entered new markets with well-designed products backed by strong advertising. In 1970 its sales were made up of 58 percent institutional customers and 42 percent homeowners. By 1978, almost 70 percent of sales came from retail sales.

They accomplished this growth despite the fact that most of CMC's financial resources over the past six years were committed to the cement division. This lack of financial resources had limited the PED's flexibility in marketing and production strategies.

One of the reasons behind the PED's strong growth was its liberal credit policy for retail accounts. The PED had found that a substantial inventory of their models at the retail level was essential to strong brand recognition and sales. Their credit policy was enacted to encourage this. The high interest rates of late 1979 and early 1980, however, encouraged retailers to take advantage of the PED's credit policy and, in some cases, to abuse it. As of April 15th, 25 percent of their 1979 Christmas orders had yet to be collected. PED's retail accounts were having trouble financing their inventories and receivables and were using the PED as a bank.

In spite of this, Sam Frankall was reluctant to advise Prescott to change the PED's credit policy. He realized that much of the division's growth—indeed, the whole strategic plan—was dependent on its liberal credit terms. As Frankall noted, "in the future we should realize that during times of inflation, the PED becomes a capital-intensive business."

1980 FORECASTS

Despite the immediate problems of the PED, the long-term prospects of the firm were good according to CMC's treasurer,

Mr. Thompson, who was responsible for translating their economic forecasts into unit and dollar sales and earnings forecasts. His translation depended on what set of economic forecasts he used, the most pessimistic of which included the worst likely recession and a minimum inflation rate. When Thompson estimated the inflation-adjusted recession pro forma income and cash flow for each division using this scenario, he found the PED's unit sales could be off by 20-percent, prices up 3 percent, and costs up 5 percent per unit. Cement sales would drop 20 percent despite the 22 percent increase already registered in the first quarter, but that return on sales would increase slightly, and total cash flows would be $132 million. These funds would have to cover any increase in working capital, taxes, interest, corporate expenses, and capital expenditures. Thompson figured that, with working capital needs expected to decrease, the $132 million would cover all these outlays with about $36 million left over to trim debt.

THE SAN DIEGO PLANT

In April of 1980 CMC was faced with an important decision. Several years earlier, it had taken an option on a possible plant site, even though it had no idea at that time whether economic conditions would support the construction of new plants. This option was soon to expire, and it was now necessary for CMC to come to a decision regarding the construction of a new plant near San Diego.

Walter Chase was convinced of the advisability of the proposed San Diego facility. He saw several compelling reasons to start construction in late 1980 or early 1981:

1. The latest economic reports suggest-

ed that the current recession would end by early 1981.

2. Other cement companies were not planning to add capacity in this market—and if CMC were to take the initiative, they would refrain from doing so.

3. Because the area imported about 25 percent of its cement requirements in 1979, almost 1 million tons, the plant could very well start up at practically capacity.

4. The greater the inflationary pressures on production costs, the greater the advantage of the new plant and, the greater the dollar margin and rate of return (if prices follow input costs).

After Prescott and Frankall listened to Chase rehearse his reasons for approval of the San Diego plant, the following conversation ensued:

Prescott: "I agree with you, Walter. The San Diego location is perfect, and there is a good chance that the plant will operate at near capacity within six months or so from start-up. It's the necessity of selling price increases, or input price increases, to provide a good return that bothers me. We need 16–17% on this kind of investment."

Frankall: "It seems to me to be very risky. The replacement cost income statements (RCI) I've prepared [Exhibit 8] show that current prices are simply too low to provide a decent return at today's cost of ca-

pacity. Negative RCI over the past five years says that our ability to replace the portion of assets used up in the production process—at today's higher prices—is shrinking. Carried to the obvious conclusion, the company won't be able to grow in the future. In fact, the company won't be able to maintain, in a real sense, its productive capacity."

Chase: "Do you have any idea what these figures look like for the other companies in the industry?"

Prescott: "They are probably worse off. And because our dividend payout ratio is below the industry average, their ability to replace capacity at today's prices is less than ours."

Chase: "I have just three comments to make. First, in order to determine depreciation expense for current cost income [Exhibit 8(a)] you used current cost of capacity times present capacity, right? Okay, that doesn't take into account the operating efficiencies that are available with the new dry process plants. Second, if everyone in the industry faces these same conditions, then doesn't the price of cement have to rise? Third, if the price of cement has to go up, then shouldn't we replace our capacity—or add to it—as soon as possible? The gain that your're ignoring—that of owning PP&E that is appreciating in value over time—is the reason to buy now."

Prescott: "You've made some good points, Walter. I should have known you would turn this around so that replacement cost income—loss, I should say—would support the new plant. One more thing, Walter, how long do we have before a decision is due on the San Diego project?"

Chase: "Well, the option expires in two months. The owners haven't made it clear to me whether we can renew it or whether they've found another buyer."

Prescott: "Okay. Well, thank you gentlemen."

This was Prescott's dilemma—he suspected that Chase was right but *knew* that the board would not cut the dividend as Frankall had suggested on the 15th. With CMC's stock at 29, only 92 percent of book value, selling new equity would be expensive.

Several members of the board were of the opinion that during times of inflation, the dividend should be increased in real terms each year, provided earnings were strong. Deceptive first quarter earnings made it unlikely that Prescott would be able to convince the board to cut the dividend (see Exhibit 9).

Prescott then remembered a conversation he had several weeks ago with CMC's investment banker who had brought up the possibility that another company might be interested in acquiring CMC's equipment division. He estimated that the after-tax proceeds from such a sale would be in the area of $120 to $150 million. "If I suggest to the board that we sell off a division," thought Prescott, "they'll throw me out in the street."

EXHIBIT 1

CMC Industries

Ten-Year Summary
(millions of dollars)

	1970	1971	1972	1973	1974	1975	1976	1977	1978	1979
Sales										
Cement Division	260.0	301.5	335.5	400.5	407.5	375.0	335.2	390.0	490.0	578.0
Power Equipment Division	65.0	72.1	88.2	103.0	125.0	145.0	135.0	160.0	225.0	350.0
Total Sales	325.0	373.6	423.7	503.5	532.5	520.0	470.2	550.0	715.0	928.0
Operating Earnings										
Cement Division	30.7	40.9	46.9	51.7	33.7	30.4	30.5	48.8	67.3	85.0
Power Equipment Division	6.5	8.3	9.2	11.8	13.5	10.3	11.4	15.0	20.8	34.0
Total Segment Earnings	37.2	49.2	56.1	63.5	47.2	40.7	41.9	63.8	88.1	119.0
Net Income	13.7	20.5	23.5	26.5	19.0	12.0	13.1	24.8	36.7	52.0

EXHIBIT 2

CMC Industries

Return on Investment in a Modern Cement Plant

Inflation complicates any return on investment calculations, especially those that require estimates of revenues and costs far into the future. No resemblance to the actual results that will occur in the future can be expected when, in an increasingly uncertain environment, one must forecast a myriad of input prices, selling prices, and, perhaps most importantly, the development and adoption of superior production processes. In developing ROI "ballpark" figures to help in planning, CMC management makes simplifying assumptions in coming up with several possibilities.

1. Operating profit margin will remain constant as a percentage of sales dollars.
2. Plant will last 25 years with no salvage value.
3. Plant will operate at 90 percent of rated capacity.
4. Taxes on income will remain at 48 percent, the investment tax credit will remain at 10 percent and will be taken in year 1.
5. Plant will cost $135 per ton of annual rated capacity.

Cement Selling Price at Startup Date	Increase in Price Per Year (%)	After-Tax Return on Investment (%)
$68/Ton	0	9.5
$68	4	12.4
$68	8	17.4
$72/Ton	0	10.0
$72	4	13.8
$72	8	19.2

EXHIBIT 3

CMC Industries

Income Statement
(millions of dollars)

	1975	1976	1977	1978	1979
Cement Division					
Sales	375.0	335.2	390.0	490.0	578.0
Cost of Goods Sold	275.2	237.4	265.1	337.5	397.6
Selling, General & Admin.	41.0	36.3	43.6	49.2	53.9
Depreciation	28.4	31.0	32.5	36.0	41.5
Operating Profit	30.4	30.5	48.8	67.3	85.0
Equipment Division					
Sales	145.0	135.0	160.0	225.0	350.0
Cost of Goods Sold	104.0	91.7	105.7	147.6	235.6
Selling, General & Admin.	29.3	30.1	37.2	54.1	76.6
Depreciation	1.4	1.8	2.1	2.5	3.8
Operating Profit	10.3	11.4	15.0	20.8	34.0
Total Operating Profit	40.7	41.9	63.8	88.1	119.0
Corporate Expenses	5.5	5.8	6.0	6.6	7.3
Interest Expense	15.3	15.1	15.3	17.9	25.1
Income Taxes	7.9	7.9	17.7	28.9	34.6
Net Income	12.0	13.1	24.8	36.7	52.0

EXHIBIT 4

CMC Industries

Balance Sheet
(millions of dollars)

	1975	1976	1977	1978	1979
Cash & marketable securities	21.3	15.3	6.1	52.6	13.6
Accounts receivable	71.0	61.2	74.0	106.5	155.8
Inventories	73.2	64.5	76.1	92.3	124.6
Other current assets	11.5	13.0	12.8	15.6	18.0
Current assets	177.0	154.0	169.0	267.0	312.0
Property plant & equipment (net)	309.5	333.2	344.4	393.6	462.9
Other noncurrent assets	27.0	29.5	30.0	36.0	38.0
Total assets	513.5	516.7	543.4	696.6	812.9
Short-term debt	50.8	14.9	23.9	26.9	63.9
Accounts payable	36.5	35.5	38.5	55.0	71.0
Current maturities of long-term debt	8.2	6.5	11.2	8.5	7.8
Other current liabilities	8.5	9.0	9.3	9.8	14.1
Current liabilities	104.0	65.9	82.9	100.2	156.8
Deferred taxes	28.5	30.2	32.1	36.8	41.9
Long-term debt	160.0	193.5	185.3	289.8	306.1
Common stock	9.5	9.6	9.7	9.9	9.9
Capital surplus	69.0	70.2	71.0	72.3	72.5
Retained earnings	142.5	147.3	162.4	187.6	225.7
Equity	221.0	227.1	243.1	269.8	308.1
Liabilities & stockholders' equity	513.5	516.7	543.4	696.6	812.9

EXHIBIT 5

CMC Industries

Operating Statistics

	1975	1976	1977	1978	1979
Performance Measures					
Overall operating margin (%)	7.8	8.9	11.6	12.3	12.8
Cement operating margin (%)	8.1	9.1	12.5	13.7	14.7
PED operating margin (%)	7.1	8.4	9.4	9.2	9.7
Return on sales (%)	2.3	2.8	4.5	5.1	5.6
Return on equity (%)	5.4	5.8	10.2	13.6	16.9
Capital Expenditures (millions)					
Cement division	$37.5	$52.5	$40.0	$75.0	$95.0
PED	$ 7.8	$ 1.5	$ 3.7	$ 7.5	$ 9.5
Capitalization Ratios					
Deferred taxes/total capital (%)	6.9	6.7	7.1	6.2	6.3
Long-term debt/total capital (%)	39.1	42.9	40.1	48.6	46.7
Equity/total capital (%)	54.0	50.4	52.8	45.2	47.0
Per Share Amounts ($)					
Earnings per share	1.26	1.36	2.55	3.72	5.23
Dividends per share	0.86	0.86	1.00	1.18	1.40
Miscellaneous					
Payout ratio (%)	68	63	39	32	27
Shares outstanding (millions)	9.53	9.64	9.72	9.86	9.94
Replacement cost of fixed assets (millions)	$ 614	$ 684	$ 755	$ 885	$1088
Imports as percent of sales (%)	4	2	8	14	12
Capacity utilization (%)	85.5	82.0	83.8	89.0	90.4

EXHIBIT 6

CMC Industries

Industry Statistics

	1975	1976	1977	1978	1979
Cement operating margin (%)	5.8	7.7	9.2	11.5	13.0
Return on sales (%)	1.6	3.8	4.8	6.1	6.3
Long-term debt/capital (%)	30	32	36	38	36
Dividend payout ratio (%)	67	62	50	43	39
Fixed asset replacement cost/ historical cost	—	—	—	—	2.85
Inflation rate (CPI) (%)	7	5.8	6.5	7.6	11.3
Average CPI	161.2	170.5	181.5	195.4	217.4
Capacity utilization (%)	—	—	—	79	81

EXHIBIT 7

CMC Industries

Margins on Domestically Produced and Imported Cement for 1979
(millions of dollars)

	Total	CMC Production	Imports
Sales	578.0	508.6	69.4
Cost of goods sold	397.6	333.6	64.0
Selling, general & administrative	53.9	49.6	4.3
Depreciation	41.5	41.0	0.5
Operating profit	85.0	84.4	0.6
% Margin	14.7	16.6	0.9

EXHIBIT 8

CMC Industries

Current Cost Income
(millions of 1979 dollars)

	1975	1976	1977	1978	1979
(A) Modern Cost of PPE[1]					
Cement Division					
Sales	505.5	427.0	466.8	544.9	578.0
Cost of goods sold	370.8	302.4	314.9	375.3	397.6
Selling, general, & administrative	55.3	46.2	52.2	54.7	53.9
Depreciation	75.9	81.1	85.3	90.1	97.5
Operating profit (loss)	3.5	(2.7)	14.4	24.8	29.0
Equipment Division					
Sales	195.5	172.0	191.5	250.2	350.0
Cost of goods sold	144.4	120.3	130.3	169.1	242.9
Selling, general & administrative	39.5	38.3	44.5	60.1	76.6
Depreciation	2.7	3.2	3.6	4.1	5.4
Operating profit	8.9	10.2	13.1	16.9	25.1
Total operating profit	12.4	7.5	27.5	41.7	54.1
Corporate expenses	7.5	7.4	7.5	7.4	7.3
Interest	20.6	19.2	18.3	19.9	25.1
Taxes	10.6	10.0	21.1	29.9	34.6
Net income (loss)	(26.3)	(29.1)	(19.4)	(15.5)	(12.9)
Gain from the decline in purchasing power of net amounts owed	13.1	12.4	12.1	21.1	28.1
Excess of specific price increases of PPE and inventory over increase due to general inflation	9.6	11.3	15.6	20.1	30.5
(B) Current Value of PPE[2]					
Net income	(11.2)	(11.9)	0.6	5.0	13.9
Excess of specific price increases of PPE and inventory over increase due to general inflation	(1.2)	(4.5)	8.0	2.6	(12.4)

[1] Replacement cost using purchased assets which are likely to be more productive.
[2] Replacement cost using purchased assets which are not likely to be more productive.

EXHIBIT 9

CMC Industries

First-Quarter Results and Balance Sheet
(millions of dollars)

		Δ1ˢᵗQ'79 (%)
Income		
Cement sales	$156.3	+22.3
Equipment sales	81.1	−3.0
Total sales	237.4	+12.2
Cost of cement sold	108.1	
Cost of equipment sold	55.5	
Selling, general and administration	31.2	
Depreciation	11.4	
Direct expenses	206.2	
Gross income	31.2	
Corporate expenses	1.9	
Interest expenses (net)	7.7	
Income taxes	9.3	
	18.9	
Net income	12.3	+14.0
Assets		
Cash and marketable securities	15.0	
Accounts receivable	151.2	
Inventories	118.3	
Other current assets	17.4	
Current assets	301.9	
Property, plant, and equipment (net)	461.5	
Other noncurrent assets	38.2	
Total assets	801.6	
Liabilities		
Short-term debt	36.4	
Accounts payable	72.5	
Current maturities of long-term debt	12.8	
Other current liabilities	15.3	
Current liabilities	137.0	
Deferred taxes	43.0	
Long-term debt	301.1	
Liabilities	481.1	
Equity		
Common stock	9.9	
Capital surplus	72.6	
Retained earnings	238.0	
Equity	320.5	
Total liabilities and equity	801.6	

CASE 42

Techtronics, Incorporated*

Robert J. Schmidt was putting the finishing touches on his annual report address for the shareholders in the annual meeting five weeks away (see Exhibit 1). He was optimistic about the future, but his concerns involved the new Scanall Corporation, which had consumed $2.5 million (if one included cost contributed from other divisions) and the vulnerability of his products to federal spending controlled by Congress. Furthermore, a staff report on the major obstacles to wide use of scanning in the supermarkets was not encouraging (see Appendix A).

With the profit picture improving since 1971, he really believed he was on the right track. However, he wondered if a movement away from government-order dependence was logical. His latest entry into the industrial field, Scanall, would use the talents of his operating companies to stimulate industrial and commercial sales.

HISTORY

Techtronics, Inc., was founded in 1947. The business began in a garage with part-time tool and die makers who performed jobs that larger firms could not profitably perform or research. It remained a small proprietorship until 1956 when it was incorporated as Precision Manufacturing Company. From 1956 to 1967 it had become a reputable producer of ultraprecision components for inertial guidance, navigational, and computer systems utilized in both government and the commercial aerospace industry.

In 1967 Precision Manufacturing Company went public, changed its name to Techtronics, Inc., and revamped its organization structure. Then a series of ac-

---

*This case was prepared by and used with the permission of Professor Charles F. Hoitash, Eastern Michigan University.

quisitions took place: McGregor Corporation was acquired for `$1.8 million and United States Spectrographic Laboratories, Inc., for $.75 million, both in 1969. In 1973 Mul-Tech Electronics Corporation in Florida was purchased in exchange for shares. DuMont Ultraspec, Inc., was purchased for $115,000 in 1973. In the spring of 1974 Scanall Corporation was formed as an industrial products division structured to manufacture and market laser scanner label-reading systems.

Scanall Corporation introduced its scanner and electronic processor at the May 1974 SMI (Supermarket Institute) annual convention, shortly after the division was formally established. The following year, the Scanall laser[1] system was to be shown as part of the NCR MODULAR 225 Point of Sale (POS), which also included the computer, electronic cash register (ECR), and the checkout counter. This system was designed for use with the Universal Product Code (UPC) developed by the supermarket industry.

GENERAL

Techtronics, Inc., was engaged in four separate lines of business (see Exhibit 2). The first, referred to as a manufacturing business, provided ultraprecision components and assemblies to primary suppliers. This type of business was carried on by the Precision Manufacturing and Systems Division and two companies in the Technological Specialization Division (TSD), DuMont Ultraspec, Inc., and

McGregor Corp. Both precision Manufacturing and Systems Division and DuMont designed and manufactured components and systems that required sophisticated engineering techniques and equipment. McGregor's business was principally related to the production of machined parts, primarily for the aircraft and defense industry, which required reasonably close tolerances.

Techtronics' second line of business was in the area of chemical analysis of a wide variety of materials for a broad spectrum of industry. The chemical analysis business was carried on through a company in the T.S. Division, U.S. Spectrographic Laboratories, Inc. Techtronics' third line of business was its electronic components and assemblies operation, which commenced with the acquisition of Mul-Tech Electronics Corporation ("Mul-Tech"), acquired in April, 1973. Techtronics' fourth line of business was industrial products, involving primarily a laser scanner label reader system, using the trade name of "Scanall." A more detailed description of each line follows.

Exhibit 3 sets forth the contributions to net sales and earnings (loss) before income taxes and extraordinary items by line of business for the five years ended January 31, 1975. Exhibit 4 contains the percentage of total sales.

MANUFACTURING SERVICES

Techtronics' manufacturing service business involved the production of products on special order to customer specifications.

---

[1] Laser is an acronym for Light Amplification by Stimulated Emission of Radiation. The laser is a device for amplifying light radiation, in which a beam of light is shot through a crystal causing the crystal to emit an intense direct light beam that is useful in micromachining, surgery, and computer design.

The Precision Manufacturing and Systems Division had two operating companies, the Precision Manufacturing Company and the Precision Systems Company.

Precision Manufacturing Company primarily manufactured components on a production basis. Its products included inertial navigation components for use in missiles, space vehicles, aircraft, ships and submarines, and other items requiring extremely close tolerances. This company also manufactured gas bearings, gyro, and accelerometer components. In July 1973 Techtronics increased its manufacturing service capability with the acquisition of DuMont, which was engaged in high-precision machining of steels, aluminums, and titaniums.

Precision Systems Company produced precision optical devices used in satellites such as the Earth Resources Technology Satellites. It also produced sensitive sensors and instruments for other outer space applications and components for nuclear applications. In addition, it designed and manufactured high-precision rotating laser and infrared scanner systems and related electronic equipment for use in communications and other applications.

In February 1969 Techtronics acquired McGregor Corporation, a firm utilizing machining processes that were numerically controlled. McGregor's capabilities were focused upon the economical mass production of structural components requiring reasonably close tolerances. McGregor served principally the commercial and military aircraft industries but also machined torpedo housings and nuclear reactor parts. This firm suffered severe losses in the four years prior to fiscal 1975 and the first quarter of fiscal 1975. Management's efforts, which had been directed toward renegotiating existing contracts and becoming more restrictive on acceptance of new contracts without adequate profit margins, had resulted in profitable operations for the last three quarters of 1975. Management believed that the past problems causing McGregor's losses had been corrected.

CHEMICAL ANALYSIS

United States Spectrographic Laboratories, Inc. (USSL), was an analytical laboratory with a capability of analyzing a broad range of materials to determine chemical composition. Analysis was accomplished by an instrumental approach using spectrographs, spectrometers, atomic absorptions, x-ray analysis, and classical chemical analysis. USSL provided support supplies to other chemical analysis laboratories and its services were utilized by industries in quality control to determine, for example, whether material alloys met required specifications or to identify causes of defects. USSL also provided analytical services in the areas of air and water pollution control, health, hygiene, and agriculture.

ELECTRONIC COMPONENTS AND ASSEMBLIES

Mul-Tech Electronic Corporation (Mul-Tech) was engaged in the manufacture of electronic components and assemblies and had a particular product line of flexible multiconductor, flat ribbon, molded electrical cable assemblies for use in computer files, business machines, guidance systems, gyro platforms, and other applications requiring high flexibility under severe operating conditions. Mul-Tech's principal customers were manufacturers of aerospace equipment, automated machinery, and business machines.

Electronic servos (a low-power device or control mechanism used to actuate or control a more complex or more powerful mechanism), digital processors, and video processors were produced at Precision Systems Company. These units were used in control and information processing mechanisms for Techtronics products and customers products.

INDUSTRIAL PRODUCTS

The efforts of Scanall Corp. (in the Technological Specialization Division) were focused upon a "front-end" for the automated checkout counters for supermarkets which would read universal product code labels on purchased goods. The Scanall system employed a laser scanner coupled with optics, video processors, and digital processors. The unit worked in conjunction with electronic cash registers and computers to automate checkout and inventory control for the supermarket industry. Prototypes of this unit had been delivered to systems manufacturers who were primarily in the computer cash register or business machine fields. Orders had been received from one systems manufacturer for production units. Deliveries under these orders were expected to commence during the fiscal year ending January 31, 1976.

In the opinion of management there was a large market potential for this device. This opinion was based on informal surveys by management; a formal market study had not been made. Other industrial products included laser measuring equipment particularly as it pertained to hardness measurement.

MARKETING

The principal customers of Techtronics were federal government prime contractors, and first-tier subcontractors that furnished services and equipment for the use of the Department of Defense, the National Aeronautics and Space Administration, and the Atomic Energy Commission. During the fiscal year ended January 31, 1975, approximately 64 percent of the sales were for the ultimate use of the government. The remainder represented sales to customers for private use, chiefly in the commercial aircraft industry. Techtronics' business with the government was obtained primarily through competitive proposals made in response to requests for bids from prime government contractors and first-tier subcontractors. Generally, the contracts were awarded on a competitive bid system.

Marketing was passive in that their business was secured through requests for bids by prime or first-tier contractors. No formal sales organization existed; however, four technical sales persons representing each line of business maintain contact with potential contractors, especially the research and development technicians. Prints were brought back from which quotes were developed and submitted.

COMPETITIVE POSITION

In view of the highly specialized fields served by Techtronics and the significance of government-sponsored programs, it was difficult to make a precise evaluation of its competitive position in the manufacturing services field. However, there were a number of large and small companies engaged in supplying services and products to the aerospace industry of the type furnished by Techtronics, and all of Techtronics' markets had been highly competitive for recent periods. The Scanall system had several known competitors, one of which was the Sperry Univac AccuScan system, a division of Sperry Rand Corporation. Some of these competitors were independent companies who had or were attempting to develop a comparable system for sale to system manufacturers. Additional competition arose from large companies (such as IBM) which had or were attempting to develop a comparable system for their own use.

The electronic components and assemblies produced by Mul-Tech had one known independent competitor.

RAW MATERIALS AND SUPPLIES

Materials purchased by Techtronics for use in the manufacture of its products consisted largely of beryllium metal, stainless steel, aluminum, ceramics, refractory metals, plastics, and chemicals purchased from many national suppliers. Electronic components such as transistors, relays, lasers, and circuit boards were also purchased from various suppliers. All of these materials and supplies were available in ample quantities.

BACKLOG

On January 31, 1975, the backlog of orders for Techtronics, Inc., and its subsidiaries was $7.1 million (a new record high) compared to $6.6 million on January 31, 1974. The backlog was reasonably expected to be filled within the current fiscal year. There were no seasonal factors affecting this amount.

RESEARCH AND DEVELOPMENT

Techtronics, Inc., made expenditures associated with the development of the Scanall system of approximately $188,000 during fiscal 1974 and $856,000 during fiscal 1975. As of January 31, 1975, there were approximately 25 full-time employees engaged in this activity. Customer-sponsored expenditures for R & D activities amounted to approximately $62,000 during fiscal 1974 and $120,000 during fiscal 1975. Prior to 1974, there were no significant research and development activities.

EMPLOYMENT

As of January 31, 1975, there were 493 persons employed by Techtronics, Inc., and its subsidiaries, compared to 450 in 1969 and 297 in 1968. Of these, approximately 138 were salaried employees. None of the hourly employees belonged to any union.

MANAGEMENT

Name	Age	Position
Robert J. Schmidt	55	Chairman of the board of directors and president
Robert J. Crowner	53	Executive vice-president
Willard C. Ursher	34	Vice-president finance and treasurer
William A. Betz	46	Vice-president marketing
Richard E. Roper	43	Vice-president industrial relations
Paul R. Trigg, Jr.	62	Secretary

There was no family relationship between any of the above persons.

Mr. Schmidt had been the chief executive officer since 1947. He held approximately 58 percent of the outstanding stock. This included the wholly owned companies of USSL, McGregor, Mul-Tech, DuMont, and Scanall, all of which were part of Technological Specialization Division.

Mr. Crowner joined the firm in September 1971 as executive vice-president. He had a Bachelor's degree from an eastern college. From 1967 until 1971 he was employed by Motorola as vice-president and general manager of one of that firm's manufacturing plants.

Mr. Ursher joined the firm in December 1974 as vice-president of finance and treasurer. He served as corporate controller from April 1970 to March 1972 and as vice-president and treasurer of Norelco to May 1974; at that time he joined Wellesly Company, as corporate controller, remaining until joining Techtronics.

Mr. Betz joined the firm in November 1971 to develop corporate planning and marketing and was named vice-president of marketing in April 1973. He graduated from an engineering college in aeronautical engineering. Like Mr. Crowner, he was employed by Motorola as manager of engineering services, marketing manager, and director of program management.

Mr. Roper joined the firm in August 1973 as director of industrial relations, to assume the position of vice-president of industrial relations in November 1974. He came to Techtronics after becoming a director of personnel in 1969 for Ken Plastics, a Division of Parke-Davis Pharmaceuticals Corporation.

Mr. Trigg had been a partner of the law firm of Trigg, Goodnow, and Smith for more than five years.

FACILITIES

Production and service facilities had been located close to their customers, or close to the home of the firm's founder and key employees. Because of the technical nature of the manufacturing services and their specialized nature, location did not present a problem in communication or cost. Exhibit 5 lists the facilities (leased and owned) their location, and approximate footage.

FINANCE

The balance sheets for 1974 and 1975 are found in Exhibit 6. The operating statements for 1971 through 1975 are in Exhibit 7, with key financial information listed in Exhibit 8. Sales and profit statistics from 1963 through 1975 are presented in Exhibit 9.

Mr. Schmidt had waived his right to any dividends since 1968, when a dividend payout ceased, and there was no intention to resume payment of them.

Net fixed assets investment was at an all-time high of $10,550 per employee.

Except for changes in the equity of the firm, net earnings had been retained entirely in the business.

Deferred income taxes were related to timing differences arising principally from the election for income tax purposes to use accelerated depreciation methods and to deduct new product development costs as incurred.

Inventories were stated at the lower of first-in, first-out cost or market.

Each year, short- and long-term debt obligations were refinanced or renewed depending on the needs and occasional restrictions on growth.

EXHIBIT 1

Techtronics, Incorporated

Report to Shareholders

Fiscal year 1975 was a year of continued growth in sales, earnings, and orders for Techtronics, Inc. Net earnings were up 60 percent to $674,000 as compared to earnings of $428,000 for fiscal year 1974. These earnings were realized on sales of $13,671,000–an increase of 16 percent over last year's level of $11,784,000.

High interest rates, during the major portion of the fiscal year, had an impact on earnings. Debt, however, increased only $285,000 in spite of a significant investment in the Scanall Corp. development of $856,000. In April of 1974 a new operation, Scanall Corp., was founded for the purpose of entering the industrial and commercial product field. The product involved was a laser point-of-sale scanner for reading the Universal Product Code. This code and scanner technique will automate the checkout counters at supermarkets. Orders were received for prototype units that were delivered during the fiscal year; and as of this point in time, tentative but as yet unconfirmed production orders have been received from National Cash Register Corporation. Negotiations are under way with other suppliers of electronic cash registers and systems to whom our product is sold. The Scanall label reader has met with exceptionally fine acceptance and, through laboratory and field tests, has proven itself to be accurate and reliable. As we are now entering the production phase of this product, no further major development investment is anticipated.

Improved performance was experienced in all entities with the exception of Precision Systems Company. Price competition in this area has become very severe. Precision Manufacturing Company saw a record year in sales and earnings as did United States Spectrographic Laboratories and DuMont Ultraspec, Inc. Mul-Tech Electronic Company and McGregor Company continued to improve in accordance with expectations.

Though the first six months of the new fiscal year will show reduced earnings because of start-up costs for Scanall Production, as well as the general decline in the economy, it is anticipated that the average growth rate experienced since fiscal 1972 will continue through fiscal 1976.

Robert J. Schmidt, President

EXHIBIT 2

TECHTRONICS, INCORPORATED
Corporate Structure by Lines of Business (1975)

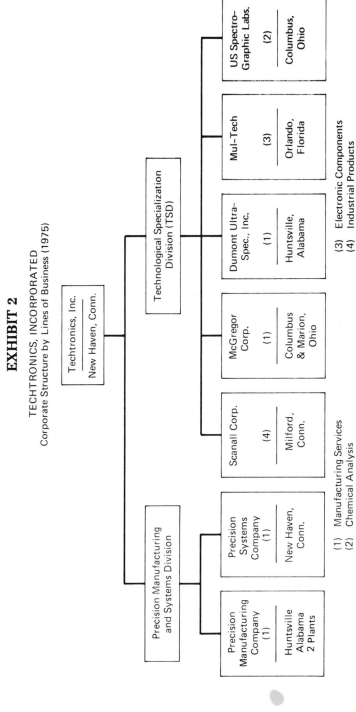

Techtronics, Inc.
New Haven, Conn.

Precision Manufacturing
and Systems Division

Technological Specialization
Division (TSD)

Precision
Manufacturing
Company
(1)

Huntsville
Alabama
2 Plants

Precision
Systems
Company
(1)

New Haven,
Conn.

Scanall Corp.
(4)

Milford,
Conn.

McGregor
Corp.
(1)

Columbus
& Marion,
Ohio

Dumont Ultra–
Spec., Inc.
(1)

Huntsville,
Alabama

Mul–Tech
(3)

Orlando,
Florida

US Spectro–
Graphic Labs.
(2)

Columbus,
Ohio

(1) Manufacturing Services
(2) Chemical Analysis
(3) Electronic Components
(4) Industrial Products

Techtronics, Inc. had no formal organization chart. Divisions have no formal status. Operating companies in the Technological Specialization Division (TSD) have functional lines of business relationships to Pre–cision Manufacturing and Systems Division operating companies.

Source: Constructed by casewriter.

479

EXHIBIT 3

Techtronics, Incorporated

Contributions to Net Sales and Earnings (Loss) Before Income Taxes and Extraordinary Items by Line of Business for the Five Years Ended January 31

	Net Sales (000's)				
	1971	1972	1973	1974	1975
Manufacturing services	$8,349	$7,349	$9,116	$10,560	$11,622
Chemical analysis	632	711	708	757	890
Electronic components and assemblies	—	—	—	467	1,009
Industrial products	—	—	—	—	150
Total	$8,981	$8,060	$9,824	$11,784	$13,671

	Earnings (Loss) Before Income Taxes and Extraordinary Item (000's)				
	1971	1972	1973	1974	1975
Manufacturing services	$(764)	$(97)	$128	$708	$1,337
Chemical analysis	205	186	159	170	286
Electronic components and assemblies	—	—	—	(75)	(23)
Industrial products	—	—	—	—	(316)
Total	$(559)	$89	$287	$803	$1,284

EXHIBIT 4

Techtronics, Incorporated

Percentage Contribution to Total Sales by Lines of Business

	1971 (%)	1972 (%)	1973 (%)	1974 (%)	1975 (%)
Manufacturing services High precision Precision mfg. systems and DuMont	80	79	78	77	71
Machining services (McGregor)	13	12	15	13	14
Chemical analysis (USSL)	7	9	7	6	7
Electronic components and assemblies (Mul-Tech)				4	7
Industrial products (Scanall)					1
	100	100	100	100	100

EXHIBIT 5

Techtronics, Incorporated

Owned and Leased Properties

Facility	Location	Approximate Square Footage
Owned		
Precision Systems Company and Corporate Headquarters	New Haven, Conn.	55,000
McGregor Company	Columbus, Ohio	30,000
Mul-Tech Electronic Company	Orlando, Florida	15,000
DuMont Ultraspec, Inc.	Huntsville, Alabama	10,800
Precision Manufacturing Company	Huntsville, Alabama	92,000
Leased (*Expiration Year)		
McGregor Company (*1987)	Marion, Ohio	34,000
United States Spectrographic Laboratories, Inc. (*1976)	Columbus, Ohio	6,500
Precision Manufacturing Company (*1977)	Huntsville, Alabama	60,000
Scanall Corp. (*Nov. 1975)	Milford, Conn.	15,000

EXHIBIT 6

Techtronics, Incorporated

Consolidated Balance Sheet
(in thousands of dollars)

Assets	Jan. 31 1975	Jan. 31 1974	Liabilities and Net Worth	Jan. 31 1975	Jan. 31 1974
Current assets			Current liabilities		
Cash	$ 246	$ 691	Notes payable		
Trade account			Bank	$ 800	$ 300
receivable	2,817	2,642	Other	0	57
Inventories			Accounts payable	688	847
Finished and In-			Employee payable	462	396
process			Property and other		
products	1,241	1,141	taxes	166	208
Raw materials	272	157	Income taxes	19	137
	1,513	1,298	Current long-term		
Prepaid expenses	50	36	debt	478	332
Total current			Total current		
assets	4,626	4,667	liabilities	2,613	2,277
Properties			Long-term debt		
Land	371	365	Notes payable to		
Buildings	2,562	1,832	bank	1,050	1,175
Machinery and			Equipment leases	285	360
equipment	5,809	6,478	Other	31	133
	8,742	8,675	Total long-term		
Less allowances			debt	1,366	1,668
for depreciation	3,539	4,122	Deferred income		
Net properties	5,203	4,553	taxes	848	333
Other Assets			Net worth		
Goodwill	450	463	Common stock	1,388	1,348
Deferred new			Paid-in surplus	2,480	2,457
product			Retained earnings	2,536	1,863
development			Total net worth	6,404	5,668
costs	895	188	Total liabilities and		
Miscellaneous	57	75	net worth	$11,231	$9,946
Total other assets	1,420	726			
Total assets	$11,231	$9,946			

EXHIBIT 7

Techtronics, Incorporated

Profit and Loss Statement
(in thousands of dollars)

	Jan. 31 1975	Jan. 31 1974	Jan. 31 1973	Jan. 31 1972	Jan. 31 1971
Net sales	$13,671	$11,784	$9,824	$8,060	$8,981
Cost of products sold	10,125	8,998	8,035	6,814	7,802
Selling and administrative	2,108	1,811	1,352	1,040	1,561
Interest	244	217	159	169	217
Total costs & expenses	12,477	11,026	9,546	8,023	9,580
Operating income	1,194	758	278	37	(599)
Other income	90	45	9	52	40
Earnings before income taxes	1,284	803	287	89	(559)
Income taxes	95	175	100	(10)	(295)
Deferred income taxes	515	205	40	35	30
Write-off of goodwill					(614)
Net profit	$ 674ª	$ 423ª	$ 147	$ 64	$ (908)

ª See note "a" on Exhibit 9

EXHIBIT 8

Techtronics, Incorporated

Key Financial Information on the Balance Sheet of
Techtronics, Inc.
(in thousands of dollars)

	1975	1974	1973	1972	1971
Current assets	4,642	4,667	3,513	3,257	3,059
Current liabilities	2,613	2,277	1,490	847	1,129
Fixed assets less depreciation	5,203	4,553	4,355	4,492	4,239
Long-term debt	1,366	1,669	1,707	2,466	2,340
Equity	6,404	5,668	4,994	4,814	4,677
Goodwill	450	463	476	488	502
Trade account receivable	2,817	2,642	1,851	1,739	1,274
Cash	246	691	659	638	977
Inventories	1,513	1,298	952	812	727
Accounts payable	688	847	1,211	792	972
Deferred income taxes	848	333	227	193	152

EXHIBIT 9

Techtronics, Incorporated

Sales and Profit Statistics from 1963 to 1975
(in thousands of dollars)

Year	Net Sales	Income Taxes	Net Profit
1975	$13,671	$610 245[a]	$674 332[a]
1974	11,784	380 285[a]	423 330[a]
1973	9,824	140	147
1972	8,060	25	64
1971	8,981	(265)[c]	(294)[b]
1970	11,572	640	652
1969	8,457	595	541
1968	7,195	420	505
1967	6,441	270	316
1966	5,221	220	261
1965	4,725	N.A.	54
1964	6,227	N.A.	129
1963	4,641	N.A.	99

[a] As required by the FASB, the company will expense expenditures for development of new products as incurred rather than the present method of deferment and amortizing such expenditures over a period not to exceed three years. Prior to 1974, expenditures of new products or capabilities were not significant and were charged to operations as incurred. By charging the development costs as incurred, the operating income was reduced as well as the affected balance-sheet entries.

[b] Before extraordinary loss item of $614,000.

[c] Tax Credit.

APPENDICES

APPENDIX A

Techtronics, Incorporated

Major Obstacles as to the Wide Use of Scanning in the Supermarket

1. At least 60 percent of the merchandise must be symbol-marked (UPC) to receive a cost benefit with the scanner. Only recently has this been accomplished.

2. Lack of satisfactory system for in-store bar-code printing and labeling for random weight merchandise.

3. Redesigned checkstands are necessary in some cases, which has been slow in coming about.

4. Electronic Cash Registers (ECR) are very expensive and are necessary to become on-line with the computer.

5. Checkout speed (15 to 20 percent faster with well-trained clerks) may not happen if it means less clerks, or if the clerk has to unload as well as load.

6. Several House bills are involved with preserving pricing of items, which makes one function of the scanner unnecessary.

7. Consumer groups have applied pressure on state and federal legislatures to write item-pricing bills so the consumer knows the price, which supermarkets claim will no longer be needed when scanners are used.

8. Union groups are not only applying pressure for item-pricing legislation but also attempting to incorporate item-pricing jobs in their contracts.

9. Initial high investment cost of ECR, checkout stand, scanner, electronic processor, and computer.

APPENDIX A (Cont.)

Present Value of $1 Received k Periods from Now Discounted at i Percent

k/i	1%	2%	3%	4%	5%	6%	7%
1	0.99010	0.98039	0.97087	0.96154	0.95238	0.94340	0.93458
2	0.98030	0.96117	0.94260	0.92456	0.90703	0.89000	0.87344
3	0.97059	0.94232	0.91514	0.88900	0.86384	0.83962	0.81630
4	0.96098	0.92385	0.88849	0.85480	0.82270	0.79209	0.76290
5	0.95147	0.90573	0.86261	0.82193	0.78353	0.74726	0.71299
6	0.94205	0.88797	0.83748	0.79031	0.74622	0.70496	0.66634
7	0.93272	0.87056	0.81309	0.75992	0.71068	0.66506	0.62275
8	0.92348	0.85349	0.78941	0.73069	0.67684	0.62741	0.58201
9	0.91434	0.83676	0.76642	0.70259	0.64461	0.59190	0.54393
10	0.90529	0.82035	0.74409	0.67556	0.61391	0.55839	0.50835
11	0.89632	0.80426	0.72242	0.64958	0.58468	0.52679	0.47509
12	0.88745	0.78849	0.70138	0.62460	0.55684	0.49697	0.44401
13	0.87866	0.77303	0.68095	0.60057	0.53032	0.46884	0.41496
14	0.86996	0.75788	0.66112	0.57748	0.50507	0.44230	0.38782
15	0.86135	0.74301	0.64186	0.55526	0.48102	0.41727	0.36245
16	0.85282	0.72845	0.62317	0.53391	0.45811	0.39365	0.33873
17	0.84438	0.71416	0.60502	0.51337	0.43630	0.37136	0.31657
18	0.83602	0.70016	0.58739	0.49363	0.41552	0.35034	0.29586
19	0.82774	0.68643	0.57029	0.47464	0.39573	0.33051	0.27651
20	0.81954	0.67297	0.55368	0.45639	0.37689	0.31180	0.25842
25	0.77977	0.60953	0.47761	0.37512	0.29530	0.23300	0.18425
30	0.74192	0.55207	0.41199	0.30832	0.23138	0.17411	0.13137
35	0.70591	0.50003	0.35538	0.25342	0.18129	0.13011	0.09366
40	0.67165	0.45289	0.30656	0.20829	0.14205	0.09722	0.06678
k/i	8%	9%	10%	11%	12%	13%	14%
1	0.92593	0.91743	0.90909	0.90090	0.89286	0.88496	0.87719
2	0.85734	0.84168	0.82645	0.81162	0.79719	0.78315	0.76947
3	0.79383	0.77218	0.75131	0.73119	0.71178	0.69305	0.67497
4	0.73503	0.70843	0.68301	0.65873	0.63552	0.61332	0.59208
5	0.68058	0.64993	0.62092	0.59345	0.56743	0.54276	0.51937
6	0.63017	0.59627	0.56447	0.53464	0.50663	0.48032	0.45559
7	0.58349	0.54703	0.51316	0.48166	0.45235	0.42506	0.39964
8	0.54027	0.50187	0.46651	0.43393	0.40388	0.37616	0.35056
9	0.50025	0.46043	0.42410	0.39092	0.36061	0.33288	0.30751
10	0.46319	0.42241	0.38554	0.35218	0.32197	0.29459	0.26974
11	0.42888	0.38753	0.35049	0.31728	0.28748	0.26070	0.23662
12	0.39711	0.35553	0.31863	0.28584	0.25668	0.23071	0.20756
13	0.36770	0.32618	0.28966	0.25751	0.22917	0.20416	0.18207
14	0.34046	0.29925	0.26333	0.23199	0.20462	0.18068	0.15971
15	0.31524	0.27454	0.23939	0.20900	0.18270	0.15989	0.14010
16	0.29189	0.25187	0.21763	0.18829	0.16312	0.14150	0.12289
17	0.27027	0.23107	0.19784	0.16963	0.14564	0.12522	0.10780
18	0.25025	0.21199	0.17986	0.15282	0.13004	0.11081	0.09456
19	0.23171	0.19449	0.16351	0.13768	0.11611	0.09806	0.08295
20	0.21455	0.17843	0.14864	0.12403	0.10367	0.08678	0.07276
25	0.14602	0.11597	0.09230	0.07361	0.05882	0.04710	0.03779
30	0.09938	0.07537	0.05731	0.04368	0.03338	0.02557	0.01963
35	0.06763	0.04899	0.03558	0.02592	0.01894	0.01388	0.01019
40	0.04603	0.03184	0.02209	0.01538	0.01075	0.00753	0.00529

APPENDIX A (Continued)

k/i	15%	16%	17%	18%	19%	20%	25%
1	0.86957	0.86207	0.85470	0.84746	0.84034	0.83333	0.80000
2	0.75614	0.74316	0.73051	0.71818	0.70616	0.69444	0.64000
3	0.65752	0.64066	0.62437	0.60863	0.59342	0.57870	0.51200
4	0.57175	0.55229	0.53365	0.51579	0.49867	0.48225	0.40960
5	0.49718	0.47611	0.45611	0.43711	0.41905	0.40188	0.32768
6	0.43233	0.41044	0.38984	0.37043	0.35214	0.33490	0.26214
7	0.37594	0.35383	0.33320	0.31393	0.29592	0.27908	0.20972
8	0.32690	0.30503	0.28478	0.26604	0.24867	0.23257	0.16777
9	0.28426	0.26295	0.24340	0.22546	0.20897	0.19381	0.13422
10	0.24718	0.22668	0.20804	0.19106	0.17560	0.16151	0.10737
11	0.21494	0.19542	0.17781	0.16192	0.14757	0.13459	0.08590
12	0.18691	0.16846	0.15197	0.13722	0.12400	0.11216	0.06872
13	0.16253	0.14523	0.12989	0.11629	0.10421	0.09346	0.05498
14	0.14133	0.12520	0.11102	0.09855	0.08757	0.07789	0.04398
15	0.12289	0.10793	0.09489	0.08352	0.07359	0.06491	0.03518
16	0.10686	0.09304	0.08110	0.07078	0.06184	0.05409	0.02815
17	0.09293	0.08021	0.06932	0.05998	0.05196	0.04507	0.02252
18	0.08081	0.06914	0.05925	0.05083	0.04367	0.03756	0.01801
19	0.07027	0.05961	0.05064	0.04308	0.03670	0.03130	0.01441
20	0.06110	0.05139	0.04328	0.03651	0.03084	0.02608	0.01153
25	0.03038	0.02447	0.01974	0.01596	0.01292	0.01048	0.00378
30	0.01510	0.01165	0.00900	0.00697	0.00541	0.00421	0.00124
35	0.00751	0.00555	0.00411	0.00305	0.00227	0.00169	0.00041
40	0.00373	0.00264	0.00187	0.00133	0.00095	0.00068	0.00013

k/i	30%	35%	40%
1	0.76923	0.74074	0.71429
2	0.59172	0.54870	0.51020
3	0.45517	0.40644	0.36443
4	0.35013	0.30107	0.26031
5	0.26933	0.22301	0.18593
6	0.20718	0.16520	0.13281
7	0.15937	0.12237	0.09486
8	0.12259	0.09064	0.06776
9	0.09430	0.06714	0.04840
10	0.07254	0.04974	0.03457
11	0.05580	0.03684	0.02469
12	0.04292	0.02729	0.01764
13	0.03302	0.02021	0.01260
14	0.02540	0.01497	0.00900
15	0.01954	0.01109	0.00643
16	0.01503	0.00822	0.00459
17	0.01156	0.00609	0.00328
18	0.00889	0.00451	0.00234
19	0.00684	0.00334	0.00167
20	0.00526	0.00247	0.00120
25	0.00142	0.00055	0.00022
30	0.00038	0.00012	0.00004
35	0.00010	0.00003	0.00001
40	0.00003	0.00001	0.00000

APPENDIX B

Future Value of $1 Received Now and Compounded Annually for k Periods at i Percent

k/i	1%	2%	3%	4%	5%	6%	7%
1	1.01000	1.02000	1.03000	1.04000	1.05000	1.06000	1.07000
2	1.02010	1.04040	1.06090	1.08160	1.10250	1.12360	1.14490
3	1.03030	1.06121	1.09273	1.12486	1.15762	1.19102	1.22504
4	1.04060	1.08243	1.12551	1.16986	1.21551	1.26248	1.31080
5	1.05101	1.10408	1.15927	1.21665	1.27628	1.33823	1.40255
6	1.06152	1.12616	1.19405	1.26532	1.34010	1.41852	1.50073
7	1.07214	1.14869	1.22987	1.31593	1.40710	1.50363	1.60578
8	1.08286	1.17166	1.26677	1.36857	1.47746	1.59385	1.71819
9	1.09369	1.19509	1.30477	1.42331	1.55133	1.68948	1.83846
10	1.10462	1.21899	1.34392	1.48024	1.62889	1.79085	1.96715
11	1.11567	1.24337	1.38423	1.53945	1.71034	1.89830	2.10485
12	1.12683	1.26824	1.42576	1.60103	1.79586	2.01220	2.25219
13	1.13809	1.29361	1.46853	1.66507	1.88565	2.13293	2.40985
14	1.14947	1.31948	1.51259	1.73168	1.97993	2.26090	2.57853
15	1.16097	1.34587	1.55797	1.80094	2.07893	2.39656	2.75903
16	1.17258	1.37279	1.60471	1.87298	2.18287	2.54035	2.95216
17	1.18430	1.40024	1.65285	1.94790	2.29202	2.69277	3.15882
18	1.19615	1.42825	1.70243	2.02582	2.40662	2.85434	3.37993
19	1.20811	1.45681	1.75351	2.10685	2.52695	3.02560	3.61653
20	1.22019	1.48595	1.80611	2.19112	2.65330	3.20714	3.86968
25	1.28243	1.64061	2.09378	2.66584	3.38635	4.29187	5.42743
30	1.34785	1.81136	2.42726	3.24340	4.32194	5.74349	7.61226
35	1.41660	1.99989	2.81386	3.94609	5.51602	7.68609	10.67658
40	1.48886	2.20804	3.26204	4.80102	7.03999	10.28572	14.97446
k/i	8%	9%	10%	11%	12%	13%	14%
1	1.08000	1.09000	1.10000	1.11000	1.12000	1.13000	1.14000
2	1.16640	1.18810	1.21000	1.23200	1.25440	1.27690	1.29960
3	1.25971	1.29503	1.33100	1.36763	1.40493	1.44290	1.48154
4	1.36049	1.41158	1.46410	1.51807	1.57352	1.63047	1.68896
5	1.46933	1.53862	1.61051	1.68506	1.76234	1.84244	1.92541
6	1.58687	1.67710	1.77156	1.87041	1.97382	2.08195	2.19497
7	1.71382	1.82804	1.94872	2.07616	2.21068	2.35261	2.50227
8	1.85093	1.99256	2.14359	2.30454	2.47596	2.65844	2.85259
9	1.99900	2.17189	2.35795	2.55804	2.77308	3.00404	3.25195
10	2.15892	2.36736	2.59374	2.83942	3.10585	3.39457	3.70722
11	2.33164	2.58043	2.85312	3.15176	3.47855	3.83586	4.22623
12	2.51817	2.81266	3.13843	3.49845	3.89598	4.33452	4.81790
13	2.71962	3.06580	3.45227	3.88328	4.36349	4.89801	5.49241
14	2.93719	3.34173	3.79750	4.31044	4.88711	5.53475	6.26135
15	3.17217	3.64248	4.17725	4.78459	5.47357	6.25427	7.13794
16	3.42594	3.97031	4.59497	5.31089	6.13039	7.06733	8.13725
17	3.70002	4.32763	5.05447	5.89509	6.86604	7.98608	9.27646
18	3.99602	4.71712	5.55992	6.54355	7.68997	9.02427	10.57517
19	4.31570	5.14166	6.11591	7.26334	8.61276	10.19742	12.05569
20	4.66096	5.60441	6.72750	8.06231	9.64629	11.52309	13.74349
25	6.84848	8.62308	10.83471	13.58546	17.00006	21.23054	26.46192
30	10.06266	13.26768	17.44940	22.89230	29.95992	39.11590	50.95016
35	14.78534	20.41397	28.10244	38.57485	52.79962	72.06851	98.10018
40	21.72452	31.40942	45.25926	65.00087	93.05097	132.78155	188.88351

k/i	15%	16%	17%	18%	19%	20%	25%
1	1.15000	1.16000	1.17000	1.18000	1.19000	1.20000	1.25000
2	1.32250	1.34560	1.36890	1.39240	1.41610	1.44000	1.56250
3	1.52088	1.56090	1.60161	1.64303	1.68516	1.72800	1.95313
4	1.74901	1.81064	1.87389	1.93878	2.00534	2.07360	2.44141
5	2.01136	2.10034	2.19245	2.28776	2.38635	2.48832	3.05176
6	2.31306	2.43640	2.56516	2.69955	2.83976	2.98598	3.81470
7	2.66002	2.82622	3.00124	3.18547	3.37932	3.58318	4.76837
8	3.05902	3.27841	3.51145	3.75886	4.02139	4.29982	5.96046
9	3.51788	3.80296	4.10840	4.43545	4.78545	5.15978	7.45058
10	4.04556	4.41144	4.80683	5.23384	5.69468	6.19174	9.31323
11	4.65239	5.11726	5.62399	6.17593	6.77667	7.43008	11.64153
12	5.35025	5.93603	6.58007	7.28759	8.06424	8.91610	14.55192
13	6.15279	6.88579	7.69868	8.59936	9.59645	10.69932	18.18989
14	7.07571	7.98752	9.00745	10.14724	11.41977	12.83918	22.73737
15	8.13706	9.26552	10.53872	11.97375	13.58953	15.40702	28.42171
16	9.35762	10.74800	12.33030	14.12902	16.17154	18.48843	35.52714
17	10.76126	12.46768	14.42646	16.67225	19.24413	22.18611	44.40892
18	12.37545	14.46251	16.87895	19.67325	22.90052	26.62333	55.51115
19	14.23177	16.77652	19.74838	23.21444	27.25162	31.94800	69.38894
20	16.36654	19.46076	23.10560	27.39303	32.42942	38.33760	86.73617
25	32.91895	40.87424	50.65783	62.66863	77.38807	95.39622	264.69780
30	66.21177	85.84988	111.06465	143.37064	184.67531	237.37631	807.79357
35	133.17552	180.31407	243.50347	327.99729	440.70061	590.66823	2465.19033
40	267.86355	378.72116	533.86871	750.37834	1051.66751	1469.77157	7523.16385

k/i	30%	35%	40%
1	1.30000	1.35000	1.40000
2	1.69000	1.82250	1.96000
3	2.19700	2.46037	2.74400
4	2.85610	3.32151	3.84160
5	3.71293	4.48403	5.37824
6	4.82681	6.05345	7.52954
7	6.27485	8.17215	10.54135
8	8.15731	11.03240	14.75789
9	10.60450	14.89375	20.66105
10	13.78585	20.10656	28.92547
11	17.92160	27.14385	40.49565
12	23.29809	36.64420	56.69391
13	30.28751	49.46967	79.37148
14	39.37376	66.78405	111.12007
15	51.18589	90.15847	155.56810
16	66.54166	121.71393	217.79533
17	86.50416	164.31381	304.91347
18	112.45541	221.82364	426.87885
19	146.19203	299.46192	597.63040
20	190.04964	404.27359	836.68255
25	705.64100	1812.77629	4499.87958
30	2619.99564	8128.54950	24201.43236
35	9727.86043	36448.68776	130161.11155
40	36118.86481	163437.13468	700037.69659

APPENDIX C

Present Value of Annuity of $1 Received for k Periods Discounted Annually at i Percent

k/i	1%	2%	3%	4%	5%	6%	7%
1	0.99010	0.98039	0.97087	0.96154	0.95238	0.94340	0.93458
2	1.97040	1.94156	1.91347	1.88609	1.85941	1.83339	1.80802
3	2.94099	2.88388	2.82861	2.77509	2.72325	2.67301	2.62432
4	3.90197	3.80773	3.71710	3.62990	3.54595	3.46511	3.38721
5	4.85343	4.71346	4.57971	4.45182	4.32948	4.21236	4.10020
6	5.79548	5.60143	5.41719	5.24214	5.07569	4.91732	4.76654
7	6.72819	6.47199	6.23028	6.00205	5.78637	5.58238	5.38929
8	7.65168	7.32548	7.01969	6.73274	6.46321	6.20979	5.97130
9	8.56602	8.16224	7.78611	7.43533	7.10782	6.80169	6.51523
10	9.47130	8.98259	8.53020	8.11090	7.72173	7.36009	7.02358
11	10.36763	9.78685	9.25262	8.76048	8.30641	7.88687	7.49867
12	11.25508	10.57534	9.95400	9.38507	8.86325	8.38384	7.94269
13	12.13374	11.34837	10.63496	9.98565	9.39357	8.85268	8.35765
14	13.00370	12.10625	11.29607	10.56312	9.89864	9.29498	8.74547
15	13.86505	12.84926	11.93794	11.11839	10.37966	9.71225	9.10791
16	14.71787	13.57771	12.56110	11.65230	10.83777	10.10590	9.44665
17	15.56225	14.29187	13.16612	12.16567	11.27407	10.47726	9.76322
18	16.39827	14.99203	13.75351	12.65930	11.68959	10.82760	10.05909
19	17.22601	15.67846	14.32380	13.13394	12.08532	11.15812	10.33560
20	18.04555	16.35143	14.87747	13.59033	12.46221	11.46992	10.59401
25	22.02316	19.52346	17.41315	15.62208	14.09394	12.78336	11.65358
30	25.80771	22.39646	19.60044	17.29203	15.37245	13.76483	12.40904
35	29.40858	24.99862	21.48722	18.66461	16.37419	14.49825	12.94767
40	32.83469	27.35548	23.11477	19.79277	17.15909	15.04630	13.33171

k/i	8%	9%	10%	11%	12%	13%	14%
1	0.92593	0.91743	0.09090	0.90090	0.89286	0.88496	0.87719
2	1.78326	1.75911	1.73554	1.71252	1.69005	1.66810	1.64666
3	2.57710	2.53129	2.48685	2.44371	2.40183	2.36115	2.32163
4	3.31213	3.23972	3.16987	3.10245	3.03735	2.97447	2.91371
5	3.99271	3.88965	3.79079	3.69590	3.60478	3.51723	3.43308
6	4.62288	4.48592	4.35526	4.23054	4.11141	3.99755	3.88867
7	5.20637	5.03295	4.86842	4.71220	4.56376	4.42261	4.28830
8	5.74664	5.53482	5.33493	5.14612	4.96764	4.79877	4.63886
9	6.24689	5.99525	5.75902	5.53705	5.32825	5.13166	4.94637
10	6.71008	6.41766	6.14457	5.88923	5.65022	5.42624	5.21612
11	7.13896	6.80519	6.49506	6.20652	5.93770	5.68694	5.45273
12	7.53608	7.16073	6.81369	6.49236	6.19437	5.91765	5.66029
13	7.90378	7.48690	7.10336	6.74987	6.42355	6.12181	5.84236
14	8.24424	7.78615	7.36669	6.98187	6.62817	6.30249	6.00207
15	8.55948	8.06069	7.60608	7.19087	6.81086	6.46238	6.14217
16	8.85137	8.31256	7.82371	7.37916	6.97399	6.60388	6.26506
17	9.12164	8.54363	8.02155	7.54879	7.11963	6.72909	6.37286
18	9.37189	8.75563	8.20141	7.70162	7.24967	6.83991	6.46742
19	9.60360	8.95011	8.36492	7.83929	7.36578	6.93797	6.55037
20	9.81815	9.12855	8.51356	7.96333	7.46944	7.02475	6.62313
25	10.67478	9.82258	9.07704	8.42174	7.84314	7.32998	6.87293
30	11.25778	10.27365	9.42691	8.69379	8.05518	7.49565	7.00266
35	11.65457	10.56682	9.64416	8.85524	8.17550	7.58557	7.07005
40	11.92461	10.75736	9.77905	8.95105	8.24378	7.63438	7.10504

k/i	15%	16%	17%	18%	19%	20%	25%
1	0.86957	0.86207	0.85470	0.84746	0.84034	0.83333	0.80000
2	1.62571	1.60523	1.58521	1.56564	1.54650	1.52778	1.44000
3	2.28323	2.24589	2.20958	2.17427	2.13992	2.10648	1.95200
4	2.85498	2.79818	2.74324	2.69006	2.63859	2.58873	2.36160
5	3.35216	3.27429	3.19935	3.12717	3.05763	2.99061	2.68928
6	3.78448	3.68474	3.58918	3.49760	3.40978	3.32551	2.95142
7	4.16042	4.03857	3.92238	3.81153	3.70570	3.60459	3.16114
8	4.48732	4.34359	4.20716	4.07757	3.95437	3.83716	3.32891
9	4.77158	4.60654	4.45057	4.30302	4.16333	4.03097	3.46313
10	5.01877	4.83323	4.65860	4.49409	4.33893	4.19247	3.57050
11	5.23371	5.02864	4.83641	4.65601	4.48650	4.32706	3.65640
12	5.42062	5.19711	4.98839	4.79322	4.61050	4.43922	3.71512
13	5.58315	5.34233	5.11828	4.90951	4.71471	4.53268	3.78010
14	5.72448	5.46753	5.22930	5.00806	4.80228	4.61057	3.82408
15	5.84737	5.57546	5.32419	5.09158	4.87586	4.67547	3.85926
16	5.95432	5.66850	5.40529	5.16235	4.93770	4.72956	3.88741
17	6.04716	5.74870	5.47461	5.22233	4.98966	4.77463	3.90993
18	6.12797	5.81785	5.53385	5.27316	5.03333	4.81219	3.92794
19	6.19823	5.87746	5.58649	5.31624	5.07003	4.84350	3.94235
20	6.25933	5.92884	5.62777	5.35275	5.10086	4.86958	3.95368
25	6.46415	6.09709	5.76623	5.46691	5.19515	4.94759	3.98489
30	6.56598	6.17720	5.82939	5.51681	5.23466	4.97894	3.99505
35	6.61661	6.21534	5.85820	5.53862	5.25122	4.99154	3.99838
40	6.64178	6.23350	5.87133	5.54815	5.25815	4.99660	3.99947
k/i	30%	35%	40%				
1	0.76923	0.74074	0.71429				
2	1.36095	1.28944	1.22449				
3	1.81611	1.69588	1.58892				
4	2.16624	1.99695	1.84923				
5	2.43557	2.21996	2.03516				
6	2.64275	2.38516	2.16797				
7	2.80211	2.50752	2.26284				
8	2.92470	2.59817	2.33060				
9	3.01900	2.66531	2.37900				
10	3.09154	2.71504	2.41357				
11	3.14734	2.75188	2.43826				
12	3.19026	2.77917	2.45590				
13	3.22328	2.79939	2.46850				
14	3.24867	2.81436	2.47750				
15	3.26821	2.82545	2.48393				
16	3.28324	2.83367	2.48852				
17	3.29480	2.83975	2.49180				
18	3.30369	2.84426	2.49414				
19	3.31053	2.84760	2.49582				
20	3.31579	2.85008	2.49701				
25	3.32861	2.85557	2.49944				
30	3.33206	2.85679	2.49990				
35	3.33299	2.85706	2.49998				
40	3.33324	2.85713	2.50000				

APPENDIX D

Future Value of Annuity of $1 Received for k Periods Compounded Annually at i Percent

k/i	1%	2%	3%	4%	5%	6%	7%
1	1.00000	1.00000	1.00000	1.00000	1.00000	1.00000	1.00000
2	2.01000	2.02000	2.03000	2.04000	2.05000	2.06000	2.07000
3	3.03010	3.06040	3.09090	3.12160	3.15250	3.18360	3.21490
4	4.06040	4.12161	4.18363	4.24646	4.31012	4.37462	4.43994
5	5.10101	5.20404	5.30914	5.41632	5.52563	5.63709	5.75074
6	6.15202	6.30812	6.46841	6.63298	6.80191	6.97532	7.15329
7	7.21354	7.43428	7.66246	7.89829	8.14201	8.39384	8.65402
8	8.28567	8.58297	8.89234	9.21423	9.54911	9.89747	10.25980
9	9.36853	9.75463	10.15911	10.58280	11.02656	11.49132	11.97799
10	10.46221	10.94972	11.46388	12.00611	12.57789	13.18079	13.81645
11	11.56683	12.16872	12.80780	13.48635	14.20679	14.97164	15.78360
12	12.68250	13.41209	14.19203	15.02581	15.91713	16.86994	17.88845
13	13.80933	14.68033	15.61779	16.62684	17.71298	18.88214	20.14064
14	14.94742	15.97394	17.08632	18.29191	19.59863	21.01507	22.55049
15	16.09690	17.29342	18.59891	20.02359	21.57856	23.27597	25.12902
16	17.25786	18.63929	20.15688	21.82453	23.65749	25.67253	27.88805
17	18.43044	20.01207	21.76159	23.69751	25.84037	28.21288	30.84022
18	19.61475	21.41231	23.41444	25.64541	28.13238	30.90565	33.99903
19	20.81090	22.84056	25.11687	27.67123	30.53900	33.75999	37.37896
20	22.01900	24.29737	26.87037	29.77808	33.06595	36.78559	40.99549
25	28.24320	32.03030	36.45926	41.64591	47.72710	54.86451	63.24904
30	34.78489	40.56808	47.57542	56.08494	66.43885	79.05819	94.46079
35	41.66028	49.99448	60.46208	73.65222	90.32031	111.43478	138.23688
40	48.88637	60.40198	75.40126	95.02552	120.79977	154.76197	199.63511

k/i	8%	9%	10%	11%	12%	13%	14%
1	1.00000	1.00000	1.00000	1.00000	1.00000	1.00000	1.00000
2	2.08000	2.09000	2.10000	2.11000	2.12000	2.13000	2.14000
3	3.24640	3.27810	3.31000	3.34210	3.37440	3.40690	3.43960
4	4.50611	4.57313	4.64100	4.70973	4.77933	4.84980	4.92114
5	5.86660	5.98471	6.10510	6.22780	6.35285	6.48027	6.61010
6	7.33593	7.52333	7.71561	7.91286	8.11519	8.32271	8.53552
7	8.92280	9.20043	9.48717	9.78327	10.08901	10.40466	10.73049
8	10.63663	11.02847	11.43589	11.85943	12.29969	12.75726	13.23276
9	12.48756	13.02104	13.57948	14.16397	14.77566	15.41571	16.08535
10	14.48656	15.19293	15.93742	16.72201	17.54874	18.41975	19.33730
11	16.64549	17.56029	18.53117	19.56143	20.65458	21.81432	23.04452
12	18.97713	20.14072	21.38428	22.71319	24.13313	25.65018	27.27075
13	21.49530	22.95338	24.52271	26.21164	28.02911	29.98470	32.08865
14	24.21492	26.01919	27.97498	30.09492	32.39260	34.88271	37.58107
15	27.15211	29.36092	31.77248	34.40536	37.27971	40.41746	43.84241
16	30,32428	33.00340	35.94973	39.18995	42.75328	46.67173	50.98035
17	33.75023	36.97370	40.54470	44.50084	48.88367	53.73906	59.11760
18	37.45024	41.30134	45.59917	50.39594	55.74971	61.72514	68.39407
19	41.44626	46.01846	51.15909	56.93949	63.43968	70.74941	78.96923
20	45.76196	51.16012	57.27500	64.20283	72.05244	80.94683	91.02493
25	73.10594	84.70090	98.34706	114.41331	133.33387	155.61956	181.87083
30	113.28321	136.30754	164.49402	199.02088	241.33268	293.19922	356.78685
35	172.31680	215.71075	271.02437	341.58955	431.66350	546.68082	693.57270
40	259.05652	337.88245	442.59256	581.82607	767.09142	1013.70424	1342.02518

APPENDIX D (Continued)

k/i	15%	16%	17%	18%	19%	20%	25%
1	1.00000	1.00000	1.00000	1.00000	1.00000	1.00000	1.00000
2	2.15000	2.16000	2.17000	2.18000	2.19000	2.20000	2.25000
3	3.47250	3.50560	3.53890	3.57240	3.60610	3.64000	3.81250
4	4.99337	5.06650	5.14051	5.21543	5.29126	5.36800	5.76563
5	6.74238	6.87714	7.01440	7.15421	7.29660	7.44160	8.20703
6	8.75374	8.97748	9.20685	9.44197	9.68295	9.92992	11.25879
7	11.06680	11.41387	11.77201	12.14152	12.52271	12.91590	15.07349
8	13.72682	14.24009	14.77325	15.32700	15.90203	16.49908	19.84186
9	16.78584	17.51851	18.28471	19.08585	19.92341	20.79890	25.80232
10	20.30372	21.32147	22.39311	23.52131	24.70886	25.95868	33.25290
11	24.34928	25.73290	27.19994	28.75514	30.40355	32.15042	42.56613
12	29.00167	30.85017	32.82393	34.93107	37.18022	39.58050	54.20766
13	34.35192	36.78620	39.40399	42.21866	45.24446	48.49660	68.75958
14	40.50471	43.67199	47.10267	50.81802	54.84091	59.19592	86.94947
15	47.58041	51.65951	56.11013	60.96527	66.26068	72.03511	109.68684
16	55.71747	60.92503	66.64885	72.93901	79.85021	87.44213	138.10855
17	65.07509	71.67303	78.97915	87.06804	96.02175	105.93056	173.63568
18	75.83636	84.14072	93.40561	103.74028	115.26588	128.11667	218.04460
19	88.21181	98.60323	110.28456	123.41353	138.16640	154.74000	273.55576
20	102.44358	115.37975	130.03294	146.62797	165.41802	186.68800	342.94470
25	212.79302	249.21402	292.10486	342.60349	402.04249	471.98108	1054.79118
30	434.74515	530.31173	647.43912	790.94799	966.71217	1181.88157	3227.17427
35	881.17016	1120.71295	1426.49102	1816.65161	2314.21372	2948.34115	9856.76132
40	1779.09031	2360.75724	3134.52184	4163.21303	5529.82898	7343.85784	30088.65538

k/i	30%	35%	40%
1	1.00000	1.00000	1.00000
2	2.30000	2.35000	2.40000
3	3.99000	4.17250	4.36000
4	6.18700	6.63287	7.10400
5	9.04310	9.95438	10.94560
6	12.75603	14.43841	16.32384
7	17.58284	20.49186	23.85338
8	23.85769	28.66401	34.39473
9	32.01500	39.69641	49.15262
10	42.61950	54.59016	69.81366
11	56.40535	74.69672	98.73913
12	74.32695	101.84057	139.23478
13	97.62504	138.48476	195.92869
14	127.91255	187.95443	275.30017
15	167.28631	254.73848	386.42024
16	218.47220	344.89695	541.98833
17	285.01386	466.61088	759.78367
18	371.51802	630.92469	1064.69714
19	483.97343	852.74834	1491.57599
20	630.16546	1152.21025	2089.20639
25	2348.80334	5176.50369	11247.19895
30	8729.98548	23221.57000	60501.08089
35	32422.86808	104136.25075	325400.27888
40	120392.88269	466960.38480	1750091.74148